LEOPOLD MOZART (*c.* 1765)

From a portrait by an unknown artist
(Mozart Museum, Salzburg)

THE
LETTERS OF MOZART
AND HIS FAMILY

Chronologically arranged, translated and edited
with an Introduction, Notes and Indexes

by

EMILY ANDERSON

Second Edition prepared by
A. HYATT KING AND MONICA CAROLAN

VOLUME I

MACMILLAN
London · Melbourne · Toronto

ST MARTIN'S PRESS
New York
1966

MACMILLAN AND COMPANY LIMITED
Little Essex Street London WC2
also Bombay Calcutta Madras Melbourne

THE MACMILLAN COMPANY OF CANADA LIMITED
70 Bond Street Toronto 2

ST MARTIN'S PRESS INC
175 Fifth Avenue New York NY 10010

Library of Congress catalogue card no. 65–7562

PRINTED IN GREAT BRITAIN

PUBLISHER'S PREFACE TO THE SECOND EDITION

THE first edition of Emily Anderson's *Letters of Mozart and his Family* was published in three volumes in 1938. Volume one went out of print in 1954 and volumes two and three in 1956. A selection of these letters, edited and introduced by the late Dr. Eric Blom with Miss Anderson's assistance, was first published by Penguin Books in 1956 under the title of *Mozart's Letters*. This was, of course, never intended to serve as more than a stop-gap. Miss Anderson had long hoped to undertake the revision of the larger work and after her translation of *The Letters of Beethoven* was published in October 1961, she returned to Mozart, but her work was cut short by her sudden and much regretted death in October 1962.

By that date, she had finished a preliminary revision of the Mozart letters, in the course of which she had noted many passages which required checking for re-translation and footnotes which were to be emended or amplified. She had also marked various points in her text at which corrections and suggestions, sent to her over the years by Mozart scholars, were to be incorporated. It was likewise her intention to translate certain passages from the original German which she had omitted from the earlier edition. The only substantial change which she envisaged was that the letters of Constanze Mozart to Johann Anton André, translated and annotated by Dr. C. B. Oldman, were to be omitted, with his consent.

In the spring of 1963, the publishers engaged Miss Monica Carolan and Mr. A. Hyatt King to complete Miss Anderson's limited revision, to prepare the copy for the printer, read the proofs, compile new indexes and see the volumes through the press. Miss Carolan, who had assisted Miss Anderson throughout her work on the Beethoven letters, had also shared the preliminary revision of the Mozart letters. She was thus familiar with her system of annotation and knew how her accumulated papers could best be used. Mr. King had been a close friend of Miss Anderson for many years and had himself specialised in Mozart.

The revised edition includes seven Letters not in the 1938 edition, namely 273,[1] 425**, 476*, 536*, 547*, 549*, 609*. Letters 96a and 273a are now published in a substantially expanded form from rediscovered autographs. (Letters 96a, 273a and 547* had previously been published in the Penguin edition.)

The following points may also be noted:

In a few Letters, passages formerly ascribed to Mozart himself have been

---

[1] The letter numbered 273 in the 1938 edition has proved to be a postscript and is now numbered 273a.

shown by Dr. Wilhelm Bauer and Professor Otto Erich Deutsch to be postscripts written by other members of his family. Here the necessary adjustment has been made. Certain changes have been made in the spelling of names in the text. The signatures of all Letters, whether abbreviated or not, are given exactly as in the originals.

The location of autographs or other sources has been brought up to date where possible.

Letters and passages in French have been kept in the original orthography.

The names of churches have been translated throughout.

In many autographs, the date is given with the writer's signature at the end. In these cases, the date has been repeated in square brackets at the head. Square brackets have also been used

(*a*) to enclose words or figures supplied in an incomplete original date,

(*b*) to enclose a conjectural date supplied to an undated letter.

Page-references to Köchel's *Chronologisch-thematisches Verzeichnis sämtlicher Tonwerke Amadé Mozarts* are to the sixth edition (1964). Traditional Köchel numbering has been retained with the numbers of the sixth edition added in square brackets.

With few exceptions, other references have been left as given in the 1938 edition, although the source referred to may now be available in a more comprehensive and easily accessible publication.[1]

We are confident that Miss Anderson would have wished us to express cordial thanks to Professor Otto Erich Deutsch. As an assiduous correspondent for two decades, he sent her a large quantity of corrections and suggestions, affecting both text and footnotes, which have been most gratefully incorporated.

Among Miss Anderson's regular correspondents during a long period were also the late Dr. Alfred Einstein and the late Professor Erich Hertzmann. The information which they gave her has likewise been gladly used. Much valuable advice and information has also been given by Dr. C. B. Oldman, who knew Miss Anderson well for nearly thirty years. Dr. Oldman has also kindly read the proofs and made various suggestions. Valuable assistance with proof-reading has also been given by Mr. H. C. Robbins Landon.

For permission to translate three previously unknown autograph letters our thanks are due to: the late Mr. S. L. Courtauld (Letter 425**),

---

[1] For instance, the entries relevant to Mozart in Count Zinzendorf's diary, mentioned on p. 5, n. 1, partially printed in the *Mozarteums Mitteilungen* for 1919, have now been included by O. E. Deutsch in *Mozart. Die Dokumente seines Lebens*; and Leopold Mozart's *Reiseaufzeichnungen* (see p. 5, n. 4, and elsewhere), edited by Schurig in 1920 and now out of print, are given throughout volumes I and II of *Mozart. Briefe und Aufzeichnungen*. For general information, it may be noted that a list of important works on Mozart issued since 1938 is given on pp. xxxv, xxxvi.

Mr. Albi Rosenthal (Letter 273) and Mr. G. M. Schnitzler (Letter 549*). Mr. Rosenthal also kindly made available another autograph in his possession, Letter 273a, which was formerly known only in the extract quoted by Nissen. Thanks are also due to the late Mr. Richard Border, who owned the autograph of Letter 425* (previously known only from Nohl and thought to be a postscript) and brought it to Miss Anderson's attention.

We would finally express our gratitude to Bärenreiter Verlag, Kassel, for permission to make the above-mentioned adjustments of some post-scripts and for permission to publish translations of Letters 235a and 536* from the text given in:

Mozart. Briefe und Aufzeichnungen — Gesamtausgabe, herausgegeben von der Internationalen Stiftung Mozarteum Salzburg, gesammelt und erläutert von Wilhelm A. Bauer und Otto Erich Deutsch. Vier Textbände, ein Kommentar-, ein Register-Band (Bärenreiter-Verlag Kassel, Basel, Paris, London, New York 1962 ff.).

———

The editors of the second edition would like to express their thanks to Mr. H. Cowdell and Mr. T. M. Farmiloe, who have lavished much pains on these volumes at all stages of their production.

PREFACE TO THE FIRST EDITION [1938]

IT is impossible to acknowledge all the obligations I have incurred in the course of preparing this work, but I wish to thank in particular: Professor Ludwig Schiedermair of Bonn University, for allowing me to use his German edition of the Mozart family letters, for assisting me during the early stages of my undertaking and for supplying me from time to time with additional material; Mr. C. B. Oldman of the British Museum, for generously consenting to the inclusion in my edition of large portions of the unpublished letters from Mozart's widow to Johann Anton André, which are in his possession and which he has translated and edited for this purpose, and for constantly contributing from his wealth of information upon all matters relating to Mozart; Dr. Alfred Einstein, for most unselfishly placing at my disposal his immense knowledge of eighteenth-century music and the results of his research work on Mozart's musical MSS., which have now been embodied in the third edition (1937) of Köchel's catalogue of Mozart's works; Dr. Bernhard Paumgartner, Director of the Mozarteum, Salzburg, for granting me free access to its collection of autographs; Dr. Georg Schünemann, Director of the Music Department of the Prussian State Library, Berlin, for permission to consult its large collection of transcripts; the Public Library of Boston (Massachusetts), Herr Braus-Riggenbach (Basel), Dr. A. Einstein, Herr H. Eisemann (London), Dr. Elmer of the Library of Prague University, Frau Floersheim-Koch (Florence), Herr Karl Geigy-Hagenbach (Basel), Dr. Karl Geiringer of the Bibliothek der Gesellschaft der Musikfreunde (Vienna), Herr Paul Gottschalk (Berlin), Herr Otto Haas (London), Dr. Robert Haas of the Vienna National Library, Herr V. A. Heck (Vienna), Herr D. N. Heineman (Brussels), Herr Henri Hinrichsen (Leipzig), Mrs. Enid Lambart, Herr Rudolf Nydahl (Stockholm), Mr. C. B. Oldman, the Historical Society of Pennsylvania, the Pierpont Morgan Library (New York City), Dr. A. Rosenthal (London), Herr Scheurleer of the Gemeentemuseum (The Hague), Dr. Richard Strauss, Mr. W. Oliver Strunk of the Library of Congress (Washington), Herr Paul Wittgenstein (Vienna), for photostats or transcripts of autographs in their possession. I wish also to express my gratitude to Herr Ernst Boucke of the Prussian State Library (Berlin), Miss Muriel Clayton of the Victoria and Albert Museum, Herr Otto Erich Deutsch (Vienna), Herr Alfred Heidl of the Mozarteum (Salzburg), Mr. R. N. Carew Hunt, Dr. Georg Kinsky (Cologne), Mr. T. O. Mabbott (New York City), Mrs. H. S. M. Stuart, Frau Eva Thurner (Salzburg), Herr Stefan Zweig, for valuable information and assistance most generously given; to Professor Ludwig Schiedermair and Dr. Henry

G. Farmer, for kindly lending me printers' blocks for illustrations; to the Podestà of Bologna, Herr Max Hinrichsen of C. F. Peters Musikverlag (Leipzig), Herr Paul Hirsch (Cambridge), M. le Chef des Services Techniques et Commerciaux du Palais du Louvre (Paris), Städtisches Schlossmuseum (Mannheim), Mr. C. B. Oldman, J. Pierpont Morgan (New York City), Internationale Stiftung, Mozart Museum (Salzburg), Stift St. Peter (Salzburg), Städtisches Museum (Salzburg), for allowing me to reproduce portraits and engravings; to Dr. Alfred Einstein, Mr. C. B. Oldman and Mr. James Turner, for assistance in reading the proofs; and finally to Mr. Harold Macmillan, for his unfailing help and interest in the production of my edition.

EMILY ANDERSON

LONDON, 1938

INTRODUCTION TO THE
FIRST EDITION

It should not be necessary to offer any apology for an English edition of the letters of Mozart and his family. The only existing translations—and those almost exclusively of the composer's letters—are to be found in two collections, one by Lady Wallace[1] and the other by M. M. Bozman.[2] But since the appearance of the former, over seventy years ago, more than a hundred letters of Mozart alone have come to light; and during the last quarter of a century the even more numerous and lengthy letters of his father, Leopold Mozart, have nearly all been collected and published in the original language. The present work is based upon the standard German edition of the Mozart family correspondence by Professor Ludwig Schiedermair, who spent many years collecting and copying the existing documents, i.e. autographs and transcripts in museums, libraries and private collections.[3] This *Gesamtausgabe*, a veritable boon to students of Mozart's life and works, completely superseded all previous texts, which apart from the one attempt of Nohl to produce a separate edition of Mozart's letters,[4] are to be found chiefly in the early biographies of the composer by Nissen,[5] Holmes,[6] Jahn,[7] in a more recent work by Schurig,[8]

[1] Ludwig Nohl, *Mozarts Briefe*, 1st edition, Leipzig, 1864, translated by Lady Wallace. Two volumes, London, 1865. This collection contains 268 letters of Mozart only.

[2] Hans Mersmann, *Mozarts Briefe in Auswahl*, Berlin, 1922, translated by M. M. Bozman. J. M. Dent and Sons, 1928. This selection contains only 141 letters of Mozart and a few extracts from those of his father.

[3] Ludwig Schiedermair, *Die Briefe Mozarts und seiner Familie*, four volumes, Munich and Leipzig, 1914. The first two volumes contain Mozart's letters, the third and fourth volumes those of his father, mother, sister, wife and cousin. The material covers the period from 1762 to 1791. A fifth volume contains reproductions of all the known portraits of Mozart and his family, of friends, statesmen, musicians and so forth, with whom he was associated, and of various places and documents of interest.

[4] See n. 1. Nohl brought out in 1877 a second edition, which has 282 letters, an addition of 14.

[5] Georg Nikolaus von Nissen, *Biographie W. A. Mozarts*, Leipzig, 1828. This biography, upon which Nissen, Constanze Mozart's second husband, was engaged at the time of his death in 1826, and for which he had full access to all the family letters and documents, was brought out by his widow with the help of a certain Dr. Feuerstein of Pirna near Dresden.

[6] Edward Holmes, *Life of Mozart*, London, 1845, 2nd edition, 1878. (Reissued by J. M. Dent and Sons in Everyman's Library, 1921.) This excellent short biography which, however, is little more than a rearrangement of Nissen's material, gives full extracts in a readable translation from the letters quoted in his work.

[7] Otto Jahn, *Wolfgang Amadeus Mozart*. Four volumes, Leipzig, 1856–1859; 2nd edition in two volumes, 1867; 3rd edition by Hermann Deiters, 1889–1891; 4th edition, 1905–1907. Jahn consulted the autographs in the Mozarteum at Salzburg and made full use of the immense collection of letters which had been copied for Aloys Fuchs (1799–1853) and which was then in Vienna. The second edition was translated into English by Pauline D. Townsend, three volumes, London, 1882.

[8] Arthur Schurig, *Wolfgang Amadeus Mozart*, two volumes, Leipzig, 1913. Schurig went to the original sources, chiefly in Salzburg and Berlin, and although his work does not profess to be an edition of the Mozart family correspondence, he in some cases gives longer extracts from Leopold Mozart's early letters (including those to his Augsburg publisher, J. J. Lotter)

and in the miscellaneous compilations of Nottebohm,[1] Nohl[2] and Leitzmann.[3] Here for the first time the reader was provided with material which enabled him to trace the development of a great composer from his earliest years (the first letter of Leopold Mozart is dated October, 1762, when his son was six) through his apprenticeship abroad to his triumphs and struggles and premature death in Vienna (Mozart's last letter is dated October, 1791).

But invaluable as is this contribution of Schiedermair to musical literature, a careful study of the correspondence and more particularly of the autographs soon led to the conviction that the proper arrangement of the material was one which would conform as far as possible to the order in which the letters were originally written. The present edition, therefore, observes a strictly chronological method, beginning with the first letters of Leopold Mozart from Vienna in 1762 and continuing up to Mozart's death in 1791.[4] Such a rearrangement has the following advantages. In the first place, as there are very few gaps in the correspondence, which covers almost the whole of Mozart's life, and forms, as it were, a continuous journal, the reader is presented with the primary sources for a biographical study. Secondly, as the Mozart family were inveterate letter-writers and indulged in a very full interchange of information and ideas (indeed most of Leopold Mozart's letters and some of Mozart's extend almost to the length of pamphlets), certain letters cannot be properly understood unless they are read in close connection with those to which they are the replies. Thirdly, as postage fees were at that time a heavy expense, Mozart, when travelling with his father or his mother, rarely troubled to write a separate

than does Schiedermair, and in many cases fuller notes. On the other hand, the spelling and punctuation are modernised, whereas in this respect Schiedermair's edition aims at an exact reproduction of the original documents. A second edition of Schurig's biography, in a smaller format, appeared in 1923.

[1] Gustav Nottebohm, *Mozartiana*, Leipzig, 1880. This little work is based upon unpublished material (not seen by Jahn) sent by Mozart's widow and sister in 1799 to the publishers Breitkopf and Härtel for a biography which was to have been written by Johann Friedrich Rochlitz (1769–1842), editor of the *Allgemeine Musikalische Zeitung*, who had met Mozart at Leipzig in 1789. It contains 42 new letters of Mozart, written chiefly during his last years in Vienna.

[2] Ludwig Nohl, *Mozart nach den Schilderungen seiner Zeitgenossen*, Leipzig, 1880. It contains one or two unpublished letters of Mozart and gives some long extracts from those of his father.

[3] Albert Leitzmann, *Mozarts Briefe*, Leipzig, 1910, a selection, based entirely on Jahn's copies of the letters in the Preussische Staatsbibliothek, Berlin. In 1926 Leitzmann brought out a work on Mozart (*Wolfgang Amadeus Mozarts Leben in seinen Briefen und Berichten der Zeitgenossen*, Leipzig, 1926), rather on the lines of Nohl's miscellany, for which he used Schiedermair's edition of the correspondence.

[4] It should be added that, like Schiedermair's edition, the present work is limited to the period of Mozart's life, 1756–1791. Thus none of Leopold Mozart's letters to J. J. Lotter of Augsburg, 1755–1756, regarding the publication of his *Versuch einer gründlichen Violinschule*, are included. For these the reader must be referred to the two editions of Schurig's biography (see p. xi, n. 8). On the other hand, as the title-page indicates, the present edition contains long extracts from letters written by Constanze Mozart to the Offenbach publisher, J. A. André, which are of special interest as dealing with the sale and publication of her late husband's musical manuscripts. [These letters have been omitted from the second edition. See p. v.].

letter, but either continued the letter which one of his parents had begun or added a postscript, or contented himself with scribbling a few lines inside the cover. Occasionally the reverse procedure was adopted; Mozart would begin the letter, and his father or his mother would finish it. Sometimes too, Mozart would take up the last words of the previous writer, use them as a theme for a variation[1] or even treat them as a peg on which to hang some comic remark.[2] In preparing this work one of the chief aims of the editor has been to present the letters as far as possible exactly as they were written.

It is hardly necessary to point out that the main purpose of this edition is to provide a complete collection of all the extant letters of Mozart himself, and that these have been treated with the same reverent care as one would treat the musical autographs of this great composer. The editor, therefore, has given every letter of Mozart in its entirety—in some cases for the first time.[3] At this point it may be appropriate to mention that Mozart's singularly outspoken letters to his cousin, Maria Anna Thekla, the so-called 'Bäslebriefe', now appear in an unexpurgated form. Even in Germany an excessive prudishness or possibly a certain unwillingness to admit that the writer, formerly regarded as the Raphael or the Watteau of music, should have been capable of expressing himself with such grossness, has hitherto prevented their publication in toto. A study of the whole correspondence, however, shows clearly that it was not only when writing to his 'Bäsle' that Mozart indulged in this particular kind of coarseness, but that on occasion he did so when writing to his mother[4] and to his sister; and that certainly his mother[5] and very probably the whole family and indeed many of their Salzburg friends were given to these indelicate jests.

In the case of Leopold Mozart's letters, however, a different method had to be adopted. Mozart's father was an indefatigable correspondent, a collector of information, a keeper of lists and diaries, who was forever exhorting his children to do likewise. Realising from the very first that his son was a genius and proposing some day to write his biography,[6] he not only kept so-called 'travel notes', most of which have been preserved,[7]

---

[1] e.g. Letters 212, 212a; 232, 232a; 249, 249a.

[2] e.g. Letters 79, 79a; 271b, 271c.

[3] For particulars of the hitherto unpublished letters or portions of letters see the List of Letters, p. xxi ff. In a few cases the only existing versions are those given by Nissen, whose ruthless manipulation of the autographs he used is well known to Mozart scholars. Facsimile no. 2 affords an example of this treatment. It is fortunate that the original documents handled by Nissen and showing the heavy strokes of his quill, are slowly coming to light.

[4] e.g. Letter 278, which is now published in its entirety. The only extant version is a copy made by Nottebohm, who must have received the autograph or perhaps only a transcript of the letter from Breitkopf and Härtel. See p. xii, n. 1.

[5] See especially Letters 209a, 214b, 219c.   [6] See Letter 51, p. 77.

[7] They have been edited by Arthur Schurig: Leopold Mozarts Reiseaufzeichnungen, 1763-1771. Dresden, 1920. The entries, a few of which were made by Mozart himself, have been transcribed and annotated, several being reproduced in facsimile.

but sent off to his landlord and later to his wife full descriptions of the countries he visited, the eminent persons he met and, not least, the triumphs of his two prodigies and of Wolfgang in particular.[1] It is possible, indeed, to trace four distinct periods in Leopold Mozart's correspondence. First of all, we have the very long letters to his landlord, Johann Lorenz Hagenauer, which give detailed accounts of his travels (1762–1768), of the courts at which his children performed, of the strange customs and habits of other nations, but which, apart from an occasional allusion to the feats of his children, couched in the language of the exultant showman, contain little matter of musical interest. Next, we have the letters written to his wife during the three journeys to Italy (1769–1773), letters which, as they were addressed to someone who shared these interests, give a most vivid description of the musical atmosphere and the social conditions prevailing in Rome, Bologna, Naples and Milan. Then a third period opens with his letters to his son, who, accompanied by his mother, has left Salzburg and gone off to seek his fortune elsewhere. These letters, particularly when they are read together with the replies from Mozart and his mother, are of very great interest. The reader finds himself at once absorbed in the most fascinating problem of the relations between father and son. In the first letters from Mozart we can almost hear his sigh of relief at having escaped from the oppressive atmosphere of the Archbishop's court and the cramping influence of an over-methodical, rather pedantic and perhaps a little too inquisitive parent; and we note his delight in his newly found freedom and his disinclination to trouble about the future. Very soon we detect in his father's letters an anxiety, a certain suspicion almost amounting to distrust, which, when he hears of his son's friendship with the Weber family, suddenly flares up in a blaze of bitter indignation and exasperation. Mozart, whose moral emancipation from his father is by this time almost complete, conceals nothing and continues to write with perfect frankness. Yet we see that a link has been broken and that behind his reluctance to accept an appointment in the Archbishop's service after his mother's death and his lamentable failure to establish himself in Paris, there lurks a kind of horror at the prospect of returning to his father's home. At the same time their all-absorbing interest in music provided a bond which was never broken. However much Mozart might feel that in other respects he was being misunderstood, in all matters relating to his art his father for many years continued to be his guide, philosopher and friend. Thus we have the illuminating correspondence about the composition of *Idomeneo*, (1780/81), which, as a revelation of a composer's method of dealing with his text and adjusting his work to the shortcomings of his singers, is almost unique in musical literature. And that he still regarded

---

[1] By order of Leopold Mozart all his letters were kept and numbered, doubtless with a view to their being used for the biography he intended to write. See Letter 77, p. 108.

his father as a friend to whom he could always unburden himself about his one passionate interest, is proved by his letters to him in regard to the composition of *Die Entführung aus dem Serail* (1781/82) and his struggles with Varesco's somewhat thankless libretto for *L'Oca del Cairo* (1783).[1] We now come to the fourth period of Leopold Mozart's correspondence (1784–1787), that is, the letters written to his daughter after her marriage.[2] These letters, while they throw much light on the worthy and rather lovable character of the writer and tell us a good deal about life in Salzburg and the comings and goings of its strange Archbishop, are on the whole of little value to the student of Mozart's life and works. For, after his final break with Salzburg and especially after his marriage to Constanze Weber in 1782, Mozart's relations with his father had become decidedly cool. The latter, it is true, still took an interest in his son's concerts, in the performances of his operas and above all in his latest compositions, some of which were duly sent off to Salzburg. But, partly on account of the estrangement which had arisen and partly owing to Mozart's own busy life which left him little time for letter-writing, Leopold Mozart, except when he encloses a letter or quotes a passage from one he has just received from Vienna, rarely refers to the doings of his son.

It soon became obvious to the editor that if Mozart was to form the centre of interest of this work and if the whole material was to be limited to three volumes, large portions of Leopold Mozart's letters, particularly of those belonging to the first and fourth periods, would have to be omitted.[3] At this point one important discovery in regard to the letters which Leopold Mozart wrote to his landlord while on his travels during the years 1762–1768, should be mentioned. As far as is known, the autographs of these letters have disappeared; but copies of them, apparently without any omissions, have been preserved in the Prussian State Library, Berlin. When checking these letters for the purpose of my edition, Herr E. Boucke, an assistant in the library, came upon the complete versions of long letters written by Leopold Mozart during the family's stay in Paris and London, 1763–1766, which appear to have been hitherto either

[1] Leopold Mozart's letters to his son after the latter's removal to Vienna in March 1781 have not been preserved. Possibly they were lost during Mozart's many moves. It is highly improbable that, as has been frequently suggested, Constanze Mozart destroyed them on account of their supposed allusions to freemasonry. She carefully kept far more outspoken and compromising letters of Mozart, which she either bequeathed to her eldest son or sent to Breitkopf and Härtel. Moreover, the letters of Mozart's sister, who appears to have written to him pretty frequently during his first years in Vienna, have also not come down to us.

[2] These 125 letters, for the most part previously unpublished, have recently been edited by O. E. Deutsch and B. Paumgartner, *Leopold Mozarts Briefe an seine Tochter*, Salzburg and Leipzig, 1936.

[3] It will be seen that only extracts have been given of nearly all these letters. In performing this pruning operation, the principle followed has been that of removing all purely extraneous and irrelevant matter, such as local gossip, rather tiresome descriptions of illnesses, long lists of greetings and so forth.

unknown or entirely neglected. This is, to say the least, surprising, for the London letters especially contain a most vivid and entertaining description of London life at that period, rivalling in its personal note the contemporary accounts of such well-known travellers as Pastor Moritz, Wendeborn and Grosley. Needless to say, it was with considerable reluctance that the editor decided to 'cut' this new material.[1]

In regard to the letters of Mozart's mother, all of which were written when she was accompanying him on his visits to Munich, Augsburg, Mannheim and Paris in search of work, it was thought advisable to give these in their entirety.[2] For, as will be seen, mother and son usually wrote on one sheet of paper; and hers are either hastily written postscripts or passages inserted in the body of Mozart's letters. Moreover, they are artless and often amusing; and their very outspokenness, verging occasionally on coarseness, throws fresh light on the home atmosphere in which Mozart grew up and explains to a certain extent a peculiar side of his nature which many readers of his letters have difficulty in connecting with the exquisite delicacy of his music.[3] On the other hand, some portions of the letters of Mozart's sister have been omitted. In the matter of letter-writing Nannerl proved to be an apt pupil of her father and, judging by the few letters which have been preserved, must have adopted his methods,[4] such as keeping a full diary of her own doings, drawing up lists of Salzburg theatrical performances and so forth.[5]

That Mozart wrote many more letters than we possess is evident from the leanness of certain years—notably the period from August 1784, the time of his sister's marriage and removal to St. Gilgen, to May 1787, the time of his father's death, for which many of the composer's letters are missing.[6] We know also, from references here and there, that other letters

---

[1] It is proposed to publish these letters in full in a separate volume, which will contain other interesting matter relating to the Mozarts' visit to England. [This proposal was never carried out.]

[2] Apart from a few sentences quoted in Eric Blom's biography of Mozart (Dent's Master Musicians series, 1935), pp. 70, 84 and 85, none of these letters have so far been translated into English.

[3] The following postscript (Letter 209a) is a specimen of Frau Mozart's grammar, spelling and punctuation: 'Von Neuigkeiten hat mir der wolfgang nichts übriggelassen, ich hoffe von dir bald einen brief zu bekomen, und mit freuden zu vernehmen, das du dich gesund befindest. wür seind gott lob wohlauf, und winschen nichts andres als das du bey uns wehrest, welches mit der hilf gottes geschehen wird, sey nur indessen ohne sorge, und schlage dir alle verdrüsslichkeiten aus dem Sinn, es wird schon alles recht werden, wann die haffel daran Komen. wür führen ein charmantes leben, früh auf spath ins beth, den ganzen dag haben wür visiten adio ben mio leb gesund, Rick den arsch zum mund. ich winsch ein guete nacht, scheiss ins beth das Kracht, es ist schon über einns. jezt kanst selber Reimen.

    an meine liebe sallerl
Catherl, nanerl bimberl alles erdenkliches.'   MARIA ANNA MOZARTIN

[4] See Letter 222, pp. 317 f.

[5] See Letter 415, p. 751, where Mozart describes his sister as 'the living chronicle of Salzburg'.

[6] It is difficult to account for the disappearance of these documents, some of which Leopold Mozart enclosed in his own letters to his daughter, who carefully kept all her father's letters (now in the Mozarteum, Salzburg). Possibly she returned them after 1787 to her brother, who may have mislaid or even destroyed them during one of his numerous moves. See Abert, vol. ii, pp. 1035 f.

must have been written. For example, a letter sent to his wife from Berlin in May 1789 (Letter 565) mentions eleven letters to her, four of which have been lost. Again, the bibliography of Nissen's Life of Mozart (Appendix, p. 217) contains the startling entry: Mozarts Briefe an die Duschek, 1781. It is extremely probable too that Mozart corresponded with the singer Anna Storace after her return to London in March 1787, the more so as at that time he was seriously contemplating a visit to England. Then there are the 'two interesting letters to Frau von Trattner about music', which Constanze Mozart mentions in a letter to Breitkopf and Härtel of November 27th, 1799,[1]—truly an irreparable loss. Yet, as new letters of Mozart are slowly coming to light, there are grounds for hope that one day some of these hidden treasures may be recovered.

It should be mentioned that the present edition does not include two letters frequently ascribed to Mozart which are of very doubtful authenticity.

(1) A letter written in 1789 to a certain Baron von P., the autograph of which is supposed to have been in the possession of Moscheles, and in which Mozart describes his method of composition. It was first published by Friedrich Rochlitz in the *Allgemeine Musikalische Zeitung*, xvii, cols. 561 ff. of 1815, and soon made its appearance in English and French reviews. From internal evidence the letter is obviously a forgery. Jahn (1st ed., vol. iii, pp. 496 ff.) treats it as such; and Nohl, although he includes it in his edition of Mozart's letters (2nd ed., pp. 441 ff.), confesses that it is spurious. Holmes, who reproduces it in his *Life of Mozart* (Everyman edition, 1921, pp. 254 ff.), does not question its authenticity, which probably explains why it has been quoted *ad nauseam* in English popular biographies. It is not included in Schiedermair's edition of the letters.[2]

(2) A short letter in Italian which Mozart is supposed to have written in September 1791 to Lorenzo da Ponte. It is included in Schiedermair's edition, vol. ii, p. 350.[3] But after careful consideration the editor decided to reject this letter on the following grounds: (*a*) the only extant version is a transcript in the Prussian State Library, Berlin, which has no signature and mentions no addressee[4]: (*b*) the internal evidence, namely, the indication of extreme depression at a time when Mozart, though in poor health, was feeling unusually stimulated and exhilarated, is a strong argument against its being a genuine document.

A few words may be necessary in regard to the treatment of the text of Mozart's letters. As has already been stated, it has been the editor's aim to

---

[1] Quoted in Nottebohm, *Mozartiana*, p. 131. Frau von Trattner was Mozart's pupil on the piano. He dedicated to her his C minor Fantasia and Sonata (K. 475 and 457).

[2] See Schiedermair, vol. ii, p. 378, n. 308 [and O. E. Deutsch, 'Spurious Mozart Letters', *Music Review*, May 1964].

[3] Nohl in his edition of Mozart's letters (2nd ed., pp. 463 f.) prints it, undated, as being the last extant letter of the composer, adding that Ludwig von Köchel discovered it in London.

[4] The transcript has the following remark in the same handwriting: In the possession of Mr Young in London.

reproduce these as faithfully as possible. Several letters, however, contain rhymed passages, either written out as verse or concealed in prose, which, if the rhyming is to be retained and the full flavour of the original preserved, defy a literal translation. Here some sort of compromise was inevitable. Again, Mozart, who was a very spontaneous letter-writer and nearly always wrote in a great hurry, frequently indulges in colloquialisms and slang, which the editor, while avoiding passing fashions of speech of the present day, has endeavoured to render into the equivalent English phraseology. Mozart's extreme liveliness and haste are reflected too in his punctuation. Very often whole letters are a series of sentences strung together by dashes. As a slavish adherence in this respect to the originals would have produced pages wearisome to the eye of the reader, the letters have been punctuated more normally and the dashes retained only when the sense demands it. The same remark applies to Mozart's lavish use of brackets, which in many cases have been replaced by commas.

Another textual peculiarity, which characterises almost the whole correspondence, requires some explanation. After the accession of Hieronymus Colloredo to the Archbishopric of Salzburg in March 1772 (and indeed intermittently during the reign of his predecessor) the Mozart family made occasional use of a simple substitution cypher (certain letters of the alphabet being replaced by others) in order to be able to express their opinions freely.[1] They adopted this device because they had good reason for believing that before their letters were delivered, the Salzburg post office sent them to the Archbishop's residence for inspection.[2] In the present translation the words, phrases and passages which in the autographs are in cypher, have been enclosed in angular brackets.[3]

To the critic who may complain that there is too much annotation, the reply is that the fullness is due to the editor's desire to remedy a defect of the German *Gesamtausgabe*, that is, to throw more light on the circumstances of Mozart's life, to recapture as far as possible the atmosphere in which he composed and to revive the forgotten or only half-remembered musicians, singers, artists, writers and men and women of note, with whom he came in contact.[4]

As to the value of Mozart's letters, their spontaneousness, their wit, their extreme gaiety, their profound poignancy, their humanity and time-

---

[1] Facsimile no. 5 affords an example of this cypher, of which the key is: for the letters m, l, o, f, h, a, e, s, i, u substitute the letters a, e, s, i, u, m, l, o, f, h. In most cases Nissen has written the solution above the encyphered passage.

[2] That this suspicion was well founded is proved by an incident described in a letter from Leopold Mozart to his daughter, 19 January 1786. See Deutsch-Paumgartner, *Leopold Mozarts Briefe an seine Tochter*, 1936, pp. 241 ff.

[3] e.g. Letter 172, p. 228.

[4] For a criticism of Schiedermair's sparse annotation of the correspondence see A. Schurig in *Mozarteums Mitteilungen*, November 1919, pp. 7–9, and E. K. Blümml, *Aus Mozarts Freundes- und Familienkreis*, Leipzig, 1923, p. vii.

lessness, there is nothing fresh to say. But long association with Mozart as a letter-writer has not failed to open up certain trains of thought which it may be of interest to indicate. In the first place, there is the strange fact that, with few exceptions, nearly all Mozart's letters are addressed to members of his family, and that, as far as we know, he never wrote to any composer or musician.[1] Then, singular as the comparison may seem, in many of his letters Mozart, while expressing himself in words, seems in reality to be thinking in terms of music.[2] Thus when we come upon passages which are curiously involved, words written backwards, phrases reversed, and other similar oddities of expression, we remember his description of how on a certain occasion he extemporised fugues on a given theme in a minor key, playing all kinds of tricks with it, reversing it, turning it into the major and so forth.[3] Again, when we take up one of Mozart's autograph letters, many of which are untidily written, larded with erasures and splashed with ink-blots, and suddenly find him weaving delicate scrolls and fantastic flourishes round a capital,[4] we remember certain themes, upon which he has embroidered a wealth of variations, deliciously interlaced and flawless in texture.[5] Then again when he describes in such masterly fashion the Langenmantels, the Auernhammers, Wieland, Grimm, and gives us the long gallery of pen-portraits with which we are familiar, we remember that these are only the rough sketches for the Don Alfonsos, the Basilios and the Marcellinas which later on will be immortalised by his music. Indeed, though the letters we possess only make us wish for more, we have here the substance of what Mozart thought about music, his ideas on the training of a pianist, his profound knowledge of the art of the singer and, if we collect the relevant passages, some indication of his own method of composition. As an autobiography their value is, if anything, greater than that of the letters of other composers, such as Beethoven, Schumann and Wagner. Lastly, it is no exaggeration to say that from a psychological and personal point of view, Mozart's letters bear comparison with those of the great letter-writers of the world.

[1] Letter 529, addressed to Joseph Haydn, is simply the dedication of his six quartets.

[2] This statement is supported by Mozart's own account of how he composed the prelude while writing down the three-part fugue of K. 394 [383a]. See Letter 447.

[3] See Letter 228b, p. 339.   [4] See Letter 236, p. 358, n. 2.

[5] e.g., the last movement of the piano concerto in C minor (K. 491), the Andante of the quintet in E♭ (K. 614), and the Andante of the divertimento in E♭ (K. 563).

LIST OF LETTERS

Owing to exigencies of space, in most cases extracts only have been given
of Leopold Mozart's letters.

VOLUME I

1762

LIST OF LETTERS

1765

1768

1770

1770

1772

1773

LIST OF LETTERS

1773

LIST OF LETTERS

1777

1777

LIST OF ABBREVIATIONS
(from the original edition)

Abert = Hermann Abert, *W. A. Mozart.* 2 volumes. Revised edition. Leipzig, 1923–1924.

AMZ = *Allgemeine Musikalische Zeitung* (Oct. 1798–Dec. 1848).

Blümml = Emil Karl Blümml, *Aus Mozarts Freundes- und Familienkreis.* Vienna, 1923.

Jahn = Otto Jahn, *Wolfgang Amadeus Mozart.* 4 volumes. Leipzig, 1856–1859.

Köchel = Dr. Ludwig Ritter von Köchel, *Chronologisch-thematisches Verzeichnis sämtlicher Tonwerke Wolfgang Amadé Mozarts.* 3rd edition, revised by Alfred Einstein. Leipzig, 1937.

Leitzmann = Albert Leitzmann, *Wolfgang Amadeus Mozarts Leben in seinen Briefen und Berichten der Zeitgenossen.* Leipzig, 1926.

MJ = *Mozart-Jahrbuch.* Herausgegeben von Hermann Abert. Munich, 1923–1924, and Augsburg, 1929.

MM = *Mozarteums Mitteilungen.* Zentralausschuss der Mozart-Gemeinde in Salzburg. November, 1918–May, 1921.

MMB = *Mitteilungen für die Mozartgemeinde in Berlin.* Herausgegeben von Rudolf Genée, 1895–1921.

Niemetschek = Franz Niemetschek, *Leben des K. K. Kapellmeisters Wolfgang Gottlieb Mozart.* Prague, 1798. (Reprinted Prague, 1905.)

Nissen = Georg Nikolaus von Nissen, *Biographie W. A. Mozarts.* Leipzig, 1828.

Nohl = Ludwig Nohl, *Mozarts Briefe.* 2nd edition. Leipzig, 1877.

Nottebohm = Gustav Nottebohm, *Mozartiana.* Leipzig, 1880.

Schiedermair = Ludwig Schiedermair, *Die Briefe Mozarts und seiner Familie.* 4 volumes. Munich and Leipzig, 1914.

Schurig = Arthur Schurig, *Wolfgang Amadeus Mozart.* 2 volumes. 2nd edition. Leipzig, 1923.

WSF = T. de Wyzewa et G. de Saint-Foix, *W. A. Mozart. Sa vie musicale et son œuvre de l'enfance à la pleine maturité, 1756–1777.* 2 volumes. Paris, 1912. The third volume of this epoch-making study of Mozart's musical development, which covers the years 1777–1783, was brought out by M. de Saint-Foix in 1936.

ZMW = *Zeitschrift für Musikwissenschaft.*

LIST OF THE PRINCIPAL BOOKS AND PERIODICALS
CONCERNING MOZART, PUBLISHED SINCE 1938

MOZART. Briefe und Aufzeichnungen. Gesamtausgabe. Gesammelt und erläutert von Wilhelm A. Bauer und Otto Erich Deutsch. 6 vols. *Kassel*, 1962 ff.

BRIEFE WOLFGANG AMADEUS MOZARTS. Herausgegeben mit Originalbriefen in Lichtdruck von Erich H. Müller von Asow. 5 vols. *Berlin*, 1942.

WOLFGANG AMADEUS MOZART. Briefwechsel und Aufzeichnungen. Gesamtausgabe herausgegeben von Hedwig und E. H. Müller von Asow. 2 vols. *Lindau in Bodensee*, 1949.

NANNERL MOZARTS Tagebuchblätter, mit Eintragungen ihres Bruders Wolfgang Amadeus. Vorgelegt und bearbeitet von Walter Hummel. *Stuttgart* [1958].

ACTA MOZARTIANA. Mitteilungen der deutschen Mozart-Gesellschaft. *Augsburg*, 1954–

BADURA-SKODA, EVA and PAUL. Mozart-Interpretation, etc. *Wien* [1957].

— Interpreting Mozart on the Keyboard. Translated by Leo Black. *London*, 1962.

DENNERLEIN, HANNS. Der unbekannte Mozart: die Welt seiner Klavierwerke. *Leipzig*, 1951.

DEUTSCH, OTTO ERICH. Mozart. Die Dokumente seines Lebens. Gesammelt und erläutert von O. E. Deutsch. *Kassel*, 1961.

— Mozart und seine Welt in zeitgenössischen Bildern. Begründet von Maximilian Zenger, vorgelegt von O. E. Deutsch. *Kassel*, 1961.

EINSTEIN, ALFRED. Mozart, his Character, his work. Translated by Arthur Mendel and Nathan Broder. *New York*, 1945.

— 2nd edition. *London*, 1956.

GIRDLESTONE, CUTHBERT MORTON. Mozart et ses concertos pour piano. *Paris*, 1939.

— Mozart's Piano Concertos. 2nd edition. *London*, 1958.

HOESLI, IRMA. Wolfgang Amadeus Mozart. Briefstil eines Musikgenies. *Zürich*, 1948.

HUTCHINGS, ARTHUR. A Companion to Mozart's Piano Concertos. Second edition. *London*, 1950.

KÖCHEL, LUDWIG *Ritter von*. Chronologisch-thematisches Verzeichnis sämtlicher Tonwerke Wolfgang Amade Mozarts. 6. Auflage. *Wiesbaden*, 1964.

KOMORZYNSKI, EGON VON. Der Vater der Zauberflöte. Emanuel Schikaneders Leben. *Wien*, 1948.

— Emanuel Schikaneder. Ein Beitrag zur Geschichte des deutschen Theaters. *Wien* [1951].

LANDON, HOWARD CHANDLER ROBBINS, and MITCHELL, DONALD (editors). The Mozart Companion. *London*, 1956.

MEDICI DI MARIGNANO, NERINA. A Mozart Pilgrimage. Being the travel diaries of Vincent & Mary Novello in the year 1829. Transcribed and compiled by N. Medici di Marignano. Edited by Rosemary Hughes. *London*, 1955.

MITTEILUNGEN DER INTERNATIONALEN STIFTUNG MOZARTEUM. (Ed. Géza Rech.) *Salzburg*, 1952–

MOZART-JAHRBUCH. 1950 [to date]. Herausgegeben von der Internationalen Stiftung Mozarteum. [Including, in most issues, a list of books and articles on Mozart.] *Salzburg*, 1950–

NEUES MOZART-JAHRBUCH. Im Auftrage des Zentral-Instituts für Mozartforschung am Mozarteum Salzburg herausgegeben von Erich Valentin. *Regensburg*, 1941–43.

SAINT-FOIX, COUNT GEORGES DE. W. A. Mozart. Sa vie musicale et son œuvre. IV. 1784–1788. V. 1789–1791. *Paris*, 1939, 1946.

SCHENK, ERICH. Wolfgang Amadeus Mozart. Eine Biographie. *Zürich*, 1955.

— Mozart and his Times. [Abridged translation.] Edited and translated by Richard & Clara Winston. *London*, 1960.

SCHENK, ERICH (editor). Bericht über den Internationalen Musikwissenschaftlichen Kongress Wien, Mozart Jahr 1956. *Graz*, 1958.

SCHNEIDER, OTTO, and ALGATZY, ANTON. Mozart-Handbuch. Chronik-Werk-Bibliographie. *Wien*, 1962.

TABLE OF MONEY VALUES

THE following table has been compiled from information contained in Muret-Sanders's German-English Dictionary, in Professor W. H. Bruford's *Germany in the Eighteenth Century* (Cambridge, 1935), p. 329 f., and in the letters of Leopold Mozart, who frequently quotes the equivalent values of foreign coins and the fluctuating rates of exchange between the various German states. As there were several standards in common use for the minting of silver coins during the latter half of the eighteenth century, the values here given are of necessity only approximate.

GERMANY AND AUSTRIA

Taking the South German kreuzer (worth 4 pfennige, slightly more than the English farthing) as the standard, the following equivalent values of silver coins are obtained:

60 kreuzer (or 16 groschen) = 1 gulden, about two shillings.
90 kreuzer (or 24 groschen) = 1 reichsthaler, about three shillings.
120 kreuzer (or 32 groschen) = 1 laubthaler or federthaler, about four shillings.

The following gold coins were in common use in Germany and Austria:

1 ducat (used all over Europe) = $4\frac{1}{2}$ gulden, about nine shillings.
1 max d'or (used chiefly in Bavaria) = $6\frac{1}{4}$ gulden, about thirteen shillings.
1 friedrich d'or (used chiefly in Prussia) = 8 gulden, about sixteen shillings.
1 pistole (used all over Europe) = $7\frac{1}{2}$ gulden, about fifteen shillings.
1 carolin (used chiefly in Southern Germany) = 9 gulden, about eighteen shillings.
1 souverain d'or (used chiefly in Austria) = $13\frac{1}{2}$ gulden, about twenty-seven shillings.

FRANCE

4 liard = 4 sous = about half-penny.
20 sous = 1 livre, about eleven pence.
1 louis d'or = 24 livres, about twenty shillings.

ITALY

1 paolo (a silver coin of Tuscany, worth originally about 56 centesimi, and used as the equivalent of half a lira) = about sixpence.
1 cigliato (or, more commonly, gigliato) = a ducat, about nine shillings.
1 zecchino (a Venetian gold coin) = about nine shillings.
1 doppio = probably a doppio zecchino, about twenty shillings.

HOLLAND

1 rijder[1] = about twenty-eight shillings.

[1] Leopold Mozart calls this coin a 'reitter'. See p. 62.

LIST OF ILLUSTRATIONS

VOLUME I

LIST OF FACSIMILES OF LETTERS

The first journey, undertaken without Frau Mozart, was to Munich, where Leopold Mozart performed with his two children before the Elector Maximilian III. They were absent about three weeks, from 12 January to the beginning of February 1762. There are no letters describing this visit.

The second journey of Leopold Mozart, this time with his whole family, was to Vienna and lasted from 18 September 1762 to 5 January 1763. The children performed several times at the Imperial Court and at concerts arranged specially for them by the Viennese nobility and foreign diplomats. This visit, towards the end of which the family also went briefly to Pressburg, is described in a series of letters from Leopold Mozart to his landlord, Lorenz Hagenauer. Letters 1-9.

(1) *Leopold Mozart to Lorenz Hagenauer,*[1] *Salzburg*

[*Extract*]   [*Copy in the Deutsche Staatsbibliothek, Berlin*]

LINZ,[2] *3 October 1762*

YOU have been thinking, haven't you, that we are already in Vienna? But we are still in Linz. Tomorrow, God willing, we shall go on to Vienna by the so-called ordinary boat. Indeed we should certainly have been there already, had we not been obliged against our will to spend five whole days in Passau. This delay, for which His Grace the Bishop of Passau was responsible, has made me lose eighty gulden, which I should have made here if I had arrived sooner, whereas I must now content myself with forty odd gulden, which *deductis deducendis*[3] remain from the concert we gave the day before yesterday. But what really took place in Passau I must postpone to a personal conversation, as it would be too lengthy to relate here. Suffice it to say that Wolfgang, but not my little girl, had the privilege of performing before His Grace and that for this he received one whole ducat, i.e. exactly four gulden, ten kreuzer. But don't tell that to anyone. Meanwhile we pray that our Archbishop[4] may live long. More when we meet.

Now let me describe our journey a little. The 20th of last month we arrived at Passau at five o'clock in the evening and left next morning with the Canon, Count Herberstein, reaching Linz at five o'clock in the evening of the same day. We are staying with people called Kiener and are very well looked after. They are two spinsters who, since the death of their parents, have taken charge of the house and who are so fond of my children that they do everything they possibly can for us. I should add that my children, the boy especially, fill everyone with amazement. Count Herberstein has gone on to Vienna and will spread in advance a sensational report about them. And yesterday Count von Schlick, Captain-General of this district, left with his wife for Vienna. Both were uncommonly gracious to us. They said that, as soon as we reached Vienna, we must go to see them; meanwhile they would speak to Count Durazzo[5] and make our arrival generally known there. To judge by appearances, everything ought to go well. May God keep us well and strong as hitherto. So far we

[1] Johann Lorenz Hagenauer (1712–1799), a Salzburg merchant, was Leopold Mozart's landlord, banker and correspondent. The Mozart family occupied the third floor of his house (since 1880 a Mozart museum) in the Getreidegasse no. 9, until they moved in 1773 to a house on their own in the Makartplatz (now Alter Markt no. 2).

[2] The Mozart family, Leopold Mozart and his wife, Nannerl and Wolfgang, had left Salzburg on 18 September.

[3] i.e. with the necessary deductions.

[4] Count Sigismund von Schrattenbach, Archbishop of Salzburg, 1753–1772.

[5] Manager of the Opera House, Vienna.

are still in good health, although I occasionally feel here and there some little twinges of gout. The children are merry and behave everywhere as if they were at home. The boy is as intimate with everyone, especially with the officers, as if he had known them all his life. I enclose my draft for this month. Please have it cashed; the tax on it, amounting to ten kreuzer, three pfennig, will have to be paid. Take your rent out of it. I should like your wife, to whom especially we send most obedient greetings, to arrange for four Masses to be said on our behalf at Maria-Plain[1] and that as soon as possible. My little girl sends greetings and would like your dear wife to know that she kept her promise at Mariahilf[2] in Passau. Yes, we all prayed for Herr Lorenz. Otherwise you are all well, I hope? That is our heart's wish. We shall soon write to you from Vienna. Perhaps before we get there we shall have some news to send; so far there is none.

(2) *Leopold Mozart to Lorenz Hagenauer, Salzburg*

[*Extract*]   [*Autograph in the Mozarteum, Salzburg*]

[VIENNA, 16 *October* 1762]

On the feast of St. Francis[3] we left Linz at half past four in the afternoon by the so-called ordinary boat and reached Mauthausen after nightfall on the same day at half past seven. At noon on the following day, Tuesday, we arrived at Ybbs, where two Minorites and a Benedictine, who were with us on the boat, said Masses, during which our Woferl[4] strummed on the organ and played so well that the Franciscans, who happened to be entertaining some guests at their midday meal, left the table and with their company rushed to the choir and were almost struck dead with amazement. In the evening we reached Stein and on Wednesday at three in the afternoon arrived at Vienna; here at five o'clock we took our midday meal and supper at the same time. On the journey we had continual rain and a lot of wind. Wolfgang had already caught a cold in Linz, but in spite of our irregular life, early rising, eating and drinking at all hours, and wind and rain, he has, thank God, kept well. When we landed, Gilowsky's servant, who was already there, came on board and brought us to our lodgings. But after leaving our luggage safely and tidily there, we soon hurried off to an inn to appease our hunger. Gilowsky himself then came to welcome us. Now we have already been here five days and do not yet know where the sun rises in Vienna, for to this very hour it has done nothing but rain and, with constant wind, has snowed a little now and then, so that we have even seen some snow on the roofs. Moreover it has been and still is very frosty, though not excessively cold. One thing I must

---

[1] Pilgrimage church, about one and a half hours' walk from Salzburg.
[2] Pilgrimage church outside Passau.   [3] 4 October.   [4] Pet name for Wolfgang.

4

(1) *Leopold Mozart to Lorenz Hagenauer,*[1] *Salzburg*

[*Extract*]   [*Copy in the Deutsche Staatsbibliothek, Berlin*]

LINZ,[2] *3 October* 1762

YOU have been thinking, haven't you, that we are already in Vienna? But we are still in Linz. Tomorrow, God willing, we shall go on to Vienna by the so-called ordinary boat. Indeed we should certainly have been there already, had we not been obliged against our will to spend five whole days in Passau. This delay, for which His Grace the Bishop of Passau was responsible, has made me lose eighty gulden, which I should have made here if I had arrived sooner, whereas I must now content myself with forty odd gulden, which *deductis deducendis*[3] remain from the concert we gave the day before yesterday. But what really took place in Passau I must postpone to a personal conversation, as it would be too lengthy to relate here. Suffice it to say that Wolfgang, but not my little girl, had the privilege of performing before His Grace and that for this he received one whole ducat, i.e. exactly four gulden, ten kreuzer. But don't tell that to anyone. Meanwhile we pray that our Archbishop[4] may live long. More when we meet.

Now let me describe our journey a little. The 20th of last month we arrived at Passau at five o'clock in the evening and left next morning with the Canon, Count Herberstein, reaching Linz at five o'clock in the evening of the same day. We are staying with people called Kiener and are very well looked after. They are two spinsters who, since the death of their parents, have taken charge of the house and who are so fond of my children that they do everything they possibly can for us. I should add that my children, the boy especially, fill everyone with amazement. Count Herberstein has gone on to Vienna and will spread in advance a sensational report about them. And yesterday Count von Schlick, Captain-General of this district, left with his wife for Vienna. Both were uncommonly gracious to us. They said that, as soon as we reached Vienna, we must go to see them; meanwhile they would speak to Count Durazzo[5] and make our arrival generally known there. To judge by appearances, everything ought to go well. May God keep us well and strong as hitherto. So far we

---

[1] Johann Lorenz Hagenauer (1712–1799), a Salzburg merchant, was Leopold Mozart's land-lord, banker and correspondent. The Mozart family occupied the third floor of his house (since 1880 a Mozart museum) in the Getreidegasse no. 9, until they moved in 1773 to a house on their own in the Makartplatz (now Alter Markt no. 2).

[2] The Mozart family, Leopold Mozart and his wife, Nannerl and Wolfgang, had left Salzburg on 18 September.

[3] i.e. with the necessary deductions.

[4] Count Sigismund von Schrattenbach, Archbishop of Salzburg, 1753–1772.

[5] Manager of the Opera House, Vienna.

3

are still in good health, although I occasionally feel here and there some little twinges of gout. The children are merry and behave everywhere as if they were at home. The boy is as intimate with everyone, especially with the officers, as if he had known them all his life. I enclose my draft for this month. Please have it cashed; the tax on it, amounting to ten kreuzer, three pfennig, will have to be paid. Take your rent out of it. I should like your wife, to whom especially we send most obedient greetings, to arrange for four Masses to be said on our behalf at Maria-Plain[1] and that as soon as possible. My little girl sends greetings and would like your dear wife to know that she kept her promise at Mariahilf[2] in Passau. Yes, we all prayed for Herr Lorenz. Otherwise you are all well, I hope? That is our heart's wish. We shall soon write to you from Vienna. Perhaps before we get there we shall have some news to send; so far there is none.

(2) *Leopold Mozart to Lorenz Hagenauer, Salzburg*

[*Extract*]   [*Autograph in the Mozarteum, Salzburg*]

[VIENNA, 16 *October* 1762]

On the feast of St. Francis[3] we left Linz at half past four in the afternoon by the so-called ordinary boat and reached Mauthausen after nightfall on the same day at half past seven. At noon on the following day, Tuesday, we arrived at Ybbs, where two Minorites and a Benedictine, who were with us on the boat, said Masses, during which our Woferl[4] strummed on the organ and played so well that the Franciscans, who happened to be entertaining some guests at their midday meal, left the table and with their company rushed to the choir and were almost struck dead with amazement. In the evening we reached Stein and on Wednesday at three in the afternoon arrived at Vienna; here at five o'clock we took our midday meal and supper at the same time. On the journey we had continual rain and a lot of wind. Wolfgang had already caught a cold in Linz, but in spite of our irregular life, early rising, eating and drinking at all hours, and wind and rain, he has, thank God, kept well. When we landed, Gilowsky's servant, who was already there, came on board and brought us to our lodgings. But after leaving our luggage safely and tidily there, we soon hurried off to an inn to appease our hunger. Gilowsky himself then came to welcome us. Now we have already been here five days and do not yet know where the sun rises in Vienna, for to this very hour it has done nothing but rain and, with constant wind, has snowed a little now and then, so that we have even seen some snow on the roofs. Moreover it has been and still is very frosty, though not excessively cold. One thing I must

---

[1] Pilgrimage church, about one and a half hours' walk from Salzburg.
[2] Pilgrimage church outside Passau.   [3] 4 October.   [4] Pet name for Wolfgang.

make a point of telling you, which is, that we quickly got through the
local customs and were let off the chief customs altogether. And for this
we have to thank our Master Woferl. For he made friends at once with
the customs officer, showed him his clavier, invited him to visit us and
played him a minuet on his little fiddle. Thus we got through. The customs
officer asked most politely to be allowed to visit us and for this purpose
made a note of our lodgings. So far, in spite of the most atrocious weather,
we have been to a concert given by Count Collalto.[1] Further, Countess
Sinzendorf introduced us to Count Wilschegg[2] and on the 11th to His
Excellency the Imperial Vice-Chancellor, Count Colloredo, where we
were privileged to see and to speak to the leading ministers and ladies of
the Imperial Court, to wit, the Hungarian Chancellor, Count Palffy, and
the Bohemian Chancellor, Count Chotek, as well as Bishop Esterházy and
a number of persons, all of whom I could not note. All, the ladies especially,
were very gracious to us. Count Leopold Kühnburg's[3] fiancée spoke to
my wife[4] of her own accord and told her that she is going to be married
at Salzburg. She is a pretty, friendly woman, of medium height. She is
expecting her betrothed in Vienna very shortly. Countess Sinzendorf is
using her influence on our behalf, and all the ladies are in love with my
boy. We are already being talked of everywhere; and when on the 10th
I was alone at the opera,[5] I heard the Archduke Leopold[6] from his box say
a number of things to another box, namely, that there was a boy in
Vienna who played the clavier most excellently and so on. At eleven
o'clock that very same evening I received a command to go to Schönbrunn[7] on the 12th. But the following day there came a fresh command to
go there on the 13th instead, (the 12th being the Feast of Maximilian and
therefore a very busy gala-day), because, I gather, they want to hear the
children in comfort. Everyone is amazed, especially at the boy, and everyone whom I have heard says that his genius is incomprehensible. Baron
Schell is using his influence on my behalf and is gratefully acknowledging
the kindnesses he enjoyed at Salzburg. If you have an opportunity, please
tell this to Herr Chiusolis with my respects. Count Daun[8] also has given
me a note for Baron Schell and has filled me with hopes that I shall leave

---

[1] On 9 October. Deutsch: *Mozart, die Dokumente seines Lebens* (Kassel, 1961), p. 17, quotes
a passage from Count Karl Zinzendorf's unpublished diary mentioning this concert:
'At eight o'clock in the evening I fetched Lamberg and we went together to Collalto
where Madame Bianchi sang and a little boy of five and a half (Mozart) played the
clavier'.

[2] i.e. Wilczek.   [3] Chief Equerry in Salzburg.

[4] This passage disproves the statements made by Schurig, *L. Mozarts Reiseaufzeichnungen*,
p. 11, and Abert, vol. i. p. 38, that Mozart's mother did not accompany her family to Vienna.

[5] Gluck's *Orfeo*.

[6] Later Leopold II, Holy Roman Emperor, [1790–1792].

[7] The Imperial summer residence outside Vienna, modelled on Versailles, where Maria
Theresia preferred to live.

[8] Chief Equerry in Munich.

Vienna fully satisfied. And so it seems, since the Court is asking to hear us before we have announced ourselves. For young Count Palffy happened to be passing through Linz as our concert was about to begin. He was calling on the Countess Schlick, who told him about the boy and persuaded him to stop the mail coach in front of the town hall and attend the concert with her. He listened with astonishment and spoke later with great excitement of the performance to the Archduke Joseph,[1] who passed it on to the Empress. Thus, as soon as it was known that we were in Vienna, the command came for us to go to court. That, you see, is how it happened.

I wrote the above on the 11th, fully intending to tell you on the 12th, after our return from Schönbrunn, how everything had gone off. But we had to drive from Schönbrunn straight to Prince von Hildburghausen, and six ducats were more important to us than the despatch of my letter. I have sufficient confidence in Frau Hagenauer[2] and trust enough to her kind friendship to know that she will accept even now our congratulations on her name-day and even in the short form of merely saying that we shall ask God to keep her and all her loved ones well and strong for many years to come and to invite us all in due course to play cards in Heaven. Now all that I have time for is to say in great haste that Their Majesties received us with such extraordinary graciousness that, when I shall tell of it, people will declare that I have made it up. Suffice it to say that Woferl jumped up on the Empress's[3] lap, put his arms round her neck and kissed her heartily. In short, we were there from three to six o'clock and the Emperor[4] himself came out of the next room and made me go in there to hear the Infanta[5] play the violin. On the 15th the Empress sent us by the Privy Paymaster, who drove up to our house in state, two dresses, one for the boy and one for the girl. As soon as the command arrives, they are to appear at court and the Privy Paymaster will fetch them. Today at half past two in the afternoon they are to go to the two youngest Archdukes[6] and at four o'clock to the Hungarian Chancellor, Count Palffy. Yesterday we were with Count Kaunitz,[7] and the day before with Countess Kinsky and later with the Count von Ulefeld. And we already have more engagements for the next two days. Please tell everybody that, thank God, we are well and happy. I send greetings and I am your old   MOZART

[1] Later Joseph II, Holy Roman Emperor, (1765–1790).
[2] Frau Maria Theresa Hagenauer (1717–1800). Her name-day was on 15 October.
[3] Maria Theresia.
[4] Francis I.
[5] Princess Isabella, daughter of Philip, Duke of Parma. She died on 27 November 1763, three years after her marriage to the Archduke Joseph.
[6] Archduke Ferdinand (1754–1806), later Governor-General of Milan, and Archduke Maximilian (1756–1801), later Elector of Cologne.
[7] Wenzel Anton von Kaunitz-Rietburg (1711–1794), Austrian Chancellor, 1753–1792. He was a great amateur of music.

(3) *Leopold Mozart to Lorenz Hagenauer, Salzburg*

[*Extract*]   [*Copy in the Deutsche Staatsbibliothek, Berlin*]

VIENNA, 19 *October* 1762

You will have received my letter by the last post. This morning I was summoned to the Privy Paymaster, who received me with the greatest courtesy. His Majesty the Emperor wanted to know whether I could not remain in Vienna a little longer, and to this I replied that I was absolutely at His Majesty's disposal. The Paymaster then paid me a hundred ducats, adding that His Majesty would soon summon us again. From whatever point of view I consider it, I foresee that we shall hardly be home before Advent. But before then I shall send in my request for an extension of leave of absence.[1] For, even if I were able to leave here in two or three weeks, I must travel slowly on account of my children, so that they may rest now and then for a few days and not fall ill. I have put the Emperor's hundred ducats, as well as another twenty ducats, to your account with Herr Peisser.[2] If I can obtain a good carriage at a decent price, I have decided to purchase one in order to give the children greater comfort. Today we were at the French Ambassador's. Tomorrow we are invited to Count Harrach's from four to six, but which Count Harrach he is I do not know. I shall see where the carriage takes us to. For on every occasion we are fetched by a servant in the nobleman's carriage and are brought home again. From six or half past six to nine we are to perform for six ducats at a big concert which a certain rich nobleman is giving and at which the greatest virtuosi now in Vienna are going to perform. The nobles send us their invitations four, five, six to eight days in advance, in order not to miss us. For instance, the Chief Postmaster, Count Paar,[3] has already engaged us for next Monday. Woferl now gets enough driving, as he goes out at least twice a day. Once we drove out at half past two to a place where we stayed until a quarter to four. Count Hardegg then fetched us in his carriage and we drove in full gallop to a lady, at whose house we remained till half past five. Thence Count Kaunitz sent to fetch us and we stayed with him until about nine. I can hardly write, for both pen and ink are wretched and I must steal time to do so. I have absolutely no news to give you, as here they talk as little about the war,[4] as if there were no war. I have never in my life heard so little news or known as little as I have during these four or five weeks since I left Salzburg. I should like to hear some news from you; I hope at least that you will have something to tell me. Has His Grace[5] returned home already? I hope that

---

[1] At that time Leopold Mozart, second violin in the Archbishop's orchestra, was both instructor in the violin to the Kapellhaus and court composer.   [2] Banker in Vienna.
[3] Wenzel Johann Josef Paar (1719–1792), created Prince in 1769. His son Wenzel (1744–1812) was a friend and patron of Mozart during his last ten years in Vienna.
[4] The Seven Years' War (1756–1763).   [5] The Archbishop of Salzburg.

he is well. Is His Excellency Count Spaur[1] in Salzburg? He must be, I
think. I wrote to him from Linz. How is our worthy Father Confessor?[2]
When you can do so, please give him my most obedient greetings. I hope
that your wife and all your dear ones are in excellent health. I send her my
greetings. Do you know whom our Estlinger[3] came across? The innkeeper at Hellbrunn.[4] He had a long talk with him. But more important
still, do you know where I am living? In the Fierberggassl, not far from
the Hohe Brücke, on the first floor of the carpenter's house.[5] The room is
a thousand feet long and one foot wide. You laugh? But it is no laughing
matter for us when we tread on one another's corns. Still less is it a laughing matter when my boy throws me and the girl throws my wife out of
our wretched beds or when they dig us in our ribs, as they do every night.
Each of our beds is, I reckon, four and a half feet wide; and this amazingly
palatial dwelling is divided by a partition into two parts for each of these
large beds. But let us be patient! We are in Vienna. My wife would
like to have her lined fur. But we think it would cost too much to send it
by the mail coach and it might get spoilt in transit. It is in the chest in the
little room. But, as I intend to have a new one made for her in Salzburg
for the festival days, it would be better to buy something for her here,
where there is plenty of choice. Would you like to know what Woferl's
costume[6] is like? It is of the finest cloth, lilac in colour. The waistcoat is
of moiré, and of the same shade as the coat, and both coat and waistcoat
are trimmed with wide double gold braiding. It was made for the Archduke Maximilian.[7] Nannerl's[8] dress was the court dress of an Archduchess
and is of white broché taffeta with all kinds of trimmings. It is a pity that
we shall only be able to make a petticoat out of it. But it has a little bodice
too. My paper is at an end and there is no more time. Give my greetings
to everyone in Salzburg.

(4) *Leopold Mozart to Lorenz Hagenauer, Salzburg*

[Extract]   *[Copy in the Deutsche Staatsbibliothek, Berlin]*

[VIENNA, *30 October* 1762]

I was beginning to think that for fourteen days in succession we were
far too happy. God has sent us a small cross and we must thank His infinite

---

[1] Leopold Maria Josef Spaur, Bishop of Brixen and member of the Salzburg Cathedral
Chapter.
[2] Abbé Joseph Bullinger, tutor to the family of Count Arco and a lifelong friend of the
Mozart family.   [3] A music copyist in Salzburg.
[4] Schloss Hellbrunn, three miles to the south of Salzburg, was formerly the summer residence of the Archbishops.
[5] Leopold wrote 'Tischler-Hause', a corruption of the name of one Ditscher.
[6] Mozart was painted in this costume in 1762. The oil painting, in life size, by an unknown
artist, is now in the Mozart Museum, Salzburg. Archduke Maximilian (1756–1801) was the
same age as Mozart.   [7] See p. 6.
[8] Pet name for Maria Anna, Mozart's only sister, born 30 July 1751. She too was painted in
her costume.

goodness that things have turned out as they have. At seven o'clock in the evening of the 21st we again went to the Empress. Our Woferl, however, was not quite as well as usual and before we drove there and also as he was going to bed, he complained a good deal of his backside and his hips. When he got into bed, I examined the places where he said he had pain and found a few spots as large as a kreuzer, very red and slightly raised and painful to the touch. But they were only on his shins, on both elbows and a few on his posterior; altogether there were very few. He was feverish and we gave him a black powder [1] and a margrave powder; [2] but he had a rather restless night. On Friday we repeated the powders both morning and evening and we found that the spots had spread: but, although they were larger, they had not increased in number. We had to send messages to all the nobles, where we had engagements for the next eight days, and refuse for one day after another. We continued to give margrave powders and on Sunday Woferl began to perspire, as we wanted him to, for hitherto his fever had been more or less dry. I met the physician of the Countess von Sinzendorf (who happened to be away from Vienna) and gave him particulars. He at once came back with me and approved of what we had done. He said it was a kind of scarlet fever rash.

Thank God he is now so well that we hope that if not tomorrow, his name-day,[3] at least on the day after tomorrow he will get up for the first time. Also he has just cut a back tooth, which has made his left cheek swell. The nobles not only enquired most graciously every day about the condition of our boy, but talked about him a great deal to our physician; so that Dr. Bernhard (that is his name) could hardly be more attentive than he is. Meanwhile, this affair has cost me fifty ducats at least. But I am infinitely grateful to God that it has turned out so well. These scarlet fever spots, which are a fashionable complaint for children in Vienna, are dangerous and I hope that Woferl has now become acclimatized. For the change of air was the main cause of the trouble. Please give my most obedient respects to your wife and tell her that I must worry her again and ask her to be so kind as to arrange for three Masses to be said in Loreto[4] at the Holy Child and three Masses in Bergl[5] at S. Francisco de Paula.[6] I shall repay everything with thanks.

PS. I beg you to use every effort to ascertain what His Grace will do eventually and what hopes I may entertain of the post of Deputy

---

[1] *Pulvis epilepticus niger*, a common remedy at that time against all kinds of disorders.

[2] A remedy discovered by the German chemist Andreas Sigismund Marggraf (1709–1782).

[3] 31 October.

[4] Convent and church of St. Clara at Salzburg, founded in 1629.

[5] Pilgrimage church near Salzburg.

[6] St. Francis of Paula (1416–1508), Calabrian hermit and the founder of the Minims.

Kapellmeister.[1] I do not ask in vain; you are my friend. Who knows what I may do! If only I knew what the future will finally bring. For one thing is certain: I am now in circumstances which allow me to earn my living in Vienna also.

However I still prefer Salzburg to all other advantages. But I must not be kept back. Once more I beg you. For otherwise I myself don't know what I may let others persuade me to do.

(5) *Leopold Mozart to Lorenz Hagenauer, Salzburg*

[*Extract*]   [*Copy in the Deutsche Staatsbibliothek, Berlin*]

VIENNA, 6 *November* 1762

I have safely received all your kind letters, and I realize fully how much I owe to your active exertions! But I know what your friendship means. You were born to render kind services to your fellow-creatures and to prove that you are a really true friend. From my last letter you will have gathered in what danger my Woferl was and in what anxiety I was on his account. Thank God, all is well again! Yesterday we rewarded our good Dr. Bernhard with a concert. He invited a number of friends to his house and sent his carriage for us. On the 4th, the festival of St. Charles, I took Woferl for the first time for a drive to St. Charles's Church[2] and the Josefstadt.[3] It was a most beautiful day. Since our arrival here we have hardly had three or four such days. Tell me, have you too had such dreadful rain in Salzburg? Here it has already begun to snow and today we are having real April weather. My wife and I send our greetings to your wife and thank her for all she has done. My wife will soon reply to her letter; and little Woferl sends most dutiful thanks for the kind remembrance of his name-day. He would have been happier, it is true, if he had not been obliged to spend it in bed, though he was better. Some of the nobles sent their congratulations and enquiries after his health; but that was all. We had enquiries from Count Ferdinand Harrach, Count Palffy, the French Ambassador, the Countess von Kinsky, Baron Pechmann, Baron Kurz and the Countess von Paar.[4] If he had not been at home for almost a fortnight, he would have come in for some presents. Well, well! Now we must see that things begin to move again. Until this

---

[1] Leopold Mozart was at this time second violinist and court composer in the Archbishop's service. G. F. Lolli had just been promoted to the post of Kapellmeister in place of J. E. Eberlin who had died in June 1762. In February 1763 Leopold Mozart was appointed Deputy-Kapellmeister.

[2] After St. Stephen's Cathedral, the most important church in Vienna. It was dedicated by Emperor Charles VI to St. Charles Borromeo after the cessation of the plague in 1713 and was completed in 1737. In the 18th century it stood in the open fields of the Wiental.

[3] A district of Vienna, then outside the walls.

[4] Antonia, née Countess Esterházy (1719–1771), wife of the Chief Postmaster.

trouble started, everything was going swimmingly.

PS. If you would be so excessively kind as to go to Lauffen,[1] it is high time to do so. For usually His Excellency Count Spaur leaves Salzburg again on November 14th, that is, the day after the Paris Anniversary.[2] If a decision is not reached now,[3] through the intervention of His Excellency and the efforts of our Father Confessor,[4] it never will be. I shall then be obliged sooner or later to alter my plan. I already have addresses in Holland and France. But I shall tell you more when we meet.

Will you also be so kind and friendly as to make emphatic representations to His Excellency Count Spaur? I have written to him and to our Father Confessor, and furthermore to His Excellency the Chief Steward[5] about permission to remain in Vienna until Advent. Perhaps if you find an opportunity, for instance, after ten o'clock Mass in the Cathedral, you might just speak to him, though it would be even better if you could go and see him. You may also tell him quite plainly about the post of Deputy Kapellmeister, for he is very partial to me. You have no idea how advantageous it would be to me if I were to obtain this post while I am still here.

When I arrived in Vienna I found myself generally regarded as the Kapellmeister of Salzburg. Indeed when the Emperor himself wanted to take me in to hear the Infanta play the violin, he came out and called: *"Where is the Kapellmeister of Salzburg?"*

Latterly, I have not added the title on purpose, for people might think it an invention.[6] Almost every day occasions arise when I am obliged to contradict such statements, for far from me be all lies and bragging. Now you understand me. I trust to your friendship.

(6) *Leopold Mozart to Lorenz Hagenauer, Salzburg*

[*Extract*]   [*From the catalogue of Leo Liepmannssohn, Berlin*]

[VIENNA, 10 *November* 1762]

The enclosed poem[7] was handed to me by Count Collalto at the concert given yesterday by the Marquise von Pacheco. A certain Puffendorf wrote the lines while listening to my boy.

---

[1] A small village, three miles from the famous health resort, Bad Ischl. The Archbishops of Salzburg often went there.

[2] 13 November was the anniversary of the election to the Archbishopric of Salzburg of Count Paris Lodron, who reigned from 1619 until 1653. He was one of the most famous ecclesiastical rulers of Salzburg. See H. Widmann, *Geschichte Salzburgs*, Gotha, 1914, vol. iii. p. 273 ff.

[3] Leopold Mozart again expresses his anxiety to obtain the post of Deputy-Kapellmeister. See p. 9.   [4] Abbé Bullinger. See p. 8, n. 2.   [5] Count von Firmian.

[6] Possibly this rather obscure statement is an allusion to the form of address of letters directed to Leopold Mozart as 'maître de chapelle de S.A.R. l'archevêque de Salzbourg'.

[7] This short poem is quoted by Nissen, p. 27, and Abert, vol. ii. p. 928.

Master Woferl thanks you for your very kind remembrance of his name-day which he had to spend in Vienna and which gave him little pleasure.

We shall bring back plenty of new concertos. Ten have already been copied.

(7) *Leopold Mozart to Lorenz Hagenauer, Salzburg*

[*Extract*]   [*Copy in the Deutsche Staatsbibliothek, Berlin*]

VIENNA, 24 *November* 1762

I have received your last letter. I would have done what you and the good friends we know of advised me, if I could have made up my mind immediately. And at last I have decided to do this on the next post-day. The causes which threw me into a certain sad state of indecision I shall tell you about later, but will it not by then be superfluous? Well, if this too fails, then I must hit on some other plan. And now for ourselves. Thank God, we are well, but we must wait patiently until we can direct our enterprise into its old successful path. For in Vienna the nobility are afraid of pockmarks and all kinds of rash. So my boy's illness has meant a set-back of about four weeks. For although since his recovery we have taken in twenty-one ducats, this is a mere trifle, seeing that we only just manage every day on one ducat, and that daily there are additional expenses. Apart from this we are in very good trim. The lady-in-waiting, the Countess Theresa von Lodron, recently conferred a great honour upon us. She gave us a box at the play (which is very difficult to get) and gave my Woferl shoe-buckles, which have little gold plates and look just like solid gold. On St. Elizabeth's day[1] we saw the gala table; and quite exceptional honours and kindnesses were bestowed on us there by the nobility. Suffice it to say that Her Majesty the Empress called out to me from the table and asked me whether my boy was now quite well. A description of St. Cecilia's Festival[2] I shall postpone until we meet. Indeed we shall need to have many long talks before we have discussed everything. On St. Cecilia's day we lunched with the Imperial Kapellmeister, von Reutter.[3] When we get home, I shall recite the menu to Frau Hagenauer. Yesterday we lunched with Herr von Wahlau and in the evening Dr. Bernhard took us to a box at the opera. And thus, God willing, one day after another passes. We have standing invitations to Herr Reutter and Herr von Wahlau. But my children's health might suffer. Moreover carriages cost

[1] 19 November.   [2] 22 November.
[3] Johann Adam Karl Georg Reutter (1708–1772) was Court and Cathedral Kapellmeister in Vienna, and a prolific composer. He was ennobled by Maria Theresia in 1740, and is best remembered for his connection with Haydn in the latter's early days.

me a good deal, for we usually take two, three and sometimes even four a day; and if we use the nobles' carriages, the tips for the coachman and the lacquey amount to as much. When shall we be home again? By Christmas or the New Year? I wish you and your wife and all your family much good fortune.

(8) *Leopold Mozart to Lorenz Hagenauer, Salzburg*

[*Extract*]   [*Autograph formerly in the possession of Dr. Ludwig Schiedermair, Bonn*]

[VIENNA, 10 *December* 1762[1]]

On the 4th I wrote to His Grace and also to our Father Confessor and both letters were composed in the way my best friends suggested. I also added a lengthy apology for not being able to return to Salzburg at the prescribed time. To put it shortly, I cannot get home before Christmas or the New Year. The reasons I shall have to explain to you later when we meet. When you read this letter you will be reminded of our Court Sculptor.[2] But perhaps you have long ago come to the conclusion that *everyone who comes to Vienna, is charmed into staying here.* So it has almost been with us. But my reasons will solve the riddle for you.

It is a good thing that we are not at home just now. We are trying to avoid smallpox; and it might find its way up to us.[3] Now you know the reason why we do not want to go home. I trust that all will turn out well.

Returning from Herr von Wahlau I have this moment received your letter of the 7th. I had really decided to leave at once and to reach Salzburg by the Feast of St. Thomas.[4] But when I saw Herr von Wahlau and told him about it, I left the matter for him to decide and he thereupon took the whole thing into his hands. He went so far as to assure me that His Grace would certainly grant an extension of a fortnight or three weeks, in order that I may fulfil the request of the Hungarian nobility. For you must know that for the last three weeks we have been worried to death with invitations to go to Pressburg[5] after the Feast of the Immaculate Conception.[6] And these became the more pressing when we met the greatest nobles of Hungary at the public banquet on the Emperor's

[1] Schiedermair (*Die Briefe Mozarts*, vol. iv, p. 394) suggests that this letter and the following one were written with a view to their being read out in Salzburg.
[2] Johann Baptist Hagenauer (1732–1810) was a distant relative of Lorenz Hagenauer, who helped him to pursue his art studies in Italy. In 1764 he was appointed Court Sculptor and Inspector of Galleries to the Archbishop of Salzburg. After the accession of Archbishop Hieronymus Colloredo in 1772 Hagenauer settled in Vienna, where he carried out certain commissions for the Emperor and eventually became Professor of Sculpture.
[3] Apparently the Hagenauer family had caught smallpox. See p. 3, n. 1.
[4] 21 December.
[5] Since 896 Pressburg (Pozsony) had belonged to Hungary, and was its capital from 1536 to 1784. In 1918 it passed to Czechoslovakia, and is now the chief Danubian port (Bratislava) of that country.   [6] 8 December.

birthday.[1] So tomorrow we are off to Pressburg. But I have not the slightest intention of staying there for more than a week. Herr von Wahlau who has taken the matter upon himself is writing in person to our Court about it. Otherwise I should have left immediately. For I really do not know whether I shall gain so very much in Pressburg. Meanwhile give my worthy and holy Father Confessor my most humble greetings and tell him that if by staying away I were to lose the favour of His Grace, I should be ready on the instant to leave by mail coach for Salzburg. At the moment there are still many things which might keep us here at least another month. For just think, Count Durazzo, who is Director of Music at this court, has not yet been able to arrange for us to play at his 'accademia' or public concert. If we agreed to do so, we could stay on until Lent and Easter and draw a nice sum every week. You will say that Vienna makes a fool of everyone. And indeed, when in certain respects I compare Salzburg with Vienna, I soon become confused. Well, if God keeps us in good health, I hope to wish you a happy New Year from my carriage. Meanwhile I wish a speedy recovery to Miss Ursula and Miss Francesca[2] and much patience to you and especially to your wife.

I am your honest friend

MOZART

(9) *Leopold Mozart to Lorenz Hagenauer, Salzburg*

[*Extract*]   [*Autograph formerly in the possession of Dr. Ludwig Schiedermair, Bonn*]

[VIENNA, 29 *December* 1762]

Homo proponit, Deus disponit.[3] On the 20th I intended to leave Pressburg and on the 26th to take our departure from Vienna in order to reach Salzburg on New Year's Eve. But on the 19th I had unusually bad toothache. I repeat, *for me unusually bad toothache*; for I had pain in the whole row of the upper front teeth which are perfectly good and otherwise healthy. During the night my whole face swelled up and on the following day I really looked like the trumpeting angel; so much so that Lieutenant Winckler, the court drummer's brother, who called on us, did not recognise me when he entered the room and thought he had lost his way. In this sad circumstance I had to console myself with the thought that in any case we were held up by the extraordinarily fierce cold weather which had suddenly come; for the pontoon was removed and it was as much as they could do to get the post-bags across the Danube by means of small boats; and the postillion had then to proceed with a field-horse. Hence I had to

---

[1] 8 December.   [2] Lorenz Hagenauer's daughters.
[3] i.e. man proposes, God disposes.

wait for news that the March[1] (which is not a wide river) was frozen. So on Christmas Eve at half past eight in the morning I said good-bye to Pressburg and, travelling by a special route, reached our lodging in Vienna at half past eight in the evening. That day our journey was not very comfortable, for, though the road was frozen hard, it was indescribably bumpy and full of deep ruts and ridges.

Immediately after our return to Vienna our landlady told me that Countess Leopold Kinsky had daily enquired as to whether we had arrived. I called on her on Christmas Day and she said she had waited most anxiously for our return and had postponed a banquet which she wanted to give for Field-Marshal Daun, who would like to make our acquaintance. This banquet she therefore gave on Monday. Now I am most certainly leaving here on Friday morning, and with God's help will reach Linz on Sunday; and on the Vigil of the Epiphany, 5th January, 1763, I hope to stand in your room. I now ask you to add the following kindness to those which you have already shown me in such numbers, and that is, to wish our gracious Father Confessor in my name the healthiest and happiest New Year and to ask him to continue his kind favours towards us. I would have written to him myself if I had not really hesitated to worry him so many times over with my letters. Give my New Year greetings too to Madame Robinig[2] and Fräulein Josepha *in optima forma*[3] and to all our excellent friends, including, of course, yourself, your wife and your whole household. Remember me also to Herr Reifenstuhl[4] and ask him to allow me to leave my carriage at his house for a few days until I find a place where I can store it. Meanwhile I trust that we shall all find one another in good health on January 5th. I am looking forward most ardently to telling you a host of things and to reminding you

that I am ever your true friend

MOZART

My wife and children send their greetings. If you could get the room heated for a few days, it would be well. Only a little fuel is necessary in the front stove.

[*Written on the cover*]

For the last few days it has been surprisingly cold here; and today it is quite extraordinarily so. Her Majesty the Empress has lost another Princess, the Princess Joanna,[5] aged thirteen, who, when we were at court, took my Woferl by the hand and led him through her rooms.

---

[1] The river Morava (or March), which now forms the frontier between Austria and Czechoslovakia, flows into the Danube about ten miles below Pressburg.

[2] Widow of a wealthy mine-owner in the Salzburg district. The Robinig family were very friendly with the Mozarts.　　　　　　　　　　　　[3] i.e. in the best style.

[4] A Salzburg merchant, who kept a shop in the Getreidegasse.

[5] Princess Joanna, who died of typhus in December 1762, was Maria Theresia's eleventh child. She had already lost an infant daughter.

The third journey, the European tour, of Leopold Mozart and his wife and two children lasted from 9 June 1763 to 30 November 1766. The family visited the chief towns of Southern Germany and the Rhineland, remained a few weeks in Brussels, spent the first winter in Paris, almost a year and a half in London, the winter 1765-66 in Holland, and returned to Salzburg by way of Brussels, Paris, Geneva, Berne and Munich. The children performed at every court and frequently gave concerts. In Paris and London Mozart met and studied the works of those composers who for a considerable time influenced his own style of writing, i.e. Schobert and Eckardt in Paris and Johann Christian Bach in London. During the winter 1763-64 he wrote his first sonatas for the clavier and during the following summer, which his family spent in Chelsea, his first symphonies. The Mozarts' long tour is described very fully in letters from Leopold Mozart to his landlord, Lorenz Hagenauer. Letters 10-46.

(10) *Leopold Mozart to Lorenz Hagenauer, Salzburg*

[*Extract*]   [*Autograph in the Mozarteum, Salzburg*]

MONSIEUR,   WASSERBURG,[1] 11 *June* 1763

That was a snail's journey.[2] But it was not our fault. Two hours outside
Wasserburg a back wheel broke in pieces and there we were stranded.
Fortunately the weather was fine and bright, and still more fortunately
there was a mill near by. The people came to our aid with a wheel which
was too small and yet too long in the hub. We had to be thankful to have
even that, although it meant hewing down a small tree to bind in front
of the wheel, so that it should not run away. We broke up the smashed
wheel in order to take away the iron with us, though we had to tie on the
hoop under the carriage-box to do so. These are only the chief circumstances which kept us for an hour on the open road. Sebastian[3] and I
covered the remainder of the distance with God's help *per pedes apostolorum*,[4]
in order that our heavy bodies should not cause the wounded carriage any
fresh casualty. Thus, while we might have reached Wasserburg at ten
o'clock, we had to content ourselves with getting there at a quarter past
twelve. The cartwright and the smith were forthwith summoned to produce a new wheel and it became necessary to feel the pulse of the other
wheel as well. The *vota unanima* of the *consilium* were to effect that this
wheel too was in an extremely dangerous condition and might collapse
at a sudden jar. I was all the more ready to believe that it would, as the
carriage doctors, even Dr. Niderl[5] himself, had foretold this the day before
our departure.

We were told that the carriage would be restored to health early this
morning, that is, in twenty-four hours. But the devil take it! Then we
hoped to get away after lunch. In vain! The cartwright chopped and
sawed, the smith singed and burnt and hammered hard. The latter would
have set the patient on his legs again at once and made him walk, if the
former could have handed him over more quickly. What were we to do
now? We could only, most reluctantly, be patient! And we still have to
do so, as I write. For the business will hardly be finished before this
evening, so that we shall have to settle down here for another night. The
most important side of the matter is the expense, for at least the honour of
feeding the horses and the driver falls to me. Yet by Heaven it is better to
lose ten wheels than a foot or a few fingers. We are well, thank God, as

---

[1] A small town in Bavaria, situated on the Inn. The Mozarts stayed at the inn 'Zum goldnen
Stern'.
[2] The Mozart family, Leopold Mozart and his wife, Nannerl and Wolfgang, had left
Salzburg on 9 June.
[3] Sebastian Winter, the Mozarts' man-servant.
[4] i.e. by means of the Apostles' feet.
[5] A Salzburg doctor and a friend of the Mozarts.

we hope that you both are and your whole household and all my good friends, to whom I send greetings.

Our hired driver would be glad if you would tell his people that he hopes to reach home next Tuesday evening; for tomorrow, God willing, we look forward to being in Munich. Hence he will probably ride home with the post-horses in two days. The latest news is that in order to amuse ourselves we went to the organ and I explained to Woferl the use of the pedal. Whereupon he tried it *stante pede*,[1] shoved the stool away and played standing at the organ, at the same time working the pedal, and doing it all as if he had been practising it for several months. Everyone was amazed. Indeed this is a fresh act of God's grace, which many a one only receives after much labour. We send our greetings and I am

your most devoted

MOZART

(11) *Leopold Mozart to Lorenz Hagenauer, Salzburg*

[*Extract*]   [*Copy in the Deutsche Staatsbibliothek, Berlin*]

MUNICH, 21 *June* 1763

We are now in Munich. We arrived on Sunday evening, June 12th. Monday was a gala-day on account of the Feast of St. Antony[2] and we drove to Nymphenburg.[3] Prince von Zweibrücken, whose acquaintance we had made in Vienna, saw us from the castle as we were walking in the garden, recognised us and beckoned to us from the window. We went up to him and, after talking to us for some time, he asked whether the Elector[4] knew that we were here. We said, No. Whereupon he immediately sent off to the Elector a courtier who was standing beside him to ask whether he would not like to hear the children? Meanwhile we were to walk in the garden and wait for the reply. Soon afterwards a footman arrived with a message bidding us appear at the concert at eight o'clock. It was then four o'clock. So we walked through the garden and visited Badenburg,[5] but were obliged by sudden rain and thunder to take shelter. To be brief, Woferl was a great success. We did not get home until a quarter past eleven, when we had some supper first and then got to bed late. On Tuesday and Wednesday evenings we were invited to visit Duke Clemens.[6] On Thursday we stayed at home in the evening on

---

[1] i.e. standing.   [2] St. Antony of Padua, 13 June.

[3] A suburb of Munich, with which it was incorporated in 1900, famous for its palace erected by Elector Ferdinand Maria (1663–1676), and its park.

[4] Maximilian III, Elector of Bavaria. He had a marked talent for music, composed church music and was a fine performer on the violoncello. The Mozarts had already performed before him in January 1762.

[5] The Elector's bath-house, built 1718–1721.   [6] i.e. of Bavaria.

account of heavy rain. Now the question is how are we to get on, seeing that here the charming custom is to keep people waiting for presents for a long time, so that one has to be contented if one makes what one spends. Tomasini[1] has been here for three weeks and has only just been paid. Tell Wenzel[2] he can imagine how overjoyed we both were to meet here unexpectedly. He recognised me first, for he has grown tall, strong and handsome. He displayed sincere gratitude for the old friendship which I had shown him in Salzburg and this touched me and proved to me that he has a good heart. He too is going on to Stuttgart[3] and Mannheim and thence back to Vienna. The Elector lunched in town on the 18th and we were at table with him. He and his sister and Prince von Zweibrücken talked to us during the whole meal. I got my boy to say that we were leaving the following day. The Elector said twice that he was sorry not to have heard my little girl. For when we were at Nymphenburg the time was too short, since the boy alone took up most of it by extemporizing and by playing a concerto for violin and clavier.[4] Two ladies sang and then the concert was over. So when the Elector said a second time: *I should have liked to hear her*, I could not but say *that it would not matter if we stayed on a few days longer*. So all that we can do is to drive over on Wednesday as quickly as possible to Augsburg. For yesterday there was hunting and today there is a French play, so that Nannerl cannot perform until tomorrow. I may thank God if I am paid on Tuesday. The Duke will not detain me; but he is waiting to see what the Elector is going to give me. Tomasini has reason to be dissatisfied with the Elector. He performed twice, had to wait for a long time and finally received eight max d'or. The Duke himself gave him a beautiful gold watch. Basta! I shall be glad if I receive what I have had to spend here and shall probably require for the journey to Augsburg. I can hardly wait for the hour to get away from Munich. I have no complaint to make about the Elector. He is most gracious and he said to me yesterday: 'Why, we are old acquaintances. We met nineteen years ago.' But the apostles only think of themselves and their purses. We lunched recently with Herr König, the Hamburg merchant, who was at our house in Salzburg. He too is lodging at Störzer's in the front part of the house, while we are two flights up in the new building. There I met a certain Johann Georg Wahler of Frankfurt, who lunched with us and gave me his address. He lives in the Römerberg[5] and is going to find private rooms for us in Frankfurt. On the same occasion

---

[1] Not the well-known Luigi Tomasini (1741–1808).

[2] Wenzel Hebelt, a Salzburg violinist who studied composition under Leopold Mozart.

[3] Leopold Mozart intended to visit Stuttgart, but had to abandon this plan. Cp. p. 23.

[4] The word 'clavier' is used when it is not certain what particular form of keyboard instrument is referred to.

[5] The centre of the old town, the market-place in front of the famous Römer, formerly the town hall of Frankfurt.

we met two Saxon councillors, De Bose and Hopfgarten, both most agreeable people. And all these persons we shall meet again, God willing, in Stuttgart or Mannheim, for they are travelling by the same route as we are.[1]

As I write a bit of this letter every day, it will be finished eventually. We leave tomorrow, June 22nd. Farewell. I remain etc.

PS.—We have now been paid and have received a hundred gulden from the Elector and seventy-five gulden from the Duke. But what our bill at the inn will be, we shall have the honour of hearing tomorrow. Herr Störzer has the reputation of giving good service, but also of writing letters and doing sums. Patience! Nannerl played before the Elector and the Duke and was warmly applauded. When we took our leave, both invited us to come again. Prince von Zweibrücken is to announce our arrival in Mannheim. He will soon be there. And Duke Clemens has provided us with a letter of recommendation to the Elector of the Palatinate.[2] Tell our friends that we are very well.

(12) *Leopold Mozart to Lorenz Hagenauer, Salzburg*

[*Extract*]   [*Autograph in the Mozarteum, Salzburg*]

LUDWIGSBURG,[3] 11 *July* 1763

I was kept in Augsburg for a long time[4] and gained little or nothing. For our takings had to be spent, as everything was uncommonly dear, although the landlord of the 'Drei Mohren', Herr Linay, the most charming man in the world, did me very well, as Herr Weiser will testify. The people who came to the concerts were almost all Lutherans. Apart from Herr Provino, who came all three times with Madame Berinet, and Herr Calligari, who appeared once *par réputation*, the only Catholic business man I saw was Herr Mayr, the master of Lisette Muralt. All the others were Lutherans. We left Augsburg on the 6th and reached Ulm[5]

---

[1] According to Leopold Mozart's *Reiseaufzeichnungen* the Mozarts met Baron de Bose and Baron Hopfgarten again in Augsburg, Ludwigsburg and Paris. See p. 42 f.

[2] Karl Theodor (1742–1799), who endeavoured at his court in Mannheim and Schwetzingen to imitate the manners and customs of the court of Louis XV at Versailles.

[3] The residence, with Stuttgart, of Duke Karl Eugen of Wurtemberg, who founded the Karlsschule, the famous military academy, where Schiller as a pupil wrote his play *Die Räuber*. The Mozarts stayed at the inn 'Zum goldnen Waldhorn'.

[4] Fifteen days. Augsburg was Leopold Mozart's native town and his two younger brothers, both bookbinders, were living there. The children gave three concerts, 28 and 30 June and 4 July, a report of which in the Salzburg *Europäische Zeitung* of 19 July 1763, is quoted by Nissen, p. 39, and Abert, vol. i. p. 43. They also met J. A. Stein, the organ builder and improver of the pianoforte, from whom Leopold Mozart bought a portable clavier (p. 28) and whom Mozart met again later (p. 315).

[5] The Mozarts stayed at the inn 'Zum goldnen Rad' and visited the Münster and its great organ.

in the evening, where we only stayed for that night and the following morning. We would not have spent the morning there had it not been that on account of horses we had difficulty in proceeding. And now for a piece of bad luck! When we arrived at the post-stage Plochingen, we heard that the Duke[1] had suddenly decided to go off on the night of the 10th to his hunting lodge Grafeneck, which is fourteen hours distant. So I quickly decided that, instead of going to Stuttgart, I would go straight to Ludwigsburg via Cannstatt in order to catch him. I arrived there late on the 9th and had just time to see a play at the French theatre. But not until the morning of the 10th was I able to see the Chief Kapellmeister Jommelli[2] and the Master of the Hounds, Baron von Pöllnitz, for both of whom I had letters from Count von Wolfegg.[3] In short, there was nothing to be done. Tomasini, who had been here a fortnight before I arrived, had not managed to get a hearing, and, as everyone tells me, the Duke has the charming habit of making people wait interminably before hearing them and then making them wait as long again before giving them a present. But I regard the whole business as the work of Jommelli, who is doing his best to weed out the Germans at this court and put in Italians only. He has almost succeeded too, and will succeed completely, for, apart from his yearly income of four thousand gulden, his allowances for four horses, wood and light, a house in Stuttgart and another one in Ludwigsburg, he enjoys to the full the favour of the Duke; and his wife is promised a pension of two thousand gulden after his death.[4] What do you think of that for a Kapellmeister's post? Furthermore, he has unlimited control over his orchestra and that explains its excellence. Indeed you can judge how partial Jommelli is to his country from the fact that he and some of his compatriots, who are ever swarming at his house to pay him their respects, were heard to say that it was amazing and hardly believable that a child of German birth could have such unusual genius and so much understanding and passion. *Ridete, amici!*[5] Well, I must get on. My prospects now seem all the worse, for the Duke has seized all the horses from the post and the hired coachmen. So I am forced to spend another day here. At the moment I am writing with constant interruptions, as I am endeavouring to beat up some horses and have sent messengers into every nook and corner of Ludwigsburg to find them. So you see that hitherto all I have gained is to have seen lands and towns and various people.

[1] Karl Eugen of Wurtemberg. The Mozarts were not invited to perform before him.
[2] Niccolò Jommelli (1714–1774) of Naples, a conspicuous representative of the Neapolitan School of operatic composers. From 1753 to 1768 he was Hofkapellmeister in Stuttgart.
[3] Count Anton Willibald Wolfegg, canon of Salzburg Cathedral.
[4] Schurig, vol. i. p. 124, note, quotes from the relevant document the conditions of Jommelli's appointment, and shows that Leopold Mozart's statement is exaggerated.
[5] i.e. Laugh, my friends.

Ludwigsburg is a very queer place. It is a town. Yet more than hedges and garden-trellises the soldiers form the walls of this town. When you spit, you spit into an officer's pocket or into a soldier's cartridge-box. In the streets you hear nothing but perpetual: '*Halt! Quick march! Right, Left*', etc., and you see nothing but arms, drums and war material. At the entrance to the castle there are two grenadiers and two mounted dragoons, with grenadier caps on their heads and cuirasses on their breasts, naked swords in their hands and overhead a fine large tin roof, instead of a sentry-box. In a word it would be impossible to find greater accuracy in drilling or a finer body of men. You see only men of the grenadier type, and every sergeant-major draws forty gulden a month. You will laugh; and really it is laughable. As I stood at the window, I thought I was looking at soldiers about to take their places in some play or opera. Just picture them to yourself. They are all exactly alike and every day their hair is done, not in ringlets but just like any petit-maître does his own—in innumerable curls combed back and powdered snow-white, with the beard greased coal-black. I shall write more from Mannheim. Now I must close. When you write, write to Mannheim and direct that the letter is to remain at the post till I fetch it. I received the music in Augsburg. If I were to write everything, I should have much more to say. But I must tell you that Wurtemberg is a very beautiful district. From Geislingen to Ludwigsburg you will see nothing to left or right but water, woods, fields, meadows, gardens and vineyards, and all these at once and mingled in the most charming fashion. Give my greetings to everyone in Salzburg and especially to our Father Confessor and Madame von Robinig and her family. Complimenti sopra complimenti. Addio!

I am your old

MOZART

My wife takes the greatest pleasure in the countryside in Wurtemberg.

[*Written on the cover*]

Tell Herr Wenzel that I have heard a certain Nardini[1] and that it would be impossible to hear a finer player for beauty, purity, evenness of tone and singing quality. But he plays rather lightly.

Herr Wodiska is still in service at Stuttgart but has not a good name on account of his childish behaviour. In Augsburg the choir master of St. Moritz, Herr Schuch, showed me a letter from Herr Meisner,[2] in which

---

[1] Pietro Nardini (1722–1793) of Tuscany, eminent violinist and composer, pupil of Tartini. Jommelli brought him in 1753 as solo violinist to the ducal court at Stuttgart, where he remained until 1768. In March 1770 he played with Mozart in Florence. See p. 125. Leopold Mozart in his *Reiseaufzeichnungen*, p. 22, mentions Nardini among the people he met in Augsburg.

[2] Joseph Meissner, a bass singer, composer and teacher of singing in Salzburg.

he signed himself Capellae Magister. I explained to him that he was 'magister' in singing, in order to excuse his childishness.[1]

(13) *Leopold Mozart to Lorenz Hagenauer, Salzburg*

[Extract]   *[Autograph in the Mozarteum, Salzburg]*

MONSIEUR!   SCHWETZINGEN,[2] 19 *July* 1763

As I was writing from Ludwigsburg, I did not dare to add that the soldiering there is driven to excess. For, in truth, twelve to fifteen thousand soldiers, who strut about every day dressed up to the nines, who can hardly walk on account of their tight gaiters and breeches made of the finest linen, all exactly alike, are too few to be taken seriously and too expensive to be joked about; consequently they are far too many. On the 12th at eight in the morning we at last got the coach-horses which had been promised us for four o'clock and, driving through Enzweihingen (entirely Lutheran and a wretched spot), we reached Bruchsal in the evening. On that day's journey we had pleasant views; and much pleasure was afforded us by a good friend, who coming from Augsburg happened to follow us. The Residenz in Bruchsal[3] is worth seeing. The rooms are in the very best taste; there are not many of them, but so noble, indescribably charming and elegant, that nothing pleasanter could be seen. Thence we drove, not to Mannheim, but straight to Schwetzingen, where the court always spends the summer. Apart from the letter of recommendation which I had brought with me from Vienna to the Director of Music, Baron Eberstein, we had already been introduced there by Prince von Zweibrücken; and in addition Prince Clemens of Bavaria had sent to the 'Drei Mohren' in Augsburg a letter of recommendation in his own hand for the Electress at Mannheim. Yesterday a concert, the second only to be held here since May, was arranged specially for us. It lasted from five to nine in the evening. Besides good male and female singers I had the pleasure of hearing an admirable flautist, Wendling[4] by name. The orchestra is undeniably the best in Germany. It consists altogether of people who are young and of good character, not drunkards, gamblers or dissolute fellows, so that both their behaviour and their playing are admirable.[5] My children have set all Schwetzingen talking. The Elector and his consort have shown indescribable pleasure and everyone has been

---

[1] At that time Giuseppe Francesco Lolli of Bologna was the Kapellmeister in Salzburg.

[2] About nine miles from Mannheim and the summer residence of the Electors. The Schloss was built by Elector Karl Ludwig in 1656 and the gardens laid out in 1753 by Elector Karl Theodor. The Mozarts arrived on 13 July and stayed at the inn 'Zum roten Haus'.

[3] An outstanding example of baroque, built 1722–1730.

[4] Johann Baptist Wendling (1720–1797), an eminent flautist, who frequently played in Paris and London. In 1754 he joined the Mannheim orchestra and in 1778 followed the Elector to Munich.

[5] See p. 562, where Mozart expresses the same opinion on the Mannheim orchestra in almost the same words.

amazed. When we leave here we shall go to Frankfurt, where our address will be: *c/o Johann Georg Wahler, auf dem Römerberg*. And now I hope that you, my valued friend, and your dearest wife and all your dear ones are in excellent health; just as we all are. For, thank God, we have not been ill for a quarter of an hour. When circumstances arise which oblige us to follow certain customs of the country which are very different from our own, we often say: '*Now Frau Hagenauer should see us*'. For indeed we see many strange and quite unusual things which we should like you to see too. At present we are staying in places where there are four religions, Catholic, Lutheran, Calvinist and Jewish. Save for the court, which accounts for a large number of the inhabitants, Schwetzingen is chiefly Calvinist. It is only a village, but it has three churches, Catholic, Lutheran and Calvinist; and the whole of the Palatinate is like this. Strange to say, since we left Wasserburg, we have not had a holy water stoup in our rooms. For, even though the places are Catholic, such things are not to be found, because many Lutherans pass through, and therefore the rooms are so equipped that all religions can live in them together. In the bedrooms too there are seldom any pictures save a few landscapes or the portrait of some old Emperor; there is hardly ever a crucifix. Fast-dishes one scarcely ever gets and they are very badly prepared, for everyone eats meat; and who knows what they have given us. Basta! It is not our fault. Our landlord here is a Calvinist. It is a good thing that this does not last long. Now I must close, for it is time to go to the French theatre, which could not be improved on, especially for its ballets and music.[1] I hope to find a letter from you in Frankfurt. I wish you good luck and good health and to all, left, right, behind and in front, I send my greetings, especially to our Father Confessor and to Madame Robinig. I am your old

MOZART

In the volume of music sent over by Madame Haffner[2] from Nuremberg there are six compositions, œuvres mêlées. Open it and give one of them to Adlgasser[3] with my compliments.

PS.—Money arrangements are surprisingly bad. In Bruchsal the Bavarian thaler already fetches only twenty-four kreuzer. The twenty-five groschen piece is twenty-four kreuzer and so on. The ducat is worth no more than five gulden. The Bavarian piece of twelve hardly fetches ten kreuzer, whereas in Augsburg the ducat fetches five gulden and twenty to twenty-four kreuzer. Herr Provino has excelled himself and has given me unasked the finest letters of credit to different places. So that thanks to him and to Herr Calligari I am well supplied with all that is necessary.

[1] For an excellent account of the French theatre and of French influences generally at the court of Karl Theodor up to 1770, see F. Walter, *Geschichte des Theaters und der Musik am Kurpfälzischen Hofe*, Leipzig, 1898.
[2] Wife of Johann Ulrich Haffner, musician and music publisher in Nuremberg.
[3] Anton Cajetan Adlgasser (1728–1777), court and cathedral organist in Salzburg.

(14) *Leopold Mozart to Lorenz Hagenauer, Salzburg*

[*Extract*]   [*Copy in the Deutsche Staatsbibliothek, Berlin*]

MAINZ, 3 *August* 1763

From Schwetzingen we drove to Heidelberg in order to see the castle and the great tun.[1]

On the whole Heidelberg is very like Salzburg, that is to say, as to its situation. The fallen-in doors and walls in the castle, which are amazing to see, show the sad fruits of the late French wars.[2] In the Church of the Holy Ghost,[3] which is famous in history on account of the struggle between the Catholics and the Calvinists, which led the Electors to transfer their residence to Mannheim,[4] our Wolfgang so astonished everyone by his playing on the organ that by order of the Town Magistrate his name was inscribed with full particulars on it as a perpetual remembrance.[5] After receiving a present of fifteen louis d'or we came on from Schwetzingen through Worms to Mainz.[6]

In Mannheim a French colonel presented a little ring to Nannerl and a pretty toothpick case to little Wolfgang.

(15) *Leopold Mozart to Lorenz Hagenauer, Salzburg*

[*Extract*]   [*Copy in the Deutsche Staatsbibliothek, Berlin*]

FRANKFURT,[7] 13 *August* 1763

The Elector[8] of Mainz was and still is suffering from a severe fever. People have been very anxious about him, as he has never yet been ill in his life. We lodged at the 'König von England' and during our stay gave a concert at the 'Römischer König'.[9] Then we left our carriage and some luggage at our lodgings and took the market boat to Frankfurt. We have been here a few days already. Next Thursday we shall give a concert, I

[1] The monster cask, capable of holding 49,000 gallons of beer, constructed in 1751 under Elector Karl Theodor.

[2] Begun in 1685, when Louis XIV laid claim to the Palatinate. In 1693 the castle was completely destroyed by Maréchal De Lorge.

[3] Built at the beginning of the fifteenth century. In 1705 the nave was separated from the choir by a wall in order that the Catholics might worship in the latter and the Protestants in the former.

[4] In 1720, owing to ecclesiastical differences with the Protestant citizens, Elector Karl Philipp moved his residence from Heidelberg (for five centuries the capital of the Palatinate) to Mannheim.

[5] The organ was taken later to the Jesuit church and the inscription was removed.

[6] The Mozarts spent eight days in Mainz and stayed at the inn 'Zum König von England'. According to a letter of Leopold Mozart of 7 December 1780 (p. 683, n. 1), they met there the famous violinist Karl Michael Esser, whom Mozart, then aged seven, rebuked for his careless playing. They also met Anna De Amicis, the famous operatic soprano, who ten years later sang in Milan in Mozart's *Lucio Silla*.

[7] The Mozarts arrived at Frankfurt on 9 August and stayed at the inn 'Zum goldnen Löwen'.   [8] Emmerich Joseph von Breidtbach.

[9] The Mozarts gave three concerts in Mainz, which brought in 200 gulden. See p. 405.

think, and then return to Mainz, for the market boats ply daily between Mainz and Frankfurt.

(16) *Leopold Mozart to Lorenz Hagenauer, Salzburg*

[*Extract*]   [*Copy in the Deutsche Staatsbibliothek, Berlin*]

[FRANKFURT, 20 *August* 1763]

We gave our concert on the 10th.[1] It went off splendidly. On the 22nd and also on the 25th or 26th we are repeating it.[2] The Imperial Envoy the Count von Pergen and his wife were there and everyone was amazed. God is so gracious that, thanks be to Him, we are well and are admired everywhere. Wolfgang is extraordinarily jolly, but a bit of a scamp as well. And Nannerl no longer suffers by comparison with the boy, for she plays so beautifully that everyone is talking about her and admiring her execution. I bought a charming little clavier from Stein[3] in Augsburg, which does us good service for practising on during our travels.

Once since we started upon them, it was in Augsburg, I think, Wolfgang, on waking up in the morning, began to cry. I asked him the reason and he said that he was sorry not to be seeing Herr Hagenauer, Wenzel, Spitzeder, Deibl, Leutgeb, Vogt, Cajetan, Nazerl[4] and other good friends.

In Mainz Nannerl was given as presents an English hat and a galanterie set of bottles (to the value of about four ducats). Here she has been given a snuff-box of vernis martin[5] and a piece of Palatine embroidery, while little Wolfgang has received a porcelain snuff-box.

(17) *Leopold Mozart to Lorenz Hagenauer, Salzburg*

[*Extract*]   [*Copy in the Deutsche Staatsbibliothek, Berlin*]

[COBLENZ,[6] 26 *September* 1763]

Before leaving Mainz I had to give another concert[7] to the nobles, after which we came on to Coblenz.

[1] Goethe, aged fourteen, was present at this concert with his father, who noted in his diary '4 gulden, 7 kreuzer pro concerto musicali duorum infantium'. In conversation with Eckermann, 3 February 1830, Goethe said, 'I still remember quite clearly the little fellow with his wig and sword' (Eckermann, *Gespräche mit Goethe*, Leipzig, 1908, ii. p. 178).
[2] It was repeated too on 30 August. Abert, vol. i. p. 46, quotes the notice of this concert, which describes enthusiastically the feats of Nannerl and Wolfgang.   [3] See p. 22, n. 4.
[4] With the exception of the first, the names enumerated are those of Salzburg musicians, i.e. Wenzel Hebelt (violinist), Spitzeder (tenor), Deibl (oboist), Leutgeb (horn-player), Vogt (viola-player), Anton Cajetan Adlgasser (first cathedral organist), Franz Ignaz Lipp (second cathedral organist).
[5] A brilliant translucent varnish, giving the effect of lacquer. It was exploited, though not invented, in the eighteenth century by four brothers Martin, and had an immense vogue for sedan-chairs, tables, fans, boxes, etc.
[6] The Mozarts arrived on the 17th in Coblenz, where they spent about ten days. They stayed at the inn 'Zu den drei Reichskronen'.   [7] See p. 27, n. 9.

On the 19th and 20th we had the most atrocious rain. The 21st was an Ember Day, on which I did not want to travel. But in order that we should not spend our time to no purpose, the few nobles who are here arranged a concert, which was held on the 21st. It did not bring in much, but it was something, and I had no expenses in connexion with it. One of the reasons why I did not leave here immediately on the 19th or 20th was that Wolfgang had catarrh or a chill, which by the evening and the night of the 22nd had turned into a proper cold. So I am obliged to wait for a few days, especially as the weather is so bad. Thus we shall hardly leave before the 25th or 26th, for I must consider the health of my children before everything else. Here I met the Baron von Walderndorf and Kopp, a priest who was formerly a steward and is now an Ecclesiastical Commissioner. The Baron von Walderndorf and the Count von Pergen, Imperial Envoy, took my children by the hand to the Elector[1] and introduced us, so that it was due to them that we were heard immediately on the 18th. We also received at once a present of ten louis d'or.

We are a great deal with the family of Baron Kerpen, who is Electoral Privy Councillor and head of the nobility. He has seven sons and two daughters, nearly all of whom play the clavier and some of whom play the violin and the violoncello and sing. After this, you will not be surprized if you hear that since we left Salzburg, we have already spent 1068 gulden. But other people have paid for this expenditure. Besides, to keep our health and for the reputation of my court,[2] we must travel 'noblement'. Moreover we only associate with the nobility and distinguished personages and receive exceptional courtesies and respect.

(18) *Leopold Mozart to Lorenz Hagenauer, Salzburg*

[Extract]   [*Copy in the Deutsche Staatsbibliothek, Berlin*]

BRUSSELS,[3] 17 *October* 1763[4]

In Coblenz we took a private boat and leaving on September 27th at ten in the morning we reached Bonn[5] that same evening in good time. Thence we travelled by mail coach through Brühl to Cologne, where we arrived early in the evening of the 28th. We spent two days in that great old town. In the cathedral[6] there is a very ancient pulpit from which Martin Luther is supposed to have preached.

[1] Johann Philipp von Walderdorf, Elector of Trier.
[2] i.e. the Archbishop's court in Salzburg.
[3] The Mozarts arrived on 4 October in Brussels, where they remained until 15 November. They stayed at the 'Hôtel d'Angleterre'.
[4] According to Leopold Mozart's statement, this letter was sealed and despatched on 4 November.
[5] Nissen, p. 44, adds: 'In Bonn the Elector (Maximilian Friedrich) was away'.
[6] In his *Reiseaufzeichnungen*, p. 26, Leopold Mozart mentions 'the dirty minster or cathedral'.

On September 30th we left Cologne by mail coach, travelling through Aachen. It was the most awful road. Now as Aachen was the most expensive place which I had so far struck during our journey, I had the honour of spending *nolens volens*[1] over seventy-five gulden there. Princess Amalia,[2] sister of the King of Prussia, was there, it is true, but she herself has no money, and her whole equipage and court retinue resembles a physician's suite as closely as one drop of water another. If the kisses which she gave to my children, and to Wolfgang especially, had been all new louis d'or, we should be quite happy; but neither the innkeeper nor the postmaster are paid in kisses. The most ridiculous thing seemed to me that she tried by every means to persuade me to go not to Paris, but to Berlin, and what is more she made to me proposals which I shall not write down here, as nobody would believe them; for I did not believe them myself, especially the particular one which she made to me.

From Aachen we drove on October 2nd to Liége, where we only arrived at nine in the evening. We left early next morning—at about half past seven. It was the most lovely day. From Liége to Paris—just think of the amazing distance!—the post road is paved like the streets of a town and planted on either side with trees like a garden walk. We spent the night in Tirlemont. On the following day we reached Louvain early and spent the morning there in order to see the town a little. The principal church was the first building we visited. Here the valuable paintings of the famous Netherland painters begin. I stood transfixed before a 'Last Supper'.[3] On October 4th we reached Brussels early in the evening. We are staying at the 'Hôtel D'Angleterre'. Quantities of white and black marble and brass and the paintings of the most famous artists are to be found here in the churches in great numbers. Day and night I have before my eyes that picture by Rubens, in the big church, in which Christ in the presence of the other apostles hands the keys to Peter. The figures are life-size. In Prince Karl's[4] rooms I found not only beautiful Dutch tapestries and paintings, but also a room with original Chinese statues, porcelain, figures and various rare pieces; above all there was a room filled with an indescribable quantity of all kinds of natural history specimens. I have seen many such collections; but it would be difficult to find such a quantity and so many species.

Prince Karl's present recreations are to lacquer, paint, varnish, eat, drink and laugh heartily, so that he can be heard three or four rooms away. The rules of the church are still taken fairly seriously here. You can see at once that this is a country which belongs to Her Majesty the Empress.

[1] i.e. willy nilly.
[2] Princess Amalia (1723–1787) was a lover and connoisseur of music.
[3] A famous triptych (c. 1464) by Dierick Bouts in the Église Saint-Pierre.
[4] Prince Charles of Lorraine, brother of Emperor Francis I and Governor of the Austrian Netherlands. He died in 1780.

But rosaries are not usual and in the churches you never see anybody praying with one. They all pray out of books and at the elevation of the Host they never strike their breasts.[1] In all the churches no chairs are to be seen, but seats can be hired for a liard, in our coinage two pfennigs.

For you alone.   BRUSSELS, 4 *November* 1763
We have now been kept in Brussels for nearly three weeks.[2] Prince Karl has spoken to me himself and has said that he will hear my children in a few days; and yet nothing has happened. Yes, it looks as if nothing will come of it, for the Prince spends his time hunting, eating and drinking, and in the end it appears that he has no money. Meanwhile in decency I have neither been able to leave nor to give a concert, since, as the Prince himself has said, I must await his decision. You can imagine that I shall in addition have a pretty bill to pay at the hotel; and for the journey to Paris I must have at least two hundred gulden in my pocket.

We have now recevied here, it is true, various handsome presents, which, however, I do not want to sell.

Little Wolfgang has been given two magnificent swords, one from Count von Frankenberg, Archbishop of Malines, the other from General Count De Ferraris. My little girl has received Dutch lace from the Archbishop, and from other courtiers cloaks, coats and so forth. With snuffboxes and étuis and such stuff we shall soon be able to rig out a stall. Indeed I hope that next Monday, when a big concert is being held, I shall haul in plenty of fat thalers and louis d'or. But as one must always be on the safe side, I beg you to be so good as to arrange through Herr Haffner or some other person that I receive another letter of credit for Paris.

If Salzburg has been surprised at my children, it will be completely amazed provided that God lets us return home. A propos, have you not yet received the portraits[3] of my children?

(19) *Leopold Mozart to Lorenz Hagenauer, Salzburg*

[*Extract*]   [*Copy in the Deutsche Staatsbibliothek, Berlin*]

PARIS, 8 *December* 1763
After giving a fine concert in Brussels at which Prince Karl was present, we left at nine in the morning on my worthy name-day[4] with four post-horses, and after taking leave early of many good friends we reached Mons in the afternoon while it was still daylight. On the second day we

---

[1] Refers to the practice which still prevails in certain Catholic countries.
[2] Leopold Mozart surely means 'five weeks', as the Mozarts arrived on 4 October.
[3] Probably the portraits of Mozart and his sister in the costumes presented to them by the Empress Maria Theresia. See p. 8, n. 6 and n. 8.   [4] 15 November.

arrived just as early in Péronne and on the third in Gournay; on the fourth, November 18th, at half past three in the afternoon, we arrived at the Hôtel of the Count van Eyck[1] in Paris. Fortunately we found the Count and the Countess at home. They gave us a most friendly welcome and have provided us with a room in which we are living comfortably and happily. We have the Countess's harpsichord, because she does not need it. It is a good one and like ours has two manuals.

You would like to know perhaps how I like Paris? If I were to tell you this in circumstantial detail, neither the hide of a cow nor that of a rhinoceros would suffice. Buy yourself for forty-five kreuzer Johann Peter Willebrandt's *Historische Berichte und Pracktische Anmerkungen auf Reisen, etc. Frankfurt und Leipzig* 1761. It will amuse you. Tomorrow we must go to the Marquise de Villeroi and to the Countess Lillibonne. The mourning for the Infanta[2] still prevents us from playing at court.

(20) *Leopold Mozart to Lorenz Hagenauer, Salzburg*

[*Autograph in the Mozarteum, Salzburg*]

[VERSAILLES, *end of December* 1763[3]]

You may read the enclosed letter, make an extract of it, seal it up and deliver it to our Father Confessor with my most humble greetings and New Year wishes; or you may let him do the sealing himself.

Madame de Pompadour[4] is still a handsome woman. She is very like the late Frau Steiner, née Therese Freysauf,[5] and she has something of the appearance of the Austrian Empress, especially in her eyes. She is extremely haughty and still rules over everything. In Versailles[6] living is expensive; and it is very fortunate that at the present time it is almost as warm as in summer, for otherwise we should be hard put to it, as every log of wood costs five sous. Yesterday my boy got a gold snuff-box from Madame la Comtesse de Tessé[7] and today my little girl was given a small,

---

[1] Bavarian minister in Paris. His wife was a daughter of Count Georg Anton Felix Arco, Chief Chamberlain in Salzburg. They lived in the Hôtel Beauvais, rue St. Antoine (now rue de François-Miron, no. 68). According to a passage in his letter from Brussels here omitted, Leopold Mozart had taken rooms in the house where Christian von Mechel was living (see p. 33), but the Van Eycks invited the family to stay with them.

[2] Princess Isabella of Parma, grand-daughter of Louis XV and Joseph II's first wife, had died on 27 November 1763.

[3] The whole letter is written on a cover, which, according to a note on the autograph in Nissen's handwriting, contained a letter reporting on the Mozart's visit to Versailles, where they stayed from 24 December 1763 until 8 January 1764. No doubt the lost letter was to be given to the Archbishop.

[4] Mlle Jeanne Antoinette Poisson, later Mme le Normant d'Etioles, subsequently Marquise de Pompadour (1721–1764), had been established at Versailles since 1745 as 'maîtresse en titre'.

[5] The Freysauf family kept a shop in the Judengasse, Salzburg.

[6] At Versailles the Mozarts lodged 'Au Cormier, rue des Bons Enfants'.

[7] Lady-in-waiting to Madame la Dauphine. She kept a salon and was famous for her wit. Mozart's second printed work was dedicated to her.

transparent snuff-box, inlaid with gold, from the Princess Carignan, and Wolfgang a pocket writing case in silver, with silver pens with which to write his compositions; it is so small and exquisitely worked that it is impossible to describe it. My children have taken almost everyone by storm. But everywhere the results of the late war are to be seen. It is impossible to write down all that one would like to describe. Wish all my good friends a happy New Year. I should like to write to everybody if I had time and if every letter did not cost twenty or thirty sous. If I had written a longer letter to His Grace, I should certainly have had to pay five livres, for they charge according to the weight and the size or the shape. Did you send me an answer? Perhaps you did and I shall find it at our Hôtel in Paris when we get back. Farewell—à Dieu! Myself, my wife and children send our greetings and wish you, your wife and all your family a happy New Year. Thank God, we are all well. You should see Wolfgang in his black suit and French hat.

(21) *Leopold Mozart to Christian von Mechel* [1]

[Autograph in the Deutsche Staatsbibliothek, Berlin]

MON AMI!   [Paris, 9 *January* 1764]

We arrived back from Versailles yesterday evening at half past eight. I called at your quarters today after one o'clock and tried both entrances. To prove this I have written my name on your blackboard. We are hoping to see you soon. Farewell. My children send greetings to you.

MOZART

I even walked to your place, a very wonderful thing for me!

A Monsieur de Mechel,
    rue St. Honoré,
        chez M. le Noir, Notaire,
            vis à vis la rue d'Eschelle.

(22) *Leopold Mozart to Frau Maria Theresa Hagenauer*

[Extract]   *[Autograph in the Städtisches Museum, Salzburg]*

MADAME!   PARIS, 1 *February* 1764

One must not always write to men but must sometimes remember the fair and devout sex. I really cannot tell you whether the women in Paris are fair; for they are painted so unnaturally, like the dolls of

---

[1] Christian von Mechel (1737–1817), a native of Basel, lived during the years 1757–1764 in Paris, where he studied copper-engraving under Wille and Delafosse. After a short stay in Italy he returned to Basel, where he founded a famous firm of art dealers.

Berchtesgaden,[1] that even a naturally beautiful woman on account of this detestable make-up is unbearable to the eyes of an honest German. As for piety, I can assure you that it is not difficult to get to the bottom of the miracles of the French women saints; the greatest of them are performed by those who are neither virgins nor wives nor widows, and they are all performed during their lifetime. Later on we shall speak more fully on this subject. But really it is extremely difficult to distinguish here who is the lady of the house. Everyone lives as he or she likes and, if God is not specially gracious, the French state will suffer the fate of the former Persian Empire.

I received safely your husband's two letters of December 20th and January 19th with the three enclosures. The most important and certainly to you the most pleasant piece of information I can give you is that, thank God, we are all well. And I too always look forward most eagerly to hearing that all of you are in good health. Since my last letter from Versailles[2] I would assuredly have written to you, only I kept on postponing this in order to await the result of our affair at Versailles and be able to tell you about it. But as everything here, even more so than at other courts, goes at a snail's pace, and since these matters have to be dealt with by the Menus Plaisirs,[3] one must be patient. If the recognition we receive equals the pleasure which my children have given this court, we ought to do very well. I should like to tell you that it is not the custom here to kiss the hand of royal persons or to disturb them with a petition or even to speak to them *au passage*, as they call it, that is to say, when they walk to church through the gallery and the royal apartments. Neither is it the custom here to do homage either by an inclination of the head or a genuflexion to the King or to members of the Royal Family. On the contrary, one remains erect and immovable, and, standing thus, one just lets the King and his family pass close by. Hence you can well imagine how impressed and amazed these French people, who are so infatuated with their court customs, must have been, when the King's daughters, not only in their apartments but in the public gallery, stopped when they saw my children, came up to them and not only allowed them to kiss their hands, but kissed them innumerable times. And the same thing happened with Madame la Dauphine.[4] But what appeared most extraordinary to these French people was that at the *grand couvert* on the evening of New Year's Day, not only was it necessary to make room for us all to go up to the royal table, but my Wolfgang was graciously

---

[1] A village in Bavaria, near Salzburg, famous for centuries for its painted carvings.

[2] Letter 20.

[3] Term given to certain Royal expenses regulated by a special administration, housed in the Hôtel des Menus Plaisirs, which dealt chiefly with the ceremonies, festivals and performances at court.

[4] Maria Josepha of Saxony, wife of the Dauphin Louis who died in 1765, and mother of Louis XVI.

privileged to stand beside the Queen[1] the whole time, to talk constantly to her, entertain her and kiss her hands repeatedly, besides partaking of the dishes which she handed him from the table. The Queen speaks as good German as we do and, as the King knows none, she interpreted to him everything that our gallant Wolfgang said. I stood beside him, and on the other side of the King, where M. le Dauphin and Madame Adélaïde[2] were seated, stood my wife and daughter. Now you must know that the King never dines in public, except on Sunday evenings when the whole Royal Family dine together. But not everyone is allowed to be present. When, however, there is a great festival, such as New Year's Day, Easter, Whitsuntide, the name-days and so forth, the *grand couvert* is held, to which all persons of distinction are admitted. There is not, however, very much room and consequently the hall soon gets filled up. We arrived late. So the Swiss Guards had to make way for us and we were led through the hall into the room close to the royal table, through which the Royal Family enter. As they passed us they spoke to our Wolfgang and we then followed them to table.

You can hardly expect me to describe Versailles to you. I can only tell you that we arrived there on Christmas Eve and attended Matins and three Masses in the Royal Chapel. We were in the Royal Gallery when the King came from Madame la Dauphine, to whom he had been breaking the news which he had just received of the death of her brother, the Elector of Saxony.[3] I heard good and bad music there. Everything sung by individual voices and supposed to resemble an aria was empty, frozen and wretched—in a word, French; but the choruses are good and even excellent. So every day I have been with my little man to the Mass in the Royal Chapel to hear the choir in the motet, which is always performed there. The Royal Mass is at one o'clock. But if the King goes hunting, his Mass is at ten o'clock and the Queen's Mass at half-past twelve. I shall tell you more about all this later. In sixteen days we were obliged to spend about twelve louis d'or in Versailles. Perhaps you think it too much and find it difficult to understand? But in Versailles there is no *carosse de remise* and no *fiacre*, only sedan-chairs. Thus for every drive one has to pay twelve sous. So now you will see that, as on many days, for the weather was always bad, we had to have at least two, if not three, sedan-chairs, they came to one laubthaler and sometimes more. If you now add four new black suits, you will not be surprised if our visit to Versailles has cost us twenty-six or twenty-seven louis d'or. Well, we must see what we shall get from the court in return. Apart from what we hope to receive, we have not taken in at Versailles more than twelve louis d'or. My Master

[1] Maria Leszczynska, daughter of the exiled King of Poland, who married Louis XV in 1725.
[2] Eldest daughter of Louis XV.
[3] Elector Frederick Christian, who died of smallpox, 7 December 1763.

Wolfgang, however, has received from Madame la Comtesse de Tessé *a gold snuff-box* and *a gold watch*, valuable on account of its smallness, the size of which I have traced here. Nannerl has been given an uncommonly beautiful, *heavy toothpick case of solid gold*. From another lady[1] Wolfgang has received a travelling writing case in silver and Nannerl an unusually fine tortoiseshell snuff-box inlaid with gold. Further, the number of our snuff-boxes has been increased by a red one with gold bands, by another

in some sort of glass material set in gold, and by a third in vernis martin, inlaid with the most beautiful flowers of coloured gold and various pastoral instruments. In addition we have received a small ring set in gold with an antique head, and a host of trifles which I do not value very highly, such as sword-bands, ribbons and armlets, flowers for caps, fichus for Nannerl and so forth. But I hope after four weeks to have a better story to tell of louis d'or, for it takes longer than to walk to Maxglan[2] before one is properly known in Paris. And I assure you that it does not require a telescope to see everywhere the evil results of the late war.[3] For the French insist on continuing their external magnificence and therefore only the fermiers are rich, while the lords are deep in debt. The bulk of the country's wealth is divided amongst about a hundred persons, a few big banquiers and fermiers généraux; and, finally, most money is spent on Lucretias, who do not stab themselves. All the same you can imagine that remarkably beautiful and precious things are to be seen here, and astonishing follies too. In winter the women wear not only fur-trimmed garments, but also neck ruffles or neckties of fur and instead of flowers even fur in their hair and fur armlets and so forth. But the most ridiculous sight is the type of sword-band, which is in fashion here, bound round and round with fine fur—an excellent idea, for the sword will not catch cold. And in addition to their idiotic '*mode*' in all things, there is their extreme love of comfort, which has caused this nation to turn a deaf ear to the voice of nature. Hence everyone in Paris sends new-born children to be reared in the country. Persons of both high and low rank do this and pay a bagatelle for it. But you see the wretched consequences of this practice. For you will hardly find any other city with so many miserable and mutilated persons. You have only to spend a minute in a church or walk along a few streets to meet some blind or. ame or limping or half-putrefied beggar, or to find someone lying on the street who has had his hand eaten away as a child by the pigs, or someone else who in childhood fell into the fire and had half an arm burnt off while the foster-father and his family were working in the

[1] Princess Carignan. See p. 33.
[2] A suburb of Salzburg, about half an hour's walk from the town.
[3] For French social life at this period see Hippolyte Taine, *L'Ancien Régime*, 1875, *passim*, and J. B. Perkins, *France under Louis XV*, 1897, vol. ii.

fields. And there are numbers of such people, whom disgust makes me refrain from looking at when I pass them. Now I am going to jump from the ugly to the charming and moreover to someone who has charmed a king. You surely would like to know what Madame la Marquise de Pompadour is like? She must have been very beautiful, for she is still good-looking. In figure she is tall and stately, stout, or rather well-covered, but very well-proportioned. She is fair and extremely like our former Therese Freysauf,[1] while her eyes are rather like those of Her Majesty the Empress.[2] She is extremely dignified and uncommonly intelligent. Her apartments at Versailles are like a paradise and look out on the gardens. In Paris she has a most splendid Hôtel, entirely rebuilt, in the Faubourg St. Honoré. In the room where the clavecin is (which is all gilt and most artistically lacquered and painted) hangs a lifesize portrait of herself and beside it a portrait of the King. Now for another matter! There is a perpetual war here between the Italian and the French music.[3] The whole of French music is not worth a sou. But the French are now starting to make drastic changes, for they are beginning to waver very much; and in ten to fifteen years the present French taste, I hope, will have completely disappeared. The Germans are taking the lead in the publication of their compositions. Amongst these Schobert,[4] Eckardt,[5] Honnauer[6] for the clavier, and Hochbrucker[7] and Mayr[8] for the harp are the favourites. M. Le Grand,[9] a French clavier-player, has abandoned his own style completely and his sonatas are now in our style. Schobert, Eckardt, Le Grand and Hochbrucker have all brought us their engraved sonatas and presented them to my children. At present four sonatas of M. Wolfgang Mozart are being engraved.[10] Picture to yourself the furore which

[1] A Salzburg acquaintance. See p. 32.
[2] Maria Theresia, Empress of Austria. See p. 32.
[3] Rousseau, who sided with the Italians, in his *Confessions*, Book 8, gives a most vivid account of this 'war'. See also his *Lettre sur la musique française*, published in 1753. See Abert, vol. i. p. 627 ff.
[4] Johann Schobert (*c.* 1740–1767), a native of Silesia, settled in Paris in 1760 in the service of the Prince de Conti. He was a famous player on the harpsichord and composed sonatas for clavier with violin accompaniment, of which the first set was published in Paris in 1764. For an excellent account of Schobert and his influence on Mozart, see WSF, vol. i. p. 65 ff.
[5] Johann Gottfried Eckardt (1735–1809), born in Augsburg. From 1758 he lived in Paris, where as a player on the harpsichord he was a rival to Schobert. He also composed for his instrument and was a painter of miniatures. Eckardt's *Six sonates pour le clavecin* were published in Paris in May 1763. According to WSF, vol. i. p. 41 ff., they influenced Mozart's first two sonatas, K. 6 and 8.
[6] Leonzi Honnauer (1717–1809), harpsichordist to Prince Louis de Rohan, spent most of his life in Paris, where a number of his harpsichord sonatas were published, 1760–1770.
[7] Christian Hochbrucker, born in Bavaria, was a virtuoso on the harp. In 1760 he settled in Paris, where some of his compositions were published. In 1792 during the Revolution he fled to London.
[8] Probably Philippe Jacques Meyer (1737–1819), a native of Strassburg, who was a famous performer on the harp. He came to London in 1780 and settled there in 1784.
[9] Le Grand was a popular harpsichord teacher and organist at St. Germain-des-Prés.
[10] K. 6, 7, 8, 9, with the title *Sonates pour le clavecin qui peuvent se jouer avec l'accompagnement de violon*. K. 6, 7. were dedicated to Madame Victoire, Louis XV's second daughter. K. 8, 9

they will make in the world when people read on the title-page that they have been composed by a seven-year-old child; and when the sceptics are challenged to test him, as he already has been, imagine the sensation when he asks someone to write down a minuet or some tune or other and then immediately and without touching the clavier writes in the bass and, if it is wanted, the second violin part.[1] In due course you will hear how fine these sonatas are; one of them has an Andante[2] in a quite unusual style. Indeed I can tell you, my dear Frau Hagenauer, that every day God performs fresh miracles through this child. By the time we reach home, God willing, he will be able to contribute to the court music. He frequently accompanies in public concerts. He even, when accompanying, transposes *a prima vista*;[3] and everywhere Italian or French works are put before him, which he plays off at sight. My little girl plays the most difficult works which we have of Schobert and Eckardt and others, Eckardt's being the most difficult, with incredible precision, and so excellently that *this mean Schobert* cannot conceal his envy and *jealousy* and is making himself a laughing-stock to Eckardt, who is an honest man, and to many others. Later on I shall tell you many things which would take too long to relate here. Schobert is not at all the man he is said to be. He flatters to one's face and is utterly false. But his religion is the religion in fashion. May God convert him! Now I have a very sad piece of news, something extremely distressing. We are all in great anxiety and very much upset. In a word, Countess Van Eyck is in a most dangerous condition, so much so that without the special grace of God she will hardly live. On Sunday we were with her before lunch, between twelve and one, and she was very cheerful. She had then been indoors for a few days owing to a cold, but that day she had been to church. As always, she talked a great deal to Wolfgang. During the night I heard a carriage enter the courtyard and then some disturbance in the house. In the morning I was told that the Countess had suddenly fallen ill and had coughed up a quantity of blood. Imagine our distress, which is all the greater as I can only look on from a distance and may perhaps never speak to her or even see her again. My children pray and shed tears, as Wolfgang loves the Countess and she loves him to distraction. I am writing this on the evening of February 1st. God grant that tomorrow morning, before I close this letter, I may be able to write more cheerfully. My wife can think of nothing else all day long but the poor Countess and indeed we are deeply concerned.

There is now little room left on this sheet of paper. I must add, however,

were dedicated to the Comtesse de Tessé. The engraver of both publications was Mme Vendôme.

   [1] Grimm, *Correspondance Littéraire*, vol. iii. p. 365, has a letter dated Paris, 1 December 1763, describing the feats of these 'vrais prodiges'.

   [2] WSF, vol. i. p. 82, suggest that Leopold Mozart is referring to the Adagio of the sonata K. 7, which was probably composed at Versailles.   [3] i.e. at first sight.

that the Archbishop of Paris has been cast out into the wilderness or, to put it mildly, has been exiled. He had a libellous pamphlet printed against the Parlement in favour of the Jesuits, which brought this punishment upon him.[1] As far as I hear, everyone blames him, for the King, who was informed that he was going to publish this piece of writing, tried in a friendly manner to dissuade him. However he persisted and thus deliberately dashed his head against the wall. The King hastened to exile him, otherwise the Parlement would have arrested him. *The secular arm is a bit too powerful here.* On the other hand the clergy go about the streets singly, lower their cowls below their shoulders, hold their hats in their hands and are absolutely indistinguishable from lay pedestrians. Farewell and thank God that I have finished writing—otherwise you would indeed have to put on your spectacles.[2] With greetings from myself, my children and my wife, I am your devoted

MOZART

How is our good Dellmor? Is he still in our neighbourhood? He will sometimes think of us when he sees nobody at our windows. Please give him my compliments and greetings from us all and especially from little Wolfgang. He is an honest man.

(23) *Leopold Mozart to Lorenz Hagenauer, Salzburg*

[*Extract*]   [*Copy in the Deutsche Staatsbibliothek, Berlin*]

MONSIEUR,   PARIS, 22 *February* 1764

The sun cannot always shine and clouds often gather, only however to be again dispersed. I did not make haste to send tidings of the sad death of Countess Van Eyck.[3] I thought it would be sufficient if I prepared the hearts of the people in Salzburg for this sad event, while leaving it to others to report the end. Nobody likes to die anywhere; but here it is doubly sad for an honest German if he falls ill or dies.

Soon afterwards a sudden and unexpected event plunged me into a certain embarrassment. My dear Wolfgang suddenly got a sore throat and a cold, so that on the 16th, the morning on which it started, he developed such an inflammation of the throat that he was in danger of choking. He also had a very high fever. After four days he got up and is now well again.

[1] Christophe de Beaumont, Archbishop of Paris, published in 1763 an *Apologie des Jésuites*, which was condemned by the Parlement. In January 1764 the King exiled him forty leagues from Paris. The *arrêt* of the Parlement suppressing the Jesuit order in France was issued in August 1762. In the previous year, 1761, their goods had been declared confiscated and their educational establishments closed. All the bishops, with one exception, were opposed to the suppression, which was, however, strongly supported by public opinion.
[2] The letter is so closely written.
[3] On February 6th.

As a precaution I wrote by local post to our friend the German Doctor Herrnschwand, who is the doctor of the Swiss Guards. But he did not have to come more than twice. Then I gave the boy a small dose of Vienna laxative water: now thank God he is well. My little girl too is suffering from a cold, but is not feverish.

And now I beg you to have four Masses said as soon as possible at Maria-Plain and one at the Holy Child at Loreto. These we promised for the sake of our children, who were both ill. I hope that the other Masses will, as I asked, always continue to be said at Loreto, for as long as we are away. The Duc d'Ayen[1] has arranged that in a fortnight at latest we shall drive out again to Versailles, in order that we may present to Madame Victoire, the King's second daughter, to whom it has been dedicated, the Œuvre 1er of the engraved sonatas of the great M. Wolfgang.[2] The Œuvre 2e will be dedicated, I think, to Madame la Comtesse de Tessé.[3] Within three or, at most, four weeks important things will have happened, if God wills. We have tilled the soil well and now hope for a good harvest. But one must take things as they come. I should have had at least twelve louis d'or more, if my children had not had to stay at home for a few days. Thank God, they are better. Do you know what people here are always wanting? They are trying to persuade me to let my boy be inoculated with smallpox.[4] But as I have now expressed sufficiently clearly my aversion to this impertinence, they are leaving me in peace. Here inoculation is the general fashion. But, for my part, I leave the matter to the grace of God. It depends on His grace whether He wishes to keep this prodigy of nature in the world in which he has placed it, or to take it to Himself. I shall certainly watch over it so well that it is all one whether we are in Salzburg or in any other part of the world. But it is this watching which makes travelling expensive.

Mr d'Hébert, Trésorier des Menus Plaisirs du Roi, has handed to Wolfgang from the King fifty louis d'or and a gold snuff-box.[5]

(24) *Leopold Mozart to Lorenz Hagenauer, Salzburg*

[*Extract*]   [*Copy in the Deutsche Staatsbibliothek, Berlin*]

PARIS, 4 *March* 1764

I ought to have written to you long ago, but the things I have had to do for some days and shall have to do until the 10th in order to make sure

---

[1] Brother of the Comtesse de Tessé.
[2] K. 6, 7. This was Mozart's first printed work.   [3] K. 8, 9.
[4] From the middle of the eighteenth century the inoculation of healthy persons from smallpox subjects was very common. But it was not until 1796 that Jenner discovered and applied his discovery of vaccine.   [5] The original of this sentence occurs in Nissen p. 59.

that between six and nine on the evening of that day I shall pocket seventy-five louis d'or, have, as you will understand, prevented me.

On the 3rd our servant Sebastian Winter[1] left here with the country coach via Strassburg for Donaueschingen. He has entered the service of Prince von Fürstenberg[2] as friseur. I have taken on another friseur, called Jean Pierre Potivin, who speaks good German and French, for he was born at Zabern in Alsace. Now I have to buy his clothes, again a heavy expense.

MADAME!

You will think perhaps that we are taking part in quite extraordinary carnival festivities? Oh, you are very much mistaken. It has never occurred to me to attend balls, which only begin after midnight. Here there are balls in every quarter; but you must know that they are for thirty or forty people and that one or, at most, two violins without a violoncello play the minuets; and what sort of minuets? Why, minuets which were danced already in the time of Henry IV; and in the whole town there are about two or three favourite minuets, which must always be played, because the people cannot dance to any save those particular ones during the playing of which they learned to dance. But, above all, contredanses[3] or what we call English dances, are danced! All this I know from hearsay only, for so far I have not seen them.

(25) *Leopold Mozart to Lorenz Hagenauer, Salzburg*

[*Extract*]   [*Copy in the Deutsche Staatsbibliothek, Berlin*]

PARIS, 1 *April* 1764

We are all well and we thank God from the bottom of our hearts. And now I have the pleasure of informing you that I hope in a few days to lodge with the bankers Turton et Baur 200 louis d'or, to be entrusted to safe hands and in due course sent off to Salzburg. On April 9th I shall again have to stand the shock which I had on March 10th. But I doubt very much whether this one will be as great as the first, for at the concert on March 10th I took in one hundred and twelve louis d'or. But fifty to sixty louis d'or are not to be despised either and, if there are more, one simply pockets them. Not a farthing is paid at the door. But whoever is without a ticket is not admitted, no matter who he is. My friends sell the tickets a week beforehand, each for a laubthaler or a federthaler, four of

---

[1] See p. 19, n. 3.

[2] Joseph Wenzeslaus, Prince von Fürstenberg, himself a performer on the clavier and violoncello, collected his own Kapelle, which Franz Anton Martelli conducted, 1762–1770.

[3] The word is a corruption of the English 'country dance'. Mozart wrote a number of contredanses, especially during the years 1788, 1789 and 1791, for the masked balls at the Viennese court.

which make a louis d'or; and they collect the money. But most of the tickets, in blocks of twelve and twenty-four, are given to ladies, who sell them the more easily, as out of politeness one cannot refuse to buy them. *Est modus in rebus*[1], or, in our language, *Frenchmen like to be fooled*. On the billet (which is written on a card and bears my seal) there are only these words: Au Théâtre de M. Félix, rue et Porte St. Honoré, ce lundi 9 avril à six heures du soir. That is a hall in the house of a distinguished gentleman, in which there is a small theatre where the nobles often act and produce plays among themselves; and I got this room through Madame de Clermont, who lives in the house. But the permission to hold the two concerts there is something quite exceptional and is directly against the privilege which the King has given to the Opera, the Concert Spirituel[2] and the French and Italian theatres; and this permission had to be obtained from M. de Sartine, Lieutenant-General of Police, by the Duc de Chartres, Duc de Duras, Comte de Tessé and many of the leading ladies who sent messengers and wrote applications in their own hand.[3]

I beg you to have a Mass said for us every day for eight days after April 10th. You can distribute them as you like, provided that four are said at Loreto at the Holy Child and four at an altar of Our Lady. I only ask you to observe for certain the days I mention. Should this letter not arrive until after April 12th, though I think it will arrive before, please see that the Masses are begun on the following day. There are important reasons.[4]

And now it is time to tell you something about my two friends from Saxony, Baron von Hopfgarten and Baron von Bose.[5] They left here for Italy about two months ago and were bound for Vienna via Carinthia or Salzburg. I gave them a short letter for you, mentioning what I now write. If they travel through Salzburg, please assist them, so that they may not only see the sights of the place but also have due honour shown to them at court. For I myself have witnessed the great honours which these gentlemen received at the courts of the Elector of Bavaria, at Ludwigsburg, at the Palatine Court at Schwetzingen, at Mainz, at Brussels from Prince Karl and here at Versailles. They have been our loyal travelling companions. Sometimes they ordered our lodgings, sometimes we ordered theirs. Here you will find two men who have everything which honest men should have in this world; and, although they are both Lutherans,

[1] i.e. there is a limit in things.

[2] A great French musical institution, founded under Louis XV in 1725, which came to an end during the Revolution. As the Opera House was closed on important religious festivals, A. D. Philidor (1681–1728) obtained permission to arrange concerts on these days, pledging himself to perform neither French nor operatic music. The number of concerts in the year never exceeded twenty-four. The 'Concert Spirituel' formed the model for other public concerts and from it the history of concert-giving in the eighteenth century developed.

[3] See Leopold Mozart's letter no. 284b, in which he goes over this incident for the benefit of his son, who is on his way to Paris.

[4] Obviously refers to the Mozarts' approaching journey to London, during which they would cross the sea for the first time.   [5] See p. 22.

yet they are Lutherans of a different type and men from whose conversation I have often profited much. When parting, Baron von Bose gave
Wolfgang as a remembrance a beautiful book containing spiritual
thoughts in verse,[1] and wrote the following lines in front:

> Take this book, little seven-year-old Orpheus, from the hand of your admirer
> and friend! Read it often—and feel its divine songs and lend them (in these
> blissful hours of emotion) your irresistible harmonies; so that the heartless
> despiser of religion may read them—and pause—may hear them—and fall
> down and worship God.
>
> FRIEDRICH KARL, Baron von Bose

These two gentlemen can tell you a hundred things about our journey,
and their company will afford you a thousand pleasures. If they go to
Salzburg they will turn up after the Ascensa[2] in Venice. The taller of the
two is Baron Hopfgarten and the little one is Baron von Bose.

We have by this time made the acquaintance of all the foreign envoys
in Paris. The English Ambassador, Mylord Bedford, and his son are very
partial to us; and the Russian Prince Galitzin[3] loves us as if we were his
children. In a few days the sonatas will be ready, which little Master
Wolfgang has dedicated to the Comtesse de Tessé. They would have been
ready before; but the Countess absolutely refused to accept the dedication
written by our best friend, M. Grimm.[4] So it had to be altered; and as she
is usually in Versailles, we have had to wait all this time for an answer. It
is a pity that this dedication was not allowed to be engraved. But the
Countess refuses to be praised; and in this dedication both she and my
boy are very vividly described. The Comtesse de Tessé has given Wolfgang another gold watch and Nannerl a gold box.

But now you must know who this man is, this great friend of mine, to
whom I owe everything here, this M. Grimm. He is secretary to the Duc
d'Orléans and he is a man of learning and a great friend of humanity. All
my other letters and recommendations brought me nothing; even those
from the French Ambassador in Vienna, the Imperial Ambassador in
Paris and all the letters of introduction from our Minister in Brussels,
Count Cobenzl, Prince Conti, Duchesse d'Aiguillon and all the others,
a whole litany of whom I could write down. M. Grimm alone, to whom
I had a letter from a Frankfurt merchant's wife, has done everything. He

[1] Nissen, p. 61, mentions Gellert's *Geistliche Oden und Lieder* (1757) as the book, Gellert
being the outstanding Protestant writer of sacred poems.
[2] The Festival of Our Lord's Ascension, 10 May 1764.
[3] Dimitri Alexeivich Galitzin (1734–1803), Russian Ambassador to France (1763) and
Holland (1769) and an intimate friend of Voltaire and Diderot.
[4] Friedrich Melchior Grimm (1723–1807) was the son of a German pastor in Regensburg.
He studied in Leipzig, came to Paris in 1748, and in 1755 became secretary to the Duc
d'Orléans. He was a friend of Diderot, d'Alembert, Rousseau, etc. He founded the famous
Correspondance Littéraire, which survived till 1790.

brought our business to court. He arranged for the first concert and he paid me on his own account eighty louis d'or, that is to say, he got rid of three hundred and twenty tickets. In addition he paid for the lighting, as more than sixty large wax candles were burnt. Well, this M. Grimm secured permission for the first concert and is now arranging for the second, for which one hundred tickets have already been sold. So you see what a man can do who has good sense and a kind heart. He comes from Regensburg. But he has been in Paris for over fifteen years already and knows how to launch everything in the right direction, so that it is bound to turn out as he wishes.

[*Written on the cover*]   [*Autograph in the Mozarteum, Salzburg*]

My children and my wife send their greetings to all. M. de Mechel,[1] a copper-engraver, is working himself to death to engrave our portraits, which M. de Carmontelle (an amateur)[2] has painted excellently well. Wolfgang is playing the clavier, I am standing behind his chair playing the violin, Nannerl is leaning on the clavecin with one arm, while in the other hand she is holding music, as if she were singing.

(26) *Leopold Mozart to Lorenz Hagenauer, Salzburg*

[*Extract*]   [*Copy in the Mozarteum, Salzburg*]

LONDON, 25 *April* 1764[3]

Thank God, we have safely crossed the Maxglanerbach.[4] Yet we have not done so without making a heavy contribution in vomiting. I, however, had the worst time of it. But we saved money which would have been spent on emetics; and, thank God, we are all well. Whoever has too much money should just take a journey from Paris to London; for his purse will certainly be lightened. We had the honour of spending four louis d'or in Calais,[5] although we did not take a single meal at home, but took them with the Procureur du Roi et de l'Amirauté, with whom we also left our carriage. As soon as you arrive at Dover, it is even worse; and when you land from the boat, you find yourself surrounded by

---

[1] See p. 33, n. 1. Possibly Mechel engraved the Carmontelle portrait under the direction of J. B. Delafosse, who signed it.

[2] L. C. de Carmontelle (1717–1806), painter and writer. He was a protégé of the Duc d' Orléans. See illustration no. 2.

[3] According to Nissen, p. 65, the Mozarts left Paris on 10 April. In his *Reiseaufzeichnungen* Leopold Mozart states that they arrived in London on 23 April. For an account of their stay of fifteen months in England see C. F. Pohl, *Mozart und Haydn in London*, Vienna, 1867, Part II. p. 93 ff.

[4] i.e. the English Channel. The allusion is to a tiny stream at Maxglan, a suburb of Salzburg. See p. 36, n. 2.

[5] Under Calais Nannerl noted in her diary (reproduced in Leopold Mozart's *Reiseaufzeich-nungen*, p. 59): 'I saw how the sea runs away and comes back again'.

twenty to forty people who are all 'your most obedient servant' and who want to snatch your luggage from your own servants in order to carry it to the inn, after which they must be paid what they demand. I had to pay three louis d'or for the crossing, for I took a boat for my family, for which one has to pay five louis d'or. I therefore took with me four other passengers, who each paid half a louis d'or. To be landed in a small boat at Dover from the large boat each person has to pay half a federthaler. So I had to pay six small or three large laubthaler, for I had two servants with me and had taken seven post-horses as far as Calais, as one servant rode. The second servant was an Italian called Porta, who has done this journey eight times already, so that all my friends in Paris advised me to take him with me. It was a very good thing too, for he arranged everything well and did all the bargaining. In London everyone seems to me to be in fancy dress; and you cannot imagine what my wife and my little girl look like in English hats and I and our big Wolfgang in English clothes. My next letter will tell you more. We greet you.

MOZART

My address is:

À Monsieur Mozart, at the house of Mr. Cousin,
haircutter in Cecil Court,
St. Martin's Lane,
at
London.[1]

(27) *Leopold Mozart to Lorenz Hagenauer, Salzburg*

[*Extract*]   [*Copy in the Deutsche Staatsbibliothek, Berlin*]

MONSIEUR!   LONDON, 28 *May* 1764

You know that the farther away an object is, the smaller does it seem to the eye; and so it is with my letters. My handwriting becomes smaller according to the distance I am from Salzburg. If we were to sail over to America, my letters would probably become quite illegible. For a mere letter without a cover the cost from here to Germany is a shilling and another shilling for the cover, so that a letter with a cover costs two shillings. A guinea is 21 shillings and is equal in value to the louis d'or, for at Dover the banker Miné, who had been recommended to me in Paris, gave me 12 guineas for 12 louis d'or. French money is not accepted here. You can work out, therefore, the value of a shilling. In her letter to Paris our most gracious Frau Hagenauer suggested: 'Perhaps even to England and Holland?' When I left Salzburg I had not quite decided to come to

---

[1] The Mozarts spent the first night at the coach-inn 'The White Bear' in Piccadilly (*Reiseaufzeichnungen*, p. 33), and then moved to their lodgings.

England. But as everybody, in Paris particularly, urged us to go to London, I made up my mind to do so. And now by the help of God we are here. But we shall not go to Holland, that I can assure everyone.[1] We still do not know how we shall fare. We really ought to have come here in winter.

On April 27th we were with the King and Queen[2] in the Queen's Palace[3] in St. James's Park; so that by the fifth day after our arrival we were already at court.[4] The present was only twenty-four guineas, which we received immediately on leaving the King's apartment, but the graciousness with which both His Majesty the King and Her Majesty the Queen received us cannot be described. In short, their easy manner and friendly ways made us forget that they were the King and Queen of England. At all courts up to the present we have been received with extraordinary courtesy. But the welcome which we have been given here exceeds all others. A week later we were walking in St. James's Park. The King came along driving with the Queen and, although we all had on different clothes, they recognized us nevertheless and not only greeted us, but the King opened the window, leaned out and saluted us and especially our Master Wolfgang, nodding to us and waving his hand.

In addition to all his kindnesses M. Grimm, our sworn friend, who did everything for us in Paris, gave Nannerl on our departure a gold watch and Wolfgang a fruit-knife such as is used in Paris with glacé fruits, the handle of which is of mother-of-pearl set in gold. It has two blades, one of gold and the other of silver. I intended to send off this letter a week ago. I was, however, not only prevented from doing so, but I wanted to wait for some news. But I have nothing more to tell, except that on May 19th we were again with the King and Queen from six to ten in the evening, when the only other people present were the two princes, who are the King's brothers, and another, the brother of the Queen. When we left the room we were again handed twenty-four guineas. If this happens every three or four weeks, we can put up with it! Now we are going to give on June 5th[5] a so-called benefit concert or *concerto al nostro profitto*. It is really not the time to give such concerts and little profit is to be expected from them, for the season is over and the expenses of an undertaking of this kind

---

[1] Leopold Mozart, pressed to do so by the Dutch minister in London (see p. 58), took his family to Holland in September 1765. They remained there until the end of April 1766.

[2] George III, then twenty-seven years old, who since 1761 had been married to Charlotte Sophie von Mecklenburg-Strelitz, then twenty-one. Both were devoted to music and the Queen sang and played on the clavier tolerably well.

[3] Buckingham House, built in 1703 by the Duke of Buckingham, and bought by the Crown in 1720.

[4] Nannerl and Wolfgang performed at court on 27 April, 19 May and 25 October. See Leopold Mozart's *Reiseaufzeichnungen*, p. 33.

[5] The *Public Advertiser* announced a concert on 17 May, in Hickford's Room, Brewer Street, Golden Square, at which Master Mozart was to appear. This concert was postponed until 22 May, and even then Mozart, who was indisposed, did not perform.

amount to forty guineas. But since the King's birthday is on the 4th, many of the nobility will come up to town from the country. So we must take the risk and make use of this opportunity to become known. Each person pays half a guinea and, if it were winter, I could certainly count on six hundred persons, that is, three hundred guineas. Now, however, they all go to the pleasure gardens and into the country. Basta! Everything will certainly succeed, if with God's help we keep well and if He only keeps our invincible Wolfgang in good health. The King placed before him not only works of Wagenseil,[1] but those of Bach,[2] Abel[3] and Handel,[4] and he played off everything *prima vista*. He played so splendidly on the King's organ that they all value his organ-playing more highly than his clavier-playing. Then he accompanied the Queen in an aria which she sang, and also a flautist[5] who played a solo. Finally he took the bass part of some airs of Handel (which happened to be lying there) and played the most beautiful melody on it and in such a manner that everyone was amazed. In short, what he knew when we left Salzburg is a mere shadow compared with what he knows now. It exceeds all that one can imagine. He greets you from the clavier, where at the moment he is seated, playing through Kapellmeister Bach's trio.[6] We also send you greetings. Not a day passes without Wolfgang's talking at least thirty times of Salzburg and of his and our friends and patrons. He has now continually in his head an opera which he wants to produce there with several young people. I have already had to count up all the players whom he has noted down for his orchestra, among whom Kolb and Ranftl are often mentioned.

(28) *Leopold Mozart to Lorenz Hagenauer, Salzburg*

[*Extract*]   [*Copy in the Deutsche Staatsbibliothek, Berlin*]

MONSIEUR!   LONDON, 8 *June* 1764

With the greatest pleasure in the world I received on June 6th your letter of May 21st, which therefore must have been wafted over by a

[1] Georg Christoph Wagenseil (1715–1777) of Vienna, organist to the Imperial court and music-master to the Empress Maria Theresia and her children.
[2] Johann Christian Bach (1735–1782), the youngest son of Johann Sebastian Bach, was trained by his brother Philipp Emanuel Bach in Berlin, then went to Milan and Bologna, where he studied under Padre Martini. In 1762 he came to London, where his operas *Orione* and *Zanaïda* were performed in 1763 and a third one, *Adriano in Siria*, in 1765.
[3] Karl Friedrich Abel (1725–1787), probably a pupil of Sebastian Bach, entered the Dresden court orchestra in 1748. He visited London in 1759 and in 1765 was appointed chamber musician to Queen Charlotte. He was a distinguished performer on the viola da gamba and founded in 1765 with J. C. Bach, with whom he lived, the famous Bach-Abel subscription concerts, fifteen concerts a year, an undertaking which lasted until 1781.
[4] George III's favourite composer.
[5] Probably Tacet, a frequent performer at the Bach-Abel concerts. See Leopold Mozart's *Reiseaufzeichnungen*, p. 34.
[6] WSF, vol. i. p. 104, suggest that this was one of the trios in J. C. Bach's Op. 2, *Six sonates pour le clavecin, accompagnées d'un violon ou flute traversière et d'un violoncelle*, published in London in 1763.

favourable wind. I am infinitely glad that my first letter reached you safely and I trust that the second one, which I sent off on the 20th, has arrived in the meantime.

I have had another shock, that is, the shock of taking in one hundred guineas in three hours. Fortunately it is now over. I have already told you that everyone is at present out of town. June 5th was the only day on which a concert could be attempted, because the King's birthday was on the 4th, and the reason why we gave it then was in order to become known. We had a week, or rather two or three days only, in which to distribute the 'billets', for before that date there was hardly anyone in London. But, although for this kind of concert four to eight weeks are usually necessary for the distribution of the 'billets', which here they call 'tickets', to the amazement of everyone there were present more than a couple of hundred persons, including the leading people in all London; not only all the ambassadors, but the principal families in England attended it and everyone was delighted. I cannot say whether I shall have a profit of one hundred guineas, as I have not yet received the money for thirty-six tickets from Mylord March[1] and for forty tickets from a friend in town and from various others; and the expenses are surprisingly great. But the profit will certainly not be less than ninety guineas. Now listen to a few details about the expenses. The hall without lighting and music-stands costs five guineas. Each clavier, of which I have had to have two on account of the concerto for two claviers, costs half a guinea. The first violin gets three guineas and so on; and all who play the solos and concertos three, four and five guineas. The ordinary players receive each half a guinea and so forth. But, fortunately for me, all the musicians as well as the hall and everything else only cost me twenty guineas, because most of the performers would not accept anything. Well, God be praised, that is over and we have made something.

My greetings to Herr Schachtner[2] and please thank him from me and from my wife and children for his friendly remembrances. I cannot send him any details other than what he will find in the newspapers, in the letters which I have written to you, and especially in my last one. What it all amounts to is this, that my little girl, although she is only twelve years old, is one of the most skilful players in Europe, and that, in a word, my boy knows in this his eighth year what one would expect only from a man

[1] William Douglas (1724–1810), 3rd Earl of March, succeeded his cousin as fourth Duke of Queensberry in 1778. He was a well-known man about town and a great patron of the turf and the opera. Later in life he was known as 'old Q', under which name he is constantly referred to by Horace Walpole.

[2] Johann Andreas Schachtner (1732–1795) had been court trumpeter in Salzburg since 1754. He was closely connected later with Mozart as the translator into German of the Italian libretto of *Idomeneo* and the author of the text of *Zaide*. After Mozart's death he wrote to Nannerl the famous letter of April 1792, describing her brother's childhood. See Abert, vol. i. p. 26 ff.

LEOPOLD MOZART WITH HIS SON AND DAUGHTER (1763)

From a water-colour painting by Carmontelle

(Musée Condé, Chantilly)

of forty. Indeed only he who sees and hears him can believe it. You yourself and all our Salzburg friends have no idea of Wolfgang's progress; for he is quite different now.

I must close, for the post is going.

I am

your obedient servant

MOZART

PS.—My wife and I, Nannerl and our all-powerful Wolfgang send greetings to you, to your whole household and to all Salzburg.

(29) *Leopold Mozart to Lorenz Hagenauer, Salzburg*

[*Extract*]   [*Copy in the Deutsche Staatsbibliothek, Berlin*]

MONSIEUR!   LONDON, 28 *June* 1764

I have much pleasure in informing you that I have again deposited with the bankers Loubier et Tessier a small sum of 100 guineas, which I could arrange to be paid to someone at Salzburg who might wish to use it in this country.

At the end of next week we are going to Tunbridge,[1] about thirty English miles from London, a distance which can be covered by the mail coach in three or four hours, for an English mile is not more than a German quarter of an hour. There are wells there and it lies in a corner between the east and the south. In July and August many of the nobility assemble in Tunbridge, for now nobody who has means and leisure remains in London.

On Friday, June 29th, that is, on the Feast of St. Peter and St. Paul, there will be a concert or benefit at Ranelagh in aid of a newly established Hôpital de femmes en couche,[2] and whoever wishes to attend it must pay five shillings entrance. I am letting Wolfgang play a concerto on the organ at this concert[3] in order to perform thereby the act of an English patriot who, as far as in him lies, endeavours to further the usefulness of this hospital which has been established *pro bono publico*. That is, you see, one way of winning the affection of this quite exceptional nation.

I send greetings, and so do my wife and Nannerl and little Wolfgang, who is always thinking of Salzburg.

I am

your old

MOZART

---

[1] Owing to Leopold Mozart's illness this plan was not carried out.
[2] Probably the Lying-in Hospital (Surrey), the foundation-stone of which was laid in 1765.
[3] The notice of this concert in the *Public Advertiser* of June 26th described Mozart as 'the most extraordinary prodigy and most amazing genius that has appeared in any age', and

(30) *Leopold Mozart to Lorenz Hagenauer, Salzburg*

[*Extract*]   [*Copy in the Deutsche Staatsbibliothek, Berlin*]

MONSIEUR,   LONDON, 3 *August* 1764

Do not be frightened! But prepare your heart to hear one of the saddest events. Perhaps you will have already noticed my condition from my handwriting. Almighty God has visited me with a sudden and severe illness which I contracted after a chill caught on my way home from a concert held at Mylord Thanet's,[1] and which I feel too weak to describe. Well! I have been clystered, purged and bled too on account of a severe inflammation of my throat. That is all over now and the doctors declare that I have no fever and tell me to eat. But I feel like a child. My stomach does not fancy anything and I am so frail that I can hardly think sensibly.

9 *August* 1764[2]

I congratulate you on your name-day. I intended to write to you immediately after I received your welcome letter. But I was far too weak. I am now in a spot outside the town,[3] where I have been carried in a sedan-chair, in order to get more appetite and fresh strength from the good air. It has one of the most beautiful views in the world. Wherever I turn my eyes, I only see gardens and in the distance the finest castles; and the house in which I am living has a lovely garden.

It depends on the grace of God whether He will preserve my life. His most holy will be done.

(31) *Leopold Mozart to Lorenz Hagenauer, Salzburg*

[*Extract*]   [*Copy in the Deutsche Staatsbibliothek, Berlin*]

CHELSEA near LONDON, 13 *September* 1764

MONSIEUR,

I notice that our letters have usually taken 16 to 17 days, for up to the present I have always received one from you on the 17th, or at any rate early on the 18th day. I thank you most humbly for having carried out so

---

stated that this boy of seven years (Mozart was then eight and a half) would perform on the harpsichord and organ works of his own composition.

[1] Sackville Tufton, 8th Earl of Thanet (1733–1786). He had succeeded to the title in 1753. C. F. Pohl, *op. cit.* p. 103, n. 2, states that the Tufton family were devoted to the arts, mentioning the fact that in 1732 six cantatas by H. Carey appeared with a dedication to the father of the eighth Earl.   [2] This letter was finished in Chelsea.

[3] Chelsea was then a village two miles from London, proverbial for its healthy situation. The Mozart family took a house belonging to a Dr. Randal in Fivefields-Row (now 182 Ebury Street), where, according to Leopold Mozart's *Reiseaufzeichnungen*, p. 34, they spent seven weeks. It was here that Mozart composed his first symphonies, K. 16 and 19.

accurately my request for Masses. I now state that every day, although my progress is slow, I am feeling a little better, so that I am confident that I have no internal disorder. So that you may know, however, how my illness started, I must tell you that in England there is a kind of native complaint, which is called a '*cold*'. That is why you hardly ever see people wearing summer clothes. They all wear cloth garments. This so-called '*cold*' in the case of people who are not constitutionally sound, becomes so dangerous that in many cases it develops into a '*consumption*' as they call it here; but I call it '*febrem lentam*';[1] and the wisest course for such people to adopt is to leave England and cross the sea; and many instances can be found of people recovering their health on leaving this country. I caught this '*cold*' unexpectedly and in the following way. On July 8th at six in the evening we were to go to Mylord Thanet's.[2] Before six I sent out to the stands where carriages are to be found, but not one was to be had. It was Sunday, so all had been hired. It was an exceedingly fine and very hot day. I sent for a sedan-chair, put my two children into it and walked behind, as the weather was unusually lovely. But I had forgotten how fast the bearers stride along here; and I soon had a taste of it. I can walk fairly quickly, as you know, and my stoutness does not prevent me from doing so. But, before we arrived at Mylord Thanet's I often thought that I should have to give up; for London is not like Salzburg. And I perspired as profusely as it is possible for a man to do. I had only a silk waistcoat on, though I was wearing a cloth coat, which I buttoned up immediately on arriving at Mylord Thanet's. But it was to no purpose. The evening was cool and all the windows were open. We stayed until eleven o'clock and I at once felt ill and engaged a second sedan-chair to take me home. Yet until the 14th, although I did not feel well, I went about and tried to cure myself by perspiring, which is the remedy generally adopted here. But it was no good.

My wife and children send their greetings. My wife has had a great deal to do lately on account of my illness, and, as you may imagine, she has had a great many anxieties. In Chelsea we had our food sent to us at first from an eating-house; but as it was so poor, my wife began to do our cooking and we are now in such good trim that when we return to town next week we shall continue to do our own housekeeping. Perhaps too my wife, who has become very thin, will get a little fatter.

You yourself will have probably gathered that I shall certainly spend at least the whole winter here, and that, God willing, I shall make in London my chief profit of some thousands of gulden. I am now in a city which no one at our Salzburg court has ever yet dared to visit and which perhaps

---

[1] i.e. a slow fever.
[2] Leopold Mozart in his *Reiseaufzeichnungen*, p. 35, mentions Mylord Thanet, Grosvenor Square.

no one will ever visit in future. *Aut Caesar, aut nihil.*[1] We have come to our long journey's end. Once I leave England, I shall never see guineas again. So we must make the most of our opportunity. If only God in His graciousness grants us good health, we need not worry about the guineas. I am only sorry that I am obliged to spend what I might have saved. But it was God's will. Both in Salzburg and in London we are in His hands. He knows how good my intentions are. During the coming months I shall have to use every effort to win over the aristocracy and this will take a lot of galloping round and hard work. But if I achieve the object which I have set myself, I shall haul in a fine fish or rather a good catch of guineas.

(32) *Leopold Mozart to Lorenz Hagenauer, Salzburg*

[Extract]   [*Copy in the Deutsche Staatsbibliothek, Berlin*]

MONSIEUR!   LONDON,[2] 27 *November* 1764

Do not be surprised that I am rather late in replying. I have more to do than most people would imagine, although the nobility are not in town and Parliament, contrary to usage, is not assembling until January 10th of next year[3] and therefore guineas are not yet flying about and I am still living on my purse. Yet it will soon be high time for me to fill it up again, for since the beginning of July I have spent over one hundred and seventy guineas. In addition I have the heavy expense of having six sonatas[4] of our Master Wolfgang engraved and printed, which (at her own request) are being dedicated to the Queen of Great Britain.

I and all my family send you and your wife millions of congratulations on the beginning of the new career of your son Cajetan.[5] I have a very good opinion of him and, since you are ever a good and sensible father, you will certainly welcome him with open arms and a smiling face when he comes home. As he has always been a quiet and placid boy, he will only do what is most wholesome for his spiritual welfare. On that account, he is doing his novitiate. Little Wolfgang wept when I read out this portion

[1] i.e. Either Caesar or nothing.

[2] On their return to town about September 25th the Mozarts took lodgings at Mr. Thomas Williamson's, 15 Thrift Street (now Frith Street), Soho. The house, which was rebuilt in 1858, occupied the site of the present no. 21, on the east side of the street. See F. G. Edwards, *Musical Haunts in London*, 1895, p. 46.

[3] The Parliament of 1765, which passed the Stamp Act, was opened by the King on January 10th.

[4] K. 10–15. They were called *six sonates pour le clavecin qui peuvent se jouer avec l'accompagnement de violon ou flaute traversière*, and the date of dedication was 18 January 1765. They were engraved at Leopold Mozart's expense. Wolfgang received from the Queen 50 guineas and the work was on sale at their lodgings from March 20th.

[5] Dominicus (Cajetan) Hagenauer entered the monastery of St. Peter at Salzburg in 1764 and in 1786 became abbot of the monastery. A Latin diary which he kept in 1769 mentions Mozart frequently. For the first Mass which Father Dominicus celebrated in October 1769, Mozart wrote his mass K. 66 (the Pater Dominicus Mass).

of your letter and, when he was asked why, he said that he was grieved, as he believed that he would never see him again. But we told him that it would not be so. He remembered that your son had often caught a fly for him and that he used to blow the organ and bring him his air-gun. As soon as he returns to Salzburg he is going to St. Peter's[1] and Mr. Cajetan is to catch a fly for him and shoot with him. So he has donned the garb of his order and entered upon his novitiate on the same day on which about seventeen years ago[2] I joined the order of patched trousers and made my profession at Aigen[3] with my wife.

(33) *Leopold Mozart to Lorenz Hagenauer, Salzburg*

[*Extract*]   [*Copy in the Deutsche Staatsbibliothek, Berlin*]

MONSIEUR!   LONDON, 3 *December* 1764

You will have received my letter of November 27th.[4] Here is the letter accompanying the sonatas.[5]

Whoever wants to buy these sonatas will have to pay forty-five kreuzer for each part, that is, one gulden, thirty kreuzer for both parts or for all four sonatas (since each part consists of two sonatas). Will you please see that a detailed notice about them is put in the Salzburg papers? In Paris the price of each part is four livres, four sous, as you will see on the title-page; a great difference from the price of forty-five kreuzer. In Frankfurt each part is being sold at one gulden, thirty kreuzer. I regret that a few mistakes have remained in the engraving, even after the corrections were made. The woman who engraved them and I were at too great a distance; and, as everything was done hurriedly, I had no time to obtain a revised proof. That is the reason why especially in Œuvre IIe in the last trio you will find three consecutive fifths in the violin part,[6] which my young gentleman perpetrated and which, although I corrected them, old Madame Vendôme left in. On the other hand, they are a proof that our little Wolfgang composed them himself, which, perhaps quite naturally, everyone will not believe. Well, it is so, all the same. My little Wolfgang sends greetings to you all and especially to Herr Spitzeder and asks him to perform these sonatas before His Grace, Wenzel playing the violin part.

[1] The famous Abbey of St. Peter in Salzburg, which was founded by St. Rupert in 696, and where the Archbishops lived until 1110.
[2] Leopold Mozart and his wife were married on 21 November 1747.
[3] A village about seven miles from Salzburg.
[4] Letter 32.
[5] Œuvre I (K. 6, 7) and Œuvre II (K. 8, 9), which had been engraved in Paris.
[6] It was in the second minuet of the fourth sonata (K. 9) that Mozart displayed his lack of experience. In subsequent editions this succession was replaced by a succession of sixths.

On October 25th, the King's Coronation Day,[1] we were with the King and Queen from six to ten.[2]

(34) *Leopold Mozart to Lorenz Hagenauer, Salzburg*

[*Extract*] [*Copy in the Deutsche Staatsbibliothek, Berlin*]

MONSIEUR, LONDON, 8 *February* 1765

On the evening of the 15th we are giving a concert, which will probably bring me in about one hundred and fifty guineas. Whether I shall still make anything after that and, if so, what, I do not know. By postponing the summoning of Parliament (which usually assembles two months earlier) the King has dealt upon the whole a severe blow at all arts and sciences.[3] To explain this would take too long.

This winter, nobody is making much money except Manzuoli[4] and a few others in the opera. Manzuoli is getting 1500 pounds sterling for this season and the money has had to be guaranteed in Italy, as the previous impresario De Giardini[5] went bankrupt last year; otherwise Manzuoli would not have come to London. In addition he is giving a benefit,[6] that is, an evening recital for himself, so that this winter he will be drawing more than 20,000 German gulden. He is the only person whom they have had to pay decently in order to set the opera on its feet again. On the other hand, five or six operas are being performed. The first was 'Ezio',[7] the second 'Berenice',[8] both so-called pasticci of different masters, the third 'Adriano in Syria', newly composed by Signor Bach.[9] And I know that a

---

[1] C. F. Pohl, *op. cit.* p. 109, draws attention to a slip of Leopold Mozart, inasmuch as it was the anniversary, not of the King's coronation (which took place on 22 September 1761), but of his accession to the throne in 1760.

[2] Although the Mozarts did not leave London until the end of July 1765, this was the last time the children performed at court.

[3] See p. 52.

[4] Giovanni Manzuoli, born 1725 in Florence, after Farinelli the most famous male soprano of his day. He sang in Madrid and Vienna and came to London for the opera season 1764–1765. Mozart took singing lessons from him and met him later in Florence.

[5] Felice De Giardini (1716–1796), born in Turin, eminent violinist. He first appeared in London in 1751. In 1756 he undertook the management of the Italian opera at the King's Theatre, Haymarket, suffered great financial losses, but retained it till 1765. Contrary to Leopold Mozart's statement, he was manager during the season 1764–1765.

[6] Manzuoli produced for his benefit Giardini's opera *Il Rè pastore* on 7 March 1765, and according to the *Gentleman's Magazine*, March 1765, made a profit of 1000 guineas. Ten years later Mozart set the same text to music.

[7] Performed 24 November 1764, a pasticcio consisting of pieces by several composers, a form of opera very common in the eighteenth century. For a repetition of *Ezio* Mozart composed his first aria 'Va, dal furor portata' (K. 21 [19c]).

[8] Performed 1 February 1765, a pasticcio of music by seven composers, including J. C. Bach, Galuppi, Vento, Abel.

[9] By Johann Christian Bach, performed 26 January 1765, 'by command of Their Majesties', and repeated seven times.

newly composed 'Demofoonte' by Vento[1] is coming, and then a few more pasticci. I shall tell you about all this later on.

I am writing this letter (to be followed by another very soon) solely in order not to miss the opportunity of sending a few sonatas[2] to Augsburg and Nuremberg. So I beg you to send thirty copies of each part, that is, sixty copies in all, to Herr Johann Jacob Lotter,[3] and the same number to Herr Haffner, lute-player in Nuremberg.[4] You will note that each part has been sold at the price of one gulden, thirty kreuzer, but, as they are a bit of a rarity, I shall let them go to the natives of Salzburg half price. Please have this inserted in our local newspapers, adding that the little composer wants to let his fellow townsmen have each part for forty-five kreuzer, or both parts for one gulden, thirty kreuzer, in order to encourage the young people of Salzburg to study music with zest.

We send our greetings to all. Oh, what a lot of things I have to do. The symphonies at the concert will all be by Wolfgang Mozart.[5] I must copy them myself, unless I want to pay one shilling for each sheet. Copying music is a very profitable business here. Our Estlinger[6] would laugh. I send him my congratulations. Addio.

(35) *Leopold Mozart to Lorenz Hagenauer, Salzburg*

[*Extract*]   [*Copy in the Deutsche Staatsbibliothek, Berlin*]

MONSIEUR!   LONDON, 19 *March* 1765

I am certain that my last short letter reached you before the end of Salzburg's Lent market and that therefore it arrived in time.[7]

My concert, which I intended to give on February 15th, did not take place until the 21st, and on account of the number of entertainments (which really weary one here) was not so well attended as I had hoped. Nevertheless, I took in about one hundred and thirty guineas. As, however, the expenses connected with it amounted to over twenty-seven

---

[1] Mateo Vento (1735–1776), born in Naples, a famous operatic composer. He was brought by De Giardini in 1763 to London, where he composed a number of operas. His *Demofoonte* was performed on 2 March 1765, and was repeated thirteen times.

[2] Mozart's Œuvre I and Œuvre II (K. 6–9).

[3] Johann Jacob Lotter, music publisher in Augsburg. He published in 1756 Leopold Mozart's *Violinschule*. Leopold Mozart corresponded frequently with him. Schurig, vol. i. pp. 58–66, gives a selection of these letters.

[4] Johann Ulrich Haffner, music publisher in Nuremberg.

[5] The concert was postponed to February 18th and again to February 21st, when it was held in the Little Theatre, Haymarket, at 6 P.M. 'in order to allow the nobility to attend other assemblies'. The notice added that 'all the ouvertures (i.e. symphonies) are by this amazing composer, who is only eight years old'. Mozart was then nine. The symphonies which were performed had been composed in Chelsea. See p. 50, n. 3.

[6] A Salzburg music copyist.

[7] Probably refers to Letter 34 and to the opportunity of sending copies of Mozart's first printed works to Augsburg and Nuremberg.

guineas, I have not made much more than one hundred guineas.[1]

I know, however, what the reason is, and why we are not being treated more generously, although since our arrival in London we have made a few hundred guineas. I did not accept a proposal which was made to me. But what is the use of saying much about a matter upon which I have decided deliberately after mature consideration and several sleepless nights and which is now done with, as I will not bring up my children in such a dangerous place (where the majority of the inhabitants have no religion and where one only has evil examples before one). You would be amazed if you saw the way children are brought up here; not to mention other matters connected with religion.

I must ask you to reply to this letter as soon as possible, for, as it is quite likely that I shall leave London at the beginning of May, I must have an answer by the end of April.

The Queen has given our Wolfgang a present of fifty guineas for the dedication of the sonatas.

Please ask our dear friend Spitzeder to forgive me for not yet replying to his very welcome letters. He will surely realise how much a man has to do, who is keeping his whole family in a town where, even with the strictest economy, it costs him 300 pounds sterling a year to do so, and where, in addition, he ought to be saving a little. Has Herr Adlgasser not yet returned to Salzburg? We send him our greetings. Why, of course we know Mr. Bach. I must close, for the post is going.

(36) *Leopold Mozart to Lorenz Hagenauer, Salzburg*

[*Extract*]   [*Copy in the Deutsche Staatsbibliothek, Berlin*]

Monsieur!   London, 18 *April* 1765

I was delighted to receive your letter. You have made most excellent arrangements. At the moment I have very little news to send you.

As for my departure, I have no more definite news; and any sensible person must realize that it is not an easy matter to decide. It will take us all our time to get away from here. The very sight of the luggage we have to pack makes me perspire. Just think! We have been in England for a whole year. Why, we have practically made our home here, so that to take our departure from England requires even more preparation than when we left Salzburg.

---

[1] The next and last concert was held on 13 May 1765. On March 11th the *Public Advertiser* had a notice that the 'prodigies of nature' were giving in six weeks a last concert before their departure from England and that every day from 12 to 3, visitors could come to Mr. Mozart's lodgings in Thrift Street, hear the prodigies perform in private, test them and buy concert tickets, now reduced to five shillings each. Leopold Mozart took the opportunity of selling copies of Mozart's sonatas and engravings of the Carmontelle painting.

(37) *Leopold Mozart to Lorenz Hagenauer, Salzburg*

[*Extract*]   [*Copy in the Deutsche Staatsbibliothek, Berlin*]

MONSIEUR!   LONDON, 9 *July* 1765

No doubt you will all be thinking that we have long ago swum over the sea. But it has been impossible to get away. We are now in London and once we leave we cannot return to England in three days. So I simply cannot hurry.

I beg you when you receive this letter to arrange immediately for six Masses to be said, two at the Holy Child at Loreto, two in the Parish and two at Maria-Plain. These are to prepare our way over the sea.[1]

I thought when I left Paris that I had requested my friend M. Grimm to send a number of the portrait engravings[2] to you at Salzburg. As I heard nothing more about this, I enquired recently from him and he replied that I had never said anything about it. I have therefore asked him to send you a large supply, so that if a parcel arrives you will know what it is. Please present a copy to our most gracious lord.[3] These copper engravings were done immediately after our arrival in Paris, when my boy was seven and my little girl eleven. Grimm was responsible for this. In Paris each engraving is sold for twenty-four sous.

(38) *Leopold Mozart to Lorenz Hagenauer, Salzburg*

[*Extract*]   [*Copy in the Deutsche Staatsbibliothek, Berlin*

THE HAGUE,[4] 19 *September* 1765

You are receiving a letter from the Haag, but not from the Haag[5] near Munich, nor from the Haag which is near Lambach[6] in Austria. No! It is from the Haag in Holland. That will indeed seem very strange to you, the more so as you may have hoped, even if you did not think it, that maybe we were not so far away. We would have been, if not near you, nevertheless already out of Holland, had not an indisposition which first affected my little Wolfgang in Lille and then myself kept us back for four weeks. But now you are going to hear all about the accident which has brought us here, seeing that I had decided to go not to Holland,[7] but to

---

[1] Leopold Mozart was proposing to leave England. The last notice in the *Public Advertiser*, July 11th, stated that the children would play every day from 12 to 3 in the 'Swan and Hoop' tavern, Cornhill, admittance 2s. 6d., and that they would play together on one clavier with the keyboard covered.

[2] See p. 44, n. 2.   [3] The Archbishop.

[4] The Mozarts arrived at The Hague on September 11th and stayed at the inn 'La Ville de Paris', described in Leopold Mozart's *Reiseaufzeichnungen*, p. 41, as 'une très mauvaise auberge'.

[5] A village 33 miles from Munich, on the road to Salzburg.

[6] A village about thirty miles from Linz, on the road to Salzburg.   [7] See p. 46.

Milan and home through Venice. The Dutch Envoy in London several times begged us to visit the Prince of Orange at The Hague. But I let this go in by one ear and out by the other. We made preparations for our departure; and so little did I think of going to Holland that I sent *all our furs* and other things in a trunk to Paris. But when on July 24th we had actually left and had driven out of London, we spent a day in Canterbury and then stayed until the end of the month at the country home of an English gentleman[1] in order to see the horse-racing. On the very day of our departure the Dutch Envoy drove to our lodgings and was told that we had gone to Canterbury for the races and would then leave England immediately. He turned up at once in Canterbury and implored me at all costs to go to The Hague, as the Princess of Weilburg,[2] sister of the Prince of Orange, was extremely anxious to see this child, about whom she had heard and read so much. In short, he and everybody talked at me so insistently and the proposal was so attractive that I had to decide to come, the more so as you know that one should not refuse anything to a woman in pregnancy. So I left England on August 1st, and sailed from Dover at ten in the morning. We had most beautiful weather and such a good wind that in three and a half hours we landed at Calais port and took our midday meal with a healthy stomach, as we had not been sick during the crossing. Our plan now was to spend the month of August in Holland, to reach Paris towards the end of September and then move gradually homewards until we should come in sight of the Untersberg.[3]

In Calais we made the acquaintance of the Duchesse de Montmorency and the Prince de Croy; thence I went to Dunkerque. We then drove to Lille, whither the Chevalier de Mezziers, Commandant in Dunkerque, had persuaded us to go. Now we have another proof that our human plans count for nothing. In Lille Wolfgang contracted a very bad cold and when after a few weeks it had improved somewhat, my turn came. This put us back four weeks and I was not very well when I left Lille[4] and was not much better when we arrived in Ghent, where we only stayed a day. Ghent is a large but not a populous town. In the afternoon Wolfgang played on the new organ at the Bernardines. In Antwerp we remained two days on account of Sunday and there Wolfgang played on the big organ in the Cathedral. I should mention that good organs are to be found in Flanders and Brabant. But a great deal could be said here

---

[1] Leopold Mozart (*Mozart. Briefe und Aufzeichnungen*, No. 99, lines 138, 139) has: 'Mr. Horatio Man Esqr.: at Bourn near Canterbury, Kent. Bourne Place, seven miles south-east of Canterbury, was the mansion house of the manor of Bishopsbourne and, according to Hasted, *History of Kent*, 1790, vol. iii. p. 746, n. (x), Sir Horace Mann resided there for several years, presumably by some arrangement with the owner, Mr. Stephen Beckington. This Horace Mann (1744–1814) was the nephew of Sir Horace Mann, British Minister in Florence and the friend and correspondent of Horace Walpole.

[2] Princess Caroline of Nassau-Weilburg.

[3] The most conspicuous mountain near Salzburg, about 6500 ft.   [4] On September 4th.

about the best of the pictures. Antwerp especially is the place for these. We have been to all the churches and I have never seen more black and white marble and such a wealth of excellent paintings, especially by Rubens, as I have seen here and in Brussels; above all, his 'Descent from the Cross' in the great church in Antwerp surpasses everything one can imagine. I left my carriage in Antwerp and hired one from the post-master to drive as far as Moerdijk. There we crossed a small arm of the sea. On the other side there are coaches ready to drive one as far as Rotterdam, where one then gets into a small boat and is taken almost to the inn. It was a good day's journey from Antwerp to Rotterdam, as it took from half past six in the morning until eight o'clock in the evening. We only spent half a day in Rotterdam, as we left in the afternoon on a trekschuit[1] for The Hague and were already there at seven o'clock. I must confess that I should have been very sorry if I had not seen Holland; for in all the towns of Europe which I have visited, everything for the most part seems to be the same, whereas both the Dutch towns and villages are quite different from all others in Europe. It would take too long to describe them, but I must say that I very much appreciate their cleanliness (which to many of us appears excessive). I should also like to add that I enjoyed seeing the statue of the famous Erasmus of Rotterdam in the square of that city. We have now been eight days at The Hague and have been twice with the Princess and once with the Prince of Orange, who had us fetched and sent home in his carriage. My daughter, however, was not with us. For now her turn has come and she has a very heavy cold on the chest, which is only now beginning to loosen. As soon as she is better, we have to go again to the Prince of Orange, the Princess of Weilburg and the Duke of Wolfenbüttel. The journey here has been paid for. But I shall have to see who is going to pay for the return journey. For I should prefer not to touch the money which is lying in wait for me at Amsterdam.

In Lille on August 26th we heard of the death of the Emperor.[2]

(39) *Leopold Mozart to Lorenz Hagenauer, Salzburg*

[*Extract*]   [*Copy in the Deutsche Staatsbibliothek, Berlin*]

THE HAGUE, 5 *November* 1765

Yes, yes! Most certainly! *Homo proponit, Deus disponit.*[3] I have a sure proof of this. Man cannot escape his fate.

I had to come to Holland against my inclination and though I have not lost my daughter, I have seen her lying well-nigh *in extremis*. Yet who

---

[1] Dutch for a 'barge'.
[2] Francis I, Holy Roman Emperor, died on 18 August 1765.
[3] A favourite quotation of Leopold Mozart. See p. 14.

urged us to come to Holland more than my daughter? Indeed she had the greatest desire to go whither her fate was driving her. You will remember that in my first letter which I wrote from here I told you that she had caught a cold on September 12th, the second day after our arrival. At first it appeared to be of no consequence and even seemed to be getting better, so she did not go to bed. But on the evening of the 26th she suddenly started to shiver and asked to lie down. After the shivering she had fever and I saw that her throat was inflamed. The following day she was no better and I sent for a doctor. To cut a long story short, at four o'clock on the evening of the 28th she was bled; and although her pulse improved somewhat, she still was a little feverish.

The doctor himself had given up hope and my poor child, feeling how weak she was, partly realised the danger. I prepared her to resign herself to God's will and not only did she receive Holy Communion but the priest found her in such a serious condition that he gave her the Holy Sacrament of Extreme Unction, for she was often so weak that she could hardly utter what she wanted to say. Whoever could have listened to the conversations which we three, my wife, myself and my daughter, had on several evenings, during which we convinced her of the vanity of this world and the happy death of children, would not have heard it without tears. Meanwhile little Wolfgang in the next room was amusing himself with his music. On October 21st, the same day on which I had the Holy Sacrament given to her at five o'clock in the afternoon, I arranged for a consultation at half past one (which they call here before mid-day). The honest old Professor Zwenke [1] (who no longer attends anybody and whom the Princess of Weilburg sent to me) showed at once that he understood the case much better. First of all he took the child's hand and felt her pulse thoroughly. He put on his glasses and examined her eyes, her tongue and her whole face. Then he had to be told the *statum morbi*. [2] This was the first time that I had especial reason to be grateful for my knowledge of the Latin tongue, for if I had not known that language, Herr Professor would have been told of quite different symptoms. For after the doctor had already been convicted by his conscience that he had made a complete blunder, he had of course to explain and describe the case in such a way as to justify the remedies he had used. But whenever he said anything which was not accurate, I contradicted him as I had already done every time he talked of the lesions, boils, pocks on the lung (or whatever he preferred to call them) which he had diagnosed. He declared more particularly that she was in pain and could not lie on both sides, which was not true and which I contradicted every time he said it.

---

[1] Thomas Zwenke, Director of the School of Anatomy and private physician to the Stadt-holder. See Scheurleer, *Mozarts Verblijf in Nederland*, 's Gravenhage, 1883, p. 76.
[2] i.e. the state of the illness.

All this time, whether asleep or awake, she was delirious and kept talking in her sleep, now in English, now in French, and now in German; and as our travels had given her plenty to chatter about, we often had to laugh in spite of all our distress. This did something to remove the sadness which Wolfgang was feeling on account of his sister.

Now it depends upon whether God will graciously allow her to recover her strength or whether some other accident will send her into eternity. We have always trusted to the Divine Will and even before we left Salzburg we prayed to God earnestly to prevent or to bless our intended journey. If my daughter dies, she will die happy. If God grants her life, then we pray to Him to send her later such an innocent and blessed death as she would have now. I hope for the latter. For on that same Sunday when she was very ill, I read the Gospel '*Domine, descende*'. 'Come, Lord! before my daughter dies.' And now on this Sunday the Gospel was: '*Thy daughter slept: thy faith hath helped thee*'. You will find it, if you look it up in the Gospel. But you can easily imagine what a time we have been having, and that all my plans have been suddenly upset. We could not and would not entrust our child to strangers, so for a long time my wife has not been going to bed until six in the morning, when I get up and look after my daughter till noon. Thus my wife and I have divided the time until midday, each of us sleeping about five or six hours. And how long will it be until my daughter, if she is to recover, will be in a fit state to travel? This is the worst season and the weather is getting more severe. Our furs were sent from Calais to Paris, for, according to my reckoning, we should have already left Holland by now. You are always asking me by what route I shall travel home. Did I not write to you that I sent a trunk from Calais to Paris? And you know that I have already left a lot of luggage there. It follows therefore that I must travel through Paris, as I want to do. I shall not lose by it. It was my intention to spend the three months, August, September and October, in Brabant, Holland and Flanders, to stay in Paris during November and to travel home in December so that I should certainly be home *ad Festum S. Thomae*.[1] Now God has upset my calculations and it no longer depends on what I wish, but on the condition of my daughter; and any reasonable person will see that, if God spares her, I cannot expose her capriciously to the obvious danger of losing her life through an inopportune journey. It is easy to understand that I have derived no advantage, but the greatest loss from this accident. And I think that there is sufficient cause for wonder (if one considers it well) how I am in a position to stand these tours and especially in the style in which we travel. For France, England and Holland are countries where one talks, not about pieces of twelve and pennies, but only about louis

---

[1] December 29th.

d'or, guineas, ducats and reitters.[1] Perhaps you do not know what a reitter is? It is a Dutch coin—a whole reitter being worth fourteen Dutch gulden, half a reitter seven Dutch gulden. I shall show them to you. My present expenses are perfectly dreadful, for here one must pay for everything. Everyone knows of course what Holland is. So heavy inroads are made on my purse. Basta! After all, what is money, if only I get away again safe and sound with my family?

Please arrange for a Mass to be said for my daughter at Maria-Plain, one at the Holy Child at Loreto, one in honour of St. Walpurgis[2] and two at Passau on the Mariahilfberg. My little girl has been thinking too of pious Crescentia[3] and has been wanting to have a Mass said in her honour as well. But, as we are not entitled to do this until our Church has come to a decision about this pious person, I leave it to your dear wife to hold a Consistorium about this with some Franciscan fathers, and so to arrange the matter that my daughter shall be satisfied and the ordinances of God and of our church shall not be offended.[4]

I have not yet been to Amsterdam. But as soon as my daughter is well enough for me to leave my wife alone with her, I am going to drive there with Wolfgang, but only to spend a few days. By the mail coach it is only a journey of six or seven hours, though it takes longer by water. These are all very curious facts and I shall talk to you about them later on. I shall not fail to do what you want in Amsterdam. In conclusion I hope that you do not think from the circumstances of my daughter's illness and treatment that I took the first doctor I could get. No indeed! He is Dr. Hayman, Physician to the Imperial, Portuguese, Spanish, French and Neapolitan Envoys, all of whom recommended him to me.

(40) *Leopold Mozart to Lorenz Hagenauer, Salzburg*

[Extract]   [*Copy in the Deutsche Staatsbibliothek, Berlin*]

THE HAGUE, 12 *December* 1765

That you may be relieved at the outset of all anxiety, I now tell you that, thank God, we are all alive. Yes, I can almost say that we are all well.

---

[1] i.e. rijder.
[2] St. Walpurgis, born in Sussex *c.* 710, went to Germany *c.* 750 with some nuns at the request of St. Boniface of Mainz. In 754 she became Abbess of the Benedictine Nunnery of Heidenheim and on the death of her brother Wunnibald, Abbot of the monastery of Heidenheim, she succeeded to his charge and governed the joint community until her death *c.* 779. In 871 her relics were removed to Eichstätt, where a church was built which became a place of pilgrimage. Her festival was celebrated at various times of the year and particularly on May 1st. Walburga was Nannerl's third Christian name. See Jahn, vol. i. p. 26, n. 1.
[3] St. Crescentia. Little is known about her. It is said that a tumulus with a stone containing an inscription about her death originally existed near Paris.
[4] St. Crescentia had not yet been canonised.

For our dear little Wolfgang has at last, with the help of God, survived his horrible struggle and is on the road to recovery.

My daughter was scarcely a week out of bed and had just begun to walk across the bedroom floor by herself, when on November 15th little Wolfgang contracted an illness which in four weeks has made him so wretched that he is not only absolutely unrecognizable, but has nothing left but his tender skin and his little bones and for the last five days has been carried daily from his bed to a chair. Yesterday and today, however, we led him a few times across the room so that gradually he may learn to use his feet and stand upright by himself. You would like to know what was wrong with him? God knows! I am tired of describing illnesses to you. It began with a fever. Our night vigils were shared, as they were during my daughter's illness; so that it is owing to the great grace of God that we, especially my wife, have been able to stand all this. But patience! What God sends must be endured. Now all that I can do is to await the time when it will please the Almighty to give my Wolfgang sufficient strength to enable us to undertake such an important journey at this season. Expense must not be considered. The devil take the money, if one only gets off with one's skin! But I will not describe to you the other circumstances in which we have found ourselves for the last three months. Had it not been for God's quite extraordinary grace, my children would not have survived these severe illnesses nor we these heavy blows.

Please have the following Masses said soon: three at the Holy Child at Loreto, one at Maria-Plain and one at Passau on the Mariahilfberg, two at St. Anne in the Parish Church of the Franciscans, one in honour of St. Walpurgis and one in honour of St. Vincent Ferrer,[1] in all nine Masses. My daughter is now so well that no trace of her illness is to be seen. I hope to God that our dear Wolfgang will also recover in a few weeks; for youth soon regains strength. I owe replies to letters from Adlgasser and Spitzeder which I shall repay in a few days. My present circumstances will excuse me. Please give our compliments to all. My children's illness, especially our Wolfgang's, has saddened not only us, but all our friends here. My daughter is not yet known in Holland, for she fell ill the day after our arrival.[2] But I cannot count my friends in this place, for people might think it boastful.

---

[1] St. Vincent Ferrer (1355–1419) was a Spanish Dominican and the most famous preacher of his generation. He was appointed by Benedict XIII master of the Sacred Palace and he played an important part at the Council of Constance (1415), where he proposed the simultaneous deposition of the three rival popes. He was canonised by Calixtus III in 1455.

[2] Mozart had performed at court alone on September 12th and 18th. On September 30th he had given a concert alone, at which all the ouvertures (symphonies) were of his composition and at which musicians were invited to give him new music to read.

(41) *Leopold Mozart to Lorenz Hagenauer, Salzburg*

[*Extract*]   [*Copy in the Deutsche Staatsbibliothek, Berlin*]

PARIS,[1] 16 *May* 1766

You will undoubtedly be more surprised than usual at not having received a letter from me for so long, and I should not have left you without any news of our condition if I had not been assured that you had heard about us at least twice from Herr Kulmann in Amsterdam. The illness of my children is the only reason why I have not yet sent you and my friends as exact a description of Holland as I have done of France and England. From Amsterdam[2] we returned to The Hague for the festival of the Prince of Orange (which took place on March 11th[3] and lasted some time), on which occasion our little composer was asked to turn out six sonatas for the clavier with violin accompaniment,[4] for the Prince's sister, Princess von Nassau-Weilburg. These were at once engraved. In addition he had to compose something for the Prince's concert and also arias for the Princess and so forth. On our arrival home you shall see them all. I have asked Herr Kulmann to send a little box to you at Salzburg. As soon as it arrives, please open it and look for the small wide parcel, which is unsealed and on which 'Music' is written. In it you will find two copies of the sonatas engraved at The Hague. Take one copy with the violin part and get the clavier and violin parts bound separately and see that these are presented most humbly to His Grace on our behalf. In the same parcel there are two sets of variations, one of which little Wolfgang had to compose on an air,[5] written on the occasion of the majority and installation of the Prince; the other set he dashed off hurriedly on another melody[6] which everybody all over Holland is singing, playing and whistling. They are trifles! But if you want to add a copy of each, you may do so, as they are unusual. I shall have the honour of showing you my 'Violinschule' in the Dutch language.[7] This book these Dutch gentlemen translated and

---

[1] The Mozarts arrived on May 10th in Paris, where they stayed until July 9th, lodging 'chez M. Brie, baigneur, rue traversière'. They spent four days, May 28th to June 1st, in Versailles.

[2] After giving a second concert at The Hague, on January 22nd, at which both Nannerl and Wolfgang performed, Leopold Mozart took his family to Amsterdam, where the children gave concerts on January 29th and February 20th. At both concerts, at which only Mozart's compositions were performed, they played works for four hands on one clavier and at the second concert works for two claviers. Probably the symphony Bb (K. 22), composed at The Hague, was performed at one of these concerts.

[3] The correct date was March 8th. Abert, vol. i. p. 71, suggests that March 11th was the day on which the Mozarts appeared at court.

[4] K. 26–31, announced in the *'sGravehaagsche Woensdagse Courant*, 16 April 1766.

[5] K. 24, harpsichord variations on an air composed for the installation of the Stadtholder by C. E. Graf or Graaf (1723–1804), Kapellmeister to the Prince of Orange.

[6] K. 25, harpsichord variations on the old national anthem of Holland, *Wilhelmus van Nassouwe*. The fugue of the 'Galimathias musicum' (K. 32) which Mozart, with his father's assistance, also composed for the festival, is on the same air.

[7] A Dutch translation of Leopold Mozart's *Versuch einer gründlichen Violinschule*, Augsburg, 1756. The copy which was presented to William V is in the Royal Library at The Hague.

produced in the same format as the original. It was dedicated to the Prince and presented to him in my presence at the festival of his installation. The edition is an uncommonly fine one, even finer than my own. The publisher (or rather, the printer in Haarlem) came to me and handed me the book in a respectful manner. He was accompanied by the organist who invited our little Wolfgang to play on the great organ in Haarlem, which is so famous. This took place on the following morning from ten to eleven. It is an extremely fine instrument with 68 stops, entirely of pewter, be it noted, for wood does not last in this damp country.

It would take too long to describe our journey from Holland through Amsterdam, Utrecht,[1] Rotterdam, across the Maas, and then across an arm of the sea at Moerdijk to Antwerp. Still more impossible would it be to describe the present sorry state of the formerly great commercial town of Antwerp and to enumerate the causes thereof.[2] Later on we shall talk about this. We travelled through Malines, where we visited our old acquaintance, the Archbishop,[3] to Brussels, where we only rested for a day and, leaving by the mail coach at nine in the morning, arrived in Valenciennes at half past seven in the evening.

In Cambrai I saw the tomb of the great Fénelon and his marble bust. He has made himself immortal by his 'Télémaque', his book on the education of girls, his dialogues of the dead, his fables, and other sacred and secular works. Then without stopping anywhere we travelled on to Paris and went to the lodgings which our friend M. Grimm had engaged for us. Thank God, we found our luggage in good condition.

As we are now dressed again in black, one can see how my children have grown. We are all well. When we get back to Salzburg nobody, at first, will recognize little Wolfgang. It is a long time since we left and meanwhile he has seen and got to know many thousands of people.

My very dear Hagenauer, we met in Amsterdam a native of Salzburg who owing to certain circumstances had become a Calvinist. My most urgent desire was to lead him back to the right path. I made every effort. That brought me back to Amsterdam[4] and kept me longer in Holland.

---

[1] The Mozarts gave another concert in Amsterdam on April 16th and one in Utrecht.

[2] The main decline of Antwerp was in the sixteenth century. About 1540 it was at the height of its importance. Then came very unhealthy speculations, leading to serious bankruptcies and unsettlement; and the political troubles made many prominent citizens take refuge in Holland. From 1580 onwards it was in decline and Amsterdam soon passed it in importance. In the eighteenth century it suffered from the closing of the Scheldt (ever since the Treaty of Münster) and it was sacked by the French in 1746. In 1780 its population was only *c.* 40,000, 12,000 of whom were living on alms.

[3] See p. 31.

[4] Probably refers to his second visit to Amsterdam in the middle of April when his children gave their third concert.

(42) *Leopold Mozart to Lorenz Hagenauer, Salzburg*

[*Extract*]   [*Copy in the Deutsche Staatsbibliothek, Berlin*]

PARIS, *9 June* 1766

Next week we are to go again to Versailles, where twelve days ago we spent four whole days.

I have not told you what our next route will be, for I think it will be more interesting if the superscription on my next letter tells it to you. Meanwhile we have had the pleasure of a visit from His Highness the Hereditary Prince of Brunswick,[1] a very agreeable, handsome and friendly gentleman. On entering the room he asked me whether I was the author of the book on the violin, and so on. He is soon to leave Paris, visit en passant forts of Metz, Strassburg and the rest, and then travel via Geneva to Turin, and so through Italy.

(43) *Leopold Mozart to Lorenz Hagenauer, Salzburg*

[*Extract*]   [*Copy in the Deutsche Staatsbibliothek, Berlin*]

LYONS, 16 *August* 1766

Do not be shocked that I am writing to you from Lyons. By the time that you receive this letter we shall have had, with the help of God, a sufficiently long opportunity of discovering what Geneva and the Genevan pocket watches are like, for in two or three days we leave here for that city. We went from Paris to Dijon[2] in Burgundy, where we spent a fortnight. We did this on account of the Prince de Condé, who had invited us there on the occasion of the assembly of the Burgundian states, which only takes place every three years.

We shall probably stay at least a fortnight in Geneva. Then we shall travel through Switzerland by way of Lausanne and Berne. But whether we shall leave Switzerland on the right by Zürich or on the left by Basel, I do not know. Thence we shall go straight through Ulm to Dischingen[3] to His Highness Prince Taxis, as we arranged with M. Becke,[4] whom we met in Paris, and who will also be there. Further, I hope to meet the Bishop of Augsburg either in Dillingen or in Augsburg and, after paying

---

[1] Karl (–1780).

[2] Leopold Mozart's *Reiseaufzeichnungen* has the entry 'Dijon', p. 40, before the second entry 'Paris', p. 47. In Dijon the Mozarts met Charles de Brosses (1709–1777), famous later for his *Lettres familières, écrites d'Italie*, 1739–40. He was a great lover of music, had associated with Hasse, Tartini, etc., and translated into French Metastasio's dramas. Leopold Mozart's criticism of the violinists in the Dijon orchestra is 'asini tutti'.

[3] A small village about thirteen miles from Dillingen, where Schloss Taxis is.

[4] Probably Johann Baptist Becke, born in 1743, flautist in the court orchestra at Munich, and later Leopold Mozart's constant correspondent.

our brief respects to His Highness the Elector of Bavaria and Duke Clemens, to congratulate Frau Hagenauer on her name-day.[1] But all this with the help of God! People have been trying hard to persuade us to proceed to the French ports of Marseilles, Bordeaux, etc. And don't you think it very heroic and magnanimous of us to have decided to abandon a trip to Turin, which lies almost in front of us? Don't you think that its proximity, our circumstances, the general encouragement to do so and our own interest and love of travel ought to have induced us to follow our noses and go to Italy and then, after witnessing the Festival of the Ascension in Venice, return home through the Tyrol? Surely you will agree that now is the time when my children on account of their youth can arouse the admiration of everyone. However, I have taken my decision. I have promised to go home and I shall keep my word.

(44) *Leopold Mozart to Lorenz Hagenauer, Salzburg*

[*Extract*]   [*Copy in the Deutsche Staatsbibliothek, Berlin*]

MUNICH, 10 *November* 1766

As far as I remember, my last letter was from Lyons, which we left after a stay of four weeks. We then went on to Geneva, where we found everything still in flames after the civil war. This, however, did not prevent us from staying three weeks. Perhaps you know that immediately outside Geneva the famous Voltaire has a castle called Ferney, where he is living.

Whoever wishes to go to Berne must travel through Lausanne. We had only intended to spend half a day there; but when we alighted from our carriages, the servants of Prince Ludwig of Wurtemberg,[2] of Madame d'Aulbonne, of Madame Hermenche, of M. de Sévery and others came up, and I had to let these distinguished personages persuade me to spend five days in Lausanne. The above-mentioned Prince was with us when we got into our carriage and, upon shaking hands with him, I had to promise to write to him very often and send him news of ourselves. From Lausanne we went to Berne and thence to Zürich. In the former town we only spent eight, in the latter fourteen days.[3] In both places we had an opportunity of getting to know men of learning; and at Zürich the two Gesners,[4] both learned persons, made our stay very pleasant and our

---

[1] Leopold Mozart hoped to be home by October 15th.
[2] Brother of Duke Karl Eugen.
[3] From September 19th to October 3rd. They gave a concert there.
[4] Johannes Gessner, physicist, and Salomon Gessner (1730–1788), poet. The latter gave the Mozarts, amongst other works, a copy of his poems with a dedication, quoted by Nissen, p. 116. Nissen adds that Salomon Gessner's wife gave the Mozarts a copy of Wieland's poetical works and her brother a German translation of Samuel Butler's *Hudibras*.

departure very sad. We took away tokens of their friendship.

Thence we proceeded through Winterthur to Schaffhausen. Here too our four days' stay was a very pleasant one and we found on our arrival in Donaueschingen Herr Meisner, who came to welcome us and helped us and our luggage out of the carriage! He remained on in Donaueschingen with us for four days longer.

His Highness the Prince welcomed us with extraordinary graciousness. It was not necessary to announce our arrival, for we were already being eagerly awaited, as Herr Meisner can testify. The Director of Music, Martelli, came at once to welcome us and to invite us to court. Well, we were there for twelve days. On nine days there was music in the evening from five to nine and each time we performed something different. If the season had not been so advanced, we should not have got away. The Prince gave me twenty-four louis d'or and to each of my children a diamond ring. Tears flowed from his eyes when we took leave of him, and truly we all wept at saying good-bye. He begged me to write to him often. Indeed our departure was as sad as our stay had been agreeable. Then we travelled at terrific speed through Messkirch to Ulm, Günzburg and Dillingen, where we only stayed two days, picked up two rings from the Prince [1] and, after spending a day in Augsburg, came to Munich where we arrived the day before yesterday and where we are staying at Störzer's. Yesterday, Sunday, we visited His Highness the Elector at table and were most graciously received. Wolfgang had at once to compose, standing beside the Elector, a piece for which His Highness hummed the beginning, or rather a few bars of the theme, and he then had to play it for him after dinner in the music room. You can easily guess how surprised everyone was to see and hear this.

That night, however, I noticed that Wolfgang was not well. He was restless and I have had to keep him in bed today, as I shall perhaps have to do for a few days more. With this weather and with the stove heating to which we have now to accustom ourselves, it is not surprising that such a delicate frame should have to suffer a little.

(45) *Leopold Mozart to Lorenz Hagenauer, Salzburg*

[*Extract*]   [*Copy in the Deutsche Staatsbibliothek, Berlin*]

MUNICH, 15 *November* 1766

If things had gone as I intended, my last letter would have begun as follows: *Here you have a letter from Regensburg*—for I should now be there,

---

[1] Prince Taxis.

in response to the insistent request of Prince Ludwig of Wurtemberg, Prince von Fürstenberg and Prince Taxis. From here it is a stone's throw and we should have gone straight home through Landshut and Alt-Ötting. This indeed is the route which we shall take on our journey and we shall doubtless still meet His Grace in Lauffen. But whether we shall now travel by way of Regensburg, I very much doubt, as I must wait until our little Wolfgang has completely recovered, and only then shall I know how soon we can get away from here. Meanwhile the weather is getting worse and worse. Our dear Frau Hagenauer will remember that after our return from Vienna [1] little Wolfgang fell ill and was very sick, so that we dreaded smallpox; and that finally the trouble settled in his feet where he complained of pains and so forth.

Now he has had a similar attack. He could not stand on his feet or move his toes or knees. No one could come near him and for four nights he could not sleep. This pulled him down a great deal and caused us all the more anxiety, since the whole time, and especially towards evening, he was very hot and feverish. Today he is noticeably better; but it will certainly be a week more before he is quite restored to health. In God's name, a hundred gulden soon disappear. I am now accustomed to this bad business.

The arrangements which we must make for our home are worrying me very much.[2] You yourself will understand this to some extent, and after our safe arrival (which God grant!) you will see it for yourself. God, who has been far too good to me, a miserable sinner, has bestowed such talents on my children that, apart from my duty as a father, they alone would spur me on to sacrifice everything to their successful development. Every moment I lose is lost for ever. And if I ever guessed how precious for youth is time, I realize it now. You know that my children are accustomed to work. But if with the excuse that one thing prevents another they were to accustom themselves to hours of idleness, my whole plan would crumble to pieces. Habit is an iron shirt. And you yourself know how much my children and especially Wolfgang have to learn. But who knows what plans are being made for us after our return to Salzburg? Perhaps we shall be received in such a way that we shall be only too glad to shoulder our bundles and clear out. But at least, God willing, I am going to bring back my children to their native town. If they are not wanted, it is not my fault. But people shall not get them for nothing. Well, I rely entirely on your sensible judgment and true friendship. Conversation will give us more pleasure. Farewell.

[1] January 1763.
[2] Probably refers to Leopold Mozart's intention to move into a house of his own.

(46) *Leopold Mozart to Lorenz Hagenauer, Salzburg*

[Extract]   [Copy in the Deutsche Staatsbibliothek, Berlin]

MUNICH, 22 *November* 1766

Now I myself am impatient. Until now Wolfgang has been unwell. He went out yesterday for the first time and today the Elector is giving a concert at which we have to appear. This impatience of mine is due to the very tiresome custom which prevails at this court, of making people wait for a very long time.[1]

[1] The Mozarts had been in Munich since November 8th and did not arrive in Salzburg until November 30th. Nissen, p. 120, adds that at Biberach Mozart competed on the organ with Sixtus Bachmann (1754–1818), later Father Sixtus of the Monastery of Marchthal, who was two years older than himself.

The fourth journey of Leopold Mozart and his wife and two children was to Vienna (their second visit), presumably in order to take part in the celebrations connected with the forthcoming marriage of the Archduchess Maria Josepha to King Ferdinand of Naples. But owing to the death of the bride in October 1767 and the prolonged court mourning, nearly all musical activities ceased for a time. Nevertheless the Mozarts remained in Vienna until January 1769. At the Emperor Joseph's suggestion Mozart wrote an opera buffa La Finta Semplice, *which however, was not performed. On the other hand, his operetta* Bastien und Bastienne *was produced at the private theatre of the famous Dr. Anton Mesmer. The visit to Vienna is described in a series of letters from Leopold Mozart to his landlord, Lorenz Hagenauer. Letters 47-70.*

(47) *Leopold Mozart to Lorenz Hagenauer, Salzburg*

[*Extract*]   [*Copy in the Deutsche Staatsbibliothek, Berlin*]

VIENNA,[1] 22 *September* 1767

On the first day we drove to Vöcklabruck; on the second in the morning to Lambach (where we took lunch in the monastery). In the evening we went on to Linz where we stayed at the 'Grüner Baum', an inn outside the town. On Sunday we did no more than walk up the Strengberg. On Monday morning we drove to Melk, where after lunch we went up to the monastery[2] and were shown the rooms. We did not disclose our identity until, when visiting the church and its organ, we gave the organist the opportunity of recognizing or rather guessing from his playing who little Wolfgang was. Immediately afterwards, however, we got into our carriage and drove to St. Pölten and on the morning of the following day to Purkersdorf and Vienna.

His Majesty[3] has only just returned from Hungary and during these days the Empress has her monthly devotions in memory of the death of the late Emperor.[4] So far I have nothing to report about our arrangements here. But every day there is either an opera seria or an opera buffa or a play.

(48) *Leopold Mozart to Lorenz Hagenauer, Salzburg*

[*Extract*]   [*Copy in the Deutsche Staatsbibliothek, Berlin*]

VIENNA, 29 *September* 1767

I have nothing to tell you except that, thank God, we are all well; and that news is quite certainly worth the postage.

Hasse's[5] opera is beautiful, but the singers, be it noted, are nothing out of the ordinary for such a festive occasion.[6] Signor Tibaldi[7] is the tenor

---

[1] The Mozarts left Salzburg on September 11th and arrived in Vienna on September 15th and took rooms in the house of a goldsmith.
[2] The famous Benedictine abbey and church.   [3] Joseph II.   [4] See p. 59, n. 2.
[5] *Partenope*, text by Metastasio, produced on 9 September 1767. The composer, Johann Adolph Hasse (1699–1783), born in Hamburg, was first a tenor. In 1724 he went to Naples to study composition under Porpora and Alessandro Scarlatti, and there wrote his first operas. Owing to his personal charm and popularity, he was known in Italy as 'Il caro Sassone'. In 1730 he married Faustina Bordoni, the famous soprano, and became Kapellmeister in Dresden. After the siege of Dresden in 1760 he and his wife moved to Vienna, where he soon became the rival of Gluck.
[6] The celebrations in connection with the betrothal of the Archduchess Maria Josepha to King Ferdinand of Naples.
[7] Giuseppe Luigi Tibaldi, a famous tenor, born 1719 in Bologna. He was a pupil of Padre Martini and during the years 1760–1772 was a leading operatic singer.

and Signor Rauzzini[1] from Munich, the leading castrato. The prima donna is Signora Teiber,[2] the daughter of a violinist at the Viennese court. But the dances are excellent, the leading dancer being the famous Frenchman Vestris.[3]

(49) *Leopold Mozart to Frau Maria Theresa Hagenauer, Salzburg*

[Extract]   [Copy in the Deutsche Staatsbibliothek, Berlin]

MADAME!   VIENNA, 14 October 1767[4]

I left Herr Estlinger certain symphonies to copy, which I hope are now ready. These are the symphonies which I have to send to Donaueschingen.[5] By the next post I shall send you a letter for the Prince which should be enclosed with the symphonies and should be sent off by the mail coach. I hope that Herr Estlinger understood what I wanted. The concertos for two claviers should be sent to Herr Gesner[6] at Zürich. The symphonies should go to Donaueschingen, and the clavier concertos, which Herr Spitzeder gave Herr Estlinger to copy, should, when copied, be delivered by him to Herr von Menhofer, who will thereupon pay him for them.

For Herr Hagenauer alone.

Do not be surprised if we draw four hundred or even five hundred gulden. *Aut Caesar aut nihil*; but not in Wenzel Hebelt's manner. Perhaps in one single day I shall pay it all back. So far we have played nowhere, for we have not yet performed at court. Later on I shall tell you some extraordinary things.

(50) *Leopold Mozart to Lorenz Hagenauer, Salzburg*

[Extract]   [Copy in the Deutsche Staatsbibliothek, Berlin]

VIENNA, 17 October 1767

The Princess bride has become a bride of the Heavenly bridegroom.[7] What an amazing change!

[1] Venanzio Rauzzini (1747–1810), born in Rome, went to Munich in 1766. He was an eminent teacher of singing and also an operatic composer.

[2] Probably Elizabeth Teiber, one of a large family of musicians in Vienna. Her sister Therese Teiber, also a famous soprano, married later the tenor Ferdinand Arnold.

[3] Vestris, a large family of Italian musicians and dancers, originally Vestri from Florence. The one mentioned here was Gaëtan Apolline Balthasar (1729–1808), who had worked under Noverre. In Paris in 1778 he danced in Mozart's ballet, written for Noverre, *Les petits riens* (K. App. 10 [299b]).

[4] A short letter from Leopold Mozart, dated 7 October 1767, says: '... That Princess Josepha, the bride of the King of Naples, has contracted smallpox, also upsets our plans to some extent. ...'

[5] See p. 68 f. K. 16, 16a, 16b [App. C. 11. 01], 19, 19a, 19b, 22, and possibly K. 76 [42a].

[6] See p. 67, n. 4.   [7] Princess Josepha died of smallpox on October 15th.

Another strange thing is that the second opera was the story of the Greek fable of Psyche. The title was: Amor e Psiche.[1]

We see a good deal of the Duke de Braganza,[2] Prince Kaunitz, M. De L'Augier,[3] and Baron Fries.[4]

Do not forget to pray for us, for if God did not watch over us, we should certainly be in a sorry plight, as you shall hear later on.

(51) *Leopold Mozart to Lorenz Hagenauer, Salzburg*

[*Extract*]   [*Copy in the Deutsche Staatsbibliothek, Berlin*]

OLMÜTZ,[5] 10 *November* 1767

Te Deum Laudamus!
Little Wolfgang has got over the smallpox safely!
And where?—In Olmütz!
And where?—At the residence of His Excellency Count Podstatzky.[6] You will have already observed from my previous letter that everything in Vienna has gone topsy-turvy. Now I must give you a few particulars which concern us alone; and from them you will see how Divine Providence links everything together, so that, if we trust to it completely, we cannot go wrong.

The elder son of the goldsmith with whom we were living, caught smallpox immediately after our arrival. We only heard of this after he had almost got over it and after the two younger children had caught it too. In vain did I search quickly for another lodging which would take us all. I was forced to leave my wife and daughter where they were and to run off with Wolfgang to a good friend. The servant remained with my wife. The only subject of conversation in Vienna was the smallpox. Of ten children whose names were put on the death register, nine had died of this disease. You can easily imagine how I felt. Whole nights were spent without sleep and during the day we had no rest.

I had decided immediately after the death of the Princess bride to go to Moravia, until the first mourning in Vienna should be over. But it was impossible to get away. For His Majesty the Emperor talked about us so often that we could never be certain when it would occur to him to

[1] An opera by F. L. Gassmann (1729–1774), who was a native of Bohemia and studied under Padre Martini of Bologna. In 1764 he was invited to Vienna as ballet composer and in 1771 was appointed Hofkapellmeister. Salieri was his pupil.
[2] Duke Johann Carl de Braganza, a famous traveller and patron of the arts.
[3] Physician to the Viennese court, at whose home scholars and artists were entertained.
[4] Baron Johann von Fries (1719–1785), a wealthy business man and banker in Vienna.
[5] The Mozarts were in Olmütz from October 26th to December 23rd. Mozart's illness lasted from October 26th to November 10th.
[6] Count Leopold Anton von Podstatzky, Dean of the Cathedral at Olmütz. His brother was a Canon of the Cathedral at Salzburg.

summon us. As soon, however, as the Archduchess Elizabeth fell ill, I let nothing more stop me, and I could scarcely wait until the hour came when I could get my little Wolfgang out of Vienna (which was by this time thoroughly infected) and into a different atmosphere.

On the afternoon of October 23rd we drove off and reached Brünn[1] on Saturday 24th. I took little Wolfgang to His Excellency Count von Schrattenbach[2] and Countess von Herberstein. They talked about a concert with a view to hearing my children and everything was already arranged. But I had a certain inner presentiment which I could not shake off and which impelled me all of a sudden to go on at once to Olmütz and hold the concert in Brünn on my return. So on Sunday evening I explained this to His Excellency, who agreed that I was acting wisely. We therefore quickly packed up our things and on Monday the 26th we left Olmütz and soon arrived there.

We put up at the 'Schwarzer Adler' and, to our annoyance, we had to take a wretched damp room, because the few other rooms were occupied. We were therefore obliged to have it heated, another cause for annoyance, because the stove smoked so that we were almost blinded and at ten o'clock little Wolfgang was complaining of his eyes. I noticed that his head was warm, that his cheeks were hot and very red, but that his hands were as cold as ice. Moreover his pulse was not right. So we gave him some black powder and put him to bed. During the night he was rather restless and in the morning he still had the dry fever. At this point we were given two better rooms, so we wrapped Wolfgang up in furs and took him into the other suite. As the fever increased we gave him some margrave powder and some black powder. Towards evening he began to rave, and all night long and during the morning of the 28th he was delirious. After church I went to His Excellency Count Podstatzky, who received me most graciously. When I told him that my small boy had fallen ill and that I feared that he might have smallpox, he told me that he would take us in, as he was not at all nervous of the disease. He sent immediately for the steward, ordered him to get two rooms ready and sent for a doctor to visit us at the 'Schwarzer Adler'. At four o'clock in the afternoon little Wolfgang was packed up in leather wrappings and furs and lifted into the carriage, and I drove with him to the Cathedral Deanery. On the 29th we saw a few little red pocks, but all the same we were not certain whether it was the smallpox, for he was no longer very ill. He took nothing but a powder every six hours and always scabious tea afterwards.

On the 30th and the 31st, his name-day, the smallpox came out completely. As soon as this happened, the fever disappeared altogether and,

---

[1] The capital of Moravia, about ninety miles from Vienna.
[2] Count Franz Anton von Schrattenbach, brother of the Archbishop of Salzburg.

thank God, he was still right in his head. He was very much inflamed and as he had swollen to a surprising extent and had a thick nose, when he looked at himself in the mirror, he said: '*Now I am like little Mayr*',[1] meaning the musician. Since yesterday the spots have been falling off here and there and two days ago all the swelling disappeared.

You will have already realised the truth of my motto: *In te, Domine, speravi, non confundar in aeternum.*[2] I leave it to you to consider in what a wonderful way our fate took us to Olmütz and how extraordinary it was that Count Podstatzky of his own accord took us in with a child who was to develop smallpox. I shall not mention with what kindness, graciousness and liberality we were waited on in every way. But I should really like to know how many people there are who would receive into their house, as he did, a whole family with a child in such a condition, and this from no other motive than fellow-feeling. This deed will do Count Podstatzky no little honour in the biography of our little one which I shall have printed later on. For from a certain aspect there begins here a new period of his life.

I am sorry that I shall have to return to Salzburg later than I intended. But at this time of the year we cannot make an early departure without endangering Wolfgang's health.

I have received your letter with the enclosure from M. Grimm in Paris. You will have seen in his letter what he has to say about the Russian Court and the Hereditary Prince of Brunswick;[3] also how and in what kind of company Herr Schobert[4] went into eternity.

Here is a reply to Herr Joseph which Wolfgang has written in bed.[5]

I still have one anxiety, which weighs heavily upon me, which is, lest my little girl should also get smallpox; for who knows whether the few pocks which she had were the real ones?

For you alone.

The six symphonies, which Estlinger has copied,[6] should be rolled up well and given to the mail coach with the address: A son Altesse Sérénissime Le Prince de Fürstenberg etc. à Donaueschingen. I shall write a letter to the Prince from here. The concerto for two claviers by Wagenseil should be added to the other printed sonatas,[7] which are to be sent to Herr Gesner in Zürich. But you will see now how topsy-turvy everything has been and how when we thought that all had gone wrong, God bestowed upon us His infinite grace and allowed our dear Wolfgang to make a

---

[1] Andreas Mayr, a member of the Salzburg court orchestra.
[2] The opening words of Psalm 71.   [3] See p. 66, n. 1.
[4] See p. 37, n. 4. Schobert died on 28 August 1767, from eating some fungi which he had gathered near Paris and which poisoned his family, his cook and three friends. His death is described by Grimm in his *Correspondance Littéraire*, vol. vii. p. 422.
[5] A letter, which is evidently lost, addressed to Joseph Hagenauer. See p. 91, n. 1
[6] See p. 74.   [7] Mozart's sonatas, K. 6-9, K. 10-15 and K. 26-31.

good recovery from his illness. But I do not mind anything so long as this is safely over. What do you say to Count Podstatzky's treatment of us? Does not such a deed deserve some sort of expression of approval, if not of thanks from His Grace, made, if not in person, at least through his brother in Brünn or through Count von Herberstein, or, at the very least, conveyed in the form of a letter from our Father Confessor, or from the Court Chancellor? I beg you to try to get something of this sort done.

(52) *Leopold Mozart to Lorenz Hagenauer, Salzburg*

[*Extract*]   [*Copy in the Deutsche Staatsbibliothek, Berlin*]

OLMÜTZ, 29 *November* 1767

I have this moment received your letter.

Iterum Iterumque

Te Deum Laudamus!

My daughter has got over the smallpox safely—a proof that the few pocks which she had in childhood were not the genuine article, as I had already suspected. She survived her attack so well that you will not notice on her any marks whatever and only a few on Wolfgang. Now I must tell you a few other things. For instance, before leaving Vienna, I wanted to let you know that Herr Haydn,[1] Herr Leutgeb,[2] Herr Franz Drasil[3] and also Herr Küffel[4] called on us. At that time I was too busy to tell you that we returned the visits of Haydn and of the above-mentioned gentlemen and that we met Theresa, Herr Haydn's lady-love.[5]

Little Wolfgang was overjoyed to receive the letter in verse from Sallerl[6] and read it out to the Count.

(53) *Leopold Mozart to Lorenz Hagenauer, Salzburg*

[*Extract*]   [*Copy in the Deutsche Staatsbibliothek, Berlin*]

VIENNA, 12 *January* 1768

That we spent a fortnight in Brünn, where we arrived on Christmas Eve, will certainly be known in Salzburg from the letters of Her Excel-

---

[1] Johann Michael Haydn (1737–1806), a younger brother of Joseph Haydn and a composer of note. In 1762 on Eberlin's death he was appointed conductor of the Salzburg court orchestra, and in 1777 after Adlgasser's death he became organist at the churches of Holy Trinity and St. Peter. In August 1768 he married the Salzburg court singer Maria Magdalena Lipp, daughter of the second organist of the Cathedral.

[2] Ignaz Leutgeb, horn-player in the Salzburg court orchestra, and later a close friend of Mozart. In 1777 he opened a cheesemonger's shop in Vienna, where he died in 1811.

[3] Franz Drasil was a horn-player in the Salzburg court orchestra. See A. J. Hammerle, *Mozart und einige Zeitgenossen*, Salzburg, 1877, p. 35.

[4] Ignaz Küffel, a cellist in the Salzburg court orchestra. See p. 93 and p. 95, n. 1.

[5] A portion of this letter which has been omitted contains an amusing description of the lady, who was the daughter of a Viennese hosier. Michael Haydn did not marry her.

[6] Rosalie Joly, a chambermaid in the household of Count Felix Arco. She was a friend of the Mozart children.

lency Countess von Herberstein. The kindnesses which we received in the home of Count Schrattenbach[1] and the special consideration shown to us by His Excellency and by the whole aristocracy of Brünn I shall not fail later on to extol in detail to His Grace, our most gracious overlord.[2] We left Brünn on the 9th. With four post-horses we succeeded in reaching Poysdorf at six o'clock on the same evening and this in spite of snow and storm. Here, however, we took six horses and on Sunday the 10th we drove off at eight in the morning and were already on the Tabor by five o'clock in the evening.[3]

(54) *Leopold Mozart to Lorenz Hagenauer, Salzburg*

[Extract]   [Copy in the Deutsche Staatsbibliothek, Berlin]

VIENNA, 23 *January* 1768

The latest news which I have to report (apart from the fact that, thank God, we are all well) is that on Tuesday the 19th we were with Her Majesty the Empress from half past two to half past four in the afternoon. His Majesty the Emperor[4] came out into the anteroom where we were waiting until Their Majesties had taken coffee, and brought us in himself. In addition to the Emperor and the Empress, Prince Albert of Saxony[5] and all the Archduchesses were present; but apart from these royal personages there was not a soul. It would take too long to describe to you all that was said and done there. I shall only say that you cannot possibly conceive with what familiarity Her Majesty the Empress conversed with my wife, talking to her partly of my children's smallpox and partly of the events of our grand tour; nor can you imagine how she stroked my wife's cheeks and pressed her hands. Meanwhile His Majesty the Emperor talked to little Wolfgang and to me about music, and many other things too, which often made Nannerl blush. Later on I shall tell you more personally. For you know me. I hate to write about things which many a puffed-up 'Gogelkopf'[6] (that is a Swabian expression), sitting behind the stove, would regard as lies. But from this extraordinary friendliness you must not conclude that we are going to be paid in proportion. I at least cannot form a favourable opinion, judging from what I see here and from the

[1] See p. 76, n. 2.
[2] The Archbishop of Salzburg. Count Franz Anton von Schrattenbach was his brother. See p. 76, n. 2.
[3] On their return from Brünn the Mozarts took rooms in a house on the Hohe Brücke. See p. 817, n. 2.
[4] Joseph II, since 1765 co-regent with his mother, the Empress Maria Theresia.
[5] Duke Albert of Saxe-Teschen, Governor of the Austrian Netherlands, who was married to Maria Theresia's daughter, Maria Christina.
[6] An idiot. Nissen, p. 128, adds: 'a Swabian and Bavarian expression'.

present conditions in Vienna. But these are things which time must show and about which we can talk more easily.

(55) *Leopold Mozart to Lorenz Hagenauer, Salzburg*

[*Extract*]   [*Copy in the Deutsche Staatsbibliothek, Berlin*]

VIENNA, 30 *January–3 February* 1768 [1]

For you alone.

It is now time to give you a fuller and clearer report of our circumstances, I know not whether they are fortunate or unfortunate, and to hear your friendly opinion. If money makes the sole happiness of man, then we are doubtless to be pitied now, seeing that, as you know, we have spent so much of our capital that there is little apparent hope of our being able to recover it. If, on the other hand, health and versatility in knowledge are a man's greatest possession, then, God be praised, we are still well off. We have weathered the biggest and most dangerous storm. By the grace of God we are all well and my children have certainly not only forgotten nothing, but, as you will see, have made great progress.

I know that what must strike you as most incomprehensible is why it is that our affairs do not improve more rapidly. I shall explain this to you as well as I can. At the same time I must omit certain things which cannot be entrusted to my pen. That the Viennese, generally speaking, do not care to see serious and sensible performances, have little or no idea of them, and only want to see foolish stuff, dances, devils, ghosts, magic, clowns, Lipperl,[2] Bernardon,[3] witches and apparitions is well known; and their theatres prove it every day. That is the first and main reason. The household organisation at court, which I cannot describe here, is an element involving many consequences, which it would take too long to explain and to illustrate by examples. That is the second reason. These two lead to countless strange things, for everything depends on chance and blind fortune and more often on some detestable meanness, which fortunately does not characterize everyone, or even on some very impudent and daring piece of bluff. To come now to our own affairs, I must tell you that many other adverse events have taken place. On our arrival, the first thing we had to do was to obtain an entry at court. But Her Majesty the Empress no longer[4] has concerts in her apartments, nor does she go either to the opera or to the play; and her manner of life is so removed from the world that it would be impossible for me to describe it adequately. She

---

[1] This long letter was finished and sent off on 3 February 1768.
[2] A diminutive of Philip and the name of a clown on the Viennese stage.
[3] A clown's part invented by the Viennese actor Joseph Felix von Kurz (1717–1783).
[4] Since the death of Francis I on 18 August 1765.

directed us to the Emperor. But as this gentleman positively abhors every-thing that might entail any expenditure, it was a very long time before he made up his mind; and in the meantime there occurred the sad death of the Princess bride and all the events of which my letters have already in-formed you. After our return from Moravia we met the Royal Family sooner than we expected. For hardly had the Empress been told of what had happened to us in Olmütz and that we had returned, when we were informed of the day and the hour when we should appear. But what was the use of all this amazing graciousness and this indescribable friendliness? What effect did it produce? None whatever, save a medal, which is, it is true, beautiful, but so worthless that I do not even care to mention its value. She leaves everything else to the Emperor, who enters it in his book of oblivion and believes, no doubt, that he has paid us by his most gracious conversations. Now you will ask me what the other nobles in Vienna do? What do they do? They all cut down their expenses, as far as possible, in order to please the Emperor. If the chief is extravagant, everyone lets things rip. But if the chief economizes, everyone wants to have the most economical household.

The members of the aristocracy are our patrons. Prince Kaunitz, the Duke de Braganza, Fräulein von Guttenberg, who is the left eye of the Empress, the Chief Equerry Count Dietrichstein, who is all-powerful with the Emperor, are our friends. But what bad luck! So far we have not been able to speak to Prince Kaunitz,[1] because his weakness is that he is so afraid of smallpox that he even avoids persons whose faces still show red spots. Hence, as little Wolfgang has still many red spots on his face, which are, it is true, small but which come out in cold weather, he merely sent us a message through our friend De L'Augier that during Lent he would look after our interests, but that just now during the carnival, the nobles could not be assembled for a function. But as I was considering this matter as carefully as I could and thinking of how much money I had already spent and that if I were now to go home without waiting for anything more, it would perhaps be extremely foolish, something quite different occurred. For I was told that all the clavier-players and composers in Vienna were opposed to our advancement, with the sole exception of Wagenseil, who, however, as he was ill at home, could not help us or contribute anything to our advantage. The chief maxim of these people was to avoid most carefully every occasion of seeing us and of admitting little Wolfgang's skill. And why? So that on the many occasions on which they might be asked whether they had heard this boy and what they thought of him, they could always say *that they had not heard him and that it could not possibly be true; that it was all humbug and foolishness; that it was all*

---

[1] Nissen, p. 131, inserts 'this time', as during their first visit to Vienna in 1762 he was one of the chief patrons of the Mozarts. See pp. 6 and 7.

*pre-arranged; that he was given music which he already knew; that it was
ridiculous to think that he could compose, and so forth.* That, you see, is why
they are keeping out of our way. For he who has seen and heard cannot
talk in such a manner without exposing himself to the danger of thereby
losing his honour. But I caught one of these people nicely. We had
arranged with someone to inform us quietly when the man in question
would be there. Our friend was then to hand this person a most extraordinarily difficult concerto, which was to be put before little Wolfgang.
So we turned up and the fellow had the opportunity, therefore, of hearing
his concerto played off by little Wolfgang as if he knew it by heart. The
amazement of this composer and clavier-player, his expressions and the
remarks he made in giving vent to his admiration, made us all realize
what I have already said above. Finally he declared: *All I can say as an
honest person is that this boy is the greatest man now living in the world. It was
impossible to believe it.* But in order to convince the public of what it really
amounts to, I decided to do something entirely out of the ordinary, that is,
to get Wolfgang to write an opera for the theatre. Can you not imagine
what a turmoil secretly arose amongst those composers? What? Today we
are to see a Gluck[1] and tomorrow a boy of twelve seated at the harpsichord and conducting his own opera? Yes, despite all those who envy
him! I have even won Gluck over to our side, though, I admit, only to the
extent that, though he is not quite whole-hearted, he has decided not to
let it be noticed; for our patrons are his also. In order to make our position
safe in regard to the actors, who usually cause the composer most annoyance, I have taken the matter up with them, and one of them has given
me all the suggestions for the work. But, in reality it was the Emperor
himself who first gave me the idea of getting little Wolfgang to write
an opera. For he asked the boy twice whether he would like to compose an opera and conduct it himself? Wolfgang said, Yes. But more than
this the Emperor could not suggest, since the operas are the concern of
Affligio.[2] The consequences of this undertaking, if God helps us to carry
it out, are so enormous, but so easy to visualize, that they require no explanation. But now I must spare no money, for it will come back to me
today or tomorrow. Never venture, never win. I must show what we can
do. We must succeed or fail. And where is my boy more likely to succeed
than in the theatre? But of course the opera will not be performed until
after Easter. I shall soon write for permission to stay here longer. It is not
an opera seria, however, for no operas of that kind are being given now;
and moreover people do not like them. So it is an opera buffa, but not a

---

[1] Since 1755 Gluck had been living almost entirely in Vienna. His operas *Alceste* (1767) and
Paride ed Elena (1770) embodied his ideas on the reform of the opera.
[2] Giuseppe Affligio was manager of the Burgtheater and the Theater am Kärntner Tor
during the years 1767–1770.

short one, for it is to last about two and a half or three hours.[1] There are
no singers here for serious operas. Even Gluck's serious opera, 'Alceste',[2]
was performed entirely by opera buffa singers. He too is now writing an
opera buffa,[3] for there are excellent singers here for works of this kind,
such as Signori Caribaldi, Caratoli, Poggi, Laschi, Polini, Signorina
Bernasconi,[4] Signorina Eberhardi, Signorina Baglioni.

What do you think? Is not the reputation of having written an opera
for the Viennese theatre the best way to enhance one's credit not only in
Germany but also in Italy? Farewell.

(56) *Leopold Mozart to Lorenz Hagenauer, Salzburg*

[*Extract*]   [*Copy in the Deutsche Staatsbibliothek, Berlin*]

VIENNA, 13 *February* 1768

I should very much like to have here the bound copy of my 'Violinschule'[5] which is standing or lying about amongst my books. When the
Salzburg delegates come here, the copy could easily come with them. I
even ought to have a few more unbound copies as well. But Heaven
knows where the copper-plates are, though I think they are below, in the
chest with the glasses. The table is probably with each book, and whatever copper-plates belong to it, will be seen from the bound copy. It ought
to be possible to find the errata-sheet and the directions to bookbinder.
If so, all the better, but if not, just send me, if you please, the bound copy.
It may also be that I have already inserted the copper-plates into the few
copies which are still there. I cannot remember. Send it open, not sealed.
I have no news to give you, except that as in Salzburg we are having
operas, redoutes, balls, plays and so forth; but at these balls some of those
who attend are without masks, while others wear some disguise but no
dominos. Wolfgang herewith sends this riddle[6] to Herr Adlgasser, since
we were so dense as not to be able to solve his riddle. We send greetings
to all our good friends.

---

[1] Mozart's *La finta semplice*. The libretto was written by Marco Coltellini, who had lived in
Vienna since 1758 and succeeded Metastasio as 'poeta cesareo'.
[2] *Alceste* was first performed on 26 December 1767.
[3] As far as is known Gluck never carried out this plan.
[4] Antonia Bernasconi, of German extraction, stepdaughter and pupil of Andrea Bernasconi,
Kapellmeister at the Munich court. She first appeared in Vienna in Gluck's *Alceste*, 1767. In
1770 she sang at Milan in Mozart's *Mitridate* and in 1783 was still singing in Vienna.
[5] Leopold Mozart's treatise on the playing of the violin, called *Versuch einer gründlichen
Violinschule*, published in 1756 by J. J. Lotter, Augsburg, won him fame during his lifetime.
A considerable number of letters written to his publisher, 1755–1756, while the work was
being printed, show his love of accuracy and his painstaking interest in the work. It went
through new editions in 1770, 1787, 1791 and 1804 and was translated into Dutch (1766),
French (1770) and Russian (1804). A selection was published in English in *c.* 1812 and a complete version by Editha Knocker appeared in 1948.
[6] Mozart was fond of sending riddles and puzzles to his friends.

(57) *Leopold Mozart to Lorenz Hagenauer, Salzburg*

[*Extract*]   [*Copy in the Deutsche Staatsbibliothek, Berlin*]

VIENNA, 30 *March* 1768

We are all in good health and, thank God, in good circumstances. The ice is broken! Not only on the Danube, but also in our affairs. Our enemies are beaten! Note well, *here in Vienna*. Nothing can happen at once. By *phlegma* I have transformed beasts into men and left them to their own confusion. The chief reason for this present letter is that I am asking you to tell Herr Wenzel Hebelt [1] to hand in to His Grace the report on the instruction in the Kapellhaus, which, in the past, I have always entrusted to him. Furthermore I ask you to explain to our Father Confessor, with the humble greetings of myself and my family, that I still hold the appointment as instructor in the violin to the Archbishop's Kapellhaus, [2] but that for the last five years, that is, since my first journey to Vienna, [3] I have left this work to Herr Wenzel. But since on account of my absence I can receive nothing from the Archbishop's exchequer, the authorities should be informed, so that someone else may be appointed *pro instructione*. [4]

Thank you for the copies of my 'Violinschule' which you sent. As the copper-plates have turned up, I should very much like to have two or three more copies of the book with the missing copper-plates and also two more copper-plates of the portrait, [5] as these are very dirty.

Last week a big concert was given for us at the house of His Highness Prince von Galitzin, [6] the Russian Ambassador. The Dean of the Cathedral and Count von Wolfegg [7] were there. The opera is getting on well. But it will probably not be performed until after the Emperor's return from Hungary.

(58) *Leopold Mozart to Lorenz Hagenauer, Salzburg*

[*Extract*]   [*Copy in the Deutsche Staatsbibliothek, Berlin*]

VIENNA, 20 *April* 1768

We had the honour and pleasure of beginning the *Salzburg wedding festivities* here. At my suggestion we held a concert and entertained the

---

[1] See p. 21, n. 2.
[2] Since 1744 Leopold Mozart, who was appointed in 1743 fourth violinist in the Hofkapelle, had been entrusted with the teaching of the violin to the boys in the Kapellhaus.
[3] September 1762.   [4] i.e. as an instructor.
[5] Leopold Mozart's book on the violin contains a portrait of himself. A facsimile of the first edition of the *Violinschule*, edited by Bernhard Paumgartner, was published in 1922 by Carl Stephenson, Vienna.
[6] Prince Dimitri Mihalovich Galitzin (1721–?) Ambassador to the Court of Vienna from 1763.   [7] See p. 23, n. 3.

wedding guests for a whole evening to the pleasure and satisfaction of everybody. We call it the beginning of the Salzburg wedding festivities, because we are natives of Salzburg.

His Majesty the Emperor has now left for Hungary or rather for the Turkish frontiers. Hence the opera will be performed in June after his return.

(59) *Leopold Mozart to Lorenz Hagenauer, Salzburg*

[*Extract*]   [*Autograph in the Mozarteum, Salzburg*]

For you alone.   VIENNA, 11 *May* 1768

I have duly congratulated His Grace on his esteemed name-day in a letter which I have just sent off. I have also written to the Chief Steward about the Archbishop's Kapellhaus. So Herr Meisner is going away? And where to? That my pay would stop at the end of March I told you already. It may be true, as people are telling me in their letters, that through the influence of His Grace's brother [1] I could once more obtain my salary as violin instructor to the Prince's Kapellhaus and as first violinist, if I were to beg for it. His brother knows this nice story, for I told it to him here. But how can I in fairness and honour obtain by begging something which I am not earning? For I am not performing my services in Salzburg, as I feel pretty sure most of the courtiers in Salzburg are saying. On the other hand this is what makes it easy for me to get permission to make a journey to Italy, a journey which, taking all the circumstances into consideration, can now be postponed no longer and for which I have received from the Emperor himself all the necessary introductions for Florence, the Imperial States and Naples. Or should I perhaps sit down in Salzburg with the empty hope of some better fortune, let Wolfgang grow up, and allow myself and my children to be made fools of until I reach the age which prevents me from travelling and until he attains the age and physical appearance which no longer attract admiration for his merits? Is my child to have taken the first step with this opera for nothing, and is he not to hurry on with firm steps along the road which is now so broad and easy to follow?

Here is the copy of the letter from the Chief Steward:

Per espresso comando di S.A. Rma: devo far sapere a V.S. qualmente il Clement^mo Principe P^re. niente abbia in contrario, che il Sgr: Mozart se ne possi restar fuori a suo piacimento sin tanto che vuole, ed inoltre gli passerà ancora questo mese di marzo il suo salario; ma in avvenire, quando non sii

---

[1] Count von Schrattenbach. See p. 76, n. 2.

attualmente presente in Salisburgo, sarà bensì mantenuto come prima nel suo servizio, ma durante la sua assenza non gli lascierà più correre il solito salario. Di tanto ho voluto rendere avvisato V: S: etc.[1]

You see, how gracious!—I can remain away as long as I like, provided I do not ask to be paid. I am quite satisfied. At least I can stay away without further reproaches. But I shall not be able to leave here for Salzburg before the end of July.[2] Our furs are now becoming a nuisance to us and I shall send them back shortly by some driver. On the other hand I must— yes, I must ask you to do me a favour. The heat is getting more and more intense, and I am becoming ashamed of appearing at my hosts' houses in cloth garments. Wolfgang too needs a lighter costume. So I beg you to send me by the next mail coach my silk suit from Lyons, my red cloth suit (which I need for the return journey) and Wolfgang's light grey camlet suit, my wife's and daughter's Persian silk dresses and a lady's hat with a veil in front, which is to be found in the large round hat-box. Please put in with the rest of the parcel pieces for patching Wolfgang's red and cherry-coloured suit and my English red-brown suit.

One thing more! I wonder if you would speak to Herr Alterdinger[3] about something? I once asked him whether he would not undertake to translate my 'Violinschule' into Italian? If he would like to do this, I will pay what he asks. He should begin with the *Preface* and the *Introductions* and then tell me candidly what he thinks I ought to pay him. But, as I wrote it in three months, I hope that it will not be difficult for him to finish the translation in the same time. You will easily guess my purpose.[4] Only I should like to remind you that, as it is a manual of instruction, it ought not to be translated in a highflown style, but, as it is in German and for the man in the street, in a style which is clear and intelligible.

I thought indeed that Herr Hartmayr would soon devise some other plan, if the redoutes were not allowed. I should still like that house; but, if God does not wish it, no more do I.[5] If I had security for my children, I could take some decision. My dear Frau Hagenauer and your family, keep well and in good health. We all send you greetings and I am

your old

MOZART

---

[1] By express command of His Most Reverend Highness I inform you that our most gracious Prince has no objection to Herr Mozart's staying away as long as he likes and will pay him his salary for the month of March, but that in future when he is not actually in Salzburg he will be retained as before in the Archbishop's service but during his absence will not be paid his usual salary. I have to acquaint you with this decision, etc.

[2] The Mozarts did not return to Salzburg until January 1769.

[3] Probably Rochus Alterdinger, administrator of the Archbishop's household.

[4] i.e. Leopold Mozart's projected visit to Italy with his son. As far as is known, his *Violinschule* was never translated into Italian.

[5] Leopold Mozart was trying to find a house for his family. See p. 69 f.

(60) *Leopold Mozart to Lorenz Hagenauer, Salzburg*

[*Extract*]   [*Copy in the Deutsche Staatsbibliothek, Berlin*]

VIENNA, 4 *June* 1768

Herr Spitzeder writes that he has had two arias copied. I should like to know how many arias Madame Wodiska sent from Munich. *There ought to be three of them in manuscript; and in addition a book with arias engraved or printed in London with the title 'Orione'.*[1] If she has not sent these, she has done me out of several arias, and this I should not like at all. That is what happens if one is *bonae voluntatis*, and cannot refuse people anything.

(61) *Leopold Mozart to Lorenz Hagenauer, Salzburg*

[*Extract*]   [*Copy in the Deutsche Staatsbibliothek, Berlin*]

VIENNA, 29 *June* 1768

I could tell you a very long story of all sorts of the most deeply laid plots and malicious persecutions. But I am too tired to go over these in my mind and would rather save them up *for our conversation, which we shall have shortly.*

Well, thank God, we are all in good health; although envy assails us from all sides. You know, however, that I hold fast to my old motto: *In te, Domine, speravi. Fiat voluntas tua.*[2] What God does not want, I do not want either.

(62) *Leopold Mozart to Lorenz Hagenauer, Salzburg*

[*Extract*]   [*Copy in the Deutsche Staatsbibliothek, Berlin*]

VIENNA, 30 *July* 1768

You have made everything all right again! We were only afraid, lest perhaps someone in your house should be unwell. On this score we are all the more happy, as we see that the cause of this silence was rather that you were very well and were enjoying the garden. Yet with regard to another matter, that is, our very long stay in Vienna, we are extremely displeased. Indeed, only our honour keeps us here! Otherwise we should have been in Salzburg long ago. But would you like everyone in Vienna to say that little Wolfgang had not been able to compose the opera; or that it turned out such poor stuff that it could not be produced; or that it was not he who

---

[1] *Orione ossia Diana vendicata*, Johann Christian Bach's first opera performed in England, was produced at the King's Theatre on 19 February 1763, and ran for nearly three months. The 'Favourite Songs' were published by Walsh in that year.
[2] A mixture of quotations from Psalm 71 and the Lord's Prayer.

wrote it, but his father? Would you wish us to look on in cold blood while such defamations should be circulated in all countries? Would this redound to our honour, nay, to the honour of our most gracious Prince? You will ask: '*What does His Majesty the Emperor say to it?*' Here I can only touch on the matter briefly, for it cannot be described in detail. But you will grasp it. Had I known all that I know now and could I have foreseen the events which have taken place, little Wolfgang would certainly never have written a note, but would have been at home long ago. The theatre is farmed out, or rather entrusted to a certain Affligio,[1] who has to pay some 1000 gulden a year to people whom the court would otherwise have to pay. The Emperor and the whole Imperial Family pay nothing for their boxes. Consequently the court cannot say a word to this Affligio, for everything is undertaken at his risk; and he is really now in danger of getting into trouble, as you shall soon hear.

His Majesty asked our Wolfgang whether he would not like to write an opera and said that he would very much like to see him at the clavier conducting it. He gave Affligio to understand that he would like this, and Affligio thereupon made a contract with us for one hundred ducats. At first the opera was to be performed at Easter. But the poet[2] was the first to prevent this, for, on the pretext of making here and there certain necessary alterations, he kept on delaying, so that by Easter we had received from him only two of the amended arias. Next, the opera was fixed for Whitsuntide and then for the return of His Majesty from Hungary. But at this point the mask fell from the face. For in the meantime all the composers, amongst whom Gluck is a leading figure,[3] undermined everything in order to prevent the success of this opera. The singers were talked over, the orchestra were worked up and every means was used to stop its performance. The singers who, moreover, hardly know their parts and one or two of whom have to learn everything entirely by ear, were now put up to say that they could not sing their arias, which they had nevertheless previously heard in our room and which they had approved of, applauded and described as quite suitable for them. The orchestra were now to say that they did not like a boy to conduct them, and a hundred similar things. Meanwhile some people spread the report that the music was not worth a fig; others said that it did not fit the words, or was against the metre, thus proving that the boy had not sufficient command of the Italian language. As soon as I heard this, I made it quite clear in the most eminent quarters that Hasse, the father of music, and the great Metastasio had stated that the slanderers who spread this report should go to them and hear out of their own mouths that thirty

---

[1] See p. 82, n. 2.   [2] Marco Coltellini. Cp. p. 83, n. 1.
[3] Undoubtedly an exaggerated statement, as Schiedermair, vol. iv. p. 396, and Abert, vol. i. p. 123, point out.

operas have been performed in Vienna, which in no respect can touch this boy's opera which they both admire in the very highest degree. Then it was said that not the boy, but his father had written it. But here too the credit of the slanderers began to fall. For they dropped *ab uno extremo ad aliud*[1] until they were in the soup. I asked someone to take any portion of the works of Metastasio, open the book and put before little Wolfgang the first aria which he should hit upon. Wolfgang took up his pen and with the most amazing rapidity wrote, without hesitation and in the presence of several eminent persons, the music for this aria for several instruments. He did this at the houses of Kapellmeister Bonno,[2] Abbate Metastasio, Hasse and the Duke de Braganza and Prince von Kaunitz. Meanwhile arrangements have been made for another opera and, as no more objections can be raised, little Wolfgang's is to be performed immediately afterwards. Hundreds of times I have wanted to pack up and go off. If this opera had been an opera seria, I should have left immediately and at the very first moment, and should have laid it at the feet of His Grace. But, as it is an *opera buffa*, and, what is more, an opera which demands certain types of *persone buffe*, I must save our reputation in Vienna, cost what it may. The honour of our most gracious Prince is also involved. His Grace has no liars, charlatans and deceivers in his service, who with his foreknowledge and permission go to other towns in order, like conjurers, to throw dust in people's eyes. No, he sends honest men, who to the honour of their Prince and of their country announce to the world a miracle, which God has allowed to see the light in Salzburg. I owe this act to Almighty God, otherwise I should be the most thankless creature. *And if it is ever to be my duty to convince the world of this miracle, it is so now, when people are ridiculing whatever is called a miracle and denying all miracles.* Therefore they must be convinced. And was it not a great joy and a tremendous victory for me to hear a Voltairian[3] say to me in amazement: '*Now for once in my life I have seen a miracle; and this is the first!*' But because this miracle is too evident and consequently not to be denied, they want to suppress it. *They refuse to let God have the honour.* They think that it is only a question of a few years and that thereafter it will become natural and cease to be a Divine miracle. So they want to withdraw it from the eyes of the world. For how could it be more visibly manifested than at a public show and in a large and populous town? But why should we be surprised at persecutions away from home, when almost the same thing has taken place in this child's native town? What a disgrace! What inhumanity! You may wonder perhaps why Prince Kaunitz and other great people, indeed His Majesty the Emperor himself, do not command

---

[1] i.e. from one extreme to another.
[2] Giuseppe Bonno (1710–1788), born in Vienna, son of one of the Imperial footmen, studied composition in Naples. In 1739 he was appointed Court Composer in Vienna, and in 1774, on the death of Gassmann, Court Kapellmeister.   [3] Probably Grimm.

that the opera be performed. First of all, they cannot command it, for it solely concerns the interest of Signor Affligio (whom some call Count Affligio). In the second place, they might perhaps command him to produce it at some other time. But it was Prince Kaunitz who, against the will of His Majesty, persuaded Affligio to bring to Vienna French players who are costing him more than 70,000 gulden a year and who are ruining him (as they are not drawing the crowds which were hoped for). So now Affligio is throwing the blame on Prince Kaunitz and because the latter, on the other hand, hoped to induce the Emperor to take an interest in the French theatre and thus defray his (Affligio's) expenses, His Majesty has not appeared at any performance for many weeks. Now you know the annoying circumstances, all of which arose simultaneously and helped to persuade Affligio to reject little Wolfgang's opera and keep his hundred ducats in his pocket. On the other hand these same circumstances prevented everyone from speaking to Affligio in a sharp, commanding and emphatic manner for fear they should have to compensate him for the 70,000 gulden. All this, of course, happened behind our backs. Affligio blamed the singers for the postponement of the opera and said that they could not and would not sing it. The singers, on the other hand, blamed Affligio and made out that he had not only said that he would not produce it, but had himself told them so. Whereas, of course, the truth is that they could always have this or that passage altered, if they so desired. So it is going to be performed. But if, as we shall soon see, some fresh obstacle begins to loom, I shall send my complaint to Their Majesties the Emperor and the Empress and demand such satisfaction as will save our honour before all Vienna and the whole honest world. For it would be no honour for us and no honour for our Salzburg court, if we were simply to allow ourselves to be driven away by persecuting envy and thus, after our departure, enable the wicked to make out to the ignorant public (as they have already done) that little Wolfgang never managed to write the opera at all or that it turned out such poor stuff that it simply could not be performed, and so forth. You see how one has to fight one's way through the world. If a man has no talents, he is unhappy enough; but if he has, envy pursues him in proportion to his ability. Moreover, in addition to all I have just told you, one of the singers, Signorina Bernasconi, has just caught a bad cold, and Signorina Baglioni is not very well. This again holds us up and will delay the business for at least three weeks. So that with extreme annoyance, such as I never elsewhere experienced on our travels, I have to await the result of this hateful affair. All sensible people must with shame agree that it is a disgrace to our nation that we Germans are trying to suppress a German, to whom foreign countries have done justice by their great admiration and even by public acknowledgments in writing. But by patience and perseverance one must convince people that our adversaries are wicked liars, slanderers and envious creatures, who would laugh in their sleeves if we were to get frightened or tired out and, by going off in a huff, give them the victory. Now, I think, you know my circumstances, although I have only described them in a general way. I should also have reported to our most gracious lord what has happened, if I had not felt some hesitation at disturbing him with such a long story in the midst of more important affairs. We all send our greetings to our Father Confessor and beg him to lay them at the feet of His Grace. Your Joseph [1] will see from this report that my enemies in Salzburg wish us well, since they are spreading the news that little Wolfgang has received 2000 gulden for the opera.

(63) *Leopold Mozart to Lorenz Hagenauer, Salzburg*

[Extract]   [Copy in the Deutsche Staatsbibliothek, Berlin]

VIENNA, 6 *August* 1768

I should never have dreamt that on the Feast of St. Laurence [2] I should still be in Vienna. My last letter explained to you very fully why I must still remain on here and what irritation it causes me.

I should be sick of the annoying circumstances which are keeping me here, if I did not know by experience that in the end many an affair takes quite a different turn from what one could ever have hoped. How often has Divine Providence clearly compelled me to go forward or has kept me back!

(64) *Leopold Mozart to Lorenz Hagenauer, Salzburg*

[Extract]   [Copy in the Deutsche Staatsbibliothek, Berlin]

VIENNA, 13 *September* 1768

It was a year ago the day before yesterday, September 11th, that we left Salzburg. Could I ever have dreamt then that I should stay a year in Vienna? But who can oppose Fate! I am so annoyed that I could foam at the mouth. The only good thing to be said is that we all, thank God, are well. But I only wish that I could let you know the happy day of our departure!

It is impossible for me to describe our affairs as fully as I should like. I have neither the time nor the patience. You will hear it all when we meet

---

[1] A son of Lorenz Hagenauer.   [2] August 10th.

91

and indeed some amazing things. As soon as our business is over we shall leave immediately.

We sometimes lunch with Father Parhammer[1] and we happened to be with him when the Emperor was laying the foundation stone for the new church.[2] On that occasion His Majesty asked Wolfgang how far he had got with his opera, and talked to him for a long time. Several people heard him do this.

(65) *Leopold Mozart to Lorenz Hagenauer, Salzburg*

[*Extract*]   [*Copy in the Deutsche Staatsbibliothek, Berlin*]

VIENNA, 14 *September* 1768

I have this very moment received your letter of the 10th. Here is my reply! The reason for my silence was as Madame Wynne has stated. I know Countess von Rosenberg and her sister-in-law. The Countess does not belong to the most select aristocracy, for she is the sister of a wealthy gentleman of private means, a Mr. Wynne,[3] a London acquaintance of mine, whose name I will show you on my list.

The brother of this Mr. Wynne fell in love with a German lady, Cronemann by name, the same who has been singing at Salzburg. Her father was a musician in Holland and her father's brother with several sons is still in Amsterdam. One son is a musician in the service of Prince Conti in Paris and came to see us with Schobert. The mother of this singer attached herself to an Italian Kapellmeister, Paradies,[4] who, after the death of her husband, took entire charge of the children. When I was in London he married off this one to Mr. Wynne, and another to Signor Paolo Mazzinghi,[5] a London violinist.

---

[1] Ignaz Parhammer (1715–1786), a famous Jesuit Father, who after the emigration of the Protestants from Salzburg in 1733 took an active part in restoring the Catholic faith. In 1758 he became Father Confessor to the Emperor Joseph and in 1759 took over the management of the Waisenhaus (Orphanage), where he introduced the teaching of music on the model of the Venetian schools of music.

[2] In summer 1768 the Emperor laid the foundation stone of the new Orphanage Church on the Rennweg.

[3] Richard Wynne, the father of Elizabeth, chief author of the Wynne diaries, edited by Anne Fremantle, London, 1935. He is not mentioned in the *Reiseaufzeichnungen* of Leopold Mozart, who must refer to some other list. His eldest sister Giustiniana married on 17 January 1758 Count Orsini von Rosenberg, Imperial Ambassador to the Venetian Republic, who died in 1765. A portion of this letter which has been omitted contains a long account of Richard's younger brother William, the 'wicked uncle' of the Wynne diaries.

[4] Pietro Domenico Paradies (Paradisi), 1710–1792, born at Naples, was trained by Porpora and made a reputation as a teacher and composer for the harpsichord. He came in 1746 to London, where he lived for many years. According to C. F. Pohl, *Mozart in London*, pp. 176–177, he married off his pupil Miss Cassandra Frederick to Thomas (*sic*) Wynne, a wealthy landowner in South Wales, and her sister to Tommaso Mazzinghi.

[5] Not Paolo, but Tommaso Mazzinghi, violinist at Marylebone Gardens, who died in 1775. He is mentioned in Leopold Mozart's *Reiseaufzeichnungen*, p. 36.

As for Wolfgang's opera all I can tell you is that, to put it shortly, the whole hell of musicians has arisen to prevent the display of a child's ability. I cannot even press for its performance, since a conspiracy has been formed to produce it, if it must be produced, extremely badly and thus ruin it. I have had to await the arrival of the Emperor. Otherwise the 'bataille' would have commenced long ago. Believe me, I shall leave nothing undone which may be necessary to save my child's honour. I knew how it would be long ago and have suspected it even longer. I even spoke to His Excellency Count von Zeill. The latter, however, believed that all the musicians were in favour of Wolfgang, because he too judged by appearances and knew nothing of the inner wickedness of these beasts. Patience! Time will clear up everything and God lets nothing happen to no purpose.

Farewell to you all. I am your old

MOZART

(66) *Leopold Mozart to Lorenz Hagenauer, Salzburg*

[Extract]   [Copy in the Deutsche Staatsbibliothek, Berlin]

VIENNA, 24 *September* 1768

I wrote today to His Grace the Archbishop. I hope that there is no foundation for the 'bruit' which you reported to me.[1] But if God has some other purpose for us, then it will not be in our power to alter it. I hope, however, that you will not leave me in ignorance for a single moment. On the morning of the 21st I had an audience with His Majesty the Emperor and handed to him my complaints about the theatrical impresario Affligio.[2] His Excellency Count Spork[3] has already been entrusted with the investigation and Affligio has been ordered to give an explanation; in addition to the hundred ducats for the opera, I am demanding repayment of the expenses which I have incurred here during all this time. But patience! We shall soon know the result. The Emperor was most gracious and promised us full justice.

Today I have had to draw money again. Heaven will repay everything.

Herr Küffel has entered the service of Prince Esterházy at Eisenstadt, where Herr Joseph Haydn is Kapellmeister.

[1] Possibly a rumour that, on account of his prolonged absence, Leopold Mozart would be asked to resign his appointments in the Archbishop's service.
[2] The autograph of Leopold Mozart's formal complaint to the Emperor Joseph II is in the Zavertal Collection of Mozart relics at Glasgow University and was published by Farmer and Smith, *New Mozartiana*, Glasgow, 1935, pp. 113-119. The petition was quite unsuccessful.
[3] Johann Wenzel Spork (1724-1804), Austrian statesman and a connoisseur of music. In 1764 Maria Theresia appointed him Director of Court and Chamber Music.

(67) *Leopold Mozart to Lorenz Hagenauer, Salzburg*

[*Extract*]   [*Copy in the Deutsche Staatsbibliothek, Berlin*]

VIENNA, 12 *November* 1768

The new church of Father Parhammer's orphanage will be blessed on the Feast of the Immaculate Conception. For this Feast Wolfgang has composed a solemn mass,[1] an offertorium[2] and a trumpet concerto for a boy,[3] and has dedicated them to the orphanage. Presumably Wolfgang himself will conduct this music.[4] There are reasons for everything.

(68) *Leopold Mozart to Lorenz Hagenauer, Salzburg*

[*Extract*]   [*Copy in the Deutsche Staatsbibliothek, Berlin*]

VIENNA, 14 *December* 1768

Only now have we been able to conclude our affairs.

The Mass, which was produced by little Wolfgang on December 7th at Father Parhammer's orphanage in the presence of the Imperial Court and which he himself conducted, has restored that reputation which our enemies, by preventing the performance of the opera, intended to destroy, and, as the throng was amazing, has convinced the court and the public of the wickedness of our adversaries. I shall give you more details when we meet.[5] And, what is more, Her Majesty the Empress has sent us a beautiful present.

(69) *Leopold Mozart to Archbishop Sigismund von Schrattenbach*

[*Autograph in the Regierungsarchiv, Salzburg*]

SALZBURG, 8 *March* 1769

YOUR GRACE, MOST WORTHY PRINCE OF THE HOLY ROMAN EMPIRE, MOST GRACIOUS PRINCE AND LORD!

When Your Grace was recently pleased to allow me most graciously to remain a few months longer in Vienna, you gave orders, however, that

---

[1] Probably K. 139 [47a] See Köchel, pp. 73, 74.
[2] Sometimes identified with K. 47: 'Veni Sancte Spiritus', but WSF, vol. i. p. 243, are inclined to doubt this.   [3] This has not been preserved.
[4] Conducting with a baton was then the custom for church music, whereas operas and orchestral works were generally conducted from the harpsichord. See G. Schünemann, *Geschichte des Dirigierens*, 1913, p. 154 f.
[5] The Mozarts arrived back in Salzburg on 5 January 1769.

until my return my pay should be withheld.[1] As my stay in Vienna has nevertheless taken place against my will and to my disadvantage and as I could not leave Vienna before without loss of my own honour and that of my child; and as, in addition, both my son and I have composed various works for the Church, and especially for use in the Cathedral,[2] I now most humbly beg Your Grace not only to pay me for the past month, but as a special favour to give your most gracious order that the sum which has been withheld should also be paid to me. The greater this favour is, the more shall I endeavour to render myself worthy of it and to pray God for Your Grace's welfare.

I and my children send our most humble greetings to Your Grace, our Prince and Lord.

Your most obedient
LEOPOLD MOZART,
Deputy-Kapellmeister[3]

(70) *Mozart to a Girl Friend*

[*Copy in the Deutsche Staatsbibliothek, Berlin*]

DEAR FRIEND,   SALZBURG, 1769[4]

Forgive me for taking the liberty of plaguing you with a few lines but as you said yesterday that you could understand everything, no matter what Latin words I might choose to write down, curiosity has got the better of me and I am writing down for you a few lines made up of various Latin words. When you have read them, please do me the favour of sending me your answer by one of Hagenauer's maids, for our Nannie cannot wait. But you must send me a letter too.

Cuperem scire de qua causa, a quam plurimis adolescentibus otium usque adeo aestimatur, ut ipsi se nec verbis, nec verberibus, ab hoc sinant abduci,[5]

WOLFGANG

MOZART

[1] See p. 85 n. 4. Schurig, vol. i. p. 188, quotes the order to the Court Pay Office, dated 18 March 1768, to the effect that 'if the court musicians, Mozart, Meisner and Küffel do not turn up in April, they are not to receive any more pay'.

[2] Apart from other works which have disappeared Mozart composed in 1767 three church sonatas, K. 67-69, [41h, 41i, 41k] and in January 1769 a mass, K. 65 [61a].

[3] The result of this application was that the 'applicant was granted his pay for the months of January and February'.

[4] The recipient is unknown. The indefinite date is an addition in a strange handwriting. This is the first letter of Mozart's which has been handed down.

[5] 'I should like to know for what reason idleness is so popular with most young people that it is impossible to draw them from it either by words or by punishments.'

Leitzmann, *W. A. Mozarts Leben*, Leipzig, 1926, p. 471 n., suggests that this Latin passage was extracted from some Latin grammar or reading-book at which Mozart was then working. And Schiedermair points out, vol. i. p. 295, n. 1, that probably Mozart was engrossed in Latin studies, seeing that in 1768 and 1769 he composed his first three masses in G major (K. 49 [47d]), D minor (K. 65 [61a]) and C major (K. 66).

Mozart's fifth journey was a visit to Italy with his father, who took him to Rovereto, Verona, Milan, Parma, Bologna, Florence, Rome, Naples, and other towns. On their return journey they spent three months in Bologna, where Mozart studied counterpoint under the learned Padre Martini, and nearly four months in Milan, where he carried out a commission to write the first opera Mitridate, Rè di Ponto *for the 1770-71 carnival season. In Italy Mozart heard several operas and made the acquaintance of the leading Italian singers. He composed too during this time several operatic arias, an oratorio* La Betulia liberata, *and his first string quartet. This tour, the first Italian journey, lasted from 12 December 1769, to 28 March 1771. It is described in letters from Leopold Mozart to his wife, Mozart occasionally adding letters or postscripts of varying length. Letters 71-137.*

(71) *Leopold Mozart to his Wife*

[*Autograph in the Mozarteum, Salzburg*]

[WÖRGL, 13 *December* 1769 [1]]

We reached Kalterl at one o'clock and had for our lunch a piece of preserved veal accompanied by a most fearful stinking smell. With this we drank a few draughts of good beer, for the wine was a laxative.

We reached Lofer after seven. When I had ordered our supper, we went to call on the prefect who was very much annoyed with us for not having gone at once to his house. So, as we had already ordered our meal in the inn, we had it brought to the prefect's house, where we supped, gossiped until ten o'clock and were given a fine room and a good bed. In the morning I drank chocolate and Wolfgang had some excellent soup. We drove until midday to St. Johann and arrived this evening at Wörgl, where I sent an invitation to the Vicar, Herr Hartmann Kehlhammer of Chiemsee. He has just come and sends you greetings. It is now ten o'clock and we must go to bed, for to morrow I have to be up at five. In spite of the roads which were, as I had been told, very bad, I slept soundly, for I saw that we had a very good driver. In these parts, especially from Lofer to St. Johann, there is an extraordinary amount of snow. Keep well and cheerful! I shall write immediately from Innsbruck.

MZT.

(71a) *Mozart to his Mother*

[*Autograph in the Pierpont Morgan Library, New York City*]

DEAREST MAMMA! [WÖRGL, 13 *December* 1769 [2]]

My heart is completely enchanted with all these pleasures, because it is so jolly on this journey, because it is so warm in the carriage and because our coachman is a fine fellow who, when the road gives him the slightest chance, drives so fast. Papa will have already described the journey to Mamma. The reason why I am writing to Mamma is to show her that I know my duty and that I am with the deepest respect her devoted son

WOLFGANG MOZART

---

[1] From internal evidence and according to Nissen's statement, p. 156, the Mozarts left Salzburg on 12 December 1769.
[2] A postscript to his father's letter.

(71b) *Mozart to his Sister*

[Autograph in the Pierpont Morgan Library, New York City]

MY DEAREST SISTER,   [WÖRGL, 13 *December* 1769[1]]

Thank God, we have arrived safely at Wörgl. To tell the truth, I must say that travelling is very jolly, that it is not at all cold and that it is as warm in our carriage as in a room. How is your sore throat? Surely our Signore Seccatore[2] turned up the very day we left? If you see Herr von Schiedenhofen,[3] tell him that I am always singing 'Tralaliera, Tralaliera' and that I need not put sugar in my soup now that I am no longer in Salzburg. At Lofer we supped and slept in the house of Herr Helmreich, who is prefect there. His wife is an excellent lady. She is the sister of Herr Moll. I am hungry. I am longing to eat something. Meanwhile, farewell. Addio.

PS.—My compliments to all my good friends, to Herr Hagenauer (the merchant), his wife, his sons and his daughters, to Madame Rosa[4] and her husband, to Herr Adlgasser and Herr Spitzeder. As for Herr Hornung,[5] ask him from me whether he has again made the mistake of thinking that I was in bed instead of you.

WOLFGANG MOZART

(72) *Leopold Mozart to his Wife*

[Autograph in the Mozarteum, Salzburg]

[INNSBRUCK, 15 *December* 1769]

Friday, at six o'clock in the evening

We have been here half an hour already. At noon we were in Schwaz. The country near Innsbruck seemed to me to resemble somewhat the road towards Hallein near Kaltenhausen; and Innsbruck itself is similarly situated. Otherwise so far I have nothing to tell. Thank God, we are well. We are lodging at the 'Weisses Kreuz'.[6] If you have anything to write to me, you can send the letter here. If in the meantime I depart, I shall first leave a message at the Post Office that letters should be forwarded to

---

[1] A second postscript, written in Italian, to his father's letter.

[2] i.e. Mr. Boring, obviously some Salzburg acquaintance.

[3] Joachim Ferdinand von Schiedenhofen (1747–1823) was a friend of Mozart's. He became later Court Councillor at Salzburg.

[4] Rosa Barducci, a portrait painter, who in 1764 married Johann Baptist Hagenauer, Court Sculptor in Salzburg, whom she had met in Florence. See p. 13, n. 2.

[5] Joseph Hornung, a baritone in the service of the Salzburg court.

[6] The information given in the letters written by Leopold Mozart and his son during their first journey to Italy is supplemented by notes kept by Mozart himself during their stay in Innsbruck, Bozen, Rovereto and Naples. The autograph of these notes, which were published by A. Sandberger, *Jahrbuch der Musikbibliothek Peters*, 1901, is in the Bavarian State Library. These notes, together with those kept by Leopold Mozart in the other Italian towns they visited, are also reproduced in A. Schurig, *Leopold Mozarts Reiseaufzeichnungen*, 1920, pp. 49–54.

Bozen. You have only to address your letters:

à Mr: Mozart, Maître de Chapelle de la Musique de S:A:S: Le Prince Archevêque de Salzbourg.

In a fit of absentmindedness I took away with me on my watch the key of our clavichord. I return it herewith, as it is unnecessary to carry it about with me so far. See that it is not lost. Farewell! Farewell to all! Wolfgang and I kiss you and Nannerl, and I am your old

MZT.

I am giving this letter now to the Vienna post.

(73) *Leopold Mozart to his Wife*

[Autograph in the Mozarteum, Salzburg]

[INNSBRUCK] 17 December [1769]
Sunday night, December 17th, I think, for
I no longer possess a calendar of this year.

His Excellency Count Spaur,[1] the brother of our Salzburg member of the Cathedral Chapter, on my announcing my arrival through my servant, not only sent his servant immediately to welcome me and to tell me that his carriage would fetch us on Saturday at two o'clock and drive us to his house, but with his wife received me most graciously and offered to place his carriage at our service, an offer which I accepted. Early on Sunday morning I received a note from him inviting us to a concert at five o'clock, which was to take place at the house of Count Leopold Künigl. Meanwhile I made use of the carriage, drove twice to Herr von Kalckhammer, then to Baron Christiani, where I chatted for three quarters of an hour about all sorts of things, then to His Excellency Baron Enzenberg, and finally at five o'clock to the concert. Wolfgang was presented with a very beautiful concerto which he played there at sight. As usual we were received with all honours and were brought home later by Count Spaur in person. In short, we are perfectly satisfied. Tomorrow I intend to pack up my things, which will not take long, as I did not unpack much, and on Tuesday, God willing, I propose to leave. Please give Herr von Schiedenhofen my obedient thanks both for the letter of recommendation which he sent me and for the kind apology which he made in my stead and which is really justified. Please ask him to give my thanks and my greetings to Herr Major. I shall write to Herr von Schiedenhofen myself as soon as I have time. I hope that you are all well. I shall write again from Bozen. You must keep all our letters. I purposely left at home the various parts of the opera,[2] even the violin parts, and only took the

---

[1] Count Franz Josef Spaur (1725–1797) was Imperial Judge of Appeal at Innsbruck.
[2] Probably Mozart's *La finta semplice*, written in Vienna 1768, and performed in Salzburg 1769.

score with me. But we forgot to take a few arias for Wolfgang. It does not matter, however, for we shall get enough arias. A certain Count Attems, who spoke to us here, is going to Salzburg with his wife. He studied there many years ago and he is an old acquaintance of mine. He will perhaps call on you in order to hear Nannerl play something to him. We kiss you and Nannerl a thousand times. Farewell to all! I am your old   MOZART

⟨The present was twelve ducats.¹⟩

(74) *Leopold Mozart to his Wife*

[*Autograph in the Mozarteum, Salzburg*]

BOZEN, 22 *December* 1769

We arrived safely at Bozen² yesterday evening. Today I took my two letters to the post and lunched with Herr Kurzweil. Tomorrow at midday we are invited to Herr Stockhammer, to whom Herr Ranftl gave us an introduction, and this evening we are going to Herr Antoni Gummer. I myself do not yet know whether we shall stay here over Christmas or leave tomorrow evening. Meanwhile, I think that you had better write to me at Rovereto, where I shall call at the post. In addition, I am leaving instructions at all Post Offices and my name as well, which is as well known everywhere as a bad half-penny. We are, thank God, in good health. Here is a sheet from the Innsbruck paper.³ I hope that you are both well. Good-bye! Our greetings to all our good friends. I write in haste and I am your old

MZT.

I and Wolfgang kiss you a thousand times.
Herr Kurzweil sends you his greetings.

(75) *Leopold Mozart to his Wife*

[*Extract*]   [*Autograph in the Mozarteum, Salzburg*]

VERONA,⁴ 7 *January* 1770

I am very sorry not to have received your first letter, which is probably lying at the Bozen Post Office. I shall make enquiries, for it will have been forwarded there from Innsbruck. *Thank God, we are well!* Let me tell you so at the outset. It would have been helpful if you had told me

---

¹ Passages in angular brackets are in cypher in the original. See p. xviii.
² In Bozen the Mozarts stayed at the inn 'Zur Sonne'.
³ Quoted by Nissen, p. 157.
⁴ The Mozarts arrived at Verona on December 27th and stayed at the 'Due Torri'.

how many letters you have received from me, for I sent you one from
Wörgl, one by the hired coachman, one from Innsbruck by post and one
from Bozen.[1] We only spent a day and a half in Bozen. We had hardly
arrived at Rovereto[2] when a certain Christiani, who took the woman's
part in the play 'The Child of Cato' at the Collegio Rupertino, turned up
at once and on behalf of his brother invited us to lunch on the following
day. And who was this brother? That very same Nicolaus Christiani who
was Ecclesiastical Commissioner in Salzburg and my pupil on the violin,
and who is now the chief man in Rovereto and the whole district, that is,
Lieutenant of the County representing Her Majesty the Empress. You
will remember him. As soon as we entered his house, he said that Wolfgang was like you, for he remembered your appearance quite well. The
nobles gave a concert in the house of Baron Todeschi. And who was this
Baron Todeschi? That same person whom Herr Giovanni once brought
to us in Vienna. You will perhaps remember him. It is hardly necessary to
mention how greatly Wolfgang has been doing himself credit. In the
afternoon of the following day we went to the organ of the principal
church, and, although only six or eight of the leading people knew that
we were coming, we found all Rovereto assembled there and some very
strong fellows had to go ahead and make way for us to the choir, where
we then had to wait for over five minutes before we could reach the
organ, as everyone wanted to get close to us. We spent four days in
Rovereto. We have standing invitations here from Marchese Carlotti and
also from Signor Locatelli.[3] We have lunched twice with Marchese Carlotti and also with Count Carlo Emily and twice with Count Giusti, who
has a beautiful garden and picture-gallery. You will perhaps find them
mentioned in Keyssler's Reisebeschreibung.[4] We dined yesterday with
Signor Locatelli and today there was absolute confusion, which I must
describe to you in greater detail. We were invited to the house of a
certain honest fellow, Signor Ragazzoni. Signor Lugiati,[5] the Receiver-
General of Venice, had asked some courtiers to request me to allow
Wolfgang to have his portrait painted.[6] Yesterday morning he had the
first sitting and today after church he was to have the second one and we
were to drive there too. Signor Lugiati himself went to Signor Ragazzoni

---

[1] Letters 71, 72, 73 and 74.

[2] The Mozarts arrived at Rovereto on December 24th and stayed at the inn 'Zur Rose'.

[3] Not the famous violinist Pietro Locatelli (1693–1764), as Abert, vol. i. pp. 177 and 331, seems to suggest.

[4] Johann Georg Keyssler, *Neueste Reise durch Deutschland, Böhmen, Ungarn, die Schweiz, Italien und Lothringen*, Hanover, 1740–1741. The Baedeker of the eighteenth century.

[5] Pietro Lugiati (1730–1802), a famous connoisseur and patron of music. Nissen, p. 197 f., quotes an Italian letter, dated 22 April 1770, which Lugiati wrote to Frau Mozart about her son, describing him as 'un portente di Natura nella musica'.

[6] This oil painting for which Mozart sat on 6 and 7 January 1770, was done by a Saverio dalla Rosa, a nephew of the Cignaroli mentioned in Leopold Mozart's *Reiseaufzeichnungen*, p. 50. See illustration no. 3.

and begged him to leave us to him, to which the latter had to agree, though most reluctantly, because Lugiati is very powerful in Venice. So this morning after church we were to go to his house to sit once more for the painter before we went on to lunch. But again an even greater person appeared, to wit, the Bishop of Verona, of the house of Giustiniani, who sent us, through Signor Locatelli, an invitation not only to call on him after church, but to lunch with him. On hearing, however, that Wolfgang's portrait was being painted and that we wanted to leave, he let us lunch with Signor Lugiati, but kept us until after one o'clock. Progress was then made with the portrait and we did not sit down to lunch until three o'clock. Afterwards we drove to St. Thomas's Church in order to play on the two organs there; and although we only decided to do this while we were at table and although only a few tickets had been sent to Marchese Carlotti and Count Pedemonte, nevertheless such a crowd had assembled that we had hardly room to get out of the coach. The crush was so great that we were obliged to go through the monastery. But in a moment so many people had rushed up to us that we should not have been able to proceed at all, if the Fathers, who were already waiting for us at the monastery doors, had not taken us into their midst. When the performance was over, the throng was even greater, for everyone wanted to see the little organist. As soon as we were seated in our carriage, I told the coachman to drive us home, where we have locked ourselves in our room and I have begun to write this letter. But I have had to tear myself away, for they would not have left us in peace long enough to finish it. We are driving out tomorrow with Signor Locatelli to see the Amphitheatre and other rare sights of the town. Then we shall lunch with him and drive round afterwards to pay farewell calls. The day after tomorrow we shall pack and on Wednesday evening, God willing, we shall travel to Mantua which, although it is near, is almost a winter day's journey on account of the filthy road. Now my paper is at an end. Farewell. I am your old

MZT.

(75a) *Mozart to his Sister*

[Copy formerly in the possession of Dr. L. Scheibler, Bonn]

DEAREST SISTER!   VERONA, 7 *January* 1770
    I have had an aching feeling, because I have been so long waiting in vain for an answer. I have had good reason too, because I have not yet received your letter. Here ends the German booby and the Italian one begins. Lei è più franca nella lingua italiana di quel che mi ho imaginato. Lei mi dica la cagione perchè lei non fu nella commedia che hanno

giocato i cavalieri? Adesso sentiamo sempre opere: una è titolata: il Ruggiero.[1] Oronte, il padre di Bradamante, è un principe (fa il signor Afferi), un bravo cantante, un baritono, ma[2] forced when he sings falsetto, but not as much as Tibaldi in Vienna. Bradamante, figlia di Oronte, innamorata di Ruggiero (she is to marry Leone, but she does not want him), fa una povera Baronessa, che ha avuto una gran disgrazia, ma non so che. Recita under an assumed name, but I do not know it, ha una voce passabile, e la statura non sarebbe male, ma distona come il diavolo. Ruggiero, un ricco principe, innamorato di Bradamante, un musico, canta un poco in the manner of Manzuoli ed ha una bellissima voce forte ed è gia vecchio, ha cinquantacinque anni ed ha una flexible throat. Leone, who is to marry Bradamante, is very rich, but whether he is rich off the stage, I do not know. Fa una donna, la moglie di Afferi. Ha una bellissima voce, ma è tanto susurro nel teatro che non si sente niente. Irene fa una sorella di Lolli,[3] del gran violinista, che abbiamo sentito a Vienna. She has a muffled voice and always sings a semiquaver too late o troppo a buon' ora. Ganno fa un signor, che non so come egli si chiama, è la prima volta che lui recita.[4] After each act there is a ballet. There is a good dancer here called Monsieur Ruesler. He is a German and dances very well. One of the last times we were at the opera (but not the very last time) we asked M. Ruesler to come up to our palco (for we have a free entrance to the palco of Marchese Carlotti, as we have the key) and there we had a talk with him. A propos, everyone is masked now and it is really very convenient when you wear your mask, as you have the advantage of not having to take off your hat when you are greeted and of not having to address the person by name. You just say, 'servitore umilissimo, Signora Maschera'. Cospetto di Bacco, what fun! But the funniest thing of all is that we go to bed between seven and half past seven. Se lei indovinasse questo, io dirò certamente che lei sia la madre di tutti indovini.[5]

[1] Probably, as Schiedermair, vol. i. p. 4, n. 2, suggests, the opera by Pietro Guglielmi (1727–1804), which had already been performed in Venice.

[2] You are more fluent in Italian than I had imagined. Please tell me the reason why you did not go to the play which the courtiers acted? At present we are always hearing operas. One of them is 'Ruggiero'. Oronte, father of Bradamante, is a prince. Signor Afferi takes this part. He is a fine singer, a baritone, but, . . .

[3] Antonio Lolli (c. 1730–1802), a famous violinist who after touring with Nardini became leader at Stuttgart and subsequently at St. Petersburg. His sister is described in the *Reiseaufzeichnungen*, p. 50, as a singer and the wife of Signor Amelli, a dancer.

[4] Bradamante, daughter of Oronte, is in love with Ruggiero, . . . Her part is sung by a poor Baroness, who has had a great misfortune, but I don't know what it was. She is singing, . . . Her voice is tolerably good and she has not a bad presence, but she sings devilishly out of tune. The part of Ruggiero, a rich prince, who is in love with Bradamante, is sung by a castrato, who sings rather in the manner of Manzuoli and has a very fine powerful voice and is already old. He is fifty-five and has, . . . His part is sung by a woman, Afferi's wife. She has a most beautiful voice, but there is so much whispering in the theatre that you can't hear anything. Irene's part is sung by a sister of Lolli, the great violinist, whom we heard in Vienna. . . . The part of Ganno is taken by someone whose name I do not know. He is singing for the first time.

[5] If you guess this I shall certainly say that you are the mother of all guessers.

Kiss my mother's hand for me. I kiss you a thousand times and assure you that I shall always remain

your sincere brother

WOLFGANG MOZART

Portez-vous bien et aimez-moi toujours.

(76) *Leopold Mozart to his Wife*

[*Extract*]   [*Autograph in the Mozarteum, Salzburg*]

MANTUA,[1] 11 January 1770

We arrived here yesterday evening and went to the opera[2] an hour later, at six o'clock. Thank God, we are well. Wolfgang looks as if he had been through a campaign, for his face is reddish-brown, especially about the nose and mouth, for instance, just like the face of His Majesty the Emperor. This is due to the air and to the open fires. My beauty has not yet suffered, or I should be in despair. I have not yet anything to write about from here. Tomorrow we are invited to lunch with Count Francesco Eugenio D'Arco and then I shall be able to let you know more about this town. Meanwhile I must tell you something about Verona. We have seen the Amphitheatre and the Geological Museum, which you will read about in Keyssler's Reisebeschreibung. I am bringing back a book on the antiquities of Verona. Herr von Helmreich, to whom I send greetings, will surely lend you the other two parts of Keyssler, so that, although you are not with us, you can at least travel at home in imagination. I should make the letters too heavy and too dear, if I were to send along the newspaper notices which have appeared about Wolfgang in Mantua and other places. But I enclose this one,[3] in which there are two mistakes, for it says 'the present *Kapellmeister*' and 'not yet thirteen years old', instead of fourteen. But you know how it is; journalists write as it occurs to them and whatever comes into their minds. I could send you along other comments too, for in Verona the poets vied with one another in composing verses about him. Here is a copy of a sonnet which a learned dilettante jotted down in our presence.[4] Kapellmeister Daniele Barba also sang extempore the most beautiful verses about Wolfgang.

On the 16th in the Hall of the Accademia Filarmonica there will be the usual weekly concert to which we are invited.[5] Then we shall leave im-

---

[1] The Mozarts reached Mantua on January 10th and stayed at the 'Ancora Verde'.
[2] For Mozart's account of the opera, which was Hasse's *Demetrio*, see p. 110.
[3] Nissen, pp. 169–170, reproduces this cutting from a Verona newspaper of January 9th.
[4] This sonnet by Signor Zaccaria Betti, described in the *Reiseaufzeichnungen*, p. 50, as 'poeta dilettante', is quoted by Nissen, pp. 162–163. Nissen, p. 163, to his version of this letter adds 'and of another poem by Meschini', and quotes the poem.
[5] For the programme of this concert and for the comment of a Mantuan newspaper, see Nissen, pp. 170–174. Rudolf Lewicki in *MM*, Nov. 1920, p. 30, gives the Italian text of the latter.

mediately for Milan and, if the weather is cold and the roads are frozen, we shall travel through Cremona.[2] If it is mild and the roads in consequence bad, we must go through Brescia. It is very quiet here and one never hears a word about anything. It is just like being in Germany. By my honour I swear I have hardly time to write this letter, and on account of it we have had to miss the opera today. As soon as we reach Milan I shall write to you again; and you must write to me at Milan. You may add below: per ricapito del Signor Troger, Segretario di S. Eccellenza il Signor Conte Carlo di Firmian.[2] Now I must go to bed. Farewell to you and Nannerl. We kiss you a thousand times. We drink your health every day. Wolfgang never forgets to do this. Good-bye. I am your old

MZT.

All kinds of greetings to all our good friends. I cannot write to anybody, for I am hustled to death. Nothing but dressing and undressing, packing and unpacking, and withal no warm room, so that one freezes like a dog. Everything I touch is as cold as ice. And if you were to see the doors and locks in the rooms! just like prisons! Post the enclosed letter to Herr Friederici[3] at Gera, so that it may be forwarded quickly and safely. It is an order for a harpsichord.

(77) *Leopold Mozart to his Wife*

[Extract]   [Autograph in the Mozarteum, Salzburg]

MILAN, 26 January 1770

I have received from Herr Troger your letter of the 12th. We reached Milan[4] at noon on the 23rd. On the 24th your letter arrived and with it your first note which, at my request, Herr Antoni Gummer called for at the Bozen Post Office and forwarded to me. You complain that for three weeks you have had no word from me. But I wrote to you from Verona and from Mantua.[5] You ought to have received my first letter from Verona, as I posted it there on January 7th. The second letter cannot have reached Salzburg yet, for I only posted it in Mantua on the 15th. At midday on the 10th we left Verona and reached Mantua in the evening, as I believe I have already told you. I wish you could see the hall where the

---

[1] The Mozarts took the route through Cremona. See *Reiseaufzeichnungen*, p. 50.
[2] Count Carlo di Firmian (1716–1774), who had been Governor-General of Lombardy since 1759, was a native of Deutschmetz in the province of Trent.
[3] Christian Ernst Friederici (1712–1779), a well-known manufacturer of claviers and the first to make upright instruments. Equally famous was his son Christian Gottlob Friederici (1750–1805).
[4] The Mozarts stayed at the Augustinian monastery of San Marco.
[5] Letters 75 and 76.

concert took place, the so-called Teatrino della Accademia Filarmonica. In all my life I have never seen anything more beautiful of its kind; and as *I hope that you are carefully collecting all our letters*, I shall describe it to you later when we meet. It is not a theatre, but a hall built with boxes like an opera house. Where the stage ought to be, there is a raised platform for the orchestra and behind the orchestra another gallery built with boxes for the audience. The crowds, the general shouting, clapping, noisy enthusiasm and cries of 'Bravo' and, in a word, the admiration displayed by the listeners, I cannot adequately describe to you.

Meanwhile some reports will doubtless have reached Salzburg not only from Rovereto but also from Verona and Mantua.

Herewith I enclose another poem composed by a lady, Signora Sartoretti, who entertained us in Mantua. On the following day her servant brought us on a beautiful plate an exceedingly fine bouquet with red ribbons below and a large piece of four ducats entwined in the ribbons; above was the poem, a copy of which I enclose.[1] I can assure you that everywhere I have found the most charming people and that in all towns we have had our particular friends, who have been with us until the last moment before our departure and have done everything to make our stay a pleasant one. I enclose a Mantuan newspaper, which we only received in Milan. Among other things you will find in it the programme of the music which was performed at the concert.[2] You must know, however, that neither this concert in Mantua nor the one in Verona were given for money, for everybody goes in free; in Verona this privilege belongs only to the nobles who alone keep up these concerts; but in Mantua the nobles, the military class and the eminent citizens may all attend them, because they are subsidised by Her Majesty the Empress. You will easily understand that we shall not become rich in Italy and you will admit that we shall do well enough if we earn our travelling expenses; and these I have always earned. But I assure you that although there are only two of us, the expenses are not small, and I fear that we have paid out about seventy ducats. It is already six weeks since we left Salzburg. Even if you live a *pasto* in Italy and hardly ever lunch at home, yet supper, room, firewood and so forth are all so dear, that after nine to eleven days in an inn you seldom get away with a bill for less than six ducats. I often thank God that I left you at home. Firstly, you would not have been able to stand the cold. Secondly, it would have cost us a great deal of money and we should not have been so free to live the way in which we now do; for here *we are staying at the Augustinian monastery of S. Marco*; not that we do so free, by any means! But we can live here comfortably and safely and we are near His Excellency Count Firmian. We have three large guest rooms. In the first we have a fire, take our meals and give audiences;

---

[1] For this poem see Abert, vol. ii. p. 932.   [2] See p. 106, n. 3.

in the second I sleep and we have put our trunk there; in the third room Wolfgang sleeps and there we keep our other small luggage. We each sleep on four good mattresses and every night the bed is warmed, so that Wolfgang, when he goes to bed, is always quite happy. We have a brother, Frater Alfonso, especially for our service and we are very well looked after. But I cannot tell you how long we shall stay here. His Excellency the Count is suffering from a cold. He wanted very much to give a concert in his house and to invite the Duke of Modena. So I have not been able to deliver the other letters of introduction, because this concert must take place first, as I think it will, on Tuesday or Wednesday next, for His Excellency is already better. I told you that Wolfgang had got red hands and a red face from the cold and the open fires. He is quite well now. Madame Sartoretti in Mantua gave him some skin cream to rub on his hands every evening, and in three days they were all right; and now he looks as he did before. *Otherwise, thank God, we have always been well*; and the change of air only gave Wolfgang a kind of dry cough which he shook off long ago. We shall hardly hear Herr Meisner sing in Florence, for not only will our stay here be a rather long one, but, as Turin is so near, we shall undoubtedly take a trip there. We are also proposing to spend a short time in Parma and Bologna, and thus we shall not reach Florence until the beginning of Lent.

Address all your letters in future to Mr. Troger, as you have been doing lately. I am your old faithful

L. MZT

We kiss you both a thousand times.

(77a) *Mozart to his Sister*

[Autograph in the Stadtarchiv, Karlsbad]

[MILAN, 26 January 1770]

I rejoice with my whole heart that you had such a good time during that sleigh-drive and I wish you a thousand opportunities of amusement so that you may spend your life very merrily. But one thing distresses me, and that is, that you have made Herr von Mölk[1] sigh and suffer so frightfully and that you did not go sleigh-driving with him, so that he might have upset you. How many handkerchiefs will he not have used that day, weeping on your account. No doubt he will have previously taken an ounce of tartar, which will have purged his wretchedly dirty

---

[1] Anton Joseph, son of Court Chancellor Felix von Mölk, was a friend of Mozart and in love with Nannerl.

body. I have no news except that Herr Gellert, the poet,[1] has died at Leipzig and since his death has written no more poetry. Just before I began this letter I composed an aria[2] from 'Demetrio',[3] which begins:

> Misero tu non sei:
> tu spieghi il tuo dolore,
> e, se non desti amore,
> ritrovi almen pietà.
>
> Misera ben son io
> che nel segreto laccio
> amo, non spero e taccio,
> e l' idol mio nol sa.

The opera at Mantua was charming. They played 'Demetrio'. The prima donna sings well, but very softly; and when you do not see her acting, but only singing, you would think that she is not singing at all. For she cannot open her mouth, but whines out everything. However, we are quite accustomed to that now. The seconda donna looks like a grenadier and has a powerful voice too, and, I must say, does not sing badly, seeing that she is acting for the first time. The primo uomo, il musico, sings beautifully, though his voice is uneven. His name is Caselli. Il secondo uomo is already old and I do not like him. His name is——. As for the tenors, one is called Otini.[4] He does not sing badly, but rather heavily like all Italian tenors, and he is a great friend of ours. I do not know the name of the other one. He is still young, but not particularly good. Primo ballerino—good. Prima ballerina—good, and it is said that she is not hideous, but I have not seen her close to. The rest are quite ordinary. A grotesco was there who jumps well, but cannot write as I do, I mean, as sows piddle. The orchestra was not bad. In Cremona it is good. The first violin is called Spagnoletto. The prima donna is not bad; she is quite old, I should say, and not good-looking; she acts better than she sings and she is the wife of a violinist called Masi, who plays in the orchestra. The opera was: La Clemenza di Tito.[5] Seconda donna, young, not at all bad on the stage, but nothing out of the ordinary. Primo uomo, musico, Cicognani—a delightful voice and a beautiful cantabile. The other two castrati, young and passable. The tenor's name is: non lo so.[6] He has a pleasant way with him, and resembles as though he were his natural son, Leroy in Vienna, who came to Geneva.

Ballerino primo, good. Ballerina prima, good but very plain. There

---

[1] Christian Fürchtegott Gellert (1715–1769), who since 1751 had been Professor of Philosophy at Leipzig University, enjoyed in his day a great reputation as a poet and man of letters. He died on 13 December 1769.

[2] This composition has not been preserved.

[3] Hasse's opera on a text by Metastasio which was performed at Mantua.

[4] Appears in the *Reiseaufzeichnungen*, p. 50, as 'Uttini'.

[5] Opera by J. A. Hasse.   [6] I don't know it.

was a woman dancer there, who did not dance badly and, what is very remarkable, was not bad-looking on the stage and off it. The others were quite ordinary. A grotesco was there too, who whenever he jumped let off a fart. As for Milan I really cannot tell you very much. We have not yet been to the opera, but we have heard that it has not been a success. Aprile,[1] primo uomo, sings well and has a beautiful even voice. We heard him in a church, when there happened to be a great festival. Madame Piccinelli from Paris, who sang at our concert, is acting in the opera. Monsieur Pick,[2] who danced in Vienna, is dancing here too. The opera is called: 'Didone abbandonata'.[3] This opera will soon come to an end and Signor Piccinni,[4] who is writing the next opera, is here. I have heard that his is called: 'Cesare in Egitto'.[5] Here there are also feste di ballo which begin as soon as the opera is over. The wife of Count von Firmian's steward is a Viennese. Last Friday we dined there and we are dining there again next Sunday. Farewell. Kiss my mother's hands a thousand times in vece mia.[6] I remain, true till death, your brother

WOLFGANG DE MOZART
The Honourable Highdale,
Friend of the Counting-house.

(78) *Leopold Mozart to his Wife*

[Extract]   [*Autograph in the Mozarteum, Salzburg*]

MILAN, *3 February* 1770

I thought that you would receive my letters gradually. I hope that by this time my letter from Mantua too and the one from Milan will have reached you. This then is my eighth letter. I have nothing to say, save that, thank God, we are well; that our hands, especially Wolfgang's, are quite all right again; that the steward's wife made the skin cream for us very successfully and according to your recipe; that yesterday we were at the dress rehearsal of the new opera, 'Cesare in Egitto'; that this opera is excellent and that we both saw and spoke to Maestro Piccinni and Madame Piccinelli; that for the last fortnight we have had the most

---

[1] Giuseppe Aprile (1738–1814), a male contralto, was trained in Naples and from 1763 onwards sang in all the principal theatres of Italy and Germany.

[2] His real name was Le Picq.

[3] The composer of this opera was Ignazio Celionat of Turin.

[4] Niccolò Piccinni (1728–1800) was for a time the most popular of Italian operatic composers. His first successes were in Naples, but he achieved a veritable triumph in Rome in 1760 with his opera buffa *La Cecchina, ossia la buona figliuola*. He moved in 1776 to Paris, where his first French opera *Roland*, produced in July 1778, brought him a crowd of admirers who ranged themselves against Gluck and his partisans.

[5] Abert, vol. i. p. 181, n. 2, points out that the original score of Piccinni's opera bears the title *Cesare e Cleopatra*.   [6] On my behalf.

beautiful weather; that every day Wolfgang looks forward to his well-warmed mattresses; that he cannot write a letter to you because he is composing two Latin motets [1] for two castrati, one of whom is fifteen and the other sixteen years old, who asked him to compose them, and to whom, as they are friends of his and sing beautifully, he could not refuse anything; that it is very distressing to me to see and hear these boys and to know that I cannot take them back to Salzburg; that I foresee that we shall stay longer in Milan than I expected; that His Excellency Count Firmian has not yet completely recovered from his cold; that during the last few days I have again found an account in the papers of how the inhabitants literally waylaid us in Bozolo, and about Wolfgang's skill and so forth; that Wolfgang sends you his thanks for your congratulations; that I and Wolfgang kiss you and Nannerl a thousand times and that I am ever your

faithful husband

MOZART

Have our two guns been cleaned? Is Nannerl practising the harpsichord regularly?

(79) *Leopold Mozart to his Wife*

[Extract]   [*Autograph in the Nationalbibliothek, Vienna*]

MILAN, 10 February 1770

You will, I hope, have received my letters of January 27th and February 3rd, and also my letter from Mantua.[2] What I certainly foresee is that we shall remain here until the end of the carnival. His Excellency Count von Firmian is now better and on Wednesday, February 7th, we had the honour of lunching with him for the first time. After lunch he presented Wolfgang with the nine volumes of Metastasio's works, the Turin edition, one of the most beautiful, and very handsomely bound. You can well imagine that this present is very welcome to me as well as to Wolfgang. His Excellency is much impressed by Wolfgang's skill and marks us out for his special courtesies and distinctions. It would take too long to describe in detail the evidence of his knowledge which Wolfgang has given in the presence of Maestro Sammartini [3] and of a number of the most brilliant people, and of how he has amazed them. You know how it is on these occasions, for you have seen it often enough.

Meanwhile we have had the opportunity of hearing various kinds of

---

[1] Probably K. 143 [73a] is one of these motets.
[2] Letters 77 (dated January 26th), 78 and 76.
[3] Giovanni Battista Sammartini (*c.* 1700–1775) was a prolific composer for instruments and voices and became maestro di cappella to more than half the churches in Milan, for which he furnished masses on all the great festivals.

church music and yesterday we listened to the High Mass or Requiem for old Marchese Litta, who to the annoyance of his enormous family died during the carnival, although they would have gladly allowed him to go on living until Lent. The Dies Irae of this Requiem lasted about three quarters of an hour. At two o'clock in the afternoon it was all over and we lunched about half past two.

You must not expect me to give you a description of the church services here. I am far too irritated to do so. They merely consist of music and of church adornment. Apart from these the most disgusting licentiousness prevails.

This very moment I have come in from a vesper service, which lasted over two hours, so that I have only had time to fetch this letter and finish writing it in the steward's quarters of Count Firmian's house. I also wanted to see whether there was not a letter from you. But I found nothing. You are very lazy. We have been here a long time and although this is the third letter which I have written from Milan, I have so far had no reply. All that I can do is not write to you for a few weeks. Wolfgang looks forward from post-day to post-day to a letter from you and yet nothing arrives. Addio. I am your old

MZT

(79a) *Mozart to his Mother and Sister*

[Autograph in the Nationalbibliothek, Vienna]

[MILAN, 10 *February* 1770[1]]

Talk of the devil and he will appear. Thanks and praise be to God, I am quite well and I can scarcely await the hour when I shall receive an answer from you. I kiss Mamma's hand and to my sister I send a pock-mark of a kiss and I remain the same old . . . old what? . . . the same old buffoon,

WOLFGANG in GERMANY, AMADEO in ITALY,

DE MOZARTINI

(79b) *Leopold Mozart to his Wife*

[Autograph in the Nationalbibliothek, Vienna]

[MILAN, 10 *February* 1770[2]]

I kiss you and Nannerl, but only once, because you do not write. Herr Troger sends greetings to you. Tell Mlle Troger that I am very much obliged to her brother for having found us such comfortable

[1] A postscript to his father's letter.   [2] A postscript added after Mozart's.

quarters, where we are well looked after and have a brother specially chosen to serve us.[1]

(80) *Leopold Mozart to his Wife*

[*Extract*]   [*Autograph in the Gemeentemuseum, The Hague*]

MILAN, 17 *February* 1770

Praise be to God, we are both well. That the winter, as you say, is not so dangerous in Italy as the summer, I can well believe. So we hope that God will spare us. And if one does not ruin one's health by irregular living and unnecessary stuffing and swilling and if one has otherwise no natural weakness, there is nothing to fear, for everywhere we are in God's hands. Wolfgang will not spoil his health by eating and drinking. You know how he controls himself; and I can assure you that I have never seen him take such care of himself as he does in this country. Whatever does not seem right to him he leaves and often he eats very little, yet none the less he is fat and cheerful and gay and jolly all day long.

The tailor has just called with cloaks and cowls which we have had to order. I looked at myself in the mirror, as we were trying them on, and thought of how *in my old age I too have had to take part in this tomfoolery*. The costume suits Wolfgang amazingly well. After having had to make this foolish expenditure, my only consolation is that one can use these costumes again for all sorts of things and can make linings, kitchen cloths and so forth, out of them.

Tomorrow the Duke and the Princess of Modena, the future bride of the Archduke Ferdinand,[2] are coming to Count Firmian's to hear Wolfgang play. In the evening we are driving en masque to the gala opera and afterwards we shall attend the ball. Then we shall drive home with our great friend, Signor Don Ferdinando,[3] who is steward to the Count. Next Friday there will be a concert for the general public and we shall then see what profit we shall make. But on the whole we shall not earn much in Italy. The main thing is that there is the greatest enthusiasm and understanding here and that the Italians see how much Wolfgang knows. Otherwise one must generally accept admiration and bravos as payment. In this connexion I must tell you that everywhere we have been received with the greatest courtesy imaginable and that on all occasions we have been asked to meet the leading nobles. Wolfgang kisses most humbly the hands of Her Excellency the Countess von Arco[4] and thanks her for the kiss she sent, which is far more precious to him than many young ones.

[1] Frater Alfonso. See p. 109.
[2] Mozart was commissioned later by the Empress Maria Theresia to compose a dramatic serenata *Ascanio in Alba* for the marriage of the Archduke Ferdinand in October 1771.
[3] Don Fernando Germani, steward to Count Firmian.
[4] Wife of Count Georg Anton Felix von Arco, Chief Chamberlain to the Archbishop of Salzburg.

(80a) *Mozart to his Sister*

[Autograph in the Gemeentemuseum, The Hague]

[MILAN, 17 *February* 1770 [1]]

Here I am, now you have me. Dear little Marianne, with all my arse I rejoice that you had such a frightfully good time. Tell Nurse Ursula, the one, I mean, with the cold arse, that I still maintain that I sent back all her songs to her. But *in any case* if, engrossed in my high and important thoughts, I swept the song off to Italy, I shall not fail, should I find it, to stuff it into a letter. Addio. Farewell, my children. I kiss Mamma's hands a thousand times and send you a hundred kisses or smacks on your marvellous horseface. Per fare il fine,[2] I am your, etc.[3]

(81) *Leopold Mozart to his Wife*

[Autograph in the Mozarteum, Salzburg]

MILAN, *Shrove Tuesday*[4] 1770

Last Saturday we had to drive unexpectedly to the opera and ball with the steward,[5] so I was not able to write to you. Our concert, which took place on Friday,[6] went off in the same way as our concerts have done everywhere, and therefore no further description is necessary. We are well, God be praised, and although we are not rich, yet we always have a little more than what is barely necessary. On Monday or Tuesday of the second week in Lent, with God's help we shall leave Milan for Parma. We should like to go off sooner, but Count Firmian wants to give a big concert for the ladies in his house in the first week of Lent;[7] and other things will have to be arranged. Here the inhabitants will still be eating meat tomorrow and on Thursday; every day operas and balls will still take place; and on Saturday the last ball will be held. This is according to the Use of St. Ambrose, which the whole town follows.[8] In the monasteries, however, they observe the Roman customs and begin Lent on Ash Wednesday. But on that day and on Thursday all the priests run out of the monasteries to their acquaintances in the town and invite themselves to eat meat. What do you think of that? Oh, later on I shall tell you a hundred nice stories of the same kind, which are not at all edifying but extremely annoying. I am quite delighted that Salzburg is so gay now and

---

[1] A postscript to his father's letter.   [2] To conclude.
[3] The autograph breaks off here.   [4] 27 February.
[5] Don Fernando Germani.   [6] 23 February.
[7] This concert was given on 12 March and is described on p. 118.
[8] In the liturgical year according to the Ambrosian rite, fasting began on the first Sunday in Lent and not on Ash Wednesday.

that you too have some entertainment. Give my best greetings everywhere. Before I leave here I shall write to the Chief Steward.[1] Go on enclosing the letters to Herr Troger even if I have left Milan, for he will certainly forward them. Farewell, I must close. Wolfgang is busy composing two arias.[2] I kiss you and Nannerl a thousand times and I remain

your old

MZT.

Basil's[3] accident not only distressed us very greatly, but cost Wolfgang many tears. You know how sensitive he is. God grant that Basil may recover. I wish it from my heart and send him our greetings.

(81a) *Mozart to his Mother and Sister*

[*Autograph in the Mozarteum, Salzburg*]

[MILAN, *Shrove Tuesday* 1770[4]]

And I kiss Mamma and you. I am utterly confused with all the things I have to do. It is impossible for me to write more.

(82) *Leopold Mozart to his Wife*

[*Extract*] [*Autograph in the Mozarteum, Salzburg*]

MILAN, 3 *March* 1770

Today, March 3rd, is the last day of carnival. Every day during the week whole companies of masqueraders have paraded through the town. Of these the most important were: firstly, the facchinata or facchinmaschera; secondly, the mascherata of the petits-maîtres; and finally, the mascherata of the so-called chicchera, which took place today and which is only another procession of the petits-maîtres, but this time they all ride either in carriages or on horseback. It was not at all a bad show. Further, there were today a number of carriages with cavaliers en masque; and a great many other masked persons were to be seen in the streets. In a word, everyone is either in the street or at a window.

Recently I had to miss a post-day and now the day of our departure is drawing near. But you will certainly receive one more letter from me from Milan, as we shall not get away from here before the 12th, 13th or 14th. You will understand that I have unpacked all our belongings and must now pack everything again. The luggage has, moreover, increased

---

[1] Count von Firmian, brother of Count Carlo di Firmian, Governor of Lombardy.
[2] Probably two of the four arias which Mozart composed for Count Firmian's concert. See p. 118, n. 1.
[3] Basilius Amann (1756–1785), son of Privy Councillor Franz Anton von Amann of Salzburg, was a friend of Mozart. [4] A postscript to his father's letter.

a good deal and I should like to send home a few things. When we left Mantua it was bitterly cold and we bought two fine foot-bags, which cost five ducats. We had to take these, as cheaper ones were not to be had. They are of grey cloth, lined with wolf's fur and trimmed with fine laces and tassels. They have done us excellent service and without them we should have fared badly in the Italian sedia.

Now I must close. Farewell. I kiss you both. My greetings to all Salzburg.

I am your old

MZT

(82a) *Mozart to his Sister*

[Autograph formerly in the possession of the Wittgenstein family, Vienna]

CARA SORELLA MIA,   [MILAN, 3 *March* 1770]

Indeed I rejoice with my whole heart that you have had such a good time. But perhaps you think that I have not been having a good time. Indeed I have, and I cannot remember how often, but I think we have been to the opera six or seven times and then to the festa di ballo which, as in Vienna, begins after the opera, but with this difference that there the dancing is more orderly. We have also seen the facchinata and the chiccherata. The facchinata is a mascherata, a beautiful sight, so called because people dress up as facchini or valets. There was a barca with a number of people in it, and many persons went on foot, and there were four to six bands of trumpeters and drummers and a few companies of fiddlers and of players on other instruments. The chiccherata which we saw today is also a mascherata. *Chiccheri* is the Milanese word for the people we call petits-maîtres or, let us say, coxcombs. They all rode on horseback and it was a charming affair. I am now as heartily glad that Herr von Amann[1] is better as I was grieved when I heard of his accident. What sort of mask did Madame Rosa wear and also Herr von Mölk and the Prince and Herr von Schiedenhofen? If you know, please write and tell me and you will do me a great favour. Today Count Firmian's steward has invited us to celebrate our last day with him, and we shall have much to chatter about. Addio. Farewell. Next post-day I shall write you a Milanese letter.

I am, etc.

WOLFGANG MOZART

3 *March* 1770

PS. Kiss Mamma's hands for me 1000000000000 times. Greetings to all our good friends and a thousand greetings to you from Catch-me-quick-and-then-you-have-me and from Don Cacarella, especially from behind and[2]

---

[1] See p. 116, n. 3.   [2] The autograph breaks off here.

(83) *Leopold Mozart to his Wife*

[*Extract*]   [*Autograph in the Mozarteum, Salzburg*]

MILAN, 13 *March* 1770

It was impossible for me to write last Saturday, because Wolfgang had to compose for the concert held yesterday at Count Firmian's, three arias and a recitative with violins,[1] and I had to copy the violin parts myself and then have them duplicated, so that they should not be stolen. Over one hundred and fifty members of the leading nobility were present, the most important of them being the Duke, the Princess and the Cardinal. We have now decided to leave Milan, God willing, on Thursday, that is, the day after tomorrow. But as we are not leaving until midday and as we are travelling in a vettura, we shall not reach Parma until Saturday morning. You will realize that I have an amazing number of things to do, the more so as on account of our long stay the whole trunk has had to be unpacked. Between this evening and tomorrow another matter has to be decided. For Wolfgang has been asked to write the first opera here for next Christmas.[2] If this is settled, you will be glad, for then, as far as we can judge, we shall certainly reach home sooner than we should otherwise have done. Indeed it will take us all our time to reach Rome for Passion week. You know that Rome is a place where one simply must stay. Then we shall go on to Naples, which is such an important centre that even if a scrittura[3] does not bring us back to Milan to write the opera, some circumstance may easily arise to keep us there during the whole of next winter. For if the scrittura is concluded, the libretto will be sent to us. Wolfgang can then think things out a little and, travelling via Loreto, we can be back in Milan by Advent. Further, as the composer is not obliged to stay on after the opera has been staged, we can then get home via Venice within a year. But I leave it all to Providence and to the ordering of God.

As this is my most strenuous week, I beg you to make excuses for me and to give my congratulations to all who are called Joseph.[4] You know how tedious, sad and trying a departure is. Please give especially my respectful greetings and apologies to our Father Confessor.[5]

Continue to address your letters, as you have done hitherto, to Herr Troger who will forward them to me safely.

As soon as I reach Bologna or Florence I shall write to you, and perhaps also from Parma.

Tomorrow we are having a farewell dinner with His Excellency,[6] who

---

[1] K. 88 [73c], 78 [73b], 79 [73d] (on texts from Metastasio's *Artaserse*) and K. 77 [73e] (on a text from Metastasio's *Demofoonte*), an aria in the grand style with an accompanied recitative.
[2] *Mitridate, Rè di Ponto.*   [3] A written contract.
[4] 19 March being St. Joseph's Day.
[5] Abbé Joseph Bullinger, tutor to the family of Count Arco, and lifelong friend of the Mozarts.   [6] Count Firmian, Governor of Lombardy.

is giving us letters of introduction for Parma, Florence, Rome and Naples. I cannot tell you how gracious he has been to us during the whole period of our stay. I would have written before now to the Chief Steward,[1] if I had not had to wait until tomorrow in order to do so more fully. I kiss you and Nannerl a thousand times and I am your old

MZT

(83a) *Mozart to his Mother and Sister*

[Autograph in the Mozarteum, Salzburg]

[MILAN, 13 *March* 1770[2]]

I send greetings and kiss Mamma and my sister millions of times, and, thank God, I am well. Addio.

(84) *Leopold Mozart to his Wife*

[*Extract*]   *[Autograph in the Mozarteum, Salzburg]*

[BOLOGNA], 24 *March* 1770

We arrived today at Bologna[3] with your last letter, which we found at the post, as Herr Troger forwarded it with some others from Count Firmian. Thank God, we are well and we live in hopes that God will keep us so. We shall not stay here more than four days and we shall only spend about five or six days in Florence. So with God's help we shall reach Rome at the latest on Tuesday or Wednesday in Passion Week; and we shall certainly see the Functiones on Holy Thursday.

I wrote from Parma to the Chief Steward, thanking him for the favours we had enjoyed in the house of Count Firmian and requesting him to tell His Grace that Wolfgang is to write the opera for Milan and asking that he should obtain leave of absence for me. I wrote to His Grace by today's post, sending him my most humble wishes for election day and asking for leave of absence on account of Wolfgang's opera. So find out whether these two letters have arrived safely. The scrittura has already been drawn up and exchanged between both parties; so all that is now required is His Grace's permission. Actually the contract was drawn up in Count Firmian's house. We are to receive 100 cigliati and free lodging. The opera is to begin in the Christmas holidays. The recitatives must be sent to Milan in October and we must be there by November 1st so that

---

[1] Count Firmian of Salzburg. No doubt Leopold Mozart was writing to ask for an extension of leave of absence, as his son had been commissioned to write the next opera for Milan.
[2] A postscript to his father's letter.
[3] The Mozarts left Milan on 15 March and travelled to Bologna by way of Lodi, Piacenza, Parma and Modena. At Lodi Mozart composed his first string quartet, K. 80 [73f].

Wolfgang may write the arias. The prima donna and seconda donna are Signora Gabrielli[1] and her sister.[2] The tenor is Signor Ettore,[3] who is now Cavaliere Ettore, as he wears a certain order. The primo uomo and the others have not yet been chosen. Perhaps Manzuoli will sing. Signora Gabrielli is known throughout Italy to be an extremely conceited fool who besides squandering all her money does the most idiotic things. We shall meet her on our travels in Rome or Naples, as she is coming up from Palermo, and we shall then do homage to her as a queen and praise her to the skies, as that is the way to curry favour. In Parma Signora Guari,[4] who is also called Bastardina or Bastardella, invited us to dinner and sang three arias for us. I could not believe that she was able to reach C sopra acuto, but my ears convinced me. The passages which Wolfgang has written down[5] occurred in her aria and these she sang, it is true, more softly than her deeper notes, but as beautifully as an octave stop in an organ. In short, she sang the trills and the passages exactly as Wolfgang has written them down, note for note. Further, she has a good deep alto down to G. She is not beautiful, and yet not ugly, but occasionally she has a wild look in her eyes, like that of people who are subject to epilepsy, and she limps with one foot. Otherwise she has a good presence, a good character and a good reputation. Count Firmian gave Wolfgang a snuff-box set in gold containing twenty cigliati.

This is the most expensive place which we have so far struck in Italy. We are staying, it is true, at the best inn, the 'Pellegrino', but we have also the honour of paying a ducat a day. The prices here have risen, because there are more people in the town than there were a few years ago. Of expelled Jesuits alone there are more than a thousand. Farewell! I am glad that Nannerl is working hard. But she must not sing more than she thinks is good for her chest. We both kiss you millions of times. Addio. I am your old

MZT

(84a) *Mozart to his Sister*

[*From Nissen, pp.* 184-186]

Oh you busy thing!   [BOLOGNA], 24 *March* 1770

As I have been idle for so long, I have been thinking that it would not be a bad idea if I did some work again for a short while. Every post-day, when letters arrive from Germany, I enjoy eating and drinking far more

---

[1] Catterina Gabrielli (1730–1796) was born in Rome and studied under Garcia and Porpora. She was a famous prima donna of her time, and toured Europe with her sister Francesca as seconda donna.   [2] Francesca Gabrielli (1735–1795).

[3] Guglielmo d'Ettore, a member of the Munich opera, who was appearing in Venice and Padua with great success.

[4] Lucrezia Agujari (1743–1783) was born at Ferrara as the natural child of a nobleman, and was always announced in the playbills as La Bastardina or Bastardella. She was celebrated for the unusual extent of her vocal range.   [5] See pp. 121, 122.

than usual. Please write and tell me who is singing in the oratorios and let me know their titles as well. Tell me also how you like Haydn's[1] minuets and whether they are better than his earlier ones. I rejoice from my heart that Herr von Amann has recovered. Please tell him to take good care of himself and to avoid violent exercise. Please do not forget this. But tell him also that I often think of him and of how in Triebenbach[2] we used to play at workmen and of how he acted the name Schrattenbach[3] by means of a bag of shot and by making the sound *sh*. Tell him also that I often remember his saying to me: 'Shall we split ourselves up?' and how I always replied: 'Good Gracious, no!' I shall soon send you a minuet which Mr. Pick danced in the theatre and which everyone danced to afterwards at the feste di ballo in Milan, solely in order that you may see how slowly people dance here. The minuet itself is very beautiful. It comes, of course, from Vienna and was most certainly composed by Deller or Starzer.[4] It has plenty of notes. Why? Because it is a stage minuet which is danced slowly. The minuets in Milan, in fact the Italian minuets generally, have plenty of notes, are played slowly and have several bars, *e.g.*, the first part has sixteen, the second twenty or twenty-four.

In Parma we got to know a singer and heard her perform very beautifully in her own house—the famous Bastardella[5] who has (1) a beautiful voice, (2) a marvellous throat, (3) an incredible range. While I was present she sang the following notes and passages:

<hr />

[1] Michael Haydn. [2] A suburb of Salzburg.
[3] An allusion to the Counts von Schrattenbach, one of whom, Sigismund, was Archbishop of Salzburg from 1753 to 1772, and another of whom, Franz Anton, the Mozarts had met at Brünn in 1767.
[4] Florian Deller (1729–1773) and Joseph Starzer (1726–1787) were well-known composers of ballet music in Vienna. [5] Lucrezia Agujari. See p. 120, n. 4.

(85) *Leopold Mozart to his Wife*

[Extract]   [Autograph in the Mozarteum, Salzburg]

BOLOGNA, 27 *March* 1770

From Parma I wrote to the Chief Steward and from here on the 24th I wrote to His Grace and to you. I await your reply as to whether all these letters have arrived safely. There was a concert yesterday at the house of Count Pallavicini, to which His Eminence the Cardinal[1] and the leading nobles were invited. I have already introduced to you Count Carl von Firmian; and now I should like you to know Count Pallavicini also. They are two gentlemen who in all respects have the same outlook, friendliness, magnanimity, placidity and a special love for and insight into all branches of knowledge. On Sunday I was privileged to pay my respects to Count Pallavicini and to hand him the letter from Count Firmian. As soon as he heard that I intended to be in Rome in Holy Week he immediately said that he would try to arrange to have the pleasure tomorrow not only of hearing this extraordinary young virtuoso himself but of granting the

[1] Cardinal Legate Antonio Colonna Branciforte.

same privilege to the leading nobles of the town. I shall not describe all the circumstances, nor how, for instance, we were fetched in His Excellency's carriage and waited upon; I shall only say that about one hundred and fifty members of the leading nobility were present. The famous Padre Martini[1] was also invited and, although he never goes to concerts, he came nevertheless to this one, which began at about half past seven and lasted until half past eleven, because the nobles refused to break up the party. Signor Aprile and Signor Cicognani sang. We are leaving the day after tomorrow, Thursday the 29th, and shall arrive in Florence on Friday evening, where we shall stay until the 5th and then continue our journey to Rome, which we hope to reach at midday on the 11th, if God places no obstacle in our way.

What especially pleases me is that we are extraordinarily popular and that Wolfgang is admired here even more than he has been in all the other towns of Italy; the reason is that Bologna is the centre and dwelling-place of many masters, artists and scholars. Here too he has been most thoroughly tested, and the fact that Padre Martini, the idol of the Italians, speaks of him with great admiration and has himself set him all the tests, has increased his reputation all over Italy. We have visited him twice and each time Wolfgang has worked out a fugue, for which the Padre had only written down with a few notes the *ducem* or *la guida*. We have also visited Cavaliere Broschi[2] or the so-called Signor Farinelli, on his estate outside the town. Here we have met Spagnoletta,[3] who is to be the prima donna in the opera, which is being performed in May, that is, instead of Gabrielli, who is still in Palermo and has let down the people of Bologna, just as she probably will let down the people of Milan also.

We have met here Signor Manfredini,[4] the castrato, who, travelling with Herr Panter from Russia by way of Vienna, came to see us in Salzburg.

A certain old Signor Abbate Zanardi sends his greetings to Herr Andrino. A few people have been asking for Kapellmeister Lolli.[5] Herr Brinsecchi and many persons have been asking for our Court Statuarius.[6]

---

[1] Giovanni Battista Martini (1706–1784), a Franciscan Father, was one of the most important scholarly musicians of the eighteenth century. In 1725 he became maestro di cappella of the church of San Francesco at Bologna, where he spent the rest of his life teaching and writing. Scholars from all parts of the world came to Bologna to consult him. In 1774–1775 he published a work on counterpoint, and at the time of his death he was working at the fourth volume of his great *Storia della musica*.

[2] Carlo Broschi, called Farinelli (1705–1782), born in Naples, was the most famous male soprano of his day. He was trained by Porpora and, after a series of triumphs in all the theatres of Italy, in Vienna and in London, and a prolonged stay at the court of Philip V of Spain, he retired in 1762 to his villa near Bologna.　　　[3] Giuseppa Useda, La Spagnoletta.

[4] He was brother to the famous Vincenzo Manfredini (1737–1799), maestro di cappella and author of the *Difesa della musica moderna*.

[5] Giuseppe Francesco Lolli of Bologna was Kapellmeister in Salzburg from 1763 until 1778.

[6] Johann Baptist Hagenauer, a relative of the Hagenauer family, was architect and sculptor to the Salzburg court. He had studied in Florence and Bologna.

All send their greetings along with mine.

We have been to the Instituto and have admired the fine statues of our Court Statuarius. What I have seen in Bologna surpasses the British Museum. For here one can see not only the rarities of nature but *everything that deserves the name of science*, preserved like a dictionary in beautiful rooms and in a clean and orderly fashion. Indeed you would be amazed. I refuse to say anything about the churches, the paintings, the fine architecture and the furnishings of the various palaces, for indeed I can hardly write for drowsiness, as it is past one o'clock. Wolfgang has been snoring for a long time and I fall asleep as I write.

I kiss you and Nannerl a thousand times. My greetings to all Salzburg. I am your faithful and sleepy husband

MZT.

It was not at all a bad idea to send the ball minuet to catch us at Bologna to be arranged for the clavier, as there is no one in Salzburg who could do this. Indeed Wolfgang was exceedingly pleased and thanks Herr von Schiedenhofen and Nannerl. He will write very soon himself. I wrote this letter yesterday after he had gone to bed and I am adding a few lines today while he is still asleep, for the post leaves almost immediately. Herewith he sends the minuet which Mr. Pick danced in the theatre in Milan. Again we send our greetings to all our good friends and I beg Herr von Schiedenhofen, Herr von Mölk and others who have written to me not to take it amiss that I do not reply. I hope they will bear in mind how much a traveller has to do, especially as I am single-handed. *Kommabit aliquando zeitus bequemus schreibendi. Nunc kopfus meus semper vollus est multis gedankibus.*[1] Wolfgang kisses you and Nannerl a thousand times.

(86) *Leopold Mozart to his Wife*

[*Extract*]   [*Autograph in the Mozarteum, Salzburg*]

FLORENCE, 3 *April* 1770

We arrived safely in Florence[2] on the evening of March 30th. On the 31st we spent the whole day indoors and Wolfgang stayed in bed until lunch, as he had caught a slight cold from the rain and the violent wind through which we drove in the mountains. I made him take tea and violet juice and he perspired a little. On the morning of April 1st we drove at ten o'clock to Count von Rosenberg,[3] who received us immediately,

---

[1] Sometime there will come a convenient time for writing. At present my head is always full of many thoughts.   [2] The Mozarts stayed at the 'Aquila'.
[3] Franz Xaver Wolf Orsini-Rosenberg (1723–1796) was Obersthofmeister at the court of Tuscany from 1766 to 1772. In 1776 he was appointed Chief Chamberlain to the Viennese court and Director of the Court Theatres, and subsequently played an important part in Mozart's life.

although more than fifty people were in the antechamber, and this because we brought a letter from Count Firmian and because he had already heard about us from the Count Joseph von Kaunitz,[1] who reached Florence the day before our arrival and is staying with him. He had dined with us in Bologna at the house of Count Pallavicini. Count Rosenberg at once sent us to the Duca de Salviati at the court with a message that he was to present us to the Grand Duke.[2] We heard the sermon and Mass in the chapel and after the service we had an audience. The Grand Duke was uncommonly gracious, asked at once for Nannerl, said that his wife was very anxious to hear Wolfgang play, and spoke to us for a full quarter of an hour. Yesterday evening, April 2nd, we were fetched and driven to the castle outside the town, where we remained until after ten o'clock. Everything went off as usual and the amazement was all the greater as Marchese Ligniville,[3] the Director of Music, who is the finest expert in counterpoint in the whole of Italy, placed the most difficult fugues before Wolfgang and gave him the most difficult themes, which he played off and worked out as easily as one eats a piece of bread. Nardini, that excellent violinist, accompanied him. This afternoon we are going to see Manzuoli, whom we met yesterday in the street and who sends you his greetings. The castrato Nicolini who was with Guadagni[4] in Vienna is here too. I am very sorry that we have to leave on Friday in order to reach Rome in time. I should like you to see Florence itself and the surrounding country and the situation of the town, for you would say that one should live and die here. During these few days I shall see all that there is to be seen. I must close, for the post is leaving. Wolfgang and I send our greetings to all; we kiss you a thousand times and I am your old

MOZART

(87) *Leopold Mozart to his Wife*

[Extract]   [*Autograph in the Nationalbibliothek, Vienna*]

ROME, 14 *April* 1770

We arrived here safely on the 11th at noon.[5] I could have been more easily persuaded to return to Salzburg than to proceed to Rome, for we had to travel for five days from Florence to Rome in the most horrible

---

[1] Imperial Ambassador successively in Stockholm, St. Petersburg and Madrid.
[2] Subsequently Emperor Leopold II, 1790–1792. He had heard the Mozart children perform in Vienna in 1762. See p. 5.
[3] Marchese Eugenio De Ligniville, Duca di Conca, who was Director of Music at the court of Tuscany from 1765 to 1790.
[4] Gaetano Guadagni (c. 1725–c. 1797), one of the most famous male contraltos of the eighteenth century. From 1748 to 1753 he sang in London in Handel's oratorios.
[5] The Mozarts, after spending a few days in an uncomfortable lodging-house, took rooms in the house of the Papal Courier Steffano Uslenghi in the Piazza del Clementino. See p. 129.

rain and cold wind. I am told here that they have had constant rain for
four months and indeed we had a taste of it, for we went on Wednesday
and Thursday in fine weather to St. Peter's and to the Sistine Chapel to
hear the Miserere during the Mass, and on our way home were surprised
by such a frightful downpour that our cloaks have never yet been so
drenched as they then were. But I will not give you a long description of
that dreadful journey. Picture to yourself a more or less uncultivated
country and the most horrible, filthy inns, where we got nothing to eat
save here and there eggs and broccoli; while on fast-days they sometimes
made a fuss about giving us the former. Fortunately we had a good supper
at Viterbo and slept well. There we saw St. Rosa of Viterbo, whose body
like that of St. Catherine at Bologna can be seen in a well-preserved condition.[1] From the former saint we took away as a remembrance a fever
antidote and relics, from the latter a belt. On arriving here on the 11th,
we went to St. Peter's after lunch and then to Mass. On the 12th we were
present at the Functiones, and when the Pope[2] was serving the poor at
table we were quite close to him, as we were standing beside him at the
top of the table. This incident was all the more amazing as we had to pass
through two doors guarded by Swiss guards in armour and make our
way through many hundreds of people. And moreover you must note
that we had as yet no acquaintances. But our fine clothes, the German
tongue, and my usual freedom of manner which led me to make my
servant order the Swiss guards in German to make way for us, soon helped
us through everywhere. They took Wolfgang for some German courtier,
while some even thought that he was a prince, which my servant allowed
them to believe; I myself was taken for his tutor. Thus we made our way
to the Cardinals' table. There Wolfgang happened to be standing between
the chairs of two Cardinals, one of whom was Cardinal Pallavicini, who
made a sign to him and said: '*Will you be so good as to tell me in confidence
who you are?*' And Wolfgang told him. The Cardinal showed the greatest
astonishment and said: '*Ah, you are the famous boy, about whom so many
things have been written to me*'. Whereupon Wolfgang asked him: '*Are you
not Cardinal Pallavicini?*' The Cardinal replied: '*Yes, I am, but why?*' Then
Wolfgang told him *that we had letters to deliver to His Eminence and that we
were going to pay him our respects.* The Cardinal appeared to be delighted,
remarked that Wolfgang spoke Italian very well and among other things
added: '*Ik kann auck ein benig deutsch sprecken*'. When we were leaving,
Wolfgang kissed his hand and the Cardinal took off his berretta and

---

[1] The body of St. Rosa (*d.* 1252), who incited the people to rise against the Emperor
Frederick II, is preserved in a side-chapel of the Church of Santa Rosa at Viterbo. That of
St. Catherine Vigri (*d.* 1463), Abbess of the Poor Clares, is in the chapel which bears her name
in the Church of Corpus Domini at Bologna.

[2] Clement XIV (1705–1774), formerly Cardinal Ganganelli. He became Pope in 1759 and
his reign was rendered famous by the dissolution of the Jesuit order.

bowed very politely. You have often heard of the famous Miserere [1] in Rome, which is so greatly prized that the performers in the chapel are forbidden on pain of excommunication to take away a single part of it, to copy it or to give it to anyone. *But we have it already.* Wolfgang has written it down and we would have sent it to Salzburg in this letter, if it were not necessary for us to be there to perform it. But the manner of performance contributes more to its effect than the composition itself. So we shall bring it home with us. Moreover, as it is one of the secrets of Rome, we do not wish to let it fall into other hands, *ut non incurramus mediate vel immediate in censuram Ecclesiae.* [2] We have already examined St. Peter's church thoroughly and we shall certainly not neglect anything that should be seen in Rome. Tomorrow, God willing, we shall see His Holiness pontificate. You cannot conceive how conceited the clergy are here. Any priest who has the slightest association with a Cardinal, thinks himself as good as he, and as each Cardinal, when on business connected with His Holiness, drives with a cortège of three or four carriages, each of which is filled with his chaplains, secretaries and valets, I am looking forward to tomorrow, when we shall walk past all these proud gentlemen and leave them in ignorance as to our identity. For we have not yet presented ourselves anywhere, because the Functiones are now taking place. On Monday we shall begin to deliver our twenty letters of introduction.

Though I am glad that neither of you undertook this journey with us, yet I am sorry that you are not seeing all these Italian towns, and especially Rome. It is useless and quite impossible to describe it in a few words. Once more I advise you to read Keyssler's *Reisebeschreibung.* Two hours after our arrival we went en passant into the German College and found there Herr von Mölk in excellent health and other acquaintances also. Out of regard for him I am going to let Wolfgang perform before the whole College, since they would like to hear him. With the help of Abbate Marcobruni we immediately took a lodging in a private house. But as there is only one room here and we must have two rooms in order to receive callers, we are going to move this evening into more spacious quarters. Today and yesterday I have been a bit of an invalid, for I have taken three digestive powders; but, thank God, I feel well. Wolfgang is splendid and sends herewith a contredanse. [3] He would like Herr Cirillus Hofmann [4] to make up the steps for it; when the two violins play as leaders, only two persons should lead the dance; but whenever the

---

[1] The Miserere of Gregorio Allegri (1582–1652). Abert, vol. i. p. 189, n. 2, draws attention to a slight exaggeration on the part of Leopold Mozart, inasmuch as according to Burney the Pope had had this beautiful Miserere copied for the Emperor Leopold I, the King of Portugal and Padre Martini, and Burney himself was handed copies in Rome and Florence. See Burney, *Present State of Music in France and Italy,* 2nd edition, 1773, p. 285 ff.

[2] i.e. so that we shall not incur the censure of the Church now or later.

[3] K. 123 [73g].   [4] Dancing master at the Salzburg court.

orchestra comes in with all the instruments, the whole company should dance together. It would be by far the best arrangement if it were danced by five couples. The first couple should begin the first solo, the second dance the second and so on, as there are five solos and five tutti passages.

Pray earnestly to God Almighty for our good health. We shall certainly do our share, for I can assure you that we take all possible care and that Wolfgang pays as much attention to his health as if he were the most grown up person. May God keep you both likewise in good health. I am your old

MZT.

Wolfgang and I kiss you and Nannerl a thousand times.

(87a) *Mozart to his Mother and Sister*

[*Autograph in the Nationalbibliothek, Vienna*]

[ROME, 14 *April* 1770][1]

Praise and thanks be to God, I and my wretched pen are well and I kiss Mamma and Nannerl a thousand or 1000 times. I only wish that my sister were in Rome, for this town would certainly please her, as St. Peter's church and many other things in Rome are *regular*. The most beautiful flowers are now being carried past in the street—so Papa has just told me. I am a fool, as everyone knows. Oh, I am having a hard time, for in our rooms there is only one bed and so Mamma can well imagine that I get no sleep with Papa. I am looking forward to our new quarters. I have just now drawn St. Peter with his keys and with him St. Paul with his sword and St. Luke with my sister and so forth. I have had the honour of kissing St. Peter's foot in St. Peter's church and as I have the misfortune to be so small, I, that same old dunce,

WOLFGANG MOZART
had to be lifted up.

(88) *Leopold Mozart to his Wife*

[*Extract*]   [*Autograph in the Mozarteum, Salzburg*]

ROME, 21 *April* 1770

Your letters of the 2nd and the 6th are, I presume, the replies to my two letters from Bologna. Meanwhile you will have received a letter from Florence and my first one from Rome, in which I gave you a hasty description of the bad weather we had and of our tiresome journey, but

[1] A postscript to his father's letter.

forgot to mention that we arrived at noon amid thunder and lightning and that the weather at a good hour's distance from Rome received us with crackling and flashes and thus accompanied us to our destination in the same way as great men are welcomed by the firing of big guns. So far we have had rain all the time and today is the first on which we have been able to visit one or two places in safety. We have met a great many Englishmen here and amongst others Mr. Beckford,[1] whose acquaintance we made at Lady Effingham's[2] in London, and with whom as well as with some other Englishmen we walked for a couple of hours this morning in the garden of the Villa Medici, which belongs to the Grand Duke of Florence. We have moved out of our first lodging and Herr Marcobruni, *who sends you his greetings*, has brought us to the house of the Papal courier, Signor Uslenghi, in the Piazza del Clementino. Here we are very comfortable and the wife and daughter of the landlord vie with one another in waiting upon us. The husband is in Portugal and so they treat me as if I were the master of the house. We all dine together and we have a large room which, as it gets the morning sun, is very healthy. When friends come to see us, all the other rooms are at our disposal and, as the daughter is beginning to learn the clavier, we have a harpsichord too. I send special greetings to Herr von Schiedenhofen and I am much obliged to him for making Nannerl play often upon the harpsichord. I shall certainly write to him soon myself. I cannot tell you anything about our affairs, for I am tired; the further we have penetrated into Italy, the greater has been the general amazement. Moreover Wolfgang's knowledge does not stand still, but increases from day to day; so that the greatest connoisseurs and masters are at a loss for suitable words to express their admiration. Two days ago we were at the house of a Neapolitan Prince San Angelo. Yesterday we were at the house of Prince Chigi, where amongst others were present the so-called King of England or Pretender,[3] and the Secretary of State Cardinal Pallavicini. Before long we are to be presented to His Holiness. But before I close I must describe a charming incident.

In Florence we came across a young Englishman, who is a pupil of the famous violinist Nardini. This boy,[4] who *plays most beautifully* and who is the same age and the same size as Wolfgang, came to the house of the

---

[1] William Beckford, of Somerley, the historian of Jamaica. This William (not to be confused with either the author of *Vathek* or with the Lord Mayor) was in Rome in the summer of 1770. See Burney, *op. cit.,* p. 268: see also C. B. Oldman, 'Beckford and Mozart,' *Music and Letters*, 1966.

[2] Elizabeth, Countess of Effingham, a sister of William Beckford, the famous Lord Mayor of London and the father of the author of *Vathek*.

[3] Charles Edward, the young Pretender (1720–1788). He was then living in Rome under the name of Count of Albany.

[4] Thomas Linley (1756–1778), eldest son of Thomas Linley, composer and singing master at Bath, at an early age displayed extraordinary skill on the violin. He studied under Nardini in Florence, and on his return to England became leader and solo-player at his father's concerts

learned poetess, Signora Corilla,[1] where we happened to be on the introduction of M. De L'Augier. The two boys performed one after the other throughout the whole evening, constantly embracing each other. On the following day the little Englishman, a most charming boy, had his violin brought to our rooms and played the whole afternoon, Wolfgang accompanying him on his own. On the next day we lunched with M. Gavard, the administrator of the grand ducal finances, and these two boys played in turn the whole afternoon, not like boys, but like men! Little Tommaso accompanied us home and wept bitter tears, because we were leaving on the following day. But when he heard that our departure would not take place until noon, he called on us at nine o'clock in the morning and gave Wolfgang with many embraces the following poem, which Signora Corilla had to compose for him on the previous evening.[2] Then he accompanied our carriage as far as the city gate. I should like you to have witnessed this scene. I now close with devoted greetings to all our friends and I am your old

MZT

We kiss you both a thousand times.

(88a) *Mozart to his Sister*

[*Autograph formerly in the possession of D. Salomon, Berlin*]

CARA SORELLA MIA!   [ROME, 21 *April* 1770]

I am delighted that you liked the minuet I sent you from Bologna,[3] I mean, the one which Signor Pick danced at Milan. I hope that you have received the contredanse which I enclosed in my first letter from Rome.[4] Do tell me quite frankly how you like it.

Please try to find the arithmetical tables. You know that you wrote them down yourself. I have lost my copy and so have quite forgotten them. So I beg you to copy them out for me with some other examples in arithmetic and send them to me here.

Manzuoli is negotiating with the Milanese to sing in my opera. With that in view he sang four or five arias to me in Florence, including some

in Bath and composed sacred and operatic music. He was drowned at the age of twenty-two. Burney, *op. cit.* p. 255, has the following remarks about Linley and Mozart: 'My little countryman, Linley, who had been two years under Signor Nardini, was at Florence when I arrived there and was universally admired. The *Tommasino*, as he is called, and the little Mozart are talked of all over Italy as the most promising geniuses of this age.'

[1] The assumed name of Maddalena Morelli, a famous poetess of her day, who was crowned on the Capitol in 1776. Burney, *op. cit.* p. 259 f., praises also her musical gifts and adds in a footnote, 'She has almost every evening a conversazione or assembly, which is much frequented by the foreigners and men of letters at Florence'.

[2] The poem is to be found in Nissen, p. 195, and Abert, vol. ii. p. 934.

[3] See p. 124.   [4] K. 123 [73g]. Cp. p. 127.

which I had to compose in Milan,[1] in order that the Milanese, who had heard none of my dramatic music, should see that I am capable of writing an opera. Manzuoli is demanding a thousand ducats. It is not known for certain whether Gabrielli will come. Some say that De Amicis will sing. We are to meet her in Naples. I should like her and Manzuoli to take the parts. Then we should have two good acquaintances and friends. The libretto has not yet been chosen. I recommended to Don Ferdinando and Herr von Troger a text by Metastasio.[2]

At the moment I am working at the aria: Se ardire, e speranza.[3]

(89) *Mozart to his Sister*

[Autograph in the Library of the Historical Society of Pennsylvania]

MY DEAR SISTER,   [ROME, 25 *April* 1770[4]]

I assure you that every post-day I look forward with an incredible eagerness to receiving some letters from Salzburg. Yesterday we were at San Lorenzo and heard vespers, and this morning the Mass which was sung, and in the evening the second vespers, because it is the festival of Our Lady of Good Counsel. During the last few days we have been to the Campidoglio and have seen several fine things. If I were to write down all that I have seen, this small sheet would not suffice. I have played at two concerts and tomorrow I am playing at another. This evening we saw a contralto singer, a castrato, who was very like Signor Meisner, whom by the way we shall have the honour of meeting at Naples. Immediately after lunch we play boccia. That is a game which I have learnt in Rome. When I come home, I shall teach it to you. Tell Signor Mölk that I am delighted and rejoice with him that his father is in better health and that I ask him to be so kind as to convey my respects to his father, his mother, his sister, his brother and his cousins and to all his relatives. Please do what I asked you to do the last time I wrote to you and please send me a reply about this. When I have finished this letter I shall finish a symphony which I have begun.[5] The aria is finished.[6] A symphony[7] is being copied (my father is the copyist), for we do not wish to give it out to be copied, as it would be stolen. My greetings to all

---

[1] See p. 118, n. 1.
[2] The text which was ultimately chosen was one by Vittorio Amadeo Cigna-Santi, a poet of Turin. It was a free adaptation of Parini's translation of Racine's *Mithridate* and had already been set to music by Quirino Gasparini and performed at Turin in 1767.
[3] K. 82 [73 o]. The words were taken from Metastasio's *Demofoonte*.
[4] This letter is in Italian.
[5] In the opinion of WSF, vol. i., p. 306 f., this symphony is K. 81 [73l]. But it may be K. 95 [73n] or K. 97 [73m]. See Köchel p. 126.
[6] K. 82 [73 o].   [7] Either K. 95 [73n] or K. 97 [73m].

my friends and please kiss Mamma's hands for me, for I am (Tra la liera)

WOLFGANGO in GERMANIA
and AMADEO MOZART in ITALIA

ROMA caput mundi,
April 25th, 1770,
and next year 1771.
Behind as in front
And double in the middle.   I kiss you both.[1]

(89a) *Mozart to Herr von Schiedenhofen*

[*Autograph in the Library of the Historical Society of Pennsylvania*]

[ROME, 25 *April* 1770[2]]

For Signor von Schiedenhofen

Please forgive me for never writing to you, but as I had no time, I could not do my duty. Here is a minuet which *Signor Pick* danced at Milan.

(90) *Leopold Mozart to his Wife*

[*Extract*]   [*Autograph in the Mozarteum, Salzburg*]

ROME, 28 *April* 1770

It is still cold, not as cold as in Salzburg, but not as warm as it ought to be in Rome, for there are always bitter winds and dull clouds. But as soon as the sun peeps out it is very hot.

We have been at the house of Principessa Barbarini, where we met Prince Xaver of Saxony[3] and, for the second time, the Pretender or so-called King of England, and Cardinal Pallavicini, and amongst others a courtier who knew us in our Paris days. Today at the house of the Ambassadore di Malta[4] we met a courtier who knew us when we were in Vienna, the Swedish envoy who met us in London and Count von Wallerstein. The Duca di Bracciano has sent us an invitation for tomorrow to the concert which is being held by the Duca di Altemps. We are

---

[1] This sentence is in Leopold Mozart's hand.   [2] This letter is in Italian.
[3] Prince Xaver of Saxony (1730–1806), who since 1769 had been living in France and Italy under the name of Comte de la Lusace, was the second son of King August of Saxony and had been Regent of Saxony from 1763 to 1768.
[4] Probably Cavaliere Santarelli, Cappellano di Malta and maestro di cappella to Pope Clement XIV. When Burney visited him in 1770 he was engaged in writing a history of church music, which, however, was never published. See Burney, *op. cit.* p. 277 ff.

lunching on Monday with the Augustinians, the same order which also has a house in Salzburg. The General will be present.[1]

With God's help we shall leave on May 12th by the procaccio[2] for Naples, where we have already ordered a lodging. For the last fortnight the roads thither have been very unsafe and a merchant has been killed. But the sbirri[3] and the bloodthirsty Papal soldiers were immediately sent out from Rome and we hear that a skirmish has already taken place in which five sbirri and three robbers were killed, four robbers taken prisoner and the rest dispersed. But they have now drawn nearer the Neapolitan borders and, if it is true that they have killed a Neapolitan courier on his way to Spain, every effort will be made from Naples to clear up the roads. I shall not leave here until I know that they are safe; and in the procaccio one is in a large company.

Thank God, Wolfgang is in good health except for a slight toothache on one side of his face as usual.

We kiss you and Nannerl a thousand times and I am your old

MZT.

(90a) *Mozart to his Mother and Sister*

[Autograph in the Mozarteum, Salzburg]

[ROME, 28 *April* 1770[4]]

I kiss my sister's face and Mamma's hands. I have not yet seen any scorpions or spiders nor do people talk or hear anything about them. Mamma will surely recognise my handwriting? She ought to let me know this quickly, or I shall sign my name underneath.

(91) *Leopold Mozart to his Wife*

[Extract]   *[Autograph in the Mozarteum, Salzburg]*

ROME, 2 *May* 1770

The latest news is that Herr Meisner arrived from Naples at midday and is off again in two days to Florence and thence straight on to Salzburg; so he will turn up there shortly. He sends his greetings to you all. I have already written to His Grace. You want to know whether Wolfgang still sings and plays the fiddle? He plays the fiddle, but not in public. He sings, but only when some text is put before him. He has grown a little. I am neither fatter nor thinner; and we have got accustomed to Italian food.

[1] His name, Padre Vasquez, appears in the *Reiseaufzeichnungen*, p. 53.
[2] A form of stage-coach.   [3] The police.   [4] A postscript to his father's letter.

We are leaving sooner than I expected, because I have the opportunity of travelling to Naples with four Augustinians. So we shall be off on May 8th. Otherwise I have nothing to write about. I trust that God will keep both you and Nannerl well and allow us not only to reach Naples in good health and return here but also to reach home safely later on. I shall not stay longer than about five weeks in Naples; then I shall travel through Loreto to Bologna and Pisa and those parts; and so spend the hottest season in the coolest and healthiest spot. We kiss you and Nannerl a thousand times and I am your old

MZT

Herr Meisner and Wolfgang performed today in the German College.[1]

(91a) *Mozart to his Mother and Sister*

[Autograph in the Mozarteum, Salzburg]

ROME, [2 May] 1770[2]

Praise and thanks be to God, I am well and kiss Mamma's hand and my sister's face, nose, mouth, neck and my bad pen and arse, if it is clean. WOLFGANGO MOZART. ROME, 1770

(92) *Leopold Mozart to his Wife*

[*Extract*]   [*Autograph in the Mozarteum, Salzburg*]

NAPLES, 19 May 1770

You will have received my last letter from Rome, dated May 2nd. I am sorry that I had to leave you without letters for such a long time, for in the meantime you will both have been very anxious. We left Rome on May 8th at ten o'clock in the morning together with three other sedie or two-seated carriages and we had a light lunch at one o'clock in the Augustinian monastery at Marino. On the evening of the 11th we were again well fed in an Augustinian monastery at Sessa and at noon on the 12th we arrived at the Augustinian monastery at Capua, intending to reach Naples in the evening. It happened, however, that on that Sunday, the 13th, the veiling of a lady was to take place in the convent, where one of my travelling companions, Padre Segarelli, had been confessor some years previously. He was to be present at this veiling and begged us to remain there too. Thus we saw the ceremony, which was very magnificent and for which a Kapellmeister with three or four carriages of virtuosi arrived

---

[1] The autograph of this letter has a short postscript added by Meisner.
[2] A postscript to his father's letter.

on the evening of the 12th and began the proceedings with symphonies and a Salve Regina. They all stayed in the Augustinian monastery, so you can imagine that on that evening we went to bed very late. The veiling, or rather the service, did not take place, however, until noon on Sunday, and the whole affair was over at about three o'clock. Apart from the ladies and gentlemen who were intimate friends no one save us two was invited to table in the convent. It would be impossible to describe everything that took place. We slept until ten o'clock next morning and after lunch we drove to Naples, where we arrived early in the evening and spent two nights in a house belonging to the Augustinian monastery of S. Giovanni a Carbonara. But we are now lodging in a house where we pay ten ducati d'argento or four ducats a month in our money. We drove yesterday to Portici to call on the minister, Marchese Tanucci,[1] and we shall drive out there again tomorrow. We had dreadful roads and a very cool breeze. We have left our fine cloth suits in Rome and have had to put on our two beautifully braided summer costumes. Wolfgang's is of rose-coloured moiré, but the colour is so peculiar that in Italy it is called colore di fuoco or flame-coloured; it is trimmed with silver lace and lined with sky-blue silk. My costume is of the colour of cinnamon and is made of piquéd Florentine cloth with silver lace and is lined with apple green silk. They are two fine costumes, but, before we reach home, they will look like old maids. Yesterday evening we called on the English ambassador, Hamilton,[2] a London acquaintance of ours, whose wife[3] plays the clavier with unusual feeling and is a very pleasant person. She trembled at having to play before Wolfgang. She has a valuable instrument, made in England by Tschudi,[4] which has two manuals and a pedal, so that the two manuals can be disconnected by the action of the foot. We found at Hamilton's house Mr. Beckford and Mr. Weis, also London acquaintances. We lunched on the 16th with Tschudi,[5] who had been in Salzburg and requested me to convey his greetings to Count Spaur and to all his good friends and very many compliments to you especially and to Nannerl. He embraced us constantly, particularly on our arrival and departure, and offered us his services on all occasions. The day before yesterday

---

[1] The Marchese Bernardo Tanucci (1698–1783), Prime Minister of the Kingdom of Naples, was famous for his long struggle against the power of the Vatican and for his active influence in securing the dissolution of the Jesuit Order in 1773. The marriage of Ferdinand IV to Caroline of Austria proved, however, his undoing. He attempted to oppose her influence and was deprived of his office in 1776. He was a man of wide interests and was responsible for the first excavations of Pompeii and Herculaneum.

[2] Sir William Hamilton (1730–1803), diplomatist and antiquarian, had been Ambassador to the Court of Naples since 1764.

[3] Sir William Hamilton's first wife, Miss Barlow, whom he married in 1758, was a gifted musician. She died in 1782. Burney, *op. cit.* p. 333, praises her performance.

[4] Burkhardt Tschudi (1702–1773), famous harpsichord-maker and founder of the house of Broadwood. The Mozarts had known him in London. See *Reiseaufzeichnungen*, p. 38.

[5] Baron Fridolin Tschudi. He is mentioned in the *Reiseaufzeichnungen*, p. 54.

we met in the street M. Meurikofer[1] from Lyons, who was looking every-where for us; he had left a card for us with his address at the Augustinian monastery and at last had run into us by chance. He came back with us to our lodging and then took us to his house. We were to have lunched with him tomorrow, but as we have to drive to Portici, we have had to cancel this arrangement. He sends cordial greetings to you all. He is in partnership here with a friend and both have offered their services to me in all eventualities. You will surely remember him, a dark young man, who often had to sing that Italian song for Wolfgang with his spectacles on his nose. I cannot yet say how long we shall stay here. The matter is entirely out of my hands. It may be five weeks or five months, but I think that it will be five weeks. It all depends on circumstances.

On the Feast of St. Philip and St. James[2] while I was hearing High Mass in the Church of the Holy Apostles in Rome, I saw before me a well-known face. Its owner came up; and who do you think he was? Why, our former servant Porta. He was neatly dressed, with lace cuffs, a gold watch and so forth. He had been with the French troops in Corsica. On the following day, just as Herr Meisner was coming in, he came to offer me his services. I refused to have anything to do with him and turned a deaf ear. Ask Herr Meisner, for he saw him. The fellow is an adventurer.

On reading the article about the Miserere, we simply burst out laugh-ing. There is not the slightest cause for anxiety. Everywhere else far more fuss is being made about Wolfgang's feat. All Rome knows and even the Pope himself that he wrote it down. There is nothing whatever to fear; on the contrary, the achievement has done him great credit, as you will shortly hear. You will see to it that the letter is read out everywhere, so that we may be sure that His Grace hears what Wolfgang has done. If the portraits are good likenesses, you may pay the painter whatever you like.

Now I must close, for we are off to the Imperial Ambassador the Count von Kaunitz. Farewell, we kiss you and Nannerl 1000 times and

I am your old

MZT

I trust that your cold left you long ago.

(92a) *Mozart to his Sister*

[Autograph in the Mozarteum, Salzburg]

CARA SORELLA MIA,   NAPLES, 19 *May* 1770

Alla vostra lettera non saprei veramente rispondere, perchè non avete scritto niente quasi. I menuetti del Signor Haydn[3] vi manderò

---

[1] A Swiss merchant in Lyons.   [2] May 1st.   [3] See p. 78, n. 1.

quando avrò più tempo, il primo già vi mandai. Ma ⟨I don't understand. You say that they have been stolen. Did you steal them? Or what do you mean?⟩

Vi prego di scrivermi presto e tutti i giorni della posta. Io vi ringrazio di avermi mandato questi arithmetical business, e vi prego, se mai volete avere mal di testa, di mandarmi ancora un poco di questi feats. Perdonatemi che scrivo si malamente, ma la ragione è perchè anche io ebbi un poco mal di testa.[1] I very much like the twelfth minuet of Haydn, which you have sent me; and you have set the bass to it exceedingly well and without the slightest mistake. You must try your hand at such things more often.

Mamma must not forget to see that both our guns are cleaned. Tell me, how is Mr. Canary? Does he still sing? And still whistle? Do you know what makes me think of him? Because there is a canary in our front room which makes a noise just like ours. A propos, I suppose Herr Johannes[2] has received the letter of congratulation which we intended to write to him? But if by any chance he has not received it, I shall tell him myself when I get back to Salzburg what would have been in it. Yesterday we put on our new clothes and we were as beautiful as angels. But I fear that they are the only beautiful things we shall bring home. Addio. Farewell. Remember me to our Nannie and tell her to pray for me earnestly.

I am

WOLFGANG MOZART

The opera, which Jommelli is composing, will begin on the 30th.[3] We saw the King and Queen at Mass in the court chapel at Portici and we have seen Vesuvius too. Naples is beautiful, but it is as crowded as Vienna and Paris. And of the two, London and Naples, I do not know whether Naples does not surpass London for the insolence of the people; for here the lazzaroni have their own general or chief, who receives twenty-five ducati d'argento from the King every month, solely for the purpose of keeping them in order.

De Amicis is singing in the opera. We have been to see her.[4] Cafaro[5]

---

[1] I really don't know how to reply to your letter, because you wrote almost nothing. When I have more time, I shall send you Herr Haydn's minuets. I have already sent you the first one. But, . . . Please write to me soon and write every post-day. Thanks for sending me that arithmetical business and, if you ever want to have a headache, please send me a few more of these feats. Forgive me for writing so badly, but the reason is that I too have had a slight headache.

[2] Johannes Hagenauer, a son of Lorenz Hagenauer.

[3] Niccolò Jommelli (1714–1774), who had been Court Kapellmeister in Stuttgart from 1753 to 1768, had returned to Italy and settled in his native village, Aversa, near Naples. The opera to which Mozart refers was *Armida abbandonata*, the first one which Jommelli composed on his return to Naples and which was performed on 30 May 1770, at the Teatro San Carlo.

[4] The autograph has 'and she recognised us at once', which Mozart struck out.

[5] Pasquale Cafaro (1706–1787), a well-known Neapolitan composer of operas and oratorios. His *Antigono* was performed in Naples on 13 August 1770.

is composing the second opera and Ciccio di Majo the third.[1] It is not yet known who is composing the fourth. Go regularly to Mirabell[2] to hear the Litanies and to listen to the Regina Coeli or the Salve Regina and sleep soundly and do not have any bad dreams. Give Herr von Schieden-hofen my fiercest greetings, 'Tralaliera, Tralaliera', and tell him to learn to play on the clavier the repeating minuet, so that he *does* not forget it. He must *do* so soon, so that he may *do* me the pleasure of accompanying him one day. *Do* remember me to all my good friends, and *do* keep well and *do* not die, so that you may *do* another letter for me and that I may *do* another for you and that we may keep on *doing* until we are *done*. For I am the man to go on *doing* until there is nothing more to *do*.

Meanwhile I *do* remain

WOLFGANG MOZART

(93) *Leopold Mozart to his Wife*

[*Extract*]   [*Autograph in the Mozarteum, Salzburg*]

NAPLES, 22 *May* 1770

In the meantime you will have received my letter of the 19th. Two days ago we went for a walk on the Molo and whom do you think we met? Why, our good friend, Mr. Donker,[3] tall, handsome Donker of Amster-dam, who for the last three years has been living here with the French consul. This consul was present on the evening when we dined with Donker in Amsterdam. We lunched with him yesterday and in the after-noon we called on the wife of the Imperial Ambassador, Countess von Kaunitz, née Princess von Öttingen. We shall soon have finished paying visits. Marchesa Tanucci, the Prime Minister's wife, sent her steward to me yesterday with a message that the latter was to be at my disposal to take us round everywhere and show us all the rare sights of Naples. This distinction amazes everyone, as this Prime Minister is really a king and has enormous influence. Yesterday Herr Meurikofer took us to the opera buffa, which is excellent. Old Principessa di Belmonte[4] saw us at once and greeted us most cordially, although our box was a good distance from hers.

I write in haste. I kiss you and Nannerl 1000 times. Herr Donker sends cordial greetings to you and to Nannerl and I am your old

MZT

[1] Francesco (Ciccio) di Majo (1740–1771), son of Giuseppe di Majo (1698–1772), had been a pupil of Padre Martini and from 1759 onwards had been composing operas regularly. *Eumene*, the last one on which he was working, was completed by Insanguine and was per-formed at Naples on 20 January 1771.

[2] Schloss Mirabell, built in 1606 by Archbishop Wolf Dietrich, was remodelled in a baroque style during the years 1721–1727. It is now divided up into private dwellings. The gardens are still kept in the style of the eighteenth century.

[3] Donker appears in Leopold Mozart's *Reiseaufzeichnungen*, p. 45.

[4] Principessa di Belmonte-Pignatelli, famous for her friendship with Metastasio.

(93a) *Mozart to his Mother and Sister*

[Autograph in the Mozarteum, Salzburg]

[NAPLES, 22 *May* 1770[1]]

Praise and thanks be to God, I am well and kiss Mamma's hands and kiss you both a thousand times.

(94) *Leopold Mozart to his Wife*

[Extract]   *[Autograph in the Mozarteum, Salzburg]*

NAPLES, 26 *May* 1770

This is the third letter which I am writing to you from Naples. The situation of this town pleases me more and more every day and Naples itself is on the whole not ugly. But I only wish that the natives were not so godless and that certain people, who do not for a moment imagine that they are fools, were not so stupid as they are.[2] And the superstition! Here it is so deeply rooted that I can say with certainty that heresy now rules supreme and that everyone treats this state of affairs with indifference. I shall explain this to you later on. I hope to bring back copper engravings of the views and rare sights of Naples, such as I already possess of Rome. God be praised, we are both well. The tailor has in hand two costumes, which I chose with the assistance of M. Meurikofer. Mine is of Pompadour, or rather, dark red shot moiré, lined with sky-blue taffeta and trimmed with silver buttons. Wolfgang's is of apple-green shot moiré, with silver buttons and lined with rose-coloured taffeta.

On Monday we are giving a concert, which the Countess von Kaunitz, the Imperial Ambassador's wife, Lady Hamilton, Principessa Belmonte, Principessa Francavilla, Duchessa Calabritta are organising and which, I think, will bring us in at least one hundred and fifty zecchini. Indeed we need money, for, if we leave, we shall have a long journey during which we shall not be able to earn anything and, if we remain, we shall have to hold out for five months. It is true that here we should always be able to earn enough for our needs, but I am still determined to leave in three weeks. We hope to be presented to the King and Queen next week.

Farewell to you and Nannerl. We kiss you both and I am your old

MZT

My greetings to the whole of Salzburg.

---

[1] A postscript to his father's letter.
[2] Abert, vol. i. p. 191, n. 1, suggests that 'certain people' is an allusion to the King and Queen of Naples.

(95) *Leopold Mozart to his Wife*

[*Extract*]   [*Autograph in the Mozarteum, Salzburg*]

NAPLES, 29 *May* 1770

I am probably writing far too often and you will be surprised to see a letter from me every post-day! But this is a precaution on my part, lest perhaps some letter should go astray. We are rather far from one another and a letter from Salzburg to Naples takes fourteen days. This is my fourth letter from here. I still intend to leave Naples on June 16th, if nothing prevents us. Yesterday we gave our concert, which was a great success and brought us in a considerable sum. The court returns to town tomorrow, May 30th, to celebrate the King's name-day with an opera and other festivities. If we leave here on the 16th we shall go to Marino and stay at the Augustinian monastery, as the Prior has begged us to do. For he wants to accompany us to Genazzano and show us the miraculous image of Our Lady of Good Counsel.[1] As it is not a long journey, I have accepted his offer in order to see this sacred image. Thus we can spend six or seven days with our friends in Rome and then start on our journey to Loreto. By leaving here at the time I have stated we shall see, so to speak, the whole of Italy. For, if we feel inclined, we shall travel on through the country beyond Loreto to Bologna or even to Florence and thence to Pisa, Lucca and Leghorn and spend the two hot months in the most suitable spot, probably going on to Milan via Genoa. If Wolfgang had not already the scrittura for the opera in Milan, he would have obtained one for Bologna, Rome or Naples, for he has received offers from all these places. So far we have not had to endure great heat, as it has been raining the whole time. Yesterday we had violent wind and heavy rain; and it is quite unusual for Naples not to have greater heat. All the same we shall return home fairly well tanned, for the air has that effect, and, as soon as the sun appears, you notice at once that you are in Naples. You yourself know that Wolfgang is always longing to be brown.

I must close, for this very moment a footman has come from the Principessa di Francavilla with an invitation to drive to her house, as she wants to see us. My greetings to all Salzburg. We kiss you and Nannerl 1000 times and I am your old

MZT

Wolfgang can hardly wait for the post-days and he begs you to write sometimes twice a week, especially if there is anything new to tell. But in Salzburg it does not take long to jot down news.

Vesuvius has not yet given me the pleasure of appearing to burn or

---

[1] Genazzano, 30 m. S.E. of Rome, is noted for its pilgrimage chapel of Our Lady of Good Counsel.

rather, to spit fire. Very occasionally you see a little smoke. But one of these days we shall inspect it at close quarters.

(95a) *Mozart to his Sister*

[*Autograph in the Library of the Historical Society of Pennsylvania*]

MY DEAREST SISTER,   [NAPLES, 29 *May* 1770[1]]
The day before yesterday we were at the rehearsal of Signor Jommelli's opera, which is well composed and which I really like. He himself spoke to us and was very polite. We have also been to a church to hear some music composed by Signor Ciccio di Majo, which was most beautiful. He too spoke to us and was most gracious. Signora De Amicis sang marvellously well. Thank God, we are in very good health, and I am especially so when a letter comes from Salzburg. I beg you to send me a letter every post-day, even if you have nothing to write about. I should like to have one merely in order to receive some letter every time the post comes in. I hope that you received my letter which contained passages in another language, which you will surely have understood or made out.[2] It would not be a bad plan if sometimes you were to send me a little note in Italian. I have nothing more to write to you about, except to ask you to give my greetings to all my friends, male and female, and especially to Herr von Schiedenhofen, who no doubt has already received the letter which my father wrote to him. Please give my greetings to Herr von Amann and ask him how he is and then let me know. Addio.
29 May 1770.

                                    WOLFGANGO AMADEO MOZART
Kiss my mother's hand for me.

(96) *Leopold Mozart to his Wife*

[*Extract*]   [*Autograph in the Mozarteum, Salzburg*]

                                    NAPLES, 5 *June* 1770
I only received today—June 5th—your letter of May 18th. You will have received by now my first four letters from here.[3] Our concert went off very well, but I cannot write anything yet about the court. The Principessa di Francavilla has given us a handsome present and we are hoping for a few more trifles. You will be very much disappointed that I do not send you more details about our takings, but I refrain from doing

---

[1] This letter is in Italian.
[2] No doubt Mozart is referring to his letter of 19 May, which has passages in Italian. See pp. 136, 137.   [3] Letters 92-95.

so on purpose, because in Salzburg only the earnings are considered and the expenses ignored and because there are very, very few people who realize what travelling costs. Let it suffice if I tell you that, thank God, we lack nothing that is necessary to enable us to continue our travels in an honourable fashion. One of the finest sights is the daily passeggio, when in a few hundred carriages the nobles go out driving in the afternoon until Ave Maria to the Strada Nuova and the Molo. The Queen too goes out driving very often, always on Sundays and on holidays. As she drives along the sea coast, guns are fired off on the ships, and on the right and on the left the carriages stop and their occupants salute her as she passes them. As soon as it is twilight, the flambeaux are lighted on all the carriages and produce a sort of illumination. Since we drive there daily and always in a carriage belonging to some lord, I have two flambeaux, that is, the servant of the lord who has sent his carriage has one and our servant has the other. However, that is no great expense, as flambeaux are very cheap here. One sees several carriages with four flambeaux carried by four footmen. Her Majesty the Queen always greets us with quite exceptional friendliness. On Whit Sunday we were at the great ball given by the French Ambassador on the occasion of the betrothal of the Dauphin.[1] Two invitation cards had been sent to us. I am still determined to leave Rome on the 16th with the procaccio, or possibly on the 20th, if I secure a private sedia in which I shall travel with the Imperial Ambassador Count Kaunitz.

I kiss you and Nannerl 1000 times and I am your old

MZT

(96a) *Mozart to his Sister*

[*Autograph formerly in possession of M. Clemendot, Dijon*]

CARA SORELLA MIA,   NAPLES, 5 *June* 1770

Vesuvius is smoking furiously today. Thunder and lightning and all the rest. We gorged ourselves today with Herr Doll.[2] He is a German composer and a fine fellow.[3] Now I shall begin to describe my way of life. Alle nove ore, qualche volta anche alle dieci mi sveglio, e poi andiamo fuor di casa, e poi pranziamo da un trattore, e dopo pranzo scriviamo, e poi sortiamo, e indi ceniamo, ma che cosa? Al giorno di grasso, un mezzo pollo, ovvero un piccolo boccone d'arrosto; al giorno di magro, un piccolo pesce; e di poi andiamo a dormire.[4] Est-ce que vous avez compris? Let us

---

[1] Louis (later Louis XVI) to Marie Antoinette of Austria.

[2] Joseph Doll was 'secondo maestro' at the Conservatorio di Sant' Onofrio in Naples, where he died in August 1774. See S. di Giacomo, *Il Conservatorio di Sant' Onofrio*, 1924, p. 159 f.

[3] These first sentences and others in this letter are in Salzburg dialect.

[4] I wake up at nine, sometimes even at ten, and then we go out, and then we lunch at an eating-house, and after lunch we write, and then we go out, and then we have supper, and what do we eat? On ordinary days half a chicken or a small slice of roast meat; on fast days a little fish; and then we go to bed.

talk Salzburgish for a change, for it is more sensible. Thank God, we are well, my father and I.

I hope that you too are well and Mamma also. If Fräulein Aloysia von Schiedenhofen comes to see you again, give her my compliments. Naples and Rome are two sleepy towns. What a beautiful handwriting mine is, is it not?

Write to me and do not be so lazy. Altrimenti avrete qualche bastonata da me.[1] Quel plaisir! Je te casserai la tête. I am already looking forward to the portraits, and I am anxious to see what they are like. If I like them I shall have similar ones done of my father and myself. Tell me, little girl, where have you been, eh? Yesterday we were in the company of Herr Meurikofer who sends his regards to you and Mamma. The opera here is one of Jommelli's; it is beautiful, but too serious and old-fashioned for the theatre. De Amicis sings amazingly well and so does Aprile, who sang in Milan. The dances are wretchedly pompous. The theatre is beautiful. The King has had a rough Neapolitan upbringing and in the opera he always stands on a stool so as to look a little taller than the Queen. She is beautiful and gracious, and on the Molo (that is a drive) she bowed to me in a most friendly manner at least six times. Every evening the nobles send us their carriages to drive out with them to the Molo. We were invited on Sunday to the ball given by the French Ambassador. I can't write anything more. My compliments to all our kind friends. Farewell.

WOLFGANG MOZART

I kiss Mamma's hand.

(97) *Leopold Mozart to his Wife*

[Extract]   [*Autograph in the Mozarteum, Salzburg*]

NAPLES, 9 *June* 1770

We shall hardly receive a letter from you here in reply to my first letter from Naples, for it is still definitely fixed that we leave either on the 16th with the procaccio or on the 22nd with the mail coach. So I shall get your letters in Rome. If you write as soon as you receive this one, I can still pick up your reply in Rome or Herr Marcobruni can forward it. Before I leave here I shall write once or twice and tell you where to send your letters. In some respects it is a pity that we cannot stay longer in Naples, for during the summer there are many pleasant things to be seen and there is a perpetual variety of fruits, vegetables and flowers from week to week. The situation of the town, the fruitfulness of the country, the liveliness of the people, the rare sights and a hundred beautiful things make me sorry

---

[1] Otherwise I shall give you a whipping.

to leave. But the filth, the crowds of beggars, the hateful and godless populace, the disgraceful way in which children are brought up, the incredible frivolity even in the churches, make it possible quite calmly to leave behind what is good. Not only shall I bring back all the rare sights in several beautiful copper engravings, but Herr Meurikofer has given me a fine collection of Vesuvius lava, not of the lava which everyone can obtain easily, but choice pieces with a description of the minerals which they contain, rare and not easy to procure. If God permits us to return home in good health, you will see many beautiful things. Keep well, both of you. We kiss you both 1000 times and I am your old

MOZART

Our servant has brought news this very moment that the sedia which we hoped to get is at my service. So I shall leave with the mail coach on the 20th and reach Rome in twenty-six hours; whereas with the procaccio I should have to spend four and a half days on the road, which, although it is very beautiful, has the most abominable inns. Our remembrances to Herr Meisner, who can describe these inns to you. The sedia belongs to the General of the Augustinian Fathers. We are lunching tomorrow at the Augustinian monastery of S. Giovanni a Carbonara, where a great feast is being held.

During the coming week we shall visit Vesuvius, the two buried cities, where ancient rooms are being excavated, then Caserta and so forth, in short, all the rare sights, of which I already possess engravings.

(98) *Leopold Mozart to his Wife*

[Extract]   [From Nissen, pp. 211-212]

NAPLES, 16 *June* 1770

We cannot leave after all on the 20th, as Count Kaunitz will not be ready by that date. On the 13th we drove in a carriage to Pozzuoli, and then took ship to Baia, where we saw the baths of Nero, the subterranean grotto of Sibylla Cumana, Lago d'Averno, Tempio di Venere, Tempio di Diana, Sepolcro d'Agrippina, the Elysian fields, the Dead Sea, where Charon was ferryman, la Piscina Mirabile, the Cento Camerelle, and so forth. On the return journey we visited many old baths, temples, underground rooms, Monte Nuovo, Monte Gauro, Molo di Pozzuoli, Colosseo, Solfatara, Astroni, Grotta del Cane, Lago d'Agnano, but especially the Grotto di Pozzuoli and Virgil's grave. We lunched today with the Carthusians on the hill of San Martino and visited all the sights and rarities of the place and admired the view. On Monday and Tuesday we are going to Vesuvius, Pompeii, Herculaneum and its excavations, Caserta and Capo di Monte. All this is going to cost money.

(98a) *Mozart to his Mother and Sister*

[From Nissen, p. 212]

[NAPLES, 16 June 1770 [1]]

I too am still alive and always merry as usual and I simply love travelling. I have now been on the Mediterranean [2] too. I kiss Mamma's hand and Nannerl 1000 times and am your Simple Simon of a son and Jack Pudding of a brother.

1770

(99) *Leopold Mozart to his Wife*

[*Extract*]   [*Autograph in the Mozarteum, Salzburg*]

ROME, 27 June 1770

We reached Rome yesterday evening at eight o'clock, having done in twenty-seven hours with the mail coach the same journey which previously took us four and a half days with the vettura. But indeed we flew. Count Kaunitz only arrived today. I thought it wise to travel by ourselves, as one often does not find enough horses at the post-stages, and thus one is given the pleasure of sitting and waiting half a day for their return. So we left Naples by ourselves and I announced everywhere that I was the steward of the Imperial Ambassador, because in these parts the stewards of such personages are very highly respected. Thus not only did I ensure a safe journey, but I was given good horses and quick service; and at Rome it was not necessary for me to go to the Customs Office for the usual examination, for at the gate I was received with a deep bow, and was simply told to drive on to my destination, at which I was so pleased that I threw a few paoli in their faces. As we had only slept for two out of the twenty-seven hours of our journey and had only eaten four cold roast chickens and a piece of bread in the carriage, you can well imagine how hungry, thirsty and sleepy we were. Our good hostess—Signora Uslenghi—gave us some nice well-cooked rice and we just ate two lightly boiled eggs each. As soon as we got to our bedroom, Wolfgang sat down on a chair and at once began to snore and to sleep so soundly that I completely undressed him and put him to bed without his showing the least sign of waking up. Indeed he went on snoring, although now and then I had to raise him and

---

[1] A postscript to his father's letter.
[2] The original text has 'Merditeranischen' in allusion to a characteristic joke in the Mozart family.

put him down again and finally drag him to bed sound asleep. When he awoke after nine o'clock in the morning, he did not know where he was nor how he had got to bed. Almost the whole night through he had lain in the same place. God be praised, we are well.

While we were in Naples the impresario Signor Amadori, who met and heard Wolfgang at Jommelli's house, made him an offer to write an opera for the Teatro Reale San Carlo, which, on account of our Milan engagement, we could not accept. Whereupon the impresario said that he quite understood that it would not be worth our while to travel as far as Naples for one single opera, but that he hoped that Wolfgang would soon write an opera in Bologna or Rome. He begged us to inform him if this should be possible, so that he might immediately send us the scrittura for the Teatro Reale. Hornung has asked us for arias. You can give him whatever he wants. You can also give Spitzeder anything he may desire. They can choose and take what they like, provided they return them eventually. You and Nannerl are well, we hope. We kiss you both 1000 times. I am

your old

MOZART

(100) *Leopold Mozart to his Wife*

[*Extract*]   [*Autograph in the Mozarteum, Salzburg*]

ROME, [30 *July or rather June*] 1770

You ask whether Wolfgang has begun his opera? Why, he is not even thinking of it. You should ask us again when we have reached Milan on November 1st. So far we know nothing either about the cast or about the libretto. But now we do know who will be the primo uomo and the tenor. Santorini, who sang during the last carnival in Turin, will be the primo uomo and Ettore will be the tenor. We found Santorini here; he called on us yesterday and said that he believed that the first opera would be 'Nitteti'.[1] Basta! We still have plenty of time.

You ask whether we played before the King of Naples? No, indeed! We did not get beyond the stock compliments which the Queen paid us wherever she met us. She has no influence and what sort of a fellow the King is it is perhaps wiser to speak of than to write about. You can easily imagine what kind of place the court is. The young violinist, Lamotte,[2] who is in the service of the Empress and has come to Italy at her command and at her expense, spent a long time in Naples and stayed on for an extra

---

[1] Composed by Johann Adolf Hasse. See Letter 106.
[2] Franz Lamotte (*c.* 1751–1781), born in Vienna, at the age of twelve played a violin concerto before the Empress, who sent him to Italy to study, and on his return in 1772 took him into the court service.

three weeks, because he was given to understand that the King and Queen would hear him. But they never did. Later on I shall tell you several amusing things about that court and you shall see the King's portrait.

I hope to be able to let you know soon what we are going to do here. I have been obliged either to stay indoors or to limp about very slowly. So I have not yet been able to pay my respects to princes and cardinals. In my first letter I did not mention this, but as the limb is now improving I shall describe my unfortunate accident. You know that two horses and a postillion are equal to three beasts. During the last stage to Rome the postillion kept on lashing the horse which was between the shafts and therefore supporting the sedia. Finally the horse reared, stuck fast in the sand and dirt which was more than half a foot deep, and fell heavily on one side, pulling down with him the front of the two-wheeled sedia. I held back Wolfgang with one hand, so that he should not be hurled out; but the plunge forward pulled my right foot so violently to the centre bar of the falling dashboard that half the shin-bone of my right leg was gashed to the width of a finger. I should mention that the dashboard could not be attached and had thus fallen back. On the following day my injury seemed rather serious, as my foot was very much swollen; and I have spent the greater part of yesterday and today in bed. But now, as I write, my leg is much better and the wound, though it is very long, looks healthy; it has almost ceased to suppurate and, what is more, I have no pain. I have only used the white ointment and shall apply nothing else. Perhaps this accident had to happen, for otherwise you would have packed the ointment and lint to no purpose. I am only sorry that there is so little plaster. By the next post please tell me how it is made. You must not worry, for with God's help the leg will heal. I am only annoyed at having to stay longer in Rome than I intended; not on account of Rome itself, which I like very much, but on account of the journey which is still before us. But God will protect us, and the great heat has not yet come.

Farewell to you and Nannerl. I kiss you both 1000 times and I am your old

MZT

(101) *Leopold Mozart to his Wife*

[Extract]   [*Autograph in the Mozarteum, Salzburg*]

ROME, 4 *July* 1770

I have nothing to write to you about except that, thank God, my foot is well. On the other hand I have slight rheumatism in my left shoulder. In eight or ten days at the latest we shall travel to Bologna by way of Loreto. This very moment a servant of Cardinal Pallavicini has invited us to lunch with His Eminence tomorrow. We are dining on Friday with

His Excellency the Tuscan Ambassador, Baron Sant' Odile. Tomorrow we are to hear a piece of news which, if it is true, will fill you both with amazement. For Cardinal Pallavicini is said to have been commanded by the Pope to hand Wolfgang the cross and diploma of an order.[1] Do not say much about this yet. If it is true, I shall write to you next Saturday. When we were at the Cardinal's house a few days ago he once or twice called Wolfgang 'Signor Cavaliere'. We thought that he was joking, but now I hear that it is true and that this is behind tomorrow's invitation. Addio! Farewell! I must hurry, for the post is going. Wolfgang cannot send you a letter, as he is writing to the son of Field-marshal Pallavicini in Bologna. We kiss you 1000 times.

MZT

Wolfgang grew noticeably in Naples.

(102) *Leopold Mozart to his Wife*

[*Extract*] [*From Nissen, p. 215*]

ROME, 7 *July* 1770

What I wrote the other day about the cross of an order is quite correct. It is the same order as Gluck's and is worded as follows: *te creamus auratae militiae equitem*.[2] Wolfgang has to wear a beautiful gold cross, which he has received. You can imagine how I laugh when I hear people calling him 'Signor Cavaliere' all the time. Tomorrow we are to have an audience with the Pope.

(102a) *Mozart to his Sister*

[*Autograph*]

CARA SORELLA MIA! [ROME, 7 *July* 1770[3]]

I am amazed to find how well you can compose. In a word, the song is beautiful. Try this more often. Send me soon the other six minuets by Haydn,[4] I beg you, Farewell.

WOLFGANG MOZART

PS.—My compliments to all my good friends. I kiss Mamma's hand: Mademoiselle, j'ai l'honneur d'être votre très humble serviteur e frere.

CHEVALIER DE MOZART

Rome 7 July 1770 Addio. Keep well, and shit in your bed make a mess of it.[5]

---

[1] The Order of the Golden Spur, which Pope Clement XIV conferred on Mozart on 8 July 1770.
[2] 'We create you a Knight of the Golden Spur'. [3] A postscript to his father's letter.
[4] Michael Haydn. See p. 78. [5] This sentence is in Italian.

(103) *Leopold Mozart to his Wife*

[*Extract*]   [*Autograph in Alfred Cortot Collection*]

BOLOGNA, 21 *July* 1770

We congratulate you on your common name-day[1] which is just past, and we wish you both good health and more especially the grace of God. For that is all we need. Everything else comes of its own accord.

We heard Mass in Città Castellana, and afterwards Wolfgang played on the organ. The day on which we performed our devotions in Loreto happened to be the 16th. I bought six little bells and various other trifles. In addition to other relics I am bringing back from Rome a piece of the Holy Cross. We visited the fair in Sinigaglia. We arrived here yesterday, having left Rome on the 10th. Count Pallavicini has offered us everything we require, and I have accepted his carriage.

If Wolfgang continues to grow as he is doing, he will be quite tall by the time we get home.

(103a) *Mozart to his Mother*

[*Autograph in Alfred Cortot Collection*]

[BOLOGNA, 21 *July* 1770[2]]

I congratulate Mamma on her name-day and I hope that she may live many hundreds of years and enjoy good health. I always ask this of God and pray for this every day and I shall always pray every day for both of you. It is impossible for me to send presents, but I shall bring home a few little bells from Loreto and candles and bonnets and fleas. Meanwhile, farewell, dear Mamma. I kiss Mamma's hands a thousand times and remain till death

her faithful son
WOLFGANG MOZART

(103b) *Mozart to his Sister*

[*Autograph in Alfred Cortot Collection*]

CARA SORELLA MIA   [BOLOGNA, 21 *July* 1770]

I hope that God will always grant you good health and will let you live another hundred years and will let you die when you have reached a

---

[1] July 16th.
[2] This note and the following one are postscripts to his father's letter. The one to his sister is in Italian.

thousand. I hope that you will get to know me better in the future and that then you will decide how much you like me. I have no time to write much. My pen is not worth a fig nor is he who is holding it. We do not yet know the title of the opera which I have to compose in Milan. Addio. Our hostess in Rome gave me as a present the 'Arabian Nights' in Italian. It is very amusing to read.

(104) *Leopold Mozart to Lorenz Hagenauer, Salzburg*

[*From Nohl, 'Mozart nach den Schilderungen seiner Zeitgenossen', pp. 112-113*]

BOLOGNA, 28 *July* 1770

If I were to observe punctiliously the rules of good behaviour, I should indeed be ashamed to appear before you with such a wretched scrap of paper. But as I am certain that you are accustomed to judge people not by their outward appearance but by their inner and true worth, I do not hesitate to wish you from an honest heart, even on this small piece of paper, thousands of pleasures, years without number and, above all, constant good health, not only on your name-day[1] but at all times. And united with all my dear ones in your friendship, which is so precious to us, I send my best greetings. God keep you for the consolation and happiness of your excellent wife, to whom I send special greetings, and for the support of your dear children, who in the future will surely bring you nothing but honour, joy and pleasure. Again, united to you and your beloved wife in friendship, I send my wishes and remain your most

obediently devoted and at the moment
limping friend

MOZART

(104a) *Mozart to Lorenz Hagenauer, Salzburg*

[*Autograph in the Deutsche Staatsbibliothek, Berlin*]

[BOLOGNA, 28 *July* 1770[2]]

I too slip in amongst the number of friends who are congratulating you and confirm all my father's cordial wishes and present my compliments to you and to dear Frau Hagenauer.

Your most obedient servant
WOLFGANGO AMADEO MOZART

---

[1] August 10th.   [2] A postscript to his father's letter.

(105) *Leopold Mozart to his Wife*

[*Extract*]   [*Autograph formerly in the possession of Messrs. Braus-Riggenbach, Basel*]

BOLOGNA, 28 *July* 1770

You will have received my first letter from Bologna, dated July 21st. I have now been nine days here and have not left my room, but have been either in bed or sitting up with my foot resting on a chair. But I hope that by the time you read this letter I shall have been out walking a few times. Well, this joke will cost me twelve ducats. For it is no fun being ill in an inn. If I had taken in a thousand doppi in Naples I could have got over this expense. All the same I still have more money than we need, and so we are content and praise God.

We received yesterday the libretto and the list of the singers. The title of the opera is: *Mitridate, Rè di Ponto*, and the text is by a poet of Turin, Signor Vittorio Amadeo Cigna-Santi. It was performed there in 1767.[1] The characters are:

Mitridate, Rè di Ponto	Il Signor Guglielmo d' Ettore
Aspasia, promessa sposa di Mitridate	Signora Antonia Bernasconi, prima donna
Sifare, figlio di Mitridate, amante d' Aspasia	Signor Santorini, soprano, primo uomo[2]
Farnace, primo figlio di Mitridate, amante della medesima Aspasia	Signor Cicognani, contra alto
Ismene, figlia del Rè dei Parti, amante di Farnace	Signora Varese, seconda donna, soprano
Arbate, governatore di Ninfea	Soprano
Marzio, tribuno romano	Tenore[3]

We knew Signora Bernasconi already. Signor Santorini sang for us in Rome. Cicognani is here and is a good friend of ours. Ettore is also here.

We like the two portraits[4] very much; but, in order to appreciate them, one must not look at them closely, but from a distance. For pastels are not like miniatures. They are rather oily; but at a distance much of the roughness disappears. Besides, we are satisfied, so that is enough. Wolfgang thanks you and his sister and all his good friends for the good wishes. We kiss you both a thousand times and I am

your old

MZT.

---

[1] Set to music by Abbate Quirino Gasparini (? –1778), who was maestro di cappella at the court of Turin from 1760 to 1770.

[2] Nissen, p. 218, in his version of this letter adds the remark 'who sang for the first time during the last carnival in Turin'. Actually the part of Sifare was taken by Pietro Benedetti. See Köchel, p. 120.

[3] Eventually the parts of Arbate and Marzio were filled by Pietro Muschietti and Gasparo Bassano respectively.   [4] These portraits have disappeared.

You can imagine what our household is like, now that I cannot get about. You know what Wolfgang is.

(105a) *Mozart to his Sister*

[Autograph formerly in the possession of Messrs. Braus-Riggenbach, Basel]

MY DEAREST SISTER,   [BOLOGNA, 28 *July* 1770 [1]]

I must confess that I am frightfully pleased that you have sent us the portraits, which I like very much. I have no more news to send you. Kiss my mother's hand a thousand times for me. I kiss you 1000000 times and remain your most humble servant

WOLFGANG AMADEO MOZART

(106) *Leopold Mozart to his Wife*

[Extract]   *[Autograph in the Mozarteum, Salzburg]*

BOLOGNA, 4 *August* 1770

I am still writing from my bed. Not that my right foot is still dangerously disabled. No, thank God, it is better, though the skin is now peeling and the leg looks as if I had had chicken-pox. But apart from my desire to spare this right foot and so prevent any fresh inflammation, I cannot get about on account of my left foot, as, during the night, I had severe pain and slight inflammation in my big toe and in the other toes of that foot, a pain rather like gout, which prevents me from walking. I shall hardly get away from this inn under twenty ducats, if that does the trick! Well, in God's name, let the devil take the money, if only one escapes with one's skin!

We have not yet had any heat and I am glad, for otherwise I should have lost heart at having to remain on my bed all this time.

During the last few days Mysliwecek [2] came to see me and so did Manfredini, the castrato, who visited us in Salzburg on his way home from Russia. His brother, Kapellmeister Manfredini,[3] has also been to see us, and a certain Schmidt, who gave a concert in Berne, whom Schulz [4]

---

[1] A postscript in Italian to his father's letter.

[2] Joseph Mysliwecek (1737–1781) was born in Prague, studied in Italy and composed several operas for Naples, Bologna and Munich. The Italians called him 'Il divino Boëmo'.

[3] Vincenzo Manfredini (1737–1799), maestro di cappella in Bologna and author of a famous work, *Difesa della musica moderna*, and many other treatises on music.

[4] There were two brothers of this name, both bassoon-players in the Salzburg court orchestra. See A. J. Hammerle, *op. cit.* p. 34.

(to whom we send our greetings) will remember well. Mysliwecek has obtained the scrittura for the first opera of the 1772 carnival in Milan, that is, a year after our Wolfgang's opera. My last letter gave you details about the first opera in Milan and the singers. The second is to be 'Nitteti'. Farewell. We kiss you a thousand times and I am at the moment your old impatient, gouty, bedridden

MZT

(106a) *Mozart to his Sister*

[Copy formerly in the Musikhistorisches Museum von W. Heyer, Cologne]

[BOLOGNA, *4 August* 1770[1]]

I am heartily sorry that Jungfrau Martha is so ill and I pray every day that she may recover. Tell her from me that she should not move about too much and that she should eat plenty of salt meats.

A propos! Did you give my letter to my dear Sigmund Robinig?[2] You say nothing about it. If you see him, please tell him not to forget me altogether. It is impossible for me to write a better hand, for this pen is for writing music and not for letters. My fiddle has now been restrung and I play every day. But I add this simply because Mamma wanted to know whether I still play the fiddle. More than six times at least I have had the honour of going alone to a church and to some magnificent function. In the meantime I have composed four Italian symphonies,[3] to say nothing of arias, of which I must have composed at least five or six,[4] and also a motet.[5]

Does Deibl[6] often visit you? Does he still honour you with his entertaining conversation? And the Honourable Karl von Vogt?[7] Does he still deign to listen to your unbearable voice? Schiedenhofen must help you to write lots of minuets; otherwise—not a single lump of sugar for him.

If I had the time, I ought to plague both Mölk and Schiedenhofen with a few lines. But, as this most necessary condition is lacking, I beg them to forgive my slackness and to allow me to postpone this honour to some future date.

[1] A postscript to his father's letter.
[2] Sigmund Robinig (1760–1823), son of Georg Joseph Robinig von Rottenfeld (1711–1760), a wealthy mine-owner in the district of Salzburg. He was a friend of Mozart's.
[3] Probably K. 81 [73l], 84 [73g], 95 [73n], 97 [73m]. See Köchel, pp. 104, 105.
[4] K. 77 [73e], 78 [73b], 79 [73d], 82 [73o], 88 [73c], 143 [73a].
[5] Possibly K. 117 [66a]. See WSF, vol. i. p. 285 f.
[6] Franz de Paula Deibl (? –1785), flautist and oboist in the Salzburg court orchestra. See A. S. Hammerle, *op. cit.* p. 35.
[7] Karl Vogt, violinist in the service of the Salzburg court. He is described in Hammerle, *op. cit.* p. 29, as 'a serious performer, who can produce a full and powerful tone'.

Opening bars of various *Cassations*:[1]

There, I have granted your request. I hardly think that it can be one of my compositions, for who would dare to pass off as his own a composition by the Kapellmeister's son, whose mother and sister are in Salzburg?[2] Addio! Farewell. My sole amusement at the moment consists in dancing English steps and in pirouetting and cutting capers. Italy is a sleepy country! I am always drowsy! Addio! Farewell.

4 August 1770.   WOLFGANG MOZART

My greetings to all my good friends! I kiss Mamma's hand!

[1] K. 63, 99 [63a], 62. 'Cassation', 'divertimento', 'serenade' and 'Finalmusik' are terms used to describe a kind of composition, often consisting of eight or ten movements, which was performed at court functions, at weddings and during banquets. The derivation of the word 'cassation' has been much discussed. WSF, vol. i. p. 201, maintain that 'cassation' is connected with 'casser', that is to say, that it was used originally for music, the movements of which need not be played in sequence.

[2] Evidently Nannerl had written to say that some Salzburg composer had passed off one of Mozart's compositions as his own.

(107) *Leopold Mozart to his Wife*

[*Extract*]   [*Autograph in the Mozarteum, Salzburg*]

A country house outside BOLOGNA, 11 *August* 1770

On the 4th, that is, the day after you wrote to me, you will have received a letter from me dated July 28th; and in the meantime my letter of August 4th will also have reached you. After hearing Mass in Bologna we arrived yesterday about noon at this country house, which is situated almost the same distance from the town as Maria-Plain is from Salzburg. At last we have now slept our fill. I need not send you a description of all the fine things here, for you can picture to yourself the rooms and the beds. Our sheets are of finer linen than many a nobleman's shirt, everything is of silver, even the bedroom sets, and the nightlights and so forth. Yesterday evening we went for a drive in two sedias, that is, Wolfgang, the Countess and the young Count in one, and I and His Excellency the Field-marshal[1] in the other. We have two servants to wait on us, a footman and a valet. The former sleeps in our anteroom in order to be at hand in case of necessity. The latter has to dress Wolfgang's hair. His Excellency has put us into the first rooms, which in Salzburg we should call the ground floor. Since in summer the upper rooms get all the heat, these are the best rooms, as we do not feel the slightest heat the whole day long nor particularly during the night. In addition to our rooms we have the *sala terrena* where we take our meals and where everything is fresh, cool and pleasant. The young Count, who is about Wolfgang's age and is sole heir to the property, is very talented, plays the clavier, speaks German, Italian and French and has five or six masters every day for lessons in various sciences and accomplishments. He is already Imperial Chamberlain. You can well believe that this young lord and Wolfgang are the best of friends. We shall remain here some time, but I do not know for how long; perhaps for the rest of the month, till the great heat is over. And my foot? Thank God, it is well. The wound has healed up completely and the skin is gradually peeling off. But since I have to use the foot during the day, however much I try to avoid doing so, the lower part, near the ankle, becomes slightly swollen by the evening. During the night, however, the swelling always disappears and it becomes less noticeable every day. My host and hostess never let me stand, but insist on my remaining seated with my foot propped up on another chair. Why, even at Mass today two chairs were put ready for me in the chapel. We have Mass daily at about noon and the young Count serves. After Mass the Rosary, the litany, the Salve Regina and the De Profundis are said.

We invite you to partake of the finest figs, melons and peaches! I am delighted to be able to tell you that, thank God, we are well. Give my

---

[1] Count Pallavicini.

greetings to Kapellmeister Lolli and tell him that I shall certainly deliver his messages and that I have already spoken to some old acquaintances of his.[1] We forgot to congratulate Nannerl on her name-day. When I was laid up with my foot my old melancholy thoughts came to me very often. It is sad to hear that living is becoming dearer in Salzburg. Are no means being devised to meet the rise in prices? Give special greetings to Schiedenhofen and his gracious mother. I shall soon reply to his letter. I must stop, for His Excellency's letters are being sent to town and this one must go with them. We kiss you and Nannerl a thousand times. Wolfgang has just now gone out driving with the Countess. We send greetings to all and I am your old

MZT.

(108) *Leopold Mozart to his Wife*

[*Extract*]   [*Autograph formerly in the possession of Oscar Bondy, Vienna*]

BOLOGNA, 21 *August* 1770

Thank God, my foot is now quite well.

We are still alla Croce del Biacco, the country house which belongs to Count Bolognetti, but which Count Pallavicini has taken for a few years. The great annual festival, which the members of the Bologna Philharmonic Society celebrate most magnificently with Vespers and High Mass, takes place on the 30th. We are going to hear it, and then we shall probably leave Bologna.

(108a) *Mozart to his Mother and Sister*

[*Autograph formerly in the possession of Otto Kallir, New York*]

[BOLOGNA, 21 *August* 1770[2]]

I too am still alive and, what is more, as merry as can be. I had a great desire today to ride on a donkey, for it is the custom in Italy, and so I thought that I too should try it. We have the honour to go about with a certain Dominican, who is regarded as a holy man. For my part I do not believe it, for at breakfast he often takes a cup of chocolate and immediately afterwards a good glass of strong Spanish wine; and I myself have had the honour of lunching with this saint who at table drank a whole decanter and finished up with a full glass of strong wine, two large slices of melon, some peaches, pears, five cups of coffee, a whole plate of cloves and two full saucers of milk and lemon. He may, of course, be following some sort of diet, but I do not think so, for it would be too much; more-

---

[1] See p. 123, n. 5.   [2] A postscript to his father's letter.

over he takes several little snacks during the afternoon. Addio. Farewell.
Kiss Mamma's hands for me. My greetings to all who know me.

WOLFGANG MOZART, 1770

PS. We have made the acquaintance of a certain German Dominican,
called Pater Cantor, who has asked me to give his kind regards to Herr
Hagenauer, the sculptor,[1] at Salzburg. He tells me that when Hagenauer
was in Bologna he always confessed to him. Addio.

(109) *Leopold Mozart to his Wife*

[Extract]   [Autograph in the Mozarteum, Salzburg]

BOLOGNA, 25 *August* 1770

I wrote to you on the 21st, and I suppose that, if letters to Germany are
delayed in Innsbruck as long as letters from Germany are, you will receive
two letters at once. We are still in the country and, thank God, we are
well. So I have no news whatever for you. You must not worry if my
letters do not arrive punctually, for, as we are out of town, it often happens
that there is no opportunity either of writing letters or of posting them.
Meanwhile continue to address yours to Bologna, although when you
receive this letter it is possible that we shall be about to leave. The weather
is beautiful, neither too warm nor too cold. As there is a Dominican
Father here, a German from Bohemia, to whom our Court Statuarius
used to confess, we performed our devotions today in the Parish Church,
which was all the more convenient as this Father accompanied us. We
were quite alone there, for the peasants attend Mass early in the morning.
We confessed and received Communion and then, having performed
together the Stations of the Cross, we returned to the castle, which is only
two hundred feet away, and where the Dominican said Mass and the
Rosary for my host. So you ought to have two fine gold halos made for
us in Salzburg; for we shall certainly return home as saints.

Thank God my foot, or rather, my feet, are well. I still keep a small
protection on the ankle of my wounded foot, more as a precaution than
as a necessity, for it still swells slightly every evening. But that is not
surprising, as during the journey I was not able to take care of it; and then
for three whole weeks it was never used and the skin had almost completely peeled off. I do not desire a repetition of this joke, especially when
travelling; indeed it was the very last thing I wanted.

I am trying hard to devise a means of lightening my luggage, which is
getting more and more bulky, for in Milan I shall be picking up a great

---

[1] Johann Baptist Hagenauer (1732–1810), a relative of the Mozart's landlord, had been
sculptor and architect to the Salzburg court since 1767.

many things which we left behind. If I can send a few articles from here to Bozen, I shall certainly do so. But I am not sure that I can. Above all, books and music, which are always accumulating, cause me much inconvenience. As soon as I reach Milan, I shall have to have nearly all Wolfgang's cravats and shirts altered. He will have to wait until then, for Frau Theresa, the wife of Count Firmian's steward,[1] can do me this service. Everything he wears is rather tight for him and he has removed all the silk threads which were wound round his diamond ring, which however still has a little wax in it. But you must not think that he has grown very tall. It is only that his limbs are becoming bigger and stronger. He has no longer any singing voice. It has gone completely. He has neither a deep nor a high voice, not even five pure notes. He is most annoyed, for he can no longer sing his own compositions, which he would sometimes like to do.

The book, my 'Violinschule,' has not yet arrived in Bologna. Perhaps Brinsecchi is to receive it in a bale of linen? Find this out from Haffner, to whom I send greetings. If it reaches me in Bologna, I shall have the pleasure of handing it to Padre Martini in person. Now I must stop, so as not to miss the post. We kiss you and Nannerl a thousand times and I am your old

L. MOZART

(110) *Leopold Mozart to his Wife*

[*Extract*]   [*Autograph in the Mozarteum, Salzburg*]

BOLOGNA, 1 *September* 1770

You will have received my letter of August 25th. Not only are we still in the country as the guests of His Excellency Count Pallavicini, but we shall very probably remain here for some time and then proceed straight to Milan via Parma. I am very sorry to have to miss Leghorn, but I still have hopes of seeing Genoa. If we have time and if I feel inclined, we can do so from Milan.

My foot has kept me for a long time in Bologna; and now it will soon be time to think rather of the recitatives for the opera than of a protracted journey and of visits to various towns. For, when you are moving from place to place, and have little or no time, you really cannot do anything. Moreover this is the season when everyone goes into the country and none of the gentry are to be found in town. So we shall arrive in Milan a little earlier, perhaps by a month, than we are due. Meanwhile, continue to write to Bologna. His Excellency arranged for us to be driven into

---

[1] Don Fernando Germani.

town on the 30th in order to hear the Mass and Vespers of the Accademia Filarmonica, which had been composed by ten different masters; that is to say, one wrote the Kyrie and Gloria, another the Credo, and so forth. Thus each psalm of the vespers was set to music by a different Kapellmeister, who in each case conducted his own composition. But they all had to be members of the Academy.[1] We lunched with Brinsecchi who did us very well. Please give my greetings to Haffner and tell him how excellently we were entertained. The weather is very mild and the great heat is over. A few days ago we had a thunderstorm and amazingly heavy rain. It was so steamy that one could hardly breathe. That was the end of the heat. I am very sorry to hear that prices are still rising in Salzburg. What will happen to all of us who have to live on our monthly pay?

Wolfgang read Nannerl's long story with much pleasure, but as he has gone out driving with the Countess, he cannot write. I have stayed indoors to write this letter and I must send one to Milan also. So I must stop. We kiss you both a thousand times and I am your old

LEOP MOZART

(111) *Leopold Mozart to his Wife*

[Extract]   [Autograph in the Mozarteum, Salzburg]

BOLOGNA, 8 September 1770

I have received your letter of August 24th and I hope that my letters of August 21st and 25th and September 1st have now reached you. Brinsecchi has not yet received my 'Violinschule'.

I shall reply later on about the other matters you mention. We are still in the country and, thank God, we are well. I have written to Milan to find out whether our rooms there are available and to ask that they be got ready, for we shall arrive there a month earlier than we expected, that is, by the beginning of October at latest, instead of at the beginning of November. And, as I have not been able to visit Leghorn, I shall take a short trip from Milan to the Borromean Islands, which are not far off and are well worth seeing.

We both kiss you a thousand times and I am your old

LEOP MOZART

---

[1] Burney, *op. cit.* p. 230 ff., gives a lengthy description of this performance. Petronio Lanzi, President of the Academy, had composed the Kyrie and Gloria, and Lorenzo Gibelli, a pupil of Padre Martini, the Credo. Burney goes on to say: 'I must acquaint my musical reader that at the performance just mentioned, I met with M. Mozart and his son, the little German whose premature and almost supernatural talents so much astonished us in London a few years ago, when he had scarce quitted his infant state'.

(111a) *Mozart to his Sister*

[Autograph in the Mozarteum, Salzburg]

[BOLOGNA, 8 *September* 1770[1]]

In order not to fail in my duty, I will add a few words myself. Please write and tell me to what Brotherhoods I belong and let me know what prayers I must offer for them. I am this moment reading 'Télémaque' and have already got to the second part. Meanwhile, farewell.

WOLFGANG MOZART

I kiss Mamma's hand.

(112) *Mozart to Thomas Linley, Florence*

[From Giulio Piccini Jarro, 'L'origine della maschera di Stentorello', 1898, pp. 5–6]

MY DEAR FRIEND,　　　　　　　　[BOLOGNA, 10 *September* 1770[2]]

Here is a letter at last! Indeed I am very late in replying to your charming letter addressed to me at Naples, which, however, I only received two months after you had written it. My father's plan was to travel to Loreto via Bologna, and thence to Milan via Florence, Leghorn and Genoa. We should then have given you a surprise by turning up unexpectedly in Florence. But, as he had the misfortune to gash his leg rather badly when the shaft-horse of our sedia fell on the road, and as this wound not only kept him in bed for three weeks but held us up in Bologna for another seven, this nasty accident has forced us to change our plans and to proceed to Milan via Parma.

Firstly, we have missed the suitable time for such a journey and, secondly, the season is over, for everyone is in the country and therefore we could not earn our expenses. I assure you that this accident has annoyed us very much. I would do everything in my power to have the pleasure of embracing my dear friend. Moreover my father and I would very much like to meet again Signor Gavard and his very dear and charming family, and also Signora Corilla and Signor Nardini, and then to return to Bologna. This we would do indeed, if we had the slightest hope of making even the expenses of our journey.

As for the engravings you lost, my father remembered you; and his order arrived in time for two other copies to be kept for you. So please

---

[1] A postscript to his father's letter.
[2] This letter and its postscript are in Italian. Jarro states that he copied them from the autograph in the possession of Novello. No doubt this is the letter to which Edward Holmes refers in his *Life of Mozart*, 1845 (reprinted by J. M. Dent, 1921, p. 54, n. 1), where he states that the late Rev. Ozias Linley, of Dulwich College, possessed a letter written by Mozart to his brother Thomas in Italian and esteemed this document, in the handwriting of the composer of *Don Giovanni*, beyond all price.

MOZART (1770)
From a portrait by Saverio dalla Rosa
(Heirs of Alfred Cortot, Paris)

let me know of some means of sending them to you. Keep me in your friendship and believe that my affection for you will endure for ever and that I am your most devoted servant and loving friend

AMADEO WOLFGANGO MOZART

(112a) *Leopold Mozart to Thomas Linley, Florence*

[*From Giulio Piccini Jarro, 'L'origine della maschera di Stentorello', 1898, p. 6*]

[BOLOGNA, 10 *September* 1770 [1]]

Please give our greetings to all our friends.

LEOPOLDO MOZART

(113) *Leopold Mozart to his Wife*

[*Extract*]   [*Autograph in the Mozarteum, Salzburg*]

BOLOGNA, 18 *September* 1770

Baron Riedheim who arrived in Bologna on the 15th left today. As I only heard this yesterday and could not go myself, I sent the footman into Bologna. Riedheim wrote a note to me and I hope to see him in Milan. We like the minuets very much. Wolfgang has no time at the moment to write to his sister, but he will do so as soon as he can. We send you both many millions of kisses and I am your old

MZT.

If you are so keen to travel to Italy, we invite you to the opera at Milan.

(114) *Leopold Mozart to his Wife*

[*Extract*]   [*Autograph formerly in the Musikhistorisches Museum von W. Heyer, Cologne*]

BOLOGNA, 22 *September* 1770

We are still in the country, but we shall certainly return to town to-morrow or Thursday. Send your next letter to Milan and to the same address, à Mr: Leopolde Troger Secretaire de la Chancellerie, intime de L : L : M : M : Imp : Roy : & apost : dans leur Lombardie à Milan.

Both here and in Rome we have been hearing lately of a great movement, the object of which is to suppress the religion of the Jesuits. The House of Bourbon absolutely refuses to be pacified and both Spain and France are still most insistently urging the Pope to dissolve the order.

A postscript to Mozart's letter.

Furthermore a violent book has appeared in Naples, the author of which is a certain Marchese Spiriti. It is a refutation of a Papalist theologian, Father Mamachi, a Dominican, who some time ago wrote a very powerful book in favour of the clergy, that is to say, on behalf of the Immunitas Ecclesiae and the right of the Church to possess property; and in it he attacked the ruling lords and their ministers rather sharply. Now this Marchese Spiriti wrote against this book in a very satirical vein, doubtless at the instigation of the Spanish, Portuguese and Neapolitan courts.[1]

Today I am not at all disposed to write as I am suffering from a pain in my shoulder, which is just as if someone had run a knife through my shoulder-blade. You and Nannerl must keep well. We send you many thousands of kisses o o o o o o o; and I am your old

MZT

(114a) *Mozart to his Sister*

[*Autograph formerly in the Musikhistorisches Museum von W. Heyer, Cologne*]

[Bologna, 22 *September* 1770[2]]

I hope that my Mamma is well, and you too; and I should like you to answer my letters more carefully in future, for it is surely far easier to reply to questions than to make up something for onself. I like Haydn's[3] six minuets better than the first twelve. We have often had to perform them for the countess.[4] We should like to be able to introduce the German taste in minuets into Italy, where they last nearly as long as a whole symphony. Excuse my wretched writing. I could do better, but I am in a hurry. We should like to have two small calendars for next year. Addio.

C: W: Mozart

I kiss Mamma's hand.

(115) *Leopold Mozart to his Wife*

[*Extract*]　　　　　　　　　　　　　　　　　　　　　　[*Autograph in the Koch Collection*]

Bologna, 29 *September* [1770]

God willing, we shall leave Bologna on October 6th or 8th. Both Wolfgang and I are dreadfully distressed about good little Martha. God give her strength! What is to be done? We cannot get her out of our

---

[1] Tommaso Maria Mamachi (1713–1792) was a great Dominican scholar and historian of Christian antiquities. His principal work was his *Originum et antiquitatum Christianorum libri XX*, Rome, 1749–1755. The writing to which L. Mozart here refers was his *Del diritto libero della Chiesa d'acquistare e di possedere beni temporali*, Rome, 1769. Mamachi was an active controversialist and his polemical writings gained him many enemies. Among these was the Marchese Spiriti, who attacked him in his *Mamachiana, per chi vuol divertirsi*, 1770.

[2] A postscript to his father's letter.　　　　　　　　　　　　　[3] Michael Haydn.

[4] Wife of Count Pallavicini.

minds all day long. Wolfgang began the recitatives for the opera today. We kiss you both 1000,000,000 times.

You will have already heard that relations between the Pope and Portugal are again on a friendly footing. But people are very much afraid that the Jesuit order will be dissolved. For Bishop Palafox,[1] who in his day was so grievously persecuted by the Jesuits, is to be beatified. I could tell you about several disputes of this kind, but they would hardly interest you. It is a great misfortune that now-a-days in Catholic countries, even in Italy, the most disgraceful pamphlets are being published against the authority of the Pope and the immunity of the clergy.

(115a) *Mozart to his Mother*

[Autograph in the Koch Collection]

[BOLOGNA, 29 *September* 1770[2]]

To make the letter a little fuller, I will also add a few words. I am sincerely sorry to hear of the long illness which poor Jungfrau Martha has to bear with patience, and I hope that with God's help she will recover. But, if she does not, we must not be unduly distressed, for God's will is always best and He certainly knows best whether it is better for us to be in this world or in the next. She should console herself, however, with the thought that after the rain she may enjoy the sunshine. I kiss Mamma's hands. Farewell. Addio.

WOLFGANG MOZART

(116) *Leopold Mozart to his Wife*

[From Mitteilungen für die Mozartgemeinde in Berlin, October 1910, pp. 230-231]

BOLOGNA, 6 *October* 1770

I received today your letter of September 14th, although I rather expected one dated the 28th. It is the fault of the Tyrolese and Italian posts that letters are delayed for a week or a fortnight. We have now been back in town for five days and have witnessed the festival of St. Petronius,

---

[1] Jean de Palafox de Mendoza (1600–1659), Spanish theologian, after serving as a layman on the Council of the Indies, took orders and was appointed in 1639 Bishop of Puebla-de-los-Angeles (Angelopolis) in Mexico, where he had certain differences with the Jesuits. The question was submitted to Pope Innocent X, and Palafox returned to Europe in 1643 to plead his cause. The King of Spain, satisfied with his conduct, gave him in 1653 the bishopric of Osma. He died a few years later, leaving a great reputation for piety. In 1694 the first steps were taken to procure his beatification. The case was not, however, introduced until 1726, when, in spite of the strong support of the Spanish Government, it was decided that this honour should not be conferred upon one who had been the declared enemy of the Jesuits.

[2] A postscript to his father's letter.

which was celebrated here most magnificently and on the occasion of which there was performed in the huge church of St. Petronius a musical work in which all the musicians of Bologna took part. We intended to leave for Milan on Monday or Tuesday. But something is keeping us here until Thursday, *something* which, if it really happens, will do Wolfgang extraordinary honour.[1] I have a great deal to do and that is the reason why I cannot write to Frau Hagenauer for her name-day, as I had intended. So I must ask you to convey our greetings. I hardly have time to scrawl this letter; and now for the next few post-days you will have no letters until you receive one from Milan.

Padre Martini has already received the book.[2] We are the best of friends. The second part of his own work is now ready.[3] I shall bring back both parts. We are at his house every day and have long discussions on the history of music.

So you have had three concerts? Well, three cheers! And you did not invite us? We should have appeared in a trice and then flown away again. We kiss you both many ten thousand millions of times and I am

your old
MZT.

(116a) *Mozart to his Sister*

[Bologna, 6 October 1770[4]]

We received your letter too late, but it does not matter, as the Italian post is extremely irregular. I rejoice from my heart that you enjoyed yourself so much and I wish that I had been there. I hope that Jungfrau Martha is better. I played the organ today in the Dominican Chapel. Congratulate Frau Hagenauer and Theresa from me and tell them that I wish from my heart that they may live to celebrate the anniversary of Father Dominic's ordination[5] and that we may all live together again very happily. It looks as though you did not receive the letter in which I enclosed a note for Sigmund,[6] for I have not had a reply. Addio. Farewell. I kiss Mamma's hand and I send congratulations to all Theresas, and greetings to all other friends in our house and elsewhere. I hope that I shall

---

[1] Leopold Mozart is referring to the prospect of his son's admission to membership of the Accademia Filarmonica of Bologna.

[2] Leopold Mozart's *Violinschule*, which was published in 1756. According to Köchel, p. 110, the autograph of Mozart's minuet K. 122 [73t], composed at Bologna in August 1770 and sent to Salzburg, contains a few lines in his father's handwriting, asking Frau Mozart to send him a copy of his treatise, which he wished to present to Padre Martini.

[3] Padre Martini's *Storia della Musica*, the first volume of which had appeared in 1757.

[4] A postscript to his father's letter.

[5] Dominicus Hagenauer, a son of the Mozart's landlord had entered the monastery of St. Peter in Salzburg, of which he became Abbot in 1786.

[6] Sigmund Robinig. see p. 153, n. 2.

soon hear those Pertl chamber symphonies and perhaps blow a little
trumpet or play on a little pipe by way of accompaniment.[1] I have heard
and seen the great festival of St. Petronius in Bologna. It was beautiful,
but very long. They had to fetch trumpeters from Lucca for the salvo,
but they played abominably.

Addio.   WOLFG. MOZART

(117) *Leopold Mozart to his Wife*

[Extract]   *[Autograph in the Mozarteum, Salzburg]*

MILAN, 20 *October* 1770

We arrived in Milan, thank God, safe and sound at five o'clock in the
evening of the 18th. We had to spend a whole day in Parma, as the
surprisingly heavy rains had made the rivers rise so high that no one could
cross them. We drove during the whole afternoon of the 14th through a
terrific thunderstorm and frightfully heavy rain; yet my luggage did not
get wet, for I had covered it well with double waterproof cloth. For nearly
three weeks I had had very painful rheumatism in my right arm; and this
pain I took with me on the journey. But so far from getting worse, it is,
on the contrary, noticeably better, although I have not yet got rid of it
completely. But note that I am not, nor have I been, treating it in any way.
It will have to go as it came. The motion of the sedia did not do it any
good. But I said to myself, evil must banish evil. So owing to the thunderstorm and heavy rain it was a rather unpleasant journey, and with my
bad arm a rather painful one.

We left Bologna a few days later than we had intended, for by a
unanimous vote the Accademia Filarmonica received Wolfgang into their
society and awarded him the diploma of Accademico Filarmonico. He
won this honour under all the normal conditions and after a previous
examination. For on October 9th he had to appear in the Hall of the
Academy at four o'clock in the afternoon. There the Princeps Accademiae
and the two Censores, who all three are old Kapellmeisters, put before
him, in the presence of all the members, an antiphon taken out of an
antiphoner, which he had to arrange for four parts in an anteroom, into
which the Bedellus led him, locking the door behind him. When Wolfgang had finished it, it was examined by the Censores and all the Kapellmeisters and Compositores. Then a vote was taken, which was done by
means of white and black balls. As all the balls were white, Wolfgang was
called in and all the members clapped their hands as he entered and congratulated him, and the Princeps Accademiae informed him, on behalf of
the company, that he had passed the examination. He thanked them and

---

[1] Mozart is referring to the informal concerts in his Salzburg home, to which his father
alludes in the last paragraph of his letter. Frau Mozart's maiden name was Anna Maria Pertl.

then the ceremony was over. Meanwhile Brinsecchi and I were locked in the library of the Academy on the other side of the hall. All the members were surprised that Wolfgang had finished his task so quickly, seeing that many candidates had spent three hours over an antiphon of three lines. For I must tell you that it is not at all an easy task, for in this kind of composition many things are not allowed and of these Wolfgang had been told previously. Yet he had finished it in less than half an hour.[1] Later the Bedellus brought the certificate to our house. It is in Latin and contains among others the following words:—*testamur Dominum Wolfgangum Amadeum etc.—sub die 9 mensis octobris anni 1770 inter academiae nostrae magistros compositores adscriptum fuisse, etc.*[2] This distinction does Wolfgang all the more credit for the Accademia Bonnoniensis is more than a hundred years old[3] and, apart from Padre Martini and other eminent Italians, only the most distinguished citizens of other countries are members of it.[4]

Farewell to both. We kiss you 100000 times and I am your old

MOZART

(117a) *Mozart to his Mother*

[*Autograph in the Mozarteum, Salzburg*]

MY DEAR MAMMA,   [MILAN, 20 October 1770[5]]

I cannot write much, for my fingers are aching from composing so many recitatives. Mamma, I beg you to pray for me, that my opera may go well and that we may be happy together again. I kiss Mamma's hand a thousand times and I have many things to say to my sister, but what? God and I alone know. If it is God's will, I shall soon, I hope, be able to tell them to her myself. Meanwhile I kiss her 1000 times. My greetings to all my good friends. We have lost our good little Martha, but with God's help we shall meet her in a better place.

(118) *Leopold Mozart to his Wife*

[*Extract*]

MILAN, 27 October 1770

You will have received my first letter from Milan, dated October 20th. By the same post I wrote to the Archbishop. Tell me whether he received

[1] Köchel, p. 112, points out that the autograph of Mozart's work (K. 86 [73v]) contains certain corrections made by Padre Martini and that the register of the Bologna Academy states that Mozart finished it 'in less than an hour'.
[2] We witness that Master Wolfgang Amadeus etc.—has been enrolled among the master composers of our academy on the 9th day of October 1770; etc. Nissen, p. 226, reproduces the text of the diploma of the Bologna Academy, dated 10 October 1770.
[3] The Bologna Academy was founded in 1666.
[4] The statutory conditions were that the candidate for membership should be not less than 20 years old and should have spent a year in the junior class of singers and players. These conditions were waived in the case of Mozart.   [5] A postscript to his father's letter.

my letter, for no doubt you will hear about it soon. Thank God, we are well. As the heavy rain has continued, we have been out of the house very little. Spagnoletta, whom you saw in Lyons, is here and is to sing in Verona during the carnival. She tells us that the tenor is coming from Germany and is in the service of a court not far from Bavaria. Perhaps it is Meisner? For I know that Meisner could have got a contract for the theatre in Verona, and I presume therefore that it is he. Let me know this at once. God willing, we shall leave here after the middle of January and travel to Venice by way of Brescia, Verona, Vicenza and Padua, in order to see the end of the carnival, which this year is very short, and to hear some of the concerts given in Lent, which, as everyone tells me, is the best season for performances. I am only sorry that afterwards we shall have a filthy and perhaps even a dangerous journey home, as it is no joke travelling through the mountains in spring, when the snow is melting. I am still thinking of leaving Italy through Carinthia, for I have now seen the Tyrol and, unless there is some necessity for it, it is no fun, I think, for me to cover the same route twice after the fashion of dogs. Meanwhile please ask Johann and Joseph Hagenauer to let me know whether I can find private rooms in some comfortable house in Venice. On my way through I shall certainly stay for a short time in Brescia, Verona and the other places which I have mentioned, in order to see the operas; and therefore I shall not arrive in Venice until February, and perhaps not even until the beginning of the week after Candlemas.

Herr Haffner, to whom I send warmest greetings, promised me to send us letters of introduction for Venice. If he still would like to do so, he could send them in advance to a friend there, so that I may find them when I arrive. When we were in Bologna Mysliwecek visited us very often and we constantly went to see him. He often mentioned Johannes Hagenauer and, of course, Herr Cröner.[1] He was writing for Padua an oratorio,[2] which he has probably finished by now. He is then going to Bohemia. He is an honest fellow and we became intimate friends.

Our lodgings here are not far from the theatre. They consist of a large room with a balcony, three windows and a fireplace, and of a bedroom about the same size with two large windows but no fireplace. So, provided we do not freeze to death, we shall be sure not to smell, for we have enough air. The bed is about nine feet wide. We are rather a long way from Count Firmian's house, but this time we have to be near the theatre.

We wish you both good health and, above all, cheaper living, as your letters always contain the sad news that prices are going up. What will become of Salzburg, if some means are not devised of establishing a sound

---

[1] Possibly one of the large family of Bavarian musicians who served the Electoral court at Munich.

[2] Einstein suggested the oratorio *Il Tobia*, which Mysliwecek wrote for Padua in 1769, or possibly his *Giuseppe riconosciuto*, of which the year of performance is not known.

régime? With the small pay we get we shall in time all be beggars. The poor court servants have hardly enough to satisfy their hunger; and their children who learn nothing, because there is no money, will grow up to be idlers, and in about twenty years the town will be full of useless people living in misery, a burden both to the court and to the whole community. In a few years' time others will have to admit that what I say is true. If everyone is to be allowed to marry and if a population is required for a town, it should be known beforehand how the means of subsistence is to be found for all these people.

We kiss you 100,000,000 times and I am your old

MOZART

(118a) *Mozart to his Sister*

DEAREST SISTER!   [MILAN, 27 *October* 1770 [1]]

You know what a great chatterbox I am—and was, when I left you. But at the moment I am talking in signs, as the son of the house is deaf and dumb from birth. Now I must work at my opera. I am heartily sorry that I cannot let you have the minuets you asked for, but, God willing, you may perhaps have them at Easter—and me too. I cannot write anything more, and I do not know what to write about, as there is no news. Farewell and pray for me. I kiss Mamma's hand, and I send greetings to all my acquaintances, and I am, as always, your brother

WOLFGANG MOZART

(119) *Leopold Mozart to his Wife*

[*Extract*]   [*From Nissen, pp. 230-231*]

MILAN, 3 November 1770

Wolfgang thanks you for your congratulations on his name-day [2] and hopes that, if God in His goodness allows us to meet again, he will be able to reward you for all your good wishes by giving you joy and pleasure.

I cannot think of anything to write to you about, except that, thank God, we are well and wish that New Year's Day or at least Christmas were here already. For until then there will always be something to do or to think about, perhaps some small worry to make one foam at the mouth and have an unpleasant time. But patience! Thanks be to God that this great undertaking is nearly over, and, God be praised, once more in honourable fashion. With His help, we shall nibble our way through these unavoidable annoyances which every Kapellmeister has to face with this canaille of virtuosi.

---

[1] A postscript to his father's letter.   [2] October 31st.

(119a) *Mozart to his Sister*

[*Autograph in the Städtisches Museum, Salzburg*]

DEAREST DARLING LITTLE SISTER, [MILAN, 3 *November* 1770[1]]

I thank Mamma and you for your sincere good wishes and I burn with eagerness to see you both in Salzburg soon again. To return to your congratulations I must say that I almost suspected that it was Martinelli who composed those Italian wishes. But as you are always such a clever sister and as you managed to arrange it so deftly by adding immediately under your Italian wishes Martinelli's greetings in the same handwriting, I simply could not detect it and said at once to Papa: 'Ah! If only I were so clever and smart!' And Papa said: 'Yes, I agree'. Then I said: 'I am sleepy'. And he said—just this very moment: 'Stop writing'. Addio. Pray to God that my opera may go well. I kiss Mamma's hand and I send greetings to all my friends and am, as always, your brother

WOLFGANG MOZART, whose fingers are
tired from writing.

(120) *Leopold Mozart to his Wife*

[*Extract*] [*Autograph in the Mozarteum, Salzburg*]

MILAN, 10 *November* 1770

I have received the miscellany which our good friends have sent us and we are both of us very glad that you had such a good time in Triebenbach. If our excellent friends sometimes add a joke to your letters, they will be doing a good deed, for Wolfgang is now busy with serious matters and is therefore very serious himself. So I am delighted when he occasionally gets hold of something really funny. By the way, I ask my friends to excuse me for not writing to anyone. I now feel less inclined to write than ever and later on you will be astounded to hear what a storm we have been through, to weather which presence of mind and constant thought were necessary. God be praised, we have won the first battle and have defeated an enemy, who brought to the prima donna's house all the arias which she was to sing in our opera and tried to persuade her not to sing any of Wolfgang's. We have seen them all and they are all new, but neither she nor we know who composed them. But she gave that wretch a flat refusal, and she is now beside herself with delight at the arias which Wolfgang has composed to suit her. So also is her maestro, Signor Lampugnani,[2] who is rehearsing her part with her and who cannot

---

[1] A postscript to his father's letter.
[2] Giovanni Battista Lampugnani (1706–1781), a prolific composer of operas.

sufficiently praise them; for when we called on her today, she happened
to be studying her first aria with him. But a second storm, which we can
already see in the distance, is gathering in the theatrical sky. Yet with God's
help and if we conduct ourselves bravely we shall fight our way through.
Do not worry, for these are unavoidable accidents which befall the greatest
masters. If only we keep well and do not get constipated, little else matters.
We must not take things too much to heart. You will hear everything in
due course. It still rains here most of the time and we have thick mists,
which, after one fine day, then settle down upon us.

We both kiss you a million times and I remain your old

LEOP MOZART

I cannot remember whether I told you that Kreusser Junior[1] looked us
up in Bologna, that is, young Kreusser of Amsterdam, whose brother is
first violin there and who came to see us constantly and wanted to travel
with us. He asked for us in Rome and Naples, but each time we had
already left. He is now returning to Holland through Turin and Paris and
he sends greetings to you both.

I have this very moment received your letter of November 2nd. Dr.
Bridi[2] of Rovereto is himself a good performer on the clavier. Count
Castelbarco I know well. I am writing this letter in the steward' squarters
of Count Firmian's house.

(121) *Leopold Mozart to his Wife*

[*Extract*]   [*Autograph in the Mozarteum, Salzburg*]

MILAN, 17 *November* 1770

In my last letter, dated November 10th, I asked you to thank all our
good friends for their very kind congratulations.[3] I have no reason to
thank you and Nannerl, for you conveyed, it is true, the good wishes of
others, but your own stuck in your pen; and Nannerl, I suppose, could
not think of a motto, for she too wrote nothing, though in the last letter
but one which she wrote, she promised her brother that she would congratulate him in her next letter. Indeed it would not have killed Nannerl
if she had written to me. Why, now I come to think of it, yes, she did

---

[1] Georg Anton Kreusser (1743–*c*. 1811), violinist and composer. After studying in Italy he
returned in 1775 to Germany and became Konzertmeister to the Elector of Mainz. His elder
brother, Adam Kreusser (1727–1791), a famous horn-player (not violinist), became Konzertmeister at Amsterdam, where the Mozarts made the acquaintance of both brothers. See
Leopold Mozart's *Reiseaufzeichnungen*, p. 45.

[2] Antonio Giacomo Bridi, who sang in the Vienna performance of *Idomeneo* in 1786. His
son Giuseppe Antonio, published in 1827 a volume of *Brevi notizie intorno ad alcuni compositori
di musica*, which mentions Mozart.

[3] Referring to a passage in his last letter, which for lack of space has been omitted.

send her brother an Italian congratulation; now I do remember. When you have several other things in your head, it is quite impossible to bear everything in mind.

Thank God, we are well. During the last few days Wolfgang has had an abscess in a tooth with a slight inflammation on one side of his face. The prima donna is infinitely pleased with her arias. The primo uomo is to arrive next week.

We have now weathered a second storm and, although a few more incidents will probably occur, I trust that with God's help all will go well. For that an opera should win general applause is a stroke of luck which in Italy is very rare, because there are so many factions and because an indifferent, indeed even a bad solo dancer has her supporters who combine to shout 'Bravo' and to make a great noise. However, we have overcome many difficulties and with God's help this undertaking too will meet with success.

You asked me lately whether we are living far from Herr Troger. It takes a quarter of an hour to Count Firmian's house and there is hardly a day that we do not walk out there after lunch for the sake of exercise, for unless it is absolutely necessary I do not want Wolfgang to compose after his midday meal. This evening we are going with Herr Troger into the country, about as far as Plain[1] is from Salzburg, and we are staying there till Monday. He has bought a vineyard and fields out there and next spring he is going to build a house on this property. Meanwhile he has rented one there. Now I have no more news for you. We kiss you both ten million times and I am your old

LEOP MOZART

(122) *Leopold Mozart to his Wife*

[Extract]   [Autograph in the Mozarteum, Salzburg]

MILAN, 24 November 1770

I have nothing to tell you, except that, thank God, we are both well. I am writing this letter in great haste at Count Firmian's house. Wolfgang has his hands full now, as the time is getting on and he has only composed one aria for the primo uomo,[2] because the latter has not yet arrived and because Wolfgang refuses to do the work twice over and prefers to wait for his arrival so as to fit the costume to his figure. I have this moment received your letter and I have read with great delight of your merrymakings.

Addio. We kiss you a hundred thousand times and I am your old

MZT.

[1] i.e. Maria-Plain.
[2] Pietro Benedetti, a male soprano, who sang the part of Sifare. He did not arrive in Milan until December 1st.

(123) *Leopold Mozart to his Wife*

[Extract]   [*Autograph in the Mozarteum, Salzburg*]

MILAN, 1 *December* 1770

I have received your letter of November 16th. I wrote on November 24th in a great hurry and so forgot to tell you that I received your letter of November 9th, filled with congratulations from you and Nannerl. When Wolfgang read it, he became rather sad and said: '*I am truly sorry for Mamma and Nannerl, because in his last letter Papa wrote such cutting remarks in jest*'. I told him that you would certainly realize that I would receive your letter very soon, which I did in fact, a few hours after mine had been handed to the post. So I send you my most solemn thanks. In the evening of November 24th, the day on which I sent you my last letter, Baron Riedheim and his tutor came to see us, and on Monday, the 26th, we met at the concert held in Count Firmian's house. He offered to take a letter for us, but, as I write every Saturday, I declined with thanks. I did intend to give him some trifles for you, which he could have easily taken, such as pieces of the Sacred Cross, some relics or a few snuff-boxes. But it has been raining so hard and the weather has been so abominable that I shall have to pay my return visit to Baron Riedheim in Salzburg. By the time you read this letter, you will have already spoken to him and heard from him that we are well. He will have told you also what a wretched orchestra performed at that concert. For these good people have all gone off to the country with their patrons and it will be eight or twelve days before they return for the rehearsals of the opera. You think that the opera is already finished, but you are greatly mistaken. If it had depended on our son alone, two operas would have been ready by now. But in Italy everything is quite mad. You will hear all about this later on, for it would take too long to tell you everything. At the time I write, the primo uomo has not yet arrived, but he will certainly arrive today. Farewell. We kiss you both a hundred thousand million times and I am your old

MZT

(123a) *Mozart to his Sister*

[*Autograph in the Mozarteum, Salzburg*]

DEAREST SISTER,   [MILAN, 1 *December* 1770[1]]

As I have not written for so long, I thought I might moderate your annoyance or disappointment with these few lines. Papa will have already informed you that we had the honour of making the acquaintance of

---

[1] A postscript to his father's letter.

Baron Riedheim. At present I have a lot of work and writing to do in connexion with my opera. I hope that with God's help all will go well. Addio. Farewell. I am, as always, your faithful brother

WOLFGANG MOZART

PS. Kiss Mamma's hands for me, my greetings to all good friends.

(123b) *Leopold Mozart to his Wife*

[MILAN, 1 *December* 1770]

As we were leaving the house yesterday, we heard something which you will think incredible and which I never imagined that I should hear, *above all in Italy*. We listened to two beggars, a man and a woman, singing together in the street and they sang the whole song together in *fifths*, and without missing a note. I have never heard this in Germany. At a distance I thought that they were two persons, each of whom was singing a different song. But when we came up we found that they were singing together a beautiful duet in perfect fifths. I immediately thought of the late Herr Wenzel, and of how, if these two beggars were to sing on his grave, he would undoubtedly rise from the dead.

(124) *Leopold Mozart to his Wife*

[*Extract*]   [*Autograph in the Mozarteum, Salzburg*]

MILAN, 8 *December* 1770

The second rehearsal of the recitatives is taking place today after the Angelus. The first went so well that only once did I take up my pen to alter a single letter, and that was, *della* to *dalla*. This achievement does the copyist great credit and has provoked general surprise, seeing that, as everyone says, an amazing number of words and notes have usually to be altered all through the text. I hope that it will be the same with the instrumental rehearsals, which, by the time you receive this letter, will perhaps have already begun. As far as I can judge without a father's partiality I consider that Wolfgang has written the opera well and with great intelligence. As the singers are good, all will depend upon the orchestra, and ultimately upon the caprice of the audience. Thus, as in a lottery, there is a large element of luck. I write this in haste. We kiss you ten million times and I am your old

MOZART

(125) *Leopold Mozart to his Wife*

[*Extract*]　　　　　　　　　　　　　　　　　　　[*From Nissen, pp. 235–236*]

MILAN, 15 *December* 1770

The first rehearsal with instruments took place on the 12th, but there were only sixteen players, and this rehearsal was held in order to discover whether the score had been copied correctly. On the 17th we shall have the first rehearsal with the full orchestra, which will consist of fourteen first and fourteen second violins, two claviers, six double basses, two violoncellos, two bassoons, six violas, two oboes and two flutes (who, if there are no flutes, always play as four oboes), four horns and two clarinets, about sixty players in all.

Before the first rehearsal with the small orchestra took place, there were plenty of people who cynically described the music beforehand as miserable immature stuff and thus prophesied its failure, because, as they maintained, it was impossible for such a young boy, and, what is more, a German, to write an Italian opera or, great virtuoso though he might be, to grasp and apply the *chiaro ed oscuro* which is necessary for the theatre. But since the evening of the first short rehearsal all these people have been silent and have not uttered a syllable. The copyist is absolutely delighted, which is a good omen in Italy, where, if the music is a success, the copyist by selling the arias sometimes makes more money than the Kapellmeister does by his composition. The singers are quite satisfied and indeed altogether delighted, and especially the prima donna and the primo uomo, who are simply enchanted with their duet. The primo uomo has actually said that if this duet does not go down, he will let himself be *castrated* again. Basta! Everything now depends on the fancy of the public. Apart from the honour, which is a small vanity, the whole business does not interest us very much. In this strange world we have already undertaken many things and God has always assisted us. We now stand on the brink of this enterprise and there are a few circumstances which do not make it easy for us. Yet this time too God will be on our side.

On St. Stephen's day, a good hour after Ave Maria, picture to yourselves Maestro Don Amadeo seated at the clavier in the orchestra and myself a spectator and a listener in a box up above; and do wish him a successful performance and say a few paternosters for him.

(126) *Leopold Mozart to his Wife*

[*Extract*]   [*Autograph in the Library of Congress, Washington*]

MILAN, *22 December* 1770

A Happy New Year!

The first rehearsal in the sala di ridotto was on the 17th and the first rehearsal in the theatre was on the 19th. The latter, thank God, went off very well. Yesterday evening we had a rehearsal of the recitatives, today after Ave Maria there will be a second rehearsal in the theatre, and on Monday the dress rehearsal will take place.

As for the 26th, the day of the performance, my one consolation is that both the singers and the orchestra are evidently quite satisfied; and, thank God, I too still have ears to hear. During the rehearsal I placed myself in the main entrance right at the back in order to hear the music at a distance; but possibly my ears were too partial! Meanwhile we hear that our good friends are hopeful and delighted and indeed they congratulate my son with genuine pleasure; on the other hand the malevolent are now silent. The greatest and most distinguished Kapellmeisters of this town, Fioroni [1] and Sammartini, are our true friends; and so are Lampugnani, Piazza, Colombo and others. Thus the envy, or rather the distrust and the wicked prejudices which some cherished in regard to our son's composition, will not be able to injure him very much. I hope at least that Wolfgang will not have the bad luck of Signor Jommelli, whose second opera at Naples [2] has failed so miserably that people are even wanting to substitute another; and Jommelli is a most celebrated master, of whom the Italians make a terrible fuss. But it was really rather foolish of him to undertake to compose in one year two operas for the same theatre, the more so as he must have realized that his first opera (which we saw) was not a great success. You now know that from the 26th we shall be in the opera house every evening from an hour after Ave Maria until eleven or twelve o'clock, with the exception of Fridays. In about a fortnight I shall be able to inform you of our departure for Turin, whence we shall proceed at break neck speed in order to be able to spend the last days of spring in Venice. Farewell. We kiss you several 100000 times and I am ever your old

MOZART

Picture to yourselves little Wolfgang in a scarlet suit, trimmed with gold braid and lined with sky-blue satin. The tailor is starting to make it today. Wolfgang will wear this suit during the first three days when he is

---

[1] Giovanni Andrea Fioroni (1704–1778) was maestro di cappella at Milan Cathedral from 1747 until his death. He was an important composer of church music.

[2] Jommelli's second opera at Naples, performed on 4 November 1770, was *Demofoonte*, which had been produced at Stuttgart in 1759. His first opera at Naples was *Armida abbandonata*, performed on 30 May 1770.

seated at the clavier. The one which was made for him in Salzburg is too short by half a foot and in any case is too tight and too small.

(126a) *Mozart to his Sister*

[MILAN, 22 *December* 1770]

Find out whether they have this symphony of Mysliwecek's in Salzburg. If not, we shall bring it back with us.

(127) *Leopold Mozart to his Wife*

[*Extract*]   [*Autograph in the Nationalbibliothek, Vienna*]

MILAN, 29 *December* 1770

God be praised, the first performance of the opera took place on the 26th and won general applause; and two things, which have never yet happened in Milan, occurred on that evening. First of all, contrary to the custom of a first night, an aria of the prima donna was repeated, though usually at a first performance the audience never call out 'fuora'. Secondly, after almost all the arias, with the exception of a few at the end, there was extraordinary applause and cries of: 'Evviva il Maestro! Evviva il Maestrino!'

On the 27th two arias of the prima donna were repeated. As it was Thursday and there was Friday to follow, the management had to try to cut down the encores; otherwise the duet would also have been repeated, for the audience were so enthusiastic. But most of the listeners wanted to have some supper at home, and it so happens that this opera with its three ballets lasts six good hours. The ballets, however, are now going to be shortened, for they last two hours at least. How we wished that you and Nannerl could have had the pleasure of seeing the opera!

Within living memory there has never been such eagerness to see the first opera as there has been this time. But there was a very great difference of opinion beforehand and whenever two persons said that it would be a fine one, ten persons at once said that they knew that it was ridiculous stuff, others that it was a horrible mixture, and others again that the music was German and barbarous. In Italy patronage does not in any way help the good reception of an opera, for everyone who goes in wants to talk, shout and criticise it as much as he likes, as he has paid for his seat. But this time protection did help us and was really necessary in order to ensure that the composition should not be rejected, or a spoke put in the wheel of our maestro while he was writing it or even during the rehearsals. Further, we had to see that he was not hindered and that no malevolent members of the orchestra or disagreeable singers should play him any tricks. I write this letter in haste, as the third performance is taking place today. You know that in Italy everyone is given a different name. For instance, Hasse is called Sassone, Galuppi [1] is called Buranello, and so forth. They have christened our son Il Signor Cavaliere Filarmonico.

We kiss you both a hundred thousand times and I am your old

MOZART

(128) *Leopold Mozart to Padre Martini, Bologna*

[Autograph in the Nationalbibliothek, Vienna]

MILAN, 2 January 1771 [2]

MOST REVEREND PADRE MAESTRO,
  MOST ESTEEMED PADRE,

While wishing you a very happy New Year I must inform you that my son's opera has been received most favourably in spite of the great opposition of his enemies and detractors, who, before hearing a single note had spread the rumour that it was a barbarous German composition, without form and content, and impossible for the orchestra to perform, so that they led half the town of Milan to wonder whether it would be anything more than a patchwork. One person had the brilliant idea of bringing the prima donna all her arias, and the duet as well, all of which had been composed by Abbate Gasparini of Turin,[3] with a view to persuading her to insert those arias and not to accept anything composed by this boy, who would certainly never be capable of writing a single good one. But the prima donna said that she would like first of all to try my son's arias; and having tried them she declared that she was satisfied and more than satisfied. Nevertheless the caluminators kept on spreading most evil reports. But the first rehearsal with instruments so effectively stopped the mouths of those cruel and barbarous backbiters that not a word more was heard. All the leading players in the orchestra swore that the opera was clear and straightforward and easy to play; and all the singers declared that they were content. It is usually the misfortune of the first opera in

---

[1] Baldassare Galuppi (1706–1785) was born on the island of Burano, near Venice. He was a successful composer of opere buffe.   [2] This letter is in Italian.
[3] Abbate Quirino Gasparini (? –1778) was maestro di cappella at the court of Turin from 1760–1770. His opera *Mitridate* had been performed there in 1767.

Milan either to fail completely or at least to draw very few spectators, as everybody is waiting for the second one. But during the six performances which have so far taken place, the theatre has always been full and every evening two arias have had to be repeated, while most of the others have been warmly applauded.

My very dear Signor Padre Maestro, we hope to have news of your good health and we still trust that we shall receive the promised Miserere, your most excellent composition, and your work for sixteen performers. Signor Giuseppe Brinsecchi will not fail to refund the expenses of having them copied. And as soon as I reach home, which will be about Eastertide, I shall not fail to send you everything which I think may please you. My son most humbly kisses your hands and, united with him in all reverence and esteem for you, I am, Reverend Father,

your most devoted and grateful servant

LEOPOLDO MOZART

(129) *Leopold Mozart to his Wife*

[*Extract*]   [*Copy in the Deutsche Staatsbibliothek, Berlin*]

MILAN, 5 *January*

behind as before and double in the middle (1771)

I can hardly find time to write to you, for every day we go to the opera and this means going to bed at half past one or even two o'clock in the morning, as we must have something to eat after the performance. So we get up late, and the day, which is short enough as it is, becomes, in consequence, even shorter. We have so many visits to pay that we do not know how we shall ever work them off. We lunched on Thursday with Madame D'Aste, née Marianne Troger, who fed us most magnificently on liver dumplings and sauerkraut, which Wolfgang had asked for, and on other good things, which included a fine capon and a pheasant. Yesterday there was a small concert at Count Firmian's, where Dr. Bridi sang a cantata and then put before Wolfgang a new and difficult concerto, which was a very beautiful one. He delivered your greetings, told us all the news and praised Nannerl very highly. Today we are again lunching with His Excellency. On the 11th or 12th we are off to Turin, but we shall only stay there for about eight days, when we shall return to Milan, pack up everything and go on to Venice. Our second stay here will not exceed four days, but we shall see a performance of the second opera. Our son's opera is still running, is still winning general applause and is, as the Italians say, *alle stelle*! Since the third performance we two have been listeners and spectators, sometimes in the parterre and sometimes in the boxes or palchi, where everyone is eager to speak to the Signore Maestro and see him at close quarters. During the performance we walk about here and there, wherever we like. For the Maestro was obliged to conduct the opera from the orchestra only on the first three evenings, when Maestro Lampugnani accompanied at the second clavier.[1] But now, as Wolfgang is no longer conducting, Lampugnani plays the first clavier and Maestro Melchior Chiesa[6] the second one. If about fifteen or eighteen years ago, when Lampugnani had already composed so much in England and Melchior Chiesa in Italy, and I had heard their operas, arias and symphonies, someone had said to me that these masters would take part in the performance of my son's composition, and, when he left the clavier, would have to sit down and accompany his music, I should have told him that he was fit for a lunatic asylum. So we see what the Almighty Power of God can make of us human beings, if we do not bury the talents which he has most graciously bestowed upon us.

I enclose the local newspapers which I have just received. You will find the opera mentioned right at the end.[3] My greetings to the whole of Salzburg. We kiss you a million times and I am your old

MOZART

Please send these newspapers to His Grace the Prince. You need only take them to His Excellency the Chief Steward.

(130) *Leopold Mozart to his Wife*

[*Autograph in the Mozarteum, Salzburg*]

MILAN, 12 *January* 1771

We are not leaving for Turin until next Monday. I must tell you that I received yesterday from Signor Pietro Lugiati the news that our son has been made a member of the Accademia Filarmonica of Verona and that the Cancelliere dell'Accademia is about to draft his diploma.[4] Thank God, the opera is drawing so well that every day the theatre is full. I remind you once more to buy some linen with which to make shirts, for I am having Wolfgang's sleeves lengthened, so that we may carry on with his little shirts until we get home. Herr Wider has written to me from Venice and I have already replied. Count Firmian has left for Parma and, as Herr Troger is with him and we are now off to Turin, we shall probably receive your letters after considerable delay. We kiss you both many million

---

[1] During the first three performances Mozart, as the custom was, conducted whilst playing the first clavier.

[2] Very little is known about Chiesa. Burney, *op. cit.* p. 113, remarks, 'Chiesa and Monza seem and are said to be the two best composers for the stage here at present'.

[3] Nissen, p. 240 f., quotes an article from a Milan paper of 2 January 1771.

[4] Nissen, p. 241 ff., gives the text of the diploma, adding a German translation.

times. I have nothing to write about and I have a great deal to do, as I have
to send off letters to half the world.

I am your old

MOZART

(130a) *Mozart to his Sister*

[Autograph in the Mozarteum, Salzburg]

DEAREST SISTER,   [MILAN, 12 *January* 1771 [1]]

I have not written for a long time, for I was busy with my opera, but
as I now have time, I will be more attentive to my duty. The opera, God
be praised, is a success, for every evening the theatre is full, much to the
astonishment of everyone, for several people say that since they have been
in Milan they have never seen such crowds at a first opera. Papa and I,
thank God, are well, and I hope that at Easter I shall be able to tell you
and Mamma everything with my own lips. Addio. I kiss Mamma's hand.
A propos! Yesterday the copyist called on us and said that he had orders
to transcribe my opera for the court at Lisbon. Meanwhile farewell, my
dear Mademoiselle sister. I have the honour to be and to remain from now
to all eternity

your faithful brother

(131) *Leopold Mozart to his Wife*

[Extract]   *[Autograph in the Mozarteum, Salzburg]*

MILAN, 2 *February* 1771

I have received four letters from you and you will have had nothing
from me for two post-days. But you will have gathered that our journey
to Turin prevented us from writing. From that very beautiful town,
where we saw a magnificent opera,[2] we returned here on January 31st.
You will hear everything in due course. Address your letters in future to
Herr Wider in Venice. We lunched today with Count Firmian. I have
hardly time to write, as I must pack.

Francesco di Majo, the Kapellmeister, has died at Naples [3] and Caratoli [4]
has travelled from Pisa into the next world.

Dr. Bridi has not said a word about the two concertos. So there is no

---

[1] A postscript to his father's letter. The signature has been cut off the autograph.
[2] WSF, vol. i. p. 332, n. 1, suggest that this opera was either Platania's *Berenice* or Paisiello's
Annibale in Torino, both of which were performed at Turin early in 1771.
[3] He died on 18 January 1771.
[4] Caratoli (1705–1772), a famous basso buffo in his day, was chosen for the part of Cassandro
in Mozart's *La finta semplice*, which was to have been performed in Vienna in 1768. The report
which Leopold Mozart mentions was false, as Caratoli died in Vienna in 1772.

hope of seeing anything of them until he returns in July from his travels for he has gone off with Count Wolkenstein to Naples or Rome.

We hope to arrive in Salzburg for the Feast of St. Joseph[1] or at latest in Passion Week. Our greetings to the whole town. We kiss you ten thousand times and I am your old

MZT.

(132) *Leopold Mozart to his Wife*

[*Extract*]   [*Autograph in the Mozarteum, Salzburg*]

VENICE, *13 February* 1771

Owing to shocking weather and a violent gale we only reached Venice early on Carnival Monday.[2] In the afternoon we managed to find Herr Wider, who, with his wife, accompanied us to the opera. On Tuesday we lunched with him and went to the opera, which began at two and went on until seven. We dined with him afterwards and about eleven or twelve o'clock by German time we were on the Piazza San Marco on our way to the Ridotto. We said to one another that at that moment both of you would probably be with Herr Hagenauer and would be little thinking that we were talking about you on the Piazza San Marco. The weather was horribly wet, but today, Ash Wednesday, it is most beautiful. God be praised, we are well. Whom do you think we met in Brescia? We were on our way to the opera buffa and ran into Signora Angelica Maggiori, prima donna, who is married to a tenor, who was also singing. She was very much surprised to see us. Tell Spitzeder that if he wants to meet his former impresario Crosa, he can find him in Milan, where he goes about begging, miserably clad and with a long beard. Thus it is that God punishes deceivers! You will have heard of the deaths of Caratoli and Laschi.[3] I have received your letter with the note from Herr von Vogt. Farewell, I must hurry. We kiss you a hundred thousand times and I am your old

MOZART

(132a) *Mozart to his Sister*

[*Autograph in the Mozarteum, Salzburg*]

DEAREST SISTER   [VENICE, *13 February* 1771[4]]

Papa will have already told you that I am well. I have nothing to write except that I kiss Mamma's hand. Farewell.

[1] 19 March.
[2] 11 February. The Mozarts remained in Venice until 12 March.
[3] A famous basso buffo, for whom Mozart wrote the part of Fracasso in *La finta semplice*, 1768.
[4] This note and the following one are postscripts to his father's letter. The second note is in Italian.

(132b) *Mozart to Johann Baptist Hagenauer*

[*Autograph in the Mozarteum, Salzburg*]

AL SIGNORE GIOVANNI.

[VENICE, 13 *February* 1771]

The particularly splendid pearl[1] and all the other pearls too admire you very greatly. I assure you that they are all in love with you and that they hope that like a Turk you will marry them all, and make the whole six of them happy. I am writing this in Herr Wider's house. He is a fine fellow, just as you told me in your letter. Yesterday we wound up the carnival at his house, dined with him and then danced and went with the pearls to the new Ridotto, which I liked immensely. When I am at Herr Wider's and look out of the window, I can see the house where you lived when you were in Venice. I have no news for you. I am charmed with Venice. My greetings to your father, mother, sisters, brothers and to all my friends. Addio.

13 February 1771   WOLFGANGO AMADEO MOZART

(133) *Leopold Mozart to his Wife*

[*Extract*]   [*Autograph in the Mozarteum, Salzburg*]

VENICE, 20 *February* 1771

Thank God, we are in good health. Since your letter of February 1st I have received nothing from you, so I do not know whether you have written or not. I am writing this letter again at Herr Wider's, where I wrote my first one, which you will have received. We have lunched with him four times already and his daughters are at the moment engaged in washing and mending my lace cuffs. The elder daughter has presented Wolfgang with a beautiful pair. It is impossible for me to say too much about the honesty of this family, all of whom send their greetings to you and especially to the whole Hagenauer household. If Johannes is always saying nice things about the Widers, I assure you that he can never say enough. I too have had some experience of people in this world, but I have met few, indeed very few, like them. For besides being willing, sincere, absolutely honest and full of human kindness, they are also courteous, they have excellent manners and are not at all puffed up by the kindnesses which they perform. We shall not get away from here before the beginning of next month. But I am still determined to be back in Salzburg if not at the Feast of St. Joseph, at any rate in Passion Week and, with God's help, by Eastertide. Otherwise I have nothing more to write

---

[1] Catarina Wider, one of six daughters of a friend of the Hagenauer family.

to you about, except that we kiss you both ten million times and that I live in hopes of seeing you soon and telling you by word of mouth that I am your old

MOZART

We shall soon have had enough of gondolas. During the first days the whole bed rocked in our sleep and the whole time I was thinking that I was in one of them. We have lunched with the brother of Signor Lugiati. Tomorrow we are lunching with Her Excellency Catarina Cornaro, on Sunday with the Patriarch, on Monday with His Excellency Dolfino, and so forth. Next week we shall be lunching for the most part with nobles.[1]

(133a) *Mozart to his Sister*

[*Autograph in the Mozarteum, Salzburg*]

[VENICE, 20 *February* 1771[2]]

God be praised, I too am still alive and well. De Amicis sang here at San Benedetto. Tell Johannes that Wider's pearls, especially Mademoiselle Catarina, are always talking about him, and that he must soon come back to Venice and submit to the *attacco*, that is, have his bottom spanked when he is lying on the ground, so that he may become a true Venetian. They tried to do it to me—the seven women all together—and yet they could not pull me down. Addio. I kiss Mamma's hand and we both send greetings to all our good friends. Farewell. Amen.

(134) *Leopold Mozart to his Wife*

[*Extract*]   [*Autograph in the Mozarteum, Salzburg*]

VENICE, 1 *March* 1771

Thank God, we are well, and we are always being invited out, now here and now there. So the gondolas of our hosts are constantly in front of our house and every day we ride on the Grande Canal. We shall leave Venice eight days later than I had intended, and we shall have to spend two or three days in Vicenza, for the Bishop, who belongs to the house of Cornaro, will not let us pass through without lunching, or as he would prefer, spending at least two days with him. Then we shall stay three days in Verona, perhaps even four. Nevertheless, unless something untoward should happen to us, which God forbid, we shall be in Salzburg before

---

[1] The last two sentences of this postscript follow 133a.
[2] A postscript to his father's letter.

Easter. I am sorry that during our journey we shall have dismal fast-days all the time. Perhaps we shall reach Reichenhall on Good Friday and hear the usual Passion Play. Later on I shall tell you in detail how I like the Arsenal, the churches, the ospedali[1] and other things, in fact Venice as a whole. Meanwhile I shall content myself with saying that beautiful and unusual things are to be seen here. My pen and ink will tell you that I am writing at the Wider's, where I have this moment received your letter with Adlgasser's enclosure. We send our greetings to him and to his wife. I shall do all he wants and answer his note by word of mouth. As for the opera, we shall not be able to bring it with us, for it is still in the hands of the copyist and he, like all opera copyists in Italy, will not let it out of his hands, as long as he can make his profit. When we left Milan, he had to make five complete copies, one for the Impresa,[2] two for Vienna, one for the Duchess of Parma and one for the Lisbon court, to say nothing of individual arias. And who knows whether the copyist has not received some more orders in the meantime. Even then he told me that I must not expect to see it before Easter, by which time I hope to be in Salzburg; but it will be sent home from Milan. We are again lunching today with Wider who, when we are not invited elsewhere, always entertains us. He and his whole family send their greetings. Indeed I owe him many kindnesses. Next Tuesday we shall give a big concert and on the Sunday before we shall be at the house of the Imperial Ambassador. Addio. Farewell to both. We kiss you many hundred thousand times. I am your old

MOZART

(135) *Leopold Mozart to his Wife*

[Extract]   [Autograph in the Mozarteum, Salzburg]

VENICE, 6 March 1771

You have to thank Wider for this letter, for he has made me write to you, as it is after lunch and I have nothing to do for a little; and besides today is post-day. Yesterday we gave a fine concert and during the last few days we have been so horribly pestered that I do not know who will win the race to secure us. So I cannot get away before Monday, the day I have now fixed for our departure. You must not think, however, that we shall not be in Salzburg by Easter. The extra days which I spend here I shall deduct from the time which I am to spend at other towns, where there will not be so much to detain us, indeed hardly anything. Thank God, we are well and are only sorry that we cannot remain here longer. It is indeed a pity, for we have got to know the whole nobility very well; and every-

---

[1] These were homes for orphans or illegitimate children, which were often great schools of music. Burney, *op. cit.* p. 145 ff., describes his visit to four famous ospedali in Venice.
[2] i.e. the management of the Ducal Theatre at Milan.

where, at parties, at table, and, in fact, on all occasions we are so over-whelmed with honours that our hosts not only send their secretaries to fetch us and convey us home in their gondolas, but often the noble himself accompanies us on our return; and this is true of the greatest of them, for instance, the Cornaro, Grimani, Mocenigo, Dolfino, Valieri and so forth. We have had some beautiful days; but today it is raining hard. I hope that this will not continue, or we shall have a dreadful drive from Padua to Vicenza. Basta! One must take things as they come; and these are matters which never disturb my peaceful sleep, if only we are in good health. After this letter you will hardly have time to send me another, unless per-haps you write to Innsbruck, where I shall call at the post.

Farewell. We kiss you ten thousand times and I am your old

MOZART

(136) *Leopold Mozart to his Wife*

[Extract] [*Autograph in the Mozarteum, Salzburg*]

VICENZA, 14 *March* 1771[1]

On Monday the —— no, on Tuesday the 12th we left Venice, but we let everybody think that we were off on Monday, in order to have one day free in which to pack in peace. Nevertheless the truth leaked out and we had to lunch with Her Excellency Catarina Cornaro, where we were given as presents for our journey a beautiful snuff-box and two pairs of precious lace cuffs. So we sailed away on the 12th. I took a barcello for ourselves and Wider, his wife and his two daughters, Catarina and Rosa; and the Abbate too came with us as far as Padua. They brought food and drink and all other necessaries and we cooked and ate on board. We spent the 13th in Padua and stayed in the Palazzo of the nobleman Pesaro. On the 14th we came on to Vicenza, and they returned to Venice. We saw as much of Padua as can be seen in a day, as there too we were not left in peace and Wolfgang had to play at two houses. Moreover he has received a commission to compose an oratorio for Padua, which he can do at his leisure.[2] We called on Padre Maestro Vallotti[3] at the church of St. Anthony and then on Ferrandini,[4] at whose house Wolfgang had to play. Finally he performed on the excellent organ in the wonderful church of San Giustino. We are spending tomorrow, the 15th, in Vicenza, and not without good reason. On the 16th, God willing, we shall go on to Verona,

---

[1] This letter, which is dated 14 March, was sent off from Verona on 18 March.
[2] *La Betulia liberata.* The text was by Metastasio. During the spring of 1771 Florian Gassmann composed an oratorio on the same text. In 1784 Mozart, hoping to have his oratorio performed in Vienna, added two numbers to his original score. See p. 881.
[3] Padre Francesco Antonio Vallotti (1697–1780), a Franciscan, was the greatest organist in Italy of his day and was maestro di cappella in Padua from 1728 until his death.
[4] Giovanni Ferrandini, a well-known composer and teacher, had just settled in Padua.

where we shall certainly remain for three days and therefore shall not get away before the 20th, when I intend to leave for Rovereto and make for home as quickly as possible. So on Good Friday we shall visit the sacred graves at Reichenhall and then hurry on to Mülln; and we shall certainly sing Alleluja with you on Easter Saturday. But if nothing occurs to hold us up on our journey, we may arrive on Thursday. Perhaps I shall be able to send you more definite news from some stage on our route. I have received your letter with the large seal. Before I saw it I heard that this letter was waiting for me and a thousand ideas occurred to me, for I suspected that it might be a communication from some important quarter.[1]

VERONA, 18 *March* 1771

We arrived here in the evening of the day before yesterday and we shall leave the day after tomorrow. Thus on account of one or two delays we shall not arrive until the afternoon or evening of Good Friday. Today I received from Venice, together with a letter from Wider, your letters with the enclosure from Schiedenhofen. We had a talk yesterday with young Kerschbaumer,[2] who sends greetings to his dear parents. He is well and happy. He came with us to Signor Lugiati's house where we are staying, saw the fine company which had assembled to hear Wolfgang perform and, being thus present, heard him play as well. He is going on to Venice and if I may advise Herr Kerschbaumer, to whom I send my greetings, he ought to entrust his son too to Johann Wider. This is the advice of an honest man. I know what is good and what is bad for young people, especially in Venice, the most dangerous place in all Italy. Yesterday I received a letter from Milan, alluding to one from Vienna, which I am to receive in Salzburg, and which will not only fill you with amazement but will bring our son imperishable honour.[3] The same letter contained another very pleasant piece of news. Farewell to all. We kiss you many hundred thousand times and I am ever your old

MZT

(137) *Leopold Mozart to his Wife*

Extract]   [*Copy in the Deutsche Staatsbibliothek, Berlin*]

INNSBRUCK, *Monday,*
25 *March* 1771

We arrived here this evening in a violent gale, in snow and horribly cold weather. God willing, we shall leave tomorrow. I hope to arrive in

[1] i.e. the Archbishop of Salzburg.
[2] Son of a Salzburg merchant, who kept a shop in the Marktplatz.
[3] The Empress Maria Theresia had commissioned Mozart to compose a dramatic serenata to be performed at Milan in October 1771 on the occasion of the marriage of her son, the Archduke Ferdinand, to Princess Maria Ricciarda Beatrice of Modena.

Salzburg on Thursday afternoon. Addio. Farewell. I must hurry, for the post is leaving.

Your old

MZT

(137a) *Mozart to his Mother and Sister*

[*Copy in the Deutsche Staatsbibliothek, Berlin*]

[INNSBRUCK, 25 *March* 1771 [1]]

I kiss Mamma's hand and I kiss Nannerl thousands of times. Thank God, I am well and I hope to see and talk to you both very soon. My greetings to all my good friends.

WOLFGANG MOZART

[1] A postscript to his father's letter.

Mozart's sixth journey was to Milan, where he carried out a commission from the Empress Maria Theresia to compose a dramatic serenata, Ascanio in Alba, for the marriage of her son, the Archduke Ferdinand, to Princess Maria Ricciarda Beatrice of Modena. He was accompanied by his father. This visit, the second Italian journey, which lasted from 13 August to 15 December 1771, is described in joint letters from father and son to Frau Mozart and Nannerl. Letters 138–158.

(138) *Leopold Mozart to his Wife*

[*Autograph in the Mozarteum, Salzburg*]

BOZEN, *16 August* 1771[1]

It is now striking twelve o'clock. We have had a light lunch and are about to start off in order to reach Trento this evening. Thank God, we are both like two deer, but, I should add, we are not in heat! Farewell to all. We kiss you ten thousand times.

MOZART

(138a) *Mozart to his Mother and Sister*

[*Autograph in the Mozarteum, Salzburg*]

[BOZEN, *16 August* 1771[2]]

I haven't time to write much. We send our greetings to all our good friends. I kiss Mamma and Nannerl many ten thousand times. Addio.

WOLFGANG MOZART

(139) *Leopold Mozart to his Wife*

[*Extract*]   [*Autograph in the Mozarteum, Salzburg*]

VERONA, *18 August* 1771

You will have received my short note from Bozen and now I am going to write to you more fully. The first day of our journey was a regular scramble. At Kaltern the postillion gave the horses some hay and while he was doing so, we ate without sitting down a few slices of boiled beef and with these we drank a measure of very good strong beer. When we reached Waidring we took some soup and some St. Johann's sherbet, which was not at all bad. We had supper at St. Johann and on the 14th we lunched at the post-station at Kundl and had supper at Innsbruck. On the 15th we lunched at Steinach and had supper at Brixen. On the 16th we lunched at Bozen and had supper at Trento. At nine o'clock in the morning of the 17th we arrived at Rovereto, intending to be in Verona that night and at noon on the following day to reach Ala, where we were to give the two Signori Piccinni a surprise. We should have done this if, firstly, we had not spent too much time with Baron Pizzini in Rovereto (where Dr. Bridi also turned up immediately) and thus only left at eleven o'clock and, secondly, we had not met with so many hindrances on the way. For, first of all Lolli, the famous violinist,[3] came to see us; then the

---

[1] The Mozarts left Salzburg on 13 August.   [2] A postscript to his father's letter.
[3] Antonio Lolli. See p. 105, n. 3.

postillions had to change their horses; and the peasants' carts kept on holding us up in the narrow roads. So we did not reach the Piccinnis' house in Ala until one o'clock in the afternoon; and long before our arrival I had decided to spend the night there, as I did not dare to go on to Verona, where the gates are closed at Ave Maria. Moreover the heat was intense and we could go to church in our travelling clothes more easily in Ala than in Verona. There too we passed the time with music, or rather, we entertained our hosts and we did not leave until seven this morning for Verona, where we arrived at Signor Lugiati's house at half past twelve and lunched at one o'clock. After lunch everyone has gone off to sleep and I am making use of the time to scribble this letter with a miserable pen and in very hot weather. With some difficulty I persuaded Wolfgang to sleep too, but he only did so for half an hour. I must tell you that in my hurry I forgot to take with me some clavier sonatas and trios for a good friend in Milan, who has rendered us many services. When Troger goes to Salzburg, ask him to take them and in the meantime get them ready. Nannerl should pick out two trios, one by Joseph Haydn in F with violin and violoncello,[1] one in C by Wagenseil (with variations, please remember) and also Adlgasser's in G; also the little Cassation by Wolfgang in C[2] and some good sonatas by Rutini,[3] for instance, in E♭, in D and so on. If Nannerl wants to play them, she has other copies, for they are amongst the sonatas by Rutini which were engraved in Nuremberg. Give our greetings to Troger and ask him to introduce you to Count Firmian, to whom you should pay your respects, for we owe him a great deal. So do not forget to do this.

I shall write from Milan as soon as possible. Keep well. We kiss you a hundred thousand times and

I am your old

MZT

What beautiful handwriting mine is!

(139a) *Mozart to his Sister*

[*Autograph in the Mozarteum, Salzburg*]

DEAREST SISTER,   [VERONA, 18 *August* 1771[4]]

I have only slept half an hour, for I do not care much about sleeping after a meal. You may trust, believe, opine, hold the opinion, cherish the

---

[1] Op. IV, no. 1, composed in 1766.   [2] There is no trace of this composition.
[3] Giovanni Marco Rutini (1723–1797), born in Florence, where after a prolonged residence in Germany and Austria he became maestro di cappella to the court. He wrote a number of operas, clavier sonatas and some church music. Seven collections of his clavier works had already been published. According to Einstein the sonatas mentioned by Leopold Mozart are Nos. 6 and 2 of Op. VI.   [4] A postscript to his father's letter.

constant hope, consider, imagine, think and be confident that we are well, but I can assure you of the fact. Well, I must hurry. Addio. My greetings to all our good friends. Wish Herr von Hefner[1] from me a prosperous journey and ask him if he has seen anything of Annamiedl? Addio. Keep well. I kiss Mamma's hand. What beautiful handwriting mine is!

WOLFGANG

(140) *Leopold Mozart to his Wife*

[*Extract*]   [*Autograph in the Mozarteum, Salzburg*]

MILAN, 24 *August* 1771

We reached Milan safely on Wednesday, August 21st, after seven in the evening, having spent the whole of Monday with Signor Lugiati in Verona, whence I wrote to you. You will no doubt have received my letter. I ought to tell you that we have not yet received from Vienna the text[2] which everyone is awaiting with great anxiety, for until it arrives the costumes cannot be made, the stage arranged nor other details settled. On October 15th the Archduke[3] will arrive in Milan, alight from his carriage at the Cathedral, enter it and get married. There will be kissing of hands and afterwards a grand supper and then good night! On the following day the celebrations will begin, which I shall describe later on. Meanwhile I have seen twenty thousand pounds of wax candles, waiting to illuminate the Cathedral, the Court and other places on October 15th.

Keep well, both of you. We kiss you many hundred millions of times and I am your old

MOZART

(140a) *Mozart to his Sister*

[*Autograph in the Mozarteum, Salzburg*]

DEAREST SISTER,   [MILAN, 24 *August* 1771[4]]

We suffered greatly from the heat on our journey and the dust worried us most impertinently the whole time, so that we should certainly have been choked to death, if we had not been too clever for that. Here it has not rained for a whole month (or so the Milanese say). Today it began to drizzle a little, but now the sun is shining and it is very hot again. What you promised me (you know what, you dear one!) you will surely

---

[1] Heinrich Wilhelm von Hefner, a son of the town magistrate, Franz von Hefner. According to Hammerle, *op. cit.* p. 8, n., he must have been slightly older than Mozart.
[2] The text *Ascanio in Alba* was by Abbate Giuseppe Parini (1729–1799), a celebrated poet and satirist of the day, who held the chair of rhetoric at Milan University. The text had to be submitted to the Viennese court for its approval.
[3] Archduke Ferdinand (1754–1806), son of the Empress Maria Theresia.
[4] A postscript to his father's letter.

do and I shall certainly be most grateful to you. The Princess[1] had an attack of diarrhœa the other day. Apart from that I have no news. Do send me some. My greetings to all our good friends, and I kiss Mamma's hand. I am simply panting from the heat! So I am tearing open my waistcoat. Addio. Farewell.

WOLFGANG

Upstairs we have a violinist, downstairs another one, in the next room a singing-master who gives lessons, and in the other room opposite ours an oboist. That is good fun when you are composing! It gives you plenty of ideas.

(141) *Leopold Mozart to his Wife*

[*Extract*]   [*Autograph in the Mozarteum, Salzburg*]

MILAN, 31 August 1771

This is the fourth letter which you are receiving from me. I must now praise my sedia, which stood this journey very well. For although we rattled along the Venetian roads from Verona and even from Peri at a terrific pace and over the biggest stones, I did not feel the slightest discomfort. Until we reached Bozen the weather was mild, but from Bozen to Innsbruck it was rather cold. The sun, which came out now and then, drew up in places mists, which collected and came down in rain, so that during our first night at St. Johann I took my flannel jerkin out of our night-bag and put it on, taking it off again at noon at our first stage outside Bozen, while the horses were being changed. Since then it has been warm. My only fear is that it may rain heavily during the marriage, and bad weather on the occasion of such festivities is certainly very inconvenient. The text has arrived at last, but so far Wolfgang has only written the overture, that is, a rather long Allegro, followed by an Andante, which has to be danced, but only by a few people. Instead of the last Allegro he has composed a kind of contredanse and chorus, to be sung and danced at the same time. He will have a good deal of work during the coming month. Hasse arrived yesterday and we are now going out to call on him.[2] We have paid our respects to Her Royal Highness the Princess, who was so gracious that she not only spoke to us for a long time and was most friendly, but, strange to say, rushed up when she saw us, took off her

---

[1] Princess Maria Ricciarda Beatrice of Modena, daughter of the hereditary Prince Ercole Rainaldo.
[2] Hasse had been commissioned to write the opera seria for this festive occasion. His *Ruggiero*, on a text by Metastasio, was performed on October 16th, the day after the Royal wedding.

glove, held out her hand and began to talk before we had time to address her.

Farewell. We kiss you many million times and I am your old

MOZART

(141a) *Mozart to his Sister*

[Autograph in the Mozarteum, Salzburg]

DEAREST SISTER   [MILAN, 31 *August* 1771 [1]]
Praise and thanks be to God, we are well. I have already eaten lots of good pears and peaches and melons for you. My only amusement is to talk the deaf and dumb language, and that I can do to perfection.[2] Hasse arrived yesterday and we are calling on him today. The libretto for the serenata only reached us last Thursday. There is little to write about. I beg you to remember the other matter, if there is nothing else to be done.[3] You know what I mean. Compliments from Herr Germani and especially from his wife who is longing to meet you, from Madame D'Aste and from her husband and from me too. My greetings to all our good friends. I kiss Mamma's hand. Addio.

WOLFGANG

(142) *Leopold Mozart to his Wife*

[*Extract*]   [*Autograph in the Mozarteum, Salzburg*]

MILAN, 7 September 1771

Heaven has refreshed us at last with a little rain which has fallen for a few days in succession. At the moment we are up to the eyes in work, for the libretto arrived late and then remained until two days ago in the poet's hands, because this passage and that had to be altered. I hope it will be a success. Wolfgang is now very busy composing, as he has to write the ballet which links together the two acts or parts.[4]

I hope you are both well. I trust that Nannerl is still taking her soup of herbs, now that she has discovered that it does her good. If Secretary Troger is still in Salzburg, give him a few boxes of Hansl Spielmann pills, which I really need, for I know that they do me good when owing to constipation I get my old giddiness. Since I left Salzburg I have had it a

---

[1] A postscript to his father's letter.
[2] The Mozarts had evidently taken rooms in the same house where they stayed during their second visit to Milan. See p. 168.
[3] Nissen, p. 253, n., mentions the fact that 'a young lady, of whom Mozart was fond, was about to get married'.
[4] Abert, vol. i. p. 276, n. 1, points out that usually the entr'acte ballets were written by some other composer.

good deal, but not so violently as to have to vomit or to be obliged to go to bed. I have only been taking the pills for three days and I notice already that my head is much clearer. But unfortunately I have only eight of them left. We kiss you many million times and I am

your old

L. Mozart

As Nannerl has not written, neither is Wolfgang writing.
Have you received my pay for the month of August?

(143) *Leopold Mozart to his Wife*

[*From Nissen, pp. 254-255*]

Milan, 13 *September* 1771

In twelve days Wolfgang, with God's help, will have completely finished the serenata, which is really an *azione teatrale* in two parts. All the recitatives with and without instruments are ready and so are all the choruses, eight in number, of which five are danced as well as sung. Today we saw the rehearsal of the dances and we greatly admired the hard work of the ballet masters, Pick and Fabier. The first scene is Venus coming out of the clouds accompanied by genii and graces.

The Andante of the symphony is danced by eleven women, that is, eight genii and three graces, or eight graces and three goddesses. The last Allegro of the symphony, which has a chorus of thirty-two voices, eight sopranos, eight contraltos, eight tenors and eight basses, is danced by sixteen persons at the same time, eight men and eight women.

Another chorus is made up of shepherds and shepherdesses, sung by different performers. Further, there are choruses of shepherds alone, tenors and basses, and of shepherdesses alone, sopranos and contraltos. In the last scene all the singers and dancers appear, genii, graces, shepherds and shepherdesses, and they dance the last chorus together. This does not include the solo dancers, Mr. Pick, Madame Binetti, Mr. Fabier and Mlle Blache. The short solo dances, which take place during the choruses, sometimes for two sopranos, sometimes for alto and soprano and so forth, are interspersed with solos for male and female dancers.

The singers in the cantata are:

La Venere,	Signora Falchini, seconda donna
Ascanio,	Signor Manzuoli, primo uomo
Silvia,	Signora Girelli,[1] prima donna

[1] Maria Antonia Girelli-Aguilar had been singing in Gluck's operas.

Aceste, sacerdote,	Signor Tibaldi, tenore
Fauno, pastore,	Signor Solzi, secondo uomo.

I am already making arrangements about Venice 1773.[1]

(143a) *Mozart to his Sister*

[*From Nissen, p. 256*]

DEAREST SISTER,   [MILAN, 13 *September* 1771[2]]

I am only writing in order to—write. But writing is indeed most tiresome, because I have a very heavy cold and a bad cough. Tell Fräulein W. von Mölk[3] that I am indeed longing to be back in Salzburg if only in order to receive once more for the minuets such a present as I was given at her concert. She will know what I mean.

(144) *Leopold Mozart to his Wife*

[*Extract*]   [*Autograph in the Mozarteum, Salzburg*]

MILAN, 21 *September* 1771

After the Angelus today there will be the first instrumental rehearsal of the opera by Signor Hasse, who, thank God, is very well; and towards the end of next week the serenata will be rehearsed. The first rehearsal of the recitatives will take place on Monday and on the following days the choruses will be rehearsed. On Monday or Tuesday at the latest Wolfgang will have finished his work. Signor Manzuoli often comes to see us, but we have only been to see him once. Signor Tibaldi comes almost every day at about eleven o'clock and remains seated at the table till about one, while Wolfgang is composing. Everyone is extremely kind and has the greatest respect for Wolfgang. Indeed we have not experienced any unpleasantness whatsoever, for all these famous singers are most excellent and sensible people. The serenata is really a short opera; indeed, as far as the music is concerned, it is very short and is only lengthened by the two grand ballets which are performed after the first and second acts, each of which will last three quarters of an hour.

There is no room on this sheet to describe the elaborate preparations for

[1] Soon after his arrival at Milan Mozart was commissioned to compose the second opera of the 1773 carnival season for the Teatro San Benedetto in Venice. Probably owing to his previous contract with the Ducal Theatre in Milan to write an opera for the same season, this commission was not carried out. The contract for Venice, signed by the impresario Michele Dall' Agata, and dated 17 August 1771, is given in Nissen, pp. 255-256.

[2] A postscript to his father's letter.

[3] Anna Barbara (Waberl) von Mölk (1752–1828), daughter of Court Chancellor Felix von Mölk. Mozart was then in love with her.

these festivities. All Milan is astir, the more so as a great deal, in fact most of the work has been postponed to the last minute. Consequently everyone is now at work. Some are getting the theatre ready, as the whole building requires to be renovated and redecorated. Others are busy preparing for the reception of His Highness, engaging lodgings and rooms, illuminating and adorning the Cathedral, obtaining garments and liveries for the servants, and horses and carriages and so forth for the balls. There are, in fact, a hundred things to do and I cannot keep them all in my mind. So everyone is frightfully busy! A few days ago Miss Davies[1] arrived here and drove past our house in the mail coach. I recognized her and she saw us, for we happened to be standing on the balcony. A few hours later I went to call on her at the 'Three Kings', which is not very far off, as I guessed that she would be staying there, since it is the most respectable inn. She, her sister, her father and her mother could hardly express their joy. I told their servant where Herr Hasse was staying and very soon his daughter appeared, who also was beside herself with delight, for they have been most cordial friends since they met in Vienna. They all asked for you at once and they send you their greetings. You will surely remember Miss Davies with her armonica? Did you see the rope-dancers when they were in Salzburg? They are now on their way here and ought to arrive very soon. Great work is in progress, for an extraordinarily large hut is being erected for them. The Italian plays came to an end two days ago, for the theatre must now be kept free for rehearsals and the painters must not be prevented from working day and night. These Italian players were uncommonly good, especially in character-plays and tragedies.

Whoever now comes to Milan to attend these wedding festivities will certainly see some fine things. A carriage for four persons would not eat up much money, but the rooms would be a very heavy item. Of course I could take one room for both of us. In the circumstances we should have to camp like soldiers for a short time and have our meals cooked at home.

I have received this very moment your letter of September 13th. In your previous letter you said that many persons have already gone crazy and now you tell me that many have died of dysentery. That is very unfortunate. For when people are attacked both in their heads and in their arses, their condition is indeed dangerous. I must have caught this disease in Salzburg, for I still have frequent attacks of giddiness. But this is not surprising, for evidently the air was already infected, and it is easy to catch

[1] Marianne Davies (1744–1792) first became proficient on the harpsichord and from 1762 onwards won a great reputation for her skill on the armonica or 'musical glasses', an instrument which had been much improved by Benjamin Franklin. In 1768 she and her sister Cecilia, an excellent singer, left England and settled for three years in Vienna, lodging in the same house as Hasse and instructing the daughters of the Empress Maria Theresia. From Vienna the sisters went to Milan, where Cecilia appeared in Hasse's opera *Ruggiero* in 1771. In 1773 they returned to London.

a complaint. That is why I wrote to you about the pills, for I want my arse to cure my head.

We kiss you both 10,000,000 times and I am your old

Lp MOZART

(144a) *Mozart to his Sister*

[Autograph in the Mozarteum, Salzburg]

[MILAN, 21 September 1771 [1]]

Praise and thanks be to God, I am well. I cannot write much, firstly, because I have nothing to say, and secondly, because my fingers ache so from composing. Farewell. I kiss Mamma's hand. I often let off my whistle, but not a soul answers me. There are now only two arias of the serenata to compose and then I shall be finished. My greetings to all my good friends. I no longer want to go home to Salzburg, for I am afraid that I might go crazy too.[2]

WOLFGANG

(145) *Leopold Mozart to his Wife*

[Extract]   [*Autograph in the Mozarteum, Salzburg*]

MILAN, 28 September 1771

This month has simply flown by with amazing rapidity, as we had first of all to wait for the text, and when it arrived, there was always something to do. Our holidays and recreation have now begun, or rather they began last Tuesday, for Wolfgang had already finished everything by Monday,[3] and so on Tuesday we resumed our walks. The first rehearsal with the whole orchestra takes place today. The choruses were rehearsed yesterday, but without the instruments. Give our greetings to Herr Spitzeder and tell him that among our choral singers is a bass, Bianchi by name, whose wife is the leading soprano. This man has twice been to see us in order to press his claims, for he takes a bass part in the Cathedral choir and would very much like to join our Archbishop's Kapelle. But as far as I know, the vacancies for voices have already either been filled or bespoken. You will be pleased to hear that I have good hopes that Wolfgang's work will win great applause; firstly, because both Signor Manzuoli and all the other singers are not only immensely pleased with their arias, but are looking forward even more than we are to hearing the serenata performed this evening with all the instruments; and secondly, because I know how good Wolfgang's work is and what an impression it will make, for it is

---

[1] A postscript to his father's letter.
[2] Mozart is alluding to the last paragraph of his father's letter.   [3] September 23rd.

more than certain that his composition is excellently adapted both to the singers and to the orchestra.

Thank God, we are well. The weather is still lovely and a few very violent storms have satisfied our longing for rain. Everyone is now happy, but we are all wishing that it may keep fine during the wedding. Please tell me in all your letters what sort of weather you are having.[1] Farewell. We kiss you both ten thousand million times and I am your old

MOZART

Our greetings to the whole of Salzburg.

(146) *Leopold Mozart to his Wife*

[Extract]   [Autograph in the Mozarteum, Salzburg]

MILAN, 5 *October* 1771

Count Firmian arrived last Tuesday about eight o'clock in the evening and will leave tomorrow for Mantua to meet His Highness the Prince and accompany him to Milan. I hear too that Count Sauerau is to arrive here shortly and also the Duke of York, who was Duke of Gloucester when we were in England and on his brother's death succeeded to his present title. He is now either in Genoa or in Turin. Yesterday we had a second rehearsal of Wolfgang's cantata, and today the opera is being rehearsed. Then we shall have two days' rest and on Tuesday the cantata will be rehearsed again. The theatre is full from eight o'clock in the morning to eleven o'clock at night, for the dancers are always there. Chaplain Troger, when handing me the pills, told me that you and Nannerl would have liked to come with us. If this was your real feeling, it was very wrong of you not to tell me so quite frankly, though the expense of the outward and return journeys alone would have meant a difference to me of at least sixty ducats. But really you need not feel any regrets, for you would have had to put up with a heat which is incredibly trying. It is true that arrangements are being made for some remarkable entertainments, but they are all shows which you have already seen better performed elsewhere and, on account of the crowd, you would only see them here at great inconvenience and, if you insisted on seeing every bit of the trash, at the risk of your life.

Perhaps some day you will have an opportunity of hearing operas in Italy; and indeed any carnival opera in Milan would be more spectacular than this one is going to be, for apart from the dances Wolfgang's has no embellishment whatsoever. I hope that I shall not need the pills. Thank God, my head is better. The trouble was simply a dreadful stuffiness which

---

[1] Nissen, p. 259, adds the remark: 'He himself always wrote about the weather at great length'.

started in my head while I was on the journey and which was brought on by the great heat. The result was that in six weeks I scarcely used three handkerchiefs, because all the moisture in my brain dried up and stuck fast, thus causing a perpetual giddiness. Foot-baths, inhaling the steam from boiling tea, and finally the change in the weather and the cool damp air have cured me. We have sunshine again and we hope that there will be no rain during the festivities. Farewell. We kiss you many hundred thousand times and I am your old

MOZART

(146a) *Mozart to his Sister*

[*Autograph in the Mozarteum, Salzburg*]

[MILAN, 5 *October* 1771[1]]

Praise and thanks be to God, I too am quite well, but always sleepy. We have been twice to see Count Castelbarco and he was present at my first rehearsal in the theatre. I have no news except that next Tuesday we shall have another rehearsal. What I was going to tell you Papa has snatched from my pen, I mean, he has already written to you. Signora Gabrielli is here and we shall very soon call on her, so that we may get to know all the leading women singers. Addio. Farewell. My greetings to all our good friends.

WOLFGANG

(147) *Leopold Mozart to his Wife*

[*Extract*]   [*Autograph in the Mozarteum, Salzburg*]

MILAN, 12 *October* 1771

Chaplain Troger has made your mouth water for Italy far too much and I agree that for people who have not seen as much of the world as you have, there are many strange things to be seen here. But for you they would not be very wonderful, and Italy can always be visited.

Yesterday the fourth rehearsal of the serenata took place; tomorrow there will be the seventh rehearsal of Signor Sassone's[2] opera and on Monday the last rehearsal of Wolfgang's.

Baron Dupin tells us that he accompanied Nannerl on the violin. The Duke of York has already arrived and also a prince of Saxe-Gotha. The Hereditary Princes, that is, the father and the mother of the Princess bride, have also arrived. Count Sauerau too is here. The crowds are enormous and people will have to see everything in the greatest discomfort. Admirable regulations have been issued, as, for instance, that commoners may

---

[1] A postscript to his father's letter.   [2] i.e. Hasse.

not bear swords or any other arms, that everyone must be identified at the gates and that all householders must hand in to a specially appointed committee a description of their tenants. No one may go about the streets at night without a light. Soldiers and sbirri patrol the town and hussars its outskirts. Everyone must have tickets for the opera, the serenata, the ball, the court banquet and all other festivities and so on.

I must close, for we have to check the two copies of the serenata, which were made in a hurry for His Majesty the Emperor and for the Archduke, and which must now be bound; and there is a great deal to correct, for Italian copyists make shocking mistakes. We kiss you both many hundred thousand times and I am your old

MOZART

Our greetings to all.

The Archduke will arrive in the evening of the 15th and the wedding will then take place. After it is over, there will be the kissing of hands at court, followed by two hours of music and a banquet. On the 16th there will be the opera, the 17th the serenata, on the 18th, 19th and 20th nothing on account of the anniversary of the death of His Majesty the Emperor.[1] On Monday the serenata will be repeated and so forth.

(148) *Leopold Mozart to his Wife*

[Extract]   [*Autograph in the Mozarteum, Salzburg*]

MILAN, 19 October 1771

Marcobruni sends greetings to you. He is with me and we are just off to the theatre. For on the 16th the opera was performed and on the 17th Wolfgang's serenata, which was such an extraordinary success that it has to be repeated today. The Archduke recently ordered two copies. We are constantly addressed in the street by courtiers and other persons who wish to congratulate the young composer. It really distresses me very greatly, but Wolfgang's serenata has killed Hasse's opera more than I can say in detail. In my next letter I shall reply to your last one and to Nannerl's postscript. You will both see Italy more pleasantly later on than you would now during this horrible rush. Addio. We kiss you both many ten thousand times. I am

your old

MZT

Pray to God and thank Him!

Troger sends his greetings, especially to you and to Nannerl who is sighing so deeply for Milan.

---

[1] Possibly the Emperor Charles VI, who died on 20 October 1740.

(149) *Leopold Mozart to his Wife*

[Extract] [*Autograph in the Mozarteum, Salzburg*]

MILAN, 26 October 1771

I have received your letter from Triebenbach and I am delighted that you both had a good time. Perhaps some report will have reached Salzburg of the tremendous applause which Wolfgang's serenata has won; for young Kerschbaumer, who is here for a few days, both saw and heard in the theatre how on October 24th, the day before yesterday, Their Royal Highnesses the Archduke and Archduchess not only caused two arias to be repeated by applauding them, but both during the serenata and afterwards leaned over from their box towards Wolfgang and showed their gracious approval by calling out 'Bravissimo, *maestro*' and clapping their hands. Their applause was taken up each time by the courtiers and the whole audience.

Today there is the opera, but yesterday, being Friday, there was no performance. Tomorrow and the day after we shall have the serenata again. The Archduke and his wife are well and very happy. This will give great pleasure to Her Majesty the Empress, for some anxiety was felt lest he should not have been pleased with his bride, because she is not beautiful. On the other hand she is unusually friendly, agreeable and virtuous, and greatly beloved by everyone; and she has completely won over the Archduke, for she has the best heart and the most pleasant manners in the world. Take care of yourselves. We kiss you a hundred million times and I am ever your faithful

MZT

If you need some clothes, get what is necessary made for you, for neither you nor Nannerl must do without necessities. What must be, must be. And do not buy inferior materials, since to buy shoddy stuff is no economy. Have a handsome dress made for festivals and put on every day the clothes which were made for you in Vienna. But do not buy woollen material, which is not worth a fig.

(149a) *Mozart to his Sister*

[*Autograph in the Mozarteum, Salzburg*]

DEAREST SISTER, [MILAN, 26 October 1771[1]]

Praise and thanks be to God, I too am well. As my work is now finished, I have more time to write letters. But I have nothing to say, for Papa has told you everything already. I have no news except that numbers 35, 59,

---

[1] A postscript to his father's letter.

60, 61, 62 were drawn in the lottery; and so, if we had taken these numbers, we should have won. But as we did not take any tickets, we have neither won nor lost, but we have had our laugh at other people who did. The two arias which were encored in the serenata were sung by Manzuoli and by the prima donna, Girelli, respectively. I hope you will have a good time at Triebenbach and get some shooting and walking too, if the weather permits. We are now off to the opera. My compliments to all our good friends. Baron Dupin is a frequent visitor at the house of the Mademoiselle who plays the clavier,[1] and so we often meet him. I kiss Mamma's hand. Farewell. I am, as always, your faithful brother

WOLFGANG

PS. Excuse this shocking writing, but I am in a hurry.

(150) *Leopold Mozart to his Wife*

[*Autograph in the Mozarteum, Salzburg*]

MILAN, 2 *November* 1771

We are delighted that you had a good time at Triebenbach and that you reached home again safe and well. I am staying indoors for a few days, because I have had very bad rheumatism all over me, which I have almost altogether steamed away simply by drinking elderberry tea. Among our medicines we had only one single black powder. Fortunately Signora d'Aste has quantities of them. As we had only one digestive powder left, she sent off the prescription, which luckily she happened to have, to the chemist and procured some more for me. This is a silly story, I admit, for when you read it, I hope that I shall not only be perfectly well, but soon quite ready to leave. So when you receive this letter, you may write to Verona, al Signor Lugiati. I have already told you that the serenata has won the day. Farewell. We kiss you both many hundred million times and I am your old

MOZART

I still have to write an answer to His Excellency Count Pallavicini, who has sent me an extremely courteous letter.

(150a) *Mozart to his Mother and Sister*

[*From Nissen, pp. 261-262*]

[MILAN, 2 *November* 1771[2]]

Papa says that Herr Kerschbaumer has undoubtedly made good use of his travels and kept his eyes open, and we can assure you that he has be-

---

[1] Probably Marianne Davies. See p. 198, n. 1.
[2] A postscript to his father's letter. Nissen, p. 261, adds that the first portion of this postscript, which he omits, is a description of all the festivities which have taken place.

haved very sensibly. He will certainly be able to tell you more about his tour than some of his friends, one of whom could not see Paris properly, because the houses there are too high. There is a performance of Hasse's opera today, but as Papa is not going out, I cannot be there. Fortunately I know nearly all the arias by heart and so I can see and hear it at home in my head.

(151) *Leopold Mozart to his Wife*

[Autograph in the Mozarteum, Salzburg]

MILAN, *9 November* 1771

I write in great haste to say that I have received your congratulations and the whole parcel of letters. Wolfgang will express his own thanks, God willing, at the end of this month or during the first days of December. Thank God, I am quite well again. We lunched yesterday with Count Firmian in the company of Hasse. Both he and Wolfgang have received beautiful presents for their compositions. Apart from the money they have got, Hasse has been given a snuff-box and Wolfgang a watch set in diamonds. I have already told you in my last letter not to send any more letters to Milan, but to write to Verona, whence you will shortly receive letters from me, telling you whether we shall go for a few days to Padua or travel straight home. Should a post-day pass without a letter from me, then you will know that I am en route and can no longer write. Addio. We kiss you many ten million times and I am ever your old

MOZART

(151a) *Mozart to his Sister*

[Autograph in the Mozarteum, Salzburg]

DEAREST SISTER,   MILAN, *9 November* 1771 [1]

I kiss Mamma's hand and send greetings to all our friends. Meanwhile I send my thanks in great haste to all who have congratulated me.[2] I shall thank them better when I see them. Farewell.

WOLFGANG

(152) *Leopold Mozart to his Wife*

[Extract]   *[Autograph in the Mozarteum, Salzburg]*

MILAN, *16 November* 1771

I have received your letter of November 8th. I hoped to leave for certain on the 18th, but His Royal Highness the Archduke now wishes to

---

[1] A postscript to his father's letter.
[2] Probably on his name-day, October 31st, as well as on the success of *Ascanio in Alba*.

speak to us when he returns from Varese in a week's time. So our stay here will have to be prolonged for more than ten days. Patience! God willing, we shall soon meet again.

Thank all our good friends for their cordial congratulations. I owe Herr von Haffner an answer; but in the meantime give him my sincere thanks and greetings. My head is full and I have more things to think of than you can guess. That the serenata was extremely successful is quite true, but I very much doubt whether, if a paid appointment is vacant, His Grace will remember Wolfgang.[1] Now I must close, for I still have to write a letter to Verona. Send your letters there, addressed to Signor Pietro Lugiati, who will give them to me. Farewell. We kiss you both ten thousand million times and I am your old

MOZART.

(153) *Leopold Mozart to his Wife*

[*Autograph formerly in the possession of Frau Jähns, Berlin*]

MILAN, 24 or 23 *November* 1771

We are still here and we shall probably stay on for another week, for the Archduke is not returning from Varese until Tuesday, when he will receive us. Yet, God willing, we shall reach home during the first fortnight of December, for, even if we break our journey on the way, we shall cover the ground from here to Salzburg in a week. Thank God, we are well. Address your next letter to Verona and I think it ought to be your last, if in the meantime you do not receive another one from me. The weather here is still cold, but very fine and it has not rained for a long time. Marcobruni, in whose room I am writing, sends his greetings to you both, and so do the Trogers and Signor and Signora d'Aste. Mysliwecek, who arrived yesterday and is writing the first opera,[2] was with us today. Herr von Mayr and Herr Chiusole[3] also send their greetings. We often meet them, and we had music for several hours yesterday in Mayr's rooms. We kiss you a hundred thousand times and I am your old

MOZART

---

[1] Mozart had been appointed Konzertmeister to Archbishop Sigismund on 27 November 1769, but, possibly owing to the former's frequent absences from Salzburg, the appointment, to which an annual salary of 150 gulden was attached, did not take effect until April 1772, after the installation of the new Archbishop, Hieronymus Colloredo.

[2] Mysliwecek's opera *Il gran Tamerlano*, on a text by Agostino Piovene, was performed on 26 December 1771.

[3] Dominicus di Chiusole—a high steward of the Prince-Archbishop.

(153a) *Mozart to his Sister*

[Autograph formerly in the possession of Frau Jähns, Berlin]

MILAN, 24 *November* 1771 [1]

Herr von Alphen [2] is here and is just the same as he was at Vienna and Paris. I have some more news too. Manzuoli, who up to the present has been generally looked upon as the most sensible of the castrati, has in his old age [3] given the world a sample of his stupidity and conceit. He was engaged for the opera at a salary of five hundred cigliati, but, as the contract did not mention the serenata, he demanded another five hundred for that, that is, one thousand cigliati in all. The court only gave him seven hundred and a fine gold snuff-box (quite enough, I think). But he like a true castrato returned both the seven hundred cigliati and the snuff-box and went off without anything. I do not know how it will all end—badly, I expect. I have no other news. I kiss Mamma's hand. I send greetings to all my good friends. Addio. Farewell. I am your true and faithful brother

WOLFGANG

(154) *Leopold Mozart to his Wife*

[Extract]   *[Autograph in the Mozarteum, Salzburg]*

MILAN, 30 *November* [1771]

I never thought that at the end of November I should still be in Milan, but circumstances have detained me. Moreover, it is Advent and in Salzburg no concerts are held at court. So the arrangement still stands that I shall arrive home during the first fortnight of December. Yes, even if I leave here on December 2nd or 3rd, I can easily reach Salzburg on the 9th or 10th. Thank God, we are well, and that is the best news I can send you. The weather here is extraordinarily cold, but very fine. I shall find your letters in Verona, if you have written; for now you may certainly go on doing so. Hoping to see you soon, we kiss you many ten million times and I am your old

MOZART

(154a) *Mozart to his Mother and Sister*

[Autograph in the Mozarteum, Salzburg]

[MILAN, 30 *November* 1771 [4]]

Lest you should think that I am unwell I am sending you these few lines. I kiss Mamma's hand. My greetings to all our good friends. I have

---

[1] A postscript to his father's letter.
[2] Eusebius Johann Alphen (1741–1772), born in Vienna, made his mark as a miniature-painter. Abert, vol. ii. p. 1037, n. 3, suggests that during the Mozart's second visit to Paris in 1766, Alphen may have done the small ivory miniature of Wolfgang and Nannerl which is now in the Mozart Museum, Salzburg.
[3] He was forty-six.   [4] A postscript to his father's letter.

seen four rascals hanged here in the Piazza del Duomo. They hang them just as they do in Lyons.

WOLFGANG

(155) *Leopold Mozart to his Wife*

[Autograph in the Mozarteum, Salzburg]

ALA, *8 December* 1771

At four o'clock in the afternoon of today we arrived here and we shall spend the night with the Piccinnis and then go on tomorrow to Trento. There we shall spend the day, for I have to carry out some commissions from Milan. I think that when you read this letter we shall be driving towards Salzburg, where we shall arrive in the evening, if not earlier. As soon as you receive it, open the small room, so that on our arrival it may not be quite cold. For as Wolfgang will sleep there and not in the back room, you should leave the door open so that the air may be warmed up. The question which you asked me in one of your four letters which I found in Verona, I shall answer when we meet. All that I can now say is that the affair is not quite hopeless. Farewell. We kiss you many million times and I am your old

MZT.

(156) *Leopold Mozart to his Wife*

[Autograph in the Mozarteum, Salzburg]

BRIXEN, 11 *December* 1771

We shall not arrive until Monday, as Count Spaur, who is keeping us here and sends you a thousand greetings, refuses to let us go. Moreover the days are short and the roads are bad, so that we really cannot leave.[1] We kiss you many hundred thousand times and I am your old

MZT.

(157) *Leopold Mozart to the Cathedral Chapter of the Archbishopric of Salzburg*

[Autograph in the Regierungsarchiv, Salzburg]

[SALZBURG, 16 *December* 1771]

MY LORDS PROVOST, DEAN, SENIOR AND
  THE WHOLE CATHEDRAL CHAPTER OF THE
    ARCHBISHOPRIC OF SALZBURG,
  Your Excellencies will be aware that Her Imperial Majesty was

[1] The Mozarts reached Salzburg on December 15th.

208

graciously pleased to summon my son to Milan to compose a dramatic
serenata for performance on the occasion of the wedding festivities there,
and that His Excellency Count Firmian in a letter to his brother the Chief
Steward endeavoured to obtain from the late Archbishop [1] permission for
me to accompany my son to Italy. His Grace gave us leave to travel but
at the same time suspended my salary which, as it is, amounts only to
28 gulden, 30 kreuzer a month, and which, through an oversight, I was
permitted to draw for a further month and a half.

His Excellency the Count von Sauerau wrote, however, to the Court
Chancellor and sent him the pleasant news of the unanimous applause and
the honour which my son had won for himself. Whereupon His Grace
immediately gave me leave to retain the sum already paid.

I am submitting, therefore, to Your Excellencies and most gracious
Lords my most humble request that the small amount deducted, that is,
59 gulden for the months of October and November, be paid to me in full.

                    I remain
                Your Excellencies' most
                obedient servant
                            LEOPOLD MOZART
                            Deputy-Kapellmeister

(158) *Leopold Mozart to J. G. I. Breitkopf, Leipzig*

[*Extract*]   [*Copy in the Deutsche Staatsbibliothek, Berlin*]

                            [SALZBURG, 7 *February* 1772]

We arrived back from Milan on December 15th. As my son has again
won great honour by his composition of the dramatic serenata, he has been
asked to write the first opera for the coming carnival in Milan [2] and
immediately afterwards the second opera for the Teatro San Benedetto
in Venice. [3] We shall therefore remain in Salzburg until the end of September and then travel to Italy for the third time.

Should you wish to print any of my son's compositions, this intervening
period would be the best time to order them. You have only to state what
you consider most suitable. He can let you have clavier compositions or
trios for two violins and violoncello, or quartets for two violins, viola and
violoncello, or symphonies for two violins, viola, two horns, two oboes
or transverse flutes, and double bass. In short, my son will write whatever

---

[1] Count Sigismund von Schrattenbach, who had been Archbishop of Salzburg since 1753,
had died that day. He was succeeded on 14 March 1772, by Hieronymus Joseph Franz von
Paula, Count Colloredo, who had been Bishop of Gurk. Mozart was commissioned to write
the festival opera *Il sogno di Scipione* to celebrate his formal installation on 29 April 1772.
[2] Nissen, pp. 264-265, quotes this contract, dated 4 March 1771, and signed by Federico
Castiglione, manager of the Ducal Theatre.
[3] See p. 197, n. 1.

kind of composition you may consider most profitable to yourself, provided you let us know in good time.

Your obedient servant

LEOPOLD MOZART

Salzburg, 7 February 1772

Have you had any news from our friend M. Grimm? Have you sold any copies of the portraits and the sonatas?

Mozart's seventh journey was again to Milan, where he carried out a commission to write the first opera Lucio Silla for the 1772–1773 carnival season. During his short stay in Italy Mozart composed six string quartets. This visit, the third Italian journey, which lasted from 24 October 1772 to 13 March 1773, is described in joint letters from father and son to Frau Mozart and Nannerl. Letters 159–176.

(159) *Leopold Mozart to his Wife*

[*Extract*]   [*Autograph in the Mozarteum, Salzburg*]

BOZEN, 28 *October* 1772

Have we not travelled a great distance, seeing that we are now in Bozen? We reached St. Johann on the first day before eight o'clock in the evening,[1] but as on the following day, which was Sunday, there was no Mass earlier than six o'clock matins, we only got away at seven o'clock, and did not reach Innsbruck until about ten o'clock. We spent Monday there and in the afternoon drove to Hall to visit the Royal Convent, where Countess Lodron, the sister of the wife of our Chief Steward,[2] showed us everything and Wolfgang played on the organ in the church. We got as far as Brixen yesterday and arrived in Bozen today at noon; and here we are staying, as otherwise we should have to drive to Trento very late at night and in the most drenching rain which began this afternoon. Nor is there on the road any convenient lodging for the night. So with God's help we shall move on there tomorrow morning at five o'clock. We called on Frater Vincenz Ranftl in the Dominican monastery of this gloomy town. He is very well and sends his greetings to the whole of Salzburg.

Thank God, my health is now more or less restored, in spite of our irregular way of living. If travelling is necessary for it, I shall try to obtain a post as courier or perhaps become a mail coach conductor. Wolfgang is well too and at the moment is writing a quartet[3] to while away the time. He sends greetings to everyone.

Farewell. We kiss you many thousand times and I am your old

MZT.

(159a) *Mozart to his Sister*

[*Autograph in the Mozarteum, Salzburg*]

[BOZEN, 28 *October* 1772[4]]

We have already reached Bozen. Already? I mean, at last. I am hungry, thirsty, sleepy and lazy, but I feel well. In Hall we visited the Convent and I played on the organ. If you see Nannerl Nader, tell her I have spoken to Herr Brindl, her beloved, who sends greetings to her. I hope that you have kept your word and that ⟨last Sunday you went to see D.N.⟩ Farewell. Let me have some news. Bozen—this pigsty.

---

[1] The Mozarts left Salzburg on Saturday, October 24th.   [2] Count Firmian.
[3] Probably either K. 155 [134a] or K. 157.   [4] A postscript to his father's letter.

Here is a poem about someone who became wild and enraged with Bozen.

> If to Bozen I must come,
> Faith, I'd rather cut my thumb.

(160) *Mozart to his Mother*

[Autograph in the Bibliothèque de Lille]

MILAN, 7 *November* 1772

Do not be alarmed at seeing my handwriting instead of Papa's. The reasons are as follows: (1) We are at Signor d'Aste's [1] and Baron Cristani is here and they all have so much to talk about that Papa simply cannot get time to write; and (2) He is too lazy. We arrived here on the 4th at noon and we are well. All our good friends are in the country or at Mantua except Signor d'Aste and his wife, who have asked me to send their greetings to you and to my sister. Mysliwecek is still here. There is no truth in the report which is being so vigorously discussed in Germany of an Italian war or of the fortifying of the castle at Milan. Excuse my wretched handwriting. When you write to us, do so direct, for it is not the custom here, as it is in Germany, for people to carry letters about, but they have to be fetched at the post and so we go there every post-day to get them. There is no news here, but we are waiting for some from Salzburg. We hope that you received our letter from Bozen. Well, I cannot think of anything else, so I shall close. Our greetings to all our good friends. We kiss Mamma 100,000 times (I did not bring any more noughts with me) and I kiss Mamma's hands and prefer to embrace my sister in person rather than in imagination.

(160a) *Mozart to his Sister*

[Autograph in the Bibliothèque de Lille]

DEAREST SISTER,   [MILAN, 7 *November* 1772 [2]]

I hope that you have been to see the lady—⟨you know who. If you see her,⟩ please give her ⟨my compliments.⟩ I hope, and indeed I do not doubt, that you are in good health. I forgot to tell you that we have run across Signor Belardo here, the dancer, whom we knew at The Hague and at Amsterdam. It was he who attacked the dancer, Signor

---

[1] The Mozarts arrived at Milan on November 4th and stayed with the d'Astes.
[2] This letter is in Italian.

Neri,[1] with his sword, because he thought that it was owing to the latter that he had been refused permission to dance in the theatre.

Addio. Do not forget me. I am ever your

faithful brother

AMADEO WOLFGANGO
MOZART

(160b) *Leopold Mozart to his Wife*

[Autograph in the Bibliothèque de Lille]

[MILAN, 7 *November* 1772[2]]

We spent Wolfgang's name-day[3] very cheerfully at Ala with the two brothers Piccinni and we also stayed at Verona. We then came on to Milan. The weather is always fine here, and indeed the only rain we have had during our journey was in the afternoon of the day after St. Simon and St. Jude.[4] That was all. Keep well! Addio!

In Verona and here too we have seen comic operas.

(161) *Leopold Mozart to his Wife*

[Extract]   *[Autograph in the Mozarteum, Salzburg]*

MILAN, 14 *November* 1772

You will have received our first letter from Milan. After three days of travelling my health is so good that I am really surprised, for we have been living very irregularly, especially on the journey from Verona to Milan. Yet now that I have been here for almost a fortnight, some trifling disorders have begun to plague me again; indeed I drop into thinking about Salzburg and, without noticing it, I go on brooding for some time. However, I quickly banish these thoughts or at least try to do so, just as I used to drive out all those wicked ideas which in my youth the devil suggested to me.

Not one of the singers has arrived yet except Signora Suarti, who sings the part of the secondo uomo, and the ultimo tenore.[5] The primo uomo, Signor Rauzzini, is expected shortly. But Signora De Amicis will not be here until the end of this month or the beginning of December. Meanwhile Wolfgang has got much amusement from composing the choruses, of which there are three, and from altering and partly rewriting the few

---

[1] Neri appears in Leopold Mozart's *Reiseaufzeichnungen*, p. 45, under 'Amsterdam'.
[2] A postscript to Mozart's letter.   [3] October 31st.   [4] October 30th.
[5] The second tenor, Giuseppe Onofrio.

recitatives which he composed in Salzburg. For the poet¹ sent the libretto to Abbate Metastasio in Vienna for his approval and the latter, after correcting and altering a good deal, added a whole scene in the second act. Wolfgang has now written all the recitatives and the overture. So Herr Leutgeb² wants to go to Rome? And I am to write and tell him whether there is an opening here? That is most difficult! If he were here during the first few days of December, there would be some hope of his being asked to accompany an aria in the opera. But, once they are written, it is too late. He ought to travel via Brescia, where he could call on Count Lecchi, who is a first-rate violinist and a great connoisseur and amateur of music, with whom we have promised to stay on our return journey. It is not so easy to give a public concert here and it is scarcely any use attempting to do so without special patronage, while even then one is sometimes swindled out of one's profits. Apart from this he would lose nothing and he could live with us and would therefore have no expenses for light and wood. I hear that M. Baudace, the Frenchman, will soon be here with his French horn. Basta! Leutgeb will not lose anything; but he will have to be here in good time if he wants to get work in the opera. So he ought to leave with the mail coach at the very beginning of December, so that he may arrive here in time; for the opera is to be produced on December 26th. What about his leave of absence?

Farewell. We kiss you many hundred million times and I am your old

L MZT

The variations are in my writing-case, where I usually write; but Nannerl must not give them away, for there are some mistakes in them.

(162) *Leopold Mozart to his Wife*

[*Extract*]   [*Autograph in the possession of the Wittgenstein family*]

MILAN, 21 *November* 1772

Thank God, we are well and strong and like fish in water, for it has rained heavily for the last week. Today is the anniversary of our wedding day. It was twenty-five years ago, I think, that we had the sensible idea of getting married, one which we had cherished, it is true, for many years. All good things take time!

The primo uomo, Signor Rauzzini, has just arrived; so now there will be more and more to do and things will become increasingly lively. But

¹ The libretto of *Lucio Silla* had been written by Giovanni De Gamerra (1743–1803) of Leghorn, who first became a priest and then a soldier. He wrote a number of dramas and even attempted to establish a national theatre at Naples. He also translated into Italian the text of Mozart's *Zauberflöte*, which was performed in his rendering at Dresden, 2 April 1794.

² See p. 78 note 2.

there will also be no lack of those charming incidents which are usual in the theatre. However, they are of little importance. The figs which Wolfgang was given when he left Salzburg have been as miraculous as the loaves and fishes in the Gospel, for they have lasted until now.

Yes indeed, there is a great deal to do at the moment. Even if it is not work, all sorts of arrangements have to be made.

(162a) *Mozart to his Sister*

[Autograph in the possession of the Wittgenstein family]

[MILAN, 21 *November* 1772 [1]]

I thank you, you know for what. I ask Herr von Hefner to forgive me for not yet replying to his letter, but it has been and still is impossible to do so, for as soon as I get home, there is always something to write; often something is already lying on the table; and out of doors, in the street, I can't possibly write. If you see him, let him read the following and tell him that he must content himself with it for the present. I shall not take it amiss that my paltry friend has not replied to me. As soon as he has time, he will surely, without doubt, doubtless, certainly, and undeniably send me an answer. My greetings to all my good friends. I kiss Mamma's hands. Well fare and news me soon some send. The Germany from post has not yet arrived.

Milano à, 2771, November 12 the. Oidda.

I usual as am

MOZART WOLFGANG

(163) *Leopold Mozart to his Wife*

[Extract]   *[Autograph in the Mozarteum, Salzburg]*

MILAN, 28 *November* 1772

I have received today your letter of the 20th. You want me to write very fully, but what is there to write about? Our best news is that, thank God, we are both well. There is no one here, for almost everyone is in the country and will not return to Milan until Christmas, when the festivities will begin with the re-opening of the theatre. Even the Archduke is out of town. As for my headache, I do not get it very often and it is only occasionally that I am seized for a few moments by my old giddiness which comes on when I turn over or raise myself in bed at night. At the same time I have a perfectly healthy appetite. But we only eat once a day, at two o'clock in the afternoon. In the evening we have an apple and a slice of bread and we drink a small glass of wine.

[1] A postscript to his father's letter.

I am writing in the house of Madame d'Aste, who sends her greetings to you. Monsieur d'Aste asks me to tell you that he is very much disappointed that you did not send greetings to him also. For I opened your last letter in their house and read it aloud. Signora De Amicis is to leave Venice today and will therefore be here in a few days; then the work will be really enjoyable. Up to the present very little has been done. Wolfgang has only composed the first aria for the primo uomo, but it is superlatively beautiful and he sings it like an angel. Addio. Farewell. We kiss you many hundred thousand times and I am your old

MZT

(163a) *Mozart to his Sister*

[Autograph in the Mozarteum, Salzburg]

[MILAN, 28 November 1772 [1]]

We both send congratulations to Herr von Amann. Please tell him from me that I am vexed that he always made a secret of it, whenever I said anything to him about his fiancée. I should have thought that he was more sincere. I have greetings to deliver from Herr and Frau von Germani. They too are sorry that they cannot be with you. One thing more. Please tell Herr von Amann that if he intends his wedding to be the real thing, he should be so kind as to wait until our return in order that what he promised me may come true, that is, that I should dance at his wedding. Farewell. I kiss Mamma's hand. My greetings to all our good friends. ⟨Tell Herr Leutgeb to take the plunge and come to Milan, for he will certainly make his mark here.⟩ But he must come soon. Do not forget to tell him this, for I am very anxious that he should come. Adieu.

(164) *Leopold Mozart to his Wife*

[Extract]

[Autograph in the Mozarteum, Salzburg]

MILAN, 5 December 1772

Signora De Amicis, who sends greetings to you both and also to Adlgasser, turned up very late last night. Her journey from Venice to Milan by mail coach with six horses took a week, as the roads were so flooded and muddy. Unfortunately poor Cordoni, the tenor, is so ill that he cannot come. So the Secretary to the Theatre has been sent off by special post-chaise to Turin and a courier has been despatched to Bologna to find some other good tenor, who, as he has to play the part of Lucio Silla, must not only sing well, but be a first-rate actor and have a hand-

---

[1] A postscript to his father's letter.

some presence. As the prima donna only arrived yesterday and as it is not yet known who the tenor will be, you will realize that the major and most important portion of the opera has not yet been composed; but now great strides will be made.

Does Kapellmeister Lolli still conduct in the Cathedral?

We both send greetings to all our good friends in the promised land of Salzburg. We kiss you ten million times through the damp air, for here the weather is rainy, and I am

your old

MZT

(164a) *Mozart to his Sister*

[Autograph in the Mozarteum, Salzburg]

[MILAN, 5 December 1772 [1]]

I still have fourteen numbers to compose and then I shall have finished. But indeed the trio and the duet might well count as four. It is impossible for me to write much, as I have no news and, moreover, I do not know what I am writing, for I can think of nothing but my opera and I am in danger of writing down not words but a whole aria. I have greetings to deliver from Herr and Frau von Germani to Mamma, to you and to Adlgasser. I have learnt a new game here in Milan, called: *Mercante in fiera*, and as soon as I come home, we shall play it. I have also learnt from Frau d'Aste a new language which is easy to speak, but troublesome though not impossible to write; it is a little bit childish, but it will do for Salzburg. Addio. Farewell. Remember me to our beautiful Nannie and to the canary, for these two and you are the most innocent creatures in our house. I suppose Fischietti [2] will soon be setting to work at an opera buffa, which, when translated, means 'crazy opera'. Addio. I kiss Mamma's hand.

(165) *Leopold Mozart to his Wife*

[*Extract*]   [*Autograph in the Mozarteum, Salzburg*]

MILAN, 12 December 1772

I received today your letter of December 4th. Thank God, we are well, myself especially. During the coming week, while this letter is wending its way to Salzburg, Wolfgang will have his heaviest work. For these blessed theatrical people leave everything to the very last minute. The tenor [3] who

---

[1] A postscript to his father's letter.

[2] Domenico Fischietti, born in 1725 at Naples, was Kapellmeister at Dresden from 1765 until 1772, when he was appointed Kapellmeister at Salzburg, a post which he held until 1783. He composed many comic operas and also oratorios.

[3] Bassano Morgnoni, who was from Lodi, not from Turin.

is coming from Turin belongs to the King's Cappella. He is expected about the 14th or 15th and not until he arrives can his four arias be composed for him. Signora De Amicis sends greetings to you both. She is very well satisfied with the three arias which she has had so far. Wolfgang has introduced into her principal aria[1] passages which are unusual, quite unique and extremely difficult and which she sings amazingly well. We are very friendly and intimate with her. I am writing with a wretched pen and very poor ink, as Wolfgang, who is composing at another table, has the good ink. The first rehearsal of the recitatives took place this morning. The second rehearsal will be held when the tenor arrives.

For some time now we have had constant rain here, but during the last three days the weather has been very fine and not at all cold, so that we have not yet had a fire in our hearth. That Wolfgang did not give the minuets to Fräulein Waberl[2] was an oversight which she will surely forgive, when she remembers that he is a careless fellow, who easily forgets things. But why he found it easier to remember Fräulein Barisani,[3] can be explained quite naturally and it is not necessary to give the reason.

We send our cordial greetings to all our good friends and we kiss you both as often as you like it and I assure you most sincerely that until death I shall ever be your admirer

L MZT

How is Mlle Zezi?[4] Does she still take lessons and does Nannerl spend much time with her? I send greetings to Nannerl and a message urging her to practise hard and to teach little Zezi conscientiously. I know well that she herself will benefit if she accustoms herself to teaching someone else very thoroughly and patiently. I am not writing this without a motive.

(166) *Leopold Mozart to his Wife*

[*Extract*]   [*Autograph in the Mozarteum, Salzburg*]

MILAN, 18 *December* 1772

My greetings to all our good friends. We kiss you both many ten thousand times and I remain your old

MZT.

I am writing this letter today, Friday the 18th, for tomorrow we shall hardly have time to write anything, because we are to have the first

---

[1] Probably Giunia's aria (no. 11) 'Ah se il crudel periglio'.
[2] See p. 197, n. 3.
[3] Therese von Barisani, a daughter of Dr. Sylvester von Barisani (1719–1810), private physician to the Archbishop of Salzburg.
[4] Barbara Zezi, whose father kept a grocer's shop in the Getreidegasse.

rehearsal with all the instruments at half past nine in the morning. During the last few days we have had three rehearsals of the recitatives. The tenor arrived only yesterday evening and Wolfgang composed today two arias for him and has still two more to do. The second rehearsal takes place on Sunday the 20th, the third on Tuesday the 22nd, and the dress rehearsal on Wednesday the 23rd. On Thursday and Friday there will be no rehearsals; but on Saturday the 26th, the very day on which you will receive this letter, we shall have the first performance of the opera. I am writing to you at eleven o'clock at night and Wolfgang has just finished the second aria for the tenor. We shall celebrate Christmas Eve at supper with Herr and Frau von Germani, who send you greetings and who wish that you were here. We are lunching tomorrow with Herr von Mayr and after lunch I shall still be able to write a few words. Addio. Farewell.

(166a) *Mozart to his Sister*

[Autograph in the Mozarteum, Salzburg]

[MILAN, 18 *December* 1772[1]]

I hope that you are well, my dear sister. When you receive this letter, my dear sister, that very evening my opera will have been performed, my dear sister. Think of me, my dear sister, and try as hard as you can to imagine that you, my dear sister, are hearing and seeing it too, my dear sister. That is hard, I admit, as it is already eleven o'clock. Otherwise I believe and do not doubt at all that during the day it is brighter than at Easter. We are lunching tomorrow, my dear sister, with Herr von Mayr, and why, do you think? Guess! Why, because he has asked us. The rehearsal tomorrow is at the theatre, but Signor Castiglione, the impresario, has begged me not to tell anyone about it; otherwise a whole crowd of people will come running in, and we do not want this. So, my child, I beg you not to mention it to anyone, my child, otherwise too many people will come running in, my child. That reminds me. Have you heard what happened here? I will tell you. We left Count Firmian's today to go home and when we reached our street, we opened the hall door and what do you think we did? Why, we went in. Farewell, my little lung. I kiss you my liver, and remain as always, my stomach, your unworthy

$$\left\{\begin{array}{l}\text{frater} \\ \text{brother}\end{array}\right.$$ WOLFGANG

Please, please, my dear sister, something is biting me. Do come and scratch me.

---

[1] A postscript to his father's letter. In the autograph every other line is written upside down.

(167) *Leopold Mozart to his Wife*

[*Autograph in the Mozarteum, Salzburg*]

[*Extract*]

MILAN, 26 *December* 1772

We have just this moment risen from table at Madame d'Aste's, with whom we have been lunching and at whose house I am now writing. She sends you greetings. The opera is to begin in about two or three hours' time. May God be gracious! The dress rehearsal the day before yesterday went off so well as to give us reason to hope for the greatest success. The music alone, without the ballets,[1] lasts for four hours. We received your letter today and enjoyed all your news. By this post I am also writing to the Chief Steward and *to the Archbishop and I am enclosing the opera text.* With regard to the ⟨letter to Florence⟩[2] there has been a serious misunderstanding. Abbate Augustini took away with him to Rome the whole parcel which he should have handed to Herr Troger here. The result has been that all these things, which have only now come back from Rome, have just been sent off to ⟨Florence⟩. Count Firmian ⟨added a good, strong covering letter, and now we must await the reply⟩. On the evenings of the 21st, 22nd and 23rd there were great parties in Count Firmian's house, at which all the nobles were present. On each day they went on from five o'clock in the evening until eleven o'clock with continuous vocal and instrumental music. We were among those invited and Wolfgang performed each evening. On the third day, in particular, Wolfgang was called upon to perform, at the request of Their Royal Highnesses, immediately after their arrival. Both of them spoke to us for a long time. On all three evenings the greatest houses of the town were illuminated with enormous torches, the bells of the churches near Count Firmian's house played melodies like the carillons in the Netherlands, and in the street there was music with trumpets and drums. This festival was held to celebrate the raising of His Eminence the Bishop of Passau to the dignity of Cardinal.

De Amicis is our best friend. She sings and acts like an angel and is extremely pleased because Wolfgang has served her extraordinarily well. Both you and the whole of Salzburg would be amazed if you could hear her. We kiss you many ten thousand times and in haste I remain

your old

MZT.

---

[1] According to Köchel, pp. 167, 168, Mozart composed for *Lucio Silla* three ballets, the first of which is his unfinished *Le gelosie del seraglio*, K. App. 109 [K. 135a].

[2] Leopold Mozart had applied to the Archduke Leopold of Tuscany, who in 1791 became Emperor Leopold II, for an appointment for his son.

(168) *Leopold Mozart to his Wife*

[*Autograph in the Mozarteum, Salzburg*]

A Happy New Year!   MILAN, 2 *January* 1773

I forgot the other day to wish you a happy New Year, because I was not only in a hurry, but in a condition of absolute confusion. I was preoccupied and absent-minded and at that very moment we were going off to the theatre. The opera was a great success, although on the first evening several very distressing incidents took place. The first hitch was that the performance, which was due to begin one hour after the Angelus, started three hours late, that is—about eight o'clock by German time. Thus it did not finish until two o'clock in the morning. It was only just before the Angelus that the Archduke rose from his midday meal and he then had to write with his own hand five letters of New Year greetings to Their Majesties the Emperor and Empress; and, I ought to mention, he writes very slowly. Picture to yourself the whole theatre which by half past five was so full that not another soul could get in. On the first evening the singers are always very nervous at having to perform before such a distinguished audience. But for three hours singers, orchestra and audience (many of the latter standing) had to wait impatiently in the overheated atmosphere until the opera should begin. Next, the tenor, who was engaged as a stop-gap, is a church singer from Lodi who has never before acted on such a big stage, who has only taken the part of primo tenore a couple of times, and who moreover was only engaged a week before the performance. At the point where in her first aria the prima donna expected from him an angry gesture, he exaggerated his anger so much that he looked as if he was about to box her ears and strike her on the nose with his fist. This made the audience laugh. Signora De Amicis, carried along by her own enthusiasm, did not realise why they were laughing, and, being thus taken aback, did not sing well for the rest of the evening. Further, she was jealous, because as soon as the primo uomo[1] came on the stage, the Archduchess clapped her hands. This was a ruse on the part of that castrato, who had arranged that the Archduchess should be told that he would not be able to sing for nervousness in order that he might thus ensure that the court would encourage and applaud him. To console Signora De Amicis the court summoned her at about noon on the following day and she had an audience with their Royal Highnesses which lasted a whole hour. Only then did the opera begin to go well; and although in the case of a first opera the theatre is usually very empty, on the first six evenings (today is the seventh) the hall was so full that it was hardly possible to slip in. Further, the prima donna is still having it all her own way and her arias have to be repeated. Madame d'Aste, at whose house I am writing,

---

[1] Venanzio Rauzzini.

sends greetings and wishes for a happy New Year. We kiss you many millions of times and I am your old

MZT.

Wolfgang sends special greetings to everyone. Thank God, we are well.

(169) *Leopold Mozart to his Wife*

[Extract]   [Autograph in the Mozarteum, Salzburg]

MILAN, *9 January* 1773

That you received no letter from me on one post-day must be due to a mistake at some post office, for I have written to you, as usual, every post-day. So you need not worry, for it may well happen that one letter goes astray. Thank God, the opera is an extraordinary success, and every day the theatre is surprisingly full, although people do not usually flock in large numbers to the first opera unless it is an outstanding success. Every evening arias are repeated and since the first night the opera has gained daily in popularity and has won increasing applause. Count Castelbarco has presented my son with a gold watch to which is attached a beautiful gold chain with a gold chaise and a gold lantern. You never told me that Prince Colloredo was so ill in Vienna. For over a week we have been told here that he was dying, but now we hear that he is somewhat better. People have doubtless kept quiet about this in Salzburg in order not to upset the arrangements for the concerts and the operas.

I am surprised that Leutgeb did not leave Salzburg sooner, if he really intended to do so. Up to the present there is no thought of our leaving here. We may do so at about the end of this month, for we want to hear the music of the second opera.[1] Thank God, we are both well, and for some time my head has been better. It began to freeze a little two days ago and now we have most beautiful weather. Monsieur and Madame d'Aste and Herr von Troger, Herr Germani and his wife and Signor Maestro Mysliwecek send greetings, and they all long to meet you. Count Castelbarco has given me special messages for both of you. We kiss you many ten million times and I am your old

MZT.

⟨I hear from Florence that the Grand Duke has received my letter, is giving it sympathetic consideration and will let me know the result. We still live in hopes.⟩[2]

---

[1] Paisiello's *Il Sismano nel Mogol*.
[2] This postscript follows Mozart's postscript to his sister.

(169a) *Mozart to his Sister*

[Autograph in the Mozarteum, Salzburg]

[MILAN, 9 *January* 1773 [1]]

When you see Madame d'Aste, Herr Troger, Herr Germani and his wife, please give them my regards. I have greetings for you from Herr von Schiedenhofen, Herr Hefner and from other good friends of blood and bone and especially from the wife of the Court Chancellor. I have no news except that Count Sauerau has been made Dean of the Cathedral.[2] Addio.

(170) *Leopold Mozart to his Wife*

[Extract]   *[Autograph in the Mozarteum, Salzburg]*

MILAN, 16 *January* 1773

His Grace the Archbishop has replied most favourably and has asked me to bring him back a few articles, which I am now procuring and about which I shall write to him by the next post.

Wolfgang's opera has now been performed seventeen times and will be performed about twenty times in all. It was arranged that the second opera was to begin on January 23rd. But as things are going so well and as the management, who at first had contracted for five hundred ducats, have now received more than a thousand, the second opera will not be produced until about the 30th. I must write quickly and only very little, because I have other letters to send off today. I am your old

LE MZT:

Monsieur and Madame d'Aste send greetings and so do Signor and Signora Germani. Herr Mysliwecek kisses Nannerl's expert hands. That was the message for her which he gave Wolfgang. Greetings too from De Amicis and her little Giuseppe, for she has been married for over five years.[3]

⟨There is little hope of what I wrote to you. God will help us. But do save money and keep cheerful, for we must have means, if we want to undertake a journey. I regret every farthing which we spend in Salzburg. Up to the present no reply has come from the Grand Duke, but we know from the Count's letter to Troger that there is very little likelihood of our getting work in Florence. Yet I still trust that at least he will recommend us.⟩ Farewell. We must go out for a drive and the carriage is at the door.

---

[1] A postscript to his father's letter. A nonsensical note, imitating perhaps the last short one he had had from Nannerl.

[2] i.e. of Salzburg.   [3] She married Buonsolazzi, a Neapolitan official.

(170a) *Mozart to his Sister*

[*Autograph in the Mozarteum, Salzburg*]

[MILAN, 16 *January* 1773[1]]

I for have the primo a uomo[2] motet compose which to tomorrow at Church the Theatine performed be will. Keep well, I you beg. Farewell. Addio. I[3] sorry to any My to our friends, am not have news. greetings all good male and Fare I Mamma's I you a female. well. kiss hand. kiss too thousand times am always faithful at and as your brother Milan.

(171) *Leopold Mozart to his Wife*

[*Extract*]   [*Autograph in the Mozarteum, Salzburg*]

MILAN, 23 *January* 1773

I am writing in bed, for during the last week I have been plagued with acute rheumatism and have had to lie up. The pain began in the joint of the left thigh, moved down after a few days to the left knee and has now settled in the right knee. The only remedy I have tried is burr root tea, three or four large glasses of which I drink every day. I have to lie on the mattress, for the room is often even colder than the street outside. The most distressing circumstance is that I have to cover these painful thighs with cloaks, furs and so forth in order to keep warm and perspire, because I have only been given one or two single blankets. So I am lying wrapped in my dressing-gown and furs in order to keep warm, and you can imagine how heavy they are on my feet and how uncomfortable it is for me when I want to move. After you receive this letter, do not write to Milan any more, because with God's help I hope to be able to leave during the first week of February, unless the copyists detain me for the music which has to be copied for His Grace and which they cannot undertake at present, as they are busy with work for the theatre. For the second opera does not begin until January 30th. Wolfgang is sorry that Leutgeb will arrive too late to hear his work. The theatre is extraordinarily crowded and the opera is being performed twenty-six times. The remaining performances will be kept for the second opera. On Fridays and on one or two holy days there are no performances. ⟨I have sent Wolfgang's opera to the Grand Duke in Florence. Even if there is no hope of obtaining anything from him, I trust that he will recommend us. But if it is all in vain, we shall not go

---

[1] A postscript to his father's letter.
[2] Mozart composed for Rauzzini the motet 'Exsultate, jubilate', K. 165 [158a].
[3] The solution of Mozart's jumble is as follows: write 'I' over 'am', 'sorry' over 'not', 'and' over 'female', 'a' over 'thousand', 'times' over 'and' and then read up and down.

under, for God will help us. I have already thought out some plans.⟩
We kiss you both many tens of thousands of times and I am your old
MZT.

(171a) *Mozart to his Sister*

[Autograph in the Mozarteum, Salzburg]

[MILAN, 23 *January* 1773[1]]
Signor and Signora d'Aste, Signor and Signora Germani, Signor
Mysliwecek and Signora De Amicis have asked me to send you their
compliments and regards. I beg you to tell Johann Hagenauer from me
not to doubt that I will certainly visit that armourer's shop and see whether
they have anything he wants and that, if I find it, I shall not fail to bring it
home with me. I am vexed that Leutgeb left Salzburg too late to see a
performance of my opera; and perhaps he will miss us too, unless we
meet on the way. The first orchestral rehearsal of the second opera took
place yesterday evening, but I only heard the first act, since, as it was late,
I left at the beginning of the second. In this opera there are to be twenty-
four horses and a great crowd of people on the stage, so that it will be a
miracle if some accident does not happen. I like the music, but I do not
know whether the public will like it, for only people connected with the
theatre have been allowed to attend the first rehearsal. I hope that my
father will be able to go out tomorrow. This evening the weather is very
bad. Signora Teiber[2] is now at Bologna. She is singing at Turin during the
coming carnival and the following year she will go and sing at Naples.
My compliments to all my friends. Kiss my mother's hands for me. I have
no more news. Farewell. Excuse my bad writing, but my pen is not worth
a straw.

(172) *Leopold Mozart to his Wife*

[Extract]　　　　　　　　　　　　　　　　[Autograph in the Mozarteum, Salzburg]

MILAN, 30 *January* 1773
We have received no letter today, unless the courier from Rome who
passes through Mantua happens to deliver something—for he sometimes
brings with him letters from Germany which have been left behind in
Mantua. If not, your letter, assuming that you wrote one, will arrive about
Wednesday. You will see from my handwriting that I am scrawling this
in bed, as I am still laid up with this accursed rheumatism and am suffering
like a dog. Patience is the patron saint of all cowards. The pious proverb

---

[1] This letter is in Italian.
[2] Elisabeth Teiber (1750– ?), one of a large family of Viennese musicians, who were the
children of Matthäus Teiber (1711–1785), a famous violinist in the service of the Austrian court.

says: Better here than there. But I say—better there than here, because a rheumaticky person who is perspiring in bed cannot appreciate a cold room, which is even colder than the street. Though indeed I should not like an overheated room either. Today the second opera is being performed for the first time, and I am very unhappy not to be able to hear it. I am sending Wolfgang to Herr Germani's box and in the meantime I myself shall have to mope at home. We have had dreadful rainy weather for some days. But yesterday, January 29th, the most beautiful weather returned and now it is more warm than cold. If my health had allowed me to do so, I should have left here during the first days of February. But now I must count myself lucky if I get away on the 10th or 12th, for this is the most dangerous season for my illness, as in the Tyrol I shall meet with more snow and fresh air than I require. Wolfgang is well, and this very moment, as I write, he is turning one somersault after another. We kiss you many hundred thousand times and I am your old

MZT.

⟨I have received no further reply from the Grand Duke in Florence. What I wrote about my illness is all quite untrue. I was in bed for a few days, but now I am well and am off to the opera this evening. You must, however, spread the news everywhere that I am ill. You should cut off this scrap of paper so that it may not fall into the hands of others.⟩[1]

(173) *Leopold Mozart to his Wife*

[*Extract*]   [*Autograph in the Mozarteum, Salzburg*]

MILAN, 6 February 1773

I had certainly hoped to leave here at the beginning of next week and thus to see you before the end of the carnival. But this accursed rheumatism has settled in my right shoulder and, as I cannot do anything for myself, I am making no progress. So you can imagine how I feel, the more so as the weather is now frightfully cold and there is a bitter wind that goes through you. We have no means of heating our room, not even a fireplace. I can only try to keep myself warm in a bed covered with fur and clothes, on which even our footbags are piled up. Nevertheless I shall endeavour, if it is possible, to leave at the end of next week and hope to be in Salzburg for the last three days of the carnival. I say, *if it is possible*, for, if my rheumatism is not completely cured, I must not attempt in this cold weather to start on so long a journey, which will take us through the Tyrol, where the cold will undoubtedly be bitter and where I must run

---

[1] Frau Mozart did not do so.

the risk of having possibly to lie up in some wretched inn on the way. Meanwhile I presume that this will be my last letter from Milan. I should like you to find an opportunity of speaking to the Chief Steward, to Count Sauerau or to Countess von Arco[1] and of informing them, with my most humble greetings, of my indisposition. This is the more important as enquiries have been made about our arrival. I shall certainly leave Milan as soon as I can.

Wolfgang is composing a quartet,[2] and I am relieved that I have written this letter. We kiss you many hundred million times and I am your old disabled

MZT

⟨Thank God, we are well. I cannot start on my journey, as I must wait the arrival of a courtier from Florence. Leutgeb has not yet reached Milan. Meanwhile you must cultivate our friendship with Count Sauerau.⟩

(174) *Leopold Mozart to his Wife*

[*Extract*]   [*Autograph in the Mozarteum, Salzburg*]

MILAN, 13 *February* 1773

My rheumatism which moved to my right shoulder has settled down there much more obstinately than when I had it in my thighs and knees. Nor have I been able to treat it so well, for in an icy cold room it is easier to keep one's feet warm in bed than one's shoulders. I was in constant dread lest I should suffer again as dreadfully as I did ten years ago when for fourteen whole weeks I had these cruel pains in both shoulders. Thank God, I trust that this attack will not be so bad, for the pains have already become less acute. But I cannot use my right arm and, as Wolfgang is not able to do much for me or even for himself, you can realize what fun we are having. I would have written to the Chief Steward and humbly requested him to apologize to His Grace for our belated return to Salzburg, but I can assure you that it is impossible for me to compose a single line of good sense without getting feverish and that I cannot even write a few words neatly. So please find an opportunity of laying our humble request before His Excellency and of assuring him that we shall leave as soon as possible.

Leutgeb arrived late one evening a week ago and on the following Sunday he came to call on us. I have not seen him for the last two days,

---

[1] Wife of Count Georg Anton Felix von Arco, Chief Chamberlain to the Archbishop.
[2] Probably K. 157 or 158.

for he is staying with the painter Martin Knoller,[1] a good quarter of an hour from this house. He pays nothing for his lodging. So far he has arranged his affairs pretty well and he will make quite a fortune here, for he is extraordinarily popular. If the concert takes place which the courtiers want to arrange for him, I wager that he will get one hundred cigliati on the spot. The Archduke too wants to hear him.

I am tired of holding my pen, and though my hands and feet are cold, my head is hot. So I must close. We kiss you many thousand times and I am your old

MZT

We are showering sugared words on the copyist to encourage him to finish the score of Wolfgang's opera, so that we may take it home with us. But we do not yet know whether we shall be so lucky.

(175) *Leopold Mozart to his Wife*

[Extract]   [Autograph in the Mozarteum, Salzburg]

MILAN, 20 *February* 1773

Alas, we are still in Milan! I sent a letter today to the Chief Steward and I found it difficult to write legibly. My rheumatism now makes me impatient. We shall have to travel through the Tyrol where I hear that the snow is very thick and I fear that we may be overwhelmed by an avalanche, as milder weather is coming. So you can understand that as soon as my health permits I shall leave. I have no more news for you except that, thank God, Wolfgang is well. I am your old

MZT

(176) *Leopold Mozart to his Wife*

[Extract]   [Autograph in the Mozarteum, Salzburg]

MILAN, 27 *February* 1773

I can only write a few words today, for it is the last day of carnival and Lent begins in March. So it is just as if everyone here were going mad. We are leaving in two or three days and I am sending you this letter as an enclosure in one to Spitzeder, so that you may say that you have received

---

[1] Martin Knoller (1725–1804) was born at Steinach in Tyrol, studied in Italy and in 1765 settled in Milan, where he made a great reputation as a painter of portraits and historical subjects. He became court painter to Count Firmian, Governor-General of Lombardy, and, with the exception of a short visit to Vienna in 1790, remained in Milan for the rest of his life. It is possible that he painted the ivory miniature of Mozart, which was formerly in the possession of the latter's sister and is now in the Mozart Museum, Salzburg.

no word from me and that therefore you think that we have probably left already. We must, and we want to arrive in Salzburg on the evening of Election day, March 13th.[1] As for the affair you know of there is nothing to be done.[2] I shall tell you all when we meet. God has probably some other plan for us. You cannot think into what confusion our departure has thrown me. Indeed I find it hard to leave Italy.

M. and Mme d'Aste send their greetings. We kiss you many 100,000 times and I am your old

MZT

I shall write to you on our journey.

[1] The first anniversary of the election of the new Archbishop, Hieronymus Colloredo.
[2] Leopold Mozart is alluding to his application to the Archduke Leopold of Tuscany.

Mozart's eighth journey was to Vienna, whither, owing to the absence from Salzburg of Archbishop Hieronymus Colloredo, his father accompanied him in the hope of obtaining for him an appointment at the Viennese court. This hope was not realized. During his two months' stay in Vienna, Mozart composed a second series of six string quartets. This visit, which lasted from 14 July to 26 September 1773, is described in joint letters from father and son to Frau Mozart and Nannerl. Letters 177–188.

(177) *Leopold Mozart to his Wife*

[*Extract*]

[*Autograph in the Mozarteum, Salzburg*]

VIENNA, 21 *July* 1773[1]

When we arrived in Vienna old Frau Fischer happened to be at table, for they take their supper at six o'clock. Her daughter and her son-in-law were at Baden[2] and only returned last Monday. She knew nothing whatever about our arrival, for the letter had been written to her daughter and lay there unopened, because so far she had had no opportunity of forwarding it to her. But the old lady was extraordinarily pleased to see us and was only sorry that you and Nannerl had not come too. She and her daughter send their greetings and, together with our own wishes, 100,000 wishes for your and Nannerl's name-day.[3] We shall drink the health of Your Highness and celebrate your name-day in the Landstrasse.[4] We have fine rooms here and everything we require. We lunched on Sunday with young Mesmer[5] in the company of Herr von Heufeld.[6] Nobody recognized Wolfgang, for each time I let him go in alone. You can picture to yourself their joy in the Landstrasse at seeing us. Everywhere it has been the same. We found Fräulein Franzl[7] in bed. She is really very much emaciated and if she has another illness of this kind, she will be done for! Herr von Bosch[8] has got a post in the War Department in Brünn. Mme von Mesmer has lost her mother-in-law.[9] She can use the interest on the whole property, but she can neither sell houses nor touch the capital. The Mesmers are all well and in good form as usual. Herr von Mesmer,[10] at whose house we lunched on Monday, played to us on Miss Davies's armonica or glass instrument and played very well. It cost him about fifty ducats and it is very beautifully made. His garden is extremely fine, with views and statues, a theatre, an aviary, a pigeon-loft and, at the top, a belvedere looking right over the Prater. We dined with them on Saturday and also on Monday. They all send their greetings. I must close, for I have

---

[1] The Mozarts left Salzburg on 14 July. [2] A watering-place near Vienna.
[3] 26 July.
[4] i.e. with Dr. Mesmer's family. They lived in a magnificent house in the Landstrasse, which belonged to his wife whose first husband was Herr von Bosch.
[5] Joseph Mesmer, a cousin of Dr. Mesmer, who founded the Vienna Reform School.
[6] Franz von Heufeld (1731–1795), a well-known dramatist and writer, who since 1769 had been manager of the Deutsches Theater in Vienna.
[7] Franziska von Osterling, who later married Mesmer's stepson, Franz de Paula von Bosch.
[8] Dr. Mesmer's stepson. [9] Frau von Eulenschenk.
[10] Dr. Franz Anton Mesmer (1734–1814), born at Iznang on Lake Constance, was educated at the Jesuit College of Dillingen and proceeded to study medicine at the Universities of Ingolstadt and Vienna. In 1768 he married a wealthy widow, Frau von Bosch, and settled in her mother-in-law's house in the Landstrasse. He soon made a tremendous reputation for cures by magnetism.

still time to write a few lines to young Herr von Andretter[1] and to send him the beginning of the Finalmusik.[2] We kiss you both many 10,000,000 times and I am your old

MZT

(178) *Leopold Mozart to his Wife*

[Extract]   [Autograph in the Mozarteum, Salzburg]

VIENNA, 12 *August* 1773

I have received all your letters.

Her Majesty the Empress was very gracious to us, but that was all. I am saving up a full account until our return, for it is impossible for me to give it in writing. His Grace[3] returns today from Laxenburg. He will spend a few days with his father in Sierndorf and then go back to Salzburg. But he will hardly leave before next Saturday or Sunday, and thus will not arrive in Salzburg until next week. You will hear by the next post when we shall leave. If we do not leave next Monday, we shall not get home before the beginning of September. I shall know today or tomorrow. Meanwhile Fräulein Franzl has again been dangerously ill and blisters had to be applied to her arms and feet. She is so much better now that she has knitted in bed a red silk purse for Wolfgang which she has given him as a remembrance. She sends greetings, as they all do, the whole litany of the Landstrasse, the two Frau Fischers and Herr Fischer, Bosch and so forth. Young Mesmer's boy is really talented, so much so that if only he were my son or at least lived with me, he would get on. As for the girl, she is none other than the daughter of Dr. Auenbrugger, or rather his elder daughter. Both of them, and in particular the elder, play extraordinarily well and are thoroughly musical. We dine with them occasionally. The family, however, do not draw a subsidy from the Empress. Young Mesmer has a good appointment. He is in charge of the organisation of the Normalschulen of all the Imperial hereditary dominions, the governor of which is a nobleman. Do you know that Herr von Mesmer[4] plays Miss Davies's armonica unusually well? He is the only person in Vienna who has learnt it and he possesses a much finer glass instrument than Miss Davies does. Wolfgang too has played upon it. How I should like to have one! On the feast of St. Cajetan[5] the Fathers invited us to luncheon and to the service; and, because the organ was not good enough for an organ concerto, Wolfgang borrowed from Herr Teiber[6] a violin and a concerto

---

[1] Cajetan Andretter, a son of Johann Ernst von Andretter, War Councillor at the Salzburg court.
[2] K. 185 [167a], written for the occasion of Cajetan Andretter's wedding.
[3] The Archbishop of Salzburg.   [4] Dr. Franz Anton Mesmer.   [5] 7 August.
[6] Probably Anton Teiber (1754–1822), the eldest son of Matthäus Teiber (1711–1785) and brother of the singers Elizabeth and Therese Teiber. Anton Teiber became a famous violinist and composer in the service of the Viennese court.

which he was impudent enough to play. On the octave of the feast of St. Ignatius[1] one of Wolfgang's masses, the Dominicus mass,[2] was performed at the Jesuits, Auf Dem Hof. I conducted it and it was very well received. We are delighted that the Finalmusik[3] went off well.

Wolfgang will express his thanks to Herr Meisner later on. Meanwhile we send him our greetings.

Now I have sent you a great deal of news. We kiss you many 100000 times and I am your old

MZT

(178a) *Mozart to his Sister*

[Autograph in the Mozarteum, Salzburg]

[VIENNA, 12 August 1773[4]]

Hodie nous avons begegnet per strada Dominum Edelbach,[5] welcher uns di voi compliments ausgerichtet hat, et qui sich tibi et ta mère empfehlen lässt. Addio.

W. M.

Landstrasse 12 August

(179) *Leopold Mozart to his Wife*

[*Extract*]   [*Autograph in the Mozarteum, Salzburg*]

VIENNA, 14 August 1773

I received today your letter of the 10th. On Tuesday His Grace will leave Sierndorf, where he is staying with his father, and will arrive here on Wednesday evening or early on Thursday. You ask when we shall return? Not yet, for His Grace has given us permission to stay on here. Von Mesmer's cousin, who is also called Mesmer, is a travelling cook in the service of the Archbishop. He arrived in Salzburg about a fortnight before the departure of the latter, and left with him at once for Vienna. He was commissioned by Herr and Frau von Mesmer to visit us in Salzburg and to deliver a thousand kind messages, but he has now excused himself on the ground that he called on us and found nobody at home. This time he will go to see you at once, as he is the bearer of innumerable messages from us all. You will notice that he is rather like young Mesmer,

---

[1] 7 August.
[2] K. 66, the Mass which Mozart wrote in 1769 for his friend, Cajetan (Dominicus) Hagenauer who had just entered the monastery of St. Peter and had to conduct his first service.   [3] K. 185 [167a].
[4] A postscript to his father's letter. 'Today we met in the street Herr Edelbach who has given us your compliments, and who asks to be remembered to you and to your mother. Farewell.'
[5] Benedikt Schlossgängl von Edelbach (1748– ?), a son of Franz Josef Schlossgängl von Edelbach, Professor of Law at Salzburg University.

that he is very refined, has an aristocratic bearing and for a cook is rather proud.

After a great deal of rain we now have fine weather at last and during these few days it has been extraordinarily warm. The Mesmers and all that gang send their greetings; likewise the two Frau Fischers and Herr Fischer. We kiss you many hundred thousand times and I am your old

MZT

The whole families of Martinez[1] and Bonno send their greetings to you, weather permitting.[2]

(179a) *Mozart to his Sister*

[*Autograph in the Mozarteum, Salzburg*]

[VIENNA, 14 *August* 1773[3]]

I hope, my queen, that you are enjoying the highest degree of health and that now and then or rather, sometimes, or, better still, occasionally, or, even better still, qualche volta, as the Italians say, you will sacrifice for my benefit some of your important and intimate thoughts, which ever proceed from that very fine and clear reasoning power, which in addition to your beauty, and although from a woman, and particularly from one of such tender years, almost nothing of the kind is ever expected, you possess, O queen, so abundantly as to put men and even greybeards to shame. There now, you have a well-turned sentence. Farewell.

WOLFGANG MOZART

(180) *Leopold Mozart to his Wife*

[*Extract*] [*Autograph in the Mozarteum, Salzburg*]

VIENNA, 21 *August* 1773

A good friend of Herr Fischer has invited him and ourselves to Baden. As we have never seen that part of the world, we are lunching today with Herr Fischer and are driving out there after lunch, returning tomorrow (Sunday) evening. We have hired two carriages, one of which will take Herr Fischer, his wife and our two selves, and the other, Herr Teiber[4] and his family.

I could not write by the last post as we had a big concert in the garden

---

[1] The family of Niccolò Martinez, master of ceremonies to the Papal Nuncio in Vienna. During his long stay in Vienna, from 1730 to 1782, Metastasio lived with this family. One of the daughters, Marianne Martinez, became an accomplished musician, whose talents are enthusiastically described by Burney, *Present State of Music in Germany, etc.*, 2nd edition, 1775, vol. i. p. 310 ff.

[2] The last two words are an addition in Mozart's handwriting.

[3] A postscript to his father's letter.

[4] Matthäus Teiber (1711–1785), violinist in the service of the Viennese court and father o Anton Teiber, violinist, Franz Teiber, organist, and the singers Elisabeth and Therese Teiber.

of the Landstrasse. Fräulein Franzl has now had a second relapse from which she has again recovered. It is amazing how she can stand so much bleeding and so many medicines, blisters, convulsions, fainting fits and so forth, for she is nothing but skin and bone. Herr von Mesmer is adding three new rooms on the ground floor in order that he may be able to live downstairs during the winter, since although an enormous amount of wood is burnt upstairs, the rooms never get warmed up. You probably did not write last post-day, as I received no letter. Today's post has not yet arrived. Let me know when the Archbishop leaves Salzburg. We kiss you 100000 times and I am your old

MZT

I have this moment received your letter.[1] If I had known Frau von Mesmer's[2] circumstances which, as you know, *were very doubtful*, I could have brought you both with us. But not only was it impossible for me to know them, but there were other difficulties. Both the Mesmers in the Landstrasse and Frau Fischer wanted to have you as their guests; but how should we have got home? You could have come to Vienna by water, or more quickly, but rather inconveniently, by mail coach. But how could you have returned? And what a fearful sensation this would have made in Salzburg! You can rest assured that your visit would have given great pleasure to us and to all our good friends in Vienna. But now it is no longer worth while and we are not in a position to meet any great expenditure. If we had had some prospects or if we had made some money, I should certainly have written to you to come. But there are many matters about which one cannot write. Moreover we must avoid anything which might create a stir or provoke any suspicion either here or, in particular at Salzburg, or which might give someone an opportunity to put a spoke in our wheel.

We do not know ourselves when we shall leave. It may be soon, but there may be some delay. It depends on circumstances which I may not enumerate. God willing, we shall certainly be home by the end of September. Things must and will alter. Be comforted and keep well! God will help us!

Should the Archbishop stay away for a long time, we shall not hurry home.

(180a) *Mozart to his Sister*

[*Autograph in the Mozarteum, Salzburg*]

[Vienna, 21 *August* 1773[3]]

If one considers the favour of Time and if at the same time one does not forget completely the respect due to the sun, then it is certain that, praise

---

[1] This postscript follows Letter 180a.   [2] i.e. Dr. Mesmer's wife, who was wealthy.
[3] A postscript to his father's letter.

and thanks be to God, I am well. But the second sentence is quite different, if for 'sun' we put 'moon' and for 'favour' we put 'art'. In this case anyone who is blessed with a little common sense will conclude that I am a fool, because you are my sister. How is Miss Bimbes?[1] Please give her all sorts of messages from me. My greetings to all my good friends. I have to deliver greetings too from Herr and Frau von Mesmer, Prean, Grill, Saliet, Steigentesch, Stesskamm Sepherl and Fräulein Franzl to Mamma and to you and to Herr von Schiedenhofen. I have all sorts of messages too from Mr. Greibich,[2] whose acquaintance we first made at Pressburg and later in Vienna, and from Her Majesty the Empress, Frau Fischer and Prince Kaunitz.

Oidda. Gnagflow Trazom.

Anneiv, Tsugua, ts12, 3771

(181) *Leopold Mozart to his Wife*

[*Extract*]   [*Autograph in the Mozarteum, Salzburg*]

VIENNA, 25 August 1773

I am astonished to hear that Madame Rosa has left for Vienna. I have not yet seen her, as I do not know where she is living; presumably with Hofvergolter. Herr von Mölk, whom I went to see today, knew as little about her as I did. But did no shimmer of an idea occur to you, prompting you to make use of this convenient opportunity to send a cloth travelling coat of mine down the river? You could have sent, for instance, my English redbrown coat with the golden paillettes and Wolfgang's grey coat. I am writing in a great hurry at young Mesmer's house, where we lunched today to celebrate the eighth anniversary of their wedding day and where we drank your healths. The Mesmers went off today to the Rotmühle. We shall visit them if we have time, and we shall bring the Teibers with us, for the daughter sings and the son plays the violin. All that Nannerl writes about corselets, caps and so forth I shall see to as far as possible, but my purse is getting emptier. As my figure becomes stouter, my purse becomes thinner, for you may well believe that I am getting visibly fatter. Take care of yourselves. We kiss you many 100000000 times and I am your old

MZT

At the moment Wolfgang is playing the clavier, so he cannot write.

We returned from Baden on Monday in time for lunch. All our friends there send their greetings to you. Fräulein Franzl has now recovered.

---

[1] Bimbes or Bimperl was the Mozart's fox-terrier bitch.
[2] Franz Kreibich, who was first violin in the Emperor Joseph II's string quartet.

(182) *Leopold Mozart to his Wife*

[*Extract*]   [*Autograph in the Mozarteum, Salzburg*]

VIENNA, 28 *August* 1773

We met Madame Rosa on Thursday evening on the Bastei, where we happened to be with Herr von Mölk. The good lady treated us very distantly, as she was arm in arm with a certain Rosa, painter of animals and inspector of picture galleries. We often go to see Mr. De L'Augier, who sends greetings to both of you. Baden is a tiny town, where there are very many baths, like those of Gastein, but built more conveniently. Most of the houses are constructed so as to have rooms which can be let to visitors who want board and lodging. Frau Schultz, whose husband, poor old blind fellow, died in Baden, and who then married some good-natured idiot, is the principal comic actress at the theatre and now acts very well, although in her youth she was very mediocre. The Mesmers are at the Rotmühle,[1] where Fräulein Franzl will probably fall ill again and possibly die. Not only she but also her sister are constantly at the Mesmers'. We kiss you many 100,000,000 times and I am your old

MZT

Tomorrow we are lunching with Herr Noverre.[2] Herr Becke, the flautist, also sends his regards.

(183) *Leopold Mozart to his Wife*

[*Extract*]   [*Autograph in the Mozarteum, Salzburg*]

VIENNA, 4 *September* 1773

Now it is all up with the poor Jesuits! I call them poor, for only those who were the leaders, I mean, the rabbis and *corpus religionis*[3] as a whole, could be called rich. The ordinary members had nothing. The Jesuit monastery Auf Dem Hof must be cleared out by September 16th. The church treasure, their wine-cellars and, in fact, their entire property have already been sealed up, for the Jesuit Order has been suppressed. But they may dress as secular priests and it is said that each priest will have three hundred gulden a year, which is not so bad. If he gets Masses as well, a young Jesuit can find a pretty room and a nice housekeeper, for otherwise he will not have very much to do, as they will no longer be allowed to

---

[1] In Rannersdorf, near Schwechat.
[2] Jean Georges Noverre (1727–1810), a famous dancer and leader of the ballet at the Opéra-Comique in Paris. From 1755 he toured in France, Germany and Italy until finally in 1776 he settled for good in Paris as maître des ballets en chef at the Paris opera. He considerably improved the ballet by introducing dramatic action. See H. Abert, *Noverre und sein Einfluss auf die dramatische Ballettkomposition*, Jahrbuch Peters, 1908.   [3] i.e. religious order.

preach or to hear confession. The public is very much distressed. I hear that a Papal Brief is to be published to the effect that on pain of excommunication no one is to write or even speak a word against their suppression.[1] On the other hand, many good Catholics are of the opinion that except in matters of faith His Holiness the Pope has no right to command and that it may truly be said that they would not have been interfered with if they had been as poor as the poor Capuchins. For in Rome they have already begun to appropriate Jesuit property *ad pias causas*; but that was an easy matter, for even if the Pope takes it for himself, it is being used *ad causas pias*. The Viennese Court would not accept the first Papal Brief,[2] because, as I hear, it contained the statement, *that the possessions of the Jesuits should be used ad causas pias*. Well, as the Court refused to have laws dictated to it, His Holiness has given His Majesty a free hand to use the possessions of the Jesuits as he likes. Everything is still in great confusion and no one knows who will get the churches and the schools. And, be it noted, the same thing applies to all the Imperial territories.[3]

Herr Gassmann[4] has been ill, but is now better. I do not know how this will affect our stay in Vienna. Fools everywhere are but fools![5] We and all the others send greetings, and I am your old

MZT

We shall not stay here much longer. By the next post I shall write more about our plans. I must close. Wolfgang has no time to scribble anything, for we are almost missing the post.

(184) *Leopold Mozart to his Wife*

[Extract]   [*Autograph in the Mozarteum, Salzburg*]

VIENNA, 8 September 1773

I am very much obliged to the citizens of Salzburg who are so anxious for my return. In that case I shall go back with greater pleasure and shall walk about the whole night in the illuminated town, so that the lights may not burn in vain. At least I shall find the lock in the hall door more easily, for I suppose that the illuminations will be so arranged that we shall have the good fortune to find a lantern at the street corner.

[1] i.e. for religious causes.
[2] Probably Leopold Mozart is referring to the famous Papal Brief 'Dominus ac Redemptor' of 21 July 1773.
[3] For a full account of the attitude of the Austrian court to the dissolution of the Jesuit order, see Ludwig Freiherr von Pastor, *Geschichte der Päpste*, 1932, vol. xvi., section 1, p. 191 ff.
[4] Florian Leopold Gassmann (1729–1774), who since 1771 had been Kapellmeister to the Viennese court, died on 20 January, 1774. His successor was Giuseppe Bonno (1710–1788).
[5] Leopold Mozart is alluding to the suspicions of some people in Salzburg who were connecting his son's visit to Vienna with Gassmann's illness.

God willing, I shall leave at the end of next week. But as I have often done this journey and have never been to Mariazell, it may be that I shall return home through that village and through St. Wolfgang,[1] in order to show our Wolfgang the pilgrimage church of his patron saint, which he has not yet seen, and St. Gilgen,[2] the famous birthplace of his mother. But whether we shall do this or not you will learn from my next letters. So, whatever happens, we shall arrive, God willing, during the week of September 24th or 25th.

(184a) *Mozart to his Mother*

[Autograph in the Mozarteum, Salzburg]

*[*VIENNA*, 8 September 1773]*

Little Wolfgang has no time to write, for he has nothing to do. He is walking up and down the room like a dog with fleas.

Concerto
per violino obbligato
e stromenti
del sig. Giuseppe Mysliwecek
detto il Boemo
= Basso =

That is what my writing-pad looks like.

(184b) *Leopold Mozart to his Wife*

[Autograph in the Mozarteum, Salzburg]

*[*VIENNA*, 8 September 1773]*

We both send greetings to all our good friends at home and elsewhere and we kiss you many 10000000 times and I remain your old

MZT

There will be some delay over the departure of the Jesuit Fathers until everything has been arranged. It is said that they may still act as Court preachers and so forth, provided that they go about as lay priests. I shall bring with me a printed copy of the Bull. The millions which the Church is getting from the Jesuits will whet its appetite and make it lay hands on the revenues of a few other religious orders.

[1] A small village on the Wolfgangsee, about 30 miles from Salzburg.
[2] Another village on the Wolfgangsee, where Nannerl went to live after her marriage in 1784.

(185) *Leopold Mozart to his Wife*

[Extract]　　　　　　　　　　　　　　　[*Autograph in the Mozarteum, Salzburg*]

VIENNA, 11 *September* 1773

The Jesuits are beginning to leave their monasteries. The Court Fathers, those who preached in the Stefanskirche, and six confessors left yesterday and will perform their duties next Sunday as usual, but in lay priests' clothes; for the order which has been issued to the higher Jesuits is that no one in the garb of a Jesuit may either hear confession or preach. Today I am too much out of humour and too stupid to write any more.[1] We kiss you many 100000 times and I am your old

MZT

(186) *Leopold Mozart to his Wife*

[Extract]　　　　　　　　　　　　　　　[*Autograph in the Mozarteum, Salzburg*]

VIENNA, 15 *September* 1773

The weather here is now becoming rather cool, especially in the morning and in the evening. On the whole, wine, fruit and vegetables have had a surprisingly good season and wine is actually being sold at six kreuzer per measure, solely in order to get empty vats. In Hungary there has been a glut of wheat, but the hay has been much poorer than usual. The Jesuit Fathers are already going about as lay priests in long black robes and cloaks with Italian collars.

His Majesty the Emperor, travelling from Poland through Moravia, arrived here last Monday morning shortly after seven o'clock. It was in a way a surprise, as he was not expected until October. It is a fact that the Russians have been thoroughly beaten a few times by the Turks, so that they now want to recall their troops in Poland.[2] Meanwhile the Prussians are to occupy the Russian portion of Poland. We and all our friends here send greetings to all of you, both at home and elsewhere. So far I have not been out to the Rotmühle, although the Mesmers have been there for a long time and Fräulein Franzl nearly died there again. We kiss you a million times and I am your old

MZT

---

[1] The first portion of this letter, which has been omitted, describes in detail the death of Dr. Niderl, a Salzburg doctor and a friend of the Mozart family, which Leopold Mozart felt very deeply.

[2] In 1773 Catherine the Great ordered Rumiantzov to cross the Danube, which he did, unwillingly, in June. He besieged Silistria but was obliged to retire and, harassed by the Turks, barely escaped disaster while recrossing the river. There is, however, no evidence for Leopold Mozart's statement that the Russians were obliged to withdraw their troops from that part of Poland which they were occupying as a result of the First Partition of 1772.

(186a) *Mozart to his Sister*

[*Autograph in the Mozarteum, Salzburg*]

[VIENNA, 15 *September* 1773[1]]

Praise and thanks be to God, we are quite well. Although we are busy, we are snatching some of our time to write to you. We hope that you are well too. Dr. Niderl's death made us very sad and indeed we wept, howled, groaned and moaned. Our regards to all good souls who praise the Lord God, and to all our good friends. We remain, yours graciously,

WOLFGANG

From our Residence, Vienna.[2]
15 September 1773.

(186b) *Mozart to Herr von Hefner*

[*Autograph in the Mozarteum, Salzburg*]

[VIENNA, 15 *September* 1773[3]]

To Herr von Hefner

I hope that we shall still find you in Salzburg,
           my friendly slug.
I hope that you are well and are not an enemy spi-
-der, for if so I'll be an enemy fly
or even a friendly bug.
So I strongly advise you to write better rhymes, for
if not, our Salzburg Cathedral will see me no more.
For I'm quite *capax*[4] to go off to Constant-
-inople, that city whose praises all chant.
And then you won't see me again nor I you; yet
when horses are hungry, some oats they get.
Farewell, my lad,   I'm ever to infinity
or else I'll go mad.   from now to all eternity.

(187) *Leopold Mozart to his Wife*

[*Extract*]   [*Autograph in the Mozarteum, Salzburg*]

VIENNA, 18 *September* 1773

For reasons which you will hear about on our arrival, we shall not be able to leave here before next Wednesday or Thursday. Thank God, we

---

[1] A postscript to his father's letter.
[2] Mozart is probably poking fun at the Salzburg Archbishop.
[3] An enclosure in his father's letter.   [4] i.e. able.

are well. The enclosure you sent me was from Mysliwecek in Naples. Nearly all the Jesuit Fathers have left their monasteries. Some brothers are already going about in lay apparel and have found employment as domestic servants. One has gone as butler to a convent, a few cleverer ones have become stewards and chamberlains, and the hunchbacked Jesuit apothecary is now apothecary in the Spanish hospital, where he is paid seven hundred gulden and is given full board.

We have not yet been able to go to the Rotmühle and I hardly think that we shall have time to do so. We kiss you many 10000000 times and I am your old

MZT

Wolfgang is composing something most enthusiastically.[1]

(188) *Leopold Mozart to his Wife*

[Extract]   [*Autograph in the Mozarteum, Salzburg*]

VIENNA, 22 *September* 1773

I see that I shall not be able to leave before Friday, or perhaps even Saturday. Today at last we drove out to the Rotmühle at about half past eleven in the morning and returned after seven in the evening. So it will be impossible to make all our arrangements tomorrow. Hence I shall probably leave on Saturday. All our friends send you their greetings! I cannot think of anything else to tell you. I am writing in great haste at the house of young Herr Mesmer, with whose wife we went to the Rotmühle.

Farewell to you all! I am hurrying so as not to miss the post. This will be my last letter. We kiss you many 10000000 times and I am your old

MZT

[1] Either his string quartet K. 172 or, more probably, the choruses for Baron von Gebler's drama *Thamos, König von Ägypten*, K. 345 [33ba], a work which Mozart took up again in Salzburg in 1779. See WSF, vol. ii. p. 98 ff.

Mozart's ninth journey was to Munich, where he carried out a commission to write an opera buffa, La finta giardiniera, for the 1774-1775 carnival season. His father accompanied him, and his sister Nannerl joined them three weeks later in order to see the first performance. This visit, which lasted from 6 December 1774 to 8 March 1775, is described in joint letters from father and son to Frau Mozart. Letters 189-203.

(189) *Leopold Mozart to his Wife*

[*Extract*]   [*Copy in the Deutsche Staatsbibliothek, Berlin*]

[MUNICH, 9 *December* 1774]

We reached Wasserburg at nine in the evening and, although we only left at eight o'clock next morning, we arrived safely in Munich on the following day, Wednesday, at about half past three in the afternoon.[1] Our lodging is small but quite comfortable. Herr von Pernat[2] shows us indeed more courtesy and honour than we deserve and it is quite evident that out of real friendship he is in many ways sacrificing his convenience to us. So far I have nothing to tell you about the opera.[3] We only made the acquaintance today of the people connected with it, all of whom, and in particular Count Seeau,[4] were very kind to us. Thank God, we are well. As to Nannerl, to whom I send greetings, I have nothing to write to you. Up to the present I have no prospect of finding a lodging for her. Besides we have been here too short a time. We kiss you both and I am your old

MOZART

(190) *Leopold Mozart to his Wife*

[*Extract*]   [*Autograph in the Mozarteum, Salzburg*]

MUNICH, 14 *December* 1774

Thank God, we are well. I have not yet been able to find a suitable lodging for Nannerl, for one has to be very careful in Munich. Another difficulty has arisen, and in this respect Munich resembles Salzburg. An opera, for which the public has to pay, cannot be performed here more than twice in succession, for otherwise the attendance would be poor. So for two or three weeks other operas have to be performed and then the first one may be trotted out again, just as is done in the case of plays and ballets. Thus the singers know the parts of at least twenty operas which are performed in turn, and at the same time they study a new one. So Wolfgang's will not be produced before Christmas and probably the first performance will be on the 29th.[5] So it is possible that Nannerl may

---

[1] The Mozarts had left Salzburg on 6 December.

[2] The Mozarts were lodging with Johann Nepomuk von Pernat, canon of the Frauenkirche in Munich, who lived in Bellvall's house.

[3] Mozart's opera buffa *La finta giardiniera*, on a text by Ranieri de' Calzabigi, Gluck's famous librettist. The libretto had already been set to music by Pasquale Anfossi and performed in Rome in 1774.

[4] Joseph Anton, Count von Seeau, Privy Councillor, was at that time Intendant or Controller of operatic and dramatic performances at the Electoral Court. From 1778 until his death in 1799 he was manager of the Munich National Theatre.

[5] *La finta giardiniera* was not performed until 13 January 1775.

not see it at all. For once the carnival is in full swing, only light and short operettas are performed on a small stage, which is rigged up in the Salle de Redoute. Here people gather in masks, here there are numbers of gambling tables and there is perpetual noise, conversation and gambling. Nothing sensible is ever performed there, because no one pays any attention. I shall tell you more about this later on. Please look up the two Litanies De Venerabili Altaris Sacramento, which are performed in the Hours. There is one of mine in D major (the score will surely be with it), a recent one which begins with the violin and double bass staccato (you know the one I mean); at the Agnus Dei the second violin has triplet notes the whole time. Then you will find Wolfgang's great Litany.[1] The score is with it, bound in blue paper. Make quite sure that all the parts are there, for these two Litanies are to be performed here in the Hours on New Year's Day. You should hand them in at the post on Saturday evening, for the mail coach leaves on Sunday. Write this address on the parcel:

À

  Monsieur Jean Nepomuc de Pernat chanoine e
          grand Custos de Notre Dame
                  à Munic

We kiss you many 1000 times and send greetings to everybody everywhere and I am your old

                                                    MZT.

(191) *Leopold Mozart to his Wife*

[Extract]   [Autograph in the Mozarteum, Salzburg]

MUNICH, 16 *December* 1774

I have now found a lodging for Nannerl, and where do you think it is? With Madame, or rather Widow von Durst, formerly the wife of a salt merchant at Reichenhall, whom Herr von Mölk drove over to visit so often and whom we frequently heard him mention. She is a young woman of about twenty-six or twenty-eight, a brunette, with dark eyes, very retiring, sensible and well read. She does not care for the society of philanderers and she is very courteous and pleasant. And who do you think helped me to find this lodging? Herr von Dufresne.[2] He asked me why I had not brought Nannerl with me and I told him that she would indeed have an opportunity of coming over to Munich with Madame von Robinig, but that, as we were now living with Herr von Pernat, I did not

---

[1] K. 125. Litaniae de venerabili altaris sacramento, composed in March 1772. It was modelled on his father's Litany.
[2] Franz Dufresne, a Munich Court Councillor.

know where to put her. He thought it over and finally said that he knew of a room in the house of Frau von Durst, that he would discuss it with her at the next opportunity and hear what she had to say, and that he was very hopeful, seeing that she lived quite alone and only received visits from her best friends and from his own parents. He then brought me the news that all would be well and that Madame Durst's only fear was lest Nannerl's presence might bring Herr von Bellvall back to her house, as she knew that he used to visit us in Salzburg; she did not mind his visiting Nannerl, but she was afraid that he might make it an excuse to start sitting on her doorstep later on. Her objection is quite justified; a young widow should not receive frequent visits from a man who is not living with his wife.

I went to see her myself today. Nannerl is to have a room of her own to sleep in, which, it is true, is rather dark, but she will spend the rest of the time in Frau von Durst's room, which looks out on the big market-place and where a harpsichord will be put for her.

Now I suppose that Nannerl will realise how silly it is not to be able to put on one's cap or make up one's face or perform other necessary duties by oneself. For one cannot always count on the services of other people. I very much suspect that Frau von Durst is accustomed to dress her own hair. So Nannerl must acquire the habit of putting on a négligé cap very neatly and of making up her face. She should also practise the clavier most diligently, especially the sonatas of Paradisi[1] and Bach,[2] and Lucchesi's[3] concerto and so forth. There is still no letter from you. We kiss you both and send greetings to all and I am your old

MZT

How is Miss Bimbes? Madame von Durst too has a small lap-dog, called, I think, Finette.

(191a) *Mozart to his Sister*

[Autograph in the Mozarteum, Salzburg]

[MUNICH, 16 December 1774[4]]

I have toothache.
Johannes Chrysostomus Wolfgangus Amadeus Sigismundus Mozartus

---

[1] Pietro Domenico Paradisi (1710–1792). His twelve *Sonate di gravicembalo* had already been printed. Cp. p. 92, n. 4.

[2] Most probably C. P. E. Bach.

[3] Andrea Lucchesi (1741–1800), a Venetian, came in 1771 to Bonn, where he was appointed Kapellmeister in 1774. He composed eight operas, some church music, symphonies and violin sonatas.

[4] A postscript to his father's letter.

Mariae Annae Mozartae matri et sorori, ac amicis omnibus, praesertimque pulchris virginibus, ac freillibus, gratiosisque freillibus

S.P.D.[1]

(191b) *Leopold Mozart resumes writing*

[*Autograph in the Mozarteum, Salzburg*]

December 17th, in the morning

Wolfgang stayed at home yesterday as he had toothache, and he is staying indoors today as his cheek is swollen.

Nannerl should find an opportunity of telling Count Sauerau that she would like to go to Munich with Madame von Robinig and Herr Gschwendner. It is important that he should know of our arrangements. Addio. I hope that I shall have a letter from you today.

(192) *Leopold Mozart to his Wife*

[*Extract*]   [*Autograph in the Mozarteum, Salzburg*]

MUNICH, 21 *December* 1774

I have today received both your letter enclosing the two Litanies and another one from you. Nannerl must certainly have a fur rug for the journey, or she will not be able to stand the cold in a half-open coach. She must wrap up her head well and she must protect her feet with something more than her felt shoes only, which after a time do not keep out the cold. She ought therefore to slip on the fur boots which she will find in the trunk under the roof. Perhaps Herr Gschwendner will also be kind enough to put a little hay in the bottom of the coach. You remember how thoroughly we protected ourselves. Just think of the quantities of clothes which we wore. I had felt shoes over my boots and we had foot-bags and even so we should not have been able to stand the cold if at the third stage, Frabertsham, I had not had a large bundle of hay put into the coach and had our foot-bags completely surrounded and covered with it. For when the journey lasts a whole day, the cold goes right through one. In addition to the sonatas of Bach and Paradisi, Nannerl might also bring copies of Wolfgang's sonatas and variations[2] and any other sonatas she likes, for they do not take up much room. She need not bring many concertos, for we have Wolfgang's concerto[3] here, and if she brings a few others, that

---

[1] Johannes Chrysostomus Wolfgang Amadeus Sigismund Mozart sends many greetings to Maria Anna Mozart, his mother and his sister, and to all his friends, and especially to pretty girls and Fräuleins and gracious Fräuleins. Salutem plurimam dicit.

[2] The five clavier sonatas, K. 279–283 [189d–h], composed in 1774, and the two sets of clavier variations, K. 179 [189a] and K. 180 [173c], composed in 1774 and 1773 respectively. See Köchel, p. 214.

[3] Probably K. 175, Mozart's first clavier concerto, which he composed in December 1773.

will be quite sufficient, for who knows whether she will use them at all. She must try to pack everything in one box, for she will not need many clothes for twelve days; and she will probably have to bring a hat-box, though indeed the latter will be a little inconvenient. However, one advantage is that women's clothes can be folded into a very small space. Wolfgang's swelling is now much better. Tomorrow, God willing, he will go out for the first time after spending six days indoors. We kiss you both and send greetings to all. Take care of yourselves. I am your old

MZT

In the writing case in the middle drawer above the desk (the drawer which does not close) you will find, I think, a little sheet of small music manuscript, on which are written only a few notes in Alle Breve time and here and there *pagina* and so on. The sheet contains a shortened form of the fugue *Pignus Futurae Gloriae* from Wolfgang's Litany.[1] If you find it, enclose it in a letter by the very next post. If you cannot find it in the drawer where the toy coach and horse are, then I do not know where it is.

I had a letter today from the Chief Steward about the commission which I received from His Grace and regarding which I have myself already written to him. The Archduke,[2] who is now in Paris, will hardly come to Munich before the end of March. The reference to Count Saurau was only if Nannerl should meet him, for I thought that he might pay you a visit. Perhaps she will come across him by chance. For that very reason no secret should be made of her visit, and you should say that Frau von Durst, widow of the salt merchant at Reichenhall, has invited her to stay with her.

(193) *Leopold Mozart to his Wife*

[Extract]   [*Autograph in the Mozarteum, Salzburg*]

[MUNICH, 28 *December* 1774]
On Holy Innocents' Day in the evening,
for the post leaves tomorrow at noon.

A Happy New Year!

On the very same day that you were both with Count Saurau, the first rehearsal of Wolfgang's opera took place at ten in the morning and was so well received that the first performance has been postponed until January 5th in order that the singers may learn their parts more thoroughly and thus, knowing the music perfectly, may act with greater confidence

---

[1] K. 125. See p. 250, n. 1.

[2] The Archduke Maximilian, the youngest son of the Empress Maria Theresia, in honour of whose visit to Salzburg in April 1775 Mozart was commissioned to write his opera *Il rè pastore*, on a text by Metastasio.

and not spoil the opera. To have got it ready by December 29th would have meant a fearful rush. As a musical composition it is indeed amazingly popular, and everything now depends on the stage production, which will, I trust, be a success, for the actors are not unfavourable to us. So it was a very fortunate occasion on which to inform Count Sauerau of Nannerl's journey and I am glad of this. I quite believe that these people are all very polite, for it is their policy to be so; but undoubtedly they suspect all sorts of things. You or Nannerl must go to Herr Hagenauer and ask him to give her a letter of credit for me to one of his agents in Munich. For even if a money present is given, it often does not come for some time and one cannot go on waiting for it. Even a present is sometimes not sent until later on. So I am not counting on getting anything, for all the arrangements here are very slow and there is often great confusion. You have only to explain this to Herr Joseph with my compliments. You will find in a leaden box some Spanish tobacco, with which Nannerl might fill a small snuff-box which she could bring with her, for my supply is coming to an end. In Wolfgang's drawer you will see an oval tobacco box, which she could use for this purpose. I again urge her to have a good fur rug and plenty of hay round her feet. Wolfgang has had to stay at home for six days with a swollen face. His cheek was swollen inside and outside and his right eye also. For two days he could only take some soup. So it is necessary to protect one's face and ears, for when you drive against the wind in a half-open coach, the air nips your face the whole time. And if you get into the coach without having your feet very warm, it is impossible to get them warm for the rest of the day. Nannerl will probably get in at Gschwendner's. So on the day before they leave, her felt boots should be brought to his house and hung up beside the stove, in order that they may be well warmed. She can then put them on when she gets into the coach. She should take some money with her for emergencies. Should anything further occur to me, you will hear it on Monday before her departure. But I cannot at the moment think of anything else. Farewell. We kiss you both and with greetings to all I am your old

MOZART

(193a) *Mozart to his Sister*

[Autograph in the Mozarteum, Salzburg]

[MUNICH, 28 December 1774[1]]

MY DEAREST SISTER,

I beg you not to forget to keep your promise before you leave, I mean, to pay the call we both know of . . . for I have my reasons. I beg

---

[1] A postscript to his father's letter.

you to convey my greetings there—but in the most definite way—in the most tender fashion—and—oh, I need not be so anxious, for of course I know my sister and how extremely tender she is. I am quite certain that she will do her utmost to do me a kindness—and for her own advantage too—but that is rather nasty. But we shall quarrel about this in Munich. Farewell.

(194) *Leopold Mozart to his Wife*

[*Autograph in the Mozarteum, Salzburg*]

MUNICH, 30 *December* 1774

When you read this letter Nannerl will have almost finished packing. So I must tell you quickly that there is something else which she will have to bring, but it is a trifle and the only condition is that it should lie flat. For I should like to have five or six copies of the copper engraving of our Paris portrait.[1] Herr von Pernat insists on having one, and so do one or two other good friends. You will find them in the drawer with all the other engravings, on the right hand side and almost on the top. But they must lie perfectly flat and not become bent. I forgot to mention too that Nannerl ought to bring a fancy dress, even if it is only a Salzburg peasant dress. I am sorry that I did not think of this sooner, but she would only be able to get a domino here. Perhaps, however, you have seen to this. We were with the Imperial Ambassador today, who was very friendly and gracious to us. You have probably sent off some New Year cards. I hope you have not forgotten Count Sauerau and Countess von Lodron. I have written to the Archbishop to wish him a happy New Year. Nannerl will arrive just in time for the opera, for she will get here on Wednesday afternoon and it is being performed on Thursday.[2] If Herr von Mölk comes too, he will see it; but if he postpones his visit, he will not do so until Easter, for after January 5th no more operas will be performed in the theatre. In the Salle de Redoute only operettas, or rather intermezzi,[3] are given, during which, however, hundreds of masks stroll around, chatter, jest and gamble at the different tables. Thus no serious work can be performed. You must know that this time last year Maestro Tozzi,[4] who this year is writing the opera seria, wrote an opera buffa, and contrived to write it so well that it killed the opera seria written by Maestro Sales.[5] Now it so happens that Wolfgang's opera is being performed

---

[1] The Carmontelle portrait of the Mozart family, painted in the autumn of 1763.
[2] 6 January. Actually Mozart's opera was not performed until 13 January.
[3] i.e. opere buffe in one or two acts.
[4] Antonio Tozzi was Kapellmeister at the Munich court. His opera seria for 1775 was *Orfeo ed Euridice*. In opinion Einstein's Tozzi's opera buffa for 1774 was probably *La serva astuta*.
[5] Pietro Pompeo Sales (1718–1797), born at Brescia, was first in the service of the Bishop of Augsburg and in 1768 became Kapellmeister to the Elector at Coblenz. He composed operas, oratorios, church music, symphonies and concertos. His opera seria for 1774 was *Achille in Sciro*.

before Tozzi's, and when people heard the first rehearsal, they all said that
Tozzi was being paid back in his own coin, for Wolfgang's opera would
certainly kill his. I do not like these bickerings. I try as far as possible to
suppress such remarks and I keep on protesting. But the whole orchestra
and all who have heard the rehearsal say that they have never listened to a
finer composition, for it is one in which all the arias are beautiful. And
wherever we go, the same thing is said. Basta! God will make everything
right. Farewell. I wish Nannerl a good journey. We kiss you both, send
our greetings to all and I am your old

MOZART

(194a) *Mozart to his Sister*

[*Autograph in the Mozarteum, Salzburg*]

[MUNICH, 30 *December* 1774[1]]

I present my compliments to Roxelana, and invite her to take tea this
evening with the Sultan. Please give all sorts of messages to Jungfrau
Mitzerl,[2] and tell her that she must never doubt my love. I see her constantly before me in her ravishing négligée.[3] I have seen many pretty girls
here, but have not yet found such a beauty. My sister must not forget to
bring with her Eckardt's variations sur le menuet d'Exaudet[4] and my
variations on Fischer's minuet.[5] I went to the theatre yesterday to see the
'Mode nach der Haushaltung',[6] which was very well acted. My greetings
to all my good friends. I hope that you will—farewell—I see you soon in
Munich to hope. I have compliments to deliver to you from Frau von
Durst. Is it true that Hagenauer has been appointed Professor of Sculpture
in Vienna?[7] Herr von Mölk said so in a letter to Father Wasenau and the
letter read out Father Wasenau to me. My mother's hand I kiss, the rest
she'll have to miss. I beg you to keep very warm on the journey, or else
for a fortnight at home you'll sit and beside the stove perspire a bit and

---

[1] A postscript to his father's letter.
[2] Fräulein Maria Raab, the owner of the Mozarts' house in the Makartplatz, into which
they had moved in 1773. She lived next door.
[3] Mozart means 'with her hair undressed'.
[4] These variations had been engraved in Paris in 1764.
[5] K. 179 [189a]. These twelve variations were composed in 1774 on a theme from the last
movement of an oboe concerto written by Johann Christian Fischer (1733–1800), a famous
oboist, who, after prolonged tours on the Continent, finally settled in London. He married
Gainsborough's daughter. Mozart heard him play in Holland in 1765 (see Leopold
Mozart's *Reiseaufzeichnungen*, p. 42), and again in Vienna in 1787. See p. 907, n. 3.
[6] Mozart is referring in jest to *Die Haushaltung nach der Mode, oder Was soll man für eine Frau
nehmen?*, a comedy written in 1765 by Franz von Heufeld (1731–1795), who in 1769 became
manager of the German theatre in Vienna. Possibly Mozart had already seen this comedy
during his family's visit to Vienna in 1768.
[7] Johann Baptist Hagenauer, court sculptor in Salzburg, had moved in 1773 to Vienna,
where he did some work for the Schönbrunn Palace and was appointed Professor of Sculpture.

not a soul will protect you one whit. But I simply refuse to have a fit; and
now the lightning's beginning to spit.

         Your Munich
brother, the 1774th day of Anno 30, Dicembre.

(195) *Leopold Mozart to his Wife*

[*Autograph in the Mozarteum, Salzburg*]

MUNICH, *5 January* 1775

Nannerl reached Munich yesterday before two in the afternoon quite
safely, but we could not be there when she arrived, as we were the guests
of Herr von Gilowsky at Störzer's, where lunch is not served until half
past one. So we first saw the Robinigs, who came to Störzer's just as we
were having our meal. But I had already sent out Herr von Pernat's
servant who was waiting for them at the bridge in the Thal[1] and brought
them straight to Frau von Durst, at whose house Herr von Dufresne
had already turned up. That evening we were with Nannerl until eight
o'clock and today I sent the servant to fetch her for coffee with us. She is
drinking some with Wolfgang this very moment, and I have been
drinking my tea. Then I am sending her back, as Frau von Durst goes to
church with her and wants to take her to a different church every day.
You will have heard from Herr Schulz that Wolfgang's opera is not being
performed until the 13th. There is a rumour here that the Archbishop is
coming over to Munich, and even Count Seeau told me this. Otherwise I
have no news. Lock up the rooms carefully so that nothing may be stolen,
for when you go out something might easily happen. My greetings to
Jungfrau Mitzerl and to everybody. We all three kiss you and I am your
old

           MOZART

(195a) *Nannerl Mozart to her Mother*

[*Autograph in the Mozarteum, Salzburg*]

[MUNICH, *5 January* 1775[2]]

I have arrived safely in Munich and was so well cared for during the
entire journey that it was impossible to feel cold. I slept with Fräulein
Louise[3] in Frau von Robinig's bedroom and we had lunch and supper en

---

[1] A street in Munich between the Isarthor and the Rathaus.
[2] A postscript to her father's letter.   [3] A daughter of Frau Robinig.

compagnie with Frau von Robinig. Meanwhile I hope that Mamma is well. I kiss Mamma's hand and with my brother, that blackguard,

I am

your most obedient daughter

MARIE ANNE MOZART

(196) *Mozart to his Mother*

[*Autograph in the Mozarteum, Salzburg*]

MUNICH, 11 *January* 1775

Thank God, all three of us are quite well. It is impossible for me to write a long letter, as I am off this very moment to a rehearsal of my opera. Tomorrow we are having the dress rehearsal and the performance takes place on Friday, the 13th. Mamma must not worry; it will go off quite well. I am very much distressed that Mamma should suspect ⟨Count Seeau,⟩ for he is certainly a charming and courteous gentleman and has more savoir vivre than many of his class in Salzburg. We were at the masked concert yesterday. Herr von Mölk was so astounded and crossed himself so often as he listened to the opera seria, that we were absolutely ashamed of him, for everyone could see quite clearly that he had never been anywhere but to Salzburg and Innsbruck. Addio. I kiss Mamma's hands.

WOLFGANG

(196a) *Leopold Mozart to his Wife*

[*Autograph in the Mozarteum, Salzburg*]

[MUNICH, 11 *January* 1775[1]]

I hope that you are quite well. I have nothing to write about except to send our greetings to everyone. We are off now to the rehearsal of the opera. It is true that the Archbishop informed the Elector that he would come, but no one knows when this will be, whether now or in the spring. Farewell. We kiss you many 10,000 times and I am your old

MZT

Up to the present it seems that there is every likelihood that Wolfgang will compose the grand opera here this time next year.

---

[1] A postscript to Mozart's letter.

(197) *Mozart to his Mother*

[Autograph in the Mozarteum, Salzburg]

MUNICH, 14 *January* 1775

Thank God! My opera was performed yesterday, the 13th, for the first time and was such a success that it is impossible for me to describe the applause to Mamma. In the first place, the whole theatre was so packed that a great many people were turned away. Then after each aria there was a terrific noise, clapping of hands and cries of 'Viva Maestro'. Her Highness the Electress and the Dowager Electress (who were sitting opposite me) also called out 'Bravo' to me. After the opera was over and during the pause when there is usually silence until the ballet begins, people kept on clapping all the time and shouting 'Bravo'; now stopping, now beginning again and so on. Afterwards I went off with Papa to a certain room through which the Elector and the whole Court had to pass and I kissed the hands of the Elector and Electress and Their Highnesses, who were all very gracious. Early this morning His Grace the Bishop of Chiemsee[1] sent me a message, congratulating me on the extraordinary success of my opera. I fear that we cannot return to Salzburg very soon and Mamma must not wish it, for she knows how much good it is doing me to be able to breathe freely.[2] We shall come home soon enough. One very urgent and necessary reason for our absence is that next Friday my opera is being performed again and it is most essential that I should be present. Otherwise my work would be quite unrecognizable—for very strange things happen here. I kiss Mamma's hands 1000 times. My greetings to all my good friends. My compliments to M. Andretter and I beg him to forgive me for not yet replying, but it has been impossible for me to find the time. However, I shall do so very soon. Adieu. 1000 kisses to Bimberl.

(197a) *Leopold Mozart to his Wife*

[Autograph in the Mozarteum, Salzburg]

[MUNICH, 14 *January* 1775[3]]

You must have received two letters from me and one from Nannerl. I do not yet know how Nannerl will return to Salzburg nor whether she

[1] Count Ferdinand Christoph von Zeill (1719–1786), Bishop of Chiemsee. He was a candidate for the Archbishopric of Salzburg in 1772, but retired in favour of Hieronymus Colloredo, Bishop of Gurk. He was a connoisseur and patron of music and was very partial to Mozart.
[2] Mozart is alluding to the tyrannical attitude of the Archbishop.
[3] A postscript to Mozart's letter.

can travel with Frau von Robinig. Perhaps she will wait and come back with us. Farewell. We kiss you many 1000000 times and I am your old

MOZART

I have received all your letters.
My greetings to all.

(198) *Leopold Mozart to his Wife*

[*Extract*]   [*Autograph in the Mozarteum, Salzburg*]

MUNICH, 18 January 1775

My last letter and other letters which must have been written to Salzburg will have told you that the opera has won general applause; and you will now have heard it from Herr Gschwendner in person. Picture to yourself the embarrassment of His Grace the Archbishop at hearing the opera praised by the whole family of the Elector and by all the nobles, and at receiving the enthusiastic congratulations which they all expressed to him. Why, he was so embarrassed that he could only reply with a bow of the head and a shrug of the shoulders. We have not yet spoken to him, for he is still too much taken up by the compliments of the nobility. He arrived about half past six in the evening just as the grand opera had begun and entered the Elector's box. It would take too long if I were to describe all the other ceremonies. The Archbishop will not hear Wolfgang's opera buffa, because, as all the other days are already filled up, it will be given on a Friday. But it cannot be performed on this coming Friday, as it is the anniversary of the death of the late Bavarian Emperor.[1] And who knows whether it can be performed on the following Friday, the 27th, as the second woman singer[2] is very ill. I am sorry that so many people have come over from Salzburg for what one may call nothing, but at least they will have seen the grand opera. It is not known yet whether the Archbishop will leave tomorrow or will stay on until next Tuesday. Addio. We kiss you many 1000000 times and I am your old

MOZART

I understand that there will be a big concert in the Kaisersaal on Saturday and that the Archbishop will probably stay on here until Monday or Tuesday.

---

[1] Emperor Charles VII, who died on 20 January 1745. He was the father of the reigning Elector Maximilian III.
[2] Possibly Teresina Manservisi.

(198a) *Mozart to his Sister*

[Autograph in the Mozarteum, Salzburg]

MY DEAR SISTER!   [MUNICH, 18 *January* 1775[1]]
Is it my fault that it has just struck a quarter past seven? It is not
Papa's fault either. Mamma will hear more news from my sister. But now
there is no pleasure in travelling because the Archbishop is not staying
here for long. It is even said that he will remain on until he leaves again.
I am only sorry that he will not see the first Ridotto. My compliments to
Baron Zemen and to all my good friends. I kiss Mamma's hands. Farewell.
I shall fetch you very soon.

Your faithful
FRANCIS WITH THE BLEEDING NOSE

Milan, 5 May 1756.[2]

(199) *Leopold Mozart to his Wife*

[Extract]   [Autograph in the Mozarteum, Salzburg]

MUNICH, 21 *January* 1775
That the gentlemen of Salzburg are gossiping so much and are convinced that Wolfgang has entered the service of the Elector, is due to our
enemies and to those whose conscience tells them that if he had done so,
it would have been with good reason. You know well that we are
accustomed to these childish stories and that such talk leaves me quite cold.
So you can tell that to everyone. His Grace will certainly not leave before
next Wednesday. The two Dukes of Zweibrücken and the Elector of the
Palatinate are coming over to Munich, so we must stay on until the opera
has been performed a second time. This morning Nannerl and a valet of
the Elector, accompanied by Barbara Eberlin and a few others, drove off
in a court carriage to Nymphenburg to see the castle rooms. They are
lunching there. Then at three o'clock Nannerl is coming with me to the
Court to see the rooms, the jewels and so forth. The Hagenauers will, no
doubt, have heard something from Munich about Wolfgang's opera. Go
and see them and give them my greetings. All possible honours are being
showered on the Archbishop and his retinue. Thank God, we are well and
we hope and trust that you are also. We kiss you many 1000000 times and
send our greetings to all and I am your old

MOZART

---

[1] A postscript to his father's letter.
[2] This postscript with its nonsensical date was really intended for his mother, as Nannerl
was still in Munich.

They rightly fear in Salzburg lest one bird after another may fly away, since Hagenauer Statuarius[1] has also taken another appointment. Addio. Farewell. Tell me everything you hear, and we shall have something to laugh about, for we know these fools.

(200) *Leopold Mozart to his Wife*

[*Extract*]   [*Autograph in the Mozarteum, Salzburg*]

MUNICH, 8 *February* 1775

Thank God, we are well. Herr Kempfer left yesterday for Augsburg after performing before the Elector and spending a week in Munich. A few rascals have been here too. One was a teacher of English, born in Silesia, Schwarz by name. He was here for almost a year and then decamped with watches and clothes, leaving many debts behind him. The other made out that he was the son of Schmittmeyer, the rich banker in Vienna, and spent a few weeks here. But he cleared out when it was discovered that he was the son of an innkeeper of Nikolsburg in Moravia. He is probably now under arrest in Augsburg. We all kiss you. Farewell. I am your old

MOZART

We send greetings to all.
Count Wolfegg is here too and the two young Counts von Zeill.

(201) *Leopold Mozart to his Wife*

[*Extract*]   [*Autograph in the Mozarteum, Salzburg*]

MUNICH, 15 *February* 1775

Thank God, all three of us are well, but I shall be glad when this carnival is over. We shall probably travel home on Ash Wednesday. A short Mass by Wolfgang was performed last Sunday in the Court chapel and I conducted it. Next Sunday another is to be performed.[2] Yesterday we had extraordinary weather, just like April, now fine now rainy. At one o'clock there was a fire alarm, for the fire was coming out of the chimney and was already very fierce. But it was put out at once by the crowd. We are not going to the Redoute today, as we really must rest. It is the first one that we have missed. Yesterday Nannerl wore the dress of an Amazon, which suited her very well. As a daily diary is being kept, you

---

[1] See p. 256, n. 7.
[2] Possibly K. 192 [186f] and 194 [186h], which were composed in 1774.

will have everything read out to you in due course.[1] Farewell. We all kiss you many 100000 times and send greetings to everyone, and I am your old

MOZART

(202) *Leopold Mozart to his Wife*

[Extract]   [*Autograph in the Mozarteum, Salzburg*]

MUNICH, 21 February 1775

I shall be delighted when this carnival is over. I am really tired out, for it is lasting far too long. Signor Tozzi,[2] who composed the opera 'Orfeo', has decamped. He had a prolonged love affair with Countess von Seefeld, whose brother, Count Sedlizky, was in the know, as was also an Italian tenor, Signor Guerrieri. The Countess left Munich six weeks ago on the pretext of visiting her estates, but what she really did was to run away from her husband and children, taking a great deal of money and jewelry with her. Thank God, we are well, and hope to be in Salzburg on the first Sunday in Lent. Farewell. We send greetings to all, kiss you many 10000000 times and I am your old

MZT

The first masked Redoute in Salzburg will have gone off well. You simply must go to one! Addio.

(202a) *Nannerl Mozart to her Mother*

[Autograph in the Mozarteum, Salzburg]

[MUNICH, 21 February 1775[3]]

Thank God we are quite well. I hope that Mamma too is very well.

A propos, are the canary, the tomtits and the robin redbreast still alive, or have they let the birds starve? We shall come home at the end of the carnival. Meanwhile my pupils must go on practising, and perhaps Herr Schulz would be so kind as to go to Barbara Zezi a few times a week, and, if he will, to Fräulein Andretter, and hear them play their pieces.

---

[1] There is evidence to show that the keeping of diaries was a habit of the Mozart family. For instance, we have Nannerl's *Reisetagebuch*, kept during their grand tour, 1763–1766, and fragments of diaries kept jointly by Nannerl and Wolfgang from 1775–1777, 1779–1780 and 1783. All this material has now been incorporated in *Mozart. Briefe und Aufzeichnungen*.

[2] See p. 255, n. 4.   [3] A short note inserted in her father's letter.

(202b) *Leopold Mozart resumes writing*

Some people have come to see us, so I can only write to you in a great hurry that I and, thank God, we all are well. I am sorry for poor Marschall.[1] Wolfgang's opera has been performed again, but on account of the woman singer who was ill, it had to be cut short. I could write a great deal about this singer, who was absolutely wretched, but I shall tell you all about her when I see you. Farewell. Do go to the ball in the Town Hall. We kiss you many 10000 times. My greetings to all. I am your old

MZT

We hope to leave here in about a fortnight. We are never at home the whole day long.

(203) *Leopold Mozart to his Wife*

[*Extract*]   [*Autograph in the Mozarteum, Salzburg*]

Ash Wednesday
[MUNICH, 1 *March*] 1775

Thank God, the carnival is over. We have now fixed our departure for Monday, the 6th, so we shall arrive in Salzburg rather late in the evening of Tuesday the 7th, for on the first day we are only travelling as far as Wasserburg. Should our arrival be postponed for a day, you will receive a letter on Tuesday or perhaps even on Monday morning. We are to bring with us from Munich a young lady, who would like to stay with us for three or four months and improve her harpsichord playing. Up to the present I have refused this. But in the meantime you might think out where we could get some bedding, for, if necessary, we shall have to put up a bed near the door in Nannerl's room, where the red sofa stands; and the sofa will have to be placed in front of the stove between your clothes-chest and the bed, so that we can put things on it. But I hope that nothing will come of this; and what I am saying is only by way of warning. If it has to be, as I hope it will not, I shall write to you by the next post. I am very much pleased that Herr Lotter has sent me something, for there is now a big hole in my purse. Otherwise, thank God, we are well; and we all three hope to see you and kiss you with delight. You may tell everyone the story of Tozzi and Countess Seefeld, so that people may realize that Italians are knaves the world over. For the last few days we have had most beautiful weather. Wolfgang's opera is to be performed on Thursday. Farewell. We all three kiss you many millions of times and I am your old

MZT

[1] Jakob Anton Marschall, a cellist in the Salzburg court orchestra, who died in January 1775. See Hammerle, *op. cit.* p. 33.

PADRE MARTINI
From a portrait by an unknown artist (*c.* 1775)
(Liceo Musicale, Bologna)

(204) *Leopold Mozart to J. G. I. Breitkopf, Leipzig*

[*Extract*]   [*Autograph in the Deutsche Staatsbibliothek, Berlin*]

[SALZBURG, 6 *October* 1775]

As I decided some time ago to have some of my son's compositions printed, I should like you to let me know as soon as possible whether you would like to publish some of them, that is to say, symphonies, quartets, trios, sonatas for violin and violoncello, even solo sonatas for violin or clavier sonatas. In regard to the latter perhaps you would like to print clavier sonatas in the same style as those of Carl Philipp Emanuel Bach 'mit veränderten Reprisen'? These were printed by Georg Ludwig Winter in Berlin,[1] and this type of sonata is very popular. I must ask you again to let me know as soon as possible and, what is more, on what conditions you would undertake to publish them, so that we may not engage in a long correspondence about a trifling business and so that, if nothing comes of my suggestion, I may apply to some other firm. I shall be very grateful if you will send me a list of all the works of Carl Philipp Emanuel Bach which you can supply.

Your obedient servant

LEOPOLD MOZART

Do you ever hear from our friend Herr Grimm in Paris? I have not had a letter from him for over a year. Have you sold the sonatas which my son composed as a child and the portraits?

(205) *Mozart to Padre Martini, Bologna*

[*MS in the Nationalbibliothek, Vienna*]

[SALZBURG, 4 *September* 1776[2]]

MOST REVEREND PADRE MAESTRO, MY ESTEEMED PATRON,

The regard, the esteem and the respect which I cherish for your illustrious person have prompted me to trouble you with this letter and to send you a humble specimen of my music, which I submit to your masterly judgment. I composed for last year's carnival at Munich an opera buffa, 'La finta giardiniera'. A few days before my departure the Elector expressed a desire to hear some of my contrapuntal compositions.

---

[1] C. P. E. Bach's *Sechs Sonaten fürs Clavier mit veränderten Reprisen* were published by Georg Ludwig Winter, Berlin, 1760.

[2] This letter is in Italian, in the hand of Leopold Mozart (see W. Plath, *Mozart-Jahrbuch* 1960/1, p. 84).

I was therefore obliged to write this motet[1] in a great hurry, in order to have time to have the score copied for His Highness and to have the parts written out and thus enable it to be performed during the Offertory at High Mass on the following Sunday. Most beloved and esteemed Signor Padre Maestro! I beg you most earnestly to tell me, frankly and without reserve, what you think of it.[2] We live in this world in order to learn industriously and, by interchanging our ideas, to enlighten one another and thus endeavour to promote the sciences and the fine arts. Oh, how often have I longed to be near you, most Reverend Father, so that I might be able to talk to and have discussion with you. For I live in a country where music leads a struggling existence, though indeed apart from those who have left us, we still have excellent teachers and particularly composers of great wisdom, learning and taste. As for the theatre, we are in a bad way for lack of singers. We have no castrati, and we shall never have them, because they insist on being handsomely paid; and generosity is not one of our faults. Meanwhile I am amusing myself by writing chamber music and music for the church,[3] in which branches of composition we have two other excellent masters of counterpoint, Signori Haydn[4] and Adlgasser.[5] My father is in the service of the Cathedral and this gives me an opportunity of writing as much church music as I like. He has already served this court for thirty-six years and as he knows that the present Archbishop cannot and will not have anything to do with people who are getting on in years, he no longer puts his whole heart into his work, but has taken up literature, which was always a favourite study of his. Our church music is very different from that of Italy, since a mass with the whole Kyrie, the Gloria, the Credo, the Epistle sonata,[6] the Offertory or Motet, the Sanctus and the Agnus Dei must not last longer than three quarters of an hour. This applies even to the most Solemn Mass said by the Archbishop himself. So you see that a special study is required for this kind of composition. At the same time, the mass must have all the instruments—trumpets, drums and so forth. Alas, that we are so far apart, my very dear Signor Padre Maestro! If we were together, I should have so many things to tell you! I send my devoted remembrances to all the members of the Accademia Filarmonica.[7] I long to win your favour and

---

[1] K. 222 [205a], 'Misericordias Domini', performed in Munich on 5 March 1775.

[2] In his reply, dated 18 December 1776, Padre Martini praises highly Mozart's composition, adding that 'it has all the qualities which modern music demands, good harmony, rich modulation, etc.' See Köchel, p. 228.

[3] During the year 1776 Mozart composed several divertimenti, church sonatas, a Litany (K. 243) and four masses (K. 262 [246a], 257, 258, 259).

[4] See p. 78, n. 1.   [5] See p. 26, n. 3.

[6] While the priest read the Epistle, the organist played softly a sonata with or without violin accompaniment. This practice, which prevailed in Italian church services, was first introduced into Austria during the reign of the Emperor Joseph II.

[7] The Accademia Filarmonica of Bologna, of which Mozart had been made a member in October 1770.

I never cease to grieve that I am far away from that one person in the world whom I love, revere and esteem most of all and whose most humble and devoted servant, most

Reverend Father, I shall always be.

WOLFGANGO AMADEO MOZART

If you condescend to write to me, please address your letter to Salzburg via Trento.

(206) *Mozart to Archbishop Hieronymus Colloredo*

[Autograph in the Regierungsarchiv, Salzburg]

[SALZBURG, 1 August 1777]

YOUR GRACE, MOST WORTHY PRINCE OF THE HOLY ROMAN EMPIRE!
    I will not presume to trouble Your Grace with a full description of our unhappy circumstances, which my father has set forth most accurately in his very humble petition[1] which was handed to you on March 14th, 1777. As, however, your most gracious decision was never conveyed to him, my father intended last June once more most respectfully to beg Your Grace to allow us to travel for a few months in order to enable us to make some money; and he would have done so, if you had not given orders that in view of the imminent visit of His Majesty the Emperor your orchestra should practise various works with a view to their performance. Later my father again applied for leave of absence, which Your Grace refused to grant, though you permitted me, who am in any case only a half-time servant, to travel alone. Our situation is pressing and my father has therefore decided to let me go alone. But to this course also Your Grace has been pleased to raise certain objections. Most Gracious Prince and Lord! Parents endeavour to place their children in a position to earn their own bread; and in this they follow alike their own interest and that of the State. The greater the talents which children have received from God, the more are they bound to use them for the improvement of their own and their parents' circumstances, so that they may at the same time assist them and take thought for their own future progress. The Gospel teaches us to use our talents in this way. My conscience tells me that I owe it to God to be grateful to my father, who has spent his time unwearyingly upon my education, so that I may lighten his burden, look after myself and later on be able to support my sister. For I should be sorry to think that she should have spent so many hours at the harpsichord and not be able to make good use of her training.

---

[1] Not extant.

267

Your Grace will therefore be so good as to allow me to ask you most humbly for my discharge, of which I should like to take advantage before the autumn, so that I may not be obliged to face the bad weather during the ensuing winter months. Your Grace will not misunderstand this petition, seeing that when I asked you for permission to travel to Vienna three years ago,[1] you graciously declared that I had nothing to hope for in Salzburg and would do better to seek my fortune elsewhere. I thank Your Grace for all the favours I have received from you and, in the hope of being able to serve you later on with greater success, I am

your most humble and obedient servant
WOLFGANG AMADE MOZART[2]

[1] Mozart is probably referring to his visit to Vienna in the summer of 1773.

[2] Possibly this letter was dictated by Mozart's father. See Fr. Pirckmayer, *Mitteilungen der Gesellschaft für Salzburger Landeskunde*, xvi, 1876. The Archbishop's minute, dated 28 August 1777, is as follows: 'To the Court Chamberlain with my decision that in the name of the Gospel father and son have my permission to seek their fortune elsewhere'. Leopold Mozart, however, was retained in his appointment. See p. 281.

In September 1777 Mozart, who, owing to his strained relations with the Archbishop of Salzburg, Hieronymus Colloredo, saw no prospect of advancement in his native town, set off with his mother on a tour of the musical centres of Southern Germany in the hope of securing commissions or possibly obtaining a permanent appointment at some court. Their first visit was to Munich, where Mozart soon realized that there was no opening for him. They left for Augsburg on October 11th. Letters 207–220.

(207) *Mozart to his Father*

[*Autograph in the Mozarteum, Salzburg*]

[WASSERBURG], 23 *September* 1777

MON TRÉS CHER PÉRE,

Praise and thanks be to God, we arrived safely at Waging, Stein, Frabertsham and Wasserburg. Now for a brief account of our journey. When we reached the town gates we had to wait for nearly a quarter of an hour until they were opened for us, for some work was being done there. Outside Schinn we came across a herd of cows, one of which was most remarkable—for she was *lop-sided*, a thing we had never seen before. At Schinn we saw a carriage which was at a standstill and behold—our postillion shouted out: 'We must change here'. 'As you like', said I. As Mamma and I were chatting, a fat gentleman, whose *symphony*[1] I recognised immediately, came up to our carriage. He was a merchant from Memmingen.[2] He looked at me for some time and finally said: 'You are Herr Mozart, are you not?' 'At your service', I replied. 'I know you too, but cannot remember your name. I saw you a year ago at a concert in Mirabell.' Whereupon he told me his name, but, thank Heaven, I have forgotten it. But I have retained one which is much more important. For when I saw him at Salzburg he had a young man with him, and on this occasion he was travelling with that young man's brother, who comes from Memmingen and is called Herr von Unhold. This young gentleman pressed me to go to Memmingen, if it were possible. We asked them to deliver 100000 compliments to Papa and to my brute of a sister, which they promised to do. This change of carriages was very inconvenient for me, for I should have liked to give a letter to the postillion to take back from Waging. After we had eaten something there, we then had the honour of continuing our journey as far as Stein with the same horses with which we had already driven for an hour and a half. At Waging I was alone for a moment with the priest, who was amazed to see us, for he had heard nothing whatever about our story.[3] From Stein we travelled with a postillion who was a perfectly dreadful phlegmaticus—*as a driver, I mean*. We thought we should never reach the next stage, but we got there eventually. As I write this letter, Mamma is already half asleep. From Frabertsham to Wasserburg everything went well. Viviamo come i principi.[4] Only one person is wanting—and that is Papa. Ah well, it is God's will. All will yet be well. I hope that Papa is well and as happy as I

[1] i.e. ensemble.   [2] Herr von Krimmel, as will be seen later. See p. 291, n. 2.
[3] i.e. the strained relations between the Archbishop and Mozart and his father.
[4] We are living like princes.

am. I am most attentive to my duty. I am quite a second Papa, for I see to everything. I have begged Mamma to let me pay the postillions, for I can deal with these fellows better than she can. At the Stern here they do you extraordinarily well. Why, I am sitting here as if I were a prince. Half an hour ago (Mamma happened to be in the closet) the porter knocked at the door and asked me about all sorts of things, and I answered him with my most serious air, looking just as I do in my portrait.[1] Well, I must stop. Mamma has now finished undressing. We both of us beg Papa to take care of his health, not to go out too early and not to worry, but to laugh heartily and be merry and always remember, as we do, that our Mufti H.C.[2] is an idiot, but that God is compassionate, merciful and loving. I kiss Papa's hands 1000 times and embrace my brute of a sister as often as I have already taken snuff today. I believe I have left my diplomas[3] at home? Please send them to me as soon as you can.

    Early in the morning, about half past six on
             September 24th.
             Your most obedient son
                       WOLFGANG AMADÉ MOZART

PS.—My pen is rough and I am not polite.
    Wasserburg, 23 September 1777.
        undecima hora nocte tempore.[4]

(208) *Leopold Mozart to his Wife and Son*

[Extract]   *[Autograph in the Mozarteum, Salzburg]*

MY TWO DEAR ONES!   SALZBURG, 25 *September* 1777

I received dear Wolfgang's letter this morning with the greatest pleasure; and just now Bullinger, who sends his greetings, has read it and laughed most heartily: When you are well I am extremely happy, and, thank Heaven, I myself am now very much better. After you both had left, I walked up our steps very wearily and threw myself down on a chair. When we said good-bye, I made great efforts to control myself in order not to make our parting too painful; and in the rush and flurry I forgot to give my son a father's blessing. I ran to the window and sent my blessing after you; but I did not see you driving out through the gate and so came to the conclusion that you were gone already, as I had sat for

[1] During the summer of 1777 a portrait of Mozart was painted by an unknown artist in Salzburg. Mozart looks very serious and rather ill. A copy of this portrait was sent to Padre Martini at Bologna. See illustration No. 5.
[2] Archbishop Hieronymus Colloredo.
[3] The diplomas of membership of the Academies of Bologna and Verona, awarded to Mozart in October 1770 and January 1771.   [4] i.e. at 11 o'clock at night.

a long time without thinking of anything. Nannerl wept bitterly and I had to use every effort to console her. She complained of a headache and a sick stomach and in the end she retched and vomited; and putting a cloth round her head she went off to bed and had the shutters closed. Poor Bimbes lay down beside her. For my own part, I went to my room and said my morning prayers. I then lay down on my bed at half past eight and read a book and thus becoming calmer fell asleep. The dog came to my bedside and I awoke. As she made signs to me to take her for a run, I gathered that it must be nearly noon and that she wanted to be let out. I got up, took my fur cloak and saw that Nannerl was fast asleep. The clock then showed half past twelve. When I came in with the dog, I woke Nannerl and ordered lunch. But she had no appetite, she would eat nothing and went to bed immediately afterwards, so that, when Bullinger had left, I passed the time lying on my bed, praying and reading. In the evening she felt better and was hungry. We played piquet and then had supper in my room. After that we had a few more games and, with God's blessing, went off to bed. That is how we spent that sad day which I never thought I should have to face. On Wednesday Nannerl went to early Mass and in the afternoon we had our shooting.[1] Bullinger won for Sallerl,[2] for he shot for both her and Mamma. So Mamma has won eleven kreuzer, but Wolfgang has lost four. Bullinger and Katherl[3] played with us until six; and that dreadful day ended with the Rosary, which I say for you daily. This morning I asked Herr Glatz of Augsburg to come and see me and we agreed that when you are in Augsburg, you should stay at the 'Lamm' in the Heiligkreuzgasse, where the tariff is thirty kreuzer for lunch, where the rooms are comfortable and where the most respectable people, both Englishmen and Frenchmen, put up. From there it is quite a short distance to the Church of the Holy Cross; and my brother, Franz Aloys,[4] also lives near by in the Jesuitengasse. So you should not say anything to Herr Albert,[5] for the 'Drei Mohren'[6] is far too expensive; the landlord asks an outrageous price for his rooms and every meal works out at about forty-

---

[1] One of the favourite recreations of the Mozart family and their friends was 'Bölzelschiessen', i.e. shooting at targets with air-guns. These shooting matches usually took place on Sunday afternoons. The 'Schützencompagnie' or company of marksmen, met at different houses, each member in turn providing a pictorial target, which had to be topical in subject and embellished with verses. The company kept a cash-box and members were allowed to shoot for absent relatives and friends.   [2] Rosalie Joly.

[3] Maria Anna Katharina Gilowsky (1750–1802), daughter of Wenzel Andreä Gilowsky von Urazowa, who held an appointment in the Archbishop's household. She was a great friend of Nannerl's.

[4] Leopold Mozart's two younger brothers, Joseph Ignaz Mozart (1725–1796) and Franz Aloys Mozart (1727–1791), were bookbinders in Augsburg. The latter, the more prosperous of the two, was the father of Maria Anna Thekla, the 'Bäsle'.

[5] Albert was the landlord of the 'Schwarzer Adler' in the Kaufingerstrasse, Munich. On account of his interest in literature and music he was nicknamed 'der gelehrte Wirt'.

[6] The Mozart family, when starting on their European Tour in 1763, had spent a fortnight at this inn at Augsburg, evidently on the recommendation of Herr Albert. See p. 22.

five or even forty-eight kreuzer a head. If you do go to Augsburg, Wolfgang should be taken at once to the organ-builder Stein[1] who will hardly recognize him, as he has not seen him since he was seven. He can tell him that he has come from Innsbruck with a commission to see his instruments. Glatz tells me that Stein, Bioley and Fingerle are in a position to arrange a very fine concert. You must also call on Christoph von Zabuesnig, a merchant and a scholar, who composed that fine German poem about you when he was in Salzburg.[2] He might get some suitable and flattering notice put into the Augsburg paper. My brother or his daughter will certainly take you to the magistrate Von Langenmantel, to whom you should deliver my very humble regards. Mamma knows that we are old acquaintances, for we travelled together to Salzburg on the occasion when Von Haffner's father[3] was also with us. When you are at Courts you must not wear the cross of your order,[4] but in Augsburg you should wear it every day, for there it will win you esteem and respect, as it will in all towns where there is no reigning lord. If you care to visit the monasteries of the Holy Cross and St. Ulrich, you should do so and try their organs. Stein will probably take you to his organ at the Franciscan Church.[5] *Hülber's*[6] *son is in the monastery of St. Ulrich.* By the way, a certain organist and composer is now in Augsburg, of whom they make a great fuss, but whose name I have forgotten. Wherever you stay, you will always, will you not, get the servant to put the boot-trees into your boots?

I intended to get up at nine o'clock this morning, but Glatz found me in bed and then Clessin,[7] the sergeant-major, came in, so that I could not get up till eleven. They all admire Wolfgang's portrait.[8] Clessin was under the impression that you were returning very soon, and so was Schiedenhofen, who was with us yesterday evening from five to seven; and indeed so is everybody. If you should leave Munich without being able to let me know, you should send a note to the Post Office saying: *If letters should arrive with the following address:* à M: Wolfgang Amadé Mozart maître de musique, please forward them to Augsburg, c/o Landlord of the Lamm, in the Heiligkreuzgasse.

　[1] Johann Andreas Stein (1728–1792), a famous organ-builder and harpsichord maker. See p. 22, n. 4.
　[2] For this poem, written in 1769, see Abert, vol. ii. pp. 929–930.
　[3] Sigmund Haffner (1699–1772), a wealthy merchant and burgomaster of Salzburg. Mozart wrote his Haffner serenade (K. 250 [248b]) for the occasion of the marriage of his daughter Marie Elizabeth in 1776 and his Haffner symphony (K. 385) when his son Sigmund (1756–1787) was granted an honorary title in 1782.
　[4] The order of the Golden Spur, conferred on Mozart by Pope Clement XIV. See p. 148.
　[5] Where Stein was organist and had built the instrument.
　[6] Joseph Hülber, violinist and flautist in the Salzburg court orchestra.
　[7] Johann Dominicus Clessin von Königsklee, sergeant-major and later captain in the Archbishop's body-guard.
　[8] The so-called Bologna portrait, painted in the summer of 1777 by an unknown artist in Salzburg. The original has disappeared, but the copy sent to Padre Martini is in the Library of the Liceo Musicale, Bologna. Mozart is wearing the cross of his order. See illustration no. 5.

You have left behind you the trousers of your pike-grey suit. If I find no other opportunity, I shall give them, together with the music for Andretter,[1] some contredanses, the Adagio and Rondo which you composed for Brunetti,[2] and anything else I may find, to the messenger who, should he miss you, can send them on to my brother in Augsburg. I believe that he does not arrive until noon on Monday.

Haydn[3] and Kapellmeister Rust[4] have had a row. The horn concerto, which has been performed once already, was to be rehearsed again after Vespers and Ferlendis[5] and Brunetti had not turned up. Haydn became very angry and said that the rehearsal was quite unnecessary and why should they wait for those Italian asses? Rust maintained that it was for him to give orders and so forth. The service lasted until a quarter to eleven and an Agnus Dei by Haydn was performed again, because Rust was not ready. The sonata was one of Wolfgang's.[6]

While you are in Munich, do not forget to ask for letters of recommendation, and especially for a letter from the Bishop of Chiemsee.[7] Count Sensheim could give you one for Würzburg, where his father's brother is bishop. Nannerl and I send greetings to Mamma and we kiss you and her millions of times.

Addio.

MOZART

(209) *Mozart to his Father*

[*Autograph in the Mozarteum, Salzburg*]

MON TRÉS CHER PÉRE,   MUNICH, 26 *September* 1777

We arrived here on the 24th at half past four in the afternoon. The first piece of news we heard was that we had to drive to the customs house accompanied by a grenadier with a fixed bayonet. And the first acquaintance we met on the way was Signor Consoli,[8] who recognized me at once and whose joy at seeing me cannot be described. He called on me the very next day. Words fail me to express the delight of Herr Albert, who is indeed a thoroughly honest man and our very good friend. After my arrival I played on the clavier till supper-time, for Herr Albert had not yet come in. But he soon turned up and we went down to supper, where

---

[1] K. 185 [167a]. See p. 236, n. 1.
[2] Antonio Brunetti was first violin and soloist in the Salzburg court orchestra. The works referred to are K. 261 and 269 [261a], both composed in 1776.   [3] Michael Haydn.
[4] Jakob Rust, who was Kapellmeister in Salzburg during the years 1777–1778.
[5] Giuseppe Ferlendis was oboist in the Salzburg court orchestra.
[6] Mozart wrote at least eight organ sonatas during the years 1776 and 1777.
[7] Count Ferdinand Zeill. See p. 259, n. 1.
[8] Tommaso Consoli (1735– ?) joined the Munich Kapelle in 1744 and became an excellent male soprano. He sang in Mozart's *Il rè pastore*, which was performed in April 1775 at Salzburg in honour of the visit of the Archduke Maximilian.

I met Mr. Sfeer and some kind of secretary, a very good friend of his, who both send their greetings to you. We got to bed late and were very tired after our journey; but all the same we got up at seven the next morning, the 25th. My hair, however, was so untidy that I did not reach Count Seeau's until half past ten and when I got there I was told that he had already gone out hunting. Patience! I then asked to be taken to Bernad, the choirmaster—but he had gone off with Baron Schmidt to his estates. I found Herr Bellvall, but he was very busy. He gave me 1000 greetings for you. During lunch Rossi made his appearance and at two o'clock Consoli turned up, and at three o'clock Becke and Herr von Bellvall. I called on Frau von Durst who is now living near the Franciscans and at six o'clock I went for a short walk with Becke. There is a certain Professor Huber here (perhaps you will remember him better than I do) who tells me that he saw me during our last visit to Vienna and that he heard me play at young Herr von Mesmer's house. He is neither very tall nor very small, pale, with whitish grey hair, and in features he somewhat resembles our Salzburg Equerry. He is a Deputy-Intendant at the theatre; his job is to read through the plays sent in for production, improve, spoil, expand them or cut them down. He comes to Albert's every evening and often has a talk with me. I was at Count Seeau's today, Friday the 26th, at half past eight in the morning. This is what happened. I walked into the house and Madame Niesser, the actress, who was just coming out, asked me: 'I suppose you want to see the Count?' 'Yes', I replied. 'Well, he is still in his garden and goodness knows when he will return.' I asked her where the garden was. 'Well,' she said, 'I too want to see him, so let us go together.' We had hardly passed the lodge gates before the Count came towards us; and when he was about twelve paces from us, he recognized me, addressed me by name, and was extremely polite. He was already acquainted with my story.[1] As we mounted the steps together very slowly, I disclosed to him very briefly the object of my visit. He said that I should ask immediately for an audience with His Highness the Elector and that if for any reason I was unable to see him, I should put my case before him in writing. I begged him to keep the whole thing secret and he promised me to do so. When I remarked that a first-rate composer was badly needed here, he said: 'I am well aware of it'. After this I called on the Bishop of Chiemsee and was with him for half an hour. I told him everything and he promised me to do his best in the matter. He was going to Nymphenburg at one o'clock and promised to speak to Her Highness the Electress without fail. The Court returns to Munich on Sunday evening. We lunched today at Rasco's with Herr von Bellvall. Rasco and his wife, Herr von Cori, Bellvall and Passauer send you their greetings. Then we went to Frau von Durst, who lives three flights up in Burgomaster

[1] See p. 271, n. 3.

Schmadl's house, where Herr von Cori lodges on the second floor. Thence Herr Siegl (who has now been married for two months) fetched us and we all went together to Frau von Hofstetten, whose husband is away but will soon return. Franz Dufresne is now Court Chancellor, but up to the present *sine auro*.[1] Afterwards Siegl took Mamma home, for she had promised Becke to go with him to the theatre, and I accompanied Frau von Durst to her lodgings and then on to the theatre, where we all met again. The play was: *Henriette, oder Sie ist schon verheiratet*.[2] This morning at half past eleven Becke and I called on the beautiful Fräulein von Seeau. Fräulein von Tosson has made a very good match. Her husband's name is Hepp and he is said to be extremely rich. Herr Johannes Cröner,[3] by being amazingly blunt, has been made Deputy-Konzertmeister. He produced two symphonies (Dio mene liberi)[4] of his own composition. The Elector asked him: 'Did you really compose these yourself?' 'Yes, Your Highness.' 'Who taught you then?' 'Oh, a schoolmaster in Switzerland. People make such a fuss about composing, but that schoolmaster told me more than all our composers here could tell me.' Count Schönborn and his wife, the Archbishop's sister,[5] arrived here today when I happened to be at the theatre. In conversation with them Herr Albert mentioned that I was here and told them that I was no longer in the Archbishop's service. They were both amazed and absolutely refused to believe that (oh, blessed memory!) my whole salary used to be twelve gulden, thirty kreuzer a month.[6] They were only changing horses, or they would have been delighted to have had a word with me; as it was, I missed them. Now at last please let me enquire after your health and condition. I hope, and so does Mamma, that you are both quite well. I am always in my very best spirits, for my heart has been as light as a feather ever since I got away from all that humbug; and, what is more, I have become fatter. Herr von Wallau spoke to me at the theatre today and I called on Countess La Rosée in her box. Well, I must leave Mamma a little room. Please deliver compliments to the whole worshipful company of marksmen from three of its members, that is, Mamma, myself and M. Novac, who comes to Albert's every day. Meanwhile farewell, my dearest Papa. I kiss your hands countless times and embrace my brute of a sister.

WOLFG: AMADÉ MOZART.

[1] i.e. without money.

[2] A comedy by G. F. W. Grossmann.

[3] Cröner was the name of a large family of musicians who all served the Electors of Bavaria and were nearly all violinists. The Deputy-Konzertmeister to whom Mozart refers was Johannes Nepomuk von Cröner, who after the death of Elector Maximilian III in 1777 was pensioned off and died in 1785.

[4] God save me from them.

[5] Maria Theresa (1744– ?), Princess Colloredo, was the second wife of Eugen Franz Erwein, Count Schönborn (1727–1801).

[6] Mozart's annual salary as Konzertmeister to the Archbishop was 150 gulden.

(209a) *Maria Anna Mozart to her Husband*

[*Autograph in the Mozarteum, Salzburg*]

[MUNICH, 26 *September* 1777[1]]

Wolfgang has left me no news to tell. I hope that I shall soon get a letter from you and hear with delight that you are well. Thank God, we are in good trim and only wish that you were with us, which, with God's help, will happen some day. Meanwhile do not worry and shake off all your troubles. Everything will come right in the end, when the hooks and eyes have been put on. We lead a most charming life—up early—late to bed, and visitors all day long. Addio, ben mio. Keep well, my love. Into your mouth your arse you'll shove. I wish you good-night, my dear, but first shit in your bed and make it burst. It is long after one o'clock already. Now you can go on rhyming yourself.

MARIA ANNA MOZART

All sorts of messages to
    my dear Sallerl, Katherl, Nannerl,
        Bimberl.

(210) *Leopold Mozart to his Wife and Son*

[*Extract*]

[*Autograph in the Mozarteum, Salzburg*]

SALZBURG, 27 *September* 1777

You will have received my letter. As yet we have had no news of you from Munich, probably because you were not able to write until Saturday. I feel somewhat better, but my cough will not leave me. I have not gone out yet, and shall not do so until tomorrow, when I shall go to the half past ten Mass in the Church of the Holy Trinity; but if I do not feel quite well, I shall not stir out. Young Herr von Unhold from Munich has just been to see me, so I had to stop writing and talk to him; and Nannerl had to play a sonata for him. My dear Wolfgang, I beg you not to write any more jokes about our Mufti. Remember that I am in Salzburg and that one of your letters might get lost or find its way into other hands. Herr von Moll spent four hours with me yesterday. He is going home on Tuesday or Wednesday of next week, and is delighted to leave Salzburg, for he has come to hate being here. In the bag containing the trousers you will find a steel button for your green summer suit and various pieces of cloth for patching, all of which I presume you will still receive in Munich, for it is possible that things may go better there than we supposed. You mention something about your diplomas, but I scarcely think that you need them. If any difficulty should arise, I can always send them and I can enclose as well a full account of the whole affair. It does our Prince no

    [1] A postscript to Mozart's letter.

credit that he gave you such a poor salary, and it does you little honour that you served him so long for that bagatelle. If anyone asks you what pay you received, *it would be better for you to say quite frankly that you only stayed in Salzburg to please your father and until you were a little older, because the pay is usually only three or four hundred gulden, except in the case of Italians, whom the Prince now remunerates more handsomely.* I trust that you have called on Woschitka[1] and flattered him. You should make friends with everybody. I wrote that sentence in the dark, but now I have a light! Yesterday little Victoria Adlgasser[2] did Nannerl's hair and this afternoon Katherl combed it out and dressed it. We played in the afternoon with Bullinger, *who always sends you his greetings.* Then Seelos,[3] who greets you, came to call on me, and Nannerl took Bimperl, who also greets you, for a walk.

My affair is again on the old footing. What is contained in my diploma, which the Privy Chancery sent to me today, is so long that I shall copy it out word for word in my next letter, which I hope to write the day after tomorrow. For I must close now and send off the parcel today to be put in tomorrow's mail coach. The reply to my petition is really comical; it is most polite and perfectly ridiculous, for it dodges the point. Mitzerl, Tresel[4] and all Salzburg send their greetings to you. Nannerl has tidied up everywhere. She sends greetings to you and kisses you and Mamma a million times. And I?—Ah, but you surely know that my whole heart is with you. God keep you in good health! My very life depends on yours. I am your old deserted father and husband

MOZART

My greetings to our good friends in Munich. Provided that both of you are well I am as gay as a lark.

(211) *Leopold Mozart to his Wife and Son*

[Extract]   [Autograph in the Mozarteum, Salzburg]

SALZBURG, 28 *September* 1777

I went out for the first time today, and to Mirabell, to hear the last Mass, and I sat up in the side oratory. During the service I saw Herr von Gilowsky with Frau von Riedel on his arm and Herr Grenier with Herr von Riedel walking into the courtyard to look at the rooms. So, when Mass was over, I crossed the landing and went there to greet them. They were very much surprised when I told them that you were both in Munich and had perhaps even left. They promised to come and see us on Monday.

---

[1] Franz Xaver Woschitka (1730– ?), leading cellist in the Munich court orchestra.
[2] Daughter of Anton Cajetan Adlgasser, court and cathedral organist in Salzburg.
[3] Jakob Seelos, tenor in the Salzburg court choir.
[4] Therese, the Mozarts' maid-of-all-work.

After lunch the marksmen came and the Paymaster contributed the target, which Bullinger won. But I won the second and, as I shot for Mamma, I made seven kreuzer for her. Wolfgang, for whom Bullinger shot, has won thirteen. Afterwards Kassl and Katherl played with us until the dress rehearsal of the French play at five o'clock, when they all three went off to the theatre. I then took Bimperl for a walk of about 100 yards from our front door and having brought her home, went on myself to the dress rehearsal. The actors were in full dress, but no other people were allowed in. Five hundred tickets are being distributed for Tuesday. The Archbishop went off to Weidwirth for a few days, but, as Count Guntacker[1] and his wife arrived this morning, he returned this evening. We are having the most lovely, warm weather and today, thank God, I am very well and have hardly coughed at all, sometimes not even three times in two hours. But I am still taking medicine to make me perspire and I shall have to speak about my health to Dr. Barisani,[2] as I have got very thin. I trust that with God's help I shall get well, for now I am more placid than I used to be and I shall take great care of myself in every way. But I beg you, dear Wolfgang, not to indulge in any excesses, for from your youth up you have been used to a regular life. And you must avoid heating drinks, for you know that you soon get hot and that you prefer cold to warmth, which is a clear proof that your blood, which has a tendency to heat, immediately boils up. Strong drinks therefore and too much wine of any kind are bad for you. Picture to yourself in what unhappiness and distress you would plunge your dear mother in a far distant country, not to mention myself. I have written very circumstantially to M. Duschek,[3] and I have added that on your journey you will find an opportunity of writing to him. Madame Duschek[4] has replied to my letter and tells me that she too has heard of our worries in Salzburg, that they both sympathize very deeply and long to see our merits rewarded and that Wolfgang, who, she supposes, must now be more of a scamp than ever, should come directly or indirectly to Prague, where he will always be given a very warm welcome. Now I must copy out for you the reply to my petition. You will see how hard they must have worked—if only to put it together.

[1] Count Guntacker Colloredo, brother of the Archbishop of Salzburg.

[2] Dr. Sylvester von Barisani (1719–1810), born in Padua, was private physician to the Archbishop. His two sons, Franz and Sigmund, became doctors, the one in Salzburg, the other in Vienna.

[3] Franz Xaver Duschek (1736–1799), born at Chotebor in Czechoslovakia, studied music in Prague and later in Vienna under Wagenseil. He settled in Prague as a teacher of music and performer on the clavier, for which he wrote a number of compositions.

[4] Josepha Duschek (1753–1823), *née* Hambacher, was born in Prague, where she became a pupil of Franz Duschek, whom she married. She became a famous singer and was called 'Bohemia's Gabrielli'. She and her husband met Mozart at Salzburg in August 1777, when he wrote for her the scena and aria 'Ah, lo previdi' from Paisiello's *Andromeda*, K. 272. An interesting account of the Duscheks, who played a praiseworthy part in Mozart's later years, is to be found in Procházka, *Mozart in Prag* (Prague, 1892), chap. i.

Ex Decreto Cels^{mi}. Principis, 26 Sept., 1777.

To signify to the petitioner that His Grace desires that there should be real harmony amongst his musicians. In gracious confidence therefore that the petitioner will conduct himself calmly and peaceably with the Kapellmeister and other persons appointed to the court orchestra, His Grace retains him in his employment and graciously commands him to endeavour to render good service both to the Church and to His Grace's person.

Did you ever in your life read such a rigmarole of nonsense? Whoever reads the petition and then the reply will be obliged to think that the Chancery Clerk attached this document to the wrong petition. Fortunately no one but Bullinger has read it, and probably nobody else will do so, for the Paymaster asked me today to send for my salary. He did not want to read anything and in any case he would not have objected to sending me the money, as he had not received any definite authority to strike me off his pay-sheet. Last Friday Herr Kolb gave a grand concert to the foreign merchants, at which Ferlendis, Ferrari,[1] Kassl, Stadler,[2] Pinzger,[3] etc. were present. He played on the fiddle your concerto[4] and your Nachtmusik[5] and, as the music was so much praised and won extraordinary acclamation and applause, he announced 'You have been hearing the compositions of a good friend who is no longer with us'. Whereupon they all cried out: 'What a pity that we have lost him!' The concert took place in Eizenberger's hall. When it was over, they all got drunk and shouldered one another in processions round the room, knocking against the lustres or rather, against the large chandelier which hangs from the middle of the ceiling, so that they smashed the centre bowl and other pieces, which will now have to be sent to Venice to be replaced. I sent off this morning the parcel with the trousers, so I hope that you have received them. If you have not, you should enquire, for parcels often go to the customs house. That was why I wrote on mine: *one worn pair of trousers and some music.*

Monday morning, September 29th

I have this moment received your first letter from Munich. Perhaps all will go well. Possibly you could get things working if you could find an opportunity of showing the Elector everything you can do, especially in fugues, canons and counterpoint compositions. You must play up all you can to Count Seeau and tell him what arias and ballets and so forth you

---

[1] Cellist in the Salzburg court orchestra.   [2] Matthias Stadler, a violinist.
[3] Andreas Pinzger (c. 1742–1817) was a violinist in the Salzburg court orchestra.
[4] During the year 1775 Mozart wrote five violin concertos, i.e. K. 207, 211, 216, 218, 219.
[5] Probably one of the virtuoso movements from Mozart's Haffner serenade (K. 250 [248b]), written for performance on the eve of the wedding of Marie Elizabeth Haffner to F. X. Späth, 22 July 1776.

are prepared to compose for his theatre, and this without asking for remuneration. You must be excessively polite to the courtiers, for each one
has a finger in that pie. Consoli could sing the new scena you wrote for
Madame Duschek[1] and you could speak to Count Seeau about her. Perhaps you could give a concert in Count Seeau's garden. If there is a ray of
hope in all this, you will have to stay on in Munich. Make good friends
with Woschitka, for he can always speak to the Elector and he is in great
favour. Should the Elector require you to write a piece for the viol da
gamba, Woschitka could tell you what it should be like and could show
you the works which he prefers, so that you may get some idea of his
taste. If you have not spoken and cannot speak to him and are thus
obliged to apply to him in writing, Herr von Bellvall will tell you who
ought to draft the letter. In conversation and in writing you may state
quite frankly both to the Elector and to Count Seeau that in regard to
your knowledge of counterpoint His Highness need only consult Padre
Maestro Martini of Bologna and Herr Hasse in Venice and hear what they
think. If you really must have them, I will send you your two diplomas
which state that when you were only fourteen you were appointed
maestro di cappella of the Academies of Bologna and Verona. I am now
quite happy; and I am delighted that Mamma, whom I kiss 1000 times, is
in good form and I can well believe that you feel lighthearted. The story
about Albert (to whom we send greetings) and Countess von Schönborn
is really killing. Our greetings to all our friends and acquaintances. So
Herr Siegl too has taken the plunge? I congratulate him most cordially!
I kiss you both most affectionately and remain the old deserted hermit
with his housekeeper

MOZART

I send you herewith the two diplomas and Padre Martini's testimonial.[2]
See that the Elector reads them. Count Seeau should read them too and
make the Elector do so. What a sensation they will make! I mean, the fact
that seven years ago you were made maestro di cappella of both Academies.

(211a) *Nannerl Mozart to her Mother and Brother*

[*Extract*]   [*Autograph in the Mozarteum, Salzburg*]

[SALZBURG, 29 September 1777[3]]

I am delighted to hear that Mamma and Jack Pudding are cheerful and
in good spirits. Alas, we poor orphans have to mope for boredom and

---

[1] K. 272. 'Ah, lo previdi', composed in Salzburg, August 1777. See p. 280, n. 4.
[2] Nissen, p. 227 f., gives the text of Padre Martini's testimonial, dated 12 October 1770. In
a footnote he adds the remark that 'it is not known why this testimonial was ever asked for
and granted'.   [3] A postscript to her father's letter.

fiddle away the time somehow or other. That reminds me, Bimperl, please be so good as to send me soon a short preambulum. But write one this time from C into B, so that I may gradually learn it by heart.

I have no good news to send you from home. So I kiss Mamma's hands and to you, you rascal! you villain! I give a juicy kiss and I remain Mamma's obedient daughter and your sister who is living in hopes—

MARIE ANNE MOZART

Miss Pimpes too is living in hopes, for she stands or sits at the door whole half-hours on end and thinks every minute that you are going to come. All the same she is quite well, eats, drinks, sleeps, shits and pisses.

(212) *Maria Anna Mozart to her Husband*

[Autograph in the Mozarteum, Salzburg]

MUNICH, 29 September 1777

Thank God, we are well and are still here. Wolfgang went today to see the Bishop of Chiemsee and tomorrow he is to pay his respects to the Elector. He was not able to do so before. Herr Woschitka had supper with us yesterday and lunched with us today and was very civil. We must wait and see how we get on. We have very many good friends who would like us to remain here.

(212a) *Mozart to his Father*

[Autograph in the Mozarteum, Salzburg]

[MUNICH, 29-30 September 1777[1]]

True enough! Any number of good friends, but unfortunately most of them can do little or nothing. I was with Count Seeau yesterday morning at half past ten and found him much more serious and not so frank as he was the first time. But it was only in appearance. Then today I called on Prince Zeill, who said to me in the most polite manner: 'I am afraid that we shall not accomplish very much here. When we were at table at Nymphenburg I had a few words in private with the Elector. He said: "It is too early yet. He ought to go off, travel to Italy and make a name for himself. I am not refusing him, but it is too soon."' So there we are! Most of these great lords are downright infatuated with Italy. Zeill advised me, however, to go to the Elector and put my case before him all the same. I had a private talk at table today with Woschitka, who told me to call at nine o'clock tomorrow morning, when he will certainly procure an audience for me. We are good friends now. He wanted absolûment to

---

[1] Mozart's letter is really a continuation of the one begun by his mother.

know who the person was,[1] but I just said: 'Rest assured that I am your friend and ever will be, and that I too am convinced of your friendship. That must suffice'. Now to return to my story. The Bishop of Chiemsee also had a word in private with the Electress, who, however, shrugged her shoulders and said that she would do her best, but was very doubtful. Now to go back to Count Seeau. When Prince Zeill had told him the whole story, he said: 'Do you know whether Mozart gets enough money from home to enable him with a small subsidy to remain on here? I should very much like to keep him.' 'I do not know', replied the Bishop, 'but I very much doubt it. However, you have only to ask him.' So that was why on the following day he was so thoughtful. I like Munich and I am inclined to think, as many of my friends do, that if only I could stay here for a year or two, I could win both profit and honour by my work and therefore would be sought after by the Court instead of having to canvass them. Since my arrival Herr Albert has thought out a scheme, which, I believe, would not be impossible of execution. It amounts to this. He wants to collect ten good friends, each of whom would fork out one ducat a month, thus making ten ducats or fifty gulden a month, or 600 gulden a year. Then if I could get 200 gulden a year from Count Seeau, I should have 800 gulden. Now what does Papa think of this idea? Is it not a proof of friendship? And should I not accept it, provided, of course, that the proposal is serious? It seems perfectly satisfactory to me. I should be near Salzburg, and if you, my dearest Papa, should feel inclined (as I heartily wish that you may) to leave Salzburg and end your days in Munich, the plan would be delightful and quite simple. For if we have had to live in Salzburg on 504 gulden, surely we could manage in Munich on 600 or 800?

Countess La Rosée has asked me to send you 100000 compliments. What a charming woman she is! and a very good friend of ours. Herr von Dufresne told me the other day that the two of them often squabbled about us with the 'Presidentess'.[2] Papa is in high favour with the Countess. She says that for a long time she has not met a man of such good sense and that you can see it in his face! I go to her every day. Her brother is not here.

(212b) *Maria Anna Mozart resumes writing*

[Autograph in the Mozarteum, Salzburg]

We lunched on Friday with Herr Bellvall and then called on Frau von Durst and went to the theatre with her. She sends greetings to you and

---

[1] Mozart is probably alluding to someone who was trying to disturb the good relations between Woschitka and himself.

[2] Probably Madame la Présidente, a lady of fashion in Munich, whose performance on the harpsichord Burney describes in *The Present State of Music in Germany, etc.*, 2nd edition, 1775, vol. i. p. 172.

Nannerl. Herr Becke went off to the country today with Countess Seeau. I am quite happy in Munich, but I should like to be able to divide myself, so that I could also be with you in Salzburg. Do take care of your health, do not go out until you are quite well again and do not let any gray hairs grow. With God's help, all will come right, as it surely must. Greetings to all my friends, that is, Frau von Moll, Frau von Gerlichs,[1] Mamsell Katherl and especially to my dearest Sallerl and Herr Bullinger, Frau Hagenauer, Jungfer Mitzerl, in a word to all who like to hear from us. I kiss Bimperl on her little tongue; but she will probably have forgotten me. Nannerl ought to look very smart indeed, as she has two lady's maids. Write and tell us all that has happened since in Salzburg. A German operetta is being performed tomorrow and we shall see it, because it is making such a sensation. It is said to be very fine. I send plenty of greetings to Thresel also. She must not feel lonely till I return and she must take out Bimbes regularly and make her perform. My greetings also to the birds. I simply cannot write much, for my pen is wretched and I cannot write at all with my gold pen. So I kiss you both many million times. Live together happily and keep well. I pray for both of you every day. Addio.

MARIA ANNA MOZART

(212c) *Mozart resumes writing*

[Autograph in the Mozarteum, Salzburg]

At nine o'clock today, the 30th, I went as arranged with M. Woschitka to Court. Everyone was in hunting dress. Baron Kern was acting chamberlain. I might have gone there yesterday evening, but I did not want to tread on the toes of M. Woschitka, who of his own accord had offered to procure me an audience with the Elector. At ten o'clock he showed me into a little narrow room through which His Highness was to pass on his way to hear Mass before going to hunt. Count Seeau went by and greeted me in the most friendly fashion, saying: 'How do you do, my very dear Mozart!' When the Elector came up to me, I said: 'Your Highness will allow me to throw myself most humbly at your feet and offer you my services'. 'So you have left Salzburg for good?' 'Yes, your Highness, for good.' 'How is that? Have you had a row with him?' 'Not at all, Your Highness. I only asked him for permission to travel, which he refused. So I was compelled to take this step, though indeed I had long been intending to clear out. For Salzburg is no place for me, I can assure you.' 'Good Heavens! There's a young man for you! But your father is still in Salzburg?' 'Yes, your Highness. He too throws himself most humbly at your

---

[1] Anna Maria von Gerlichs, widow of the Salzburg Privy Councillor Gerhart von Gerlichs, who died in 1763.

feet, and so forth. I have been three times to Italy already, I have written three operas, I am a member of the Bologna Academy, where I had to pass a test, at which many maestri have laboured and sweated for four or five hours, but which I finished in an hour. Let that be a proof that I am competent to serve at any Court. My sole wish, however, is to serve your Highness, who himself is such a great——' 'Yes, my dear boy, but I have no vacancy. I am sorry. If only there were a vacancy——' 'I assure your Highness that I should not fail to do credit to Munich.' 'I know. But it is no good, for there is no vacancy here.' This he said as he walked away. Whereupon I commended myself to his good graces. Herr Woschitka has advised me to put in an appearance at Court as often as I can. This afternoon I went to see Count Salern.[1] The Countess, his daughter, is now a maid of honour. She had gone out hunting with the rest. Ravani and I were in the street when the whole company passed by. The Elector and the Electress greeted me in a most friendly manner. Countess Salern recognised me at once and waved her hand to me repeatedly. Baron Rumling, whom I saw beforehand in the antechamber, has never been so *civil* to me as he was on this occasion. How I got on with Salern I shall tell you in my next letter. It was quite satisfactory. He was very polite—and frank.

PS. Ma très chère sœur. I shall send you very soon a letter all for yourself. My greetings to A.B.C.M.R. and more letters of the alphabet of that kind. Addio. I do beg you to take great care of your health. I kiss Papa's hands 100000 times and always remain your most obedient son

WOLFGANG AMADÉ MOZART

Someone built a house here and wrote on it:

> To build a house is good fun, 'tis true.
> That 'twould cost so much I never knew.

During the night someone scrawled underneath:

> That to build a house would cost so much brass
> You ought to have known, you silly ass.

(213) *Leopold Mozart to his Son*

[*Extract*]   [*Autograph in the Mozarteum, Salzburg*]

SALZBURG, [30 *September*] 1777

MON TRÉS CHER FILS!

There was a rehearsal in the theatre this morning. Haydn[2] had to provide entr'acte music for 'Zaïre.'[3] At nine o'clock already one performer

---

[1] Count Joseph von Salern (1718– ?), chief manager of the opera in Munich.
[2] Michael Haydn.   [3] Incidental music for a performance of Voltaire's *Zaïre*.

after the other began to turn up; the rehearsal started at ten and they were not finished until about half past eleven. Of course the Turkish music was included and a march too. Countess von Schönborn came to the rehearsal driven in a chaise by Count Czernin.[1] The music is supposed to suit the action very well and to be very fine. Although it was entirely for stringed and wind-instruments, the court harpsichord had to be brought over and Haydn played on it. On the previous evening Hafeneder's[2] Finalmusik was performed at the back of the pages' garden, where Madame Rosa used to live. The Archbishop had supper in Hellbrunn and the play began after half past six. We saw from our window the attendance, which, however, was not so large as I had expected, for almost half the ticket-holders had stayed away.[3] People say that it is to be performed very often, so I shall be able to hear the music whenever I like. I have seen the dress rehearsal. The play was already over by half past eight, so that the Prince and all the company had to wait half an hour for their carriages. Half a company of grenadiers were parading in the square and the Prince walked up and down the garden.

October 1st. Is not Baron Dürnitz[4] in Munich? Then he is probably on his estates. What is Herr von Dufraisne, the priest, doing? Yesterday I received quite unexpectedly a letter from Mysliwecek, which I am quoting for you.

> Diversi ordinari sono ch'io ricevei avviso da Napoli che per diversi impegni fortissimi hanno dovuto prendre un certo Maestro Valentini[5] per l'opera di carnevale, nonostante però s'accorderanno cigliati 100 al Signor figlio per un' opera l'anno venturo. Ma vogliono l'impresario, cioè, il signor *Don Gaetano Santoro,* che V.S. gli scriva che per meno di 100 cigliati non può venire, ma con i 100 d'esser pronto di accettar l'opera che si destinerà. Io sono tanto tormentato da cotesti impresari che assolutamente vogliono ch'io ne scriva due l'anno venturo: e a momenti aspetto la scrittura. Già a me toccheranno gli siti più cattivi, non importa. Io in Napoli sono conosciuto, e ne scrissi sei. Perchè so che vogliono che io scrivessi la prima, e probabilmente la terza. Io consiglio sempre, per maggior sicurezza, l'opera del carnevale. Dio sa, se ci potrò andare, ma già che vogliono così, accetterò la scrittura, se non potrò, la rimanderò. V.S. dunque da me sarà avvisato quali opere me deveno toccare. Ed allora potrà Lei scrivere al Signor Don Gaetano Santoro circa il prezzo e circa l'opera

---

[1] Count Johann Rudolf Czernin, brother of the Countess Lützow and nephew of the Archbishop.

[2] Joseph Hafeneder, violinist and composer, was a member of the Salzburg court orchestra.

[3] The Mozarts' house in the Makartplatz had a good view of the Salzburg theatre.

[4] Baron Thaddäus von Dürnitz (? –1803), a well known-patron of music and a good performer on the clavier and the bassoon. He commissioned Mozart after the latter's arrival in Munich in December 1774 to write various works, including the clavier sonata, K. 284 [205], for which, however, he never paid him.

[5] There were several operatic composers of this name in the latter half of the eighteenth century, chief of whom were Giovanni Valentini and Michael Angelo Valentini.

addirittura, ovvero mandarmi la lettera, che io l'invierò. Frattanto mille saluti a tutta la stimatissima famiglia e mi do l'onore, etc., etc.[1]

You see from this letter that I cannot answer it at once, because I still have to wait to hear from him what operas he is going to compose. Moreover, he does not seem to have the faintest idea that you are in Munich. So I am waiting for a letter from you, which I hope to receive tomorrow morning, and then I shall be able to take a decision; for one must be guided by circumstances. The journey to Naples is too far and too expensive, especially if you decide to go beyond Munich. Our object is now quite a different one; and should you have the good fortune, which is hardly likely, to get an appointment in Munich, you could not run away during the first year. But in that case you could draft the letter to Santoro to the effect that the offer brings you honour and ensures a contract for an opera in Naples for some other year, when it would be more convenient and practicable. If in the meantime Mysliwecek hears or has heard that you are in Munich, your excuse, if you do not wish to visit him, will have to be that your Mamma forbids you to do so and that other people have persuaded you, and so forth. It is indeed a pity. But, if he is sensible, he will appreciate the point and will not nourish a grievance against a mother. Even if he does manage to reach Naples, what sort of figure will the poor fellow, who is now without a nose, cut in the theatre? But *propriâ culpâ haec acciderunt.*[2] Where does the blame lie, but on himself and on the horrible life he has led? What a disgrace he is before the whole world! Everybody must fly from him and loathe him. It is indeed a real calamity, which he has brought on himself.

Thursday, October 2nd. I was at the Thursday service today, where I heard that the play is to be repeated on Saturday, and that on Sunday there will be a ball, probably a subscription affair. Haydn's interlude was so good that the Archbishop honoured him by saying at table *that he never would have thought that Haydn was capable of composing such music and that instead of beer he ought always to drink burgundy.* What kind of talk is that!

---

[1] Some posts ago I received the news from Naples that owing to several important commitments the authorities have had to engage a certain Maestro Valentini for the carnival opera. Nevertheless they will undertake to pay 100 cigliati to your son for an opera for next year. But the impresario Don Gaetano Santoro would like you to write, refusing to allow your son to go for less than 100 cigliati, but stating that for this sum he will compose whatever opera is allotted to him. Indeed I am worried to death by those impresarios who insist on my writing two operas next year; and at the moment I am awaiting the contract. I shall have the worst of the bargain, but no matter. I am well known in Naples and have written six operas. So I know that they will want me to write the first and probably the third. For greater safety I always advise the carnival opera. Heaven knows whether I shall be able to go to Naples, but as they wish it, I shall accept the contract. If I cannot go, I shall return it. I will inform you in due course what operas have been allotted to me. Then you may write to Don Gaetano Santoro about the fee and the opera itself, or send me your letter which I shall forward to him. Meanwhile, a thousand greetings to your whole most esteemed family, and I have the honour, etc., etc.   [2] i.e. but this happened through his own fault.

After the service I went straight home, as I was expecting a letter from you. But although it is now midday, no letter has arrived yet. Meanwhile I must tell you that I feel very much better, but that I still have a slight cough and a stinking expectoration. Moreover, two days ago a slight rheumatism developed in my left shoulder; but I have kept warm and yesterday afternoon I went for a walk with Nannerl and Pimperl in the hot sun. I let it grill me, got some fresh air and felt so well that I longed to be able to get into a coach and clear out of Salzburg. As it is now past four o'clock and too late for your letter to come, I shall close mine and go for a walk with Nannerl and Pimpes! Everybody sends greetings, especially Frau Hagenauer, to whom I have just been talking in the street and who sends us invitations every day or invites herself to our house. Nannerl and I kiss you millions of times, we wish you luck 1000 times and especially good health; and, hoping to receive a letter tomorrow, I am the old grass widower, bereft of wife and child,

MOZART

If you can perform something before the Elector, you will—or you may—at least get a present, that is, if there is nothing else for you to do.

(214) *Mozart to his Father*

[*Autograph in the Mozarteum, Salzburg*]

[MUNICH, 2 *October* 1777]

Yesterday, October 1st, I called on Count Salern again and today, the 2nd, I actually lunched there. During the last three days I have had quite enough playing, I think, but I have thoroughly enjoyed it. Papa must not suppose that I like to go to Count Salern's on account of ——. Not at all, for unfortunately, she is in service at Court and therefore is never at home. But about ten o'clock tomorrow morning I shall go to Court with Madame Hepp, née Tosson, and shall then see her. For the Court leaves on Saturday and will not return until the 20th. I am lunching tomorrow with Frau and Fräulein De Branca,[1] who is now half my pupil, as Siegl seldom turns up and Becke, who usually accompanies her on the flute, is not here. At Count Salern's during those three days I played several things out of my head, and then the two Cassations I wrote for the Countess[2] and finally the Finalmusik with the Rondo,[3] all from memory. You cannot imagine how delighted Count Salern was. But he really understands music, for all the time he kept on shouting 'Bravo', where

[1] Wife and daughter of Privy Councillor De Branca. Frau De Branca was a Frenchwoman.
[2] K. 247 and 287 [271H], two Divertimenti written in 1776 and 1777 for Countess Antonia Lodron.
[3] Probably K. 250 [248b], the Haffner serenade, composed in 1776.

other noblemen would take a pinch of snuff, blow their noses, clear their throats—or start a conversation. I said to him that I only wished that the Elector could be there, for then he might hear something. As it is, he knows nothing whatever about me. He has no idea what I can do. Why do these gentlemen believe what anyone tells them and never try to find out for themselves? Yes, it is always the same. I am willing to submit to a test. Let him get together all the composers in Munich, let him even summon a few from Italy, France, Germany, England and Spain. I undertake to compete with any of them in composition. I told Salern what I had done in Italy and I begged him, whenever the conversation should turn on me, to trot out these facts. He said: 'I have very little influence, but what I can do, I will do with my whole heart'. He too is strongly of the opinion that if I could stay on here for a time, the problem would solve itself. If I were here alone, it would not be impossible for me to manage somehow, for I should ask for at least 300 gulden from Count Seeau. As for food, I should not have to worry, for I should always be invited out, and whenever I had no invitation, Albert would only be too delighted to have me at table. I eat very little, drink water, just at dessert I take a small glass of wine. I should draw up a contract with Count Seeau (all on the advice of my good friends) on the following lines: to compose every year four German operas, some *buffe*, some *serie*; and to be allowed a *sera* or benefit performance of each for myself, as is the custom here. That alone would bring me in at least 500 gulden, which with my salary would make up 800 gulden. But I should certainly make more, for Reiner,[1] the actor and singer, took in 200 gulden on the occasion of his benefit; and I am *very popular* here. And how much more popular I should be if I could help forward the German national theatre? And with my help it would certainly succeed. For when I heard the German sing-spiel, I was simply itching to compose. The leading soprano is called Mlle Kaiser.[2] She is the daughter of a cook by a count here and is a very attractive girl; pretty on the stage, that is; but I have not yet seen her near. She is a native of the town. When I heard her, it was only her third appearance. She has a beautiful voice, not powerful but by no means weak, very pure and her intonation is good. Valesi[3] has taught her; and from her singing you can tell that he knows how to sing as well as how to teach. When she sustains her voice for a few bars, I have been astonished at the

---

[1] Franz von Paula Reiner (1743–?) lived from 1767 to 1778 in Munich, where he introduced the operetta.

[2] This singer performed in Munich until 1784 and then moved to Vienna.

[3] Johann Evangelist Wallishauser (1735–1811), a Bavarian, had at first great successes as a singer. The Duke of Bavaria sent him to study in Padua, where he adopted the name of Valesi, and in 1771 he sang in opera at Florence, and subsequently in all the leading theatres of Italy. In 1776 he returned to Munich for good, and eventually devoted himself entirely to training singers. Two of his most distinguished pupils were Valentin Adamberger and Carl Maria von Weber.

beauty of her *crescendo* and *decrescendo*. She still takes her trills slowly and I am very glad. They will be all the truer and clearer when later on she wants to trill more rapidly, for it is always easier to do them quickly in any case. People here are delighted with her—and I am delighted with them. Mamma was in the pit. She went in as early as half past four in order to secure a seat; but I did not turn up until half past six, as I have the entrée to all the boxes, for I am so well known. I was in the Brancas' box and I kept my opera-glasses on Mlle Kaiser and she often drew a tear from me. I kept on calling out 'Brava, Bravissima', for I could not forget that it was only her third appearance on the stage. The play was 'The Fisher-maiden', a very good translation of Piccinni's opera.[1] As yet they have no original plays. They would like to produce a German opera seria soon, and they are very anxious that I should compose it. Professor Huber, whom I have already mentioned, is one of the people who want this. Now I must go to bed, for I have come to an end of my tether. It is ten o'clock sharp.

Baron Rumling paid me a compliment the other day by saying: 'I *love* the theatre, good actors and actresses, good singers, and, last but not least, a first-rate composer like yourself'. Only words, it is true, and it is very easy to talk. But he has never spoken to me before in such a flattering manner. I wish you good night—tomorrow, God willing, I shall have the honour of talking to you again, my dearest Papa, in writing.

October 2nd. Number four on the second floor.

(214a) *Maria Anna Mozart to her Husband*

[*Autograph in the Mozarteum, Salzburg*]

[MUNICH, 2 *October* 1777]

Wolfgang is lunching today with Madame Branca and I have lunched at home; but as soon as three o'clock strikes I am going to Frau von Tosson, who is sending someone to fetch me. Herr von Krimmel[2] turned up again yesterday with Herr von Unhold. He is a good friend of ours and is trying hard to persuade us to go to Memmingen and to give a first-class concert, as he assures us that we shall make more there than at a court. I quite believe it, for, as hardly anybody goes to such a place, the people there are glad when they can get anyone at all. Now how is your health? I am not really satisfied with your letters. I don't like that cough, which is lasting far too long. You ought not to have anything wrong with you at all. I beg you to use the sago soon, and the sooner the better, so that you may regain your strength as quickly as possible. We received the parcel

[1] Piccinni's *Le Pescatrice*, produced in 1766. Burney saw it in Florence in 1770. See Burney, *Present State of Music in France and Italy*, 2nd edition, 1773, p. 241 ff.
[2] See p. 271, n. 2.

by the mail coach and the other one too by the ordinary post. I send greetings to Nannerl. Please tell her not to get cross with you and to take good care that you have no worries and to help you to pass the time so that you do not get melancholy. Bimperl, I trust, is doing her duty and making up to you, for she is a good and faithful fox terrier. I send greetings to Tresel also and should like you to tell her that it is all one whether

(214b) *Mozart resumes writing*

[*Autograph in the Mozarteum, Salzburg*]

I shit the muck or she eats it. But now for something more sensible.

I am writing this on October 3rd. The Court is leaving tomorrow and will not return until the 20th. If it had stayed, I should have kept on hammering and I should have stayed on myself for some time. As it is, I hope next Tuesday to continue my journey with Mamma, but the position is this: in the meantime the company, about which I wrote to you the other day, will be formed; so that, when we are tired of travelling, we shall have a safe place to return to. Herr von Krimmel was with the Bishop of Chiemsee today; he had a good many things to settle with him, including that matter of the salt. Von Krimmel is a curious fellow. Here they call him 'Your Grace', I mean, the flunkeys do. He would like nothing better than that I should remain here, and spoke about me very warmly to the Prince.[1] He said to me: 'Just leave it to me. I shall talk to the Prince. I know how to deal with him, as I have often been of service to him.' The Prince promised him that I would *certainly* be taken into the Court service, but added that things could not be done quite so quickly. As soon as the Court returns, he will speak most seriously and earnestly to the Elector. At eight o'clock this morning I saw Count Seeau. I was very brief and merely said: 'I have come, Your Excellency, solely in order to explain myself and produce my credentials. It has been cast up at me that I ought to travel to Italy. Why, I have spent sixteen months in Italy and, as everyone knows, I have written three operas. My other achievements Your Excellency will learn about from these papers.' I then showed him my diplomas and added: 'I am showing these to Your Excellency and I am telling you all this so that, if ever my name is mentioned and any injustice should be done to me, you may be justified in taking my part'. He asked me if I was now going to France. I replied that I was staying on in Germany. But he thought I meant Munich and asked with a pleasant smile: 'What? So you are staying on here?' 'No', I said, 'I should have liked to; and, to tell the truth, the only reason why I should have been glad of a

[1] i.e. the Bishop of Chiemsee.

292

subsidy from the Elector is that I might have been able to serve Your Excellency with my compositions and without asking for anything in return. I should have regarded it as a pleasure.' At these words he actually raised his skull-cap. At ten o'clock I was at Court with the Countess Salern, who has already received the arias. The Robinigs just say, of course, whatever comes into their heads. Afterwards I lunched with the Brancas. Privy Councillor von Branca had been invited to the French Ambassador's, and so was not at home. He is addressed as 'Your Excellency'. His wife is a Frenchwoman, who hardly knows a word of German, so I spoke French to her all the time, and I talked quite boldly. She told me that I did not speak at all badly and that I had one good habit, that is, of talking slowly, which made it quite easy to understand me. She is an excellent woman with the most charming manners. Her daughter plays quite nicely, but her time is still poor. I thought at first that it was due to her own carelessness or that her ear was at fault, but I can now blame no one but her teacher, who is far too indulgent and is satisfied with anything. I made her play to me today. I wager that after two month's lessons from me she would play quite well and accurately. She asked me to send her greetings to you and to the whole Robinig family. She was at the convent at the same time as Fräulein Louise. Later in the day a certain Fräulein Lindner, who is now at Count Salern's as governess to the two young countesses, also requested me to send all sorts of messages to the Robinigs and to Fräulein Louise von Schiedenhofen, with whom she was at the same convent. At four o'clock I went to Frau von Tosson, where I found Mamma and Frau von Hepp. I played there until eight o'clock and then we went home. About half past nine in the evening a small orchestra of five players, two clarinets, two horns and one bassoon, came up to the house. Herr Albert (whose name-day is tomorrow) had ordered this music in his and my honour. They did not play at all badly together. They were the same people who play in Albert's dining-hall during the meals. But you can tell at once that Fiala[1] has trained them. They played some of his compositions and I must say that they were very pretty and that he has some very good ideas.

Tomorrow we are going to have a little scratch-concert among ourselves, but, I should add, on that wretched clavier. Oh! Oh! Oh! Well, I wish you a very restful night and I improve on this good wish by hearing to hope soon that Papa is well quite. I forgiveness your crave for my disgraceful handwriting, but ink, haste, sleep, dreams and all the rest. . . . I Papa your, my hands kiss, a thousand times dearest, and my embrace, the

---

[1] Joseph Fiala (*c.* 1754–1816) was a noted performer, first on the oboe and later on the cello and viola da gamba. He was a member of the orchestra at Donaueschingen until 1774 when he joined the orchestra at Munich. From 1778 onwards he was oboist at Salzburg where he became friendly with the Mozart family.

heart, sister I with all my brute of a, and remain, now and for ever, amen,

WOLFGANG most obedient your
AMADÉ MOZART son

Munich, 3 October 1777.

To all good friends, to all bad friends, good friends, bad friends, all sorts of messages.

(215) *Leopold Mozart to his Son*

[*Extract*]   [*Autograph in the Mozarteum, Salzburg*]

MON TRÈS CHER FILS!   SALZBURG, 4 *October* 1777

I have no great hopes of anything happening in Munich. Unless there is a vacancy, the Elector is bound to refuse to take anyone and, moreover, there are always secret enemies about, whose fears would prevent your getting an appointment. Herr Albert's scheme is indeed a proof of the greatest friendship imaginable. Yet, however possible it may seem to you to find ten persons, each of whom will give you a ducat a month, to me it is quite inconceivable. For who are these philanthropists or these music-lovers? And what sort of undertaking or what kind of service will they require from you in return? To me it seems far more likely that Count Seeau may contribute something. But unless he does, what you may expect from Albert would only be a mere trifle. If he could make the arrangement even for a year—that is all I will say for the moment—then you could accept an offer from Count Seeau. But what would he demand!—perhaps all the work which Herr Michl[1] has been doing? Running about and training singers! That would be a dog's life and quite out of the question! In short, I cannot see where these ten charming friends are to come from. Further, Albert may not be able to see them at once, as some of them are perhaps out of town. Moreover, I should prefer merchants or other honest persons to these courtiers, for a great deal would depend on whether they would keep their word and for how long. *If the arrangement is immediately practicable, well and good, and you*

---

[1] Joseph Michl (1745–1810), a nephew of another Bavarian composer of the same name, was educated and trained in Munich. In 1776 he became composer of chamber music to the Bavarian court, but lost this appointment after the Elector's death in 1777. He wrote a great many compositions solely for performance in Munich. Burney heard one of his works performed in 1772. See Burney, *Present State of Music in Germany, etc.*, 2nd edition, 1775, vol. i. p. 172.

ought to accept it. But if it cannot be made at once, then you simply must not lounge about, use up your money and waste your time. For in spite of all the compliments and shows of friendship which you are receiving, you cannot hope to make a farthing in Munich. So, if the whole scheme cannot be set going now, then let Albert and our other good friends continue their efforts and do you continue your journey and wait until you hear from him. For the stage for these Italians does not extend very much further than Munich and practically comes to an end there. In Mannheim, for instance, everyone except a few castrati is already German, and in Trier at the court of His Royal Highness the Elector, Prince Clement of Saxony, you will only find Maestro Sales; all the rest are Germans. In Mainz they are all Germans, and in Würzburg I only know of Fracassini,[1] a violinist, who is now Konzertmeister, I think, or perhaps Kapellmeister. But these posts he obtained through his German wife, a singer and a native of Würzburg. At the courts of all the less important Protestant Princes you will not find a single Italian. I am writing in haste, for Herr Lotter wants to take my letter. I am enclosing the chorale melodies, which here or there you may find useful and perhaps even necessary, for one should aim at knowing everything. I have just been to see the Chief Steward, who is paying me a special visit one of these days in order that I may tell him everything in detail. For there is no peace at his house; someone is always being announced or else his Countess comes rushing in. He loves you with his whole heart. Before he heard our story, he had already bought four horses and was looking forward to the pleasure he would give you by turning up with one of them for you to ride on. When, however, he heard about our affair, he simply could not express his annoyance. He was paying his respects one day to the Archbishop, who said to him: '*Now we have one man less in the orchestra*'. Firmian replied: '*Your Grace has lost a great virtuoso*'. '*Why?*' asked the Prince. The reply was: '*Mozart is the greatest player on the clavier whom I have ever heard in my life; on the violin he rendered very good services to Your Grace; and he is a first-rate composer*'. The Archbishop was silent, for he had nothing to say. Now I must close because I have no more room. When writing you should at least mention *whether you have had such and such a letter*. You must surely have received by now the parcel containing the roll with the diplomas and Padre Martini's testimonial. We kiss you millions of times and I am your old

MOZART

Be careful not to lose Padre Martini's testimonial.

---

[1] Aloisio Lodovico Fracassini (1733–1798), a pupil of Tartini, became solo violinist to the Bishop of Bamberg in 1757. The Bishop's court was sometimes in Würzburg and sometimes in Bamberg. In 1764, two years after his marriage to the soprano singer of the Würzburg Hofkapelle, Anna Katharina Boyer, Fracassini became Konzertmeister in Würzburg.

(215a) *Nannerl Mozart to her Mother and Brother*

[*Extract*]   [*Autograph in the Mozarteum, Salzburg*]

[SALZBURG, 4 *October* 1777[1]]

DEAREST MAMMA AND DEAREST BROTHER!

I am very glad that you are both well and in good trim. Since you left I have not yet sent you an account of my daily routine; so I shall begin today. The day you left, September 23rd, I spent chiefly in bed, for I was vomiting and had a horrible headache. On the 24th, at half past seven I went to early Mass in Holy Trinity. In the afternoon we had a shooting match. Papa will have told you who won.

On the 25th I went to the half past ten Mass. Herr Glatz and Herr Clessin came to see us in the morning and Herr Bullinger in the afternoon.

On the 26th little Victoria Adlgasser dressed my hair in the morning and Barbara Eberlin was with us. I went to the half past ten Mass and in the afternoon from four to five I took Pimperl for a walk. Then Herr Moll spent the evening with us and stayed until nine o'clock.

On the 27th I went to the half past eleven Mass in Mirabell and in the afternoon I went to market with Katherl Gilowsky. Afterwards we played cards until four o'clock with Abbé Bullinger. Then Katherl combed my hair and I took Pimperl for a walk. Later in the day Herr Unhold came to see us and delivered messages from you.[2]

Today, October 4th, Victoria did my hair. I went to the half past ten Mass and now I shall take Pimperl for a walk and then go to the play with Papa. Keep well. I kiss Mamma's hands and I beg you not to forget me.

MARIA ANNA MOZART

(216) *Leopold Mozart to his Wife and Son*

[*Extract*]   [*Autograph in the Mozarteum, Salzburg*]

SALZBURG, 6 October 1777

I received your letter of October 3rd at a quarter to ten this morning, while I was still in bed, for we were at the ball last night until half past twelve. I quite agree that if you were alone, you could live in Munich. But it would do you no honour, and how the Archbishop would laugh! *You can live in that way anywhere, not only in Munich. You must not make yourself so cheap and throw yourself away in this manner, for indeed we have not yet come to that.* Mamma must make her mind easy, for I am much

---

[1] A postscript to her father's letter.
[2] Nannerl continues this diary up to October 4th. For lack of space it has had to be omitted.

MOZART, WEARING THE ORDER OF THE GOLDEN SPUR (1777)

From a portrait by an unknown artist
(Liceo Musicale, Bologna)

better and this afternoon I am going to take some sago, which has just been got ready. I went to the ball for the sake of some recreation and got a great deal of fun out of it, for nobody recognised me and I quizzed people most dreadfully. With God's help you will now continue your journey. When you reach Augsburg, stay at the 'Lamm' in the Heilig-kreuzgasse, which all the merchants from that town have recommended so highly. Everything else I have already written to you. If anything further should occur to you which you would like to have, I can still send it to Augsburg, as it is not too far. I understand that the Bishop of Chiemsee is to be here tomorrow evening. He will therefore be leaving Munich this evening. He has to take a confirmation at Werfen and it is impossible to say whether he will return to Munich in the immediate future, for the Archbishop does not like him to be there. On Saturday I was at the play. As there was a French epilogue, Brunetti had to play a concerto while the actors were changing dresses, and he played your Strassburg concerto [1] most excellently. But in the two Allegros he played wrong notes occasionally and once nearly came to grief in a cadenza. Haydn's intermezzi [2] are really beautiful. After the first act there was an Arioso with variations for violoncello, flute, oboe and so forth; and incidentally, preceding a variation which was piano, there was one on the Turkish music, which was so sudden and unexpected that all the women looked terrified and the audience burst out laughing. Between the third and fourth acts there was a cantabile movement with a continuous recitative for the cor anglais. Then the Arioso came in again, which, together with the preceding sad scene with Zaïre and the following act, affected us very much. I must add that the orchestra performed your concerto amazingly well. I hear that one more oboist is coming from Italy as secundarius, but nothing more is being said about the castrato. The Chief Steward has had to tell Meisner, who could not sing on one or two occasions because of a cold, that he must sing and perform regularly in the church services or else he will be dismissed. Such is the great favourite's reward! I kiss you both millions of times, with my whole heart I am ever with you, and I remain your old husband and father

MOZART

You say nothing about Mysliwecek, as though he were not in Munich. How then am I to reply to his letter? I suppose that he will have heard that you are there. *Please give Herr Albert my most cordial and sincere greetings and my thanks for all his kindnesses to you, for his friendly support, his interest and his efforts. Indeed I urge him most insistently to care as a true friend for your*

---

[1] Mozart's violin concerto in D major (K. 218), composed in 1775, the last movement of which has a theme reminiscent of a Strassburg dance. See Köchel, p. 243.
[2] The incidental music which Michael Haydn wrote for Voltaire's *Zaïre*. See p. 302, n. 3.

welfare. Basta! He is one of the most honest men and the lover of mankind which I have always thought him to be. What grieves me now and then is that I no longer hear you playing on the clavier or the violin; and whenever I enter our house a slight feeling of melancholy comes over me, for, as I approach the door, I think that I ought to be hearing you play.

Our maid Tresel finds it extraordinarily funny that Nannerl should be for ever poking her nose into the kitchen and scolding her daily about its dirty condition. For Nannerl does not overlook the least thing; and when Tresel tells a lie, Nannerl at once points out to her that it is an untruth. In short, Tresel's eyes are getting wider and wider, for Nannerl says everything to her without mincing matters, though indeed she becomes quite calm again after it is all over.

Addio, keep well! But do take care of your health, for illness would be the worst thing that could befall you. And save as much money as you can, for travelling is expensive.

(216a) *Nannerl Mozart to her Mother and Brother*

[Extract]   *[Autograph in the Mozarteum, Salzburg]*

SALZBURG, 5 *October* 1777[1]

Today, October 5th, we had shooting in our house. Papa supplied the target. I shot for Mamma, who has lost nine kreuzer. Katherl shot for you and won the most. Barbara Eberlin is with me at the moment and sends you her greetings. She wants to take me off to her garden. So farewell. I kiss Mamma's hands and am

your old grandmother

MARIA ANNA MOZART

It would not do you any credit to stay on in Munich without an appointment. It would do us far more honour if you could succeed in obtaining a post under some other great lord. You will surely find one.

(217) *Mozart to his Father*

[Autograph in the Mozarteum, Salzburg]

MON TRÉS CHÉR PÉRE   MUNICH, 6 *October* 1777

Mamma cannot begin this letter; firstly, because she won't be bothered; and secondly, because she has a headache! So I have to rise to the occasion. I shall be going off in a moment with Professor [Huber] to

---

[1] A postscript to her father's letter.

call on Mlle Kaiser. Yesterday, Sunday, October 5th, we had a religious wedding or *altum tempus ecclesiasticum*[1] in this house and there was dancing. I only danced four minuets and by eleven o'clock I was back in my room, for among fifty ladies there was only one who could keep in time; and that was Mlle Käser, a sister of the secretary of that Count Perusa who was once in Salzburg. The Professor has been kind enough to let me down. So I have not been able to go to Mlle Kaiser, as I do not know her address.

(217a) *Maria Anna Mozart to her Husband*

[*Autograph in the Mozarteum, Salzburg*]

MUNICH, 6 *October* 1777

Herr Lotter brought us your letter today and assured us that you are well, news which greatly delighted us. We have received safely all your letters and the parcels. This I wrote in my last letter. I don't know whether we shall stay on here for the rest of the week, but we shall know this in three or four days' time. Herr Albert is making great efforts and he hopes to arrange something, if he can only get the people together. He has eight subscribers already. Every week, that is, every Saturday, there is a concert in his hall. Herr von Düssen has also put in an appearance and some other good people. They all want us to stay on for the winter at least, and Prince Zeill would also like it. The latter is going off to Salzburg the day after tomorrow, but he will only stay there for a day. He too is taking an interest in Wolfgang and has already spoken to Count Sensheim and Count Bergheim, who have promised him to do their very best. He is exceptionally popular here and can do a great deal. One must just be a little bit patient. That is why Herr Albert thinks that if we could only hold out for this winter, we should not have to spend our capital; for the concerts begin next month, on November 1st, and go on until May. So far he is not at all anxious, for all his friends have not yet turned up. I send greetings to Nannerl and by the next post I shall send her the silks. My compliments to Sallerl and to Herr Bullinger, Frau Hagenauer and Herr Gött and other good friends, Mlle Katherl, Tresel, Pimperl and so forth.

I remain your miserable grass widow
MARIA ANNA MOZART

(217b) *Mozart resumes writing*

[*Autograph in the Mozarteum, Salzburg*]

The day before yesterday, Saturday the 4th, on the solemn festival of the name-day of His Royal Highness Archduke Albert[2] we had a little

---

[1] i.e. an old religious occasion.
[2] i.e. the landlord of the 'Schwarzer Adler'. See p. 275, n. 5.

concert here, which began at half past three and finished at about eight.
M. Dupreille,[1] whom Papa will probably remember, was also present.
He was a pupil of Tartini. In the morning he was giving a violin lesson to
Albert's youngest son Carl, when I happened to come in. I had never
thought much of Dupreille, but I saw that he was taking great pains over
the lesson, and when we started to talk of the fiddle as a solo and orchestral
instrument, he made quite sensible remarks and always agreed with me,
so that I went back on my former opinion and was convinced that I should
find in him an excellent performer and a reliable orchestral player. I asked
him therefore to be so good as to come to our little concert in the afternoon. We first played Haydn's two quintets,[2] but to my dismay I found
that I could hardly hear him. He could not play four bars in succession
without going wrong. He could not find his fingering and he knew
nothing whatever about short rests. The best one can say about him is that
he was very polite and praised the quintets; apart from that—Well, I said
nothing at all, but he kept on exclaiming: 'I beg your pardon. I have lost
my place again! It's ticklish stuff, but very fine.' I kept on replying: 'Do
not worry. We are just among ourselves.' I then played my concertos in
C, B♭ and E♭,[3] and after that my trio.[4] There indeed I had a fine accompaniment! In the Adagio I had to play his part for six bars. As a finale
I played my last Cassation in B♭.[5] They all opened their eyes! I played as
though I were the finest fiddler in all Europe. On the following Sunday at
three o'clock we called on a certain Herr von Hamm. I have simply no
time to write more, otherwise Herr von Kleinmayr[6] will not be able to
take the letter. The Bishop of Chiemsee left today for Salzburg. I send my
sister herewith six duets for clavicembalo and violin by Schuster,[7] which
I have often played here. They are not bad. If I stay on I shall write six
myself in the same style, as they are very popular here.[8] My main object
in sending them to you is that you may amuse yourselves à deux. Addio.

---

[1] Charles Albert Dupreille (1728–1796), violinist in the Munich court orchestra.
[2] Probably quintets by Michael Haydn.
[3] K. 246, 238, 271. The first two clavier concertos were composed in 1776, the third in
1777.
[4] K. 254, a clavier trio, composed in 1776.
[5] K. 287 [271H]. See p. 289, n. 2.
[6] Johann Franz Thaddäus von Kleinmayr (1733–1805), Secretary to the Salzburg Court
Council.
[7] Joseph Schuster (1748–1812), Kapellmeister to the Dresden court. In 1765 he and his friend
Seydelmann went with Naumann to Italy to study composition, and remained there until
1768. In 1772 both were appointed church composers to the Elector of Saxony. Schuster
wrote several Italian and German operas, oratorios, symphonies and chamber music. It has not
yet been discovered to which works of Schuster Mozart is referring. See Köchel, pp. 297, 298
and 887.
[8] Mozart carried out his intention at Mannheim, where he composed the five sonatas
for violin and clavier, K. 296, 301-303, 305 [293a-d]. Abert, vol. i. pp. 623-626, points out how
greatly Mozart's sonatas show the influence of Schuster's. See also Saint-Foix, vol. iii. p.
38 ff.

I kiss your hands 1000 times. And I beg you, Nannerl, to wait patiently a little longer.[1]

I am your most obedient son
WOLFGANG AMADÉ MOZART

Munich, 6 October 1777.[2]

(218) *Leopold Mozart to his Son*

[*Extract*]   [*Autograph in the Mozarteum, Salzburg*]

MON TRÈS CHER FILS!   SALZBURG, 9 *October* 1777

As I assume that you have now left Munich, I am writing to Augsburg and am enclosing a letter for Herr Stein, in which I urge him very strongly to arrange one or two concerts and tell him that you will inform him in person of the atrocious treatment which we have been receiving in Salzburg.[3] Do yourself credit on his organ, for he values it very highly; and, moreover, it is a good one. Write and tell me *what instruments he has.* When you were in Munich, you probably did not practise the violin at all? But I should be sorry to hear this. Brunetti now praises you to the skies! And when I was saying the other day that after all you played the violin *passabilmente,* he burst out: 'Cosa? Cazzo! Se suonava tutto! Questo era del Principe un puntiglio mal inteso, col suo proprio danno.'[4] Herr Glatz will bring you a pair of white silk stockings, which I have picked out for you. I put them on for the ball and found them far too tight. You will find too a book of small music paper, which I have put in, in case you should care to write a preambulum for your sister, for this kind of paper is thinner and more convenient for enclosing in a letter. When you talk to Herr Stein, you must not mention our instruments from Gera, for he is jealous of Friederici. But if this is impossible, you should say that I took over the instruments belonging to Colonel Count Prank, who left Salzburg on account of his epilepsy. You should add that you know nothing about the other instruments, as you were too young to notice such things. The Archbishop goes off to Lauffen today and will be away for about a fortnight. Countess Schönborn has left and has taken with her the present for your sonatas. I am still finding one or two little things which you need, so you will be glad when you are further away, for if I am always sending you something, your luggage will become more and more bulky. There is a whole music score for the wind-instruments of

---

[1] Mozart is referring to the composition she had asked for. See p. 283.
[2] The autograph of this letter has the following postscript by the Munich musician Siegl, first published in *MM*, Nov. 1920, p. 32: 'I, Siegl, now a thoroughly trained husband, send my most humble greetings to the Papa of the cher fils!'
[3] Leopold Mozart is referring to their strained relations with the Archbishop.
[4] What? Nonsense! Why, he could play anything! That was a mistaken idea the Prince ersisted in, to his own loss. See letter 266.

the Court orchestra and the score of the Adagio you wrote specially for
Brunetti, because he found the other one too artificial.[1] Perhaps I shall
copy it out on small paper and send it bit by bit. I do not know whether
you will be able to arrange more than one concert in Augsburg, for the
natives there have had an overdose of them. I read in a paper the other day
that Baumgartner, the cellist,[2] and four other musicians gave a concert
there together. When you perform something, and especially if it is a
clavier concerto, take care to see, when the concert is over, that you have
collected all the parts, since you have no scores with you. If you find that
you cannot give more than one good concert in Augsburg, it would be as
well not to stay there too long. I must close, for the post will soon be
going. We did not expect a letter today, for the Munich people always
give theirs to the Reichenhall post, which does not arrive until tomorrow.
Keep well! We are in good health and I seem to get better every day. I
sleep fairly well, my cough is disappearing and I look better. Ah, but
you and Mamma are ever in my mind. We both kiss you many
1000000000000000 times and I am your old faithful, honest husband and
father

                                                            MOZART

I hear that for his fine composition[3] Haydn only received from the
Archbishop six Bavarian thalers (che generosità!)[4]

(219) *Mozart to his Father*

[Autograph in the Mozarteum, Salzburg]

MON TRÉS CHER PÉRE!   [MUNICH, 11 *October* 1777]

Why have I said nothing so far about Mysliwecek? Because it was a
relief not to have to think of him for a while. For whenever he was
mentioned, I was obliged to hear how highly he has been praising me and
what a good and true friend of mine he is! At the same time I felt pity and
sympathy for him. People described his appearance to me and I was nearly
distracted. Was I to know that Mysliwecek, so good a friend of mine, was
in a town, even in a corner of the world where I was and was I not to see
him, to speak to him? Impossible! So I resolved to go and see him. But on
the previous day I went to the Governor of the Ducal Hospital and asked
him whether he could not arrange for me to talk to Mysliwecek in the
garden, since, although everyone, even the doctors had assured me that
there was no longer any danger of infection, I did not want to go to his

---

[1] K. 261, an Adagio written in 1776 to replace the original Adagio of K. 219, Mozart's
violin concerto in A major, composed in 1775.
[2] Johann Baptist Baumgartner (? –1782), born in Augsburg, was a member of the Stockholm court orchestra in 1775.
[3] i.e. the incidental music for Voltaire's *Zaïre*.   [4] How generous!

room, as it was very small and smelt rather strongly. The Governor said that I was perfectly right and told me that Mysliwecek usually took a walk in the garden between eleven and twelve and that if I did not find him there, I was to ask whether he would not come down. I went therefore on the following day with Herr von Hamm, Secretary for War, (about whom I shall have something to say later on) and with Mamma to the hospital. Mamma went into the church and we walked into the garden. Mysliwecek was not there; so we sent him a message. I saw him coming across the garden towards us and recognised him at once by his walk. I should say here that he had already sent me his compliments through Herr Heller,[1] the cellist, and had begged me to be so kind as to visit him before my departure. When he came up to me, we shook hands in the most friendly fashion. 'You see', he said, 'how unfortunate I am!' These words and his appearance, which Papa already knows about, as it has been described to him, so wrung my heart that all I could say half sobbing was: 'With my whole heart I pity you'. '*My dear friend*', he said, for he saw that I was moved and began at once to speak more cheerfully, '*do tell me what you are doing. I was told that you were here, but I could hardly believe it. Was it possible that Mozart was in Munich and had not visited me all this time?*' I replied: 'Indeed I must crave your forgiveness. I have had so many calls to pay. I have so many true friends here.' '*I am sure that you have very true friends here, but none so true as I, that I can assure you.*' He asked me whether I had not heard from Papa about a letter—'Yes', I interrupted, 'he wrote to me (I was so distracted and trembled so in every limb that I could hardly speak), but not in detail.' Mysliwecek then told me that Signor Gaetano Santoro, the Naples impresario, had been obliged owing to *impegni* and *protectione*[2] to give the carnival opera this season to a certain Maestro Valentini, but that next year he would have three to distribute, one of which would be at his disposal. '*So*', said Mysliwecek, '*as I have already composed six times for Naples, I have not the slightest objection to taking on the less important opera and giving you the better one, I mean, the one for the carnival. God knows whether I shall be able to travel. If I cannot, then I shall just return the scrittura. The cast for next year is excellent; they are all singers whom I have recommended. My credit in Naples, you see, is so high that when I say, 'Engage this man', they engage him at once.*' The primo uomo is Marchesi,[3] whom he praises very highly and so does the whole of Munich. Then there is Marchiani, a good prima donna, and, further, a tenor, whose name I have forgotten, but who, as Mysliwecek says, is now the

---

[1] Gaudenz Heller (1750– ?), born at Politz in Czechoslovakia, became a famous cellist. He first held an appointment under the Bavarian Elector, and in 1780 settled in Bonn.

[2] i.e. obligations and patronage.

[3] Ludovico Marchesi (1755–1829), of Milan, was a famous male soprano. He made his début in Rome in 1774 and two years later entered the service of the Elector of Bavaria. After the latter's death in 1777 Marchesi returned to Italy, had a two years' engagement at the Teatro San Carlo in Naples, and continued to sing until 1806.

best tenor in Italy. '*I implore you*', he urged, '*go to Italy. There one is really esteemed and valued.*' And I am sure he is right. When I think it over carefully, I have to admit that in no country have I received so many honours, nowhere have I been so esteemed as in Italy; and certainly it is a real distinction to have written operas in Italy, especially for Naples. He told me that he would draft a letter to Santoro for me, and that I was to come to him on the morrow and copy it. But I could not possibly bring myself to go to his room; and yet if I wanted to copy it, I should have to do so, for I could not write in the garden. So I promised him to call without fail. But on the following day I wrote to him in Italian saying, *quite frankly*, that it was impossible for me to come to him, that I had eaten nothing and had only slept for three hours, and in the morning felt like a man who had lost his reason, that he was continually before my eyes, and so forth— all statements which are as true as that the sun can shine. He sent me the following reply:

> Lei è troppo sensibile al mio male. Io la ringrazio del suo buon cuore. Se parte per Praga, gli farò una lettera per il Conte Pachta.[1] Non si pigli tanto a cuore la mia disgrazia. Il principio fu d'una ribaltata di calesse, poi sono capitato nelle mani dei dottori ignoranti. Pazienza Ci sarà quel che Dio vorrà.[2]

He has sent me the following draft of a letter to Santoro:

> La brama ch'ebbi già da tanto tempo di servire V.S. Ill. e codesto rispettabilissimo pubblico di Napoli, colle mie debolezze di produrmi in codesto Real Teatro, è il motivo ch'io (non riguardando il lungo e dispendioso viaggio) condiscendo e mi contento di scriver l'anno venturo in codesto Regio Teatro una opera per 100 cigliati, pregandola però se possibile fosse che mi fosse confidata l'ultima, cioè, quella del carnevale, perchè i miei interessi non mi permetteranno di poter accettare una opera prima di quel tempo. Già tanto spero dalla sua grazia ed, avendo l'approvazione Reale per me, prego di mandar la scrittura al Maestro Mysliwecek, che così mi sarà sicuramente ricapitata. Frattanto anzioso d'imparar a conoscere persona di tanto merito, mi do l'onore di protestarmi per sempre etc.[3]

[1] Count Johann Pachta belonged to the Prague nobility, and was a devoted lover of music. During his first visit to Prague in 1787 Mozart was commissioned by him to compose some country dances, and wrote for him six German dances (K. 509).

[2] You feel my suffering too keenly. I am grateful for your good heart. If you go to Prague, I shall give you a letter for Count Pachta. Do not take my misfortune so much to heart. My illness began as the result of a carriage accident and then I fell into the hands of ignorant doctors. Patience, God's will will be done.

[3] The longing I have had for a considerable time to serve your illustrious person and that most worthy public of Naples by appearing with my humble works in your Royal Theatre, is the reason why (disregarding the long and expensive journey) I agree and am willing to compose an opera next year for the Royal Theatre for 100 cigliati. But, if possible, I should like to have the contract for the last one, I mean, the carnival opera, because my interests will not allow me to accept a commission before that time. I trust that you will be so gracious as to agree and that, when you have received the Royal approval, you will send the written contract to Maestro Mysliwecek, through whom I shall safely receive it. Meanwhile, longing to make the acquaintance of such a distinguished person, I have the honour to assure you that I am ever, etc.

Mysliwecek showed me too some letters in which my name was frequently mentioned. I am told that he has expressed great surprise when people here have talked about Beecke[1] or other clavier-players of the same kind, and has always exclaimed: 'Make no mistake. No one can play like Mozart. In Italy, where the greatest masters are to be found, they talk of no one but Mozart. When he is mentioned, everyone is silent.' I can now write the letter to Naples when I choose, but the sooner the better. First, however, I should like to have the opinion of that very wise Court Kapellmeister, Herr von Mozart!

I have an inexpressible longing to write another opera. It is a long way to go, it is true, but it would be a long time before I should have to write it. Many things may happen before then. But I think that I ought to accept it. If in the meantime I fail to secure an appointment, eh bien, then I can fall back on Italy. I shall still have my certain 100 ducats at the carnival and once I have composed for Naples, I shall be in demand everywhere. Moreover, as Papa is well aware, there are also opere buffe here and there in the spring, summer and autumn, which one can write for practice and for something to do. I should not make very much, it is true, but, all the same, it would be something; and they would bring me more honour and credit than if I were to give a hundred concerts in Germany. And I am happier when I have something to compose, for that, after all, is my sole delight and passion. And if I secure an appointment or if I have hopes of settling down somewhere, then the scrittura will be an excellent recommendation, will give me prestige and greatly enhance my value. But all this is only talk—talk out of the fulness of my heart. If Papa can prove conclusively that I am wrong, well, then I shall acquiesce, although unwillingly. For I have only to hear an opera discussed, I have only to sit in a theatre, hear the orchestra tuning their instruments—oh, I am quite beside myself at once.

Tomorrow Mamma and I are taking leave of Mysliwecek in the garden. For only the other day, when he heard me say that I had to fetch my mother in the church, he said: 'If only I were not such a sight, I should very much like to meet the mother of such a great virtuoso'. I implore you, my dearest Papa, to reply to Mysliwecek. Write to him as often as you have time. You can give him no greater pleasure. For the man is completely deserted and often no one goes to see him for a whole week. 'I assure you', he said, 'it seems very strange that so few people come to see me. In Italy I had company every day.' If it were not for his face, he would be the same old Mysliwecek, full of fire, spirit and life, a little thin, of course, but otherwise the same excellent, cheerful fellow. All Munich is talking about

[1] Ignaz von Beecke (1733–1803) was adjutant and Kapellmeister to Prince Krafft Ernst von Öttingen-Wallerstein. He was an excellent pianist and composed several works for the clavier.

his oratorio 'Abramo ed Isacco', which he produced here.[1] He has now finished, except for a few arias, a cantata or serenata for Lent. When his illness was at its worst he composed an opera for Padua.[2] But nothing can help him. Even here they all say that the Munich doctors and surgeons have done for him. He has a fearful cancer of the bone. The surgeon Caco, that ass, burnt away his nose. Imagine what agony he must have suffered. Herr Heller has just been to see him. When I wrote that letter to him yesterday, I sent him my serenata which I composed in Salzburg for Archduke Maximilian;[3] and Heller gave it to him with the letter.

Now for something else.

(219a) *Maria Anna Mozart to her Husband*

[Autograph in the Mozarteum, Salzburg]

[MUNICH, 11 *October* 1777]

There is a Secretary for War here, Herr von Hamm by name, about whom Wolfgang has already written to you. He has a daughter who plays the clavier but who has not been well taught. He would like to send her to you in Salzburg for a year in order that she might perfect her playing. She is thirteen and, as she is an only child, she has been brought up rather indulgently. He is spending a lot of money on her. He is going to write to you himself, so we have had to give him your address. He is the most honest man in the world. He is completely wrapt up in his daughter. I have only written this to you so that you may know about it in advance and decide what you want to do. We are travelling from here to Augsburg tomorrow, October 11th, so I am busy packing, and this gives me a great deal of trouble, for I am doing it all by myself, since Wolfgang cannot help me the least little bit. He and I were with Mysliwecek today from eleven until half past twelve. He is indeed to be pitied. I talked to him as if I had known him all my life. He is a true friend to Wolfgang and has said the kindest things about him everywhere. Everyone has told us so.

(219b) *Mozart resumes writing*

[Autograph in the Mozarteum, Salzburg]

Herr von Hamm's address is as follows:

A Monsieur Monsieur de Hamm, secretaire de guerre de
S.A.E. Sérénissime de Baviére, à Munic.

Immediately after lunch yesterday I went with Mamma to a coffee

---

[1] It was written in 1775 for Florence.
[2] Possibly his *Atide*, produced at Padua in 1774.
[3] *Il rè pastore*, composed in 1775 on the occasion of a visit of the Archduke Maximilian, Maria Theresia's youngest son.

party at the two Fräulein Freysingers'. Mamma, however, drank no coffee, but had two bottles of Tyrolese wine instead. She went home at three o'clock to put a few things together for our journey. I went with the two young ladies to the said Herr von Hamm, where the three ladies each played a concerto and I played one of Eichner's[1] at sight and then went on improvising. Miss Simplicity von Hamm's teacher is a certain clergyman of the name of Schreier. He is a good organist, but no cembalist. He kept on staring at me through his spectacles the whole time. He is a dry sort of fellow, who does not say much: but he tapped me on the shoulder, sighed and said: 'Yes—you are—you know—yes—that is true— you are first-rate'. A propos. Does Papa not recall the name Freysinger? The Papa of the two beautiful young ladies whom I have mentioned says that he knows Papa quite well, and was a student with him. He still remembers particularly Wessobrunn, where Papa (this was news to me) played on the organ amazingly well. *'It was quite terrifying'*, he said, *'to see how rapid your Papa was with his feet and hands. Indeed he was absolutely amazing. Ah, he was a great fellow. My father thought the world of him. And how he fooled the clerics to the top of their bent about becoming a priest![2] You are the very image of him, as he then was, absolutely the very image. But when I knew him, he was just a little shorter.'* A propos. Now for something else. A certain Court Councillor, Öfele by name, who is one of the best Court Councillors here, sends his most humble greetings to Papa. He could have been Chancellor long ago, but for one thing—his love of the bottle. When I first saw him at Albert's, I thought, and so did Mamma, 'Goodness me, what a superlative idiot!' Just picture him, a very tall fellow, strongly built, rather corpulent, with a perfectly absurd face. When he crosses the room to go to another table, he places both hands on his stomach, bends over them and hoists his belly aloft, nods his head and then draws back his right foot with great rapidity. And he performs the same trick afresh for every person in turn. He says he knows Papa infinitely well. I am now off to the theatre for a while. Later on I shall write more. I simply cannot do so now, for my fingers are aching horribly.

(219c) *Maria Anna Mozart resumes writing*

[Autograph in the Mozarteum, Salzburg]

[MUNICH, 11 *October* 1777]

And I am sweating so that the water is pouring down my face, simply from the fag of packing. The devil take all travelling. I feel that I could

[1] Ernst Eichner (1740–1777), born in Mannheim, became a distinguished bassoon and oboe player. He lived for a time in Paris and in London and then went to Potsdam, where he entered the service of the Prussian Crown Prince. His compositions are typical of the Mannheim school.

[2] Leopold Mozart was intended for the Church, but after two years' study at the University of Salzburg he decided to take up music as a profession.

shove my feet into my mug, I am so exhausted. I hope that you and Nannerl are well. I send most cordial greetings to my dear Sallerl and Monsieur Bullinger. Please tell Nannerl not to give Bimperl too much to eat, lest she should get too fat. I send greetings to Thresel. Addio. I kiss you both millions of times.

MARIA ANNA MOZART

Munich, [October] 11th, at eight o'clock in the evening, 1777.

(219d) Mozart resumes writing

[Autograph in the Mozarteum, Salzburg]

MUNICH, 11 October [1777]

I am writing this at a quarter to twelve at night. I have just been to the Lipperl Theatre.[1] I only went to see the ballet, or rather pantomime, which I had not yet seen. It was called: *Das von der für girigaricanarimanarischaribari verfertigte Ei*. It was excellent and very good fun. We are off to Augsburg tomorrow, for Prince Taxis is not at Regensburg, but at Dischingen. At the moment, it is true, he is at one of his summer residences, but it is not more than an hour from Dischingen. In Augsburg I shall follow Papa's instructions to the letter. I think it would be best if Papa were now to write to us at Augsburg and direct his letters to be delivered at the 'Lamm'. I shall write again as soon as we decide to move on. What a clever suggestion that is, isn't it? Herr von Bellvall, who came to see us this evening at Albert's, sends 100000 greetings to Papa and to my sister. I enclose four praeambula[2] for her. She will see and hear for herself into what keys they lead. I hope that you received the Schuster duets. My greetings to all my good friends, especially to young Count Arco,[3] to Miss Sallerl, and to my best friend Herr Bullinger, whom I will get you to ask to be so good as to make at the eleven o'clock concert next Sunday an authoritative pronouncement in my name, presenting my compliments to all the members of the orchestra and exhorting them to be diligent, lest I be proved a liar one of these days. For I have extolled these concerts everywhere and shall continue to do so. I kiss Papa's hands and I am his most obedient son

WOLFGANG MOZART

---

[1] Probably the Kasperle-Theater, a popular playhouse near the Isartor.
[2] There is no trace of these works.
[3] Count Leopold Arco, son of Count Georg Anton Felix von Arco, Chief Chamberlain at the Salzburg Court. Abbé Bullinger had been his tutor.

(220) *Leopold Mozart to his Son*

[*Extract*]   [*Autograph in the Mozarteum, Salzburg*]

MON TRÈS CHER FILS!   SALZBURG, 12 *October* 1777

I hope that both you and Mamma are very well and that you have received the letter which I enclosed to my brother Franz Aloys. Thank God, we are both in excellent health. As the weather is fine, we take an early walk every day with our faithful Bimperl, who is in splendid trim and only becomes very sad and obviously most anxious when we are both out of the house, for then she thinks that because she has lost you two, she is now going to lose us as well. So when we went to the ball and she saw us masked, she refused to leave Mitzerl, and, when we got home, she was so overjoyed that I thought she would choke. Moreover, when we were out, she would not stay on her bed in the room, but remained lying on the ground outside the porter's door. She would not sleep, but kept on moaning, wondering, I suppose, whether we should ever return.

People here are gossiping and saying that you have got such a handsome present from the Elector that you have enough money with which to travel for a whole year and that as soon as there is a vacancy he will take you into his service. Well, I prefer that people should say something amiable and flattering rather than something unpleasant—especially on account of the Archbishop! I suppose that the Bishop of Chiemsee's household have been spreading rumours of this kind in order to spite the Archbishop. How I hope that the weather will remain as fine as it is for your journey.

October 13*th*

We received, not, as we had hoped, from Augsburg, but once more from Munich, your letter which says that you were going to Augsburg on Saturday the 11th; and by mistake you both dated your letter the 11th instead of, as it should have been, the evening of the 10th. But by Heaven, if you stayed so long, almost three weeks, in Munich, where you could not hope to make a farthing, you will indeed get on well in this world! That Prince Taxis is at Dischingen and not at Regensburg was no news to me. But you must find out at the Head Post Office in Augsburg, where my brother's daughter[1] is very well known, how long he is staying at Dischingen, for to go off to Regensburg would mean a very considerable détour. He will probably return to Regensburg after All Saints'; so you should arrange your stay at Augsburg accordingly. Not far from Dischingen and close to Donauwörth is the famous Imperial Monastery of

---

[1] Maria Anna Thekla (1758–1841), the only surviving child of Leopold Mozart's brother, Franz Aloys. See p. 273, n. 4. For an account of Mozart's 'Bäsle', see *MMB*, March 1904, p. 245 ff., and Abert, vol. ii. pp. 959–975.

Kaysersheim,[1] whose Abbot, I hear, is a great patron of virtuosi and where you will receive all kinds of honours. But you must do yourself credit and set a high price on your talent. You will find out all this in Augsburg and Herr Stein will be an excellent guide and will obtain letters for you to various places. I do not know whether you would do better to go first to Wallerstein or to Kaysersheim; I mean, of course, after you have been to Prince Taxis. Kaysersheim lies to the right and Wallerstein to the left, so I think you should go first to Kaysersheim and then the Abbot could let his horses take you to Wallerstein. Prince von Öttingen-Wallerstein will perhaps be in his castle at Hohenaltheim, which is close to Wallerstein. You can find all this out in Augsburg and later on in Dischingen. You will remember that *the Prince, who was that handsome young gentleman in Naples, invited you to visit him*; and you can make this the reason why you are paying him your respects. It used to be possible to get work at the Margrave's in Anspach and with the Commandant at Mergentheim or Mergenthal. Thus your journey to Würzburg should be so arranged as to take in Anspach and Mergentheim on your way. You will easily ascertain whether these places are still good for your purpose. But you must not believe every ass, for even if here and there many people are not very highly esteemed and have therefore become discontented, yet great virtuosi are regarded quite differently. If at some particular place the whole orchestra, I say, *the whole orchestra* have been dismissed, that, I admit, is a sign that no more money is to be made there, and if you can find no players to accompany you, of course it would be impossible to perform. From Würzburg to Mannheim you go through Heidelberg. Other places worth visiting are Darmstadt, Frankfurt, Mainz and Coblenz. Now that it occurs to me, I must remind you (as you pay little attention to these things) that the Pope, who conferred that order on you, was the famous Pope Ganganelli, Clement XIV. You must wear your cross in Kaysersheim. What you write about the opera in Naples *I myself thought of long ago*. Did Mysliwecek give you Don Santoro's address? You may now send him the letter from Augsburg or enclose it to me; it does not matter, provided it is written clearly and intelligibly. If you have not got his address, then you must send me the letter. I will correspond with Mysliwecek and set things going; but everything depends on the address. Meanwhile what could I have written to Mysliwecek when I did not know whether you had seen him or not? Moreover, I could not send you my opinion upon the matter, as I did not know what might lie behind it. For I was convinced that Mysliwecek knew that you were in Munich, since you both arrived there on the 22nd and he did not write to me until the 28th. About the whole history of his illness I shall write more fully

---

[1] Kaysersheim (now Kaisheim), a Cistercian monastery, founded in 1132 by Count Heinrich von Lechsmünd.

some other time. He is indeed to be pitied! Only too well do I understand your fright and your terror, when you saw him. I should have felt exactly the same. You know how tender-hearted I am!

Mamma writes about the daughter of War Secretary von Hamm. It is quite possible that he may write to me; and, if he does, I shall be exceedingly embarrassed. First of all, you know that we live very frugally and that these people are used to good living. But that is not the main reason. You both say that she has had a very stupid upbringing. So I presume that she has little talent for music, and, if this is so, she would not do me any credit. The wrong position of her hands is not very important, for that can be remedied. But if she has no ear and therefore no sense of time, then I must humbly refuse the honour. In order to find this out, you should give her a short test, which would be quickly done. You have only to play two simple bars to her and see whether she can play them *a tempo*, that is, whether, once she knows the notes of the two bars, she can imitate the time also. So write by the next post and say whether she has any ear or not; for at present it is very difficult for me to decide. It is quite true that Herr Freisinger was a fellow-student of mine; but I never knew that he heard me play the organ so admirably in Wessobrunn monastery. So nothing can be kept secret. You know how often I have said to you: *Murder will out.* You ask whether I know Court Councillor Öfele? Do I not? He was married to the handsome daughter of Lepin, a merchant, in the Abbot's chapel and by the Abbot himself, and I, being then a descanter in the monastery of St. Ulrich, sang a cantata at the Nuptial Mass. His wife not only sang well but was a good performer on the harpsichord and she brought him a dowry of 30,000 gulden. I saw him afterwards in Munich quite frequently when he had become a Court Councillor. *Sic transit gloria mundi!*[1] Drink has been the ruin of him. His excessive devotion to music has undoubtedly contributed to it.

I well believe that dear Mamma finds packing a troublesome job. Oh, how gladly would I do it for her and relieve her. I kiss her many million times and wish her health and patience. It is more difficult for me to be patient. Nannerl thanks you for the praeambula. The whole company o marksmen, Hagenauer, Schiedenhofen and so forth, Mitzerl and all Salzburg send their greetings. We kiss you both most cordially and I am your old

MOZART

You ask whether we received Schuster's duets? Not a trace of them! Could you not have added 'which I sent by Tom, Dick or Harry'? Where are we to make enquiries? Who was to deliver them? Indeed I must say that you are sometimes very slap-dash!

[1] i.e. so passes the glory of the world.

At Augsburg, his father's native town, Mozart gave a concert which, however, brought in very little money. After a fortnight's stay, during which he tried for the first time the new Stein pianoforte and made the acquaintance of his cousin, Maria Anna Thekla, Mozart and his mother left for Mannheim. Letters 221-231.

(221) *Maria Anna Mozart to her Husband*

[*Autograph in the Mozarteum, Salzburg*]

AUGSBURG, 14 *October* 1777

We left Munich on the 11th at noon and arrived safely in Augsburg at nine in the evening; and this journey we did in nine hours with a hired coachman who, moreover, fed his horses for an hour.

(221a) *Mozart continues the letter*

‡[*Autograph in the Mozarteum, Salzburg*]

[AUGSBURG, 14 *October* 1777]

So we did not make a mistake about the date; for we wrote in the morning; and we shall be off again, I think, next Friday, that is, the day after tomorrow. For just hear how kind and generous these good Augsburg gentlemen have been! In no place have I been overwhelmed with so many marks of honour as here. My first visit was to the magistrate, Longotabarro.[1] My uncle, a most excellent and lovable man and an honourable townsman, accompanied me and had the honour of waiting upstairs on the landing like a lackey until I should come out of the Arch-Magistrate's room. I did not forget to deliver at once my Papa's most humble respects. He was so good as to remember our whole history and asked me: '*How has he fared all this time?*' Whereupon I at once replied: 'Very well, thanks and praise be to God. And I trust that you too have fared very well?' After that he began to unbend, and addressed me in the second person, while I continued to address him as 'Your Highness', as I had done from the very first. He would not let me go and I had to follow him upstairs to his son-in-law (on the second floor); and meanwhile my uncle had the honour of waiting, seated on a stool in the lobby. I had to restrain myself, most manfully, otherwise I should have said something quite politely, of course. Upstairs I had the honour of playing for about three quarters of an hour upon a good clavichord by Stein in the presence of the dressed-up son and the long-legged young wife and the stupid old lady. I improvised and finally I played off at sight all the music he had, including some very pretty pieces by a certain Edelmann.[2] They were all exceedingly polite and I too was very polite. For it is my custom to treat

[1] Von Langenmantel. See p. 274.
[2] Johann Friedrich Edelmann (1749–1794), born in Strassburg, went to Paris with his pupil Baron Dietrich and became a popular clavier-player and composer. When Baron Dietrich became Mayor of Strassburg, Edelmann returned with him to his native town, where both were guillotined during the French Revolution.

people as I find them; it pays best in the end. I told them that after lunch I was going to see Stein. The young gentleman of his own accord offered to take me there. I thanked him for his kindness and promised to call again at two o'clock, which I did. We all set off together, accompanied by his brother-in-law, who looked the perfect student. Although I had asked them to keep my identity a secret, yet Herr von Langenmantel was so thoughtless as to say to Herr Stein: 'I have the honour of introducing to you a virtuoso on the clavier', and began to snigger. I at once protested and said that I was only an unworthy pupil of Herr Siegl in Munich, who had asked me to deliver 1000 compliments to him. He shook his head— and said finally: 'Is it possible that I have the honour of seeing Herr Mozart before me?' 'Oh, no,' I replied, 'my name is Trazom and I have a letter for you.' He took the letter and wanted to break the seal at once. But I did not give him time to do so and asked: 'Surely you do not want to read that letter now? Open the door, and let us go into your room. I am most anxious to see your pianofortes.' 'All right,' he said, 'just as you wish. But I feel sure that I am not mistaken.' He opened the door and I ran straight to one of the three claviers which stood in the room. I began to play. He could scarcely open the letter in his eagerness to make sure. He only read the signature. 'Oh,' he cried and embraced me. He kept crossing himself and making faces and was as pleased as Punch. I shall tell you later on all about his claviers. He then took me straight to a coffee-house. When I entered I thought that I should drop down, overcome by the stink and fumes of tobacco. But with God's help I had to stand it for an hour; and I pretended to enjoy it all, though to me it seemed as if we were in Turkey. He then talked a great deal about a certain composer, called Graf, who, however, has only written flute concertos. He said 'Now Graf [1] is something quite exceptional', and all that kind of *exaggerated* talk. I was sweating with fright, my head, my hands and my whole body. This Graf is a brother of the two who live at The Hague[2] and at Zürich respectively. My host would not let me off, but took me to him at once. Graf is indeed a most noble fellow. He had a dressing-gown on, which I should not be ashamed to be seen wearing in the street. His words are all on stilts and he generally opens his mouth before he knows what he wants to say; and often it shuts again without having done anything. After many compliments he performed a concerto for two flutes. I had to play the first violin part. This is what I think of it. It is not at all pleasing to the ear, not a bit natural. He often plunges into a new key far too brusquely and it is all quite devoid of charm. When it was

[1] Friedrich Hartmann Graf (1727–1795), born in Rudolstadt, went to Hamburg in 1759 as a flute virtuoso and toured as flautist and conductor until 1772, when he became Kapellmeister in Augsburg. In his day he was regarded as a composer of outstanding merit, who did not write only for the flute, as Mozart's description would seem to imply.
[2] See p. 64, n. 5.

over, I praised him very highly, for he really deserves it. The poor fellow must have taken a great deal of trouble over it and he must have studied hard enough. At last a clavichord, one of Stein's, was brought out of the inner room, an excellent instrument, but covered with dust and dirt. Herr Graf, who is Director here, stood there transfixed, like someone who has always imagined that his wanderings from key to key are quite unusual and now finds that one can be even more unusual and yet not offend the ear. In a word, they were all astounded. Now I must close, or else I shall miss the post which leaves at four o'clock. The next time I shall tell you the whole story about Augsburg. I kiss your hands 1000 times and

I am

WOLFGANG MOZART

(221b) *Mozart to his Father*

[Autograph in the Koch Collection]

[AUGSBURG, 14 October 1777 [1]]

I gave the Schuster duets to Herr von Kleinmayr to take with him to Salzburg, and with them I also wrote a letter in which I explained that he was taking charge of them. My greetings to all my good friends, especially to Herr Bullinger. Please send me the Bishop of Chiemsee's address. Do not forget it!

(221c) *Maria Anna Mozart to her Husband*

[Autograph in the Koch Collection]

[AUGSBURG, 14 October 1777][2]

All sorts of messages from me to all my good friends.

MARIA ANNA MOZART

(222) *Leopold Mozart to his Son*

[*Extract*]   [*Autograph in the Mozarteum, Salzburg*]

MON TRÉS CHER FILS!   SALZBURG, 15 *October* 1777

Including the letter which I enclosed to my brother, this is the third which you will receive from me in Augsburg. I foresee that you will not

---

[1] A postscript to the above letter.
[2] A postscript to Mozart's letter.

be able to give a concert before next Sunday, as it has always to be announced a week in advance. I must remind you of something which you can make use of, if circumstances permit. If you find that you are warmly applauded and are very highly esteemed, I should like *a special article, praising your gifts, to appear in the Augsburg papers, after you have left*, an article which my brother could perhaps dictate to Herr Stein or which Herr Glatz could draft and Herr Stein could arrange to have published. You know why! It would make someone here very angry,[1] but Herr Stein and some other Evangelicals would get a lot of fun out of it. You know, of course, that the Lutherans should be called *Evangelicals*, for they do not like to be called Lutherans. Thus, for instance, you should talk of an *Evangelical Church* and not of a *Lutheran Church*; similarly the Calvinists like to be called *Protestants* and not Calvinists. It has just occurred to me that I ought to tell you this, for no more than a single wrong word may often lead to an unpleasant experience with some irritable person, though, of course, sensible people pay no attention to such formalities. Now for your journey. I quite agree with what you say about the opera in Naples, that is, that you should endeavour to obtain the scrittura. Yes; and if the Naples plan does not come off, I am quite prepared to approach Michele Dall'Agata[2] once more, for it is always well to have a contract in the offing. You both stayed in Munich far too long, so you must now give one or two concerts in Augsburg in order to earn something, *be it ever so little*. Flattering words, praises and cries of 'Bravissimo' pay neither postmasters nor landlords. So as soon as you find that there is no more money to be made, you should try to get away at once. There is usually an opera in Mannheim on November 4th, the Feast of St. Charles; and the question now is, whether you propose to be there by that date? Why, it is almost impossible! Prince Taxis and Prince von Öttingen-Wallerstein sometimes go there to see the opera; and, fortunately, neither of them live very far from Augsburg. So, unless you find that it is clearly to your advantage to do so, you must not stay on there for a minute longer than is absolutely necessary. The opera which is being performed in Mannheim for the Feast of St. Charles *will be repeated during the carnival*. So, if you can win the favour of Prince Taxis, you ought not to hurry away to Mannheim, *for you can see the operas there later on*. Moreover, if you want to be in Mannheim by November 4th, it is quite out of the question to go on to Würzburg from Wallerstein. No, you would have to travel straight to Mannheim, which is a good distance from Wallerstein, about twenty miles, or a two days' journey. *Mamma will find the route on the postal maps.* A great deal, of course, depends on whether the roads are good and on

---

[1] Archbishop Hieronymus Colloredo.
[2] Michele Dall'Agata, impresario of the Teatro San Benedetto in Venice. He did not reply to Leopold Mozart's two applications.

whether the route is circuitous. From Wallerstein to Würzburg is a stretch of only fifteen miles and the distance from Würzburg to Mannheim is the same. The days are now beginning to get shorter. So you should always try to leave *early in the morning* in order not to have to travel late at night. You can get fuller information about all this from our good friends in Augsburg and especially, I believe, from the Director of the Post Office, who knows my brother's daughter very well and who will perhaps give you letters of introduction to the Court of Prince Taxis. When talking to strangers who happen to be staying at your inn, you should not be too outspoken about your journey, for there are many rascals and adventurers about. Be sure to remember to ask *Prince Taxis and Prince von Öttingen-Wallerstein for letters of introduction to Mannheim.*

When you were leaving, there were a thousand necessary matters which I simply could not talk over with you, because I was ill, confused, out of humour, depressed and very sad; because, moreover, speaking hurt my chest very much, and because the packing and hoisting of your luggage on the coach in the early morning gave me a number of things to think about. Had this not been so, I should have told you that immediately after your arrival in Munich, you should try to find a copyist and that you should do this wherever you stay for any length of time. For you must really endeavour to get ahead with your composition, and that you can do if you have in readiness copies of symphonies and divertimenti to present to a Prince or to some other patron. The copying should be arranged so that *the copyist writes out at your lodgings and under your supervision at least the violino primo or some other leading part.* The rest he can copy out at home. It is absolutely essential that you should have something ready for Prince Taxis and you should therefore give the oboe-, horn- and viola-parts of six *good symphonies* at once to one or, better still, to *several copyists* (in order to speed up matters). You would thus be in a position to present to the Prince the whole score of a symphony and still have the duplicated violin and bass parts to be used on some other occasion, as, for example, at Würzburg, to which you would only have to add the parts for oboe, horn and viola. The divertimenti can be copied very quickly, even though it is true that yours have a number of parts and are rather long. Basta! Wherever you are, you must look about immediately for a copyist, or else you will lose a great deal! For if you do not do this, of what use to you will be all the music which you have taken away? You really cannot wait until some patron has them copied; and, now that I come to think of it, he would thank you for allowing him to do so and would not pay you a farthing. It is far too laborious to have your compositions copied from the score, and a thousand mistakes will creep in unless the copyist works the whole time under your supervision. But he could come *for a few mornings*, when you happen to be in, copy out *the chief parts* and then write out the remainder at home. *Your main object, however, should now be to have something ready for Prince Taxis*; and, if you had a copy of your oboe concerto,[1] Perwein[2] might enable you to make an honest penny in Wallerstein. Further, the Abbot of Kaysersheim would certainly reward you well for your music; and there you would have the no small advantage of not having to pay anything for food, drink and the rest, in respect of which landlords' bills usually make heavy inroads on one's purse. Now you understand me. *These steps are really necessary and are to your interest*. All the compliments, visits and so forth are only incidental and should not be taken seriously. For you must not lose sight of your main object, which is to make money. All your endeavours should thus be directed to earning money, and you should be very careful *to spend as little as possible*, or you will not be able to travel in an honourable fashion, and may even have to remain rooted to one spot and there run up debts. After all, you can find copyists everywhere. You should get the copyist first of all to show you a specimen of his writing, and also the kind of paper he uses, which should resemble that which you have already used. In a word, it is necessary to take thought for everything, so that no fatal mistake is made; and this it is possible to do, if you have your head screwed on. And another idea occurs to me. You took with you the big Latin prayer book, which you will find very useful, not only because it has all the Psalms and other Church texts,—Mamma has the German version of the Psalms in her big service-book—, but also because it will help you *to keep up your Latin*. You should sometimes for a change say your morning and evening prayers out of it. These are easy to understand and you might add some confession and communion prayers.

My brother will gladly bind for you the scores which are still on loose sheets, but you should remind him that *the edges must not be clipped*. He need only look at the other bound scores. When you are in Augsburg, my brother or his daughter or his wife (to all of whom I send my greetings) will certainly help you to pack. Baron Dürnitz[3] was in Munich, was he not? You could easily have used that money for the journey. *How much had you to pay at Albert's?*

The preludes[4] which you sent Nannerl are superlatively beautiful and she kisses you a million times in gratitude for them. She plays them very well already. I shall write by the next post to Venice and see whether you cannot secure the opera for Ascension. Mysliwecek has informed me with

---

[1] Köchel (p. 295, 296) suggests that Leopold Mozart is referring to an oboe concerto which his son had composed for Giuseppe Ferlendis and which he rewrote later in Mannheim as a flute concerto for De Jean (K. 314 [285d]).

[2] An oboist in the Archbishop's service who in 1777 joined the orchestra of Prince von Öttingen-Wallerstein.

[3] He owed Mozart a fee for composing the clavier sonata, K. 284 [205b], and possibly some other works. See p. 287, n, 4.

[4] See p. 283.

the greatest delight that, although he never expected it, he had the pleasure of seeing both you and Mamma, *la quale*, he writes, *è veramente una signora di garbo, degna del Signor Mozart.*[1] He tells me that he has now sent twelve symphonies and six quintets with oboe obbligato to the Archbishop and he asks me to arrange for their performance and to endeavour to make the Archbishop remember him for his earlier music and this present contribution: *producir di rammentar al Principe la musica vecchia e moderna che gli mando, per interesse mio. Sono viaggiatore* and so forth.[2] He adds at the end: *Alla signorina figlia manderò delle suonate per cembalo.*[3] I shall be very curious to hear what will happen about the Naples scrittura which we are hoping to obtain, while in the meantime we must try to secure the contract for Ascension. You must think ahead and aim at getting on. Should you obtain a good appointment in Mannheim or in some other centre, this will not prevent you from undertaking a journey to Italy, for every great lord, who really loves music, regards it as a personal honour if someone in his service makes a reputation for himself. I shall send my next letter franco to my brother's address in Augsburg. He will be able to forward it, if you have left, as he will know your route. I am inclined to think, however, that it will still catch you in Augsburg. You really should not worry about the opera in Mannheim, for you can see it during the carnival. *But you must make a point of visiting Prince Taxis on his estates;* and when you are there, you will have to be guided by circumstances. How you should set things going I shall let you know some other time. We have not yet received the Schuster duets, but perhaps they will come by today's mail coach. Thank God, we are well; and I should be even better, if I were one of those light-hearted fathers who can forget their wives and children in three weeks. That I could not do in a hundred years, nay, even during my lifetime. Nannerl and I kiss you a million times and, alive and dead, I am your old honest husband and father

MOZART

Many of my questions receive no answer; on the other hand, you will notice that I reply to all yours. Why? Because when I have written to you about all sorts of important items, I then put your letter before me—read it through and, whenever you ask a question, I answer it then and there. Furthermore, I always keep a slip of paper on my table, and whenever anything occurs to me, which I want to tell you about, I jot it down in a few words. Thus when I begin writing, it is impossible for me to forget anything. I am sending you this rather long letter with some music, for I

[1] Who is truly a charming lady, worthy of Herr Mozart.
[2] Endeavour to remind the Prince in my interest of my earlier music and the compositions which I am now sending him. I am a traveller and so forth.
[3] I shall send some cembalo sonatas to your daughter.

could not refrain from letting you have these works.[1] Sometimes an opportunity occurs of composing in the same style; and these are still very good models.

The Hagenauers (yesterday all the Theresas received shoals of congratulations), Fräulein Sallerl, Count Arco, our ever faithful Bullinger, who came to see us yesterday evening at half past six when Nannerl and I were practising the clavier as usual, Fräulein Mitzerl, Ferlendis and Ferrari, Mme Gerlichs, Court Councillor von Mölk, who did not even know that Mamma was away, and Tresel, who is just the same as ever, except that, instead of sitting in the kitchen in the evenings, she now has to spin, and last Friday had to do in one day what she has taken two days to get through up to the present (however, she is in good form and is better tempered than she used to be)—all of the above and many others, whom I cannot think of at the moment, send their greetings. Addio!

(223) *Mozart to his Father*

[*Autograph in the possession of John Bass, New York*]

[AUGSBURG, 16 *October* 1777[2]]

Mr. Novac, who arrived here today, sends greetings to all and especially to Mlle Katherl. I shall write a more amusing letter next time. Next Wednesday I am giving a sort of a concert in Count Fugger's drawing-room.[3] My dear cousin also sends you her love. The three of us are now going to Herr Stein's where, we are lunching. The only thing I have to worry about is how I shall be accompanied at my concert, for the orchestra here is execrable. I must close now, for it is already eleven o'clock. I kiss Papa's hands 10000 times and embrace my sister in a manner most bold,

and I am, behold,

neither warm nor cold,

your most obedient son

W: A: MOZART

Our compliments
    a tutti, tutti, tutti.

---

[1] According to Köchel, p. 768, this collection (K. App. 109^{VI} [A. 71–88]) is a copy made by Leopold Mozart of eighteen church works by Ernst Eberlin and Michael Haydn. It is now in the British Museum.

[2] These lines are written on a cover which, as Schiedermair suggests (vol. i. p. 298, n. 80), may belong to Letter 224.

[3] Probably the famous Fuggerhaus in Augsburg, the town house of Prince Fugger von Babenhausen, built 1512–15.

(224) *Mozart to his Father*

[Autograph in the Mozarteum, Salzburg]

[AUGSBURG, 16 October 1777]

MON TRÉS CHER PÉRE,

All that I can say about the daughter of Hamm, the Secretary for War, is that she undoubtedly must have a gift for music, as she has only been learning for three years and yet can play several pieces really well. But I find it difficult to give you an idea of the impression she makes on me when she is playing. She seems to me so curiously affected. She stalks over the clavier with her long bony fingers in such an odd way. It is true that she has not yet had a really good teacher, and if she stays in Munich she will never, never become what her father is so anxious that she should be: and that is, a first-rate performer on the clavier. If she comes to Papa at Salzburg, her gain will be twofold; both in musical knowledge and in intelligence, which is not exactly her strong point at present. She has made me laugh a great deal already at her expense and you would certainly get plenty of entertainment for your pains. She would not eat much, for she is far too simple. You say that I ought to have tested her playing. Why, I simply could not do so for laughing. For whenever, by way of example, I played a passage with my right hand she at once exclaimed Bravissimo! in a tiny mouse-like voice. I will now finish the account of my Augsburg adventures as briefly as I can. Herr von Fingerle, to whom I delivered Papa's compliments, was also present at Director Graf's. Everyone was extremely polite and talked the whole time of getting up a concert. They all declared: 'It will be one of the most brilliant concerts we have ever had in Augsburg. Your acquaintance with our magistrate Langenmantel will be a great point in your favour. Besides, the name of Mozart carries great weight here.' We parted in very good spirits. Now Papa must know that at Herr Stein's young Herr von Langenmantel had declared that he would undertake to get up a concert in the Stube[1] for the patricians alone, as a special honour for me. You can scarcely imagine how earnestly he spoke and with what enthusiasm he promised to take up the matter. We arranged that I should call on him the next day and hear the decision. I went. This was October 13th. He was very polite, but said that he could not tell me anything definite yet. I played to him again for about an hour and he invited me to lunch on the following day, the 14th. In the morning he sent a message asking me to come at eleven o'clock and bring some music, as he had invited some of the orchestra and they would like to play something. I sent him some music at once and arrived myself at eleven o'clock. He mumbled a whole string of excuses

---

[1] A local term for the large hall in the Augsburg Rathaus.

and remarked quite coolly: 'Look here, a concert is quite out of the question. Oh, I assure you, I lost my temper yesterday on your account. The patricians told me that their funds were very low and that you were not the type of virtuoso to whom they could offer a souverain d'or.' I smiled and said 'I quite agree'. *He is Intendant of the orchestra at the Stube and his old father is the magistrate!* But I did not let it worry me. We went up to lunch. The old man was also at table; he was very polite, but did not say a word about the concert. After lunch I played two concertos, improvised something and then played the violin in one of Hafeneder's trios. I would gladly have done some more fiddling, but I was accompanied so badly that it gave me the colic. He said to me in a very friendly manner: 'You must spend the day with us and we will go to the play and then you will come back to supper with us'. We were all very merry. When we got back from the theatre, I played again until we went to supper. He had already questioned me in the morning about my cross and I had explained quite clearly how I had got it and what it was.[1] He and his brother-in-law kept on saying: 'We must get our crosses too, so that we may belong to the same body as Mozart'. But I took no notice. They also addressed me repeatedly: 'Hallo, you fine gentleman, Knight of the Spur'. I said nothing; but during supper things really got beyond a joke. They asked me 'About how much does it cost? Three ducats? Must one have permission to wear it? Does this permission cost something too? We really must send for our crosses.' A certain Baron Bagge, an officer, who was there, called out: 'Come! You ought to be ashamed of yourselves. What would you do with the cross?' That young ass, von Kurzenmantel,[2] winked at him. I saw him and he knew it. Then we had a little peace. He offered me snuff and said: 'There, take a pinch'. I still said nothing. At last he began again in a jeering tone: 'Well, tomorrow I shall send someone to your inn and perhaps you will be so kind as to lend me the cross just for a moment. I shall return it immediately. I only want to have a word with our goldsmith. He is quite a character and I am sure that if I ask him what its value is, he will say: 'About a Bavarian thaler'. And it is not worth more, for it is not gold at all, only copper. Ha! Ha!' 'You are wrong there', I said, 'it is tin. Ha! Ha!' I was burning with anger and rage. 'But do tell me', he said, 'I suppose that, if necessary, I can leave out the spur?' 'Oh, yes,' I replied. 'You do not need one, for you have one in your head already. I have one in mine too, but of a very different kind, and indeed I should not care to exchange it for yours. Here, take a pinch of snuff.' I offered him some. He turned rather pale, but began again: 'The other day—your order looked fine on that grand waistcoat of yours'. I said nothing. At length he called out to the servant: 'Hi, there, you will

---

[1] See p. 148, n. 1.
[2] Another pun of Mozart's on the name Langenmantel. See p. 315.

have to show more respect to my brother-in-law and myself when we wear the same cross as Herr Mozart. Here, take a pinch of snuff.' 'That is really very strange,' I began, as though I had not heard what he said, 'but it would be easier for me to obtain all the orders which it is possible for you to win than for you to become what I am, even if you were to die twice and be born again. Take a pinch of snuff on that.' With that I stood up. They all got up too and were exceedingly embarrassed. I took my hat and sword and said: 'I shall have the pleasure of seeing you tomorrow'. 'Oh, I shall not be here tomorrow.' 'Well, then, the day after, if I am here myself.' 'Why, you surely do not mean to——' 'I mean nothing. You are a lot of mean pigs. Good-bye for the present.' And off I went. The next day, the 15th, I told the whole story to Herr von Stein, Herr Geniaux [1] and Director Graf—not about the cross, but how utterly disgusted I was that such fine promises had been made to me about a concert and that nothing had come of them. 'That is what is called playing the fool with people and letting them down', I said. 'I am heartily sorry that I ever came here. I should never in my life have believed that in Augsburg, my father's native town, his son would have been so insulted.' You cannot imagine, dear Papa, how sorry and angry the three of them were. 'Oh,' they said, 'you really must give a concert here. We can do without the patricians.' But I stuck to my decision, and said: 'Well, I shall give a small farewell concert at Herr von Stein's for my few good friends here, who are connoisseurs'. The Director was quite distressed. 'It is abominable,' he cried, 'it is a scandal. Who would have thought it of Langenmantel? Pardieu, if he had really wanted it, it would have gone off well'. We parted. The Director in his dressing-gown accompanied me downstairs to the front door. Herr Stein and Herr Geniaux, who sends greetings to Papa, walked home with me. They urged us to decide to stay here for a while, but we were adamant. Now Papa must know that yesterday young Herr von Langenmantel, after coolly stammering out his nice bit of news about my concert, told me that the patricians had invited me to their concert on the following Thursday. 'I shall come and listen', I replied. 'Oh, but you will give us the pleasure of hearing you play?' *Well, who knows? Why not?* But after being so grossly insulted on the following evening, I resolved never to go to him again but to let the whole company of patricians lick my arse and to leave the place. On Thursday, the 16th, I was called out from table and found one of Langenmantel's servants, who had brought a message asking whether I was going along with him to the concert, and, if so, would I please go to him immediately after lunch. I sent him my humble regards, but said that I

---

[1] Christof Gignoux, an Augsburg organ-builder. He appears in Leopold Mozart's *Reiseaufzeichnungen*, p. 22, after Stein, as Gingeoux. So the Mozarts met him in 1763. See *ZMW*, Jan. 1934, p. 43.

was not going to the concert and that I could not go to him, as I was
already engaged, *which was in fact the case,*—but that I would call on the
morrow to take my leave of him, as I should be leaving Augsburg on
Saturday at the latest. Meanwhile Herr von Stein had rushed off to the
other patricians of the Evangelical persuasion and had given them such a
fearful talking-to that these gentlemen were quite uneasy. 'What,' they
said, 'are we going to let a man who does us so much honour go away
without even hearing him? Herr von Langenmantel thinks no doubt that
because he has heard him, that is enough.' Enfin, they became so excited
about it that our good young Herr von Kurzenmantel himself had to
look up Herr von Stein and entreat him on behalf of all the patricians to
do his utmost to persuade me to attend the concert, but to add that I was
not to expect anything first-rate and so forth. So after much hesitation I
went along with him. The leading nobles were very polite to me,
especially a certain Baron Relling, an officer, who is also a Director or
some such animal. He himself unpacked my music. I had brought a
symphony too, which was performed and in which I played the fiddle.
But the Augsburg orchestra is enough to give one a fit. That young puppy
von Langenmantel was quite polite, though he still had a sneer on his face.
'I really thought you would slip away from us', he said; 'I even thought
that perhaps you might have taken offence at our joke the other day.'
'Not at all', I said, 'you are still very young. But I advise you to be more
careful in future. I am not used to such jokes. And the subject you were
joking about does you no honour at all, and has served no purpose, for I
still wear my cross. It would have been better to have tried some other
joke.' 'I assure you', he said, 'it was only my brother-in-law who——'
'Well, let us say no more about it', I said. 'We were nearly deprived of
the pleasure of seeing you', he added. 'Yes', I said, 'if it had not been for
Herr von Stein, I should certainly not have come. And, to tell you the
truth, I have only come so that you, gentlemen of Augsburg, may not be
laughed at in other countries, when I tell people that I spent a week in the
town where my father was born without anyone taking the trouble to
hear me.' I played a concerto which, save for the accompaniment, went
very well. Finally I played another sonata.[1] Baron Relling, on behalf of
the whole company, thanked me most politely, asked me to take the will
for the deed and gave me two ducats. They have not yet left me in peace,
for they want me to give a public concert before next Sunday. Perhaps I
will. But I have already had such a sickener of it that I can hardly express
what I feel. I shall be honestly glad to go off again to a place where there
is a court. I may say that if it were not for my good uncle and aunt and
my really charming cousin, I should have as many regrets at having come
to Augsburg as I have hairs on my head. I must now say a few words

[1] K. 283 [189h]. See p. 329, n. 3.

about my dear little cousin. But I shall save that up until tomorrow, for one must be in very good spirits if one wants to praise her as she deserves.

On the morning of this day, the 17th, I write and declare that our little cousin is beautiful, intelligent, charming, clever and gay; and that is because she has mixed with people a great deal, and has also spent some time in Munich. Indeed we two get on extremely well, for, like myself, she is a bit of a scamp. We both laugh at everyone and have great fun. I beg you not to forget the address of the Bishop of Chiemsee. I shall probably send off to Mysliwecek today the letter for Gaetano Santoro, as we arranged. He has already given me his address. I beg you to write soon to poor Mysliwecek, because I know that your letter will give him great pleasure. Next time I shall give you an account of Stein's piano-fortes and organs and tell you about the concert in the Stube. A great crowd of the nobility was there: the Duchess Smackbottom, the Countess Makewater, to say nothing of the Princess Dunghill with her two daughters, who, however, are already married to the two Princes Potbelly von Pigtail. Farewell to all. I kiss Papa's hands 100000 times and I embrace my brute of a sister with a bearish tenderness and remain your most obedient son

WOLFGANG AMADÉ MOZART

Augsburg, 17 October 1777.

(224a) *Maria Anna Thekla Mozart, the 'Bäsle', to her Uncle*

[Autograph in the Mozarteum, Salzburg]

[AUGSBURG 16 October 1777 [1]]

MY PARTICULARLY LOVABLE UNCLE,

It is impossible for me to express the great pleasure which we have felt at the safe arrival of my aunt and of such a dear cousin and indeed we regret that we are losing so soon such excellent friends, who show us so much kindness. We are only sorry that we have not had the good fortune to see you here with my aunt. My parents send their humble greetings to you both, my uncle and my cousin Nannerl, and they hope that you are well. Please give my greetings to my cousin Nannerl and ask her to keep me in her friendship, since I flatter myself that I shall one day win her affection. I have the honour to send you my greetings and I remain with much respect

your devoted servant and niece

M. A. MOZART

---

[1] A separate letter sent in the same cover as Mozart's.

Augsburg, 16 October 1777.

My father cannot remember whether he informed you that on 31 May, 1777, he gave Herr Lotter four copies of your 'Violinschule', and two more on 13 August 1777.

(225) *Mozart to his Father*

[*Autograph in the Mozarteum, Salzburg*

[AUGSBURG, 17 *October* 1777]

MON TRÉS CHER PÉRE!

This time I shall begin at once with Stein's pianofortes. Before I had seen any of his make, Späth's[1] claviers had always been my favourites. But now I much prefer Stein's, for they damp ever so much better than the Regensburg instruments. When I strike hard, I can keep my finger on the note or raise it, but the sound ceases the moment I have produced it. In whatever way I touch the keys, the tone is always even. It never jars, it is never stronger or weaker or entirely absent; in a word, it is always even. It is true that he does not sell a pianoforte of this kind for less than three hundred gulden, but the trouble and the labour which Stein puts into the making of it cannot be paid for. His instruments have this special advantage over others that they are made with escape action. Only one maker in a hundred bothers about this. But without an escapement it is impossible to avoid jangling and vibration after the note is struck. When you touch the keys, the hammers fall back again the moment after they have struck the strings, whether you hold down the keys or release them. He himself told me that when he has finished making one of these claviers, he sits down to it and tries all kinds of passages, runs and jumps, and he shaves and works away until it can do anything. For he labours solely in the interest of music and not for his own profit; otherwise he would soon finish his work. He often says: 'If I were not myself such a passionate lover of music and had not myself some slight skill on the clavier, I should certainly long ago have lost patience with my work. But I do like an instrument which never lets the player down and which is durable.' And his claviers certainly do last. He guarantees that the sounding-board will neither break nor split. When he has finished making one for a clavier, he places it in the open air, exposing it to rain, snow, the heat of the sun and all the devils in order that it may crack. Then he inserts wedges and glues them in to make the instrument very strong and firm. He is delighted when it cracks, for he can then be sure that nothing more can happen to it. Indeed he often cuts into it himself and then glues it together again and

---

[1] Franz Jakob Späth (1714–98), a famous manufacturer of organs and claviers at Regensburg. Like Stein he also made pianofortes, and Mozart evidently possessed one of these.

strengthens it in this way. He has finished making three pianofortes of this kind. Today I played on one again.

We lunched today, the 17th, with young Herr Gassner, a handsome young widower, who has lost a pretty young wife. They had only been married two years. He is a very fine, polite young fellow. We were most royally entertained. At lunch there was also a colleague of Abbé Henri, Bullinger, and Wishofer, an ex-Jesuit, who is now Kapellmeister in the Augsburg Cathedral. He knows Herr Schachtner very well, for he was his choir-master at Ingolstadt. His name is Pater Gerbl, and he asked me to send his greetings to Herr Schachtner. After lunch Herr Gassner, one of his sisters-in-law, Mamma, our little cousin and I went to see Herr Stein. At four o'clock the Kapellmeister turned up and so later on did Herr Schmittbauer, organist at St. Ulrich, a nice, oily, old gentleman. There I just played at sight a sonata by Beecke, which was rather hard and *miserabile al solito*.[1] Really I cannot describe the amazement of the Kapell-meister and the organist, who kept crossing themselves. Here and at Munich I have played all my six sonatas by heart several times.[2] I played the fifth, in G,[3] at that grand concert in the Stube. The last one in D,[4] sounds exquisite on Stein's pianoforte. The device too which you work with your knee is better on his than on other instruments. I have only to touch it and it works; and when you shift your knee the slightest bit, you do not hear the least reverberation. Well, tomorrow perhaps I shall come to his organs—I mean, I shall come *to write about them*; and I am saving up his little daughter for the very last. When I told Herr Stein that I should very much like to play on his organ, as that instrument was my passion, he was greatly surprised and said: 'What? A man like you, so fine a clavier-player, wants to play on an instrument which has no douceur, no expression, no piano, no forte, but is always the same?' 'That does not matter', I replied. 'In my eyes and ears the organ is the king of instruments.'

'Well,' he said, 'as you like.' So off we went together. I noticed at once from what he said that he thought that I would not do much on his organ; that I would play, for instance, in a thoroughly pianistic style. He told me that he had taken Schubart[5] at his own request to this same organ. 'I was rather nervous,' he said, 'for Schubart had told everyone and the church was pretty full. For I thought of course that this fellow would be all spirit, fire and rapid execution, qualities which are not at all suited to

---

[1] Wretched as usual.
[2] K. 279-284 [189d-h, 205b], of which the last one was written for Baron von Dürnitz. See p. 287, n. 4.   [3] K. 283 [189h], composed in 1774.
[4] K. 284 [205b], the so-called 'Dürnitz sonata', composed in 1775.
[5] Christian Friedrich Daniel Schubart (1739–91), a Swabian by birth. In 1768 he became organist at Ulm, but moved about from Mannheim to Munich and Augsburg. He founded in 1774 the *Deutsche Chronik*, and for his revolutionary opinions was imprisoned for ten years, 1777–87, at Hohenasperg. See *ZMW*, Jan. 1934, p. 43.

the organ. But as soon as he began I changed my opinion. All I said to Stein was: 'Well, Herr Stein, do you think that I am going to canter about on your organ? 'Ah, you, he replied, 'that is quite another matter.' We reached the choir and I began to improvise, when he started to laugh; then I played a fugue. 'I can well believe', he said, 'that you like to play the organ, when you play so well.' At first the pedal seemed a bit strange to me, as it was not divided. It started with C, and then D and E followed in the same row. But with us D and E are above, as E♭ and F♯ are here. But I soon got the hang of it. I have also been to St. Ulrich to play on the old organ there. The staircase there is perfectly dreadful. I begged them to get someone to play on the organ, saying that I should like to go down and listen, for up above it produces no effect whatever. But I could form no opinion, for the young choirmaster, a priest, rushed up and down the keyboard in such a fashion that one could not get the least idea of anything. And when he wanted to play a few chords, the result was simply discords, for the notes did not harmonize. Afterwards we had to go off to a wine-shop, as my Mamma, my little cousin and Herr Stein were with us. A certain Father Emilian, a conceited ass and a sorry wit of his profession, was very sweet on my little cousin and wanted to jest with her, but she made fun of him—finally when he was a bit tipsy, which soon happened, he began to talk about music and sang a canon, saying: 'In my life I have never heard anything more beautiful'. I said: 'I am sorry that I cannot join in, but nature has not bestowed on me the gift of intoning'. 'That does not matter', he said. He began. I took the third voice, but I invented quite a different text, i.e., 'Pater Emilian, oh, you idiot, you, lick my arse. I beg you'. All this, *sotto voce*, to my cousin. Then we laughed together for another half-hour. He said to me: 'If only we could be together longer, I should like to discuss composition with you'. 'Then', I replied, 'we should soon have dried up.' *On the scent*, Towser. To be continued in my next.

W: A: MOZART

(226) *Leopold Mozart to his Son*

[Extract]   *[Autograph in the Mozarteum, Salzburg]*

SALZBURG, 18 *October* 1777

MON TRÈS CHER FILS!

I received yesterday your letter from Augsburg, dated October 14th, which must have been sent off on the 15th. First of all, *with regard to October* 11th, *I must finish my case for the prosecution.* I know that I am right and that you made a mistake, for the letter was signed by my dear spouse with these unmistakeable words—'*Munich, October 11th, at eight o'clock in the evening*'. Then my son and heir steps in and writes the following words: '*Munich, October 11th. I am writing this at a quarter to twelve at night, and so on*'.[1] So you were then already in Augsburg? Who is right now? I guessed, of course, that the letter did not leave Munich until midday on Saturday, at the same time that you did. *Toot, toot!* We did not receive the Schuster duets until yesterday evening, for Herr von Kleinmayr's luggage only came by the last mail coach. We lit our candles at once and to my delight Nannerl played them off, yes, to my great astonishment, without the slightest hesitation and on the whole performed her part in the Adagio with taste and expression. Herr Bullinger, who was with Abbé Henri, came in just as we were unpacking them and we were glad that you mentioned in the letter you enclosed that Herr von Kleinmayr was bringing them, or we should never have believed the servant who delivered them. Oh, how Herr Bullinger laughed! I am glad that you danced at the *altum tempus ecclesiasticum*[2] and I am only sorry that owing to the lack of good partners you had such a poor time. It is quite possible that the Bishop of Chiemsee has spoken to Counts Sensheim and Bergheim and, if so, no harm has been done. *Non si deve lasciare strada intentata,*[3] and so on. The Bishop went off at once to a confirmation in Werfen; he is then going to his bishopric for a visitation and later on to Bischofshofen to see the new building. As soon as he returns I shall pay my respects to him. The concert on Albert's name-day must have sounded very strange with a violinist like Dupreille, who is so sure of his time! Count Seeau probably knows all about him, which explains why he asked Johannes Cröner[4] to lead the orchestra for your opera buffa.[5] I am not surprised that when you played your last Cassation they all opened their eyes. You yourself do not know how well you play the violin, if you will only *do yourself credit and play with energy, with your whole heart and mind, yes, just as if you were the first violinist in Europe.* You must not play carelessly, or people will think that from some foolish conceit you consider yourself to be a great player, seeing that many people do not even know that you play the violin, since you have been known from childhood as a clavier-player. So whence could you draw the grounds for such conceit and presumption?—Say these words first: '*I really must apologize, but I am no violinist*'. Then play with your whole mind and you will overcome all difficulties. Oh, how often you will hear a violinist play, who has a great reputation, and feel very sorry for him! What you tell me about Augsburg and your visit to the Magistrate Longotabarro is precisely what I expected. That letter of yours made me and all of us laugh very heartily, and not least Herr

---

[1] See p. 308.   [2] See 290, n. 1.   [3] We must leave no avenue unexplored.
[4] See p. 277, n. 3.
[5] *La finta giardiniera*, which Mozart composed for the Munich carnival season, 1775.

Bullinger. Whenever I thought of your journey to Augsburg, Wieland's Abderiten [1] occurred to me. How often does one not experience in real life some circumstance of which one has read and which at the time seemed utterly impossible! Herr Longotabarro was extraordinarily clever at his studies, but he never got beyond Salzburg and Innsbruck, where he was obliged to continue them and where he became Juris Utriusque Doctor. He was then immediately appointed to the lowest post in the magistracy, served through all the grades in the Augsburg municipality, and finally became Magistrate, which is the highest rung in the ladder. He has therefore seen nothing of the world. You may have thought it strange that my brother had to wait in the lobby, but he will not have thought so. All the citizens of Salzburg, even the leading merchants, must appear in their cloaks at the Town Syndicate, and the Syndic makes them, and particularly the ordinary citizens, wait for hours in the lobby; yet, after all, the Syndic is only a syndic and not the reigning prince. On the other hand the Magistrate of Augsburg is their little king. Moreover the natives are accustomed to treatment of this kind, for they have the most extraordinary respect for their Syndic, because they have no greater lord.

Monday, October 20th

I have just received your letter of the 17th and I am very curious to read the continuation of the Augsburg story. Everyone knows about the beggarliness of the patricians and every honest man there laughs about it. That is why they are *in the pay of the rich merchants*, who can get anything for money from their hungry superiors. As for young Herr von Longotabarro, he has not had to go in search of his love of quizzing and jeering, for his cher père was also given to it. It is thus due to his upbringing; and indeed this is the sole privilege which the young patricians have ever claimed and still do claim—to jeer at others, whenever an opportunity presents itself. Therein consists their great nobility. But the effect of anyone lowering himself to their vulgar level is at once to make them drop into their jeering habits, which they usually adopt only towards people of their own class. You made yourself too cheap with that fellow. You went to the theatre together! You were merry! You were not sufficiently reserved, you were far too familiar! In short, you were far too free and easy with such a *puppy*, and he thought, of course, that he could make fun of you. Let that serve as a lesson to you *to associate freely and naturally with grown-up people* rather than with such ill-bred, unfledged boys whose only boast is that their father is the magistrate of the town. *Such fellows should always be kept at arm's length; their society should be*

---

[1] Christoph Martin Wieland (1733–1813), a native of Wurtemberg, enjoyed a great reputation in his day as a poet and man of letters. He published in 1774 *Die Abderiten, eine sehr wahrscheinliche Geschichte*, an admirable satire on German provincialism and one of his most attractive prose writings.

avoided and, still more so, their intimate companionship. One thing is quite certain—*they would have had great difficulty in dragging me to their beggarly concert.* Basta! You did it to please Herr Stein and I take it that by now you will have given a public concert and have left Augsburg or at least be about to leave it. I sent off to you by the last post a very big letter franco, in which there is a collection of good scores, and which by this time you will have received.

I have told you that I wrote to Mysliwecek. When you reach Mannheim, the principal person, and one whom you can trust absolutely, is *Signor Raaff,*[1] an honest *God-fearing* man, who loves German musicians and can give you very valuable help and counsel. Would that he could arrange for the Elector[2] to retain you for the winter in order to find out what you know and to give you an opportunity of displaying your powers! Anyhow, Signor Raaff can give you the best advice and you should ask for a special interview with him. Herr Danner,[3] the violinist, who is an old friend and acquaintance of ours, will introduce you to him. But you must say no word of your intentions to anyone but Signor Raaff, who will tell you whether you should have an audience with the Elector, and who can perhaps arrange one for you himself. *At first you should only endeavour to get a hearing. Afterwards you should have an audience and set things going.* Even if nothing more can be done, you will still get some fine present. *When you have given your performance, you should present one of your compositions to the Elector, and finally you yourself should ask him to test you more thoroughly and give you an opportunity of showing your ability in all kinds of composition, especially in church music.* You must make a point of going to the chapel and observing the style employed there—length, shortness and so forth. For these lords always consider the one style to which they are accustomed to be the best. *Consuetudo est altera natura*[4]! I believe that there is in Mannheim a better composer of church music than in Munich, probably some good old fellow. In Mannheim, too, there is an opportunity of writing for the German stage. But see to it that you do not confide in anybody. For many a one says: '*I should like you to remain here*', in order to worm your intention out of you and then work against you. Basta! Common sense! And reserve! May God give you good

---

[1] Anton Raaff (1714–1797), one of the most famous tenors of the eighteenth century. He was born at Gelsdorf, near Bonn, where the Elector Clemens August had him trained as a singer. Raaff studied at Bologna under Bernacchi, and returned to Germany in 1742. He then had long residences abroad, 1752–1755 in Lisbon, 1755–1759 in Madrid under Farinelli and 1759–1769 in Naples. He again returned to Germany in 1770 and took an appointment at Mannheim under the Elector Karl Theodor. His last public performance was in 1781 in Mozart's *Idomeneo*. The remaining years of his life were spent in retirement in Munich. For a full account of his career, see Heinz Freiberger, *Anton Raaff*, Bonn, 1929.

[2] Karl Theodor, Elector of the Palatinate.

[3] Christian Danner (1745–c. 1807). According to Leopold Mozart's *Reiseaufzeichnungen*, p. 22, the Mozarts met the Danner family at Schwetzingen in 1763.

[4] Custom is second nature.

health. I, thank God, am a hundred per cent better; my cough has gone and with God's help I hope to come in for what will be better times for poor fools like ourselves. Hold fast to God, I beg you, Who will see to everything. For all men are villains! The older you become and the more you associate with people, the more you will realize this sad truth. Just think of all the promises, flatteries and the hundred circumstances we have already experienced, and draw for yourself the conclusion as to how much one can build on human aid, seeing that in the end everyone always finds, or invents some plausible excuse for throwing the failure of his good intentions on the shoulders of a third person. I kiss Mamma, wish her patience and urge her to protect herself well against the cold. I kiss you and beg you to think over courageously everything you are about to do and not to give your friendship and your full confidence to every flatterer so readily. God bless you on your journey, and, while I kiss you both a million times, I am your old

MOZART

(226a) *Nannerl Mozart to her Brother*

[*Extract*]   [*Autograph in the Mozarteum, Salzburg*]

DEAREST BROTHER!   [SALZBURG, 20 *October* 1777[1]]

I am glad that, praise and thanks be to God, and you Mamma are well. I am sorry that I cannot write more often; but firstly, I have no time, and secondly, when I have leisure to do so, Papa always happens to be writing. I thank you for the Schuster duets, which are very pretty and attractive. Who gave them to you? Must we copy them and return them to you? We had some shooting yesterday at home. Next Sunday Mamma is to provide the target and, as you told me to let you know when your turn would come, I should like you to write at once and give me your idea for a target. Then I could let the others know immediately and it could be got ready in a fortnight. I kiss Mamma's hands and I embrace you.

(226b) *Leopold Mozart resumes writing*

[*Autograph in the Mozarteum, Salzburg*]

Greetings from us both to my dear brother, to my sister-in-law and to your little cousin. I am altogether delighted to hear that my niece is beautiful, sensible, charming, clever and gay, and so far from having any objection to make, I should like to have the honour of meeting her.

---

[1] A postscript to her father's letter.

Only it seems to me that she has too many friends among the priests. If I am mistaken, I shall be charmed to beg her pardon on bended knee. But I only say: *it seems to me*. For appearances are deceptive, particularly at such a distance as Augsburg is from Salzburg, and particularly at this season when mists are falling so thickly that it is impossible to see further than thirty feet. Now you can laugh as much as you like! I am quite pleased to hear that she is a bit of a scamp, but these ecclesiastical gentlemen are often far worse. I am waiting for the continuation of your story about Stein's instruments and the Duchess Smackbottom and the rest.

(227) *Leopold Mozart to his Wife*

[*Extract*]   [*Autograph in the Mozarteum, Salzburg*]

MY DEAR WIFE!   SALZBURG, 23 *October* 1777

Tell Wolfgang that the Court Baker's saucer-eyed daughter who danced with him at the Stern, who often paid him friendly compliments and who ended by entering the convent at Loreto, has returned to her father's house. She heard that Wolfgang was going to leave Salzburg and probably hoped to see him again and to prevent him from doing so. Will Wolfgang be so kind as to refund to her father the money which the pomp and all the fine preparation for entering her convent cost him! You are still in Augsburg? Bravissimo! My last letter to you was enclosed in one to my brother, as I thought that you might by now have cleared out over hedges and ditches. I see however that you will not get away before the 24th or 25th, and that you are therefore staying for a fortnight. Of course, if you want to give a concert, you must make it known several days in advance. I only hope that it may be profitable! Though I doubt whether it will bring in much. Everyone who comes will probably pay one gulden, twelve kreuzer; but will a great many turn up? *I am very curious to hear all about it.* I knew already that the orchestra was very poor; it is indeed disappointing. *Herr Hagenauer has just sent me the news sheet and Frau von Gerlichs has this moment brought the paper; both contain an announcement of your concert.* It is all to the good that you have left two items free.[1] The concert is very well announced. So you are going to play the clavier concerto for three harpsichords?[2] Perhaps Herr Stein's little daughter is going to play? Perhaps she will play on the first harpsichord, you on the second and Father Stein on the third? This is only guess-work on my part! By the time you read this letter the concert will be over *and I hope to have*

---

[1] Leopold Mozart means that no works are mentioned. Probably Mozart intended to improvise.
[2] K. 242, composed in 1776 for the Countess Antonia Lodron and her two daughters Aloisia and Josepha.

a few words of news as to how it went off. I am glad that Herr Stein's piano-fortes are so good, but indeed they are expensive. Herr Gasser (not Gassner) has only just lost his pretty young wife, as I read in a letter which he sent a short time ago to Herr Hagenauer. So he entertained you in princely fashion? He is indeed an uncommonly helpful and pleasant man. You have also called on Herr von Zabuesnig, for he mentioned it in a letter to Johannes Hagenauer, adding that he would gladly have invited you to his home, had not his wife been approaching her confinement, but that he would be delighted to go to your concert. Now do not forget to make careful preparations for your departure, for the cold is becoming more and more bitter. Thank God I am well. I have neither a pain in my chest nor a cough and I have made a complete recovery. By this time you will probably have become more accustomed to walking than you were in Salzburg, as you have now to walk for a quarter, or as much as half an hour when you go to St. Ulrich or when you visit Herr Stein, that is, if he still lives on the Lech, outside the town. With all this exercise I trust that you are well. God keep you both. I am your old

MOZART

MON TRÈS CHER FILS!

I am to wish you happiness on your name-day! But what can I now wish you that I do not always wish you? And that is, the grace of God, that it may follow you everywhere, that it may never leave you. And this it will never do, if you are diligent in fulfilling the duties of a true Catholic Christian. You know me. I am no pedant and no praying Peter and still less am I a hypocrite. But surely you will not refuse the request of a father, that you should take thought for your soul's welfare so that in the hour of his death you may cause him no anxiety, and that in that dread moment he may have no reason to reproach himself for not having watched over your soul's salvation. Farewell! Be happy! Be sensible! Honour and care for your mother, who in her old age is having much anxiety. Love me as I love you. Your truly affectionate father

LEOP. MOZART

(227a) *Nannerl Mozart to her Brother*

[*Extract*]   [*Autograph in the Mozarteum, Salzburg*]

DEAREST BROTHER!   [SALZBURG, 23 *October* 1777 [1]]

I wish you all happiness and blessings and that God may ever keep you in good health. When things fare well or badly with you, think of us, who are obliged to live sadly here, separated from you both. I only wish that

---

[1] A postscript to her father's letter.

FRAU ANNA MARIA MOZART (*c.* 1775)

From a portrait by an unknown artist
(Mozart Museum, Salzburg)

what Herr Cassel[1] came to congratulate us about were true, that is, that you and Papa were appointed to Munich and were to draw 1600 gulden. I am sure that it is Haydn's wife[2] and her vulgar set who concoct these lies. For they would like to see Papa leave Salzburg, so that her husband might be certain of the post of Kapellmeister.

Katherl Gilowsky sends her greetings to Mamma and congratulations to you on your name-day. As the Chamberlain is back again, she never has time to visit us except on Sundays. Tresel and Bimperl also send you their congratulations. Farewell and keep in good health. I kiss Mamma's hands and I give you a smacking kiss.

(228) *Mozart to his Father*

[*Autograph in the Mozarteum, Salzburg*]

[AUGSBURG, 23 *October* 1777]

MON TRÉS CHER PÉRE!

My concert duly took place yesterday, Wednesday, the 22nd. Count Wolfegg[3] was very active in connection with it and brought several highborn elderly ladies with him. During the first days of our stay I called at his lodgings to pay my respects to him, but he was away. He returned a few days ago and when he heard that I was here, he did not wait for me to call on him, but came in at my door just as I was taking my hat and sword to visit him. But before I come to the concert, I must give you some account of our first few days. As I have already written, I went last Saturday to St. Ulrich. A few days before, my uncle had taken me to see the Abbot[4] of the Holy Cross Monastery, an excellent, honest old man, and on the Saturday before my visit to St. Ulrich I again went to the Holy Cross Monastery with my cousin, as the Dean and the Procurator were not there on the former occasion and my cousin said that the latter was such a jolly fellow.

(228a) *Maria Anna Mozart to her Husband*

[*Autograph in the Mozarteum, Salzburg*]

[AUGSBURG, 23 *October* 1777]

Today, the 23rd, Wolfgang is lunching again at the Holy Cross Monastery and I too was invited, but as the cold has given me pains in

---

[1] Johann Thomas Cassel played the violin (and occasionally the double bass) in the Salzburg court orchestra.
[2] Maria Magdalena, wife of Michael Haydn. She was the daughter of Franz Ignaz Lipp, organist in the Salzburg Cathedral, and was a singer.
[3] Count Anton Willibald Wolfegg, canon of Salzburg Cathedral.
[4] Bartholomäus Christa was Abbot of the Holy Cross Monastery from 1760 to 1780. Mozart gave him copies of his masses, K. 192 [186f] and K. 220 [196b].

my belly, I have stayed at home. Is it as cold at Salzburg as it is here, where everything is frozen hard just as if it were midwinter? If nothing prevents us, we intend to leave for Wallerstein[1] on the day after tomorrow Saturday. The concert here was an amazing success. The papers will tell you more. Herr Stein took infinite trouble and rendered us many kindnesses. You must write him a letter and thank him. I hope that you and Nannerl are in good health, but somehow I am dreadfully anxious lest you should be unwell, as we have not had a line from you this week. Do write to me soon and relieve me of my anxiety. I am very much surprised that you have not received the Schuster duets—

(228b) *Mozart resumes writing*

[*Autograph in the Mozarteum, Salzburg*]

Why, of course he has received them.

Mamma. Not at all, he has kept on writing that he has not yet received them.

Wolfgang. I detest arguing. He has certainly got them and that's an end of it.

Mamma. You are wrong, Wolfgang.

Wolfgang. No, I am right. I will show it to Mamma in black and white.

Mamma. Where then?

Wolfgang. There, read that.

Mamma is reading your letter now. Last Sunday I attended Mass in the Church of the Holy Cross and at ten o'clock I went to Herr Stein. That was on the 19th. We rehearsed a few symphonies for the concert. Afterwards I lunched with my uncle at the Holy Cross Monastery. During the meal we had some music. In spite of their poor fiddling I prefer the monastery players to the Augsburg orchestra. I performed a symphony and played Vanhall's violin concerto in Bb,[2] which was unanimously applauded. The Dean, who is a cousin of Eberlin,[3] by name Zeschinger, is a fine, jolly fellow and knows Papa quite well. In the evening at supper I played my Strassburg concerto,[4] which went like oil. Everyone praised my beautiful, pure tone. Afterwards they brought in a small clavichord and I improvised

---

[1] A small suburb of Nördlingen, and the residence of Prince Krafft Ernst of Öttingen-Wallerstein, an enthusiastic patron of music.

[2] Johann Baptist Vanhal or Wanhal (1739–1813) was born in Czechoslovakia of Dutch extraction. In 1760 he was taken to Vienna where he was trained as a violinist by Dittersdorf. After a prolonged stay in Italy he settled in Vienna. He was a most prolific and popular composer of symphonies, string quartets and all kinds of church music.

[3] Johann Ernst Eberlin (1702–62), a former court organist and Kapellmeister in Salzburg and an eminent composer of sacred music.

[4] K. 218. See p. 297, n. 1.

and then played a sonata[1] and the Fischer variations.[2] Then the others whispered to the Dean that he should just hear me play something in the organ style. I asked him to give me a theme. He declined, but one of the monks gave me one. I put it through its paces and in the middle (the fugue was in G minor) I started off in the major key and played something quite lively, though in the same tempo; and after that the theme over again, but this time arseways. Finally it occurred to me, could I not use my lively tune as the theme for a fugue? I did not waste much time in asking, but did so at once, and it went as neatly as if Daser[3] had fitted it. The Dean was absolutely staggered. 'Why, it's simply phenomenal, that's all I can say,' he said. 'I should never have believed what I have heard. You are a first-rate fellow. My Abbot told me, it is true, that he had never in his life heard anyone play the organ so smoothly and so soundly.' (For he had heard me a few days before, when the Dean was away.) At last someone produced a sonata in fugal style and wanted me to play it. But I said: 'Gentlemen, this is too much. Let me tell you, I shall certainly not be able to play that sonata at sight.' 'Yes, that I can well believe', said the Dean very pressingly, for he was my strong supporter. 'It is too much to expect. No one could tackle that.' 'However,' I said, 'I should like to try it.' I heard the Dean muttering behind me all the time: 'Oh, you little villain, oh, you rascal, oh, you——!' I played until eleven o'clock, for I was bombarded and besieged with themes for fugues. When I was at Stein's house the other day he put before me a sonata by Beecke—I think that I have told you that already. That reminds me, now for his little daughter.[4] Anyone who sees and hears her play and can keep from laughing, must, like her father, be made of stone.[5] For instead of sitting in the middle of the clavier, she sits right up opposite the treble, as it gives her more chance of flopping about and making grimaces. She rolls her eyes and smirks. When a passage is repeated, she plays it more slowly the second time. If it has to be played a third time, then she plays it even more slowly. When a passage is being played, the arm must be raised as high as possible, and according as the notes in the passage are stressed, the arm, not the fingers, must do this, and that too with great emphasis in a heavy and clumsy manner. But the best joke of all is that when she comes to a passage which ought to flow like oil and which necessitates a change of finger, she does not bother her head about it, but when the moment arrives, she just leaves out the notes, raises her hand

---

[1] Probably one of his clavier sonatas, K. 279-284 [189d-h, 205b].
[2] K. 179 [189a]. See p. 256, n. 5.   [3] A Salzburg tailor.
[4] Maria Anna (Nanette) Stein (1769–1838) was the infant prodigy of Augsburg, where she had given her first recital in 1776, at the age of seven. After her father's death in 1792 she managed his business. In 1794 she married Johann Andreas Streicher, a piano-maker from Stuttgart, famous for his friendship with Schiller. The Streichers moved to Vienna, where they established a piano factory and where in later years Nanette proved a staunch friend to Beethoven.   [5] Mozart puns on the word 'Stein', which means 'stone'.

and starts off again quite comfortably—a method by which she is much more likely to strike a wrong note, which often produces a curious effect. I am simply writing this in order to give Papa some idea of clavier-playing and clavier-teaching, so that he may derive some profit from it later on. Herr Stein is quite crazy about his daughter, who is eight and a half and who now learns everything by heart. She may succeed, for she has great talent for music. But she will not make progress by this method—for she will never acquire great rapidity, since she definitely does all she can to make her hands heavy. Further, she will never acquire the most essential, the most difficult and the chief requisite in music, which is, time, because from her earliest years she has done her utmost not to play in time. Herr Stein and I discussed this point for two hours at least and I have almost converted him, for he now asks my advice on everything. He used to be quite crazy about Beecke; but now he sees and hears that I am the better player, that I do not make grimaces, and yet play with such expression that, as he himself confesses, no one up to the present has been able to get such good results out of his pianofortes. Everyone is amazed that I can always keep strict time. What these people cannot grasp is that in tempo rubato in an Adagio, the left hand should go on playing in strict time. With them the left hand always follows suit. Count Wolfegg and several other passionate admirers of Beecke, publicly admitted at a concert the other day that I had wiped the floor with him. The Count kept running about in the hall, exclaiming: 'I have never heard anything like this in my life'. And he said to me: 'I really must tell you, I have never heard you play as you played today. I shall tell your father so too as soon as I return to Salzburg.' Now what does Papa think that we played immediately after the symphony? Why, the concerto for three claviers.[1] Herr Demmler[2] played the first, I the second and Herr Stein the third. Then I gave a solo, my last sonata in D, written for Baron Dürnitz,[3] and after my concerto in B♭.[4] I then played another solo, quite in the style of the organ, a fugue in C minor and then all of a sudden a magnificent sonata in C major, out of my head, and a Rondo to finish up with. There was a regular din of applause. Herr Stein was so amazed that he could only make faces and grimaces. As for Herr Demmler, he couldn't stop laughing. He is a quaint fellow, for when he likes anything very much, all he does is to burst into fits of laughter. In my case he even started to curse. Addio. I kiss Papa's hands and embrace my sister with my whole heart. I am your most obedient son

WOLFGANG AMADÉ MOZART

24 October, 1777. Augusta Vindelicorum.

[1] K. 242, composed in 1776.
[2] Johann Michael Demmler (? –1784), organist at Augsburg Cathedral.
[3] K. 284 [205b]. See p. 287, n. 4.　　[4] K. 238, a clavier concerto composed in 1776.

(229) *Mozart to his Father*

[*Autograph in the Mozarteum, Salzburg*]

[AUGSBURG, 25 *October* 1777]

The concert, before expenses were deducted, brought in ninety gulden. So, adding the two ducats I was given in the Stube, we have now taken in one hundred gulden. The expenses of the concert amounted to about sixteen gulden, thirty kreuzer. I had the hall for nothing; and many of the performers, I think, will have given their services *free*. *Altogether* we are now twenty-six or twenty-seven gulden out of pocket; which is not too bad. I am writing this letter on Saturday, the 25th. I received this morning your letter containing the sad news of the death of the wife of the Chief Purveyor.[1] Fräulein Tonerl can now point her snout—and perhaps she will have to open it very wide—and then close it without having snatched *anything*. As for the Court Baker's daughter, I have no objection whatever to raise. I saw all this coming long ago and that was the reason why I was so reluctant to leave home and why I felt our departure so keenly. But I hope the story is not known all over Salzburg? I implore Papa most earnestly to keep it quiet as long as possible and for Heaven's sake to refund on my behalf the expenses which her father incurred in connection with her magnificent entry into the convent; pending my return to Salzburg when (like Father Gassner in his little monastery) quite naturally and without any sorcery I shall make the poor girl first ill and then well again and restore her to her convent for life. I kiss Papa's hands and thank him most humbly for his congratulations on my name-day. Papa must not worry, for God is ever before my eyes. I realise His omnipotence and I fear His anger; but I also recognize His love, His compassion and His tenderness towards His creatures. He will never forsake His own. If it is according to His will, so let it be according to mine. Thus all will be well and I must needs be happy and contented. I too will certainly endeavour to follow most strictly your counsel and the advice which you have been good enough to give me. I thank Herr Bullinger 1000 times for his congratulations. I shall write to him soon and express my gratitude. Meanwhile I can only assure him that I know of and possess no better, no more sincere or faithful friend than he is. To Sallerl, whom I also thank most humbly, I shall enclose in my letter to Herr Bullinger some verses of thanks. I also thank my sister, who, by the way, may keep the Schuster duets and must not worry about anything in future. I wrote Gassner as the merchant's name and not Gasser on purpose, for everyone here calls him by that name. In his first letter Papa says that I made myself cheap with that young von Langenmantel. Not at all. I was just natural, that

---

[1] Leopold Mozart's letter of 23 October contains a full account of her fatal illness, which for reasons of space has had to be omitted.

was all. I think Papa imagines that he is still a boy. Why, he is twenty-one or twenty-two and a married man. Is it possible to remain a boy when one is married? Since that episode I have not gone near them; but today as a parting message I left two cards at the house and apologized for not going up, explaining that I had too many important calls to pay. Now I must close, for Mamma insists *absolument* on our going to table and then packing. Tomorrow we shall travel straight to Wallerstein. I think it will be best if Papa continues to address his letters to my uncle, until we have settled down somewhere, but not in prison, of course.[1] My dear little cousin, who sends greetings to you both, is not at all *infatuated with priests*. Yesterday, to please me, she dressed up as a Frenchwoman. When she does so, she is five per cent prettier. Well, addio. I again kiss Papa's hands and embrace my sister and send greetings to all my good friends; and now off to the closet run I, where perchance shit some muck shall I, and ever the same fool am I.

WOLFGANG and AMADEUS MOZARTY

Augsburg, 25 Octobery, seventeen hundred and seventy-seveny.

(230) *Nannerl Mozart to her Mother and Brother*

[*Extract*]   [*Autograph in the Mozarteum, Salzburg*]

[SALZBURG, 27 *October* 1777]

MY DEAREST MAMMA AND MY DEAR BROTHER,

Not a single letter! And we were looking forward to hearing how the concert had gone off. We hope that you are both in good health. Thank God, we are well.

A castrato,[2] who happened to be passing through, sang yesterday at Court. Papa was there and heard him, but he did not like his singing particularly, for he has a rather nasal voice and is a long-legged fellow with a long face and a low forehead. All the same, he sings far better than Madame Duschek. As the Archbishop is of the same opinion, perhaps he will take him into his service, for Signor Caselli,[3] who was offered 2000 gulden but no leave of absence during the carnival, is not coming. Otherwise I have no news. We hope to hear something from you soon. By the way, do not forget your target. I kiss Mamma's hands and wish you both good health and great success.

I am

your devoted sister

MARIE ANNE MOZART

[1] Mozart is playing upon the two meanings of the word *sitzen*.
[2] Francesco Ceccarelli. He was appointed soon afterwards to the Archbishop's service for six years at an annual salary of 800 gulden.
[3] Probably Vincenzo Caselli, a male soprano, whom the Mozarts met at Mantua in 1770. See Leopold Mozart's *Reiseaufzeichnungen*, p. 50.

(230a) *Leopold Mozart to his Wife and Son*

[Extract]   [*Autograph in the Mozarteum, Salzburg*]

[SALZBURG, 27 October 1777[1]]

It is never more necessary to write than when one is about to leave a place, even if the note consists only of two lines. We had not the slightest doubt that we would have received a letter from you today; yet nothing has come. If you have left Augsburg, my brother could or ought to have told us so. You are most fortunate in having very fine weather. Today, the 27th, it is most beautifully warm. I do not yet know the name of the castrato,[2] but I gather that Rust wrote to him in confidence that he ought to come for an audition, for he now praises him and shoves him forward on every possible occasion. He sings rather through his nose, and produces some notes in his throat, and his voice is not at all strong; but if he does not cost much, he is quite good enough. The choral singer Egger has died.[3] Probably Hofstettner will take his place as tenor in the Church of the Holy Trinity. You must always leave a note at post offices, so that letters may be forwarded; otherwise they will be lost. This is the third letter which I am addressing to my brother. You will have received, no doubt, the parcel containing the scores of Eberlin's works, which I sent to the landlord of the Lamm. If you are in good health, all is well. God keep you! Lately dear Mamma has added nothing to your letters. I hope that the exercise which this journey involves will be good for her. Did she not buy herself some felt shoes in Augsburg? She has left her knickers behind as well. I, of course, was ill at the time, or I should have attended to a hundred things. You should examine your carriage very carefully and particularly the wheels; and, if there is little rain, you should often have them wetted. You ought to have *a second coachman* at your disposal, for if you lose one on the way, *there you are high and dry*! And this can happen to you any moment, for from now on you will have bad roads. Be sure *not to travel late at night*; it is far better to get up early in the morning, and, if you can avoid doing so, never mention at the inns *whither* and *when* you are travelling; for sometimes some bad fellow overhears these remarks and makes use of the information. Now I must close. I kiss you both a million times and, while I am always wishing to be with you, I assure you from the bottom of my heart that I am until death

your old husband and father

LEOPOLD MOZART

I must tell you that in everything which has to do with the house Nannerl is extraordinarily industrious, hard-working and amazingly

---

[1] The continuation of Nannerl's letter.   [2] See p. 342, n. 2.
[3] Joseph Egger, a tenor in the Salzburg court choir.

attentive; besides which she plays as much as she can and is an excellent accompanist. Every evening we practise for two, or two and a half hours at least. Addio.

(231) *Leopold Mozart to his Son*

[*Extract*]   [*Autograph in the Mozarteum, Salzburg*]

MON TRÉS CHER FILS!   SALZBURG, 29 *October* 1777

Up to the present I have written to you by every post and although I read in Mamma's letter of October 23rd that she was anxious because she had received no letter from me that week, I hope and, judging by what you wrote about that Langenmantel boy, I assume that my letter, which I sent off from Salzburg on October 20th, has by this time reached you. Actually I have already addressed three letters to my brother and this is the fourth. I trust that you will write from every town you stay in and inform me, if possible, when you leave. If it is not possible to do so, then you must leave the name of the place on a card at the Post Office and thus no letter will be lost. The above is an extremely necessary precaution and you should make a point of doing this in person, for we have known of hundreds of instances of hired servants and valets who intercept letters when they arrive and open them in the hope of finding a credit note or draft; and of innumerable letters, which were to have been taken to the post, but were kept back by the servant who pocketed the six kreuzer which he should have paid for the postage. This last is a very common trick. God be thanked that your concert in Augsburg went off so well. I long from my heart to read an account of it in tomorrow's papers, and I may say that all Salzburg is of the same mind. *You know, of course, why.* The whole town was delighted when they read the notice, which was worded so nicely, and after the concert everyone was anxious to see Thursday's and Friday's papers, which arrived here on Sunday, for they thought that something further would have been published in them, which, of course, was impossible. In Wednesday's paper there was only a notice at the foot of the page to the effect that the concert would begin at six o'clock. I know only too well that the Dean at Holy Cross is a gay fellow. He ought to have put before you his little galanterie pieces for the clavier which he had printed by Lotter eighteen or nineteen years ago. Then you would have found out the name of the author, who was such a sly rascal that he published his works under the name of Reschnezgi.[1]

As for Herr Stein's little daughter, I am glad that her father is becoming sensible and that all who are in favour of making grimaces are beginning to think better of it. I suggested her for the first clavier, because you had

---

[1] i.e. Zeschinger. See p. 338.

not said very much about her; so I thought that perhaps she played very well. If you have an opportunity, try to find out (who Herr Beecke's father was. He was born at Wallerstein or somewhere in that district and his father was a schoolmaster or an organist.[1] Tell me also how Beecke behaves to you).

October 30th. This very moment, at half past eleven in the morning, I have received four letters—one from your little cousin, one from Herr Stein, one from Herr von Hamm and the fourth from Mysliwecek. Your cousin is very sad at your departure, for her distress at parting from Mamma will not have been anything out of the ordinary. Moreover she solemnly protests against the accusation of being *too friendly with priests.* Herr Stein's letter is full of your praises and he even maintains that I myself never heard you play as you played at that concert. Tell me whether I shall find more about it in the papers and whether you left on Sunday and whether your parting from your cousin was very sad and distressing. Herr von Hamm writes from Munich that he would like to send me his daughter in the spring. Herr Mysliwecek sends me six short clavier pieces for Nannerl, and his letter is *in forma ostensiva*[2] a polite and concise reminder about the music which he sent some time ago to the Archbishop. So I shall show this letter to the Countess.[3] *I had advised him to adopt these tactics.* If the Countess refuses to deal with the matter, then I shall take it up with the Chief Steward. I should like Mysliwecek to be paid decently. The letter is drafted quite clearly; he mentions that the copying and binding of both batches of musical scores cost him about ten ducats.

I have just received a paper which contains a splendid article about your concert. I gather from your letter that from Wallerstein you will go straight to Mannheim; and Herr Stein tells me the same. I suppose therefore that Prince Taxis has already gone to Regensburg; and I imagine that you have been given a letter to his Director of Music,[4] as you have mentioned nothing more about Dischingen. Thus owing to your long stay in Munich and Augsburg you have used up over 100 gulden, while, if you had remained for a shorter time in Munich, you would now have a surplus. But we can get over that, as something has been set going there— although really all you got there was *flattery* and expressions of good intentions. To some extent Augsburg has made up for your losses. Now you must be well on your guard, for Mannheim is a dangerous spot as far as money is concerned. Everything is very dear. You will have to move heaven and earth to obtain a hearing, then wait interminably for a

---

[1] Ignaz von Beecke (1733–1803) was born at Wimpfen im Tal on the Neckar. His father was warden of the Military College. See L. Schiedermair, 'Die Blütezeit der Öttingen-Wallersteinschen Hofkapelle' in *Sammelbände der Internationalen Musikgesellschaft*, IX, 107 f.
[2] i.e. in a presentable form.   [3] Countess Lodron, the Archbishop's sister.
[4] Joseph Riepel (1708–1782), Kapellmeister to Prince Thurn and Taxis at Regensburg. He composed church music, operas, chamber music and wrote works on the theory of music. See Burney, *Present State of Music in Germany, etc.*, 2nd edition, 1775, vol. ii. p. 320.

present and in the end receive at most ten carolins—or 100 gulden, a sum which by that time you will have probably spent. The Court is packed with people who look on strangers with suspicion and who put spokes in the wheels of the very ablest. Economy is most necessary. If Herr Danner or some other friend could take you from your inn to a private lodging, you would save half your money. You must consider carefully whether you ought to offer your services to the Elector, with a view, that is, to obtaining an appointment. For my part, I should say no! since he only offers a miserable remuneration. But if it can be arranged that the Elector shall test your knowledge and if no one in the orchestra thinks that you are looking for an appointment or trying to fly over the heads of others, then something may be arranged; and this you should discuss in confidence with the Elector, telling him frankly *that you are coming straight to him, because you are well aware that through other channels matters are frequently represented to the reigning lord in an unfavourable light and that the talents of the young are almost invariably kept back.* Now I must close. God keep you well. We kiss you both most cordially. Take care of your health. We are well. Do not leave us without letters. If you cannot do so, for you have to run about a great deal, perhaps Mamma could undertake to write to me when you arrive at some destination. Nannerl and I, alive and dead, are the old faithful, abandoned orphan and grass widower and everything that is sad.

MOZART

*Mozart and his mother spent the next four months at Mann-
heim, which possessed one of the finest orchestras in Europe
and where German opera was being gradually established.
Here Mozart formed friendships with Cannabich, the two
Wendlings and the Weber family, and met Vogler,
Holzbauer, Raaff and Wieland. But all his efforts to interest
the Elector in his future met with no response. His position
soon became precarious and his prospects of making both ends
meet very uncertain. Urged by his exasperated father, who
was obliged to run up debts in order to provide money for the
travellers and was beginning to doubt his son's capacity to
meet life's responsibilities, Mozart reluctantly decided to try
his luck in Paris. During his stay at Mannheim Mozart's
chief compositions were three flute quartets and a flute concerto
written to order, two clavier sonatas, four violin sonatas and
three arias. Letters 232–297.*

(232) *Maria Anna Mozart to her Husband*

[*Autograph in the Mozarteum, Salzburg*]

MY DEAREST HUSBAND, MANNHEIM, 31 *October* 1777

Thank God, we both arrived here safe and sound yesterday, the 30th, at six o'clock in the evening. We left Augsburg last Sunday, the 26th, lunched at Donauwörth and drove in the afternoon to Nördlingen. At seven o'clock we reached Hohenaltheim, where the Prince of Wallerstein is staying and where we lodged in a wretched inn. We would have started off again on the following day, had I not caught a heavy cold which obliged us to spend two nights and one whole day there. Herr Perwein was with us most of the time. The Prince of Wallerstein is greatly to be pitied, for he is in the deepest melancholy and cannot look at anybody without bursting into tears. Wolfgang had a talk with him, but the Prince is so absent-minded that he asked him four or five times about the same thing. He refuses to listen to music and spends all his time with his child. We therefore left for Nördlingen on Tuesday, the 28th, St. Simon and St. Jude's day, at seven in the morning. Captain Beecke had given us our route, a horrible road to Ellwangen, and so through Schwäbisch-Hall and Heilbronn to Heidelberg and Mannheim. But the postmaster in Ellwangen strongly advised us not to go by this route, which, he said, nobody ever took when driving, but only if they were going on horseback. We thereupon drove from Ellwangen, to Aalen, Schwäbisch-Gmünd, Schorndorf, Cannstatt, Enzweihungen, Kündlingen, Bruchsal, Wagheussel, Schwetzingen and thence to Mannheim, this route being longer by only one stage and a half. Wolfgang has gone to see young Herr Danner, who is already married, although he is a year younger than my son. Old Herr Danner is not here, but will return from his estate in the country on Monday. Meanwhile his son is taking Wolfgang to meet Messieurs Raaff and Cannabich.[1] We were only a few yards from Bruchsal yesterday when Herr von Schmidt, who was coming from Speyer, met us on the road. He recognised us, as Wolfgang did him. He got out of his coach at once and, shouting out 'Halt', came up to our carriage and spoke to us. He was uncommonly glad to see us and was sorry not to be in Mannheim. He also advised us to take rooms at the 'Pfälzischer Hof', where he always

---

[1] Christian Cannabich (1731–1798), born in Mannheim, was trained as a violinist by Johann Stamitz, a pioneer of the famous Mannheim school. He studied in Italy under Jommelli and in 1759 became leader of the Mannheim orchestra, and in 1775 conductor along with Holzbauer. In 1778 he followed the Elector Karl Theodor to Munich. Cannabich was a composer of note, but his chief merit lies in his work as leader of the Mannheim orchestra, solo violinist and teacher. In his day he trained nearly all the violinists of the Mannheim orchestra. According to Leopold Mozart's *Reiseaufzeichnungen*, p. 47, the Mozart family met Cannabich in Paris during their second visit in May 1766.

stays. So we are there and not at the 'Prinz Friedrich', which is much dearer. If we find that we have to stay on for a good while, we shall go to some private house, for living in inns is far too expensive. I hope that you and Nannerl are well. And what is my Bimperl doing? I have not heard anything of her for a long time. I am sorry from my heart that the Chief Purveyor's wife died so suddenly. Fräulein Tonerl's mouth will probably water. Wolfgang is writing today to my brother-in-law in Augsburg to tell him to forward the letters he has received, for we told him to keep them until we should send him our address. So Wolfgang will hardly be able to write to you today, for he is at the rehearsal of the oratorio, moreover the post goes at six o'clock and it is already half past four. So you will have to put up with my humble self.

(232a) *Mozart to his Father*

[Autograph in the Mozarteum, Salzburg]

[MANNHEIM, 31 *October* 1777]

And please put up with my very mediocre self. I went with Herr Danner today to M. Cannabich, who was exceedingly courteous. I played to him on his pianoforte, which is a very good one, and we went together to the rehearsal. I thought I should not be able to keep myself from laughing when I was introduced to the people there. Some who knew me by repute were very polite and fearfully respectful; others, however, who had never heard of me, stared at me wide-eyed, and certainly in a rather sneering manner. They probably think that because I am little and young, nothing great or mature can come out of me; but they will soon see. Herr Cannabich himself is taking me tomorrow to Count Savioli,[1] the Intendant of the orchestra. It is a good thing that the Elector's name-day falls very soon. The oratorio, which is being rehearsed, is by Handel,[2] but I did not stay to hear it, for, before it came on, they rehearsed a Psalm—a Magnificat—by Vogler, the Deputy-Kapellmeister here,[3] and it lasted almost an hour. Now I must close, for I have still to

---

[1] Count Louis Aurèle de Savioli.

[2] Handel's *Messiah*, Part I, was performed on 1 November. Vogler conducted it. Berlin and Hamburg had already given performances of this oratorio.

[3] Abt Georg Joseph Vogler (1749–1814), born in Würzburg, was the son of a violin-maker. He first studied law in Bamberg, but in 1773 the Elector Karl Theodor provided him with funds to study music under Padre Martini at Bologna. Vogler proceeded instead to Padua and became a pupil of Vallotti. He was ordained a priest in Rome. In 1775 he returned to Mannheim, was made Court Chaplain and became a famous teacher. Owing to his peculiarities he made many enemies as well as devoted friends. In 1780 Vogler followed the Electoral Court to Munich, where he trained the celebrated singer Aloysia Weber-Lange. He soon set out, however, on his many travels abroad, which included a visit to England in 1790. He was a prolific composer and writer of books on musical theory, but his fame rests on his success as a teacher of famous composers, such as Weber and Meyerbeer. See Schaf häutl, *Abt Georg Joseph Vogler*, Augsburg, 1888.

write to my little cousin. I kiss Papa's hands and my sisterly beloved I embrace shortly and sweetly, as is proper.

Joannes*** Chrisostomus sigismundus**
Wolfgang* gottlieb Mozart

*Today is my name-day! **That is my confirmation name!
***January 27th is my birthday!

Our greetings to all our acquaintances, and particularly to Count Leopold Arco, Herr Bullinger, Mlle Katherl and the whole company of shitters.

À Mademoiselle Rosalie Joli
A thousand thanks, dear Sally, for your wishes.
Now in your honour I shall drink whole dishes
Of coffee, tea, and even lemonade,
Dipping therein a sticklet of pomade,
And also—Oh! It's striking six o'clock!
Whoe'er denies it, well, he's just a—block.

To be continued in my next.

(233) *Mozart to his Cousin, Maria Anna Thekla Mozart, Augsburg*

[*Autograph formerly in the possession of Richard Strauss*]

[Mannheim, 31 *October* 1777[1]]

50 *October* 1777.[2]

How very odd! I am to write something sensible and not one sensible idea occurs to me. Do not forget to remind the Dean to send me that music soon. Do not forget your promise; I shall certainly not forget mine. How can you doubt me? I shall send you very soon a whole letter in French, which you can then get Herr Forstmeister to translate for you. I hope that by this time you have started to learn French? Well, I have too little space left to jot down any more sensible remarks. Besides, too much sense gives one a headache. In any case my letter is full of sensible and learned stuff, as you must acknowledge if you have read it; and if you have not yet read it, please do so quickly, for you will draw a great deal of profit from it and some lines in it will make you shed bitter tears.

---

[1] The version of this letter is that given in Nottebohm, *Mozartiana*, p. 71.
[2] A nonsensical date was one of Mozart's favourite jokes. See p. 261.

(234) *Leopold Mozart to his Son*

[*Extract*]   [*Autograph in the Mozarteum, Salzburg*]

MON TRÈS CHER FILS!   SALZBURG, 1 *November* 1777

I have this moment come in from the Cathedral service, during which
Haydn's oboe mass[1] was performed, he himself conducting it. He had
also composed the offertory and, instead of a sonata, he had set to music
the words of the graduale, which the priest has to say. The mass was
rehearsed yesterday after Vespers. The Prince did not conduct the service,
but Count Friedrich Lodron took his place, as the Bishop of Chiemsee,
Breuner and Dietrichstein are in Augsburg for the All Saints Peremptorio
and were therefore not available. I liked the whole mass very much, as
there were six oboists, three double basses, two bassoons and the castrato
who has been taken on for six months at one hundred gulden a month.[2] Ferlendis
and Sandmayr played the oboe solos. The oboist at Lodron's, a certain
student, the chief watchman and Oberkirchner[3] were the oboists in the
orchestra. Cassel and the choirmaster Knozenbry were the double basses,
seated near the organ and beside the trombones; Estlinger was there with
his bassoon; Hofner and Perwein were seated beside the oboists on the
violinists' platform. What I particularly liked was that, since oboes and
bassoons resemble very much the human voice, the tutti seemed to be a
very strongly supported chorus of voices, as the sopranos and altos,
strengthened by the six oboes and the alto trombones, admirably balanced
the number of tenor and bass voices; and the pieno was so majestic that I
could have easily done without the oboe solos. The whole affair lasted an
hour and a quarter and I found it far too short, for it is really an excellent
composition. It all flows along naturally; the fugues, and particularly the
Et vitam etc. in the Credo, the Dona Nobis and the Hallelujah in the
offertory are worked out in a masterly fashion, the themes being most
natural and without any exaggerated modulations or too sudden transi-
tions. The graduale, which was performed instead of the sonata, is a piece
of pure counterpoint throughout *in pieno*.[4] The voice of the castrato did
on the whole good service here. If some time or other I can obtain this
mass, I shall certainly send it to you. I should mention that Brunetti stood
behind Ferlendis, Wenzl Sadlo[5] behind the bassoon-players and Hafeneder
behind the other oboists. They watched Haydn throughout the performance and beat time on their shoulders; otherwise it would have really
gone higgledy-piggledy in places and particularly in the fugues and in the

---

[1] Michael Haydn's mass which Leopold Mozart praises so highly is his so-called
Hieronymus mass in C major, finished on 14 September 1777.
[2] Francesco Ceccarelli. See p. 342, n. 2.
[3] Johann Michael Oberkirchner, a native of Donauwörth. See Hammerle, *op. cit.* p. 35.
[4] i.e. in full.
[5] Wenzl Sadlo played the horn in the Salzburg court orchestra. See Hammerle, *op. cit.*
p. 35.

running bass-accompaniments. The result may be at last an appointment as Cathedral Kapellmeister or Deputy-Kapellmeister, for which Haydn has been working for so many years. But there are great difficulties. For you must know that Rust[1] is in wretched health; so much so that Dr Barisani has told him that he must leave Salzburg as soon as possible unless he wants to leave his bones here this winter.

Sunday, November 2nd. The graduale was not by Haydn but by an Italian. Haydn had got it from Reutter[2] some time or other. I was with Countess von Lodron today from a quarter to eleven until after noon. She was, of course, very polite and said that she had read in the papers that you were in Augsburg and that she was sure that you would go to Mannheim not only on account of its great opera but because German operas are always performed there and the Elector values people of talent. This, it should be noted, tallies with a remark which she made at lunch yesterday and which Abbé Henri passed on to me: '*Mozart*', she said, '*will go to Mannheim and, whatever happens, I am persuaded that the Elector will retain him.*' She talked a great deal and, upon her asking me about Stein's pianoforte, I told her what you had written to me about it. She said that you were right, judging by the approval of Countess Schönborn,[3] who had told her that she had travelled through Augsburg on purpose in order to see these instruments and, finding them infinitely better than Späth's, had ordered one for herself at the cost of 700 gulden. I am surprised that Herr Stein said nothing to you about this. When we came to speak of Haydn's mass, I mentioned what I have just told you, and she immediately interrupted me: '*Yes,*' she said, '*that was precisely the Archbishop's opinion. Haydn did not understand him properly. He told me so the first time the Kyrie and Gloria were rehearsed, but he added; 'I did not want to say anything more to him, so as not to make him confused and out of humour, as he has begun it like that*''.' The Countess tried to get me to allow Nannerl to pay her a visit in order that she should play the clavier rondo which Mysliwecek has sent her. The object of my visit was in fact mainly on account of Mysliwecek's letter. She assured me that by the last post the Archbishop had sent to him at Munich a draft for twenty-five or thirty ducats. She invited me several times to visit her more often and she ended by asking me to send you her greetings. Then Count Potbelly[4] and their son and heir Sigerl both shouted out: 'From me too! From me too!' She even asked me how Count Leopold Arco was getting on, a thing she has never yet done, and I praised him in appropriate fashion. By the way, Abbé Henri came to congratulate you on your name-day. You promised to write to him and you should do so when you get a free moment.

[1] See p. 275, n. 4.   [2] See p. 12, n. 3.
[3] Countess von Lodron and Countess Schönborn were sisters of the Archbishop.
[4] Count Ernst Lodron, Marshal of the district of Salzburg. Sigmund Lodron was his only son.

Monday, November 3rd. I have this moment come in from the Requiem, in which Signor Ceccarelli sang, as it was Festum Praepositum. He lives in the wig-maker's house, where Ferrari used to live at first. He is a good sight-reader and his method is excellent. He asked me all about you and said that he was sorry to have missed meeting a virtuoso, of whom he had heard such extraordinary accounts both in Italy and at Salzburg. I have invited him to see your portrait. Now I have something to tell you which will certainly infuriate you, for it has annoyed me very much. It is hardly believable, but on the day on which you gave your concert, our best friend, M. Grimm, arrived at the 'Drei Mohren', next to the Concert Hall. I have read in the Augsburger Intelligenzblatt that *Herr von Grimm, envoy of Saxe-Gotha, was due to arrive from Saxony by the mail coach on the 22nd and would stay at the 'Drei Mohren'.* Is it not maddening? I presume that he arrived late in the evening and left again on the following morning; otherwise he would have read the announcement or would have heard people talking about you. Where on earth is he now? God knows. Perhaps you will run into him somewhere. Well, now you know at any rate that he is travelling. How delighted this man would have been and both you and Mamma also, if he had arrived *a tempo* and had been present at the concert. We had our usual shooting yesterday. Next Sunday we shall have as a target the sad parting of two persons dissolving in tears, Wolfgang and the 'Basle'. Where will you be reading this letter? Probably in Mannheim. For this is the second post-day on which we have received no letters. I hope that you will get something to do in Mannheim, where they are always performing German operas. Perhaps you will get a contract to compose one. If you do, you know that I need not urge you to imitate the natural and popular style, which everyone easily understands. The grand and sublime style is suited to grand subjects. Everything in its place. I hope that you are both well. That is our first wish and it should be your principal care. I am always a little bit worried about Mamma. You, dear Wolfgang, should keep to your usual diet, which is very important for your health. I need not be anxious about Mamma, if she only keeps warm. Now farewell. God preserve you, God bless you. Nannerl and I kiss you both a million times and I am your old

TRAZOM

(235) *Mozart to his Father*

[*Autograph in the Mozarteum, Salzburg*]

[MANNHEIM, 4 *November* 1777]

MONSIEUR MON TRÉS CHER PÉRE,

We wrote the day before we left Augsburg. It looks as though you haven't received the letter yet.[1] I shall be sorry if it is lost, for it is a long

[1] Possibly Letter 228.

one and in it I described my concert very fully. It also contains something about Stein's daughter, and, further, my thanks for the congratulations on my name-day. But I hope that by now you have received it. This is my second letter from Mannheim. I am with Cannabich every day. Mamma too came with me today to his house. He is quite a different person from what he used to be and the whole orchestra say the same thing. He has taken a great fancy to me. He has a daughter who plays the clavier quite nicely;[1] and in order to make a real friend of him I am now working at a sonata for her, which is almost finished save for the Rondo.[2] When I had composed the opening Allegro and the Andante I took them to their house and played both to them. Papa cannot imagine the applause which this sonata won. It so happened that some members of the orchestra were there, young Danner, a horn-player called Lang,[3] and the oboist[4] whose name I have forgotten, but who plays very well and has a delightfully pure tone. I have made him a present of my oboe concerto,[5] which is being copied in a room at Cannabich's, and the fellow is quite crazy with delight. I played this concerto to him today on the pianoforte at Cannabich's, and, although *everybody knew that I was the composer*, it was very well received. Nobody said that it was not *well composed*, because the people here do not understand such matters—they had better consult the Archbishop, who will at once put them right.[6] I played all my six sonatas[7] today at Cannabich's. Herr Kapellmeister Holzbauer[8] himself took me today to Count Savioli, the Intendant, and Cannabich happened to be there. Herr Holzbauer spoke to the Count in Italian, suggesting that the Elector ought to grant me the favour of a hearing. He added that I had been here fifteen years ago, when I was seven, but that now I was older and more developed in music as well as in body. 'Ah,' said the Count, 'that is——' Goodness knows who he thought I was. But Cannabich stepped in at once, and I pretended not to hear and fell into conversation with some other people. I noticed, however, that he was speaking to the Count about me with an earnest expression. The latter then said to me: 'I hear that you play the clavier quite passably'. I bowed.

Now I must tell you about the music here. On Saturday, All Saints' Day, I was at High Mass in the Kapelle. The orchestra is excellent and very strong. On either side there are ten or eleven violins, four violas, two

---

[1] Cannabich's eldest daughter Rosa.
[2] K. 309 [284b]. For the identification of this clavier sonata see Köchel, p. 289.
[3] Franz Lang (1751– ?). He and his younger brother, Martin Lang (1755– ?), were horn-players in the Mannheim orchestra.
[4] Friedrich Ramm (1744–1811) was appointed in 1759 oboist in the Mannheim orchestra, which he followed to Munich in 1778.
[5] K. 314 [285d]. See p. 320, n. 1.   [6] This is ironical.   [7] K. 279–284 [189d–h, 205b].
[8] Ignaz Holzbauer (1711–1783), born in Vienna, became Kapellmeister at Mannheim in 1753 and held this appointment until the Elector's death in 1777. He composed eleven Italian operas, a famous German opera *Günther von Schwarzburg*, produced at Mannheim in 1777, oratorios, symphonies, masses and a great deal of church music.

oboes, two flutes and two clarinets, two horns, four violoncellos, four bassoons and four double basses, also trumpets and drums. They can produce fine music, but I should not care to have one of my masses performed here. Why? On account of their shortness? No, everything must be short here too. Because a different style of composition is required? Not at all. But because, as things are at present, you must write principally for the instruments, as you cannot imagine anything worse than the voices here. Six sopranos, six altos, six tenors and six basses against twenty violins and twelve basses is just like zero to one. Is that not so, Herr Bullinger? The reason for this state of affairs is that the Italians are now in very bad odour here. They have only two castrati, who are already old and will just be allowed to die off. The soprano would actually prefer to sing alto, as he can no longer take the high notes. The few boys they have are miserable. The tenors and basses are like our funeral singers. Deputy-Kapellmeister Vogler, who had composed the mass which was performed the other day, is a dreary musical jester, an exceedingly conceited and rather incompetent fellow.[1] The whole orchestra dislikes him. But today, Sunday, I heard a mass by Holzbauer, which he wrote twenty-six years ago, but which is very fine. He is a good composer, he has a good church style, he knows how to write for voices and instruments, and he composes good fugues. They have two organists here who alone would be worth a special visit to Mannheim.[2] I have had an opportunity of hearing them properly, for it is not the custom here to sing the Benedictus, but during that part of the service the organist has to play the whole time. On the first occasion I heard the second organist and on the second, the first organist. But in my opinion the second is even more distinguished than the first. For when I heard him, I enquired: 'Who is playing the organ?' I was told, the second organist. He played abominably. When I heard the other one, I asked: 'Who is playing now?' I was told, our first organist. He played even more wretchedly and I think that if they were thrown together, something even worse would be the result. To watch these gentlemen is enough to make one die of laughing. The second, when seated at the organ, is like a child at stool, for his face tells you what he can do. The first, at any rate, wears spectacles. I went and stood at the organ and watched him in the hope of learning something from him. At every note he lifts his hands right up in the air. His forte is to play in six parts, but chiefly in five and eight parts! He often leaves out the right hand for fun and plays with the left hand alone. In short, he can do just what he likes, for he is completely master of his instrument. Mamma asks me to tell Nannerl that the lining for the coat is at the very bottom of the

[1] Mozart had already sided with Vogler's opponents. For a good account of Mozart's relations with Vogler see Abert, vol. ii. p. 982 ff.

[2] Nikolaus Bayer and Anton Marxfelder. The latter was organist in Mannheim from 1745 until 1778.

large box on the right hand side. She will find all sorts of bits for patching, black, white, yellow, brown, red, green, blue and so forth.

Mamma sends her greetings to all. It is impossible for her to write, for she still has to say her office, as we were very late getting home from the rehearsal of the grand opera. The cotton is not in skeins, but in a ball, wrapped up in a blue cloth. Yes, that is how it is and not otherwise! After High Mass tomorrow I have to go to that stern Electress, who *insists* on teaching me to knit. I am dreadfully nervous, as both she and the most honourable Elector want me to knit in public at the grand gala concert on Thursday evening. The young princess here, who is a natural child of the Elector, also knits very nicely. The Duke and Duchess of Zweibrücken arrived here punctually at eight o'clock. A propos, Mamma and I beg Papa very earnestly to be so good as to send a souvenir to our dear cousin, for we both regretted that we had nothing with us to give her; but we promised to write to Papa and to ask him to send her something, or rather two things, one from Mamma, a double fichu like her own, and one from myself, a trinket, such as a box or toothpick case, or whatever you like, so long as it is pretty, for she deserves it. She and her father took a great deal of trouble and wasted much time in our company. Moreover my uncle took in the money at my concert. Addio. Baccio le mani di vostra paternità ed abbraccio con leggiertà la mia sorella e facendo i miei complimenti da per tutto sono di tutto cuore.[1]

Wolfgango Amadeo Mozart

Mannheim, li 4 di novembre 1777.

(235a) *Postscript written by Maria Anna Mozart to her Husband on the cover*

A certain Signor Gervasio and his wife, who knew you in Holland, send their congratulations to your son the virtuoso. He plays the mandolin and she sings: they gave a concert to-day. Our greetings to the whole of Salzburg, Herr Bullinger, Jungfrau Sallerl.

(235b) *Postscript written by Mozart on the cover*

Gilowski Katherl, fr: v: Gerlisch, h: von Heffner, fr: v: Heffner, fr: v: Schidenhofen, h: Geschwendner, h: Sandner and all who are dead. As for the targets, if it is not too late, this is what I would like. A short man with fair hair, shown bending over and displaying his bare arse. From his mouth come the words: 'Good appetite for the meal'. The other man to be shown booted and spurred with a red cloak and a fine

---

[1] I kiss my father's hands and embrace my sister tenderly. I send greetings to everyone and remain with all my heart. . . .

fashionable wig. He must be of medium height and in such a position that he licks the other man's arse. From his mouth come the words: 'Oh, there's nothing to beat it'. So, please. If not this time, another time.

(236) *Mozart to his Cousin, Maria Anna Thekla Mozart, Augsburg*

[*Autograph in the possession of the Heirs of Stefan Zweig*]

DEAREST COZ FUZZ!   [MANNHEIM, 5 *November* 1777[1]]

I have received reprieved your dear letter, telling selling me that my uncle carbuncle, my aunt can't and you too are very well hell. Thank God, we too are in excellent health wealth. Today the letter setter from my Papa Ha! Ha! dropped safely into my claws paws. I hope that you too have got shot the note dote which I wrote to you from Mannheim. If so, so much the better, better the much so. Now for some sense. I am very sorry to hear that the Abbot rabbit has had another stroke so soon moon. But I trust that with God's cod's help it will have no serious consequences excrescences. You say lay that you will keep the compromise[2] which you made me before I left Augsburg and that you will do so soon boon. Well, that will certainly be a shock to me. You write further, you pour out, disclose, divulge, notify, declare, signify, inform, acquaint me with the fact, make it quite clear, request, demand, desire, wish, would like, order me to send lend you my portrait. Eh bien, I shall certainly despatch scratch it to you. Oui, par ma foi. I shit on your nose and it will run down your chin. A propos. Have you got that Spuni Cuni business? Do tell me! Do you still love me? I am sure you do! If so, so much the better, better the much so!

Well, so it is in this world, I'm told. One has the purse and another has the gold. Whom do you hold with? Surely with me—I am certain you do. But now things are more difficult. A propos. Would you not like to go and see Herr Goldschmidt again soon? . . . But, you ask, what for? What for?—Why, nothing at all—beyond asking about that Spuni Cuni business. Well, well; that's all right. Long live all those who . . . how does it go on? Well, I wish you good night, but first shit into your bed and make it burst. Sleep soundly, my love, into your mouth your arse you'll shove. Now I'm off to fool about and then I'll sleep a bit, no doubt. Tomorrow we'll talk sensibly for a bit vomit. I tell a things of lot to have you, you imagine can't simply how have I much say to; but hear all tomorrow it will you. Meanwhile, good-bye. Oh, my arse is burning like fire! What on earth does it mean?—Perhaps some muck wants to come

---

[1] The autograph of this letter, a facsimile of which was published for private circulation by Herbert Reichner, Vienna, 1931, shows a tremendous flourish round the first letter of 'Allerliebstes Bäsle Häsle'.

[2] Mozart uses instead of *Versprechen* (promise) the word *Verbrechen* (crime).

out? Why yes, muck, I know, see and smell you . . . and . . . what is that?
—Is it possible . . . Ye gods!—can I believe those ears of mine? Yes indeed,
it is so—what a long melancholy note! Today letter the writing am 5th
this I. Yesterday I had to talk with the formidable Electress and tomorrow,
the 6th, I am playing at the great gala concert; and afterwards I am to play
again to her in private, as she herself told me. Now for some real sense.

No. 1. A letter or letters addressed to me will reach you, which I must
ask you to—to what? Why, a fox is no hare, well . . . Now, where was
I . . . Yes, of course, at reach. Yes, they will reach you—well, what will?
—Why, now I remember. Letters, why, letters will reach you . . . But
what sort of letters?—Why, of course, letters addresed to me, which I
must ask you to forward without fail. I shall let you know where I go on
to from Mannheim.

Now for No. 2. I must ask you, why not?—I must ask you, dearest
dunce, why not?—if you happen to be writing to Madame Tavernier at
Munich, to send my regards to the two Misses Freysinger, why not?—
Strange!—Why not? And say that I beg the youngest one, Fräulein
Josepha, to forgive me, why not?—Why should I not beg her to forgive
me? Strange! Why should I not? Say that she must forgive me for not
having yet sent her the sonata[1] I promised her and that I shall send it as
soon as possible. Why not?——What?—Why not?—Why should I not
send it?—Why should I not despatch it?—Why not?—Strange! I don't
know why I shouldn't—Well then—you will do me this favour.—Why
not?—Why should you not do it?—Why not?—Strange! I shall do the
same for you, when you want me to. Why not? Why should I not do it
for you? Strange! Why not?—I can't think why not?

Do not forget also to send my compliments to the Papa and Mamma of
the two young ladies, for it is a gross fault to forget must shall will have
one's duty to father and mother. When the sonata is finished, I shall send
it to you and the letter as well; and you will be good enough to send it on
to Munich. Now I must close, though it makes me morose. Dear Uncle,
let us go at once to the Holy Cross Monastery and see if anyone is still
up? We shall not stay long, we shall just ring the bell, that is all. Now I
must tell you of a sad thing which has happened just this very moment.
As I was doing my best to write this letter, I heard something on the
street. I stopped writing—I got up—went to the window . . . and . . . the
sound ceased. I sat down again, started off again to write—but I had
hardly written ten words when again I heard something. I got up again—
As I did, I again heard a sound, this time quite faint—but I seemed to
smell something slightly burnt—and wherever I went, it smelt. When I
looked out of the window, the smell disappeared. When I looked back

[1] Saint-Foix, vol. iii. p. 18, suggests that this clavier sonata is K. 311 [284c], begun in
Munich and finished in Mannheim.

into the room, I again noticed it. In the end Mamma said to me: 'I bet you have let off one'. 'I don't think so, Mamma', I replied. 'Well, I am certain that you have', she insisted. Well, I thought 'Let's see', put my finger to my arse and then to my nose and—Ecce, provatum est. Mamma was right after all. Well, farewell. I kiss you 1000 times and remain, as always, your little old piggy wiggy

WOLFGANG AMADÉ ROSY POSY

A thousand compliments from us two travellers to my aunt and uncle. My greetings bleatings to all my good friends sends. Addio, booby looby.

♡ 333 to the grave, if my life I save.
Miehnnam, Rebotco eht ht5, 7771.

(237) *Leopold Mozart to his Wife and Son*

[*Extract*]   [*Autograph in the Mozarteum, Salzburg*]

SALZBURG, 6 *November* 1777

MY DEAR WIFE AND MY DEAR SON!

Thank God that you have arrived safely in Mannheim! I do not know, it is true, and I very much doubt whether Wolfgang will find there all those things which he has imagined and the great advantages which several people may perhaps have described to him. That long journey from Augsburg to Mannheim will have made heavy inroads on your purse and Mannheim will hardly fill it again. Basta! You are there, however. Herr Beecke will indeed be glad that neither Prince Taxis nor the Abbot at Kaysersheim heard you play. Thus he is still cock of the walk in his country and the clavier-god of his admirers. Herr Vogler is the person who, as far as I know, has published a treatise on musical composition.[1] He is well versed in counterpoint and in algebra and he has under his control the school of music or academy for young people. If, as is usually the case with courts of that kind, you are likely to be kept waiting, arrange for some other lodgings. Perhaps Wolfgang will be able to obtain from the Elector a commission to write a German opera. *I am indeed anxious*, for Mannheim is an expensive place. You know how we are placed at the moment. I hope that Herr Danner, to whom I send most polite greetings, will assist and guide you and I trust that Wolfgang will endeavour by ingratiating politeness to make friends of everybody. Deputy-Kapellmeister Vogler must be a very clever man, for the Elector thinks very highly of him. I am anxious to hear whether you gain the favour of Herr Raaff, to whom I send my humble greetings. He has always been praised to me as a very honest Christian. I wrote to Mysli-

---

[1] *Tonwissenschaft und Tonsetzkunst*, Mannheim, 1776.

MARIA ANNA THEKLA MOZART, THE 'BÄSLE' (1778)

From a drawing by an unknown artist
(Mozart Museum, Salzburg)

wecek and asked him to write to Raaff about you. Now I hope that you are both well and that Mamma's cold is better. Thank God, we are both in good health and Pimperl is too, for she has never been so fresh as she is now. Keep well. We both kiss you a million times and I am your old.

MOZART

(238) *Maria Anna Mozart to her Husband*

[Autograph in the Mozarteum, Salzburg]

MY DEAREST   MANNHEIM, *8 November* 1777

We have received safely your last letter of October 29th and all the others; but it is absolutely impossible to answer all your questions as accurately as we should like to, for we can only steal the time and we generally write at night. We never get to bed before one o'clock, we get up late the following morning and we are just ready in time for lunch. After lunch we go to Herr Director Cannabich and at nine o'clock we come home to supper. The gala days are now over. On the first there was a service at eleven o'clock, during which cannons and rockets were fired off. Afterwards Wolfgang had to go to the Electress to whom the Intendant, Count Savioli, had introduced him. She remembered that he had been here fourteen years ago, but she did not recognize him. After that there was a splendid banquet and during the evening a magnificent reception. On the second day the grand German opera, entitled 'Günther von Schwarzburg', was performed.[1] It is very beautiful and the music is incomparably fine. There was also a marvellously beautiful ballet.[2] On the third day there was a grand concert at which Wolfgang played a concerto; then, before the final symphony, he improvised and gave them a sonata. He won extraordinary applause from the Elector and Electress and from all who heard him. On the fourth day there was a gala play, which we went to see with Monsieur and Madame Cannabich. We both lunched with Herr Cannabich on the day of the concert, and my son is lunching alone with him today, as immediately after their meal he is going with him to the ⟨Elector's children⟩. He was there yesterday and the ⟨Elector⟩ was present the whole time. There are four children and two of them play the clavier.[3] ⟨The Elector is immensely attached to them,⟩ and commanded the Intendant to arrange that Wolfgang should be taken to them. He is to play once more quite alone, for the Electress has promised this, so we must wait until she sends a command. Meanwhile, my dear husband, I wish you 1000 happinesses for your coming name-day, and I hope that you may enjoy everything beneficial to your soul

---

[1] The text was by Professor Anton Klein and the music by Ignaz Holzbauer.
[2] The ballet was designed by Lauchéry and set to music by Cannabich.
[3] They were the four children, one son and three daughters, of Countess Haydeck, née Seuffert, who had been an actress. The son later became Prince von Bretzenheim.

and body, and constant good health. Above all I wish I were with you to congratulate you in person. But, as this is not possible now, we shall drink your health in a good Rhine wine (which we only wish from our hearts that you had) and we shall always think of in the most pleasant hope of meeting again, if it be God's will, and then remaining together. I send my greetings to Nannerl. Please ask her whether her cousin has already sent her the silks, for she promised me to forward them to her at once. Baron Schafmann[1] and Herr Dehl called on us yesterday morning and left today for Wetzlar.

(238a) *Mozart to his Father*

[Autograph in the Mozarteum, Salzburg]

I wrote out at Cannabich's this morning the Rondo to the sonata for his daughter, with the result that they refused to let me go. The Elector, the Electress and the whole Court are very much pleased with me. At the concert, on both occasions when I played, the Elector and the Electress came up quite close to the clavier. After the concert Cannabich arranged for me to speak to them. I kissed the Elector's hand. He remarked: 'I think it is about fifteen years since you were here last'. 'Yes, Your Highness, fifteen years since I had the honour of——' 'You play admirably.' When I kissed the Princess's hand she said to me: 'Monsieur, je vous assure, on ne peut pas jouer mieux'. I went yesterday with Cannabich on the visit Mamma has already referred to and there I talked to the Elector as to an old friend. He is a most gracious and courteous gentleman. He said to me: 'I hear that you have written an opera at Munich'. 'Yes, your Highness,' I replied, 'I commend myself to Your Highness's good graces. My dearest wish is to write an opera here. I beg you not to forget me utterly. Thanks and praise be to God, I know German too',[2] and I smiled. 'That can easily be managed', he answered. ⟨He has a son and three daughters. The eldest girl and the young Count⟩ play the clavier. The Elector put some questions to me in confidence about his ⟨children⟩, and I expressed myself quite frankly, but without disparaging their ⟨teacher⟩. Cannabich too was of my opinion. On leaving, the Elector thanked me very graciously. After lunch today at about two o'clock I went with Cannabich to Wendling, the flautist.[3] There they were all extremely polite to me. The daughter,[4] ⟨who was at one time the Elector's mistress⟩, plays the clavier very charmingly. I then played myself. I was in such excellent spirits

---

[1] Franz Felix Josef von Schafmann, Baron von Hammerles and Kanösowitz, Chief Magistrate of the Abtenau district.

[2] Mozart's Munich opera *La finta giardiniera* was on an Italian text.

[3] The Mozarts had heard Wendling play in 1763 when they visited Schwetzingen, the summer residence of the Elector. See p. 25, n. 4.

[4] Augusta Wendling, who was then twenty-one.

today—words fail me to describe my feelings. I improvised and then I played three duets with violin accompaniment which I had never seen and the composer of which I had never even heard of. They were all so delighted that I had to kiss the ladies. In the daughter's case this was no hardship, for she is not at all bad-looking. Afterwards we went back ⟨to the Elector's natural children⟩. There I played again with my whole heart. I played three times. The Elector himself kept on asking me for more. He sat down each time beside me and did not move a inch. I also asked a certain Professor to give me a theme for a fugue which I proceeded to develop. Now for my congratulations:—

DEAREST PAPA!

I cannot write in verse, for I am no poet. I cannot arrange the parts of speech with such art as to produce effects of light and shade, for I am no painter. Even by signs and gestures I cannot express my thoughts and feelings, for I am no dancer. But I can do so by means of sounds, for I am a musician. So tomorrow at Cannabich's I shall play on the clavier a whole congratulatory composition in honour of your name-day and of your birthday. All I can do today is to wish you, mon très cher Père, from the bottom of my heart what I wish you every day, both morning and evening; health, long life and good spirits. I hope too that you have now less cause for annoyance than when I was in Salzburg. For I must admit that I was the sole cause of it. They treated me badly and I did not deserve it. You naturally sympathised with me—but too feelingly. Believe me, that was the chief and most important reason for my leaving Salzburg in such a hurry. I hope too that my wishes have been fulfilled. I must now conclude with a musical congratulation. I wish you as many years of life as years will be needed until nothing new can be produced in music. Now farewell. I beg you most humbly to go on loving me just a little and in the meantime to put up with these poor congratulations until I get new drawers made in my small and narrow brain-box, into which I can put that wisdom which I intend yet to acquire. I kiss Papa's hands 1000 times and remain until death, mon trés cher Pére,

your most obedient son
WOLFGANG AMADÉ MOZART

Mannheim, 8 November 1777.

(239) Leopold Mozart to his Son

[Extract]   [Autograph in the Mozarteum, Salzburg]

MON TRÉS CHER FILS!   SALZBURG, 10 *November* 1777

In the greatest hurry I write to say that I received your letter of November 4th on my way to the service at the Cajetans, as today is the Feast of

St. Andrew Avellino. I lunched there; and then I had to run to Vespers in the Cathedral on account of St. Martin,[1] and now I have an hour left in which to write, for the post goes at five o'clock.

I should like you to win the Elector's favour and to be able to show what you can do *on the organ and in composition*. Indeed they need a good organist in Mannheim. I hope that you will send *your sister the sonata, which you have composed for Mlle Cannabich, copied out on small paper*. Did I not tell you recently that the Italians are not in favour at Mannheim? Why, I knew it! I hear that Vogler is a musical theorist, so he may well be ⟨a *fool* or a comedian⟩. I have not seen any of his compositions. Herr Holzbauer was always an excellent, honest fellow. Please give my compliments to him and to Cannabich. You tell me nothing whatever about the grand opera and the theatre. Perhaps you will do so in your next letter. Are there no actors in Mannheim? Are German operas being performed? If you get an opportunity of really showing what you can do, then you have hopes of remaining there; for just to play a concerto and nothing else is something which anyone can do who has practised it. I am sorry that we are now so far from one another. By the time I write to you about any matter, it is all over as far as you are concerned. Have you not tried to leave your inn and get private rooms and cheaper board? Herr Cannabich will surely advise and help you. I shall certainly send your cousin something and I shall write to her today about it in the letter to her which I began yesterday. We two and Bimperl and Theresa are well, as I hope and trust that you both always are. We kiss you both a million times and I am your old husband and son

MOZART

(240) *Leopold Mozart to his Son*

[*Extract*]   [*Autograph in the Mozarteum, Salzburg*]

MON TRÈS CHER FILS!   SALZBURG, 13 *November* 1777

I think that I have told you that Mysliwecek wrote a letter to me *in forma ostensiva*[2] (as I had asked him to, in order that I might show it to the person in question), in which he urged me to find out whether the music he sent both some years ago and again recently had been delivered to the Archbishop. As a result, he was sent a draft for twenty-five ducats. He now informs me that he received it on November 8th and that on his doctor's advice he will remain a while longer in Munich for the benefit of his health, which is improving, and so that he may be able to travel in

---

[1] 12 November.   [2] See p. 345, n. 2.

greater safety. He adds that he is going to present to the Elector a cantata (Enea negl'Elisi) which, he feels sure, will be performed together with Monza's opera,[1] as the Elector has ordered the score to be copied immediately. He tells me, further, that, as I requested, he has written to Signor Raaff, that he has received his own scritture for the operas for May 30th and November 4th and that he is now waiting for the scrittura for you, which, however, cannot arrive for another month. As soon as he receives it, he will forward it to me at Salzburg. To tell the truth I am really not counting on this contract, for you know what excuses these Italians make and what tangles of wires there are at Naples. I heard today that the Archbishop commissioned Brunetti yesterday to write to Mysliwecek and order some concertoni, which may or may not be included in the twenty-five ducats. The graduale in counterpoint which I liked so much was by the famous Maestro Lotti, who died a long time ago.[2] As for your resignation from the Archbishop's service, Herr Duschek has been strongly suspected of having influenced both yourself and the rest of us, and this suspicion has now been extended to Counts Hardik and Lützow. Duschek told me this himself. Certainly, if you had gone to Prague, the Archbishop would have been convinced that his suspicions were justified! But, as it is, he is simply being made a fool of. On St. Martin's Day I lunched in the priests' house and the healths of both of you were drunk. Nannerl invited herself that day to old Hagenauer's and he has told her that whenever I lunch out, she must take her meal with them.

My dear Wolfgang, in your last letter of November 4th, signed on St. Charles's day, there is so much confusion that it is impossible for me to know when this and that took place. You keep on saying, *'Today I played my six sonatas at Cannabich's. Herr Holzbauer took me today to Count Savioli. But today, being Sunday, I heard the mass by Holzbauer. Mamma cannot write—we got home very late from the rehearsal of the opera. Tomorrow after High Mass I have to go to the Electress'*—and all this, *according to your signature, happened, it seems, on November 4th, St. Charles's day.* Surely the opera, and not the rehearsal took place on that day? So my common sense tells me that you did not write the letter on November 4th, but only closed it on that day. Why can you not do as I do? When I break off writing and go on the next day, I set down whether it is Sunday or Monday. It is then possible to tell in what order things have happened; and it may sometimes be important to have this information. Meanwhile

---

[1] *Attilio Regolo*, by Carlo Monza (1740–1801), who in 1787 became maestro di cappella in Milan Cathedral, and was already an operatic composer of note. According to Leopold Mozart's *Reiseaufzeichnungen*, p. 51, the Mozarts had met him in Milan in 1770.

[2] Antonio Lotti (c. 1607–1740), an eminent Venetian composer, who in 1704 became organist at St. Mark's, Venice. He wrote a number of operas, one of which, *Giustino*, was produced in Venice when he was 16. After 1719 he only composed church music.

I had already written to Herr Pfeil and Herr Otto in Frankfurt to find out about winter concerts and whether you could not obtain a well-paid appointment there, such as Meisner and Reiner used to have. I received an answer at once, written on November 4th, which arrived at the same time as your letter, and in which, in the most sincere and friendly manner and to his great regret, Herr Pfeil informed me on behalf of old Otto that nothing could be done. He added that of course you could give a private concert on your own, but that the music-lovers were so apathetic and so few in number that you would run the risk of not even making your expenses. Thus, much as he would like to have you, he would not advise you in your own interest to make a special journey to Frankfurt. But if your tour were to bring you there, your visit would give him infinite pleasure, and he said that you would find at his house a collection of instruments which would mean for you an embarrassment of choice. He mentioned that in addition to his large Friederici harpsichord with two manuals like our own, he had a perfectly new and very large forte-piano in mahogany, which he described at length and with the greatest enthusiasm. Further, he has a clavichord also in mahogany, which he would not sell for 200 gulden, as he says that this instrument simply has not got its equal; that the descant sounds like a violin being played softly, and the bass notes like trombones. In addition, he has a number of fortepianos all made by Friederici, as he deals in these. He regrets that his large collection of clavier music contains no composition of yours. As far as I can see, most of it comes from Lang in Coblenz, to whom he offers to give you letters of introduction. He closes with the remark: 'How are your dearest wife and your daughter? Tell your son that if he is travelling through Frankfurt, he must not forget me, for I shall show him how much I loved him as a child and how much I love him still.' So in this direction little or nothing can be done. I am really at a loss as to how to advise you, for, if there is no prospect of your remaining in Mannheim, you will surely go on to Mainz, and from there it is only a short trip to Frankfurt. Returning, you could then go on to Coblenz and call on the Elector of Trier, who is Prince Clement of Saxony. You will remember that seated at table between him and the Elector of Bavaria you once wrote a composition in pencil when we were passing through Munich on our way back from England.[1] But whither could you go after that? To the Elector of Cologne, at Bonn, where Lucchesi is still Kapellmeister? That visit would not even pay the expenses of your journey and, besides, it would take you too far to the right of the direct route to Holland through the Netherlands—and so to Paris? What a fearful distance! Where on earth would you raise the money for such a journey? Indeed I did not think that you would decide on going to Mannheim immediately, as you never

[1] See p. 68.

even mentioned it to me, which you ought to have done from Augsburg, the more so as I wrote to you on purpose, saying that I would send you my considered opinion as to what steps you should take there. I know well that I wrote to you very fully, but I was proposing to send you a written statement, a document which you could have handed to the Elector.

You say that after the service you were summoned to the Electress. There you had an opportunity of ingratiating yourself and, if circumstances permitted, of making a beginning with the plan you have in mind. But why should I trouble to write at length! Who knows whether this letter will reach you in Mannheim? And even if you are still there, I do not know how things are in that town. Mannheim has poor organists. If there is no hope of your getting an appointment there, the Elector might keep you for a year, or at least for this winter, the more so as *you could give as a good excuse to the Electress your mother's age and the strain of a winter journey, which would be very uncomfortable indeed for an elderly woman.* If you have to stay there, you will not lack opportunities of showing what you can do in every branch of music and of making yourself popular. Then, if you must leave in the spring or summer, you have only to go to Spa, which is swarming with English people. In a word, if you do not ask for a *permanent* appointment, an Elector who so loves and values talents, will give you an opportunity for a short time at least of displaying your genius at his Court, that famous Court, whose rays, like those of the sun, illumine the whole of Germany, nay even the whole of Europe. Herr Cannabich would gain a great deal if you were to help his daughter *without getting in the way of her teacher.* But everything will depend on your audience with the Elector and the Electress and on the skill with which you address them. Women sympathize with one another, and Her Highness knows what old age means. Count Savioli must not be pushed aside, but by treating him respectfully you should make a friend of him, which is your duty and at the same time good diplomacy. All this is neither intrigue nor deception, but is the way which will enable you to gain sufficient time to display your gifts in all directions. For your youth and your appearance prevent people from realizing the wealth of the Divine grace which has been bestowed on you in your talents. You have left behind you many places, where people never got to know half of what you can do. I have nothing more to say, as I have received no letter today, and so I do not know how you are getting on. Perhaps, as has often happened already, I shall receive a letter tomorrow by the extra post. But in that case I cannot reply until Monday. I repeat, however, that I do not doubt but that the Elector will keep you for the winter and perhaps even longer, if Mamma represents to the Electress the discomfort of a journey. ⟨If you do spend a winter there, I feel sure that you will be appointed permanently and with a good salary.⟩ I hope that you are both well, as, thank God, we are. Nannerl and

I kiss you cordially a million times. I shall write every post-day, as I have always done, and I am your old husband and father

MOZART

I repeat that *on your departure you should leave at the post office a note stating to what address your letters should be forwarded*. Herr Bullinger and all Salzburg send their greetings. I am exceedingly anxious to hear whether this letter reaches you in Mannheim. We are now separated by a very great distance, for a letter takes six days, and if you do not write every post-day, we have no idea where you are or what you are doing. Do but write '*we are well*', nothing more—and surely my dear wife, who will sometimes be alone at home, can do that.

(241) *Mozart to his Father*

[*Autograph in the Mozarteum, Salzburg*]

[MANNHEIM, 13 *November* 1777]

MON TRÉS CHER PÉRE!

We have received your last two letters dated October 29th and November 6th. I must now answer all your questions. I did not get the letter in which you asked me to find out ⟨about Beecke's parentage⟩, until I had reached Mannheim, consequently too late for me to do so. It would never have occurred to me to do anything of the sort, as it really does not concern me in the least. Well, would Papa like to know how Beecke received me? Why, very favourably and most politely. He asked me where I was going. I said that, as far as I knew, it was to Paris. He then gave me a good deal of advice, remarking that he had just been there himself. 'You will make heaps of money by giving lessons,' he added, 'for in Paris they are very fond of the clavier.' He at once arranged for me to be taken to the officers' mess and took steps to secure me an audience with the Prince.[1] He expressed great regret that he himself happened to have a sore throat (which was perfectly true) and that he could not therefore take me out himself, and entertain me. He was sorry too that he could not arrange some music in my honour, but on that very day most of the performers had taken a holiday and gone out walking to some place or other. At his request I had to try his clavichord, which is a very good one. He frequently exclaimed, 'Bravo!' I improvised and played my sonatas in B♭ and D.[2] In short, he was very polite and I was the same, but perfectly serious. We fell to talking of various things, amongst others of Vienna, and how the Emperor was no great lover of music. 'That is true,' he said; 'he knows

---

[1] Prince Krafft Ernst von Öttingen-Wallerstein. Mozart is describing their visit to Hohenaltheim, of which his mother had already written a short account. See p. 349.

[2] Probably K. 281 [189f], 284 [205b].

something about counterpoint, but that is all. I can still remember (here he rubbed his forehead) that when I had to play to him, I had not the least idea what to play. So I started to play fugues and such-like foolery, and all the time I played I was laughing up my sleeve.' When I heard this, I was scarcely able to contain myself and felt that I should love to say to him: 'Sir, I well believe that you laughed, but surely not as heartily as I should have done, had I been listening to you'. He then went on to say (something which is quite true) that music is performed in the Imperial apartments which would drive a dog away. I remarked that whenever I heard that kind of music and could not get away from it, it always gave me a headache. 'Oh, it does not affect me at all', he retorted. 'Bad music never gets on my nerves; on the other hand, beautiful music does; and then I sometimes do get a headache.' Once more I thought to myself: 'Yes, a shallow pate like yours no doubt begins to ache when it hears something which it cannot understand'.

Now for some news from Mannheim. Yesterday I had to go with Cannabich to Count Savioli, the Intendant, to fetch my present. It was just as I had expected. No money, but a fine gold watch. At the moment ten carolins would have suited me better than the watch, which including the chains and the mottoes has been valued at twenty. What one needs on a journey is money; and, let me tell you, I now have five watches. I am therefore seriously thinking of having an additional watch pocket on each leg of my trousers so that when I visit some great lord, I shall wear both watches (which, moreover, is now the 'mode') so that it will not occur to him to present me with another one. I see from Papa's letter that he has not seen Vogler's book.[1] I have just read it, as I borrowed it from Cannabich. Let me give you a short history of Vogler. He came here, absolutely down and out, performed on the clavier and composed a ballet.[2] People took pity on him and the Elector sent him to Italy.[3] When the Elector happened to be in Bologna,[4] he asked Padre Vallotti about him and received this reply: 'O altezza, questo è un gran uomo!'[5] He also asked Padre Martini, who informed him: 'Altezza, è buono; ma a poco a poco, quando sarà un poco più vecchio, più sodo, si farà, si farà, ma bisogna che si cangi molto'.[6] When Vogler returned to Mannheim, he took orders and was immediately made Court chaplain.[7] He produced a Miserere which, everyone tells me, simply cannot be listened to, for it sounds all wrong. Hearing that his composition was not receiving much praise, Vogler went to the Elector and complained that the orchestra were

---

[1] See p. 360, n. 1.   [2] In 1771.   [3] Early in 1773.
[4] The Elector Karl Theodor went to Italy in 1774. The conversation must have taken place in Padua, where Vallotti had been maestro di cappella since 1730.
[5] Oh, Your Highness, he is a great man!
[6] Your Highness, he is good; and gradually, as he becomes older and surer of himself, he will improve. But he will have to change considerably.   [7] In 1775.

playing it badly on purpose. In a word, he was so clever at pulling strings (he had had more than one naughty little affair with women, who were useful to him) that he was appointed Deputy-Kapellmeister. But he is a fool, who imagines that he is the very pitch of perfection. The whole orchestra, from A to Z, detest him. He has caused Holzbauer a great deal of annoyance. His book is more useful for teaching arithmetic than for teaching composition. He says he can turn out a composer in three weeks and a singer in six months, but so far no one has seen him do it. He disparages the great masters. Why, he even belittled Bach[1] to me. Bach has written two operas here, the first of which was more popular than the second, 'Lucio Silla'. Now, as I too had composed a 'Lucio Silla' in Milan, I wanted to see Bach's opera and I had heard from Holzbauer that Vogler possessed a copy. So I asked him for it. 'Delighted,' he said. 'I shall send it to you tomorrow. But you will not make head or tail of it.' When he saw me a few days later, he asked me with an obvious sneer: 'Well, do you find it beautiful? Have you learnt anything from it?—It has one fine aria. Let me see, what are the words?' He turned to somebody who happened to be standing beside him. 'What sort of aria?' asked his companion. 'Why, of course, that hideous aria by Bach, that filthy stuff— yes, yes, *Pupille amate*,[2] which he certainly wrote in his cups.' I thought I should have to seize his front hair and pull it hard, but I pretended not to hear him, said nothing and walked off. He has had his day with the Elector. My sonata for Mlle Rosa Cannabich is now finished. Last Sunday I tried the organ in the chapel for fun. I came in during the Kyrie and played the end of it, and, when the priest had finished intoning the Gloria, I played a cadenza. As my performance was so different from what they are accustomed to here, they all looked round, especially Holzbauer. He said to me: 'If I had known this I should have put on another mass'. 'Yes,' I replied, 'so that you could have caught me out!' The elder Toeschi[3] and Wendling were standing beside me all the time. The people were splitting with laughter. Now and then the music was marked pizzicato and each time I just touched the keys very lightly. I was in my very best spirits. Instead of a Benedictus the organist has to play here the whole time. So I took the theme of the Sanctus and developed it as a fugue. Whereupon they all stood gaping. Finally, after the *Ita missa est*, I played a fugue. The pedal there is different from ours, which put me out a bit at first; but I soon got the hang of it. Now I must close. Papa should continue to write to us at Mannheim. It is safer. I shall see that we get his letters all right. I

---

[1] Johann Christian Bach, whose operas *Temistocle* and *Lucio Silla* had been performed at Mannheim in 1772 and 1774.
[2] The aria 'Pupille amate' in *Lucio Silla*.
[3] Carlo Giuseppe Toeschi (c. 1724–1788), a pupil of the great Johann Stamitz, became a violinist in the Mannheim orchestra in 1752, and in 1759 Konzertmeister in Mannheim. He was a prolific composer in all branches of orchestral and chamber music.

know what Mysliwecek's sonatas are like, for I played them at Munich. They are quite easy and pleasing to the ear. I should advise my sister, to whom I send my most humble greetings, to play them with plenty of expression, taste and fire, and to learn them by heart. For they are sonatas which are bound to please everyone, which are easy to memorize and very effective when played with the proper precision. I kiss Papa's hands and remain his obedient son

WOLFGANG AMADÈ MOZART

Mannheim, 13 November 1777.

(241a) *Maria Anna Mozart to her Husband*

[Autograph in the Library of the University of Prague]

[MANNHEIM, 13 November 1777[1]]

Today, the 13th, we received your letter of November 1st, which therefore arrived a post-day later than your last letter. Thank God, we are well. Wolfgang has received from the Elector a watch of the finest workmanship, small but beautifully designed. The day before yesterday, being the feast of St. Martin, we lunched with old Herr Danner and yesterday with young Herr Danner. We and especially my son have also lunched very often with Herr Cannabich. I too am with them every day and they are extremely courteous to us. Herr Danner sends you his greetings and longs to see you. Wolfgang wants to know whether the Bishop of Chiemsee has arrived in Munich, for he would like to write to him. *I must close, for Wolfgang must go out and he has to write the address and take the letter to the post.* I kiss you and Nannerl many 1000 times and I send greetings to the whole of Salzburg. I remain your faithful wife

MARIA ANNA MOZART

(242) *Mozart to his Cousin, Maria Anna Thekla Mozart, Augsburg*

[Autograph in the Heineman Foundation]

[MANNHEIM, 13 November 1777]

Now do send her a sensible letter for once. You can make jokes in it all the same. But tell her that you have received all your letters which she forwarded, so that she may no longer worry and fret.[2]

---

[1] A postscript to Mozart's letter on the cover.
[2] The autograph of this letter begins with this apparently disconnected sentence. Mozart evidently jotted down what his mother happened to say to him.

Ma trés chére Niéce! Cousine! fille! Mére, Sœur, et Épouse!

Bless my soul, a thousand curses, Croatians, damnations, devils, witches, sorcerers, hell's battalions to all eternity, by all the elements, air, water, earth and fire, Europe, Asia, Africa and America, Jesuits, Augustinians, Benedictines, Capuchins, Minorites, Franciscans, Dominicans, Carthusians and Brothers of the Holy Cross, Canons regular and irregular, all slackers, knaves, cowards, sluggards and toadies higgledy-piggledy, asses, buffaloes, oxen, fools, nit-wits and dunces! What sort of behaviour is that, my dears —four smart soldiers and three bandoliers? . . . Such a parcel to get, but no portrait[1] as yet! I was all eagerness—in fact, I was quite sure—for you yourself had written the other day that I was to have it soon, very, very soon. Perhaps you doubt that I shall keep my word? Surely you do not doubt me? Well, anyhow, I implore you to send me yours—the sooner, the better. And I trust that you will have it done, as I urged you, in French costume.

How do I like Mohmheim?[2] As well as I could like any place without my little cousin. Forgive my wretched writing, but the pen is already worn to a shred, and I've been shitting, so 'tis said, nigh twenty-two years through the same old hole, which is not yet frayed one whit, though I've used it daily to shit, and each time the muck with my teeth I've bit.

On the other hand, I hope that, however that may be, you have received all my letters, that is, one from Hohenaltheim[3] and two from Mannheim; and this one, however that may be, is my third letter from Mannheim, but the fourth in all, however that may be. Now I must close, however that may be, for I am not yet dressed and we are lunching this very moment, so that after that we may shit again, however that may be. Do go on loving me, as I love you, then we shall never cease loving one another, though the lion hovers round the walls, though doubt's hard victory has not been weighed and the tyrant's frenzy has crept to decay; yet Codrus, the wise philosopher, often eats soot instead of porridge, and the Romans, the props of my arse, have always been and ever will be— half-castes. Adieu. J'espère que vous aures déjà pris quelque lection dans la langue française, et je ne doute point que—céoutes—que vous saures bientôt mieux le français, que moi; car il y a certainement deux ans que je n'ai pas écrit un môt dans cette langue. Adieu cependant. Je vous baise vos mains, votre visage, vos genoux, et votre—enfin, tout ce que vous me permettes de baiser. Je suis de tout mon cœur

votre tres affectionné Neveu et Cousin

WOLFG: AMADÉ MOZART

Mannheim, le 13 Nomv: 1777.

---

[1] The 'Bäsle' sent Mozart her portrait in February 1778. It is a pencil drawing, which is now in the Mozart Museum, Salzburg. See illustration no. 7.
[2] i.e. Mannheim.   [3] This letter is lost.

(243) *Maria Anna Mozart to her Husband*

[*Autograph in the Mozarteum, Salzburg*]

MOHMHEIM, 14 *November* 1777

DOMMSCHLEIM [1]

MY DEAR HUSBAND,

I sent you off a letter only yesterday and I am begining another one again today. You asked in yours whether Wolfgang has gained the favour of Herr Raaff. Well, all I can tell you is that Raaff is a good, honest fellow, but all the same he can do nothing. He's been singing in the opera here. You can see that he must have been a good singer in his time; but he is packing up like Herr Meisner, to whom by the way I much prefer to listen. But Raaff is the most honest fellow in the world. I spoke to him at the concert and he congratulated me on my son's ability and seemed to be absolutely amazed at him; likewise Herr Kapellmeister Holzbauer, who has a great opinion of my son.

(243a) *Mozart to his Father*

[*Autograph in the Mozarteum, Salzburg*]

[MANNHEIM, 14 *November* 1777]

I, Johannes Chrysostomus Amadeus Wolfgangus Sigismundus Mozart, hereby plead guilty and confess that yesterday and the day before (not to mention on several other occasions) I did not get home until midnight; and that from ten o'clock until the said hour at Cannabich's house and in the presence and company of the said Cannabich, his wife and daughter, the Treasurer,[2] Ramm and Lang I did frequently, without any difficulty, but quite easily, perpetrate—rhymes, the same being, moreover, sheer garbage, that is, on such subjects as muck, shitting and arse-licking—and that too in thoughts, words—but not in deeds. I should not have behaved so godlessly, however, if our ringleader, known under the name of Lisel (Elisabetha Cannabich),[3] had not egged me on and incited me; at the same time I must admit that I thoroughly enjoyed it. I confess all these sins and transgressions of mine from the bottom of my heart and in the hope of having to confess them very often, I firmly resolve to go on with the sinful life which I have begun. Wherefore I beg for the holy dispensation, if it can be easily obtained; if not, it's all one to me, for the game will go on all the same. *Lusus enim suum habet ambitum,*[4] as the late Meisner, the singer, says (chap. 9, p. 24); so does Saint Ascenditor too, patron of burnt soup coffee, musty lemonade, almondless milk of almonds and, more particularly, of strawberry ice full of bits of ice, as he himself is a great connoisseur and artist in ices. As soon as I can, I shall have the

---

[1] This word is in Mozart's hand.
[2] Gres, who appears to have held an official appointment at the Mannheim court.
[3] Cannabich's second daughter.   [4] For the game has its own bounds.

sonata which I have written for Mlle Cannabich copied out on small paper and shall send it to my sister. I began to teach it to Mlle Rosa three days ago. We finished the opening Allegro today. The Andante will give us most trouble, for it is full of expression and must be played accurately and with the exact shades of forte and piano, precisely as they are marked. She is very smart and learns very easily. Her right hand is very good, but her left, unfortunately, is completely ruined. I can honestly say that I often feel quite sorry for her when I see her struggling, as she so often does, until she really gets quite out of breath, not from lack of skill but simply because she cannot help it. For she has got into the habit of doing what she does, because no one has ever shown her any other way. I have told her mother and I have told her too that if I were her regular teacher, I would lock up all her music, cover the keys with a handkerchief and make her practise, first with the right hand and then with the left, nothing but passages, trills, mordants and so forth, very slowly at first, until each hand should be thoroughly trained. I would then undertake to turn her into a first-rate clavierist. For it's a great pity. She has so much talent, reads quite passably, possesses so much natural facility and plays with plenty of feeling. They both said that I was right. Now for the opera, but quite briefly. Holzbauer's music is very beautiful. The poetry doesn't deserve such music. What surprises me most of all is that a man as old as Holzbauer should still posses so much spirit; for you can't imagine what fire there is in that music.[1] The prima donna was Mme Elizabeth Wendling, not the flautist's wife, but the fiddler's.[2] She is always indisposed and, what is more, the opera was not written for her, but for a certain Danzi, who is at present in England;[3] consequently it is not suited to her voice but is too high for her. On one occasion Raaff sang four arias, about 450 bars in all, in such a fashion as to call forth the remark that his voice was the strongest reason why he sang so badly. Anyone who hears him begin an aria without at once reminding himself that it is Raaff, the once famous tenor, who is singing, is bound to burst out laughing. It's a fact. I thought to myself: 'If I didn't know that this was Raaff, I should double up with laughing'. As it is, I just pull out my handkerchief and hide a smile. Moreover, he has never been, so people here tell me, anything of an actor; you'd only have had to hear him, without even looking at him; nor has he by any means a good presence. In the opera he had to die, and while dying sing a very very very long aria in slow time; well, he died with a grin on his face, and towards the end of the aria his voice gave out so

---

[1] Holzbauer was sixty-six when he composed his opera *Günther von Schwarzburg*, which was performed on 5 January 1777, and was still running.

[2] Elizabeth Augusta Wendling, *née* Sarselli (1746–1786), wife of Franz Anton Wendling, brother of Johann Baptist Wendling and a violinist in the Mannheim orchestra.

[3] Franziska Danzi (1759–1791), daughter of the Mannheim cellist, Innocenz Danzi, became a famous prima donna. In 1778 she married the Mannheim oboist, Ludwig August Le Brun.

badly that one really couldn't stand it any longer. I was sitting in the orchestra beside Wendling the flautist. He had objected beforehand that it was unnatural for a man to keep on singing until he died, as it was too long to wait. Whereupon I remarked: 'Have a little patience. He'll soon be gone, for I hear it.' 'So do I', he said and laughed. The second female singer is a certain Mlle Strasser (not a street walker, in spite of her name) who sings very well and is an excellent actress.[1] There is a permanent German National Theatre here as in Munich. German Singspiele are performed occasionally, but the singers in them are wretched. I lunched yesterday with Baron and Baroness von Hagen. The Baron is Master of the Hunt. Three days ago I went to see Herr Schmalz, the merchant, to whom I had a letter of introduction from Herr Herzog, or rather from Nocker and Schiedl. I expected to find a very amiable and honest man. I handed him the letter. He read it through, made me a slight bow and— said nothing. At length (after many apologies for not having paid my respects to him long ago) I mentioned the fact that I had played before the Elector. 'Really?'—*altum silentium!*[2] I said nothing. He said nothing. At last I said: 'I shall not trouble you any longer. I have the honour——' At this point he interrupted me: 'If I can be of any service to you, please——' 'Before I leave I shall take the liberty of asking you——' '*For money?*' 'Yes, if you will be so kind as to——' '*Oh! that I cannot do. There is nothing in the letter about money. I cannot give you any money. But if there's anything else——?*' 'But there is *nothing else* you can do for me, nothing whatever that I know of. I have the honour to take my leave of you.' Yesterday I wrote the whole story to Herr Herzog in Augsburg. We must now wait for an answer. Consequently Papa can go on writing to Mannheim. Please remember me to all my good friends. I kiss Papa's hands 100,000 times and embrace my sister with all my heart, and I am your young brother and father,

WOLFGANG GOTTLIEB MOZART

because Papa wrote in his last letter 'I am your old husband and son'.

On this day, the 16th, I finished this letter, this letter, otherwise Papa will not know when it was sent off. Have you finished it?—the letter? . . . Yes, Mamma, it's finished now, the letter.[3]

(244) *Leopold Mozart to his Wife and Son*

[*Extract*]   [*Autograph in the Mozarteum, Salzburg*]

SALZBURG, 17 *November* 1777

MY DEAR WIFE! AND MY DEAR SON!

I received only today, November 17th, your letter of the 8th. So it

---

[1] Barbara Strasser. She married later Karl Ludwig Fischer, one of the most celebrated bass singers of his day and the original Osmin in Mozart's *Entführung aus dem Serail*.
[2] Profound silence.   [3] Mozart jots down the remarks he is exchanging with his mother.

must have been sent to the post too late or have been left lying there. I thank you both for your congratulations and wish you both good health and happiness and that we shall meet again joyfully—and possibly over a glass of Rhine wine! Anyone who reads your letters of congratulation and this reply of mine, would think that we are constantly handling full glasses, as we talk so glibly about Rhine wine. Meanwhile you will have received my letters of the 3rd, the 6th, the 10th and the 13th. In the last one I was a little bit peevish, as I had had no news from you. I sent you my views about Mannheim, but perhaps they will arrive too late. I admit that your letter of the 8th, to which I am now replying, raises my hopes, as ⟨you are going to have an opportunity of speaking to the Elector and also, if necessary, of playing to him.⟩ If you can only remain there for six months and ⟨show what you can do in all styles of music, you will certainly be appointed—especially if there are such wretched organists there⟩. Have you not played ⟨the organ⟩ as well? My dear spouse complains that the only time she can write is at night. I can believe it, as I know only too well how it is on journeys, especially when you want to write a letter at a moment's notice—anywhere if need be. But if *every evening* you write down, *just as Wolfgang used to do at home*, what has happened on that day, even a few words, then on the post-day you need only finish the letter and everything has been put in. Do not be annoyed with me, my dear ones. For tell me, what entertainment have Nannerl and I in Salzburg now, except—the post-days! As it is, I am never sure whether a letter will reach you in the same place. We are very far apart and I think I can and ought to hope that you will be able to stay in ⟨Mannheim⟩. Basta! God in His most holy providence will guide both you and ourselves along the true path. Herr Wolfgang Mozart contributed a charming target to our shooting yesterday. An Augsburg maiden stood on the right and handed a parting bouquet to a young man in riding boots and about to leave; in the other hand she held an enormous linen cloth which trailed along on the ground and with which she was drying her weeping eyes. The young dandy was dragging a similar linen sheet with which he was doing the same, and in the other hand he held his hat containing the bull's eye, which could be spotted there more easily than on the bouquet. Above were the words:

Adieu, my pretty cousin!
Adieu, my gallant cousin!
I wish you good luck on your journey, good health and fine weather!
We have spent very nicely and gaily a fortnight together.
'Tis this that makes parting so sad for us twain.
These dear ones we welcomed must leave us again.
Hateful Fate! Now I weep bitter tears, but in vain!

The weather was dreadful, so we stayed at home and played cards until five o'clock with Katherl Gilowsky and Cajetan Andretter, who send their greetings to you. The rest of the evening we two spent at the clavier as usual. We are alone every day and if we go on practising during the winter, Nannerl will be able to accompany everything, figured or unfigured, in the easiest or the most difficult keys, and, what is more, with the most unexpected changes of key. For in this respect your compositions afford her ample opportunity to perfect herself. Moreover we always choose the most difficult ones and especially your works in C major and F major with the minor movements,[1] which we often pick out to practise.

As for Hagenauer, the architect, things are now moving forward a bit. He wants to get away, but the Prince keeps on trying to detain him by offering him all kinds of jobs and by flattering him. So nothing has been decided. When I hear these things, it always pleases me to think that you are far away from this worry. You are quite right. I did feel the greatest annoyance at the mean treatment you had to put up with. It was that which gnawed at my heart, which kept me awake at night, which was ever on my mind and finally consumed me. My dear son, if you are happy, then I am too and your mother, and your sister and all of us. And you must be so, I trust, if you rely, as I do, on God's grace and on your own sensible behaviour. Thank God, we are well. I trust that you are both in good health. If so, all is well. What will and must be will happen. It is enough if with your common sense you contribute your quota to your own happiness. I for my part shall never cease to care for the welfare of my children, teach them what I can and, as I have done hitherto, use all my efforts on their behalf until I die.

Your old faithful husband and father

MOZART

Francesco von Barisani,[2] who is sitting beside me, sends his greetings to you both. ⟨The Elector's natural children may be a fortunate circumstance for you.⟩

(244a) *Nannerl Mozart to her Mother and Brother*

[Autograph in the Mozarteum, Salzburg]

[SALZBURG, 17 November 1777[3]]

I kiss Mamma's hands and I embrace you. I am glad that you are both in good health. Thank God, we too are well. Pimperl, who is quite fit and jolly, curls herself up at the feet of both of you and so does Theresa. Barbara Eberlin, the Adlgassers, the Hagenauers, Katherl Gilowsky, the Andretters, Bawanzky and all Salzburg send their greetings to you both.

---

[1] Mozart's clavier sonatas K. 279 [189d] and K. 280 [189e], the slow movements of which are in minor keys.

[2] Son of Dr. von Barisani, the Archbishop's private physician. He too became a doctor.

[3] A postscript to her father's letter.

(245) *Mozart to his Father*

[*Autograph in the Mozarteum, Salzburg*]

MANNHEIM, 20 *November* 1777

MON TRÉS CHER PÉRE

I must be quite brief today, as I have no more paper in the house. Yesterday, Wednesday, the 19th, the gala began again. I went to the service, brand new music composed by Vogler. I had already been to the afternoon rehearsal the day before yesterday, but went off immediately after the Kyrie. I have never in my life heard such stuff. In many places the parts simply do not harmonize. He modulates in such a violent way as to make you think that he is resolved to drag you with him by the scruff of the neck; not that there is anything remarkable about it all to make it worth the trouble; no, it is all clumsy plunging. I will not say anything about the way in which the ideas are worked out. I will only say that it is impossible that a mass of Vogler's should please any composer who is worthy of the name. To put it briefly, if I hear an idea which is not at all bad—well—it will certainly not remain *not at all bad* for long, but will soon become—beautiful? God forbid!—bad and thoroughly bad; and that in two or three different ways. Either the idea has scarcely been introduced before another comes along and ruins it; or he does not round it off naturally enough to preserve its merit; or it is not in the right place; or, finally, it is ruined by the instrumentation. That's Vogler's music. Cannabich is now a much better composer than he was when we knew him in Paris.[1] But what Mamma and I noticed at once about the symphonies here is that they all begin in the same manner, always with an introduction in slow time and in unison. I must now tell Papa something about the Holy Cross Monastery in Augsburg, which I have kept on forgetting to mention.

I received a great many kindnesses there and the Abbot is the best man in the world, an excellent old dunce, who, however, is likely to pop off at any moment, as he is very short of breath. For instance, he had a stroke quite recently, in fact on the very day we left. He, the Dean and the Procurator made us swear that if ever we came to Augsburg again we would drive straight to the Monastery. The Procurator is a jolly fellow like Father Leopold at Seeon. My cousin had told me beforehand what he was like, and so at our first meeting we were on as good terms as if we had known one another for twenty years. I left with them there my mass in F, the first of the short masses in C and my contrapuntal Offertory in D minor.[2] My cousin is acting agent-in-chief for me. I have got back safely the Offertory, which I asked to be returned first. Now they have all plagued me, including the Abbot, to give them a litany *De Venerabili.*

---

[1] In 1766, when Mozart was ten years old. See p. 349, n. 1.

[2] K. 192 [186f], 220 [196b], 222 [205a].

I told them that I hadn't one with me; and as a matter of fact I was not quite sure whether I had. I looked for it, but couldn't find it. But they wouldn't leave me in peace, they thought I was just trying to put them off. So I said: 'Look here, I haven't got it with me, it's at Salzburg. Write to my Papa. It's for him to decide. If he sends it to you, well and good. If not, I can do nothing.' So I expect that a letter from the Dean to Papa will soon make its appearance. Do just as you like. If you want to send them one, send them my last one, in E♭.[1] For they can provide the full forces needed, since a great many performers turn up at that time. They even engage them, as it is their chief festival. Adieu. I kiss Papa's hands 100,000 times and embrace my sister with all my heart and remain your most obedient son

Wolfgang Amadé Mozart

(245a) *Maria Anna Mozart to her Husband*

[Autograph formerly in the Musikhistorisches Museum
von W. Heyer, Cologne]

[Mannheim, 20 November 1777[2]]

Our greetings to all our acquaintances, especially to Herr Bullinger, Jungfer Sallerl, Jungfer Mitzerl, Katherl Gilowsky, Herr Gött. I send greetings too to Theresa. Thank God, we are well. Today the grand opera is being performed again. Yesterday, on the feast of St. Elizabeth Wolfgang and I lunched with Herr and Madame Wendling, I mean, the flautist. Wolfgang is a tremendous favourite with them. They have an only daughter who is very beautiful and whom that Bach[3] in England wanted to marry. She has been delicate for more than a year and a half as she never recovered completely from a fever. It is a pity about the creature. Addio. Take care of yourselves. I kiss you and Nannerl several thousand times and remain your faithful

old wife

Frau Mozart

(246) *Leopold Mozart to his Son*

[*Extract*]   [*Autograph in the Mozarteum, Salzburg*]

Mon très cher Fils!   Salzburg, 20 *November* 1777

As much as your letter of November 8th filled me with a certain hope and delighted all of us, especially Herr Bullinger, so much were we distressed by your letter of the 13th, which to our great surprise we received on the evening of the 18th, that is on the fifth day after its dispatch, whereas all the others took six days at the very least. It would

---

[1] K. 243, composed in 1776.
[2] A postscript to Mozart's letter, written inside the cover.
[3] Johann Christian Bach.

have been very much better, I admit, if you had received fifteen louis
d'or instead of a watch, which you say has been valued at twenty louis
d'or, since for travelling money is very necessary, indeed indispensable.
Where will you read this letter, I wonder? Probably in Mainz. For the love
of Heaven, ⟨you really must try to get some money⟩. You will not have
received my letter of the 13th in Mannheim, as probably you had left
already. I had planned everything in advance, and in regard to Frankfurt
I reported to you in detail what Leopold Heinrich Pfeil wrote to me.
What earthly use was all the information I made a point of sending you!
However, what is done cannot be helped. Further, I was never privileged
to hear why you had to hurry off immediately to Mannheim. I presume
that it was at the urgent persuasion of various people who thought they
knew better, and possibly in order not to miss the fine German opera.
But indeed your journey was not a direct one, for Herr Beecke *in his
malevolence* sent you off on a roundabout track, since, as Bullinger says,
everyone there knows that the way to Mannheim is by Cannstatt and
Bruchsal and *not by the other route*, which people sometimes choose. And,
pray, has Herr Beecke himself never travelled to Mannheim? That tiresome journey to Ellwagen was all to no purpose; and again you have to
thank Herr Beecke's kindness for this unnecessary expenditure. And had
Prince Taxis already returned to Regensburg? Well! It can't be helped!
But now you must see to it not only that the *Elector of Mainz* hears you
play but that you receive a present of money and, if it is at all possible,
give a concert in the town as well. For Mainz is the centre of a great
aristocracy and the seat of the government, which is not true of Mannheim,
as the government and people of importance there reside in Dusseldorf.
Konzertmeister Kreusser is the best person to help you in all these matters
and to arrange everything. For in regard to your first object, he himself
knows as a traveller that money is necessary; and when you have played
before the Elector, you can tell him everything quite frankly, the more
so as in Mannheim you only received a galanterie. As for your concert,
Kreusser can do a great deal, for he is popular in Mainz. If he is not there,
then the leading singer, Franziska Ursprünger, to whom I send most
devoted greetings, will tell you to whom you should apply—perhaps to
the cellist Schwachhofen junior, to whom I send my regards, who could
also introduce you to Prince von Biberach who lives close by and takes
lessons from him. I am talking at random about Mainz, simply because I
presume that you are there, although you do not say a single word about
where you are going to. But Mainz is the nearest Court; and to reach it
may have cost you ten to eleven gulden in coach fares and tips. There you
will have an opportunity of presenting Choirmaster Stark with clavier
compositions, which, after simplifying their difficult passages, he can
then hand on to his pupils. Why did you not make a point of giving the

Elector of Mannheim some of your compositions? I sent you that enclosure not only *for your own purpose* but in order that *you should make your compositions known,* for there is such an excellent orchestra there. Well, probably you had no time to think of this. Where are you going to now? To Paris? What route will you take? Are you making for Paris without any introductions? What route will you choose so as to be able to make some money on the way? You must make some, for you doubtless appreciate what a sum will be necessary for this terrific journey. And when you reach Paris, to whom will you apply? Surely you must have enough money in your pocket to enable you to live until you have made the necessary acquaintances who will help you to earn something? You can do a great deal in Paris by giving lessons. That is quite certain. But no one obtains pupils at once; and are people going to dismiss their own teachers immediately and take a stranger who has only just arrived? A great deal of money can be made by having your compositions engraved and sold. Yes, but for all these schemes it is necessary to have some patron, a friend or two, a subscription list; and does not all this presuppose that you have already made a number of acquaintances?—Well, let us drop this for the moment. It is quite certain that the journey and the first period of your stay in Paris will necessitate a well-filled purse. ⟨You know that we owe Herr Bullinger three hundred gulden and Herr Weiser more than a hundred. I forget how much we owe Kerschbaumer, but it probably amounts to forty gulden. In the New Year I shall be getting bills from the dressmaker and the tailor, not to mention other trifling accounts *of a few gulden* and our daily unavoidable expenses. Food does not cost much, but there are many other expenses, *especially now in the winter, what with wood, candles* and many other small items, so that I have to rack my brains to fit them all in.⟩ Nevertheless I am willing, if you really wish to go to Paris, to arrange for you to draw there *an advance of twenty or thirty louis d'or* in the hope that this sum will come back to me doubled and trebled. But is our good friend Grimm there now? Why would ill luck have it that you were both quite close to one another in Augsburg without knowing it? Perhaps he is in Paris? Perhaps when he was in Augsburg he was about to leave for Paris? But who knows? How would it be if Wolfgang were to write now to M. Grimm, Envoyé de S. A. Sérénissime, Le Duc de Saxe-Gotha, à Paris? In this letter he could tell him about his journey and express his regret that they should have been so close to one another in Augsburg, where Wolfgang's concert took place on the very evening when Grimm turned in to the 'Drei Mohren'. You must send him an address to reply to, possibly Coblenz or wherever you may be going to. And, as a note left behind at the Post Office on your departure will ensure that your letters are forwarded, you will certainly have a reply from him, if he is in Paris. If not, it does not matter if the letter is lost, as there will be nothing compromising in it. It would be wiser, however, not to put your signature too low down or to leave too much empty space, for, if a letter of this kind were to fall into unknown and evil hands, some rascal might cut out the name and write in the space above a demand for a few louis d'or. I have already reminded you twice that by means of a note left behind giving your address, you are sure to receive your letters, for it is in the interest of the Post Office to forward to its destination *a letter which has not yet been paid for*. Good friends, whom you might ask to do this, might forget it. So when you arrive at some town, you must enquire several times at the Post Office. What I have said about a money advance in Paris ⟨*cannot be arranged, if you now proceed to draw money in Frankfurt*. Therefore you really must *endeavour to obtain a present of money*⟩ or at any rate see that some lady shall undertake ⟨*to exploit*⟩ your ⟨*watch*⟩ among the nobility, as Lamotte did in Prague with all the galanteries he had received there. Herr von Dalberg's[1] handsome wife could do that for you. Herr Krauser knows best how to arrange it. But that is not all! When I ask Mamma about the journey to Paris, she will say: 'But how shall we travel?' *Why, you must take the same old road as we took many years ago*. Mamma will remember that there are thirty-four stages. But I must remind you that you cannot use our chaise any longer, since four horses and two postillions are necessary. I beg you to send me your ideas as to how you are really thinking of continuing your journey.

The Prince of Chiemsee has had an attack of gout at Zeill in Swabia. Otherwise he would have been in Munich long ago. But if you write to him now at Munich, he will certainly have got there by this time. You seem to like Munich better than Mannheim. I too should prefer Munich, in spite of the fact that the orchestra in Mannheim is excellent. But Mannheim has no singers and every year they make changes in the singers and maestri at the opera. Would you not write to Prince Zeill and ask him to suggest to the Elector and Count Seeau that they should take you on for a year or two, as the latter usually does with his castrati? Say that you will not ask for a certificate of appointment, that you are a young man who is not yet trying to get established, but has still time to make his fortune in the world—but that you have a great desire to serve the Elector for any period of time he may choose. You could write *a separate letter* to the Prince, mentioning that His Excellency Count Seeau would not lose by this arrangement, seeing that you would undertake to touch up his German Singspiele and that you would give an assurance, perhaps even a written undertaking, that you will not beseech or worry the Elector to retain you any longer than the period arranged for, unless of

---

[1] Baron W. Heribert von Dalberg (1750–1806), manager of the Mannheim Theatre and later Schiller's active patron.

course he himself wishes to do so. What I feel is that if you were in Munich, you would be nearer Italy. Then, if you obtained a scrittura, he would let you go and your salary would continue. And even if you do not obtain a scrittura now, your work in Munich would be the best way to obtain one eventually and, in addition, a hundred other things which I need not mention. There are an amazing number of castles of the nobility and monasteries in the neighbourhood of Munich and, once you are known, there will always be plenty of amusement to be had, what with hunting, riding and driving. There will also be countless opportunities to compose for the church and the theatre, besides more entertainments in winter than in any other place I know of. I must close. We both kiss dear Mamma and yourself and I am your old husband and father

MOZART

We had no letter from you today. Perhaps we shall get one by Friday's post. About that German opera you mentioned, who composed it? Who sang and how? *Not a word!* And that concert you mentioned, who played, sang, blew and whistled? Was the music good? *Not a word!* You are nice people indeed! Ah yes, Mamma *did say that the music of the opera was fine.* That is so—but for the rest—we may whistle for it! What sort of people played the violin concertos there? Herr Fränzl?[1] We may whistle! And what about that ancient philosopher and mummified Raaff? We may whistle indeed!

(247) *Mozart to his Father*

[*Autograph in the Mozarteum, Salsburg*]
MANNHEIM, 22 *November*, 1777
In the evening, or rather, *nocte temp ris,*
Puncto and *accur t* on the stroke of ten.

MON TRÉS CHER PÉRE!

(I nearly dropped into the feminine.)

First of all I must inform you that my most truthful letter to Herr Herzog in Augsburg, puncto Schmalzii,[2] has had a very good effect. He has written a most polite letter to me in reply and expressed his annoyance that I got such a cold reception from the said Herr Butter. He sent me the other day a sealed letter for Herr Milk, together with a draft for 150 gulden on the said Herr Cheese. You must know that although I had only spoken to Herr Herzog on one single occasion, I couldn't refrain from

---

[1] Ignaz Fränzl (1736–1811), a famous violinist, who became a member of the Mannheim orchestra in 1747 and its leader in 1774. When the court was transferred to Munich in 1778, Fränzl remained in Mannheim and was musical director of the Hoftheater from 1790 to 1803.
[2] On the subject of Herr Schmalz see p. 375. Mozart proceeds to pun on his name, which means 'lard'.

asking him in my letter to be so kind as to send me a draft on Herr Schmalz, alias Butter, Milk, Cheese or on anyone else he chose. A ça, apparently the joke came off. So there's no need to knock and offer sympathy. This morning, the 21st, we received your letter of the 17th. I was not at home but at Cannabich's, where Mr. Wendling was rehearsing a concerto which I had scored for him. At six o'clock today the gala concert took place. I had the pleasure of hearing Herr Fränzl (who is married to a sister of Mme Cannabich) play a concerto on the violin. I like his playing very much. You know that I am no great lover of difficulties. He plays difficult things, but his hearers are not aware that they are difficult; they think that they could at once do the same themselves. That is real playing. He has too a most beautiful, round tone. He never misses a note, you can hear everything. It is all clear cut. He has a beautiful staccato, played with a single bowing, up or down; and I have never heard anyone play a double trill as he does. In a word, in my opinion he is no wizard, but a very sound fiddler. If I could only get rid of this habit of slanty writing! I am very sorry that I was not in Salzburg during Madame Adlgasser's sad experience, so that I might have consoled her.[1] For I'm very good at that—especially with such a pretty woman as Mme Nadlstrasser.[2] All that you write about ⟨Mannheim⟩ I know already— but I never like to write about anything prematurely. Everything will be all right. In my next letter I may perhaps be able to tell you something *very good* for you, but only *good* for me, or something *very bad* in your eyes, but *tolerable* in mine; or it may be something *tolerable* for you, but *good, precious and valuable* for me! Rather in the style of an oracle, is it not? Well, it is obscure, yet intelligible. Remember me to Herr Bullinger. I feel ashamed, whenever I get a letter from you, as there is generally some message from him in it; and when I think that I have not yet written to the man who is my best and truest friend, and who has shown me so much kindness and sympathy! But—I shall make no excuses—No. I shall ask him instead to make my excuses for me as far as he can and I promise to write to him as soon as I feel *settled*. Up to the present I have never been so. For as soon as I know that as likely as not and in all probability I shall have to leave a place, then I simply cannot settle down. And although I now have just a faint hope, I still can't feel settled until I know where I am. Part of the oracle must come to pass. I think it will be either the middle section or the third. It's all the same to me. For it's all one at all times whether I gobble up the dirt or Papa chews it. Bother, I can't say it properly! I meant to say: it's all one whether Papa chews the dirt or I gobble it up. Well, I would rather chuck it. I can see it's no use. A propos. Did you reply to Herr von Hamm at Munich? Are you taking on his

---

[1] Mozart refers to a story in his father's letter of 17 November, which for lack of space has had to be omitted.   [2] Mozart is punning on the name Adlgasser.

daughter? I hope I told you that Holzbauer's grand opera is in German? If not, I am telling you now. It is entitled 'Günther von Schwarzburg', but not our worthy Herr Günther, Barber and Councillor of Salzburg. During the next carnival 'Rosemunde' will be performed, a new text by Wieland with new music by Schweitzer.[1] Both of them are coming here. I have already seen some of the opera and played it on the clavier, but I will not say anything about it yet. The target you had painted for me as Master of the Shoot is superb and the verses are incomparable. Well, there's nothing left for me to write except to wish you all a thoroughly good rest and that you will all sleep soundly until I wake you up with this present letter. Adieu. I kiss Papa's hands 100000000 times and embrace my sister, that darling blister, with all my heart, until I smart, just a little or not at all, and remain your most obedient son, hoping away you will not run,

WOLFGANG AMADÉ MOZART

Knight of the Golden Spur and, as soon as I marry, of the Double Horn, Member of the Grand Academies of Verona, Bologna. Oui, mon ami!

(247a) *Maria Anna Mozart to her Husband*

[*Autograph in the Mozarteum, Salzburg*]

MY DEAR HUSBAND,   MANNHEIM, [23 *November* 1777[2]]

We have received all your letters safely and, thank God, we are well, and I am glad that you are both in good health. We are still in Mannheim and you may go on sending all our letters here. If we leave, we shall certainly make arrangements to have them forwarded. I am very sorry for poor Martinelli. What on earth will Lenerl do now, for the inheritance will probably not be very large? You do not tell us very much about Salzburg. Are there no players there? Are no operas being performed? Is Dr. Barisani still out of favour? Does our Chief Purveyor still pay attention to Fräulein Tonerl? I should like to know all these things in detail. We send special greetings to Mlle Sallerl and M. Bullinger. Please tell them that we think of them every day. This very moment Nannerl will please lay aside whatever she is doing and give Bimperl a kiss on her little paws and make it smack so loudly that I can hear it in Mannheim.

[1] Anton Schweitzer (1735–1787) was first Kapellmeister of Seyler's theatrical company in Hildburghausen, which performed German singspiele. After studying in Italy he became musical director at the Ducal Theatre in Weimar, for which he composed *Alceste*, on a text by Wieland. This opera was performed at Mannheim in 1775, and he and Wieland were commissioned by the Elector to write an opera for the 1778 carnival.
[2] A postscript to Mozart's letter.
[3] Frau Mozart is referring to a passage in her husband's letter of 17 November, which for lack of space has had to be omitted.

Remember me to the Hagenauers, Robinigs, Frau von Gerlichs, the Barisanis, Jungfer Mitzerl, Katherl Gilowsky, to whom we send congratulations on her coming name-day. Remember us too to Theresa. Now I think I have sent greetings to all and our compliments and thanks. Keep well, both of you, and think of us, as we do of you. Then we and you shall all be happy. Addio. I kiss you and Nannerl many 100 000 000 000 times without number, and remain your faithful wife,

both in body and soul,

FRAU MARIA ANNA MOZART

(248) *Leopold Mozart to his Son*

[*Extract*] [*Autograph in the Mozarteum, Salzburg*]

MON TRÈS CHER FILS! SALZBURG, 24 *November* 1777

Indeed I do not know what to say to you. I am so amazed at your last letter of November 16th, in which you inform me *with the greatest sans-gêne* that Herr Schmalz, probably the father, brother or friend of Herr Schmalz of the leather-shop at Munich, or possibly even he himself, excused himself by saying that he had no instructions to provide you with money. That I can well believe and he was quite right. You ought to have asked Herr Herzog or somebody in the firm of Nocker and Schiedl to arrange for you to have a small credit elsewhere, *as I used to do*. For these people had no orders from Hagenauer to extend this credit to other houses, and no true business man exceeds his literal orders. But they would have done so if you had asked them beforehand. This incident, however, was described to me as frankly and coolly as if I had chests full of money and as if I were going to be horribly annoyed that payment had not been made to you at once. I shall not waste time with a lengthy description of our circumstances, for you yourself know them and so does Mamma. In my letter of the 20th I enumerated our chief debts and even so forgot to mention a ⟨*rather large sum which we owe*⟩ to Hagenauer, and which at the moment ⟨*we are not reducing by a single farthing.*⟩ What astonished me most of all in your last letter was that all of a sudden you trotted out this story, without mentioning a word about it in your previous one, in which you just said that for your journey money would be more necessary and more welcome than a present, although you both knew at the time that financially you were in very low water. So, if Herr Schmalz had obliged you, I should have been saddled with a bill, *without having received the slightest warning from you beforehand, and that too at a time when it was the last thing I expected.* Very nice of you, indeed! I leave it to you to think over, bearing in mind all my circumstances. You wrote to me from Augsburg that you were only 27 gulden on the wrong side. I have now worked out that if you were 30 gulden on the wrong side, you would still have 170 gulden; and if that silly trip to Mannheim through Wallerstein cost you 70 gulden, you should still have 100 gulden. Even if it cost you more, *have you still not enough* to take you both to Mainz? There you would be near Frankfurt and, if it were absolutely necessary, you could draw a little with your second letter of credit from Herr Bollongari. Then you would only have to apply to some merchant in Mainz who is in touch with Herr Bollongari and who would undertake to send him the letter of credit and give you the sum you require. Would that not be more sensible than to sit down in Mannheim and use up your money to no purpose, particularly as with this sum you could meet the expenses of the journey which costs only about 15 to 16 gulden? For the distance to Worms is only 1¼ stages, to Oppenheim 2 and to Mainz 1, that is, only about 3¾ stages in all. And if on your arrival you had little or no money, we have acquaintances there who would stand by you; and no gentleman need be ashamed if he has not a farthing in his pocket, provided he can produce a letter of credit. For to be short of money can happen to the wealthiest and most respectable people. Why, it is even a maxim when travelling, only to carry, if possible, the sum that is absolutely necessary. I keep on talking at random about Mainz, all pure supposition, as you have not done me the honour of telling me in a single letter where you are thinking of going. You wrote to me from Augsburg at the very last moment: 'We are off to Wallerstein tomorrow'; and Herr Stein wrote to me: 'They left for Wallerstein and Mannheim at 7.30 on Sunday'. Surely you should let me know your arrangements some time beforehand, as now and then I might make useful preparations and send reminders, as I endeavoured to do for Frankfurt by writing to Otto and Pfeil.—But indeed your journey does not concern me! Is it not so? As it is, you could have taken quite a different route from Mannheim, I mean, to Würzburg, and thence to the Margrave of Darmstadt and on to Frankfurt and Mainz. But how can I fathom your intentions, or make any suggestions, seeing that I am never consulted and was never told how things were progressing in Manheim? On the contrary I got a different impression from your letter ⟨in which you mentioned an opportunity of a heart-to-heart talk with the Elector⟩, and thought that you would be staying there for a long time. All your plans and views, inclinations, intentions and so forth, whatever they may be, you ought to have reported candidly and in good time, as even by the quickest and safest route it takes *twelve days* to receive a letter from you and answer it. This too, however, you did not take the trouble to consider, seeing that in your last letter, dated the 16th, you told me *that I could go on writing to Mannheim*, although you could only receive this letter after 12 days at the earliest that is, not before the 28th. But I did not receive your letter until

Friday, 21st, as a present on *our wedding day*, and thus could not reply before the 24th. So you will read this letter—God knows where, on the 1st or 2nd of December. You must not think that I do not realise how many incidental expenses crop up on journeys and how money disappears, especially if one is too generous or too kind-hearted. My dear wife prided herself on getting up early, on not dawdling and on doing everything briskly and economically. *But 16 days in Munich, 14 days in Augsburg*, and now, to judge by your last letter of November 16th, *17 days in Mannheim*, which, if you await the reply from Augsburg, will be prolonged to three weeks—that is lightning speed, in truth! You have now been away eight weeks, that is, two months, and have already reached Mannheim! How amazingly quick! When we travelled to England we spent nine days in Munich, where we performed before the Elector and Duke Clemens and had to wait for a present. We spent a fortnight in Augsburg, but we gave three concerts there, on June 28th and 30th and July 4th. We left Salzburg on June 9th and only arrived in Munich on the 12th, because in Wasserburg we had to have new wheels put on our carriage. Yet we reached Schwetzingen on July 13th, although we stopped at Ulm, Ludwigsburg and Bruchsal. So you see that your long and quite unnecessary sojourn has ruined all your prospects; the most beautiful autumn within living memory has gone by and so far you have just had a holiday and have spent the time in enjoyment and amusement. Now the bad weather, short days and the cold have arrived and these conditions will become worse, while our prospects and purposes become more costly and more distant. You cannot go on travelling the whole winter, and if you want to make a stay, you ought to do so in a large town where there is a society and where merit has hopes and opportunities of being rewarded—and where is there such a place abroad? Nowhere except Paris. But if you want to live in Paris, you must adopt quite a different manner of living and an entirely different outlook. There must be attention and daily concentration on earning some money and you must cultivate extreme politeness in order to ingratiate yourself with people of standing. I shall write more about this in my next letter, in which I shall put forward my ideas about another route which you could take in order to reach Paris more quickly. Meanwhile, whatever route you take, see that you get letters of recommendation to Paris from anyone who will give them, merchants, courtiers and so forth. And is there no French Ambassador or Resident in Mainz or Coblenz? No, I think not. You have no letters of introduction—whereas I had lots of them. These are absolutely essential if you want to procure patrons and acquaintances at once. A journey of this kind is no joke. As yet you have had no experience of it. You should have more important things in your mind than practical jokes; you should be endeavouring to arrange a hundred things in advance, or you will find yourself suddenly

in the soup, and without money—and where there is no money, friends
are no longer to be found, and that too even if you give a hundred lessons
for nothing, compose sonatas and, instead of occupying yourself more
profitably, play the fool every evening from ten o'clock until midnight.
Then ask for money credit! Suddenly jokes will cease, and in a moment
the most laughter-raising countenance will certainly become serious. I
do not blame you at all for putting the Cannabich household under an
obligation to you by your friendly kindness. That was a sensible thing to
do. But you might have devoted a few idle hours in the evening to your
father who is so anxious about you and you might have sent him not
just a rigmarole dashed off in a hurry, but a proper, confidential and
detailed report of the expenses incurred on your journey, of the money
you still have in hand, a few particulars about the journey you are going
to undertake and about your intentions with regard to Mannheim; and
then you would have had advice from him. I hope that you yourself will
have the good sense to see this. For in the long run everything recoils on
your poor old father. As I said above, I received your letter on the 21st,
but I could not reply to it before today. Yesterday, the 23rd, I made my
confession at Holy Trinity and with weeping eyes recommended you
both to the protection of Almighty God. Bullinger, who sends you his
greetings, was rather surprised at your letter and, in view of our serious
circumstances, did not appear to relish your joke about your open confession. At 5.30 I went to see Hagenauer to ask *that if Nocker and Schiedl
did not inform him by post that they had given you a draft, he might have a letter
to this effect sent by today's post to Augsburg.* This morning I again went to
the shop and saw Herr Joseph and found that, although they had had
letters from Nocker and Schiedl, no mention had been made of you. He
promised me to write today. Now I have seen to everything and trust
that in the meantime you will have got some money. The firm of Nocker
and Schiedl will not report until they know how much money you have
drawn. Remember, it is always better, whenever you draw money, to do
so, not in guldens, but piecemeal, for instance, six or seven louis d'or,
carolins or whatever the coinage may be. I have now unburdened my
whole heart to you and in the light of truth, such as is pleasing to God.
Experience will teach you that it is no joke to undertake such a journey
and to have to live on whatever sums you happen to make, and that above
all you must pray earnestly to God for good health, protect yourself carefully against wicked people and earn money by every means you know
of and can use, and spend it with the greatest economy. I prefer when
travelling that a man to whom I have perhaps given very little and whom
I may never see again in this life, should say of me that I am a skinflint,
rather than that he should laugh at me behind my back for giving him
too much. The page is full and I am tired, my eyes especially. Nannerl

and I wish you the best of health and kiss you cordially a million times and I am your old husband and father, but not your son

MOZART

I hope that you received my letter of the 20th in which I told you to write to M. Grimm in Paris, and also what you ought to write to the Prince of Chiemsee in Munich. By the next post I shall send you particulars of all the stages to Paris and my ideas and so forth, and also the list of our former acquaintances there. Addio.

(249) *Maria Anna Mozart to her Husband*

[Autograph in the Mozarteum, Salzburg]

MY DEAR HUSBAND,   MANNHEIM, 26 *November* 1777

You want to know why we came here in such a hurry? Well, first of all, I must tell you that Prince Taxis was no longer at Dischingen and that some time before he left, he sent off his orchestra to Regensburg. Then, when we were in Hohenaltheim, Prince Taxis was staying with some other noble family on their estate. So where should we have gone? Perhaps to Würzburg? But the Bishop was then in Bamberg. And when we left Würzburg we should have had to travel through the Forest of Spessart. So we preferred to come to Mannheim.

(249a) *Mozart continues the letter*

[Autograph in the Mozarteum, Salzburg]

And, moreover, everyone who knows it, the gentry included, advised me to come to Mannheim. The reason why we are still here, is that I am thinking of staying on for the winter. I am only waiting for a reply from the Elector. Count Savioli, the Intendant, is a very honest gentleman, and I told him to be so kind ⟨as to tell the Elector that, as in any case the weather is at present bad for travelling, I should like to stay here and teach the young Count.⟩ He promised me to do his best, but begged me to have patience until the gala days were over. All this took place with the knowledge and *at the instigation* of Cannabich. When I told him that I had been to Savioli and what I had said to him, he remarked that he would sooner believe that it would happen than that it would not. Cannabich had himself mentioned the matter even before ⟨the Count spoke to the Elector.⟩ I must now wait and see. Tomorrow I shall draw my 150 gulden from Herr Schmalz, as I have no doubt that our landlord would rather hear the sound of money than of music. I never imagined I should get a watch for a present here, but such is the case. I should have left long ago if they hadn't all said: 'Where will you spend the winter then?—It's a very bad time of the year for travelling. Stay where you are.' Cannabich is very anxious for me to stay on. So I have now put out a feeler, and, as a affair of this sort cannot be hurried up, I must just wait patiently. I hope soon to be able to send you really good news. I already have two pupils in view (not counting my Archpupil),[1] who will most probably give me a louis d'or each per month. But without the Arch-one, it is true, it can't be managed. Now do let me drop all that, how it is and how it will be. What is the use of needless speculation? What will happen we know not—and yet we do know! It is God's will. Cheer up then, Allegro, non siate sì pegro.[2] If after all we do leave Mannheim, we shall go straight to—where do you think?—to Weilburg or whatever the place is called, to the Princess, the sister of the Prince of Orange, whom we knew so well à la Haie.[3] And there we shall remain, that is to say, as long as the officers' table is to our taste; and we shall get at least six louis d'or. Herr Sterkel[4] came here from Würzburg a few days ago. The day before yesterday, the 24th, Cannabich and I lunched again with Herr von Hagen, Chief Master of the Hunt, and I spent the evening at Cannabich's *al solito*.[5] Sterkel came in. He played five duets, but so fast that it was hard to follow them, and not at all clearly, and not in time. Everyone said the same. Mlle Cannabich played the sixth and, to tell the truth, better than Sterkel. Now I must close as I have no room for more, for I can't write in bed, and it is an effort to stay up, as I'm so sleepy. I shall write more the next time, but I can't today, for lack of space, I mean. I will have a large supply of paper for my next letter. Adieu. Confound it! There's still some more to write. I kiss Papa's hands and embrace my sister with all my heart and am ever

your faithful son
WOLFGANG AMADÉ MOZART

Mannheim, 26 November 1777.

If I could find some more room, I would send 100,000 compliments from us 2, I mean, from us two, to all our good friends: particularly to the A's:—the Adlgassers, Andretters and Arco (Count); B's:—Herren Bullinger, Barisani and Berantzky; C's:—Czernin (Count), Cusetti and

---

[1] i.e. the young Count.   [2] Don't be so lazy.
[3] Princess Caroline von Nassau-Weilburg, to whom Mozart dedicated in 1766 his clavier sonatas, K. 26-31.
[4] Abt Johann Franz Xaver Sterkel (1750-1817) born at Würzburg, was a distinguished clavier-player and a very prolific and popular composer. In 1778 he became chaplain and organist to the Elector of Mainz, in whose service he remained until 1805.
[5] i.e. as usual.

the three organ blowers (Calcanten); D's:—Herren Daser, Deibl and Dommeseer; E's:—Mlle Barbara Eberlin, Herr Estlinger and all the asses (Eseln) in Salzburg; F's:—Firmian (Count and Countess and their little molly-coddle), young Franz and the Freihof of St. Peter's; G's:—Mlle, Mme and the two MM. Gilowsky and the Councillor too; also Herren Grétry and Gablerbrey; H's:—the Haydns, Hagenauers, Theresa Höllbrey: J's:—Joli (Miss Sallerl), Herr Janitsch the fiddler and Hagenauer's Jakob; K's:—Herr and Frau von Küsinger, Count and Countess Kühnburg and Herr Kassel; L's:—Baron Lehrbach, Count and Countess Lützow, Count and Countess Lodron; M's:—Herren Meisner, Medlhammer and Moser-brey; N's:—Nannerl, our Court ninny, Father Florian, and all night watchmen; O's:—Count Oxenstirn, Herr Overseer and all the oxen in Salzburg; P's:—the Prexes, Count Prank, the Lord High Cook, and Count Perusa; Q's:—Herren Quilibet, Quodlibet and all quakers; R's:—Father Florian Reichsigel, the Robinigs and Maestro Rust; S's:—Herren Suscipe, Seiffert and all the sows in Salzburg; T's:—Herr Tanzberger, our butcher, Theresa and all trumpeters; U's:—the towns of Ulm and Utrecht and all the clocks (Uhren) in Salzburg, especially if you put an H in at the beginning;[1] W's:—the Weisers, Hans the Wurst-maker and Woferl; X's:—Xantippe, Xerxes and all whose names begin with an X; Y's:—Herr Ypsilon, Herr Ybrig and all whose names begin with a Y; and, lastly, Z's:—Herr Zabuesnig, Herr Zonca and Herr Zezi[2] at the Castle. Addio. If I had room I would write something more, at least my compliments to my good friends. But it is impossible, for I don't know where I could work them in. I can't write anything sensible today, as I am rails off the quite. Papa be annoyed not must. I that just like today feel. I help it cannot. Warefell. I gish you nood-wight, Sound sleeply. Next time I'll sensible more writely.

(250) *Leopold Mozart to his Son*

[Extract]   [Autograph in the Mozarteum, Salzburg]

Mon trés cher Fils!   SALZBURG, 27 *November* 1777

I received on the 25th, five days after its despatch, your letter of the 20th, written on a scrap of paper, *as you had no more in the house*. But, as usual, there was not a word in it as to whether in the meantime you had had a letter from me, although you must have received the one I wrote on the 13th, seven days previously. Besides I have already told you that up to the present I have written every post-day; and as you are aware that

---

[1] Mozart's joke is that by prefixing an H to 'U(h)ren', one obtains the word 'Huren' (whores).

[2] The personal names in this list are partly those of persons known to the Mozart family, partly those of persons not known to them, and partly those of imaginary persons.

the Salzburg post goes on Mondays and Thursdays only, you may know for certain whether you have received all my letters; and surely it is not much trouble for you to mention at the beginning of yours: 'I have received your letter of the ——'. Further, there is *not a word* about where you are going to or what plans you are thinking of making. Although I keep on hoping from one letter to another, yet every time there is— *nothing—not a single word*! The object of your journey, the very necessary object was and is and must be, to obtain ⟨an appointment or to make money.⟩ So far I see little prospect of the one or the other; unless, of course, it has to be kept a secret from me. You sent me from Munich most detailed news about everything. Thus I knew how matters stood, and up to the present I have still been able to arrange things and think out what measures you might adopt in order to get something done. From Augsburg too you sent me a full report—my only objection being that both in Munich and Augsburg you stayed too long—but at least ⟨*something to your credit appeared in the papers.*⟩ I was expecting, however, a reply to my suggestions about your journey, to know whither you were travelling, and why this plan—and not that—but—not a word—and then you write to me from Mannheim ⟨about a watch and no money.⟩—A pretty kettle of fish; and yet not a syllable about your plans for your next journey. I keep on racking my brains—and write myself blind. I do want to arrange things in advance. You, however, make light of everything, you are indifferent, you tie my hands when I want to advise and help, since you do not say a word about where you are going to next. I shall give you a clear instance of an unpardonable piece of thoughtlessness on your part. As you do not mention anything ⟨about your wish to remain in Mannheim⟩ or that ⟨you have told the Elector⟩ or that you have taken any further steps on these lines, I am driven to think that you are planning another journey. So, as I mentioned in previous letters, you will probably be thinking of going on to Paris. Now, whatever route you choose, *you cannot hope to earn enough money* on the way to defray the expenses of this costly journey. Did it never occur to you both that at some point on this long route a credit would have to be arranged? ⟨*You have only reached Mannheim*⟩ and you are already in that predicament. When you leave Mainz, you cannot draw any more money in Frankfurt. If you draw some now in Mannheim, then, in the name of Heaven, you must not draw any more in Frankfurt, where, to be sure, you cannot make any. So it is to be hoped that in Mainz, Coblenz and Bonn you will make enough money out of the three Electors to take you to Brussels. During our grand tour we travelled from Bonn to Cologne through Jülich to Aachen, from Aachen to Liège; thence through Tirlemont to Brussels. Aachen and Liège are expensive places and in the winter the former is empty. I see on my map, *on which all the routes are marked*, that your most direct one is from Cologne straight to Maastricht, a distance of 14 German miles at most. From Maastricht the route proceeds through Tongres (or Tongern in German)—St. Trond—Tirlemont—and Louvain direct to Brussels. From Maastricht to Brussels is a distance of not more than 14 German miles. Hence the whole route from Cologne to Brussels is 28 German miles, that is, 3 miles more than from Salzburg to Augsburg, which is 25 miles. So there is not much difference. As you are travelling by post-chaise and can stop wherever you like, Maastricht and Louvain are two places, especially the latter, which is a well-populated town with a great University, where you could perhaps give a concert. It could be arranged in this way. First find out from your landlord who is the *Kapellmeister or Music Director* of the place, or, if there is none, *who is its leading musician.* Arrange to be taken to him, or, if he is not too grand a person, ask him to call on you. You will then know at once whether giving a concert there is an expensive business, whether you can count on having a good harpsichord, whether an orchestra is available and whether there are many lovers of music. Perhaps you might be introduced to someone who from a love of music would interest himself in your undertaking. In short, you must find out quickly whether something can be done or not—and you should do this on your arrival and without unpacking anything: just put on a few fine rings and so forth, in case when you call you should find a harpsichord there and be asked to perform. As great violinists are rarely to be found in towns of that size, you might play a violin concerto which can be easily accompanied. *But no doubt your violin is having a rest!* That I can well imagine. I should be more inclined to count on Louvain, where we turned in at the 'Wilder Mann' and were very well done; I only paid 2 gulden 30 kreuzer for lunch for five people. I don't think that there is much to be made in Maastricht.

To return to our discussion about a credit. You ought to have written to me about continuing your journey—for you surely realize that you must get credit in Brussels, since it is impossible to foretell all eventualities and the distance is extraordinarily great. It might not be possible to arrange to give a concert quickly and you would then run the risk of having to sit there for two or three weeks and spend money to no purpose. *I dare not advise you* to choose the other route through Trier and Luxemburg, which I mentioned the other day, for things might not turn out well and, moreover, I do not know whether money is to be made in either of these centres; whereas on the Rhine route you will find *three Electors*; and in Brussels and Louvain perhaps something might be done. A little thought and common sense should convince you that it is most necessary to think things out and to take these wearisome and constant precautions and that fruitless over-anxiousness is not prompting me to write as I do,

nor timorous melancholy imaginings, but simply experience. I am longing
to hear where you are and to know whither you are going, so that I may
make further arrangements. My dear wife always writes very little; but
as she does tell us where she is being invited to lunch, we know at least
that she is in good health. God bless you and keep you well! We too are
flourishing, thank God, and jog along as well as we can. Nannerl attends
to everything and I spend my day, partly with my numerous services in
the churches, and partly with my pupils, with writing to you and sitting
with Nannerl at the clavier from 5.30 to 8.30 in the evening. All our
friends send their greetings, and so do Bullinger and Gött, who are with
me at the moment; and also Jungfer Sallerl, Mitzerl, the Hagenauers,
Andretters, Katherl Gilowsky, Frau Moshammer, I mean, Marianne, the
wife of the Contrôleur, who did not even know that you had left Salzburg.
We kiss you a million times and I am ever your old husband and father
MZT

The copy of your portrait, which is a splendid likeness, is being sent to
Bozen by Herr Triendl on December 3rd or 4th and thence to Bologna.[1]
Your portrait has already been framed in a black frame with thick gold
beading.

(251) *Mozart to his Father*

[Autograph in the Mozarteum, Salzburg]

MANNHEIM, 29 *November* 1777
In the evening

MON TRÉS CHER PÉRE!
Your letter of the 24th reached me safely this morning. I see from it
that you would never be able to adapt yourself equally to good fortune
or bad fortune, if perchance some adversity should befall us. Up to the
present all four of us, as things are, have been neither fortunate nor
unfortunate, and I thank God for that. You make many reproaches to us
both—all quite undeserved. We spend nothing beyond what is necessary;
and what is necessary when travelling you know as well as we do and
even better. That we stayed so long in Munich was entirely due to *me*;
and if I had been alone, I should most certainly be there still. Why did we
spend a fortnight in Augsburg? I am almost driven to think that you never
received the letters I sent from there. I wanted to give a concert. I was let
down. In this way I lost a week. I wanted absolument to leave. They
wouldn't let me. They wanted me to give a concert. I wanted them to

---

[1] i.e. the copy sent to Padre Martini. See p. 272, n. 1.

press me to do so; which they did. I gave a concert. That accounts for
that fortnight. Why did we make straight for Mannheim? That I answered
in my last letter. Why are we still here? Well—do you really believe that
I would stop anywhere without a reason? But I might have told my father
—very well, you shall hear the reason and, what is more, the whole
course of events. But God knows that I did not want to say anything
about it, simply because I could give you no details (any more than I can
now) and because I know you well enough to realize that a *vague* account
would only cause you worry and anxiety; and this I have always tried to
avoid. But if you attribute it to my negligence, thoughtlessness and laziness,
I can only thank you for your good opinion of me and sincerely regret
that you do not know your own son.

I am not careless, I am simply prepared for anything and am able, in
consequence, to wait patiently for whatever may come, and endure it—
provided that my honour and the good name of Mozart are not affected.
Well, as it must be so, so let it be. But I must beg you at the outset not
to give way prematurely to joy or sadness. For come what may, all is
well, so long as a man enjoys good health. For happiness consists—simply
in imagination. Last Tuesday week, November 18th, the day before
St. Elizabeth's Day, I went to Count Savioli in the morning and asked
him whether it wasn't possible ⟨that the Elector might keep me here this
winter? I would like to teach the young Count.⟩ He said: 'Yes, I will
⟨suggest it to the Elector;⟩ and, if it rests with me, it will certainly be
arranged'. In the afternoon I was at Cannabich's. As I had gone to the
Count on his advice, he asked me at once whether I had been there. I
told him everything. He then said: 'I should very much like you to ⟨stay
with us for the winter,⟩ but I should like it still more ⟨if you could get a
permanent post'.⟩ I replied that it was my dearest wish to be near them
always, but that I really did not know how it would be possible for me
to be so ⟨permanently.⟩ I added: 'You have ⟨two Kapellmeisters⟩ already,
so I don't know ⟨what I could be.⟩ I shouldn't like to be subordinate to
⟨Vogler'.⟩ 'That you shan't', he rejoined. 'None of the ⟨musicians⟩ here
are inferior to the ⟨Kapellmeister,⟩ or even to the ⟨Intendant. Why, the
Elector could make you his chamber composer.⟩ Just wait, I will ⟨discuss
it with the Count.'⟩ On the following Thursday there was a grand
concert. When ⟨the Count⟩ saw me, he apologized to me for not having
yet mentioned the matter: ⟨the gala⟩ was still in progress, but as soon
⟨as it was over,⟩ that is on Monday, he would ⟨certainly put in a word.⟩
I waited for three days and, as I had heard nothing whatever, I went to
him to inquire. That was yesterday, Friday. 'My dear Mr. Mozart,' he
said, 'there was a ⟨hunt⟩ on today, ⟨so it was not possible for me to
speak to the Elector.⟩ But this time tomorrow ⟨I shall certainly be able
to give you an answer.'⟩ I begged him not to forget. To tell the truth I

was rather annoyed when I left him and I decided to take my six easiest variations on Fischer's minuet [1] (which I had copied out here expressly for this purpose) ⟨to the young Count⟩ in order to have an opportunity ⟨of speaking to the Elector in person.⟩ You can hardly imagine how delighted ⟨the governess⟩ was to see me. I was received most courteously. When I pulled out the variations and told her that ⟨they were for the Count,⟩ she said: 'Oh, that is good of you; but have you something for ⟨the Countess too?⟩' 'Not yet,' I said, 'but if I stay here long enough to have time to compose something, then I shall——' 'A propos', she said, 'I am glad to hear ⟨that you are staying for the winter.⟩' 'What? That is the first I have heard of it!' 'You surprise me. How very strange. ⟨The Elector told me so himself⟩ the other day, "A propos," he said, ⟨"Mozart is staying here for the winter."⟩' 'Well, if you heard it from him, you heard it from the one person who has the right to say it. For without ⟨the Elector⟩ I naturally ⟨cannot stay here.⟩' I then told her the whole story. We arranged that the next day (that is today) I should come some time after four o'clock and bring with me something for ⟨the Countess.⟩ In the meantime ⟨she would speak to the Elector,⟩ who would ⟨still be there when I came.⟩ I went there today, but he had not arrived. But I shall go again tomorrow. I have composed a Rondo [2] for ⟨the Countess.⟩ Now, tell me, have I not reason enough to stay here and await the result? Should I go off now, just when I have taken the most important step? I now have the chance of ⟨speaking to the Elector in person.⟩ I shall in all probability ⟨stay here for the winter. For the Elector likes me, thinks highly of me and knows what I can do.⟩ In my next letter I hope to be able to give you some good news. But once more I beg you neither to rejoice nor worry too soon, and to take no one but Herr Bullinger and my sister into your confidence. I send her herewith the Allegro and Andante of the sonata for Mlle Cannabich.[3] The Rondo will follow the next time. It would have made the packet too thick to send them all together. You must put up with the original. You can have it copied for six kreuzer the sheet more easily than I can for twenty-four. Don't you think that's dear? Adieu. I kiss your hands 100,000 times and embrace my sister with all my heart and remain your most

obedient son

WOLFGANG AMADÉ MOZART

You may have heard something of my sonata, for at Cannabich's it is sung, strummed, fiddled or whistled at least three times a day! only *sotto voce*, of course!

---

[1] K. 179 [189a], composed in 1774.   [2] There is no trace of this composition.
[3] K. 309 [284b].

(251a) *Maria Anna Mozart to her Husband*

[*Autograph in the Mozarteum, Salzburg*]

MY DEAR HUSBAND,   [MANNHEIM, 29 *November* 1777 [1]]

I kiss you and Nannerl many 1000 times and beg you to give our greetings to all our acquaintances. I shall write more the next time. But now it is midnight already. Addio. I remain your faithful wife

MARIA ANNA MOZART

(252) *Leopold Mozart to his Son*

[*Extract*]   [*Autograph in the Mozarteum, Salzburg*]

MON TRÉS CHER FILS!   SALZBURG, 1 *December* 1777

Yesterday, Friday, in the morning old Fräulein von Küfstein passed over into eternity, and in the afternoon, when Bullinger was with us as usual, we received your letter of the 23rd. *Blast your oracular utterances and all the rest!* I hinted in my last letter that there must be secrets which I am not allowed to know. You are perfectly right. Whether they turn out well or ill, I shall hear them soon enough. In the same letter I could only write in pure supposition and as cautiously as possible: and I must confess that as I could not find any facts in your letters except your approaching journey and your ⟨lack of money,⟩ I was naturally extremely anxious. Moreover as I know the world better than either of you, and how few, yes, most certainly, how few ⟨true friends⟩ are to be found, my hope hangs by ⟨a very slight thread.⟩ Still you must ⟨have found a friend in Herr Cannabich, for on account of his daughter, it is to his interest⟩ to be one. Really I do not know ⟨what to say.⟩ But if in this instance ⟨nothing should come⟩ of it all? Well, let us leave ⟨it to Almighty God!⟩

What you wrote about the Litany for the Church of the Holy Cross you could have done without so much circumlocution, *ad captandam benevolentiam.*[2] Besides I should not have been opposed to it, as I know that usually they choose this kind of Litany. But as for engaging people to play in the orchestra, I know perfectly well that *that is not so.* I was a descanter there myself for a while and used to sing, standing on the steps beside the organ. They engage the *town musicians* and the *court trumpeters*, when the latter happen to be there. So far I have heard nothing from Augsburg. I should prefer to send them a copy of the parts rather than the

---

[1] A postscript to Mozart's letter, written on the cover.
[2] For the sake of winning goodwill.

score in your handwriting, for many years ago the Dean, who was then organist, held on to one of my scores for three years, before I could get it back. Besides I could have it copied here much more satisfactorily than they would, if they let their students play about with it and smudge it. Moreover you are aware that to one who is not in the habit of reading your scores, many passages in them are difficult to make out. So I prefer to have it copied neatly and without untidy corrections and possibly fresh errors.

I had a letter some time ago from Herr von Hamm, Secretary for War, and sent him a reply, asking him to state what he would be willing to pay me for boarding and teaching his daughter. He then wrote again to say that he hoped I would be content with 150 gulden a year inclusive, that is, 12 gulden 30 kreuzer a month; but he did not forget to mention that her daily breakfast should consist of a small bowl of coffee and a white roll. I have not yet replied, as I have not had time. Besides there is no hurry, for in his first letter he said that he would not send his daughter until next spring and repeated this in his second letter, in which he talked about travelling in winter and added that first of all she would have to be well supplied—or rather equipped with everything. So I take it that her trousseau has to be collected first. Perhaps I am even to marry her! In accordance with her father's proposal I should thus have the honour of giving Fräulein von Hamm for 25 kreuzer a day her board and drink, breakfast, lodging and instruction in every subject. I shall write to him soon again and point out carefully that it is impossible for me to take her under 200 gulden a year. Well, before next spring there will have been many a snowstorm and much water will have flowed under the bridges. Herr Leutgeb, who has now bought in a suburb of Vienna a cheese-monger's shop (the size of a snail's shell), wrote to us both after your departure, promised to pay me in due course, and asked you for a concerto. But he must know by now that you are no longer in Salzburg. Mme Duschek wrote to me the other day. She and her husband want to know where you are and how you are getting on. In conclusion, I should like to hear whether Baron Dürnitz paid you in Munich? or whether you made him a present of your composition?[1]—or whether you or I ought not to remind him? I think that is all. Nannerl is at the Hagenauers at the moment and is then going on to the Robinigs where I shall join her, as Fräulein Louise wants to hear us play Schuster's duets. Keep in as good health as we are. We kiss you both many 100000000000 times and I am ever, like those innocent angels who puff along without joy and sorrow, your husband and father

MZT

---

[1] Probably K. 284 [205b], the clavier sonata written for Baron Thaddäus von Dürnitz. See p. 287, n. 4.

(253) *Mozart to his Father*

[*Autograph in the Mozarteum, Salzburg*]

MANNHEIM, 3 *December* 1777

MONSIEUR MON TRÉS CHER PÉRE,

I can still write nothing definite about my position here. Last Monday, after going for three days in succession, morning and afternoon, ⟨to his natural children,⟩ I had at last the good fortune to meet ⟨the Elector.⟩ We all thought indeed that once more our efforts were to be in vain, as it was then quite late. ⟨But at last we saw him coming. The governess⟩ at once told ⟨the Countess⟩ to seat herself at the clavier and I placed myself beside her and gave her a lesson; and that was how ⟨the Elector found us when he came into the room. We stood up but he told us to go on.⟩ When the Countess had finished playing, the governess was the first to speak and said that I had composed a very fine Rondo. I played it and he liked it very much. At length he asked: 'But will she be able to learn it?' 'Oh yes,' I replied. 'I only wish ⟨that I might have the good fortune to teach it to her myself.' He smiled and said: 'I should like it too. But would not her playing be spoilt if she had two different masters?' 'Oh no, Your Highness', I replied. 'All that matters is whether she has a good one or a bad. I hope Your Highness will not doubt—and will have confidence in me.'⟩ 'Oh, most certainly', ⟨he replied. The governess then said:⟩ 'See, Herr Mozart has also written some variations on Fischer's minuet for ⟨the young Count'.⟩ I played them and ⟨he liked them⟩ very much. He then began to jest ⟨with the Countess.⟩ I thanked him ⟨for his present.⟩ He said: 'Well, ⟨I shall think it over. How long are you going to stay here?'⟩ *My reply:* ⟨'As long as your Highness commands. I have no engagements whatsoever: I can stay as long as Your Highness requires.'⟩ That was all. I went there again this morning. I was told that yesterday ⟨the Elector⟩ had again remarked: ⟨Mozart is staying here for the winter'.⟩ Well, we are now in the thick of it and I am bound to wait. Today, for the fourth time, I lunched with Wendling. Before we sat down, Count Savioli came in with Kapellmeister Schweitzer, who had arrived the night before. Savioli said to me: ⟨'I spoke to the Elector again yesterday, but he hasn't yet made up his mind'.⟩ I told him that I should like to have a word with him, and we went to the window. I told him about ⟨the Elector's⟩ hesitation and complained that things were dragging on so long. I said that ⟨my expenses here were already heavy⟩ and I begged him ⟨to persuade the Elector to grant me a permanent appointment,⟩ as I feared that ⟨he would give me so little during the winter that I should probably not be able to stay on.⟩ 'He ought', I said, ⟨'to give me some work. I like work.'⟩ Savioli said that ⟨he would certainly suggest it to the Elector⟩ but that he could not do so this evening, ⟨because the Elector is not going to Court today;⟩ but he promised to give me ⟨a definite answer tomorrow.⟩ Well, I'm prepared for anything now. ⟨If he does not retain me, I shall press for a *contribution towards my travelling expenses*, for I don't intend to make him a present of the Rondo and the Variations.⟩ I assure you that it is because I am convinced that, whatever happens, things will certainly turn out well that I am so calm about it all. I have resigned myself entirely to the will of God.

We received yesterday your letter of November 27th. I hope you got the Allegro and Andante of my sonata! Here is the Rondo. Herr Kapellmeister Schweitzer is a good, worthy, honest fellow, dry and smooth like our ⟨Haydn,⟩ but better-spoken. There are some very beautiful passages in his new opera and I do not doubt that it will be a real success. His 'Alceste',[1] which is not half as fine as 'Rosemunde',[2] was very popular. The fact that it was the first German Singspiel had, of course, a lot to do with it. It no longer makes so strong an impression on people who are only carried away by novelty. Herr Wieland, who wrote the libretto, is also coming here this winter. I should like to meet him. Who knows? Perhaps—by the time Papa reads this, it will all, with God's will, be settled. ⟨If I stay here, I am to go to Paris in Lent⟩ in the company of Wendling, Ramm, who plays very beautifully, and Lauchéry, the balletmaster.[3] Wendling assures me that I shall never regret it. He has been twice to Paris and has only just returned. He maintains that it is still the only place where one can make money and a great reputation. He said: 'Why, you are a fellow who can turn your hand to anything. I will tell you the way to set about it. You must compose all sorts, opera seria, opéra comique, oratorio, everything, in fact. Once a man has written a couple of operas in Paris, he is sure of a settled yearly income. Then there is the *Concert Spirituel* and the *Académie des Amateurs*, which pay five louis d'or for a symphony. If you take pupils, the usual fee is three louis d'or for twelve lessons. Further, you can get sonatas, trios and quartets engraved *par souscription*. Cannabich and Toeschi send a great deal of their music to Paris.' Wendling is an experienced traveller. Please let me have your views about this scheme, which strikes me as being useful and sensible. I shall be travelling with a man who knows Paris (present-day Paris, for it has changed considerably) thoroughly. My expenses will

---

[1] *Alceste*, for which Wieland had written the text, was performed at Weimar on 28 May 1773, with tremendous success, and soon found its way to other theatres. The Elector Karl Theodor had it performed in Schwetzingen on 13 August 1775.

[2] After the successful performance of *Alceste* in Mannheim, the Elector commissioned Wieland to write a new German opera, for which Schweitzer was to compose the music. *Rosemunde* was to have been performed on 11 January 1778, but, owing to the death of the Bavarian Elector on 30 December 1777, and the immediate departure of the Elector Karl Theodor for Munich, the performance was dropped. The opera was given in Mannheim on 20 January 1780. See F. Walter, *Geschichte des Theaters und der Musik am Kurpfälzischen Hofe*, Leipzig, 1898, p. 246 ff.

[3] Étienne Lauchéry, who since 1774 had been maître de ballet at the Mannheim theatre.

be no greater. Indeed I don't think that I shall spend half as much, as I shall only have myself to pay for, since Mamma would stay here, probably with the Wendlings. Herr Ritter,[1] a fine bassoon-player, is off to Paris on December 12th. Now if I had been alone, this would have been an excellent opportunity for me. He mentioned it to me himself. Ramm, the oboist, is a very good, jolly, honest fellow of about 35, who has already travelled a great deal, and consequently has plenty of experience. The chief and best musicians here are very fond of me and show me great respect. They never call me anything but 'Herr Kapellmeister'. I may say that I very much regret not having a copy of at least one mass with me. I should have certainly had one performed, for I heard one of Holzbauer's recently and it is quite in our style. If only I had the 'Misericordias'[2] copied out. But it cannot be helped now. There's no altering it. I would have decided to have one copied, but copying is much too expensive here and I might not have got as much for the mass as it would have cost me to have it copied. They are not very generous here. Now please remember me to all my good friends, especially Count Arco, Mlle Sallerl, Herr Bullinger and the whole company of marksmen. I kiss Papa's hands 100000 times and embrace my sister with all my heart and hope that my sonata will please you, my sister and Herr Bullinger and all who hear it as much as it has pleased all who have heard it here. Adieu. I am your most obedient son

WOLFGANG AMADÉ MOZART

(253a) *Maria Anna Mozart to her Husband*

[Autograph in the Mozarteum, Salzburg]

MY DEAR HUSBAND,   [MANNHEIM, 3 *December* 1777[3]]

You see that I can't write very much to you, as Wolfgang has left me no room. In any case he has told you all there is to tell, so that I have no more news for you about our affairs. Often I just wish that I could spend at least one day with you, so that I could talk to you about all the things we cannot write about. To do so is quite impossible, for the letters would be far too long. We write to you twice every week, so you ought to get as many letters as we do. Addio. Keep well. I kiss you both many 100000 times and remain your faithful wife

MARIA ANNA MOZART

All sorts of messages to all our acquaintances.

[1] Georg Wenzel Ritter (1748–1808), bassoon-player, was appointed in 1768 to the Mannheim orchestra, which he followed to Munich in 1778. In 1788 he took an appointment under King Frederick William II of Prussia.   [2] K. 222 [205a], composed in 1775.
[3] A postscript to Mozart's letter, written on the cover.

(254) *Mozart to his Cousin, Maria Anna Thekla Mozart, Augsburg*

[Copy in the Mozarteum, Salzburg]

[MANNHEIM, 3 *December* 1777]

MA TRÈS CHÈRE COUSINE!

Before I write to you, I must go to the closet. Well, that's over. Ah!
At last I feel lighter, a weight is off my heart; and now I can guzzle again.
Oh, oh, when you've emptied yourself, life is far more worth living.
Your letter of November 25th would have reached me safely, if you
hadn't written that you had had pains in your head, throat and arms; but
as you say that now, at the moment, for the present, for the nonce, at
this instant you feel no more pains, I have safely received your letter of
November 26th. Yes, yes, my dearest Miss Cousin, thus has it been since
days of old, Tom has the purse and Dick has the gold; and what do you
hold it with? with your 🖎, don't you? Huzza, copper-smith, come,
be a man, catch if you can, lick my arse, copper-smith. Yes, and true it is
that whosoever believes it, is happy and whosoever does not, will go to
Heaven, but straight, and not in the way I am writing. You see now that I
can write just as I like, both fair and untidy, both straight and crooked.
The other day I was in a bad humour and I wrote a fair, straight and
serious hand; today I am in good spirits and I am writing an untidy,
crooked and jolly one. So all depends now on what you prefer. You
must make the choice (I have no medium article to offer you) between
fair and untidy, straight and crooked, serious and jolly, the three first or
the three last. I expect to hear your decision in your next letter. My decision is taken; when it's necessary, I go somewhere; but it all depends on
circumstances. If I have diarrhœa, I run: and if I can't contain myself any
longer, I shit into my trousers. God preserve thee, foot, on the window-
sill lies the hamstring. I am much obliged to you, my dear Miss Cousin,
for the compliments from your Fräulein Freysinger, which your dear
Fräulein Juliana has been so kind as to send me. You say: 'I could tell you
a great deal more, but too much is more than enough'. In *one* letter it is
too much, I admit, but one can write a great deal by instalments. You
see what I mean? As for the sonata,[1] she must possess herself in patience
for a little longer. If it had been for my dear coz, it would have been
finished long ago. Who knows whether Mlle Freysinger hasn't forgotten
all about it? All the same I'll get it done as soon as possible, write a letter to
accompany it and beg my dear coz to deliver them safely. A propos, since
I left Augsburg, I have not taken off my trousers, except at night before
going to bed. What will you think when you hear that I am still in

---

[1] See p. 359, n. 1.

Mannheim, dug in? It is due to my not having left and gone somewhere else! But now I think that I shall soon leave Mannheim. Yet Augsburg, through you, can continue to write to me and address letters to Mannheim until further notice. My uncle, my aunt and my cousin send their greetings to my Mamma and to me. They were very anxious about us and thought that we must be ill, as they had received no letter from us for so long. But at last to their delight they received the day before yesterday our letter of November 26th, and today, December 3rd, they have had the pleasure of replying to me. So I am to keep my promise to you? Ah, you are glad to hear this. Be sure you don't forget to compose the Munich for sonata, for what one has once performed, one must promise, one must always be a word of one's man. Well, let's be serious.

I must tell you something very briefly. I did not lunch at home today, but with a certain Mr. Wendling. Now you must know that he always takes his lunch at two o'clock, that he is married and has a daughter who, however, is always ailing. His wife is singing in the new opera and he plays the flute. Well, can you believe it, but when it was half past one we all, except the daughter who stayed in bed, we all, I say, sat down to table and began to eat.

Please give a whole arseful of greetings from us both to all our good friends. Our remembrances to your parents will be found on Page 3, line 12. Well, I've no more news to give you, save that an old cow has shit some new muck. So now adieu, Anna Maria Schlosser, née Schlüsselmacher. Take care of yourself and continue to love me. Write without delay, for it is cold today and keep your promise too or else forsooth I'll spue. Adieu, mon Dieu, I send you a great dollop of kisses, slap bang wollop!

Mannheim	Ma très chère cousine,
without slime,	Were you never in Berlin?
The 3rd of December,	Your cousin of virtues rare
Today's not an Ember,	In weather foul or fair
1777 in dark obscurity,	W. A. Mozart,
From now to all eternity	Who shits without a fart.
Amen.	

(255) *Leopold Mozart to his Wife and Son*

[*Extract*]   [*Autograph in the Mozarteum, Salzburg*]

SALZBURG, *4 December* 1777

MY DEAR WIFE AND DEAR SON!

That you have had to await the result of what you wrote to me about I quite understand. Further, you need not have troubled to describe all that happened contrary to what I was expecting and to what would have been to our advantage, as it is all over now and can no longer be remedied. But that you, my son, should tell me *that all planning is needless and useless, since after all we do not know what is going to happen,* argues indeed a scattered brain; and you must have written that quite thoughtlessly. No sensible man, I need hardly say, no Christian will deny that *all things will and must happen in accordance with the will of God.* But does it follow therefore that on all occasions we are to act blindly, ever live carelessly, make no plans and merely wait until something drops down from the sky of its own accord? Does not God himself and do not all sensible folk require that in all our actions we should consider, as far as our human reason enables us to, their consequences and their result, and should endeavour to see as far ahead as we can? Now if this is essential in all our actions, how much more necessary is it not in your present circumstances and on a journey? Surely you have already experienced some of the consequences of your actions? Or do you really think that it is enough to have made that démarche ⟨to the Elector with a view to spending the winter in Mannheim?⟩ Surely you must think out, as you ought to have done long ago, a plan which you can adopt, if this present business should not come off. And surely you ought to have told me about it long ago and obtained my views. And now you write—what? 'If after all we do leave Mannheim we we shall go straight to Weilburg, to the Princess of Nassau-Weilburg (for whom you wrote the sonatas in Holland).[1] And there we shall remain as long as the ⟨officers' table⟩ is to our taste,'[2] What sort of a yarn is that? Those are the words, as are indeed all the remarks which precede them, of a man ⟨who has lost his reason⟩ and who is trying to delude himself and me. But ⟨you still hope⟩ to get six louis d'or, and that will make everything right. I should now like to enquire whether you know for certain that the Princess is there; if she is, there must be a special reason, seeing that her consort, on account of his military profession, has to reside at The Hague. Surely you ought to have told me this long ago? There is another question—whether you would not do better to go to Mainz— and thence to Weilburg via Frankfurt; for if you now go straight to Weilburg, you will strike the road to Frankfurt; and as you are not staying in Weilburg for good, the road to Mainz will take you back through Frankfurt. But if you go to Mainz first and from there to Weilburg, you will have a short distance to go from Weilburg to Coblenz via Nassau. But perhaps you want to give up Mainz, where we have so many good friends and where we took in from three concerts 200 gulden, although we did not play before the Elector, who happened to be ill. Tell me, my dear son, do you really think now that these are useless

[1] K. 26-31, six sonatas for the clavier with violin accompaniment, written for and dedicated to the Princess Caroline of Nassau-Weilburg in 1766. [2] See p. 391.

speculations? Our dear good Mamma promised: 'I shall keep a careful account of our expenses'. Excellent! I do not ask and have never dreamt of asking you to produce detailed statements of your expenditure. But when you reached Augsburg, you might have written to say, 'We paid out so much at Albert's in Munich, and so much slipped away in travelling expenses, so that we now have such and such a sum'. You wrote to me from Augsburg that in spite of what you took in at your concert you were about twenty gulden on the wrong side. You ought to have told me at least in your second letter from Mannheim that the journey cost you so much and that now you stood as follows . . . and then I should have made arrangements in time. But perhaps you think that my plan to provide you with a letter of credit for Augsburg was also an unnecessary precaution? Do you imagine that Herr Herzog, *who is a good friend of mine*, would in response to all your letters from Mannheim have provided you with money? Far from it! The most he might have done would have been to make enquiries from me first. Why was I not to hear from you that you needed money, until you were absolutely down and out? ⟨*You wanted to wait and see what the Elector would give you.*⟩ Your object in acting thus was to prevent me from worrying. But it would have cost me far less anxiety if I had been told everything quite frankly and in good time. For I know even better than you do that on such journeys a man must be prepared for all emergencies, if he is not to be unpleasantly embarrassed at some moment when he is least expecting it. In such moments all one's *friends* disappear! *One should be cheerful and enjoy oneself, I admit*. But at other times *one should be serious*; and travelling is a serious occupation, during which not a day should be wasted. The days which at this season are short and moreover cost money in an inn, slip away rapidly. Good God! You ask me not to plan ahead, although ⟨*it is solely on your account that I am in debt to the extent of 450 gulden;*⟩ and you think perhaps to put me in a good humour by sending me a hundred silly jokes. I am delighted when you are in good spirits; but instead of the greetings you sent in the form of an alphabet,[1] I should have been better pleased if you had sent me the reasons for your proposed journey to Weilburg. In a word, this is not unnecessary circumspection. Whoever acts otherwise is a stupid, careless fellow who, particularly *in the world as it is today*, with all his cleverness will always be left behind, and may even meet disaster, the more so as he is sure to be taken in by flatterers, fawners and back-biters. Mark well, my son, that *to find one man in a thousand*, who is your true friend from unselfish motives, is to find *one of the greatest wonders of this world*. Think of all those who call themselves or seem to be your friends and you will surely detect some reason why they act thus. If they are not self-interested themselves, then probably they are professing

[1] See pp. 391, 392.

friendship in the interest of some other friend, who is necessary to them; or they keep up their friendship with you in order by picking you out, to cause a third person annoyance. If this letter does not reach you in Mannheim, that is, if you are in Weilburg already, I cannot help you. But if you are still at Mannheim and have to leave, then Mamma will see on the map that your best move is to go to Mainz first, or else Mainz will have to be omitted or you will have to come back a bit on your route. Remember that in Weilburg, where everyone is ⟨either Lutheran or Calvinist,⟩ you will not find ⟨a Catholic church.⟩ So I do not want you ⟨to stay there too long.⟩

And who informed you, pray, that from Würzburg to Mannheim would take you through the Forest of Spessart, which, as everyone knows, is near Aschaffenburg and between Fulda and Frankfurt? It was probably Herr Beecke who told you that cock and bull story. Why, Aschaffenburg and Würzburg are ten miles apart.

You must now seriously consider how you are going to deal with your present difficulties, travel with all possible economy and make sensible plans. Under no circumstances must you sell our chaise. God keep you both and myself. Nannerl and I kiss you many 100000000 times and I am your old husband and father

MZT

Count Czernin asks me to send you his greetings. There was a rumour the other day that the Archbishop was not only sending Haydn to Italy but that he had wanted to send him off to Bozen with Triendl, who, however, had got out of it. My dear Wolfgang, I beg you to think out your plans and to give up writing to me about matters which are over and done with. Otherwise we shall all be most unhappy.

(256) *Mozart to his Father*

[Autograph in the Mozarteum, Salzburg]

MANNHEIM, 6 December 1777

MON TRÉS CHER PÉRE!

I can still tell you nothing more. I'm beginning to get sick of this joke. I am only curious now as to how it will end. ⟨Count Savioli⟩ has already spoken three times ⟨to the Elector and each time his reply has been⟩ a shrug of the shoulders and the remark that he would certainly ⟨give me an answer, but that he had not yet made up his mind.⟩ My good friends quite agree with me that all this hesitation and reserve is rather a good sign than a bad one. ⟨For if the Elector had no intention of taking me on

at all, he would have said so at once; as it is,⟩ I attribute this delay to—
⟨denari siamo un poco scrocconi.⟩[1] Moreover I know for a fact that ⟨the
Elector likes me.⟩ A buon conto, we must just wait a little longer. I may
say at once that I should be glad ⟨if the affair turned out well,⟩ as otherwise I should regret ⟨having sat about here for so long and wasted our
money.⟩ However, come what may, it can never be bad, if it is in accordance with God's will; and that it may be so is my daily prayer. Papa is
right in his guess as to the chief reason ⟨for Herr Cannabich's friendship.⟩
But there is one other little matter for which ⟨he can make use of me.⟩
He has to produce selections of all ⟨his ballet music,⟩ but these must be
arranged for ⟨the clavier.⟩ He is quite unable to transcribe them in such a
way as to render them effective and at the same time easy. So he finds me
very handy ⟨for this,⟩ as he did on one occasion already when I arranged
a contredanse for him.[2] He has been away hunting for the last eight days
and doesn't return until next Tuesday. Such things, of course, contribute
⟨a good deal to a close friendship,⟩ but all the same I do not think, to say
the least, that he ⟨would work against me;⟩ for he has altered considerably.
When a man reaches a certain age and sees his children growing up, his
ideas are bound to change a little. His daughter who is fifteen, his eldest
child, is a very pretty and charming girl. She is very intelligent and steady
for her age. She is serious, does not say much, but when she does speak,
she is pleasant and amiable. Yesterday she again gave me indescribable
pleasure; she played the whole of my sonata—excellently. The Andante
(which must *not be taken too quickly*) she plays with the utmost expression.
Moreover she likes playing it. I had already finished the Allegro, as you
know, on the day after my arrival, and thus had only seen Mlle Cannabich
once. Young Danner asked me how I thought of composing the Andante.
I said that I would make it fit closely the character of Mlle Rosa. When I
played it, it was an extraordinary success. Young Danner told me so
afterwards. It really is a fact. She is exactly like the Andante. I hope that
you received the sonata safely. Your letter of December 1st reached us
this morning. Today I lunched with Wendling for the sixth time and
with Schweitzer for the second. Tomorrow for a change I shall lunch
there again. I go there regularly for meals. But now I must go to bed.

I wish you both good night.

(256a) *Maria Anna Mozart to her Husband*

[Autograph in the Mozarteum, Salzburg]

[MANNHEIM, 7 *December* 1777]
Wolfgang is lunching with Herr Wendling today, December 7th. So
I am at home alone, as I usually am, and have to put up with the most

---

[1] We are a little stingy with the cash.   [2] There is no trace of these compositions.

horrible cold. For even if they light a small fire, they never put any more coal on it, so that when it burns out, the room gets cold again. A little fire of this kind costs twelve kreuzer. So I make them light one in the morning, when we get up, and another in the evening. During the day I have to put up with dreadful cold. As I write I can hardly hold my pen, I am freezing so. You must not be so accommodating about Herr Hamm. As it is, 200 gulden is little enough, for that will include her laundry. You must bear in mind all our expenses. In a convent she would have to pay 100 gulden for food and drink alone, and that would not include a teacher and other extras. So charge him what is right and see that you make some profit for your trouble. Only death costs nothing—and even that's not true. I am really delighted that you have given Jungfer Sandl[1] that room, for she is a good girl and will not give you much trouble. Up to the present we have not been to any balls and only to one gala play, for the tickets are very expensive. You have to pay 45 kreuzer in the parterre and 1 gulden in the cheaper boxes, and besides you have to get there early, if you want to be sure of a good seat. So we have not bothered. No one gets in free. Everyone has to pay, both performers in the orchestra and those connected with the theatre, for the Elector pays them all and gives them large salaries. The leading actor in the theatre, Herr Marshall, gets 3000 gulden a year, and the most wretched singer, even a beginner, gets 600. In the orchestra too they get fine salaries. Herr Cannabich as Director now draws 1800 gulden, Herr Fränzl as Konzertmeister 1400 gulden, Kapellmeister Holzbauer almost 3000 gulden, and in addition they get presents for any new compositions. Rather different this from ⟨Salzburg.⟩ It makes your mouth water. We are now relying on that God who, if it is His divine will, will see to it that the ⟨Elector⟩ will retain us. Things are moving a bit slowly. We must just wait and see, and be grateful for the time being that he has not refused altogether.

(256b) *Mozart resumes writing*

[Autograph in the Mozarteum, Salzburg]

I have just this moment come back from Wendling's. As soon as I have taken this letter to the post I shall run off there again, for they are going to rehearse the opera[2] *in camera caritatis.*[3] At 6.30 I am going on to Canna-bich's to give my usual daily lesson on the clavier.

A propos. I must correct a statement I made. I told you yesterday that Mlle Cannabich was 15; she is, however, only 13, though she is getting

---

[1] Sandl Auer was a poor cap-mender to whom Leopold Mozart had offered a room at the back of his house. He had mentioned this in Letter 252 (portion omitted).
[2] Schweitzer's *Rosemunde*.   [3] i.e. between ourselves.

on for 14. Our greetings to all our good friends, especially to Herr Bullinger. Mamma is burning with indignation, rage and jealousy at the thought that all that Papa has to do is to move the chest and open the door in order to get to that pretty young chambermaid.[1] I assure you that I deeply regret that I am away from Salzburg, as this would have been a splendid opportunity for me to forget all my troubles in the arms of such a beautiful, charming, blue-nosed maiden. But so it had to be. I must just console myself with the thought that there are many women quite as fair. Now I must close, or else I shall miss the post. Hoping (for the third time!) that in my next letter I really shall have some news to tell you, whether it means a fulfilment of our hopes or not, I kiss your hands 1000 times and remain, as always,

your{most obedient son / faithful wife

WOLFG:AMADÉ MOZART
MARIA ANNA MOZART[2]

My sister,
Who sleeps at Sylvester,
I do embrace with all my might
In Lent as well as on Carnival night.

(257) *Leopold Mozart to his Son*

[*Extract*]   [*Autograph in the Mozarteum, Salzburg*]

MON TRÈS CHER FILS!   SALZBURG, *8 December* 1777

It is evident that we have not understood one another. The step you took was, in my opinion, well taken and my letters told you so. But did you write to tell me whether you had made any plans or not? And as to whether the step you took led to anything? Not a single word! But suddenly I get your letter, saying: ⟨'*The present was a gold watch. In view of our journey I should have much preferred some money.*'⟩ Then you go on to say: 'I called on Herr Schmalz ⟨*who excused himself by remarking that he had orders to give me money*'.⟩ What else could I gather from these statements but that ⟨you wanted to leave and could not do so for lack of money?⟩ Surely you must understand my astonishment at having news like this dumped on me when I was least expecting it, and particularly as you had never prepared me for it. How?—What?—Why?—Whither? If you had only said that you were staying on, ⟨that you were *intending to spend the winter in Mannheim*, that you had *approached* the Elector or were proposing to do so,⟩ then Nannerl, Bullinger and I would have understood

---

[1] Sandl Auer, see p. 409, n. 1.   [2] This signature is in Mozart's handwriting.

everything quite clearly and would not have been anxious. At the same time I was aware that a prolonged stay in any one centre meant money. So naturally I was plagued by a thousand thoughts and I had to write a great many things to you which I otherwise should not have written.

You are convinced that I should *never be able to adapt myself equally to good fortune or bad fortune*. True, for there is only one occasion when I *can* adapt myself, and that is, when in spite of all the preparations which I have made, ill luck comes upon me. Then I have nothing with which to reproach myself. When I was dangerously ill in England,[1] I had thought out already the arrangements for entrusting you to safe hands in the event of my death. And during the dangerous illnesses of yourself and Nannerl at The Hague[2] and at Olmütz,[3] Mamma and I managed to comfort one another. But the fact remains that in all our misfortunes we always knew where to get money. However, my mind is now at rest and I am prepared for any eventuality. Your anxiety that your affairs should be kept secret is quite unnecessary. For do you imagine for one moment that I would give ⟨the Archbishop, *who seems to hear everything, an opportunity of laughing at us,*⟩ if nothing should come of your scheme? Can you believe this of me? I have not yet told you that after you left, everybody kept on asking me, *where you were going to*? I always replied, as I still do, that I did not know myself. Indeed I could say so truthfully, as at the time I did not know. They read about Augsburg in the papers and Baron Schafmann wrote about Mannheim. When people ask me with a significant look why you are still in Mannheim, I always say that I myself do not know whether you are still there. You stayed on there for the Elector's name-day and perhaps you may not leave now until after his birthday, which is December 12th. For, if I remember rightly, he was born on 10 or 12 December, 1724.[4] Well, enough of this. But nothing makes my heart so heavy or makes me feel so restless as *ignorance and doubt* and anxiety for those who are more precious to me than *life itself*. I should like you to remain in Mannheim for the winter, particularly as a long journey at this time would not be very suitable for Mamma. So I have been wondering what better arrangement could be made. ⟨*If you are appointed to instruct the young Count,*⟩ you will have ample opportunity ⟨*of ingratiating yourself with the Elector;*⟩ and I need hardly tell you ⟨*that you must make a good friend of the governess too.*⟩ The last point in your letter about which I have something to say is your wild statement that *happiness consists only in imagination.* I quite agree. But would you apply your dictum so universally that, for instance, a traveller who is ⟨stranded in an inn or a post-house without money with which to proceed on his journey⟩ and who is exposed, in consequence, to the rude taunts ⟨of a landlord or a postmaster,⟩

---

[1] In 1764. [2] In 1765. [3] In 1767.
[4] The Elector Karl Theodor was born on 1 December 1724.

ought to console himself with the thought that happiness consists only in imagination?—My dear Wolfgang, this dictum is a moral saw only applicable to people who are perpetually discontented. Most of us, nay almost all of us, are never content, and everyone considers his neighbour to be more fortunate than himself. So this saying is to instruct, guide, and remind us that everyone should be content with his station in life and should not envy his neighbour, whom he probably never would envy, if he were thoroughly well acquainted with the private circumstances of the latter. For we always judge by appearances, and most people are careful to hide their real misfortunes.

There is a rumour that a handsome winter suit has been ordered in the guardarobba for Herr Haydn on the occasion of his journey to Italy. How I should like to hear him talking to the Italians in Italy! They will certainly exclaim: 'Questo è un vero tedesco!'[1] Now I must close, for the sheet is really covered, quite seriously—not, as it was in your case, to provide a joke. If you stay on in Mannheim, I shall send you the two sonatas a quattro mani,[2] copied out on small paper for your two pupils. We kiss you both with all our hearts and wish you good health and so forth and along with Nannerl I am your young husband and father

MZT

Greetings upon greetings!—you must imagine them yourselves, for there are so many of them that I have not been able to make a note of them, remember them and write them down. Bimperl is barking and drowning them all with the row she is making at the moment.[3]

(257a) *Nannerl Mozart to her Mother and Brother*

[Autograph in the Mozarteum, Salzburg]

[SALZBURG, 8 *December* 1777[4]]

I am really delighted that, thank God, you are both well. We are as fit as one can be in this dull Salzburg. Thanks for the first movement and the Andante of your sonata which I have already played through. The Andante requires indeed great concentration and exactness in playing. But I like the sonata very much. One can see from its style that you composed it in Mannheim. I am now looking forward to the Rondo. The wife of Anton Lodron, the Marshal of the Court, has died. There is no other news. I do hope that you will be able to stay in Mannheim for the winter, as it would be too trying for Mamma to have to travel at this

---

[1] He's a real German!
[2] Probably K. 381 [123a] and 358 [186c], composed in 1772 and 1774 .
[3] This postscript follows Nannerl's letter.   [4] A postscript to her father's letter.

time of the year. Keep well, both of you, and do think of us very often. I kiss Mamma's hands and embrace my brother.

(258) *Mozart to his Father*

[*Autograph in the Mozarteum, Salzburg*]

MANNHEIM, 10 *December* 1777

MON TRÉS CHER PÉRE!

There's nothing to be hoped for at present ⟨from the Elector⟩. The day before yesterday I went to the concert at Court to get ⟨his answer. Count Savioli⟩ studiously avoided me, but I made my way up to him. When he saw me, he shrugged his shoulders. 'What,' I said, 'no answer yet?' 'Please forgive me,' he replied, 'unfortunately none.' '*Eh bien*,' I said, 'the Elector might have told me so before.' 'True,' he said, 'but he would not have made up his mind even now, if I had not prodded him and pointed out that you had been hanging on here for such a long time and were using up all your money at the inn.' 'That's what worries me most of all', I retorted. 'It's not at all nice. However, I am very much obliged to you, Count (we don't address him as Your Excellency), for having taken such an interest in me, and I beg you to thank ⟨the Elector⟩ on my behalf for his gracious though belated reply and to say that I can assure him that he would never have regretted it if he had taken me on.' 'Oh,' he replied, 'I am surer of that than you think.' I then told Wendling about the decision. He went quite red in the face and remarked very angrily: 'We must find some way out. You must stay here, at least for the next two months until we can go to Paris together. Cannabich returns from his hunting tomorrow. We can then discuss the matter further.' Whereupon I left the concert and went straight to Madame Cannabich. Our Treasurer came with me. He is an excellent fellow and a good friend of mine. On the way I told him what had happened. You cannot imagine how wild the fellow became. When we entered the room, he burst out at once: 'Well, here's another who has been favoured with the usual nice treatment they deal you out ⟨at Court.⟩' 'What,' exclaimed Madame, 'so nothing has come of it?' I told them the whole story. They then told me about all kinds of pretty pranks which have been played on people here. Mlle Rosa was three rooms off and busy with the laundry at the time. When she had finished she came in and said to me: 'Are you ready to begin?' For it was time for our lesson. 'I am at your service', I replied. 'But we must have a really serious lesson today', she said. 'We certainly must,' I rejoined, 'for we shan't have the chance much longer.' 'Why? What's this?' She went up to her mother who told her. 'What?' she said, 'is it really true? I can't believe it.' 'Yes, yes, quite true', her mother said. Thereupon Mlle Rosa played my sonata very seriously. I assure you, I couldn't keep from weeping. In the end the mother, the daughter and the Treasurer all had tears in their eyes. For she had been playing my sonata, which is the favourite of the whole house. 'I say', said the Treasurer, 'If the Kapellmeister (they never call me anything else here) leaves us, he will make us all weep.' I must say that I have some very kind friends here. Indeed it is at times like these that one gets to know their worth. For they are friends not only in words but in deeds.

Let me tell you just one thing more. The other day I went to lunch at Wendling's as usual. 'Our Indian', he said, meaning a Dutchman,[1] a gentleman of means and a lover of all the sciences, who is a great friend and ⟨admirer⟩ of mine, 'our Indian is really a first-rate fellow. He is willing to give you 200 gulden if you will compose for him three short, simple concertos and a couple of quartets for the flute. Through Cannabich you can get at least two pupils who will pay well. You can compose duets for clavier and violin here and have them engraved *par souscription*. Your lunch and supper you can always have with us. You can lodge at the Privy Court Councillor's.[2] All that will cost you nothing. For your mother we shall find some cheap lodging for the next two months until you have written home about all our plans. Your Mamma can then travel home and we can go on to Paris.' Mamma is quite satisfied with this arrangement and it only remains for you to give your consent. I am so certain of it that if it were now the time to travel, I should go off to Paris without waiting for an answer. For no other answer could be expected from a father who is so sensible and has shown himself up to the present so anxious for the welfare of his children. Herr Wendling who sends you his compliments is a bosom friend of our bosom friend Grimm. The latter, when he was here, said a good deal about me to Wendling, I mean, when he came here after seeing us in Salzburg. As soon as I get your reply to this letter I shall write to him, for I have it from a stranger, whom I met at table here, that he is now in Paris. As we shall not be leaving before March 6th, I should also be glad if, through Herr Mesmer in Vienna or somebody or other, you could possibly arrange for me to get a letter to the Queen of France—but only if there's no difficulty about it; it's really of no great importance, though undoubtedly it would be better to have it. This was also a suggestion of Herr Wendling's'. I can magine that what I have written will seem strange to you, living as you are in a town where one is accustomed to having stupid enemies or weak and silly friends who, because ⟨Salzburg's⟩ stodgy bread is indispensable to them, are always toadying and are consequently one thing one day and another the next. You see, that was just the reason why I have kept on

---

[1] De Jean (or Dechamps).   [2] Serrarius.

writing childish nonsense and jokes to you and have rarely been serious. I wanted to wait for the upshot of the whole affair here in order to save you from worry and to spare my good friends, on whom (though they are quite innocent) you are perhaps throwing all the blame, as though they had been working against me in secret. That is certainly not the case. I know well enough who was the cause! However, your letters have compelled me to tell you the whole story. But I implore you, for Heaven's sake do not upset yourself about it; God willed it so. Bear in mind this only too certain truth that it is not always possible for a man to do what he proposes. He often thinks—'This would be very pleasant, and that would be very bad and undesirable'; and when it comes about, he often finds it is just the opposite. Well, I must go to bed now. I shall have quite enough to write during the next two months, three concertos, two quartets, four or six duets for the clavier. And then I have an idea of writing a new grand mass and presenting ⟨it to the Elector.⟩ Adieu. Please reply at once to all my questions. I kiss your hands 100000 times and embrace my sister with all my heart and remain your most obedient son

WOLFGANG AMADE MOZART

Baron Dürnitz was not in Munich when I was there. I shall write to Prince ⟨Zeill⟩ on the next post-day and ask him to ⟨push on with⟩ my Munich scheme. If you would write to him too, I should be very glad. But be short and to the point; and let there be ⟨no cringing,⟩ for I cannot bear that. One thing is quite certain, if he wants to, he can ⟨fix it up;⟩ for all ⟨Munich⟩ told me so.

(258a) *Maria Anna Mozart to her Husband*

[*Autograph in the Koch Collection*]

[MANNHEIM, 11 *December* 1777]

MY DEAR HUSBAND,

You insist on knowing how much we have spent on our journey. We told you about Albert's account and that our bill in Augsburg was 300 gulden. Wolfgang told you that we were 24 gulden on the wrong side; but he forgot to include the expenses of the concert, which were 16 gulden, and also our landlord's account. Thus by the time we got to Mannheim we had only about 60 gulden in all. So if we had gone off again after a fortnight, we should not have had much left. For travelling expenses have gone up a lot since everything has become so dear. It is not anything like what it used to be, you would be surprised. As for Wolfgang's journey to Paris, you must think it over and let us know if you approve. At this time of the year Paris is the only place where there is anything doing. Monsieur Wendling is an honest fellow, as everybody knows. He has travelled far and wide and has been to Paris thirteen times already. He knows every stick and stone there; and then our friend Herr Grimm is his best friend and has done a lot for him. So make up your mind and whatever you decide will suit me. Herr Wendling has assured me that he will be a father to Wolfgang, whom he loves as if he were his own son; and Wolfgang will be looked after as well as if he were with me. As you may imagine, I myself do not like to let him go, nor do I like to have to travel home alone, it is such an awful distance. I can't bear to think of it. But what can we do? I am too old to undertake such a long journey to Paris and besides it would cost too much. To travel à quatre is much cheaper than to meet all one's expenses oneself. I shall write more next post-day. Today I have a headache and I think I am in for a cold. It is bitterly cold here. I am so frozen that I can hardly hold my pen. Wolfgang has gone out to look at lodgings. The cheap ones are very scarce here, but there are plenty of expensive ones. Tell Nannerl that people do not wear jackets here except indoors. Out-of-doors they wear chiefly cloaks and capes. The caps they wear are much prettier than what we wear in Salzburg and quite different—their frisure is quite wonderful, nothing piled up at all. The women are very smartly dressed. If it were not such a distance, I would send Nannerl a cap and a Palatine. Addio. Keep well, both of you. I kiss you many 1000000 times and remain your faithful wife

11 December 1777   MARIA ANNA MOZART

All sorts of messages to all our good friends, especially to Bullinger, Jungfer Sallerl, Katherl Gilowsky, the Andretters, Hagenauers, Robinigs, Frau von Gerlichs, the Schiedenhofens, Mölks, Junfrau Mitzerl, Herr Gött, Jungfrau Sandl, Theresa.

A kiss for Bimperl.

(259) *Leopold Mozart to his Son*

[*Extract*]   [*Autograph in the Mozarteum, Salzburg*]

SALZBURG, 11 *December* 1777

MON TRÉS CHER FILS!

I received safely on the 9th your letter of the 3rd. It is a great pity that all your letters reach us on *Tuesdays and Fridays*, since we cannot reply to them before Thursdays and Mondays. Nannerl plays your whole sonata excellently and with great expression. If you leave Mannheim, *as I now presume you will*, I shall have it copied and enclose a small sheet in every letter, so that you may have it again. Your sonata is a strange composition. It has something in it of the *rather artificial* Mannheim style, but so very little that your own good style is not spoilt thereby. I am assuming that you will leave Mannheim, for you ⟨told Count Savioli⟩ that you feared that the Elector ⟨would give you so little during the winter that it would be impossible for you to stay.⟩ But though he does not intend ⟨to appoint you permanently,⟩ he may be wondering whether you may not stay on after all and he may therefore be hesitating to take a decision. So the logical conclusion ⟨is that *he is not going to retain you.*⟩ Basta! Well, it is all over now and God knows where you will be reading this letter. Your next one which I am expecting tomorrow will surely tell me. If you had thought things out a bit beforehand, you would have taken with you your testimonials and so forth from Padre Martini and shown them to the Elector. You must surely know that he thinks the world of Padre Martini and that he sent Herr Ritschel,[1] whom he afterwards appointed his Deputy-Kapellmeister, to be trained by him, and after Ritschel's death, Vogler also. Besides you surely know that Martini dedicated Part II of his book to the Elector?[2] You ought at least to have shown Count Savioli your diplomas from the Academies and your testimonials, the more so as Italians are always impressed by these public tributes from their fellow-countrymen. For even though you may have convinced all the leading musicians in Mannheim of your knowledge of composition, does it follow that the Elector is aware of it? Have these gentlemen an opportunity of telling him? *And would they want to tell him?* The Elector knows that you are a *competent clavier-player*, but he has had no opportunity of hearing *what you can do* in the way of composition. I am not going to say anything more about having your works copied, which you ought to have arranged during your long visits to Munich and Augsburg, since the farther you travel the more expensive does copying become. You will remember, however, that I was very much against your taking so many symphonies with you. I just picked out a good number of them, but I naturally thought that you would leave some of them behind. Yet instead of putting several aside, you added to them others, and thus made such an enormous pile that you could not pack any of your church music. If I had not been so ill that I could hardly speak, I should not have let you take more than about four or six symphonies with the parts doubled for concert use, and all the others in single parts or in their original scores. Could you not have performed in Mannheim your Haffner music,[3] your concertone[4] or one of your Lodron serenades?[5] I suppose that the Elector never has music except when there is a gala concert—and that Herr

---

[1] Probably Franz Ritschel, who in 1756 was court organist at Mannheim.
[2] Part II of his *Storia della musica*, published in 1770.   [3] K. 250 [248b], written in 1776.
[4] K. 190 [186e], for two violins and orchestra, written in 1773.
[5] K. 247 and 287 [271h]. See p. 289, n. 2.

Cannabich has already provided for such occasions.

If you have left Mannheim, I trust that before your departure you got Herr Wendling *to give you a few letters of introduction or some addresses in Paris*—and that you have found out from him where *he lived*—and where *he used to lunch*. If you have not done so, write to him at once and ask him *for all these*. You must make a point of getting hold of some honest person who will direct you immediately to a comfortable and inexpensive lodging, so that you may not have to stay at an inn nor, if possible, even have to put up at one at all. Your conscience, if you will hear its voice, must be reminding you that you have kept on postponing many things which you ought to have done. For example, you ought to have had your 'Misericordias'[1] copied, as soon as it was returned to you from Augsburg, since it is not a big work; you ought to have enquired whether the court copyist would not copy one of your masses for the Elector, as was done with your 'Misericordias' in Munich; you ought to have hit on the idea ⟨*about his natural children, your variations and your Rondo*⟩[2] much earlier and immediately after you received his present—and indeed many other things which the above remarks and my frequent questions must recall to your mind. Your idea about travelling to Paris with Herr Wendling is not to be rejected entirely. There is time to think it over. It all depends where you will be in Lent. I fully realize how much money can be made in Paris and told you this in my last letter. If M. Grimm is there, then your fortune is made. If not, no doubt you will make fresh acquaintances. If you have left Mannheim, you ought to go straight to Paris and I shall fire off at once a letter to M. Grimm and send you particulars of all our old acquaintances there. If you are in Mainz, you will know from one of my letters what you can do there. I now close with the hope that God may keep you in good health, for which I pray to Him constantly, and with the earnest reminder that you must take the greatest care of it. For a break-down would be our most crushing misfortune and would plunge us all into the deepest misery. I dare not remember that I ⟨now owe more than six hundred gulden⟩—or else—

Nannerl and I kiss you millions of times. We both send you our greetings and I remain your old husband and father

                                                          MZT

The castrato[3] is now living at the fencing-master's and goes to Varesco[4] for his meals. Addio!

[1] K. 222 [205a]. See pp. 378 and 402.
[2] This rather obscure passage is an allusion to Mozart's Letter 251, in which he tells his father that he made a present of these two compositions to the Elector's children.
[3] Francesco Ceccarelli.
[4] Abbate Giambattista Varesco, who since 1766 had been court chaplain in Salzburg. He wrote the Italian libretti for Mozart's opera seria *Idomeneo*, 1781, and for his unfinished opera buffa *L' oca del Cairo*, 1783.

My dear Wife,

I am delighted to hear that you are well, but I am rather anxious as to whether you have really left Mannheim, for travelling in winter must be very uncomfortable for you. You must protect yourself from the cold as well as you can and it would be better to buy another large fur. You did not take a foot-bag with you, although we have two. You say that if you were to tell me everything, your letters would be too long. But you see that I take a whole sheet, and that I write all over it and only leave room for the seal. I do this simply in order to tell you a great many things, and I write twice as much as you write to me—and yet I only pay six kreuzers. I trust that you too only pay six kreuzers for my very long letters. You see that I do not use separate covers and that I fill in all the empty spaces with writing. Indeed I too should like to talk to you. Oh, sometimes I cannot get you out of my head the whole day long, especially when I think of you, travelling in this cold weather—and of other things—which ought to have turned out very differently. God, however, will provide! But we human beings must also take thought; and in this world it is impossible by honest expedients only, to get on at Court. All sorts of ways and means have to be adopted. I well know how expensive a journey can be, and my oft-repeated reminders that you ought to look about for private rooms will have told you that I foresaw that your stay in Mannheim would be a long one. I realized what you wanted to do and suspected at the same time that the fulfilment of your plan might be delayed and perhaps in the end come to nothing. Inns are expensive, especially if you take supper there, though indeed, if you are frequently invited to a late lunch at a good table, you can content yourself with soup at night. As it is, these landlords ask quite enough for a room and so forth. Farewell. I try to comfort myself as well as I can and I remain your

honest husband

MZT

(260) *Maria Anna Mozart to her Husband and Daughter*

[Autograph in the Mozarteum, Salzburg]

MANNHEIM, 14 December 1777

My dear Husband and Nannerl,

Thank God, we have left the inn at last and have a nice room now with two fine beds and an alcove in the house of a Privy Court Councillor.[1] I don't yet know his name. He has an excellent wife and a Mademoiselle of fifteen, who has been playing the clavier for eight years already and to

---

[1] Serrarius. See p. 414.

whom Wolfgang has to give lessons. For this we get free lodging, including wood and light. Wolfgang has his meals at Monsieur Wendling's and I go for mine to young Herr Danner's, who in return for this takes lessons in composition from my son. That is our present arrangement. Wolfgang has such an awful lot to do that he really doesn't know whether he is standing on his head or his heels. He lunched today with the wealthy Dutchman[1] who is giving him 200 gulden for some compositions. He hasn't come back yet and if he doesn't soon, I shan't be able to send off this letter. It is almost four o'clock now. I could not write before, as I was not lunching at home. I have not yet got our landlord's account. You cannot imagine in what high favour Wolfgang is here both with the orchestra and with other people. They all say that there is no one to touch him. They absolutely idolize his compositions. Often I do not see him all day long. I am at home alone most of the time, for on account of the cold and wet weather I cannot go out much, as I have no umbrella to put up when it snows or rains. The old and young Herren Danner send their greetings to you; and Wolfgang and I send our compliments to the whole population of Salzburg. I wish I could be with you just for one day so that I could have a chat with you, for in a letter it is impossible to describe everything in detail. Well, I shall close this letter, for Wolfgang will not be able to write a great deal today. The post will be off in a moment. Addio. I kiss you and Nannerl many 1000 times and remain your faithful wife

MARIANNA MOZART

(260a) *Mozart to his Father*

[Autograph in the Mozarteum, Salzburg]

[MANNHEIM, 14 *December* 1777]

I can only write a few words. I did not get home until four o'clock, and had to give a lesson at once to the daughter of the house.[2] It is almost half past five now and therefore time to close this letter. I shall tell Mamma always to start writing a few days in advance, so that I shan't have a dozen things to do at once. For it's no longer easy for me to see to this; what little time I have for writing I must devote to composition, as I have a lot of work before me. As for my journey to Paris I implore you to let me have an answer quickly. I played through my concertone[3] to Herr Wendling on the clavier. He remarked that it was just the thing for Paris.

---

[1] De Jean (or Dechamps). See p. 414.   [2] Therese Pierron Serrarius.
[3] K. 190 [186e], composed in 1773.

When I play it to Baron Bagge,[1] he's quite beside himself. Adieu.

A fine handwriting and a glorious rigmarole, eh? I kiss your hands 100000 times and embrace my sister with all my heart and remain your most obedient son

WOLFGANG AMADÉ MOZART

My greetings to everyone in Salzburg and especially to Herr Bullinger.

(261) *Leopold Mozart to his Son*

[Extract]   *[Autograph in the Mozarteum, Salzburg]*

MON TRÈS CHER FILS!   SALZBURG, 15 *December* 1777

In the name of Heaven! Patience! For I too have nothing to say. Surely your business must be over by now—not at the moment of writing, but by the time you read this letter, which will be about the 21st. Almighty God grant that in accordance with His most holy will everything has turned out well. ⟨*If you have not been retained then you will have surely received a handsome sum for your travelling expenses.*⟩ I take it that you used your ⟨expenses in the inn⟩, your *total* expenses, as an excuse? ⟨*It would have pleased me best of all if you had been able to settle in Mannheim.*⟩ If I had been in your shoes, ⟨I should have *gone on teaching the Rondo and the variations to the children*. For, even if the Elector had not *given you a large salary now*, he would *soon have raised it.*⟩ Enough! We must resign ourselves to the will of God. But we must always do our best, and for that reason must always ⟨*take thought.*⟩ Have you ⟨*finished composing the ballets for Herr Cannabich?*⟩[2] I should have left myself plenty of time for that. From the very first moment when you told me of this business, I formed the opinion, and still hold it, that the only way to achieve success was ⟨through the children, or rather through the governess, and by thus *obtaining the opportunity of speaking to the Elector himself.* For although *Count Savioli*⟩ may mean well as far as you are concerned (a thing about which one can never be too sure in this wicked world), yet ⟨he may *not have the opportunity*⟩ of raising the matter very often or even have the courage to do so. Now I have nothing more to write about. I pity you, my dear wife, for having to suffer so from the cold, although you pay 24 kreuzer a day for heating. And it must be even worse now, as we too have been having for some time the most extraordinarily cold weather. If I were you, I should look up and visit somebody who has a warm room, and whenever

---

[1] Baron Karl Ernst von Bagge (1718–1791), whose musical salon in Paris was famous. The Mozart family had met him in Paris in 1764. See Leopold Mozart's *Reiseaufzeichnungen*, p. 29. For a study of Baron Bagge see G. Cucuel, 'Le Baron de Bagge et son temps', in *L'Année Musicale*, no. 1, 1912.   [2] See p. 408.

I had to be at home, I should get into bed, rest my back against the pillows and cover myself up to the waist and then read or knit or sew or even play cards, or tell my fortune with the cards. If anyone should chance to call, you could say that you have a slight headache or make some other excuse. I should certainly do this rather than suffer from cold. You have both been away now for three months, that is, a quarter of a year. To me it already seems a year.

Is it necessary for me to ask whether Wolfgang is not getting a little lax perhaps ⟨about confession?⟩ God must come first! From His hands we receive our temporal happiness; and at the same time we must think of our eternal salvation. Young people do not like to hear about these things, I know, for I was once young myself. But, thank God, in spite of all my youthful foolish pranks, I always pulled myself together. I avoided all dangers to my soul and ever kept God and my honour and the consequences, the *very dangerous consequences* of foolishness, before my eyes. We have no news at all. We and all our good friends send you our greetings. We kiss you millions of times and while awaiting news from you constantly—and patiently, I remain your husband and father

MZT

Your daughter and sister

NANNERL

Nothing more is being said about Haydn's journey. We still have time to wish you a Happy New Year.

A propos!—Is Wolfgang's beard going to be cut off, singed off, or shaved off?

(262) *Leopold Mozart to his Son*

[*Extract*]   [*Autograph in the Mozarteum, Salzburg*]

MON TRÉS CHER FILS!   SALZBURG, 18 *December* 1777

The news contained in your letter of the 10th about the unfavourable result of your famous affair did not find me quite unprepared, for I had already hinted as much to Bullinger and your sister, and indeed I never expected anything else. You too will have gathered this from my letters. It is true that I should have been glad if you had been successful, for you could have undertaken other journeys from Mannheim from time to time just the same. Further you will have noticed in all my letters that I have been keeping my eye on Paris. I must now write to you very fully. You know that for many years certain people[1] in Salzburg have been trying our patience and you know how often you and I have longed to clear out. No doubt you still remember what objections I used to raise

---

[1] i.e. the Archbishop.

to our doing this, and how I would point out that it would be impossible for us all to leave. You now realize these difficulties, that is, the great expenses of travelling and the impossibility of making enough money to defray them, especially with a whole family. I could not let you travel alone, because you were not accustomed to attend to everything or to be independent of the help of others and because you knew so little about different currencies and nothing whatever about foreign money. Moreover you had not the faintest idea about packing nor about the innumerable necessary arrangements which crop up on journeys. I used to point out to you that, even if you were to remain in Salzburg until you were a little over twenty, you would not necessarily be wasting your time, which you could spend in dipping into other useful branches of knowledge and in training your reason by reading good books in several languages. Further, I used to remind you that it takes time for a young man, even one of such extraordinary gifts that he surpasses all other masters, to win the esteem which he deserves. Indeed several years are necessary; and as long as the young man is under twenty, his enemies and persecutors will certainly attribute his possible lack of success to his youth and slight experience. Have you the slightest doubt that such considerations were put forward to ⟨*the Elector in regard to the instruction of his natural children?*⟩ I am indeed as little fond of cringing as you are; and you will remember that while you were in Munich, I told you that you should not make yourself *so cheap*; and that all those attempts to collect ten persons who would so arrange matters that you might stay on there, seemed to me *far too cringing*. But kind-hearted and well-meaning friends persuaded you to do so—fires of straw, I call them, which quickly flare up—and end in smoke. Yet doubtless it was well meant! It is true that I should like you to have an appointment, but only one, such as you might find in Munich or Mannheim, which would enable you to travel from time to time. And I think too that you should not make a contract for life. Now for your journey to Paris, where indeed I wish you were already. This was precisely my objection to your disastrously long stay at Mannheim. It is only natural that the gentlemen with whom you are going to travel to Paris should not let you go on without them. They need a fourth; and where will they get such *a fourth* as you are? That Herr Wendling is your friend, that he means well, that he knows Paris, that he will take great care of you —all that I do not doubt for a moment. And that he will try to arrange for you to be supported in Mannheim until March, I do not doubt that either. For it is very important that he should have your company. All friendships have their motives. If this Dutch gentleman[1] gives you 200 gulden, then you can keep going in Mannheim, especially if you go to Wendling's for lunch. Supposing Mamma spends 3 gulden a week for

---

[1] De Jean (or Dechamps).

food, that is 12 gulden a month; or perhaps Cannabich or Wendling would feed her at the rate of 4 gulden a week, which would be 16 gulden a month—then how much does a room cost by the month? If you get 200 gulden from your Dutchman and together you spend 50 gulden a month, that is, 100 gulden in two months; and if you can get a couple of pupils, you will still have 100 gulden to spare; and if you have free board, how can you each spend 50 gulden a month? In short! I quite approve of your present arrangement. But that you should be living with a Court Councillor[1]—whose name you do not seem to know—and that Mamma should have to live alone, *that I simply will not have*. As long as Mamma is in Mannheim, you and she must live together. *You should not and must not leave Mamma alone and at the mercy of other people*, as long as she is with you. However small her room may be, space can surely be found for a bed for you—and in any case why not take a larger room? It will cost a couple of gulden more, of course, but that is no great expense for two months and will certainly be only half the amount that you were paying at the inn. If only you had done what I told you in my letters to Augsburg and in subsequent ones, that is, that on reaching Mannheim *you should look for a private room at once*, you would have saved a good deal of money. Mamma ought to remember how we travelled long ago. I never used to stay at inns in towns where I thought we were going to make a long sojourn. For instance, I know nothing about inns in Paris, London, Vienna, or even Brünn. You will realize that Mamma cannot leave Mannheim now that really cold weather is setting in. Besides, I must think out the easiest and most convenient way to bring her home. In the meantime be sure you stay with her and care for her, so that she may lack nothing, for indeed she cares for you. But if the 200 gulden, which the Indian[2] is going to give you, have turned out to be only another fire of straw which has flamed up in the first excitement of friendship and has already ended in smoke, then pack up and go. But if they are genuine gulden, then set to and carry out his commission; and I agree that it would be a very good thing if you were to write a new grand mass for the Elector. So during the next two months you will have to be methodical with your time. ⟨It would be well for you to write to Prince Zeill and say that you are not asking the Elector to give you a permanent appointment, but that *you would like him to take you on for a couple of years*, so that you might have the opportunity and the privilege of serving him and giving him proofs of your *talent*.⟩ I shall write also by the next post. Then you must write to Herr Grimm as I shall too. Herr Bullinger and all our good friends send their greetings. Nannerl and I kiss you millions of times and I am your devoted father

MZT

---

[1] Serrarius.   [2] De Jean (or Dechamps).

We send our regards to the whole Cannabich and Wendling households.

MY DEAR WIFE!

My letter above contains my reply about the question of this journey to Paris with Herr Wendling. But I want you and Wolfgang to live together, provided that it is all right about the 200 gulden. If there is any uncertainty, however, and no guarantee, then pack up and go off to Mainz at once. On your arrival in Mannheim you ought with the help of young Herr Danner or someone else to have looked about at once for private rooms. You ought to have done this and disregarded the objections of other people. I mentioned it so often—and yet you did not do it and as a result it has been to our loss. You say that you sent me Albert's account. *Not a trace of it!* It is quite evident from your letters that you both always scribble them off in a hurry, at night and when you are half asleep, and that you just jot down whatever occurs to you at the moment. Probably you yourself, therefore, do not remember what you have written, and I wager that you hardly ever read a letter which Wolfgang has written to me. By Heaven! You are nice folk! I can well believe that the price of food has gone up with the general rise; but postal fees have remained the same. I myself had already worked out that you must have spent a great deal of money. Well, well! If you had read my letters carefully, you would have known what to do, even if you had arrived in Mainz without a farthing. However, it can't be helped. ⟨*Nobody worked against Wolfgang more than Vogler.*⟩ I said so long ago to Bullinger and Nannerl. If it is true that you are to get 200 gulden from the Dutchman, then I shall have to think out how you can come home later on. For you could not do so now; it would be far too cold for you, particularly as the cold generally becomes most severe at Christmas and Twelfth Night. Besides, how are you going to travel? In our chaise? And quite alone? This all requires very careful consideration. Once you reach Augsburg, it will be easy. Do you think that Wolfgang will now attend to his affairs? I hope he has got accustomed to doing this and that his head is not always full of music. Farewell to you both. I am

your old husband

MZT

(263) Maria Anna Mozart to her Husband

[Autograph in the Mozarteum, Salzburg]

MY DEAR HUSBAND,   MANNHEIM, 18 *December* 1777

We have received all your letters safely and up to the present have not missed a single one. But the postage fee here is much higher than in

Salzburg. We have to pay twelve kreuzers for every letter we receive or send, and eighteen kreuzers if it is a large one. Since our arrival we have already spent more than six gulden on postage. For things are done here in the French style. We now have a perfectly splendid room with two beautiful beds and full service. The Privy Court Councillor's name is Serrarius. His wife is very charming to us. I have supper with them every evening and chat to the wife and daughter until half past ten. They would like me to spend every afternoon with them. I cannot tell you what a high opinion they have of my son. They only regret that he cannot spend all his time with them. A distinguished Lutheran came to see us today and has invited Wolfgang most courteously to try the new organ in the Lutheran church. All the Kapellmeisters who are in Mannheim are to be present. He is to try it at three o'clock this afternoon. He has so much to do that he really doesn't know whether he is standing on his head or his heels; what with composing and giving lessons he hasn't time to visit anybody. So you see we can stop here for the winter quite comfortably, and all this is due to Monsieur Wendling, who loves Wolfgang as his own son. The inkeeper's bill, which has pretty well emptied our purses, amounted to 111 gulden, and I gave 3 gulden in tips to the waiters and maids. It would have been better, of course, if we had taken rooms sooner, but they are very dear here. A furnished room alone costs three to four gulden a week and on top of that other necessities have to be purchased. And our affairs have always been so unsettled that we have never known from one day to another whether we are leaving or staying on. It would not have been worth our while to move out for three or four days. All this time I have been worried and anxious about living in this uncertainty and being bottled up in an inn. Every day I wanted to go to some other house. We still have 72 gulden left of our whole capital. We drew 150 gulden from Herr Schmalz; otherwise we could not have paid our landlord. With this sum and what Wolfgang is going to make during the winter we must meet our travelling expenses. For, as you are already aware, one needs a lot of money in Paris. Even here our expenses are quite heavy enough, and that too although we have free board and lodging. For there is our laundry, which is very expensive in Mannheim shoes, hair powder, pomade and other trifles which I cannot recall at the moment, but all of which cost money, so that the whole time one has to keep forking out. I really don't know how I could live more economically. Since I left Salzburg I have only had one cap made and not a single pair of shoes. I never took wine at the inn unless Wolfgang was having a meal there, and then we had a glass together. Yet our account has mounted up to such a figure. The room, fire and candles alone came to 30 gulden for the six weeks; and our room was under the roof and had two wretched beds; my feet were never warm the whole day long and I used to sit in my fur and my felt shoes. So you can imagine how happy I am to be able to lie in comfort for once and to have a fine warm room, praise and thanks be to God. I trust that Almighty God who has ordered everything so well will give us all the other things we desire, if they are good for us. Everything has been arranged so satisfactorily—when we were least thinking that it would. I promised a Holy Mass at the Holy Child of Loreto, and also in Maria-Plain, which I beg you to have said, perhaps at the Child of Loreto at once and later on in Maria-Plain when the weather is warmer, so that Nannerl can go out there. Both of these are for my protection on our journey and I put my whole trust in them, for I shall certainly not be forsaken. I have no other news beyond what you must know already, that is, that the English have suffered a crushing defeat at the hands of the Americans and that a whole regiment has been captured.[1] Schweitzer's new opera[2] is being rehearsed every day. Wolfgang does not like it at all. He says there is nothing natural about it, that it is all exaggerated and that it is not composed to suit the singers. We must wait and see whether the performance will be a success. I wish you and Nannerl a happy Christmas and New Year. I have to write in good time, since you always get our letters so late. Keep well and cheerful until our next joyful meeting. Please give my compliments to all our good friends, especially to Monsieur Bullinger and Mlle Sallerl. I have greetings to deliver from our acquaintances here, some of whom you know and some of whom you do not. Addio. I kiss you both many 10000 times and remain as always your faithful wife until death

MARIANNA MOZART

I send warm greetings to Theresa.

Pimperl, I suppose, is still quite well. Has she never been snarly since we left? Has she never had an attack of hydrophobia? I was indoors all day today, as I had a heavy cold and could only take some soup, which Herr Danner sent in to me. I hope to get out tomorrow, if it is God's will. Addio. I kiss you both again.

(263a) *Mozart to his Father*

[Autograph in the Mozarteum, Salzburg]

[MANNHEIM, 18 *December* 1777]

At top speed and in the greatest hurry. The organ in the Lutheran church which has just been tried today is very good, both in the full and

---

[1] Probably a reference to Burgoyne's unsuccessful operations against Gates in September and October, which led to the surrender of the former at Saratoga on 17 October 1777. The French immediately concluded a treaty with the revolted colonies, which was, however, not signed until 6 November 1778.   [2] *Rosemunde.*

in single stops. Vogler played it. He is, to put it bluntly, a trickster pure and simple. As soon as he tries to play maestoso, he becomes as dry as dust; and it is a great relief that playing upon the organ bores him and that therefore it doesn't last long. But what is the result? An unintelligible muddle. I listened to him from a distance. He then began a fugue, in which one note was struck six times and presto. Whereupon I went up to him. Indeed I would much rather watch him than hear him. There was a whole crowd of people there, including many of the musicians, Holzbauer, Cannabich, Toeschi and so forth. I shall soon have finished one quartet[1] for the Indian Dutchman,[2] that true friend of humanity. A propos, Herr Wendling told me yesterday that he had written to you by the last post. Addio. My greetings to everyone in Salzburg. I kiss your hands 100000 times and embrace my sister with all my heart. Oh what a fine handwriting! I am your most obedient son

WOLFGANG AMADÉ MOZART

I had to conduct the opera[3] at Wendling's the other day with a few violins, in place of Schweitzer who was indisposed.

(264) *Maria Anna Mozart to her Husband*

[*Autograph in the Mozarteum, Salzburg*]

MY DEAR HUSBAND,   MANNHEIM, 20 *December* 1777

I have received this very moment your letter of the 15th and am delighted to hear that you are both well. Thank God, we are too. Wolfgang is out and therefore will not read your letter until eleven o'clock tonight when he gets home. I wrote to you on the 10th that all was well with us. These last two days I have not been out of doors, for the weather has been both wet and cold. Wolfgang and I are lunching, tomorrow, Sunday, with our landlord, Privy Court Councillor Serrarius; so that is why I am writing today. If I left it until tomorrow, we might get away too late for us to write, for the post leaves at six o'clock in the evening. What you say about confessing, we already did at the Feast of the Immaculate Conception. We rarely hear Mass during the week, I must admit, for daylight is so late now that it is impossible for us to get out in time and the last Mass is at eleven o'clock and the church is a good distance from this house. But on Sundays and Holy days we can go to the Pfarrkirche. Indeed Wolfgang goes every Sunday to High Mass at the Hofkirche in order to hear the music. I have no news whatever for you, for during the last two days nothing has happened. From now on I

---

[1] K. 285.   [2] De Jean (or Dechamps).   [3] Schweitzer's new opera *Rosemunde*.

shall write once a week, which is much more sensible, because every letter, big or small, costs twelve kreuzers; and moreover the post-days, which are Thursday and Saturday, are so close together that it is much simpler to write once only. We have not yet called in the barber to deal with Wolfgang's beard: we have just been cutting it with scissors. But this will not do much longer and the barber will soon have to tackle it. We send all sorts of messages to Sallerl and to our best friend Herr Bullinger.

(264a) *Mozart to his Father*

[Autograph in the Mozarteum, Salzburg]

[MANNHEIM, 20 *December* 1777]

I wish you, dearest Papa, a very happy New Year, and hope that every day your health, which is so precious to me, may get better and better, to the advantage and delight of your wife and children, to the satisfaction of your true friends and to the vexation and annoyance of your enemies! I beg you during the coming year to love me with the same fatherly affection as you have shown me hitherto! I for my part shall endeavour to my utmost to deserve more and more the love of so excellent a father. Your last letter, dated December 15th, gave me the greatest pleasure, as it told me that, praise and thanks be to God, you are quite well. We two, God again be thanked, are in excellent health. I can't help being so, for I certainly get enough exercise. I am writing this at eleven o'clock at night, for it is the only time I am free. We can't get up before eight o'clock, for until half past eight there is no daylight in our room, which is on the ground floor. I dress in haste and at ten I sit down to compose until about twelve or half past twelve. Then I go to Wendling's, where I again compose a little until half past one, when we have lunch. Thus the time passes until three, when I go off to the Mainzischer Hof (an inn) to a Dutch officer[1] to give him a lesson in galanterie and thoroughbass, for which I receive, if I am not mistaken, four ducats for twelve lessons. At four I must be home again to instruct the daughter of the house. We never begin our lesson before half past four, as we have to wait for the lights. At six I go to Cannabich's and give Mlle Rosa her lesson. I stay there to supper, after which we talk or occasionally someone plays. If it is the latter, I always take a book out of my pocket and read—as I used to do in Salzburg. I have just said that your last letter gave me great pleasure. That is true! But one thing upset me a little bit—your enquiry as to whether I wasn't perhaps getting a little lax about confession. I have nothing to say to this; but just let me ask you one thing, and that is, not

---

[1] De La Pottrie.

to have such a bad opinion of me. I like to enjoy myself, but rest assured that I can be as serious as anyone else can. Since I left Salzburg (and even in Salzburg itself) I have come across people who, although they are ten, twelve and thirty years my senior, have talked and behaved in such a way as I should blush to imitate. So once more I beg you most humbly to think better of me. Please give my greetings to Herr Bullinger, my very best friend, and convey to him my heartiest wishes for the New Year. Remember me to all my good friends, and particularly to Father Dominic.[1]

My dearest Rosie, O sweetheart mine,
My dearest Nan, O sister mine.
Angel, a thousand thanks for your excellent wishes.
And here is one from Mozart, that queerest of fishes.
Good luck and happiness, if such things be, to you.
I trust you will love me, as Woferl loves you too.
And truthfully I tell you that you he does admire
And, if you were to ask him, would rush into the fire.
Exactly as he says them, his words do I impart,
And I see it all so clearly, that passion in his heart
For his sweet Rosie Joli and his dear sister Nan.
Ah, come away, you darlings! A dance for maid and man!
Long life to all you dear ones, Papa and my Mamma,
My sister and her brother! Hey sassa! Houp sassa!
And Woferl too and also the mistress of his heart.
And this for evermore, my dears, as long as he can fart,
As long as he can piddle and shit it with the best,
So long will he and Rosie and Nan and all be blest—
A charming crew! Alas, to bed I now must creep,
For I hear it stricking midnight, when we all should be asleep.

WOLFGANG AMADÈ MOZART
MARIA ANNA MOZART[2]

(265) *Leopold Mozart to his Wife and Son*

[Extract]   [Autograph in the Mozarteum, Salzburg]

SALZBURG, [21]-22 *December* 1777

MY DEAR WIFE AND DEAR SON!

I sent you in my last letter my views about your journey to Paris. I am delighted to see from your letter of December 14th that you have left

---

[1] Dominicus Hagenauer, who in 1764 had become a priest and for whom Mozart wrote in 1769 his mass K. 66.
[2] Her signature is in Mozart's handwriting.

the inn and are now well provided for on the whole for the next two months. Herr Wendling, to whom I was going to write by this post, has anticipated me. I had no time to write to him last post-day, as I had to write to Padre Maestro Martini, to tell him about the portrait which I had already dispatched.[1]

I wrote the above yesterday, Sunday, December 21st, on my return home after the Horary Service, when your mass in B flat major[2] was performed, in which the castrato[3] sang most excellently. In the evening Johannes Hagenauer came to tell me that Count Castelbarco had arrived at the 'Schiffwirth' that very moment. I went off there at once, but was told that he had just gone out and would be leaving again in an hour to join his brother, the officer, in Schwanenstadt, but that he would be back again in Salzburg in five or six days, when he would be staying for some time. The servant, on hearing my name, which I was asked to leave, exclaimed: 'Oh, lo conosco, il padre di quel giovane che ha scritto tre opere in Milano. Non manchèro di presentare i suoi rispetti ed attenzioni al mio padrone.'[4]

Adlgasser, who died today, is to be buried tomorrow night, and on the 24th there will be a service at St. Sebastian's.[5] Who will be the new organist, I wonder? Who will teach in the Kapellhaus? And who will instruct the Countess's[6] daughters? I am thankful that neither Nannerl nor I have had anything to do with them. She will probably try to find an opportunity of speaking to me. His Excellency the Chief Steward[7] sent for me today after my lesson at Arco's.[8] He wanted to see me, because he likes you so much and was wondering whether he ought not to put your name forward to the Archbishop for the post of organist. I thanked him for his kind proposal, which I declined, and said that it was quite out of the question and explained a good deal to him. He replied that he was very much relieved and that he now had a load off his mind. You will both understand that *I must postpone my answer to Herr Wendling, to whom I send my most humble greetings*. The Adlgasser incident has prevented me. I must now go off to their house, help these people and make arrangements about the music for the service. God protect you. Mamma ought to write a good deal to us, but Wolfgang only a little, because he has so much to

---

[1] Leopold Mozart's letter to Padre Martini about his son's portrait is dated 22 December. See letter 266. He may refer to another letter which has been lost, but this is not likely.

[2] K. 275 [272b], composed in 1777.   [3] Francesco Ceccarelli.

[4] Oh, I know you, for you are the father of the youth who wrote three operas at Milan. I shall certainly present your respects and regards to my master.

[5] A portion of this letter, which has been omitted, contains a long description of Adlgasser's fatal seizure while playing the organ during a Vesper Service in the cathedral.

[6] Countess Lodron, the Archbishop's sister.

[7] Count von Firmian.

[8] Leopold Mozart taught the violin to Count Leopold Arco, son of Count Georg Anton Felix Arco, Chief Chamberlain to the Archbishop.

do. Nannerl plays his sonata[1] with the greatest expression. We kiss you millions of times and I am your old

MZT

(265a) *Nannerl Mozart to her Mother and Brother*

[Autograph in the Mozarteum, Salzburg]

[S<small>ALZBURG</small>, 22 December 1777[2]]

Since you have now become so distinguished and your time is so much taken up that you cannot write to me, probably you will have no time to read a few lines from me either. So with your permission I shall take the liberty of talking quite alone to Mamma. Besides it is going to be women's chat. I trust that you are both well and happy. Mamma was kind enough to tell me that the frisures and caps they wear in Mannheim are much prettier and that the women dress much more smartly than in Salzburg. That I can well believe. And if I am going to be fortunate enough to have my Mamma back here in two months, then I should like to ask her to be so good as to watch closely how that frisure is made and to bring a toupee cushion with her and whatever else is necessary for it and, if possible, a cap in the very latest fashion and anything else she may like to bring. If only I could make money by giving lessons as I did some time ago, I should love to have my garnet-red gown made into a Bolognese and trimmed with lawn. In that case, I might perhaps find a cheaper lawn in Mannheim. But I must banish all thoughts of new fashions like these. I am delighted that you now have a comfortable room and I trust that Mamma no longer suffers from the cold as she did at the inn. I must stop now, otherwise Papa will have no more room. I wish you both continual good health and I kiss Mamma's hand and embrace my brother.

(266) *Leopold Mozart to Padre Martini, Bologna*

[Autograph in the Deutsche Staatsbibliothek, Berlin]

[S<small>ALZBURG</small>, 22 December 1777[3]]

M<small>OST</small> R<small>EVEREND</small> P<small>ADRE</small> M<small>AESTRO</small>,
    M<small>OST</small> <small>ESTEEMED</small> F<small>ATHER</small>,

Tandem aliquando![4] For the last year my son has owed you a reply to your very kind letter of 18 December 1776, in which you were good enough to express your approval of his motet for four voices[5] and at the same time your desire to have a portrait of him and of myself. So far I

---

[1] K. 309 [284b], written for Rosa Cannabich.   [2] A postscript to her father's letter.
[3] This letter is in Italian.   [4] At last!
[5] K. 222 [205a], composed early in 1775 at Munich. See p. 266, n. 1.

have hesitated to send you these for lack of a competent artist, such as is not to be found in this part of the world. I kept on postponing it in the hope that, as sometimes happens, some good painter would pass through Salzburg. In the end, however, I had to make up my mind quickly and commission one of our own painters to carry out the work. Now listen to our story. For the last five years my son has been serving our Prince for *a miserable pittance* in the hope that his efforts and his slight knowledge coupled with his very great zeal and uninterrupted studies would in time be appreciated. But we were wrong! I refrain from giving you a full description of the manner in which our Prince prefers to think and act. Suffice it to say that he was not ashamed to declare that *my son knew nothing and that he ought to betake himself to some conservatorio of music at Naples and study music*. And why? Simply in order to make it quite clear that a young man in a subordinate position should not be so foolish as to feel convinced that he deserved better pay and more recognition, since he had heard that decisive statement from the lips of a Prince. The rest of the story will gradually find its way to Italy, where possibly it may be known already. This disappointment made me decide to allow my son to resign from the service and go off elsewhere. So he left Salzburg on September 23rd and after spending a short time at the Electoral Court of Munich he proceeded to Mannheim, where he is at present and in excellent health and whence he sends you his most devoted regards. He will remain there until the beginning of March, that is, until the carnival is over; and, God willing, he will be in Paris at the beginning of Lent. This is the reason which determined me to have the portrait painted before his departure and thereby to serve our dear Signor Padre Maestro. If with your usual goodness of heart you would be so kind as to send to His Highness the Elector a true account and a favourable description of my son, you would be performing a very fine act, the more so as two words from you are worth more than the warmest recommendation from a king. I flatter myself that possibly you may do so, when you are writing to Mannheim for the New Year. But, if the painting has not yet reached you, you will ask, where is the portrait? I gave it to the firm of Sigmund Haffner, merchant of Salzburg, who took it on the occasion of the Fair of St. Andrew to Bozen, whence he will endeavour to send it to you, addressed probably to Signor Brinsecchi at Bologna. The painting is of no great value as a work of art, but I assure you that it is an excellent likeness. My son is exactly like that. I have jotted down at the back of the portrait his name and his age. I now have another idea, and that is, to send you the beginnings of my son's compositions, starting with the cembalo sonatas written for Madame Victoire[1] and engraved in Paris *when he was seven years old*; then the sonatas he composed *when he was*

[1] K. 6, 7.

eight for the Queen of England,[1] which were engraved in London; then those he composed *at the age of nine* for the Princess of Nassau-Weilburg,[2] which were engraved in Holland, and so forth. To these I might add a short account of his travels and any noteworthy incidents. As for my portrait, I do not think that my snout deserves to be placed in the company of men of talent. If, however, you desire it, I shall endeavour to fulfil your wish, but solely on account of this one merit of mine, namely, that I have done my duty in the matter of cultivating the talent which God in his goodness has bestowed on my son. I beg you to continue to grant us your favour and protection, to take great care of your health and to remember that I am ever at your command and that I remain, most Reverend Padre, your command and that I remain, most Reverend Padre, your most humble, devoted and grateful servant

LEOPOLD MOZART

Salzburg, 22 December 1777.

I have mentioned the New Year and have almost forgotten to send you my wishes. But what would you like me to say? *I wish you good health*—that is all you need. May God say: Amen!

(267) *Mozart to his Father*

[Autograph in the Mozarteum, Salzburg]

MANNHEIM, 27 *December* 1777

MON TRÈS CHER PÉRE!

Fine paper this, isn't it? Indeed, I only wish I could produce something better! But it's too late now to get any other. You know already from our previous letters that Mamma and I now have excellent lodgings. I never intended that she should take rooms apart from me. But when Privy Court Councillor Serrarius was so kind as to offer to house us, *I naturally thanked him*; but that was all. I didn't accept. The other day I called on him with Herr Wendling and M. Dechamps, the valiant Dutchman, and just waited until he should start the subject again. At length he renewed his proposal and I thanked him and replied as follows: 'I realize how kind it is of you to honour me with an invitation to lodge with you, but I regret that unfortunately I cannot accept your generous offer. You will not take it amiss if I tell you that I do not like my Mamma to be separated from me without good cause, and, as things are, I know no reason why she should live in one part of the town and I in another. If I were to go to Paris, it would naturally be a very great advantage for me if she were not with me. But for the two months we shall be here, a few

[1] K. 10-15.   [2] K. 26-31.

gulden more or less will make no difference.' With this speech I achieved a *complete* fulfilment of my wishes, that is, that board and lodging for the two of us should not make us a penny the poorer. Well, I must now hurry upstairs to supper. We have been playing cards until this very minute, that is, half past ten. I went the other day with M. De La Potrie, the Dutch officer, who is my pupil, to the Reformed Church, and played on the organ for an hour and a half. I put my whole heart into it. Some time soon we, that is, the Cannabichs, Wendlings, Serrariuses and Mozarts, are going to the Lutheran church, where I shall have some good fun on the organ. I tried the full organ before during that test, about which I wrote to you, but didn't play much, only a prelude and a fugue. I have now added Herr Wieland to the list of my acquaintances.[1] But he doesn't know as much about me as I know about him, for he has never heard any of my compositions. I had imagined him to be quite different from what I found him. He strikes you as slightly affected in his speech. He has a rather childish voice; he keeps on quizzing you over his glasses; he indulges in a sort of pedantic rudeness, combined occasionally with a stupid condescension. But I am not surprised that he permits himself such behaviour here, even though he may be quite different in Weimar and elsewhere, for people stare at him as if he had dropped from Heaven. Everyone seems embarrassed in his presence, no one says a word or moves an inch; all listen intently to every word he utters; and it's a pity they often have to wait so long, for he has a defect of speech that makes him speak very slowly and he can't say half a dozen words without stopping. Apart from that, he is what we all know him to be, a most gifted fellow. He has a frightfully ugly face, covered with pock-marks, and he has a rather long nose. In height he is, I should say, a little taller than Papa. You must have no doubt about the Dutchman's 200 gulden. Well, I must close now, as I want to go on composing for a little while. One thing more. I suppose I had better not write to ⟨Prince Zeill⟩ just yet? You probably know the reason already, since Munich is nearer to Salzburg than to Mannheim, and therefore you must have heard ⟨that the Elector is dying of smallpox.⟩ It is quite true. This is bound to upset things a bit. Now, farewell. As for Mamma's journey home, I think it could most easily be arranged during Lent and in the company of some merchants. That's merely what I think; what I know beyond all question is that what meets with your approval will be the best for us, for you are Court Kapellmeister and a paragon of intelligence! Madame Robinig has said so. I kiss Papa's hands—you know Papa?—1000 times and embrace my sister with all my heart and in spite of my scratchy writing I remain your most obedient son and true and faithful brother

WOLFGANG AMADÉ MOZART

[1] Wieland arrived at Mannheim on 21 December.

(267a) *Maria Anna Mozart to her Husband*

[*Autograph in the Mozarteum, Salzburg*]

MANNHEIM, 28 *December* [1777]

I have received this very moment your letter of December 22nd. I am truly sorry about Herr Adlgasser's sad and rapid death, which was indeed very sudden and gave me a great shock.[1] The poor wife and children are greatly to be pitied. She will be inconsolable, for I know her, as you do too, and also the reason why she will be inconsolable.[2] We did not write to you last post-day. The last time I told you that, thank God, we were very well. I usually spend the whole afternoon with the wife of the Privy Court Councillor and have supper with them every evening. Everyone thinks the world of Wolfgang, but indeed he plays quite differently from what he used to in Salzburg—for there are pianofortes here, on which he plays so extraordinarily well that people say they have never heard the like. In short everyone who has heard him says that he has not got his equal. Although Beecke has been performing here and Schubart too, yet everyone says that Wolfgang far surpasses them in beauty of tone, quality and execution. And they are all positively amazed at the way he plays out of his head and reads off whatever is put before him. Please tell Nannerl that lawn is not at all cheap in Mannheim and also that no coloured lawn is worn, only white. I shall see whether I can bring the cap with me. The trimming here is very charming and will certainly please her. Greetings to all our acquaintances and friends, especially to Herr Bullinger and Jungfer Sallerl, from myself and Wolfgang. I send greetings to Theresa and my compliments too to Herr Gött. And once more I wish you a happy New Year, a better one than the last, and especially that you, my dear husband, may keep well and live happily, and that we may have a joyful meeting in the coming year. Addio. I kiss you many 1000 times and I remain as always your faithful wife

MARIA ANNA MOZART

(268) *Leopold Mozart to his Wife and Son*

[*Extract*]   [*Autograph in the Mozarteum, Salzburg*]

SALZBURG, 29 *December* 1777

MY DEAR WIFE AND DEAR WOLFGANG,

We both wish you a very happy New Year! God grant that the year 1778 may bring us more happiness than the last. We trust to God's grace

---

[1] See p. 431, n. 5.
[2] Obviously a reference to the small pension which Frau Adlgasser would receive from the Archbishop.

and mercy and to the talent, industry and intelligence, but particularly to the good heart, of our dear Wolfgang, who will certainly do his utmost to win glory, honour and money in order to help us and to save his father from the scornful mockery and sneers of certain persons, whose names I dare not mention, but whose ridicule would, as you know, most certainly send me to my grave. Wolfgang's good fortune and success will be our sweetest revenge, of which, as you will see, we are already tasting a little. Count Starhemberg[1] happened to be with Count Arco the other day. The conversation turned on Adlgasser's death. *Count Arco.* You are in a fix, are you not? Young Mozart would now have rendered you good service. *Count Starhemberg.* Very true. He ought to have had patience a little longer. *Count Arco.* Patience? How absurd! Who could have foreseen this sudden death—and besides, what would you have given him apart from his few dirty gulden? It is a good thing for him that he has cleared out. You have all treated him abominably quite long enough. *Count Starhemberg.* Yes, I admit, he was treated very badly. Everyone allows that he is the most competent clavier-player in Europe. But all the same he could have waited a little longer. *Count Arco, very heatedly.* Well, let's chuck it! He is quite happy in Mannheim, where he has found good companions with whom he is going off to Paris. You will never get Mozart back again. And serve you right! You will have precisely the same experience with Hagenauer.[2] *Count Starhemberg.* Hagenauer is to have a salary from the beginning of next year. *Count Arco.* A fine salary it'll be, to be sure—and even if he gets one, you have made sport of him and led him by the nose quite long enough. Then the conversation turned on myself—in which connexion Count Starhemberg declared that he believed *that no more competent teacher could be found.* You will notice that Count Arco kept on saying 'You—you—' that is, he lumped Count Starhemberg and company together in order not to have to mention the Prince.

Who do you think has been made organist at Holy Trinity? Herr Haydn! Everybody is laughing. He will be an expensive item, as after every Litany he swills a quart of wine and sends Lipp,[3] who is also a tippler, to do the other services. Meanwhile Spitzeder is to instruct the chapel boys in the clavier until something definite has been decided. We now kiss you millions of times, the sheet is full and I am your old

                             MZT

[1] Count Josef Starhemberg, canon of Salzburg Cathedral.
[2] Johann Baptist Hagenauer, architect to the Salzburg court. He settled later in Vienna.
[3] Franz Ignaz Lipp, second organist in the Cathedral and father-in-law of Michael Haydn.

(268a) *Nannerl Mozart to her Mother and Brother*

[*Autograph in the Mozarteum, Salzburg*]

[SALZBURG, 29 *December* 1777[1]]

I wish Mamma and my dearest brother a joyful New Year, good health and happiness. I hope that Mamma will soon return to us in good health; and as for you, my dear brother, I wish that, wherever you may go, you may be successful and also enjoy good health; and as for myself, I should like to have the pleasure of seeing you soon again, provided it is not in Salzburg. I send greetings to Mamma as her obedient daughter and to my brother as his faithful sister and friend. Katherl Gilowsky sends New Year wishes to you both. We had our shooting yesterday. Bullinger contributed the target which the Paymaster won. On New Year's Day Mamma is to provide the target. As cashier for us both I should state that I am quite satisfied with my cash-box, for until Mamma returns, her losses will not have been very great. Please forgive me for not writing more often or more fully; but, as you see, Papa hardly leaves me any room and, when he does, it is only a tiny bit.

(269) *Maria Anna Mozart to her Husband*

[*Autograph in the Mozarteum, Salzburg*]

MANNHEIM, 3 *January* 1778

I received yesterday, January 2nd, the letter you enclosed to Herr Wendling and was delighted to hear that you are both well. Thank God, we also are in good health. But on account of the death of the Elector of Bavaria[2] everyone here is in the deepest mourning; there are no operas (for which I am truly sorry); all plays, balls, concerts, sleigh-drives, music, everything has been stopped. The courier arrived from Munich at seven o'clock on the evening of the 31st with the sad news that the Elector had died at one o'clock on the previous afternoon. Our Elector left for Munich at ten o'clock on the evening of New Year's Day and has arrived there long since. God grant that everything may turn out well and that no troubles may come. I wish it with all my heart, for he is a very good ruler. Here it is deadly quiet and thoroughly boring, and in Munich it must be even more so. That I can well imagine. Salzburg will be a much jollier place this winter, for the carnival will last a long time. Well, how is Frau Adlgasser? Remember me to her. I sympathise with her with my whole heart. Those poor children are to be pitied. Victoria

---

[1] A postscript to her father's letter.
[2] The Elector Maximilian III had died on 30 December 1777.

will probably not stay with her, and indeed who could blame her? *Today, Sunday, January 4th.* I received yesterday evening your letter of December 29th and was delighted to read how old ⟨Count Arco⟩ gave Count ⟨Starhemberg⟩ such a fine dressing-down. He really wishes us well, I believe. It does my heart good to hear that they are realizing at last what they have lost in Wolfgang. It was ⟨very mean⟩ of Herr Haydn to take the post of organist at Holy Trinity. I thought he went to Italy in order to become a Kapellmeister. What is Kapellmeister Rust doing? Is he still in Salzburg? Has he recovered or not? Is Herr von Schiedenhofen not getting married this carnival to Fräulein Nannerl and Herr von Mölk to Fräulein Josepha? Is Franz Barisani still in Salzburg? Give him our best regards. People are anxiously awaiting today a courier from Bavaria to hear whether the Elector arrived safely and what is happening there. God grant that everything may turn out well. I wish it with all my heart. Please give Katherl Gilowsky my New Year wishes and greetings and the same to all my other good friends. It would indeed be a very good thing if you could arrange for a letter of introduction from someone in Vienna to the Queen.[1] I have no more news to send you, for I am not very well known here, and there is very little in Mannheim that could interest you. But I know everyone and everything in Salzburg. So you can write and tell me all that is happening; and there is far more news there than here. Addio. Keep well, both of you. I kiss you many 100000 times and remain as always your old faithful wife

MARIANNA MOZART

Wolfgang has not come home yet. Whether he will get back in time to add a few lines I really don't know. He has a lot of composing to do, time simply flies and he has, as it were, to steal it. For how can it be otherwise when he must go to one place for his meals, to another to compose and give lessons, and to yet another when he wants to sleep?

(269a) *Mozart to his Father*

[Autograph in the Mozarteum, Salzburg]

[MANNHEIM, January 4 1778]

I hope that you are both quite well. I am in excellent health, thank God. As you may readily imagine, I am greatly distressed at the death of the Elector of Bavaria. All that I hope is that the Elector here will succeed to the whole of Bavaria and move to Munich. I think that you too would be quite satisfied with such an arrangement. At noon today Karl Theodor was proclaimed here at court Duke of Bavaria. In Munich

---

[1] Marie-Antoinette.

too, immediately after the death of the Elector, Count Daun, the Chief Equerry, claimed allegiance on behalf of our Elector and got the dragoons to ride round the whole town with trumpets and drums, shouting 'Long live our Elector Karl Theodor'. If all goes well, as I hope it will, Count Daun will get a rather pretty present. His adjutant, a certain Lilienau whom he sent here with news of the death, got 3000 gulden from the Elector. Now farewell. I kiss your hands 1000 times and embrace my sister with all my heart and remain

WOLF: MOZART

A tous mes amis des compliments.

(270) *Leopold Mozart to his Son*

[Extract]   [Autograph in the Mozarteum, Salzburg]

MON TRES CHER FILS!   SALZBURG, 5 *January* 1778

On the 30th the Elector of Bavaria passed over into eternity. In the afternoon of the same day His Highness the Elector of Mannheim was proclaimed Duke of Bavaria, and on the following day all government departments and the army had to take the oath of allegiance. Meanwhile news has come that on Friday, January 2nd, the Elector of Mannheim arrived in Munich very quietly and quite alone, that is to say, accompanied only by a courtier, Count or Baron Vieregg. You can easily imagine that here too people are wishing that things may remain as they are. I had to laugh very heartily today, for it was rumoured in town that the Elector was going to appoint you Kapellmeister in Munich, as old Bernasconi[1] is no longer able to perform his duties. It is said here that news has come from Vöcklabruck that the ⟨Imperial soldiers⟩ who are encamped there and also near Wels, have received orders to ⟨get ready to march:⟩ moreover, Trumpeter Schwarz's son is said to have written something to the same effect from Bohemia. God preserve us! that would be a nice business![2] But we shall soon know. In regard to Mamma's return journey I have been thinking for some time that the most convenient way would be for her to travel in one of the empty coaches which come to fetch merchants in Salzburg. But the problem is, *how is she to travel from Mannheim to Augsburg?* If she could find some suitable means, our chaise could be sold

---

[1] Andrea Bernasconi (1706–1784) had been Kapellmeister at the Munich court since 1755. He was the stepfather and teacher of the famous singer Antonia Bernasconi.

[2] The outcome of these events was the war of the Bavarian Succession. As the Bavarian line of Electors had died out, Karl Theodor, as head of the elder dynasty of the House of Wittelsbach and in consequence of certain agreements, became the lawful heir to the Bavarian territories. He came to an agreement with the Emperor Joseph II (the Pact of Vienna, signed on 15 January 1778), which Frederick the Great regarded as an infringement of his rights. With Saxony as his ally, Frederick invaded Bohemia in July 1778. After the Peace of Teschen, May 1779, the Pact of Vienna was annulled.

in Mannheim. If not, she will have to travel in the chaise to Augsburg and leave it at the Holy Cross Monastery until my brother finds an opportunity of selling it. For, as you will be four people on your journey to Paris, you will not be able to use it. At the same time it would fetch a better price in Mannheim, where everything is dear. From Augsburg Mamma will be able to reach Salzburg in three days. Some of the hired coachmen leave there on March 9th, some on the 10th, to fetch the merchants; and she could travel very comfortably in a closed glass-windowed coach for four. I once did the journey home for a max d'or. If she prefers to travel with the merchants when they come to Salzburg, it may be a little difficult to arrange, as they generally make up parties of four. But whatever she chooses, I can in any case settle it through my brother. The main question, however, is, *which is the best way for her to travel from Mannheim to Augsburg?* The other portion of the journey I can arrange, provided we think about it in good time. *Time flies*; and I should much prefer her to make the fourth in a party travelling to Salzburg. *I could then let you know at what date she ought to be in Augsburg.* As for the chaise, I paid *about* 80 *gulden* for it, but you will surely find some friend to value it for you; and if Mamma cannot use it, mind you sell it as advantageously as possible. In Mannheim, at least, people surely cannot buy much of a carriage for eight louis d'or. If, however, Mamma has no suitable opportunity of travelling to Augsburg, then some *honest* traveller might perhaps be glad to accompany her in her comfortable chaise and she could charge him his post-chaise fare. But you would, of course, have to know something about him. Further, if, as I wish and hope, the Elector remains in peaceful possession of his new dukedom, somebody will be travelling from time to time from Munich to Mannheim, whom she could accompany; and once she is in Munich, she can then hire a coachman and drive home. But everything depends on how you think that she can get to Augsburg, since the remainder of the journey will have to be arranged accordingly. Only I must remind you not to leave anything to the last moment. Mamma should make a list of *your linen, stockings and so forth*, in good time, and indeed of *all your clothes, so that you may know what you have with you.* That reminds me, what are you going to do about the trunk? Possibly one of you can make use of it. But I think that it would be too big for either of you. These points must be settled in good time. If Mamma prefers to bring it back, she could of course fill it up with straw, as her clothes take up so little space. *Wolfgang could more easily use it. Basta! Be sure and settle these matters well in advance.*

When Adlgasser died, I said to Nannerl: 'You bet that the Archbishop will get the Countess[1] to write to Joseph Arco, the Bishop of Königgrätz, to get his organist, that grubby Hasse or Hass, or whatever he is called,

---

[1] The Countess Lodron.

to come'. You will remember that the Countess once mentioned this to you? He is the dirty old fellow who tested you at Prince Pugiatowsky's in Vienna with the theme of Scarlatti's fugue. And it really is a fact that the Archbishop has already written about him. Meanwhile I have been twice already to the Lodron ladies. On New Year's Eve the Countess sent her manservant to ask me to come. She informed me with her usual insincere friendliness that she had a request to make, which, however, if it was inconvenient to me, I was to refuse quite frankly, as she did not wish to embarrass me; which, to my mind, was as much as to say that she fully realized that I was under no obligation to her. She then asked me to take on the teaching of her daughters, though she was well aware that I had very little time and did not like to be bothered. I made a few objections and finally said that I would come on one day at eleven in the morning and on the next at four in the afternoon. Whereupon she was delighted, talked a lot and said a number of nice things about you both. She was in the room on Friday when I came to teach the young ladies. I have just received your letter of December 27th. *I did not write to you on New Year's Day*, for on the eve and on the day itself I was busy with congratulations. I am positively delighted that you are now in such a comfortable house, that you are in good health and that you, my dear wife, have a nice warm room. The portrait you sketched of ⟨Wieland⟩ for my benefit I too could almost have given you, although I have never seen him. For M. Grimm and the two Romanzows gave me a most minute description of him during a walk which we all took together over the Mönchsberg. Philosophical birds of his type usually have something odd about them. You must not be in the least distressed that I enquired about your ⟨confession.⟩ I shall answer your quession another time. But surely you will be able to supply the answer yourself, if you will just put yourself in my place, or indeed in the place of any father. Could Mamma bring with her a Mannheim Court calendar? And I should very much like to know the title of *Vogler's book*[1] *and how much it costs*? If Wolfgang can remember how I set to work about these things, he will procure both very cheaply. He must not laugh, however, but preserve a very serious expression. I must certainly close now, for the paper is becoming blacker and blacker. Do take care of your health. Nannerl and I kiss you a million times and I am your old

MZT

(271) *Maria Anna Mozart to her Husband*

[*Autograph in the Mozarteum, Salzburg*]

MY DEAR HUSBAND,   MANNHEIM, 10 *January* 1778
I received today your letter of the 5th and am delighted to hear that you are both well. Eternal thanks be to God, we too are in good health.

---

[1] *Tonwissenschaft und Tonsetzkunst*, Mannheim, 1776.

We had heard some of your news about Bavaria, but not in such detail. People here are not suspecting any action on the part of ⟨Austria,⟩ but some folks are rather afraid of ⟨Prussia.⟩ Indeed there is a frightful lot of talk, mostly lies and nothing definite to report. Everyone is absolutely silent about the real truth, whatever it may be. God grant that everything may remain peaceful. I wish it with all my heart. As for my return journey, do not worry, for we shall think out the easiest way to arrange it. I am quite willing to travel in the company of merchants, if it can be arranged. But it is not so easy to settle from Mannheim that I should be in Augsburg at the very time that they would want to leave. If we still have peace, then it is quite probable that somebody may be going from here to Munich. We must make lots of enquiries so that we do not get in too late. I shall probably have to bring home the trunk with me, for it is too big for Wolfgang to use, since there will be four of them, each with his luggage, and the trunk would be far too heavy. But all this we shall find out when the time comes. May God but grant us the blessing of peace.

(271a) *Mozart to his Father*

[Autograph in the Mozarteum, Salzburg]

[MANNHEIM, 10 *January* 1778]

Indeed, I wish it with all my heart. What I really should like to see, you will have already gathered from my last letter. As for Mamma's journey home it is high time that we began to think about it; for although there have been rehearsals of the opera all the time, it is not at all certain whether it will be performed;[1] if it isn't, we shall probably leave on February 15th. If there weren't so many preparations to make, it would be easy enough. I shall make full enquiries. I shan't want the big trunk. My idea is to take as little luggage with me as possible and to leave all the things I don't want, such as that stack of symphonies, etc., and a few clothes besides, with the Privy Court Councillor here, where they are sure to be well looked after. Then again, as soon as I have heard your advice about this, I shall follow the opinion and practice of my travelling companions and have a black suit made for me, as they have done, and keep for Germany my braided clothes, which in any case are no longer the fashion in Paris. In the first place, a black suit is an economy (which is my chief consideration on my journey to Paris), and, secondly, it looks well and is suitable for both country and drawing-room wear; with a black coat you can go anywhere. The tailor has just brought Herr

---

[1] *Rosemunde*, which was to have been performed on 11 January 1778, was not given in Mannheim until 20 January 1780.

Wendling his suit today. The clothes I intend to take with me are my brown puce-coloured Spanish coat and the two waistcoats. Please tell me in your next letter whether I ought to do so. Well, let's change the subject. Now that he has heard me twice, Herr ⟨Wieland⟩ is quite enchanted with me. The last time after showering compliments on me he said: 'It is a real piece of good fortune that I have found you here', and he pressed my hand. Today there was a rehearsal of 'Rosemunde' in the theatre. It is—good, but ⟨nothing more.⟩ If it were bad, they couldn't produce it, could they?

Just as one can't sleep without lying in bed! Yet there's no rule without an exception. I myself have come across some instances of this. So goodnight!

(271b) *Maria Anna Mozart resumes writing*

[Autograph in the Mozarteum, Salzburg]

[MANNHEIM, 11 *January* 1778]

I lunched today, [January] 11th, with Herr Danner as usual. They both asked me to send their most devoted greetings to you and Nannerl. They are both excellent people and are exceedingly kind to me. I am not at all pleased that you have taken on the ⟨Countess's daughters.⟩ She isn't worth so much trouble on your part and doesn't deserve such a return for her deceitfulness.

(271c) *Mozart resumes writing*

[Autograph in the Mozarteum, Salzburg]

[MANNHEIM, 11 *January* 1778]

Particolarmente per un zecchino il mese.[1] Now for some sensible talk. I know for a fact that ⟨the Emperor⟩ is proposing to ⟨establish German opera in Vienna⟩ and that he is making every effort ⟨to find a young Kapellmeister⟩ who understands the ⟨German language,⟩ is talented and is capable of striking out a new line. ⟨Benda[2] of Gotha⟩ is applying, but ⟨Schweitzer⟩[3] is determined to get it. I think it would ⟨be a good thing for me⟩—provided, of course, that ⟨the pay⟩ is good. ⟨If the Emperor will give me a thousand gulden, I will write a German opera for him: if he won't have me,⟩ it's all the same to me. Please write to all ⟨our friends in Vienna⟩ you can think of and tell them ⟨that it is in my power

[1] Particularly for a zecchino a month.

[2] Georg Benda (1722–1795), the most distinguished member of a family of Czech musicians, was Kapellmeister to the Duke of Gotha from 1750 until 1778. He composed sacred and instrumental music and several operettas. His fame, however, rests on his two duodramas *Ariadne auf Naxos*, 1774, and *Medea*, 1775.

[3] Anton Schweitzer had been musical director of the Seyler theatrical company in Gotha since 1774.

to do honour to the Emperor.⟩ If he won't take me on any other terms, then let him ⟨try me with an opera⟩—after that he can do what he likes for all I care. Adieu. But please set the ball rolling *at once*, or ⟨someone may forestall me.⟩ I kiss your hands 1000 times and embrace my sister with all my heart and remain

WOLFGANG MOZART

(271d) *Maria Anna Mozart resumes writing*

[Autograph in the Mozarteum, Salzburg]

[MANNHEIM, 11 *January* 1778]

Wolfgang is now composing six new trios[1] and is going to have them engraved by subscription. When they are finished he'll send you six copies, so that you may sell them in Salzburg. Addio. Keep well. I remain as always your wife faithful unto death

MARIANNA MOZART

All sorts of messages to all our acquaintances.
My kindest regards to Bimperl.

(272) *Leopold Mozart to his Wife and Son*

[Extract]   *[Autograph in the Mozarteum, Salzburg]*

MY DEAR ONES!   SALZBURG, 12 *January* 1778

I didn't write to you last post-day and I too shall write only once a week, unless something special happens. I have received your letter of the 3rd and am delighted that you are well. We too are in good health, except that Nannerl has had a cold in her head for some days and I am not letting her go out. We have had no more letters from Munich. Perhaps my correspondent[2] has no definite information—or perhaps he does not dare to write. All that people know here is that the new Imperial Ambassador to Munich is the Imperial envoy Baron Lehrbach, District Commandant of Ellingen, and an uncle of our Lehrbach here. An officer and 28 men of the Taxis regiment have moved into Reichenhall. Cornet Andretter has written home for money, but doesn't yet know where he has been ordered to. Otherwise everything is quiet and I trust that it may remain so. Mysliwecek has written to say that at the Prince's request he composed two concertoni which he sent to Brunetti, but has had no

---

[1] K. 301-306 [293a–c, 300c, 293d, 300l], six sonatas for clavier and violin, four of which Mozart composed in Mannheim. They were published in November 1778 by Sieber in Paris and were dedicated to the Electress Marie Elizabeth of the Palatinate. Frau Mozart calls them trios, as they could be performed with a cello obbligato.

[2] Leopold Mozart's correspondent was Johann Baptist Becke, flautist in the Munich court orchestra.

reply. I have written to tell him that he will get nothing for them, as they were probably included in the former payment, but that he ought to go on reminding Brunetti until the latter gets tired of paying the six kreuzer postal fee and sets things going. We are to have only five or six balls at the Town Hall. The actors are wretched, are drawing very small audiences and are much to be pitied. We have not yet seen any of their performances. They say that after Easter the Archbishop would like to bring over the opera buffa from Munich and pay the company 50 ducats a month out of his own pocket. His Excellency the Chief Steward has just told me that His Grace commanded him to ask *Haydn and me* whether we knew of a *very good organist* who must, however, be a *first-rate clavierist*, and at the same time *of good appearance and presence, as he will be giving lessons to the ladies.* 'What?' I asked, 'did His Grace mention me too?' 'Yes, you in particular', he replied and laughed. I said: 'I know nobody who has all these qualities. *If there is such a person in Mannheim, then he can make his fortune.*' The Prince booked Walter's room at the Andretters for a new Italian secretary and had it heated for a week. But the latter having only got as far as Rovereto, already began to sniff the air of Salzburg, and this brought on such a violent fever that he turned back home, and although he had only been away for three days, he looked so ill that, as letters about him state, he was absolutely unrecognizable. Wolfgang will laugh when he hears that Fehlacher of Lauffen has applied for the post of Court Organist. Rust never goes out now. He is setting the 'Parnasso confuso'[1] to music for the consecration of the new Bishop of Olmütz. But, as Spitzeder and the copyists tell me, he is for the most part using arias taken from his own scores. I must close now. We kiss you both a million times. Nannerl is better—and we are your old

MZT

All—Herr Bullinger especially, send you their greetings. Addio! I am enclosing only one page of your sonata,[2] so that the letter may not be too bulky. I shall return it bit by bit.[3]

(273) *Maria Anna Mozart to her Husband*

[*Autograph in the possession of A. Rosenthal, Oxford*]

MANNHEIM, 17 *January* 1778

MY DEAR HUSBAND,

I was delighted to receive today your letter dated the 12th. I am sorry that so many people are ill. No doubt this is due to the bad weather. Here

---

[1] A text by Metastasio.
[2] K. 309 [284b], written for Rosa Cannabich, which Leopold Mozart was having copied in Salzburg.   [3] These last two sentences are written on the wrapper.

we have had a lot of rain and now it is rather warm for the season and very unhealthy. One never hears any news here and everything is very quiet. There has already been a rumour that the Imperial soldiers have marched into Bavaria. But no one really knows anything for certain. I think that if the Emperor were planning something against the Elector, the Elector would not stay so long in Munich but would return to Mannheim. We know, of course, that Baron Lehrbach is the Imperial envoy and we know him quite well. He is an excellent gentleman and he has been here. We had a letter to him from the Baron Lehrbach at Salzburg. Wolfgang handed him the letter here at our inn. May God but grant that everything may remain peaceful. My journey home would not be at all enjoyable if there were soldiers round about. God protect me from such a thing. I should certainly die of fright. Meanwhile I live in hopes that events will very soon show what turn they are going to take.

(273a) *Mozart to his Father*

[*Autograph in possession of A. Rosenthal, Oxford*]

[MANNHEIM, 17 *January* 1778]

Next Wednesday I am going for a few days to Kirchheim-Bolanden to visit the Princess of Orange.[1] People here have said such nice things to me about her that I have at last decided to go. A Dutch officer,[2] a good friend of mine, got a terrible scolding from her for not bringing me with him when he went to offer her his New Year wishes. I shall get eight louis d'or at least, for, as she is passionately fond of singing, I have had four arias copied for her and, as she has a nice little orchestra and gives a concert every day, I shall also present her with a symphony. Moreover the copying of the arias will not cost me much, for it has been done by a certain Herr Weber,[3] who is accompanying me there. I don't know whether I have already written about his daughter[4] or not—She sings indeed most admirably and has a lovely, pure voice. The only thing she lacks is dramatic action; were it not for that, she might be the prima

---

[1] Princesse Caroline of Nassau-Weilburg, sister of William of Orange. See p. 391, n. 3.
[2] Probably De La Pottrie.
[3] Fridolin Weber (1733–1779), uncle of Karl Maria von Weber, composer of *Der Freischütz*, was first a notary. In 1765 he accepted an ill-paid post as bass singer at the Mannheim court and manged to eke out an existence by prompting and copying. He and his family followed the Electoral Court to Munich in 1778, but soon moved to Vienna, where his second daughter, Aloysia, had obtained an appointment at the Opera. He died in October 1779. For a full account of the Weber family see Schurig, vol. ii. pp. 463–465; E. K. Blümml, *Aus Mozarts Freundes- und Familienkreis*, 1923; F. Hefele, *Die Vorfahren Karl Maria von Webers*, 1926.
[4] Aloysia (*c.* 1760–1839), Fridolin Weber's second daughter. She was then about seventeen.

donna on any stage. She is only sixteen. Her father is a thoroughly honest German who is bringing up his children well, and for that very reason the girl is persecuted with attentions here. He has six children, five girls and one son.[1] He and his wife and children have been obliged to live for fourteen years[2] on an income of 200 gulden and because he has always attended carefully to his duties and has provided the Elector with a very talented singer, who is only sixteen, he now gets in all—400 gulden. She sings most excellently my aria written for De Amicis with those horribly difficult passages[3] and she is to sing it at Kirchheim-Bolanden. She is quite well able to teach herself. She accompanies herself very well and she also plays galanterie quite respectably. What is most fortunate for her at Mannheim is that she has won the praise of all honest people of good will. Even the Elector and the Electress are only too glad to receive her, provided it doesn't cost them anything. She can go to the Electress whenever she likes, even daily; and this is due to her good behaviour.

Do you know what I should like to ask you to do?—To send me whenever you have an opportunity, *but as soon as possible*, let us say, bit by bit, the two sonatas for four hands[4] and the Fischer variations![5]—For I could make good use of them in Paris.

I think that we shall leave here on February 15th at latest, as there is no opera here. Now for something else. Last Wednesday there was a big party at our house to which I too was invited. There were fifteen guests and in the evening the young lady of the house[6] was to play the concerto[7] I had taught her. About eleven in the morning the Privy Councillor came to see me and brought Herr Vogler who by the way wanted absolument to make my closer acquaintance. I just can't tell you how often he had bothered me to go to him. At least he had overcome his pride and paid me the first visit. Besides, people tell me that he is now quite different, since he is no longer so much admired; for at first they made an idol of him. So we at once went upstairs together, the guests began to arrive by degrees and we did nothing but chatter. After dinner, however, he sent to his house for two claviers, tuned to the same pitch, and also for his tedious engraved sonatas. I had to play them while he accompanied me on the other clavier. At his urgent request I had to send for my sonatas also.[8] I should mention that before dinner he had scrambled through my concerto[9] at sight (the one which the daughter of the house plays—written for Countess Lützow[10]). He took the first movement *prestissimo*, the Andante *allegro* and the Rondo, believe it or not, *prestississimo*. He

---

[1] We only know of four daughters, Josefa Hofer, Aloysia Lange, Konstanze Mozart and Sophie Haibel.   [2] Twelve years. Fridolin Weber had moved from Zell to Mannheim in 1765.
[3] Giunia's aria no. 11, 'Ah, se il crudel', in Mozart's opera *Lucio Silla*, composed 1772.
[4] K. 358 [186c] and K. 381 [123a].   [5] K. 179 [189a].   [6] Therese Pierron Serrarius.
[7] K. 246.   [8] Probably K. 279-284 [189d-h, 205b].   [9] K. 246.
[10] Wife of Count von Lützow, commandant of the castle Hohensalzburg.

generally played the bass differently from the way it was written, invent-
ing now and then quite another harmony and even melody. Nothing else
is possible at that pace, for the eyes cannot see the music nor the hands
perform it. Well, what good is it?—That kind of sight-reading—and
shitting are all one to me. The listeners (I mean, of course, those who
deserve the name) can only say that they have seen music and piano-
playing. They hear, think and—feel as little during the performance as
the player himself. Well, you may easily imagine that it was unendurable.
At the same time I could not bring myself to say to him, *Far too quick!*
Besides, it is much easier to play a thing quickly than slowly: in certain
passages you can leave out a few notes without anyone noticing it. But
is that beautiful?—In rapid playing the right and left hands can be changed
without anyone seeing or hearing it. But is that beautiful?—And wherein
consists the art of playing prima vista? In this; in playing the piece in the
time in which it ought to be played, and in playing all the notes, appog-
giaturas and so forth, exactly as they are written and with the appropriate
expression and taste, so that you might suppose that the performer had
composed it himself. Vogler's fingering too is wretched; his left thumb
is just like that of the late Adlgasser and he does all the treble runs
downwards with the thumb and first finger of his right hand. In my
next letter I shall tell you more about this. For in the meantime Vogler
has invited me to a musical party. So after all I must stand high in his
favour. Addio. I kiss your hands 100,000 times and embrace my sister
with all my heart. Our best regards to all our good friends and especially
to Herr Bullinger and Mlle. Sallerl.

WOLFGANG AMADÈ MOZART

Please copy out for me a beautifully written A B C with both capital
and small letters, and send it to me.

(274) Leopold Mozart to his Son

[*Extract*]   [*Autograph in the Mozarteum, Salzburg*]

SALZBURG, 19 January 1778

You say that on your journey to Paris you intend to take as little
luggage as possible. That is very sound. But it would be a mistake to
leave anything behind in Mannheim. I have had experience of this and
have a thousand times regretted that I have left things behind, thus
obliging me to return to the place or to have them sent on at great risk
and expense or perhaps abandon them altogether. I should never have
made our second journey to Paris from England, if I had not left a

number of things there, and I should have saved a great deal of money in Holland, if I had not sent our furs and other things from Calais to Paris. For how could I foresee that my children would fall ill in Holland and that I should be forced to remain there and buy a lot of things over again at a very high price? So you must take your clothes with you. You cannot and must not do the same as your travelling companions, for your circumstances are very different from theirs. These gentlemen are only going to Paris for a short time, so it is to their interest not only to take very little luggage, but to save up their fine clothes for the gala-days in Mannheim. They can't go about in Paris in an ordinary everyday costume, such as they wear at home, just as we used to wear daily in other places the clothes which we wore in Salzburg on Sundays. If they were to wear their fine clothes every day in Paris, they would be faced with the sad necessity of having to purchase more fine clothes with which to appear at Court at home. Now as the attire which does one most honour in Paris and elsewhere is a black suit with a richly worked waistcoat for special occasions, it is quite true that their preparations are perfectly sound. But your circumstances are quite different. It would be very foolish for you to travel to Paris merely in order to put in an appearance and then return to Mannheim with these gentlemen. I well believe that they all want to have you back. I need not tell you the reason, for you know it. But as you must now endeavour to make greater strides, to win for yourself, as far as in you lies, glory, honour and a great name, and thus make money also, you have a purpose which cannot be achieved in a few months, still less in a few weeks. So to my mind economy demands that you should take your clothes with you. As for your music, you must leave nothing behind you in Mannheim. Carriers will surely be going to Paris. You could pack everything into a small box (but not your principal scores) and send them on to Paris. *Write on the box the address at which it should be delivered and that it contains music.* You will be able to make use of it all in Paris. If this doesn't work (though if it were myself, it would *have* to work!), then Mamma must bring home your music. Nothing must be left in Mannheim. I shall write about everything else next time.

I sent off at once full details of what ⟨*you told me about the Emperor's German opera*⟩ to Heufeld,[1] and begged him most urgently to send ⟨*a petition to the Emperor and Empress immediately.*⟩ I am writing by the next post to the Chief Equerry Count Dietrichstein, to the wife of Dr. Vaugg and to a few other people who, I think, can do something. All our Salzburg friends send their greetings to you both, and Nannerl and I kiss you many 1000 times and I remain ever your old

MZT

---

[1] Franz von Heufeld, who had great influence in the theatrical world in Vienna. Leopold Mozart's letter is lost.

I shall write again by the next post and enclose a little more of your sonata; to do so now would make this letter too bulky. By that time I shall have more to say ⟨about the prospects of a war.⟩

(275) *Maria Anna Mozart to her Husband*

[*Autograph in the Mozarteum, Salzburg*]

MY DEAR HUSBAND,   MANNHEIM, 24 *January* 1778

I was delighted to receive today your letter of the 19th, and the news it contains has given me much pleasure. For one hears nothing at all here; it is as quiet as if one were no longer in the world. People only sigh and long to have ⟨the Elector⟩ back. His absence means a great loss to the town, for no visitors come here, as there is nothing to see. The towns-people have generally made their biggest profits during the carnival, when they are able to fleece visitors properly; but this year their prospect of doing so is spoiled. Wolfgang went off yesterday morning with Herr Weber and his daughter to Kirchheim-Bolanden to visit the Princess of Weilburg.[1] I hardly think that she will let them go before the week is out, for she is a passionate lover of music and plays the clavier and sings. Wolfgang took with him a supply of arias and symphonies to present to her. The place is only a ten hours' drive from here, that is, a short day's journey. The Princess is nearly always there and only goes to Holland for about two months of the year in order to visit her brother. Meanwhile I have persuaded Wolfgang to change his mind about his clothes, which he is now going to take with him; and I shall persuade him to take the big trunk, for if he packs into it all his clothes and all his music, which made up three huge parcels, it will certainly be full enough; and as I hear that they are going to travel by the mail coach (which, by the way, starts from here and does not travel at night), it is much better for him to have all his luggage together in one trunk. You have not yet had a reply from Herr von Grimm. I think you would have done better to send your letter to his old address, for if he has left it, the people would doubtless know where he has moved to. It was a good plan to write those letters to Vienna, but I ought to remind you that it would do no harm if you were to write to Count Thun also, who has so much influence ⟨with the Emperor⟩ and had such a liking for Wolfgang. There is a singer at the opera here, Hartig[2] by name, who is so affectionate and friendly with us that he never calls me anything but his dear Mamma. Without knowing you he sends you his warmest greetings. He called on me today to see

---

[1] See p. 447.
[2] Franz Christian Hartig (1750–*c.* 1812), a tenor at the Mannheim opera. He was being trained by Raaff.

how I was getting along without Wolfgang. When he heard that I was writing home, he at once asked me to convey his most devoted compliments.

Our hostess, the wife of the Privy Court Councillor, also sends you her greetings. She is indeed an excellent woman. I have to spend the whole afternoon and evening until half past ten with them. As soon as I get home after lunch, the young lady comes to our room and makes me go upstairs to them. We do needlework until it gets dark and after supper we play 'fire and murder' (which I have taught them) at twenty counters for a kreuzer. So you can work out how much we can lose. Addio. Keep well, both of you. I kiss you both 1000 times and remain as always your faithful wife

MARIA ANNA MOZART

Please give my best greetings to all our good friends, especially to Monsieur Bullinger and Mlle Sallerl.

A kiss for Bimperl.

(276) *Leopold Mozart to his Wife and Son*

[Extract]   [Autograph in the Mozarteum, Salzburg]

MY DEAR ONES!   SALZBURG, 25, 26 *January* 1778

My last letter, a very long one, was dated the 19th and I did not write on the 22nd. I have received your letter of the 17th. Thank God that you are well. We too are in good health. Padre Maestro Martini has replied, but he had not yet received the portrait which was packed with other goods and will have travelled very slowly by carriers. He sends Wolfgang a thousand greetings and says that he is going to write to Signor Raaff and ask him to say on his behalf all sorts of nice things to the Elector about you and your merits. Herr Janitsch,[1] the violinist, and a cellist[2] from Wallerstein have arrived in Salzburg and came to see me at once. They brought a letter for Count Kühnburg from Beecke, who has gone on to Vienna. The Archbishop is not going to hear them play at Court. He said that if they liked they could give a concert, but he did not offer to go to it. The upshot of all this and the information which I have got from them I shall tell you next time I write. Beecke must be very jealous of Wolfgang, for he tries to belittle him as much as possible. I have sent

---

[1] Anton Janitsch (1753–1812), a member of the orchestra of Prince Krafft Ernst von Öttingen-Wallerstein. See p. 338, n. 1.

[2] Joseph Reicha (1746–1795), a Czech, was cellist in the Wallerstein orchestra, and in 1785 was appointed musical director to the Elector of Cologne. His nephew was the well-known Czech composer, Anton Reicha (1770–1836).

off my second letter to Vienna about that matter and a letter to the wife
of Dr. Vaugg, which contains the fullest and most vivid description of
our affair. People of his type generally get a thing done more easily than
the very great, with whom you can never be sure as to whether they are
not already interested in someone else. I put forward most insistently my
requests—⟨both about the *German opera* and about the *recommendation to
Paris.*⟩ By the next post I shall write to a different quarter. Grimm has
not yet replied, which is rather disappointing for me. I shall send you the
sonatas for four hands[1] and the variations.[2] Mysliwecek wrote again the
other day to say that he was hoping to receive shortly your scrittura from
Naples. But I regard it as an excuse, for he only makes an announcement
like this when he wants me to do something for him. By the way, I stick
to my opinion that Wolfgang should leave nothing behind him in
Mannheim. It is high time that Mamma got ready for her journey, for a
good opportunity may perhaps present itself for her to reach Augsburg
or even Munich. Ah, my dear Wolfgang, I must not brood on the whole
business, for if I do, the heaviest sadness comes over me. Nannerl sends
you greetings and kisses Mamma's hands. We kiss you a million times and
I am your old

MZT

Wolfgang will have returned from Kirchheim by now. Mlle Weber
and her father will have had the same experience as others. *Propheta non
acceptus in patria!*[3]

The two gentlemen from Wallerstein[4] insisted on hearing Nannerl
play. It emerged that their sole object in so doing was that they might
guess from her style of playing what yours was like; and they were
particularly anxious to hear one of your compositions. She played your
Mannheim sonata[5] most excellently and with all the necessary expression.
They were amazed at her performance and at the composition, saying
that they had never heard any of your works and that this one had
some entirely new and original ideas; and Reicha, the cellist, who is
an excellent clavierist and who had previously been playing on our
harpsichord very smoothly and in the style of the organ, remarked
several times that *it was a very sound composition.* After that they accompanied Nannerl most excellently in your clavier trio in B♭.[6]

I have just this moment heard that Count Daun, canon of our Cathedral,
has stated that the Elector is to remain in Munich and that he is going to
have his orchestra brought over after Easter. The first is quite possible, for

---

[1] K. 381 [123a], composed in 1772, and K. 358 [186c], composed in 1774. See p. 412, n. 2.
[2] The variations are probably K. 179 [189a], twelve variations on a minuet by Fischer.
See p. 256, n. 5.   [3] A prophet has no honour in his own country.
[4] Anton Janitsch and Joseph Reicha.   [5] K. 309 [284b].   [6] K. 254, composed in 1776.

he must himself take stock of the government, introduce law and order and wrest it from the claws of those vultures, a task which he can entrust to no one else. The second may be a natural consequence of the first. What do you think of this letter? Have I left a single white spot uncovered?

Addio.

(277) *Leopold Mozart to his Son*

[*Extract*]   [*Autograph in the Mozarteum, Salzburg*]

MON TRÉS CHER FILS!   SALZBURG, 29 *January* 1778

Here is Herr von Heufeld's letter.[1] To tell the truth, I did not expect much from the whole business, ⟨for the Emperor⟩ seems to me to be like our Archbishop, that is to say, he declares, '*I must have something very good but as cheaply as possible*'. I don't want the letter back, so Mamma may keep it. Enclosed with it was a note from Director Mesmer,[2] which runs as follows:

> DEAREST FRIEND,
>
> I cannot understand how it is that you have not had a reply to your letter to me, for I certainly wrote to you after my illness, though rather late, it is true. I wonder whether my wife, who was very anxious at the time about her Joseph, could have forgotten to post my letters? My cousin, Dr. Mesmer, who is leaving one of these days for Paris and intended to introduce my son to you on the way through, was to have reproached you with the same kind of slackness. Well, the plan has been dropped, as your son is no longer in Salzburg. You may rest assured that I have a warm affection for you and take an interest in everything which concerns your family. Why did you not send your son straight to Vienna? And why are you not sending him now? I promise you faithfully that he can have free board, lodging and everything else with us as long as he likes, and that all your friends in Vienna, myself included, will endeavour to obtain some good appointment for him. But unless he comes here, it is impossible to do anything for him. There is plenty of room in Vienna for a great talent, but these things cannot be arranged in a trice. With the help of good friends, however, it would be possible for him to achieve his object; and, after all, Vienna is the best place to live in. You know all about your Swabian friends and the advantages of this capital. So choose—and let me know. I remain your old friend
>
> MESMER

---

[1] Heufeld's letter, which gives an interesting account of theatrical conditions in Vienna, is printed in *Mozart. Briefe und Aufzeichnungen*, vol. ii, pp. 235–237. Heufeld held out little hope of an appointment for Mozart, but suggested that he should compose a German opera, send it to the Emperor and, if possible, come to Vienna. He mentioned the advantage of having the support of Wieland, who, however, had strongly recommended Schweitzer.

[2] See p. 235.

If our good Mesmer had replied or if his wife had not kept back the letters, I should doubtless have considered sending you to Vienna, for you would have been very well treated in his house. If you decide to take this path, it is still open to you. You will see that Herr von Heufeld, who, as we know, is not a very ardent Christian, says nevertheless that he trusts you to hold to the good principles inculcated by your parents and to guard yourself against evil company. Count Kühnburg, Chief Equerry, who, as is well known, lays no claim to saintliness, talked to me a few days ago in the same vein and expressed extreme anxiety about Paris, which he knows thoroughly. He said that you should be on your guard against its dangers and that you should refrain from all familiarity with young Frenchmen, and even more so with the women, who are always on the look-out for strangers to keep them, who run after young people of talent in an astonishing way in order to get at their money, draw them into their net or even land them as husbands. God and your own good sense will preserve you. Any such calamity would be the death of me! Janitsch and Reicha went off to Linz this morning by the mail coach. They will have taken in about 70 gulden at their concert, although the Archbishop only forked out eight. They are both very fine players; they have an extraordinary facility and lightness in their bowing, sure intonation and a beautiful tone, and they play with the greatest expression. Reicha is a first-rate fellow. Janitsch plays in the style of Lolli,[1] but his adagio playing is infinitely better. Indeed I am no lover of excessively rapid passages, where you have to produce the notes with the half tone of the violin and, so to speak, only touch the fiddle with the bow and almost play in the air. On the other hand his cantabile playing is very poor, for he is inclined to make sharp jerks and to indulge in allegro fireworks which to an understanding listener are really most offensive. Reicha has a better cantabile. Both, however, have Becke's[2] fault of dragging the time, of holding back the whole orchestra by a nod and then returning to the original tempo. They ended by playing a duet in *contrattempo*[3] and with the most astounding execution and precision. But the tempo of their playing was altogether in the manner of the two Besozzi[4] of Turin, who

---

[1] The famous eighteenth-century violinist and teacher, Antonio Lolli (*c.* 1730–1802).

[2] Probably the Munich flautist, Johann Baptist Becke, Leopold Mozart's friend and correspondent.

[3] Leopold Mozart may mean 'broken time', which he discusses fully in his *Violinschule*, chap. xii. § 16. (See facsimile edition by B. Paumgartner, Vienna, 1922, p. 26.) Certainly the expression can be used to indicate either 'with syncopation' or 'in florid counterpoint', i.e. with one part playing rapid passages while the other proceeds steadily.

[4] The Besozzi were an Italian family of distinguished wind-instrument players. The two brothers to whom Leopold Mozart refers were probably Alessandro (1700–1775), a remarkable oboist, who in 1731 joined the court orchestra at Turin, and Hieronimo (1713–1778), a famous bassoon-player. Hieronimo was the special associate of Alessandro, and their beautiful duet performances aroused Burney's enthusiasm (*Present State of Music in France and Italy*, 1773, p. 69).

by the way are both dead now.[1] Reicha and Janitsch spent the whole of yesterday afternoon until six o'clock at our house. Your sister had to play your clavier concertos[2] from the original score and some other pieces. We played their violin parts. They liked your compositions immensely. Reicha played a concerto of his own which was quite good, with some new ideas and rather after your style. Haydn liked it too. If you are really leaving on February 15th, then I have only two more post-days left. So, in order to let you have all the music, I must send a rather heavy letter each time. It will be expensive for you, but you really need the sonatas for four hands and the variations.[3] Who will comb Wolfgang's hair now? Is his head ⟨free of lice?⟩ Oh, indeed I have a great many things to think of ! If only Herr Grimm had replied; that would have taken a heavy load off my heart. All send their greetings. Nannerl and I kiss you millions of times and I am your old

MZT

(278) *Mozart to his Mother at Mannheim*

[*Copy in the Mozarteum, Salzburg*]

[Worms, 31 *January* 1778]

Oh, mother mine!
Butter is fine.
Praise and thanks be to Him,
We're alive and full of vim.
Through the world we dash,
Though we're rather short of cash.
But we don't find this provoking
And none of us are choking.
Besides, to people I'm tied
Who carry their muck inside
And let it out, if they are able,
Both before and after table.
At night of farts there is no lack,
Which are let off, forsooth, with a powerful crack.
The king of farts came yesterday
Whose farts smelt sweeter than the may.
His voice, however, was no treat
And he himself was in a heat.
Well, now we've been over a week away
And we've been shitting every day.
Wendling, no doubt, is in a rage
That I haven't composed a single page;

---

[1] Alessandro died in 1775, but Hieronimo was still living.
[2] Probably K. 238, 246 and 271.   [3] See p. 453.

But when I cross the Rhine once more,
I'll surely dash home through the door
And, lest he call me mean and petty,
I'll finish off his four quartetti.[1]
The concerto[2] for Paris I'll keep, 'tis more fitting.
I'll scribble it there some day when I'm shitting.
Indeed I swear 'twould be far better fun
With the Webers around the world to run
Than to go with those bores, you know whom I mean,
When I think of their faces, I get the spleen.
But I suppose it must be and off we shall toddle,
Though Weber's arse I prefer to Ramm's noddle.
A slice of Weber's arse is a thing
I'd rather have than Monsieur Wendling.
With our shitting God we cannot hurt
And least of all if we bite the dirt.
We are honest birds, all of a feather,
We have summa summarum eight eyes together,
Not counting those on which we sit.
But now I really must rest a bit
From rhyming. Yet this I must add,
That on Monday I'll have the honour, egad,
To embrace you and kiss yours hands so fair.
But first in my pants I'll shit, I swear.

Worms, January 1778th   Your faithful child,
      Anno 31.   With distemper wild.
                              TRAZOM

(279) *Maria Anna Mozart to her Husband*

[Autograph in the Mozarteum, Salzburg]

MY DEAR HUSBAND,   MANNHEIM, 1 *February* 1778

I have received your letter of the 25th and am delighted to hear that you are well. Wolfgang has not yet returned from Kirchheim and will probably not come back until next Wednesday. Herr Weber has written to his wife that the Princess will not let them go before then. So I too must be content, I suppose. But about his journey to Paris, I am every bit as anxious as you are. If only Monsieur Grimm were there, I shouldn't

[1] Wendling had obtained for Mozart a commission to write three easy flute concertos and two flute quartets for De Jean. See p. 414. Actually Mozart wrote three flute quartets in Mannheim, K. 285, K. 285a and K. App. 171 [285b]. See p. 481.

[2] Mozart composed one flute concerto, K. 313 [285e], in Mannheim and probably rewrote for De Jean his oboe concerto, K. 314 [285d], written in 1777 for Ferlendis. See p. 320, n. 1.

worry at all, for he could perhaps take him into his house or help him to make his fortune in some way or another. Grimm has certainly been a true friend to us and one on whom we can rely. I have just this moment had a letter from Wolfgang, who is in Worms and will get back here tomorrow. How glad I shall be to see him again. The Privy Court Councillor invariably copies out the news which you send me from Salzburg and the articles about the war, and always looks forward most eagerly to my getting your letter, for everything is kept very quiet here and the rumours we hear are lies. Thus whatever you tell us we regard as articles of faith. The people of the Palatinate say that ⟨the Elector⟩ cannot possibly remain ⟨in Munich⟩. In short, they consider ⟨Mannheim and the Palatinate to be far superior to and finer than Bavaria and Munich.⟩ It is all right for you to house the opera-singers, provided they do not spoil the stove in our new room by heating it too much, and that they do not behave like a lot of pigs as Italians generally do.[1] You need not worry about Wolfgang taking all his things with him. He must take everything and the big trunk as well. I shall see that he does. A smaller trunk will do for me. The list of marksmen will be shorter when the two gentlemen from Wallerstein go off again.[2] I can well believe that Captain Beecke is trying to belittle Wolfgang, for up to the present he has been looked up to as a god in his own district and in the neighbourhood of Augsburg. But when people heard Wolfgang, they immediately exclaimed: 'Why, he knocks Beecke into a cocked hat. You simply can't compare them.' All sorts of messages to all our good friends, and especially to Monsieur Bullinger and Mlle Sallerl. I kiss you both a million times and remain your faithful wife

MARIANNA MOZART

I wanted very much to write more. But they have already sent for me to go upstairs, for I have to spend the whole day with them and never get back to my room until half past ten. Addio. Once more, do keep well.

(280) *Leopold Mozart to his Wife*

[Extract]   [Autograph in the Mozarteum, Salzburg]

MY DEAR WIFE!   SALZBURG, 2 *February* 1778

I have received your letter of January 24th. Wolfgang will have long since returned and I hope that he has received a handsome present. You will need money for the journey. I have just received two New Year ⟨accounts from tailors,⟩ I mean, from Daser and Amman. The first, for Wolfgang's suit and waistcoats, amounts to 15 gulden, the second, for

[1] Frau Mozart is referring to a passage in her husband's letter of 25 January, which for lack of space has had to be omitted.
[2] Anton Janitsch and Josef Reicha had joined the Mozarts' shooting parties.

yourself, amounts to 6 gulden 24 kreuzer. ⟨I don't know how I am going to pay them⟩ and they will ⟨have to be paid⟩ before our Salzburg fair. ⟨Moreover, Theresa wants her wages⟩ to buy things for herself. Then there is our ⟨house rent,⟩ though that sum I shall be able to raise; but, by Heaven, I do not know how I am going to meet the other bills. Mannheim will probably have to sigh and groan, for not only now, when circumstances require his presence, but in the future too, the Elector will assuredly spend most of his time in Munich. You will have gathered from Herr von Heufeld's letter that introductions, especially from the great ones of this world, sometimes do more harm than good. But Dr. Vaugg's wife, to whom I wrote a most pressing letter, will certainly be able to make use of the fact that people have not forgotten our Wolfgang. I have now fired off replies to the Honourables Heufeld and Mesmer. If Wolfgang were to go to Vienna today, he knows of one safe haven into which he can turn. Please give my most devoted greetings to the wife of the Privy Court Councillor, her husband and daughter, to Herr Hartig, Herr Wendling and all the other gentlemen. I know that you will have done so very often even if I did not mention it, just as I always deliver greetings here from you. *Bring back with you any old stockings, silk or otherwise, and anything else belonging to Wolfgang which he doesn't want; also any old linen of his or other articles,* for no doubt he will require a supply of new things. You and I can make use of some of his old clothes. When I close the letter, I shall *probably* put in all the music which I have to send to Wolfgang. I have bought something for his cousin, but I have not yet found a safe means of dispatching it to her. She has sent Wolfgang her portrait, for which he was always asking her.[1] Why did he put her to this expense? After all it is probably a miniature and possibly not even a good likeness. Nannerl kisses your hands and embraces her brother with all her heart. I am your old

                                                                    MZT

How are you going to travel home? I shall write another letter to Herr Grimm and address it: rue Neuve Luxembourg. Nannerl asks you not to forget to bring her *the kind of cap that is in fashion.*

(281) *Mozart to his Father*

[*Autographs in the Mozarteum, Salzburg, and in the Library of the Paris Conservatoire*]

MONSIEUR   [MANNHEIM, 4 *February* 1778]
    MON TRÉS CHER PÉRE!

I simply cannot wait as I usually do until Saturday, because it is too long already since I have had the pleasure of talking to you in a letter.

[1] See p. 371, n. 2.

The first thing I want to tell you about is how I and my good friends got on at Kirchheim-Bolanden. Well, it was just a holiday trip—nothing more. We set off from here at eight o'clock on Friday morning, after I had breakfasted with Herr Weber. We had a smart covered coach which held four and we reached Kirchheim-Bolanden at four o'clock. We had to send a list of our names at once to the castle. Early next morning Herr Konzertmeister Rothfischer[1] called on us. He had already been described to me in Mannheim as a most honest fellow; and I found him so. In the evening, Saturday evening, we went to Court, where Mlle Weber sang three arias. I say nothing about her singing—only one word, excellent! I wrote to you the other day about her merits; but I shall not be able to close this letter without telling you something more about her, for only now have I got to know her properly and as a result to discover her great powers. We had to dine afterwards at the officers' table. We were obliged to walk a good distance to church next day, for the Catholic church is rather far off. That was Sunday. We lunched again with the officers, but they had no concert in the evening, as it was Sunday. So they have only 300 concerts in the year. We could have dined at Court in the evening, but we did not wish to do so, preferring to remain in the inn by ourselves. We would have unanimously and with heartfelt gladness done without the meals at Court, for we never enjoyed ourselves better than when we were alone. But we had to think a little about economy—for, as it was, we had quite enough to pay for. The following day, Monday, we again had a concert, and also on Tuesday and Wednesday. Mlle Weber sang thirteen times in all and played the clavier twice, for she does not play at all badly. What surprises me most is her excellent sight-reading. Would you believe it, she played my difficult sonatas[2] at sight, *slowly* but without missing a single note! On my honour I would rather hear my sonatas played by her than by Vogler! I played a dozen times in all, and once by request on the organ in the Lutheran church. I presented four symphonies to the Princess and received ⟨only seven louis d'or in silver,⟩ mark you, and my poor dear Mlle Weber only ⟨five.⟩ Really it was the last thing I expected. I was not hoping for much, but at least I thought that each of us would receive ⟨eight louis d'or.⟩ Basta! We have lost nothing by it, however, for I still have a profit of 42 gulden and moreover the inexpressible pleasure of making the acquaintance of a thoroughly honest, good Catholic Christian family. I am truly sorry that I did not get to know them long ago. I am now coming to an important point, about which I want you to reply at once.

Mamma and I have talked the matter over and are agreed that we do not like the sort of life the Wendlings lead.

---

[1] Paul Rothfischer, a violinist in the service of the Princess of Nassau-Weilburg.
[2] Probably the clavier sonatas of the series K. 279–284 [189d–h, 205b].

Wendling is a thoroughly honest, excellent fellow, but unfortunately he has no religion whatever; and the whole family are the same. It is enough to say that his daughter has been somebody's ⟨mistress.[1]⟩ Ramm is a decent fellow, but a libertine. I know myself, and I am positive that I have enough religion never at any time to do anything which I could not do openly before the whole world; but the mere idea of being, even though it is only on a journey, in the society of people whose way of thinking is so entirely different from my own (and from that of all honourable people), horrifies me. But of course they can do as they please. I have not the heart to travel with them, I should not have a single happy hour, I should not know what to talk about. For, in a word, I do not fully trust them. Friends who have no religion cannot be our friends for long. I have already given them a slight hint in advance by saying that during my absence three letters have arrived, about which all that I can tell them is that it is unlikely that I shall be able to travel with them to Paris, but that perhaps I shall follow them—or perhaps go elsewhere; and that they must not count on me. My idea is as follows:

I propose to remain here and finish entirely at my leisure that music for De Jean, for which I am to get 200 gulden. I can stay here as long as I like and neither board nor lodging costs me anything. In the meantime Herr Weber will endeavour to get engagements here and there for concerts with me, and we shall then travel together. When I am with him, it is just as if I were travelling with you. The very reason why I am so fond of him is because, apart from his personal appearance, he is just like you and has exactly your character and way of thinking. If my mother were not, as you know, too *comfortably lazy* to write, she would tell you the very same thing! I must confess that I much enjoyed travelling with them. We were happy and merry; I was hearing a man talk like you; I had nothing to worry about; I found my torn clothes mended; in short, I was waited on like a prince.

I have become so fond of this unfortunate family that my dearest wish is to make them happy; and perhaps I may be able to do so. My advice is that they should go to Italy. So now I should like you to write to our good friend Lugiati, and the sooner the better, and enquire what are the highest terms given to a prima donna in Verona—the more the better, one can always climb down—perhaps too it would be possible to obtain the Ascensa in Venice.[2] As far as her singing is concerned, I would wager my life that she will bring me renown. Even in a short time she has greatly profited by my instruction, and how much greater will the improvement be by then! I am not anxious either about her acting. If our

---

[1] See p. 362, n. 3.
[2] i.e. the contract to sing in the opera performed on the occasion of the Festival of the Ascension.

plan succeeds, we, M. Weber, his two daughters[1] and I will have the honour of visiting my dear Papa and my dear sister for a fortnight on our way through Salzburg. My sister will find a friend and a companion in Mlle Weber, for, like my sister in Salzburg, she has a reputation for good behaviour, her father resembles my father and the whole family resemble the Mozarts. True, there are envious folk, as there are in Salzburg, but when it comes to the point, they have to speak the truth. Honesty is the best policy. I can say that I shall look forward immensely to going to Salzburg with them, if only that you may hear her sing. She sings superbly the arias which I wrote for De Amicis, both the bravura aria and 'Parto, m'affretto' and 'Dalla sponda tenebrosa'.[2] I beg you to do your best to get us to Italy. You know my greatest desire is—to write operas.[3]

I will gladly write an opera for Verona for 50 zecchini, if only in order that she may make her name; for if I do not compose it, I fear that she may be victimized. By that time I shall have made so much money on the other journeys we propose to undertake together, that I shall not be the loser. I think we shall go to Switzerland and perhaps also to Holland. Do write to me soon about this. If we stay anywhere for long, the eldest daughter will be very useful to us; for we could have our own ménage, as she can cook. A propos, you must not be too much surprised when you hear that I have only 42 gulden left out of 77. That is merely the result of my delight at being again in the company of honest and like-minded people. I paid one half of the expenses, for I could not do otherwise, but I shall not do so on our other journeys and I have already told them so; I shall then pay only for *myself*. After we left, we stayed five days at Worms, where Weber has a brother-in-law, who is the Dean of the Monastery. I should add that he is terrified of Herr Weber's sarcastic quill. We had a jolly time there and lunched and dined every day with the Dean. I may say that this little journey gave me fine practice on the clavier. The Dean is an excellent and sensible man. Well, it is time for me to stop. If I were to write all I think, I should have no paper left. Send me an answer soon, I beg you. Do not forget how much I desire to write operas. I envy anyone who is composing one. I could really weep for vexation when I hear or see an aria. But Italian, not German; seriosa, not buffa. You should not have sent me Heufeld's letter, which caused me more annoyance than pleasure. The fool thinks that I shall write a comic opera; yes, and write one on chance and at my own risk. I think too that he would not have disgraced his title of 'Honourable',[4] if he had written 'der Herr Sohn'

---

[1] Josefa and Aloysia.
[2] Arias sung by De Amicis, who took the part of Giunia in *Lucio Silla*, composed in 1772. See p. 448, n. 3.
[3] The autograph in the Mozarteum, Salzburg, ends here. The autograph of the remaining portion of this letter is in the library of the Paris Conservatoire.
[4] Franz von Heufeld had recently received from the Emperor the Austrian title of 'Edler'.

and not 'Ihr Sohn'. But what is he after all but a Viennese booby; or perhaps he thinks that people remain twelve years old for ever? I have now written all that is weighing on my heart. My mother is quite satisfied with my ideas. It is impossible for me to travel with people—with a man—who leads a life of which the veriest stripling could not but be ashamed; and the thought of helping a poor family, without injury to myself, delights my very soul. I kiss your hands a thousands times and remain until death your most obedient son

WOLFGANG AMADÉ MOZART

Mannheim, 4 February 1778.

My greetings to all our good friends, and particularly to my best friend—Herr Bullinger.

(281a) *Maria Anna Mozart to her Husband*

[*Copy in the Deutsche Staatsbibliothek, Berlin*]

MY DEAR HUSBAND!   MANNHEIM, *5 February* [1778]
You will have seen from this letter that when Wolfgang makes new acquaintances, he immediately wants to give his life and property for them.
    True, she sings exceedingly well; still, we must not lose sight of our own interests. I never liked his being in the company of Wendling and Ramm, but I never ventured to raise any objections, nor would he ever have listened to me.
    But as soon as he got to know the Webers, he immediately changed his mind. In short, he prefers other people to me, for I remonstrate with him about this and that, and about things which I do not like; and he objects to this. So you yourself will have to think over what ought to be done. I do not consider his journey to Paris with Wendling at all advisable. I would rather accompany him myself later on. It would not cost so very much in the mail coach. Perhaps you will still get a reply from Herr Grimm. Meanwhile we are not losing anything here. I am writing this quite secretly, while he is at dinner, and I shall close, for I do not want to be caught. Addio.
    I remain your faithful wife

MARIA ANNA MOZART

(282) *Leopold Mozart to his Son*

[*Extract*]   [*Autograph in the Mozarteum, Salzburg*]

MY DEAR SON!   SALZBURG, *5 February* 1778
    As in all probability this will be the last letter which will reach you at Mannheim, it is addressed to you alone. My heart is heavy indeed, now

that I know that you will be still farther away from me. True, you can realise this to some extent, but you cannot feel the burden of grief which is weighing down my heart. If you will take the trouble to remember what I undertook with you two children in your tender youth, you will not accuse me of cowardice, but will admit, as others do, that I always have been and still am a man who has the courage to dare all. Yet I managed everything with the greatest caution and consideration that was humanly possible—for no one can prevent accidents—as only God knows what the future will bring. Up to the present, it is true, we have been neither happy nor unhappy; things have been, thank God, half and half. We have done everything to make you happier and through you to bring happiness to ourselves and to set your future at least on a firm footing. But Fate has willed that we should not achieve our purpose. As you are aware, owing to our last step I am now in very deep waters. As you know, ⟨*I am now in debt* to the extent⟩ of about 700 gulden and ⟨*haven't the faintest idea how I am going to support myself, Mamma and your sister on my monthly salary;*⟩ for as long as I live I cannot now hope ⟨*to get another farthing from the Prince.*⟩ So it must be as clear as noonday to you that the future of your old parents and of your good sister who loves you with all her heart, is entirely in your hands. Since you were born or rather since my marriage it has been very difficult for me to ⟨*support*⟩ a wife, seven children,[1] two maids and Mamma's own mother ⟨*on my monthly pay* of about 20 gulden⟩, and ⟨*to meet the expenses*⟩ of child-births, deaths and illnesses. If you think it over, you will realise that not only have I never spent a farthing on the smallest pleasure for myself but that without God's special mercy I should never have succeeded in spite of all my efforts ⟨*in keeping out of debt;*⟩ and yet ⟨*this is the first time I have got into debt.*⟩ When you were children, I gave up all my time to you in the hope that not only would you be able to provide later on for yourselves, but also that I might enjoy a comfortable old age, be able to give an account to God of the education of my children, be free from all anxiety, devote myself to the welfare of my soul and thus be enabled to meet my death in peace. But God has ordained that I must now take on again the *wearisome task* of giving lessons and that too in a town where this heavy work is so wretchedly paid that it is impossible to ⟨*earn enough each month to support oneself and one's family;*⟩ yet one has to be thankful to have any work, though one has to talk oneself hoarse if one is ⟨*to make even a pittance.*⟩ My dear Wolfgang, not only do I not distrust you in the very slightest degree; on the contrary, I place all my trust and confidence in your filial love. Our future depends on your abundant good sense, if

---

[1] Jahn, vol. i. p. 26, and Abert, vol. ii, p. 904, give particulars of Leopold Mozart's seven children, only two of whom survived, i.e. Nannerl, the fourth, born in 1751, and Wolfgang, the youngest, born in 1756.

you will only hearken to it, and on more fortunate circumstances, which, it is true, we cannot command. You are going off now to an entirely different world. Please do not think that prejudice makes me regard Paris as a very dangerous place; au contraire—from my own experience I have no reason whatever to think Paris so very dangerous. But my situation then and your present one are entirely different. On our first visit we stayed at the house of an ambassador and the second time in a self-contained lodging.[1] I had a certain position and you were children. I avoided all acquaintances and, mark you, *particularly all familiarity with people of our own profession*; you will remember that I did the same in Italy. I made the acquaintance and sought only the friendship of people of position—and, what is more, among these I associated with older people, never with young fellows, not even if they were of the highest rank. I never invited anyone to visit me constantly in my rooms, as I wanted to be quite free. Besides I thought it was more sensible to visit others when it suited me. For if I do not like the man or if I have work or business to do, I can stay away; whereas if people come to see me and don't know when to leave, it is difficult to get rid of them; and a person who is otherwise a welcome visitor may well hinder me when I have work on hand which must be done. You are but a young man of twenty-two; so you cannot have that settled gravity which might discourage any young fellow, of whatever rank he may be, an adventurer, jester or deceiver, old or young, from seeking your acquaintance and friendship in order to draw you into his company and then by degrees bend you to his will. One drifts imperceptibly into these traps and then one cannot get out. I shall say nothing about women, for where they are concerned the greatest reserve and prudence are necessary, Nature herself being our enemy. Whoever does not use his judgement to the utmost to keep the necessary reserve with them, will exert it in vain later on when he endeavours to extricate himself from the labyrinth, *a misfortune, which most often ends in death*. But how blindly we may often be led on by seemingly meaningless jests, flatteries and fun, for which Reason, when she reawakens later, is compelled to blush, you yourself may perhaps have learnt a little by experience. However, I do not want to reproach you. I know that you love me, not merely as your father, but also as your truest and surest friend; and that you understand and realize that our happiness and unhappiness, and, what is more, my long life or my speedy death are, if I may say so, apart from God, in your hands. If I have read you aright, I have nothing but joy to expect from you, and this alone must console me when I am robbed by your absence of a father's delight at hearing you, seeing you and folding you in his arms. Live like a good Catholic. Love and fear God. Pray most ardently to Him in true devotion and put

[1] Leopold Mozart is referring to their visits to Paris in 1763 and 1766.

your trust in Him; and lead so Christian a life that, if I should see you no more, the hour of my death may be free from anxiety. From my heart I give you my paternal blessing and remain until death your faithful father and your surest friend

LEOPOLD MOZART

Here is a list of our Paris acquaintances, who will all be delighted to see you.[1]

(282a) *Leopold Mozart to his Wife*

[*Extract*]   [*Autograph in the Mozarteum, Salzburg*][2]

MY DEAR WIFE,   [SALZBURG, 5 *February* 1778]
As you will receive this letter on the 11th or 12th and as I doubt whether a letter will still reach Wolfgang in Mannheim, I will say good-bye to him with this enclosure! I write this with tears in my eyes. Nannerl kisses her dear brother Wolfgang a million times. She would have added a few words of farewell to him, but the paper was already filled up and, besides, I did not let her read my letter. We entreat Wolfgang *to take great care of his health and too keep to the diet he has been accustomed to at home*. If not, he will *have to be bled* as soon as he arrives in Paris. All *heating food* disagrees with him. He will surely take with him *our big Latin prayer-book*, which contains all the psalms in the full office of Our Lady. If he decides to buy the German version of this office of Our Lady in Mannheim, he ought to try to get a copy in the very smallest format. The Latin psalms are difficult to read and a German translation would be helpful. Learned contrapuntal settings of the psalms are performed at the Concert Spirituel; and one can acquire a great reputation by this means. Perhaps Wolfgang could have his 'Misericordias'[3] performed there as well. You have received, I hope, the two sonatas for four hands, the Fischer variations and the Rondo,[4] which were all enclosed in one letter? Farewell. We kiss you millions of times.

MZT.

(283) *Maria Anna Mozart to her Husband*

[*Autograph in the Mozarteum, Salzburg*]

MY DEAR HUSBAND,   MANNHEIM, 7 *February* 1778
You will have seen from Wolfgang's last letter of February 4th that he is quite determined not to go to Paris with ⟨Wendling.⟩ He has told you the reasons, and it is true that those fellows would be ⟨bad company

---

[1] Leopold Mozart encloses a long list, which is almost the same as the lists entered in his *Reiseaufzeichnungen*, pp. 29–32, 47–48.
[2] This undated Postscript is written on the cover of Letter 282.   [3] K. 222 [205a].
[4] K. 358 [186c], 381 [123a], 179 [189a], and probably the rondo of Mozart's clavier sonata, K. 309 [284b], which Leopold Mozart was having copied and returning bit by bit.

for him and might lead him astray.⟩ But do write all the same to Herr von Grimm, whom Wolfgang trusts absolutely. He can always go to Paris later on and meanwhile he is losing nothing by staying here, for it is costing him nothing he can finish his compositions, which he ought not to hurry over.[1] As far as news is concerned, I must tell you that next week the plays and balls are to begin again, for the townspeople would lose far too heavily if the mourning were to last any longer. I can well believe that things are in a sad state in Salzburg; if this goes on, ⟨the whole country will probably be ruined. I pity all good folks who have to live there under such a monster.⟩ I wish Herr von Schiedenhofen a thousand happinesses and blessings on his marriage; and indeed he will need them. Does not Fräulein Louise come to see us any more and is Nannerl Kranach still at home? How is our Chief Purveyor and does he still pay attention to Fräulein Antonia and Herr von Mölk to his Josepha?

(283a) *Mozart to his Father*

*[Autographs in the Mozarteum, Salzburg, and in the possession of
A. Rosenthal, London]*

[MANNHEIM, *7 February* 1778]

Herr von Schiedenhofen might have let me know long ago through you that he was getting married soon, and I should have composed new minuets for the occasion.[2] I wish him joy with my whole heart; but his, I daresay, is again one of those money matches and nothing else. I should not like to marry in this way; I want to make my wife happy, but not to become rich by her means. So I shall let things be and enjoy my golden freedom until I am so well off that I can support a wife and children. Herr von Schiedenhofen was obliged to choose a rich wife; his title demanded it. People of noble birth must never marry from inclination or love, but only from interest and all kinds of secondary considerations. Again, it would not at all suit a grandee to love his wife after she had done her duty and brought into the world a bouncing son and heir. But we poor humble people can not only choose a wife whom we love and who loves us, but we may, can and do take such a one, because we are neither noble, nor highly born, nor aristocratic, nor rich, but, on the contrary, lowly born, humble and poor; so we do not need a wealthy wife, for our riches, being in our brains, die with us—and these no man can take from us unless he chops off our heads, in which case—we need nothing more. We received safely your letter of February 2nd. I had already told you in my previous letter my chief reason for not going to Paris with those people. My second reason is that I have thought over carefully what I should have

---

[1] The works ordered by De Jean. See p. 414.
[2] Mozart's friend, Joachim Ferdinand von Schiedenhofen (1747–1823), married Anna Daubrawa von Daubrawaick (1759–1818), the daughter of the Chief Magistrate of Salzburg.

to do there. I could not get on at all without pupils, which is a kind of
work that is quite uncongenial to me—and of this I have an excellent
example here. I could have had two pupils. I went three times to each,
but finding one of them out, I never went back. I will gladly give lessons
as a favour, particularly when I see that my pupil has talent, inclination
and anxiety to learn; but to be obliged to go to a house at a certain hour
—or to have to wait at home for a pupil—is what I cannot do, no matter
how much money it may bring me in. I find it impossible, so must leave
it to those who can do nothing else but play the clavier. I am a composer
and was born to be a Kapellmeister. I neither can nor ought to bury the
talent for composition with which God in his goodness has so richly
endowed me (I may say so without conceit, for I feel it now more than
ever); and this I should be doing were I to take many pupils, for it is a
most unsettling métier. I would rather, if I may speak plainly, neglect
the clavier than composition, for in my case the clavier with me is only
a side-line, though, thank God, a very good one. My third reason is that
I do not know for certain whether our friend Grimm is in Paris. If he is,
I can always follow in the mail coach; for a capital one goes from here
through Strassburg. We had intended in any event to have gone by it.
They too are travelling in this way. Herr Wendling is inconsolable at
my not going with them, but I believe that this proceeds more from
self-interest than from friendship. In addition to the reason which I gave
him (about the three letters that had come during my absence), I also
told him about the pupils and begged him to procure something *certain*
for me, in which case I should be delighted to follow him to Paris (for I
can easily do so)—especially if I am to write an opera. Writing operas is
now my one burning ambition; but they must be French rather than
German, and Italian rather than either. The Wendlings, one and all,
are of the opinion that my compositions would be extraordinarily
popular in Paris. I have no fears on that score, for, as you know, I can
more or less adopt or imitate any kind and any style of composition.
Shortly after my arrival I composed a French song[1] for Mlle Gustel (the
daughter), who gave me the words; and she sings it incomparably well.
I have the honour to enclose it to you. At Wendlings it is sung every day,
for they are positively crazy about it. Now here is a satire which was
written in Munich. I do not know whether you know it or not, but at
any rate here it is:—

THE KIND AUSTRIANS

Our frontiers to powerfully defend,
But not to do us any harm,
Good Joseph his soldiers doth send

[1] K. 307 [284d], an arietta, 'Oiseaux, si tous les ans', written for Augusta Wendling, daughter
of the flautist Johann Baptist Wendling.

That obstreperous Fritz to alarm.
From eastwards these neighbours have come
And as friends they have filed through our gates,
Both outposts and guards; and no sum
In return our good Joseph awaits.
Our hearths and our homes he's protecting,
So let's give him full use of our land
And, no evil purpose suspecting,
Our welfare entrust to his hand.
But if they too long should remain
And if, after all, 'twere deceit,
The intruders we'll drive out again,
For us no impossible feat.
'Tis true, we possess few soldati,
They're rather a costly affair;
But look at our dancers, castrati,
And of clerics we've more than a pair,
Not to mention those companies grand,
Money-lenders—and huntsman and hound.
Why, Joseph, if these made a stand,
They'd surely dash you to the ground.
Some generals too we possess,
More numerous perhaps than your own,
The piper you'll pay, you confess;
Then leave us in peace and alone.
We hope it—we're just sitting tight.
Oh, do keep those Prussians away!
We hate them, but don't want to fight.
Guardian angel, protect us, we pray.[1]

Joseph's declaration follows in the cover:

Joseph's declaration
In a tone of exaltation.

Bavaria, keep calm! I come to defend,
But what I defend, I'll grab in the end.

In my last letter I forgot to mention Mlle Weber's greatest merit, which
is her superb cantabile singing. Please do not forget about Italy. I commend this poor, but excellent little Mlle Weber to your interest with all
my heart, *caldamente*[2], as the Italians say. I have given her three of De

---

[1] The autograph in the Mozarteum, Salzburg, ends here. The autograph of the remaining
portion of this letter, written inside the cover, is in the possession of A. Rosenthal, Oxford.
[2] i.e. warmly.

Amicis's arias,[1] the scena I wrote for Madame Duschek[2] (to whom I shall be writing soon) and four arias from 'Il Rè pastore'.[3] I have also promised her to have some arias sent from home. I hope you will be kind enough to send them to me, but send them *gratis*, I beg you, and you will really be doing a good work! You will find the list of them on the French song which her father has copied out, and the paper is part of a present from him; but indeed he has given me much more. Now I must close. I kiss your hands a thousand times and embrace my sister with all my heart. Our compliments to all our good friends, especially to Herr Bullinger. Addio. I am your most obedient son

WMZT

Thanks for the sonatas for four hands and the Fischer variations.

(284) *Leopold Mozart to his Wife*

[*Extract*]   [*Autograph in the Mozarteum, Salzburg*]

MY DEAR WIFE!   SALZBURG, *9 February* 1778

People in Mannheim will know enough by this time about conditions in Bavaria, since the Austrian manifestoes have appeared in the papers. Wolfgang ought to be in Munich at the moment, for he could have a word with Baron Zemen, who was and perhaps still is Saxon envoy to Bavaria.

So far I have not heard a word about the preparations for your journey, but perhaps your next letter will tell me something. Here is another sheet of music for Wolfgang, which I trust will still reach him. If, however he has left already, you had better keep it until he has sent you his address in Paris. Possibly, however, Madame Wendling knows it, and, if so, you can send a letter along with the music. But I hope he will not have left before this letter reaches you. Commend our son to Herr Wendling once more and most warmly, and may God protect him! I felt sure that your last letter would have something more to tell, but as Wolfgang wrote to you from Worms, you had naturally nothing new to report. It would have been well if Wolfgang could have found an opportunity of getting someone to remind the Elector about him. However, there is time enough for that. Farewell. We kiss you both millions of times and I remain your old

MZT

---

[1] Giunia's arias in *Lucio Silla*. See. p. 448, n. 3.   [2] K. 272.
[3] Probably nos. 2, 3, 8 and 10.

(284a) *Nannerl Mozart to her Mother and Brother*

[Autograph in the Mozarteum, Salzburg]

[SALZBURG, 9 *February* 1778[1]]

Papa never leaves me room enough to write to Mamma and yourself.
I hope to see her soon and I beg her not to forget me when she is leaving
Mannheim. I wish you a pleasant journey to Paris and the best of health.
I do hope, however, that I shall be able to embrace you soon. But God
alone knows when that will happen. We are both longing for you to
make your fortune, for that, I know for certain, will mean happiness to
us all. I kiss Mamma's hands and embrace you and trust that you will
always remember us all and think of us. But you must only do so when
you have time, say, for a quarter of an hour when you are neither composing nor teaching.

(284b) *Leopold Mozart to his Son*

[Extract]   *[Autograph in the Mozarteum, Salzburg]*

MY DEAR SON!   SALZBURG, 9 *February* 1778

You will have received no doubt the small scores, which I made up in
a neat parcel, and also my letter with the list of our acquaintances in Paris.
The most important people are M. Grimm and Madame la Duchesse de
Bourbon, formerly Mademoiselle d'Orléans, with whom we found
Paisible[2] on the two occasions when we visited her in the convent, and
who dedicated to you a little piece for the clavier, which she had composed
herself. Her husband is the son of Prince Condé and is only 22, whereas
she is 28. ⟨She is not happily married; and I believe that they are not
living together.⟩ Her brother, the Duc de Chartres, is about 31. It was he
who got permission from M. de Sartine, then Lieutenant de la Police, for
us to give those two concerts which brought us in so much money. Then
there is Madame la Comtesse de Tessé, to whom you dedicated your
sonatas,[3] and who is a great patroness of all branches of knowledge. She
took a great fancy to you and gave you the little watch and your sister
the gold toothpick case. I hope she has returned to Paris. She and her
husband, who have been travelling a great deal, were in Italy some time
ago and in Sicily too, I understand. You must make a point of finding out

---

[1] A postscript to her father's letter.
[2] Louis Henri Paisible (1745–1782), born in Paris, became a famous violinist. He was a pupil
of Gaviniès, through whose influence he became a member of the orchestra of the Concert
Spirituel and one of the musicians attached to the household of the Duchesse de Bourbon.
He soon threw up these posts and started travelling in the Netherlands, Germany and Russia,
where, disheartened by failure, he shot himself in St. Petersburg. He composed a few works
for the violin.   [3] K. 8 and 9.

whether the Duc de Braganza may not perhaps be in Paris. He left
Vienna last autumn in order to return to Lisbon, where as a result of the
death of the King of Portugal there is now a government more favourable
to him. I know that he broke his journey in Paris, but possibly he has left
by this time. He would be a useful person for you to know. I must not
forget Madame d'Épinay,[1] a very intimate friend of M. Grimm, who
gave Mamma that beautiful fan. That reminds me, the Comtesse de Tessé
would procure you, I am sure, through her father the Duc d'Ayen, who
took us to Versailles, an introduction to Madame Victoire, who would
be only too glad to see you, as she was so gracious and friendly to you
when you were a child. I should mention too Madame la Duchesse
d'Enville, La Duchesse d'Aiguillon, La Duchesse de Mazarin, La
Comtesse de Lillebonne, Madame de St. Julien, Madame la Princesse de
Robeck, Madame la Comtesse de Wall. In short! All the people on that
list are people of rank, who are sure to remember you and on whom you
must not hesitate to call and, with a certain dignified courtesy and ease of
manner, ask for their protection. I assure you that this will be no easy
task for any one like your self, who is not always associating with the
aristocracy; but it is of the utmost importance that you should do so.
This politesse is extraordinarily efficacious in winning over the French
and will at once secure for you the friendship of all these great ones and
their many acquaintances. *Mark you, you must do this at once*, and you must
let nothing put you off. As it is, you are arriving in Paris rather late, too late
in fact, for in the summer everyone goes into the country. Grimm, if he
is there, will endorse my views and give you all the help you require. You
can tell him all that I have written to you. If he is not in Paris, Madame
d'Épinay will assist you in every way or introduce you to one of her
friends, that is, if you can manage to find her at once. Meanwhile Baron
Bagge will probably be able to give you the addresses of one or two
people. Herr Wendling or somebody else will be able to tell you how
much you should pay for a fiacre. Whenever you walk, be very careful,
for in wet weather the paving-stones in Paris, which are rather like
rounded squares, are extremely slippery, so that one is constantly tripping.
Well, I had better send you a few more names of other people whom
we knew long ago, namely, M. l'Abbé Gauzargue,[2] Kapellmeister in
the Royal Court Chapel at Versailles, a most worthy man, with whom we
had lunch; M. Eckardt, clavierist; M. Gaviniés,[3] violino; Hockbrucker,

[1] Louise Tardieu d'Esclavelles d'Épinay (1726–1783), a French writer, well known on
account of her *liaisons* with Rousseau and Grimm and her friendships with Diderot, d'Alembert and other French men of letters. Her *Mémoires*, a sort of autobiographical romance, were
published in Paris in 1818.

[2] Abbé Charles Gauzargue (? –1799). He wrote a *Traité de composition*, Paris, 1797.

[3] Pierre Gaviniés (1728–1800), an eminent violinist, called the French Tartini. He appeared
in 1741 at the Concert Spirituel, which he subsequently directed, 1773–1777; and when the
Paris Conservatoire was founded in 1794, he was appointed to a professorship of the violin.

harpist. The latter, as you know, is a cheerful fool, but *you must avoid having anything to do with him*, for he has *a very bad reputation* on account of his dissolute life; moreover, he is a coarse fellow and runs up debts. M. du Borde,[1] a very conceited violoncellist; M. le Tourneur,[2] court organist; M. Molitor, who plays the French horn at Versailles; M. Haranc,[3] violino; M. Besson, violino; M. le Grand, clavierist; M. Jélyotte,[4] chanteur au théâtre; M. Mayer, harpist; M. Henno, who plays the French horn at Prince Conti's; M. Duni,[5] maître de chapelle, who has written some comic operas; M. Canévas,[6] violoncellist, whose daughter married Herr Cramer and died at Mannheim; M. le Duc,[7] violino; Mlle Fel,[8] an old singer in the French theatre; M. Cahaut,[9] joueur de la lute chez le Prince Conti; M. Honnauer, clavecin; M. Philidor,[10] compositeur, and so forth. I need hardly tell you, for you know this quite well yourself, that with *very few exceptions* you will gain nothing by associating with these people, and that to be intimate with them may even do you harm. If Gluck and Piccinni are there, you will avoid their company as much as possible; and you must not form a close friendship with Grétry [11] De la

[1] Jean Pierre Duport (1741–1818), one of two brothers who were eminent violoncellists. He was in the orchestra of Prince Conti until 1769, then paid several visits to London, travelled to Spain in 1771 and finally, on the invitation of Frederick the Great, settled in Berlin as first violoncellist in the king's orchestra, his pupil being the future king, Frederick William II.

[2] In Leopold Mozart's *Reiseaufzeichnungen*, p. 30, le Tourneur is described as 'claveciniste de la cour'.

[3] Louis André Haranc (1738–1805) became in 1770 first violin in the court orchestra and in 1775 Director of the court music to the Queen.

[4] Pierre de Jélyotte (1713–1787), a French tenor and composer. He was trained at Toulouse, first appeared in the Paris opéra in 1733, soon took part in all the important productions and continued to sing until 1779. The Mozarts had met him in Paris in 1764. Leopold Mozart's entry in his *Reiseaufzeichnungen*, p. 32, is 'chanteur renommé en France, c'est-à-dire, pour leur goût'.

[5] Egidio Romoaldo Duni (1709–1775), composer of Italian and French light operas. He was born and studied in Naples and had his first triumph in Rome with his opera *Nerone*. After several travels abroad he was appointed tutor to the court of Parma. At the Duke's suggestion he composed a French opera *Ninette à la cour*, which was so popular that in 1757 he settled in Paris, where he wrote twenty operas, most of which were outstanding successes. He is regarded as the founder of the French opéra-comique.

[6] Canavas. In his *Reiseaufzeichnungen*, p. 32, Leopold Mozart adds the remark 'Sa femme et sa fille qui joue du clavecin fort bien et qui chante bien'.

[7] Either Simon Leduc (1748–1787), soloist in violin concertos at the Concert Spirituel and a well-known music publisher, or his younger brother, Pierre Leduc (1755–1816), who was also a violinist at the Concert Spirituel and subsequently took over Simon's publishing business.

[8] Marie Fel (1713–1794), a famous high soprano, who made her début in 1734 at the opera and the Concert Spirituel, but had to retire in 1758 owing to bad health.

[9] Joseph Kohaut (*c.* 1736–1793). He also wrote operas for the Comédie-Italienne. A second entry in Leopold Mozart's *Reiseaufzeichnungen* has the remark 'honnête homme'.

[10] François André Danican Philidor (1726–1795), an eminent composer and a distinguished chess-player. He at first supported himself in Paris by giving lessons and copying music. He then travelled and wrote books on chess. Diderot and other friends brought him back to Paris, where he started to compose sacred and operatic music and from 1759 onwards won great successes with his comic operas. He is generally regarded as Duni's successor.

[11] André Ernest Modeste Grétry (1741–1813), born at Liège, an eminent composer of operas. He very soon discovered that comic opera was his true vocation and from 1768 onwards won outstanding successes in Paris. He has been called the 'Molière of music'. His literary activity too was very great, though the value of his works as contributions to the study of music is small.

politesse et pas d'autre chose. *You can always be perfectly natural* with people of high rank; but with everybody else *please behave like an Englishman.* You must not be so open with everyone! You should not let a friseur or any other domestique see your money, rings or watch; still less should you leave them lying about. ⟨Even your friends should not know when you receive money or how much you have in hand.⟩ If you have any cash, take it to the bankers Turton et Baur. I only kept out what I really needed and gave them the remainder, for which they handed me a receipt. Thus I could be sure that my money would not be stolen, while, if anyone wanted to borrow from me, I could make the excuse that I had sent off my earnings to Salzburg. Never go out walking at night. And finally, remind yourself every day what you owe to God, who has bestowed such extraordinary talents upon you. Do not get annoyed with me for telling you this so often. Surely you realise my responsibility as a father? You were vexed when I reminded you the other day ⟨*about confessing.*⟩ But put yourself in my place and then tell me whether it is my duty to do so or not? Oh, Heaven! When shall I see you again? I kiss you millions of times and remain your surest and truest friend and father

L:MZT

(285) *Leopold Mozart to his Son*

[Extract]   [*Autograph in the Mozarteum, Salzburg*]

MY DEAR SON!   SALZBURG, [11]–12 *February* 1778

    I have read your letter of the 4th with amazement and horror. I am beginning to answer it today, the 11th, for the whole night long I was unable to sleep and am so exhausted that I can only write quite slowly, word by word, and so gradually finish what I have to say by tomorrow. Up to the present, thank God, I have been in good health; but this letter, in which I only recognise my son by that failing of his which makes him believe everyone at the first word spoken, open his kind heart to every plausible flatterer and let others sway him as they like, so that he is led by whimsical ideas and ill-considered and impracticable projects to sacrifice his own name and interests, and even the interests and the claims of his aged and honourable parents to those of strangers—this letter, I say, depressed me exceedingly, the more so as I was cherishing the reasonable hope that certain circumstances which you had had to face already, as well as my own reminders, both spoken and written, could not have failed to convince you that not only for the sake of your happiness but in order that you may be able to gain a livelihood and attain at length the desired goal in a world of men in varying degrees good and bad, fortunate and unfortunate, it was imperative for you to guard your warm heart by the strictest reserve, undertake nothing without full consideration and never let yourself be carried away by enthusiastic notions and blind fancies. My dear son, I implore you to read this letter carefully—and take time to reflect upon it. Merciful God! those happy moments are gone when, as child and boy, you never went to bed without standing on a chair and singing to me *Oragna fiagata fa*,[1] and ending by kissing me again and again on the tip of my nose and telling me that when I grew old you would put me in a glass case and protect me from every breath of air, so that you might always have me with you and honour me. Listen to me, therefore, in patience! You are fully acquainted with our difficulties in Salzburg—you know my wretched income, why I kept my promise to let you go away, and all my various troubles. The purpose of your journey was twofold—either to get a good permanent appointment, or, if this should fail, to go off to some big city where large sums of money can be earned. Both plans were designed to assist your parents and to help on your dear sister, but above all to build up your own name and reputation in the world. The latter was partly accomplished in your childhood and boyhood; and it now depends on you alone to raise yourself gradually to a position of eminence, such as no musician has ever obtained. You owe that to the extraordinary talents which you have received from a beneficent God; and now it depends solely on your good sense and your way of life whether you die as an ordinary musician, utterly forgotten by the world, or as a famous Kapellmeister, of whom posterity will read,—whether, captured by some woman, you die bedded on straw in an attic full of starving children, or whether, after a Christian life spent in contentment, honour and renown, you leave this world with your family well provided for and your name respected by all. You took that journey to Munich—with what purpose you know—but nothing could be done. Well-meaning friends wanted to keep you there and you wished to remain. Someone hit on the idea of forming a company—but I need not recapitulate everything in detail. At the time you thought the scheme practicable. I did not. Read the letter I sent you in reply. You have a sense of honour. Would it have done you honour, assuming that the scheme had been carried out, to depend on the monthly charity of ten persons? At that time you were quite amazingly taken up with the little singer[2] at the theatre and your dearest wish was to forward the cause of the German stage; now you declare that you would not even care to write a comic opera! No sooner had you left the gates of Munich behind you than (as I prophesied) your whole company

---

[1] For the melody, which, as Abert (vol. i, p. 28, n. 1) points out, is a variation of an old Dutch folk-song 'Willem von Nassau', see Leitzmann, p. 12. In the material which Nissen collected for his biography of Mozart, and which is now in the Mozarteum, Salzburg, there is a statement that Mozart often hummed a tune to the nonsensical words 'Nannetta Nanon, puisque la bedetta fa, Nannetta, inevenedetta fa Nanon'. See *MM*, November 1919, p. 30.

[2] Mademoiselle Kaiser. See p. 290, n. 2.

of subscribers had forgotten you. What would be your lot were you in Munich now?—In the end one can always see the providence of God. In Augsburg too you had your little romance, you amused yourself with my brother's daughter, who now must needs send you her portrait. The rest I wrote to you in my first letters to Mannheim. When you were at Wallerstein[1] you caused the company great amusement, you took up a violin, and danced about and played, so that people described you to absent friends as a merry, high-spirited and brainless fellow, thus giving Herr Beecke the opportunity of disparaging your merits although your compositions and your sister's playing (for she always says '*I am only my brother's pupil*') have since made these two gentlemen regard you in another light, so that they now have the very highest opinion of your art and are indeed more inclined to run down Herr Beecke's poor compositions. When you were in Mannheim you did well to win the good graces of Herr ⟨*Cannabich*⟩. But you would have gained nothing, had he not been seeking a double advantage therefrom. I have already written to you about the rest. Next, Herr ⟨Cannabich's⟩ daughter was smothered in praises, her temperament was recorded in the Adagio of a sonata, in short, *she* was now the reigning favourite. Then you made the acquaintance of Herr Wendling. *He* was now the most honourable friend—and what happened next, I need not repeat. Suddenly you strike up a new acquaintanceship—with Herr Weber; all your other friends are forgotten; now *this family* is the most honourable, the most Christian family and the daughter is to have the leading role in the tragedy to be enacted between your own family and hers! In the transports into which your kind and too open heart has thrown you, you think all your ill-considered fancies as reasonable and practicable as if they were bound to be accomplished in the normal course of nature. You are thinking of taking her to Italy as a prima donna. Tell me, do you know of any prima donna who, without having first appeared many times in Germany, has walked on to the stage in Italy as prima donna? In how many operas did not Signora Bernasconi sing in Vienna, and operas too of the most passionate type, produced under the very severe criticism and direction of Gluck and Calzabigi?[2] In how many operas did not Mlle Teiber[3] sing in Vienna under Hasse's direction and taught by that old singer and very famous actress, Signora Tesi,[4] whom you saw at Prince Hildburghausen's[5] and whose negress

[1] Leopold Mozart had evidently heard an account of his son's doings from Anton Janitsch and Joseph Reicha.

[2] Raniero da Calzabigi (1715–1795), famous in musical history as the librettist of Gluck's three great Italian operas, *Orfeo ed Euridice* (1762), *Alceste* (1767) and *Paride ed Elena* (1770).

[3] Elizabeth Teiber. See p. 74, n. 2.

[4] Vittoria Tesi-Tramontini (1700–1775), a celebrated singer. She was born in Florence and in her youth sang chiefly in Italy. In 1747 she settled in Vienna where she opened a school of singing.

[5] Prince Joseph Friedrich von Sachsen-Hildburghausen, Imperial Field-marshal, famous in musical history as the patron of Gluck.

you kissed as a child?[1] How many times did not Mlle Schindler[2] appear in Italian opera at Vienna, after making her début in a private production at Baron Fries's country seat under the direction of Hasse and Tesi and Metastasio? Did any of these people dare to throw themselves at the head of the Italian public? And how much patronage, what powerful recommendations did they not need before they were able to attain their object? Princes and counts recommended them, famous composers and poets vouched for their ability. And now you want me to write to Lugiati! Your proposal is to compose an opera for fifty ducats, although you know that the Veronese have no money and never commission a new opera. I am now to remember the Ascensa, although Michele Dall' Agata has not even replied to my two previous letters. I am quite willing to believe that Mlle ⟨Weber⟩ sings like a Gabrielli; that she has a *powerful voice* for the Italian stage; that she has the build of a prima donna and all the rest; but it is absurd of you to vouch for her capacity to act. Acting calls for more than these qualities. Why, old Hasse's childish, albeit most kindly meant and good-natured efforts on behalf of Miss Davies[3] banished her for ever from the Italian stage, where she was hissed off on the first night and her part given to De Amicis. Even an experienced male actor, let alone a female, may well tremble during his first appearance in a foreign country. And do you think that is all?—By no means!—Ci vuole il possesso del teatro.[4] This is particularly true of a woman, who has in addition to consider the way in which she dresses and adorns herself. You yourself know all this, if you will but think it over. I know that serious reflection on all these points will convince you that, kindly as your plan is meant, it needs *time* and *much preparation* and must be approached in a very different way if it is ever to be carried out. What impresario would not laugh, were one to recommend him a girl of sixteen or seventeen, who has never yet appeared on a stage! As for your proposal (I can hardly write when I think of it), your proposal to travel about with Herr ⟨Weber⟩ and, be it noted, his two daughters—it has nearly made me lose my reason! My dearest son! How can you have allowed yourself to be bewitched even for an hour by such a horrible idea, which must have been suggested to you by someone or other! Your letter reads like a romance. For could you really make up your mind to go trailing about the world with strangers? Quite apart from your reputation—what of your old parents and your dear sister? To expose me to the mockery and ridicule of the Prince and

---

[1] During Mozart's first visit to Vienna in 1762.

[2] Katharina Leithner-Schindler (1755–1788) was a well-known singer at the Italian opera in Vienna. In 1777 she married the theatrical manager J. B. Bergopzoomer. In 1783 she joined the Prague opera.

[3] Cecilia Davies (1738–1836), the younger sister of Marianne Davies, the armonica-player. She was an excellent singer and was fairly successful in Italy, where she was called 'L'Inglesina'. In 1771 she appeared in Hasse's opera *Ruggiero* in Milan.

[4] One must have the stage presence.

of *the whole town which loves you?* Yes, to expose me to mockery and yourself to contempt, for in reply to repeated questions, I have had to tell everyone that you were going to Paris. And now, after all, you want to roam about with strangers and take your chance? Surely, after a little reflection you will give up all idea of doing so! But that I may convince you of your rash precipitancy, let me tell you that the time is now coming when no man in his senses could think of such a thing. Conditions are now such that it is impossible to guess where war may break out, for everywhere regiments are either on the march or under marching orders. —To Switzerland?—To Holland? Why, there is not a soul there the whole summer; and at Berne and Zürich in winter one can just make enough not to die of starvation, but nothing more. As for Holland they have things to think of there besides music; and in any case half one's takings are eaten up by Herr Hummel[1] and concert expenses. Besides, what will become of your reputation? Those are places for lesser lights, for second-rate composers, for scribblers, for a Schwindel,[2] a Zappa,[3] a Ricci[4] and the like. Name any one great composer to me who would deign to take such an abject step! *Off with you to Paris!* and that soon! Find your place among great people. *Aut Caesar aut nihil.* The mere thought of seeing Paris ought to have preserved you from all these flighty ideas. *From Paris the name and fame of a man of great talent resounds throughout the whole world. There the nobility treat men of genius with the greatest deference, esteem and courtesy; there you will see a refined manner of life, which forms an astonishing contrast to the coarseness of our German courtiers and their ladies; and there you may become proficient in the French tongue.* As for the company of ⟨Wendling⟩ and his friends, you do not need it at all. You have known them for a long time—and did your Mamma not realize what type of men they were? Were you both blind?—Nay, but I know how it was. You were set upon it, and she did not dare to oppose you. It angers me that both of you should have lacked the confidence and frankness to give me circumstantial and detailed information. You both treated me in the same way over that matter of the ⟨Elector,⟩ and yet in the end it all had to come out. You want to spare me anxiety and in the end you suddenly overturn a whole bucketful of worries on my head, which almost kill me! You know, and you have a thousand proofs of it, that God in his goodness

[1] Johann Julius Hummel (? –1798), a music publisher at Amsterdam (from *c.* 1766) and Berlin (from 1774), who published many important works. The business was dissolved in 1821.

[2] Friedrich Schwindel (1737–1786) was a skilful player on the violin, flute and clavier. As a composer he was a follower of the Mannheim school. From 1765 onwards his numerous symphonies, quartets and trios were performed in Amsterdam, Paris and London.

[3] Francesco Zappa of Milan was a famous violoncellist in his day and composed several works, chiefly for his instrument.

[4] Abbate Pasquale Ricci (*c.* 1733– ?) was born in Como, where he eventually became maestro di cappella of the cathedral. He travelled widely. Many of his numerous compositions were published and were well received in other countries.

has given me sound judgement, that I still have my head screwed on, and that in the most tangled circumstances I have often found a way out and foreseen and guessed aright. What has prevented you then from asking my advice from always acting as I desired? My son, you should regard me rather as your most sincere friend, than as a severe father. Consider whether I have not always treated you kindly, served you as a servant his master, even provided you with all possible entertainment and helped you to enjoy all honourable and seemly pleasures, often at great inconvenience to myself! I presume that Herr ⟨Wendling⟩ has left already. Though half-dead, I have managed to think out and arrange everything connected with your journey to Paris. Herr Arbauer, a well-known merchant of Augsburg and Frankfurt, is now there with his German agent and is staying for the whole of Lent. I shall send off a letter to him on the 23rd and by the same post I shall write to you very fully and tell you what you have to do and how much approximately the journey will cost you; and I shall enclose an open letter which you must deliver to Herr Arbauer (I understand that he was at your Augsburg concert), who will be expecting it. This wretched business has cost me a couple of sleepless nights. As soon as you receive this letter, I want you to write and tell me *how much money you have in hand*. I trust that you can count for certain on those 200 gulden. I was amazed to read your remark that you would now finish that music for M. De Jean at your leisure. It seems then that you have not yet delivered it. Yet you were thinking of leaving on February 15th?—You even went on a trip to Kirchheim—even taking Mlle ⟨Weber⟩ with you, with the result that of course you received less money, as the Princess had two people to reward, a present which otherwise you might have had for yourself. However, that does not matter. But, Good God! Suppose Herr ⟨*Wendling*⟩ were now to play a trick on you and M. De Jean were ⟨to break his word,⟩ for the arrangement was that you were to wait and travel with them. Do send me news by the next post, so that I may know how things are. Well, I am going to tell you what you *can* do for Mlle Weber. Tell me, who are the people who give lessons in Italy? Are they not old maestri, and generally *old tenors*? Has Signor Raaff heard her sing? Have a word with him and ask him to hear her perform your arias. *You could say that you would like him to hear a few of them.* In this way you could use your influence with him later on her behalf. However he may sing now, he knows his job, and if she impresses him, she can count on making a good impression on all the Italian impresarios who knew him in his prime. Meanwhile she could surely find an opportunity of getting on the stage in Mannheim where, even if it is unpaid work, she would be gaining experience. Your desire to help the oppressed you have inherited from your father. But you really must consider first of all the welfare of your parents, or else your soul will go to the devil. Think of me as you saw me when you left us, *standing beside the carriage in a state of utter wretchedness.* Ill as I was, I had been packing for you until two o'clock in the morning, and there I was at the carriage again at six o'clock, seeing to everything for you. Hurt me now, if you can be so cruel! Win fame and *make money* in Paris; then, *when you have money to spend,* go off to Italy and get commissions for operas. This cannot be done by writing letters to impresarios, though I am prepared to do so. Then you could put forward Mlle ⟨Weber's⟩ name, which can be the more easily done if you do so personally. Write to me by the next post without fail. We kiss you both a million times and I remain your old honest husband and father

                                                                    MZT

Bullinger sends his greetings.

Nannerl has wept her full share during these last two days. Addio. Mamma is to go to Paris with Wolfgang, so you had better make the necessary arrangements.

(286) *Maria Anna Mozart to her Husband*

[*Autograph in the Mozarteum, Salzburg*]

MY DEAR HUSBAND,   MANNHEIM, 13 *February* 1778

We know only too well what the situation is in Bavaria. But as for the Electress of Saxony's claims we have not yet heard anything about them. That would really be too much. In the end the Elector would have nothing left of his whole inheritance. Everything is very quiet here and there seems to be nothing but secrets. The papers only talk about matters of indifference; there is not a single thing about Bavaria. As for my journey to Salzburg I do hope that we shall hit on something suitable, for the weather is still too cold and raw for me to sit all day in an open carriage. Really it would be too uncomfortable. And after all if I had wanted to travel in winter, it would not have been necessary for us to stay here so long. Moreover, when the weather gets milder, we shall more easily find some opportunity for me to travel in company. I do not mind a bit, provided I have not got to travel alone to Augsburg. I am not at all nervous about the journey on to Salzburg. I shan't forget Nannerl. In the meantime I send my greetings to her, and also to all our good friends. Addio. Keep well, both of you. I kiss you both many 100000 times and remain your faithful wife

                                                          MARIANNA MOZART

In the meantime you will have received our letter and decided what is to be done.

FRIEDRICH MELCHIOR GRIMM (1778)

From a water-colour painting by Carmontelle
(Musée Condé, Chantilly)

(286a) *Mozart to his Father*

[Autograph in the Mozarteum, Salzburg]

MONSIEUR   [MANNHEIM, 14 *February* 1778]
MON TRÉS CHER PÉRE!

I see from your letter of February 9th that you have not yet received my last two letters. Herr Wendling and Herr Ramm are leaving early tomorrow morning. If I thought that you would be really displeased with me for not going to Paris with them, I should regret having stayed here; but I hope it is not so. The road to Paris is still open. Herr Wendling has promised to make enquiries immediately about M. Grimm and to send me information at once. If I have such a friend in Paris, I shall certainly go there, for he will assuredly arrange something for me. The main cause of my not going with them is that we have not yet been able to arrange about Mamma returning to Augsburg. How on earth could she have stayed here in the house without me? I do implore you just to give a little thought to her journey from Augsburg to Salzburg; once I know about this, I shall arrange for her to get to Augsburg comfortably. If there is no other way, I shall take her there myself. We can lodge at the Holy Cross Monastery. But the essential thing to know is whether she will be then travelling home with one or more persons? And whether, if they are only two, there will be a chaise there already, or whether she ought to use ours? This last we can settle quite well later on. The main thing is to get her safely on the road from Augsburg to Salzburg. The journey to Augsburg will not cost much, for no doubt there are drivers here who can be engaged at a cheap rate. By that time, however, I hope to have made enough to pay for Mamma's journey home. Just now I really do not know how it would be possible. M. De Jean is also leaving for Paris tomorrow and, because I have only finished two concertos[1] and three quartets[2] for him, has sent me 96 gulden (that is, 4 gulden too little, evidently supposing that this was the half of 200); but he must pay me in full, for that was my agreement with the Wendlings, and I can send him the other pieces later. It is not surprising that I have not been able to finish them, for I never have a single quiet hour here. I can only compose at night, so that I can't get up early as well; besides, one is not always in the mood for working. I could, to be sure, scribble off things the whole day long, but a composition of this kind goes out into the world, and naturally I do not want to have cause to be ashamed of my name on the title-page. Moreover, you know that I become quite powerless whenever I am obliged to write for an instrument which I cannot bear. Hence as a

[1] K. 313 [285c] and 314 [285d]. See p. 457, n. 1.
[2] K. 285, 285a and K. App. 171 [K. 285b]. See p. 456.

diversion I compose something else, such as duets for clavier and violin,[1] or I work at my mass.[2] Now I am settling down seriously to the clavier duets, as I want to have them engraved. If only the Elector were here, I should very quickly finish the mass. But what can't be, can't be. I am much obliged to you, my dear Papa, for your fatherly letter; I shall put it by among my treasures and always refer to it. Please do not forget about my mother's journey from Augsburg to Salzburg and let me know the precise time; and please remember the arias I mentioned in my last letter. If I am not mistaken, there are also some cadenzas which I once jotted down and at least one aria cantabile with coloratura indications.[3] I should like that first of all, for it would be good practice for Mlle Weber. I only taught her the day before yesterday an Andantino Cantabile by Bach,[4] the whole of it. Yesterday there was a concert at Cannabich's, where all the music was of my composition, except the first symphony, which was his own. Mlle Rosa played my concerto in B♭,[5] then Herr Ramm (by way of a change) played for the fifth time my oboe concerto written for Ferlendis,[6] which is making a great sensation here. It is now Ramm's cheval de bataille. After that Mlle Weber sang most charmingly the aria di bravura of De Amicis.[7] Then I played my old concerto in D major,[8] because it is such a favourite here, and I also extemporized for half an hour; after which Mlle Weber sang De Amicis's aria 'Parto, m'affretto'[9] and was loudly applauded. Finally my ouverture to 'Il Rè pastore' was performed. I do entreat you most earnestly to interest yourself in Mlle Weber; I would give anything if she could only make her fortune. Husband, wife and five children on an income of 450 gulden! —On my own account too, don't forget about Italy. You know my great longing and my passion. I hope that all will go well. I have placed my trust in God, Who will never forsake us. Now farewell, and don't forget all my requests and recommendations. I kiss your hands 100000 times and remain your most obedient son

WOLFGANG GOTTLIEB MOZART

Mannheim, 14 February 1778.

I embrace my sister with all my heart. My greetings to all our good friends and especially to Herr Bullinger. A propos, how do you like the French aria?[10]

[1] The violin sonatas K. 301-306 [293a–c, 300c, 293d, 300l], two of which, K. 304 [300c] and 306 [300l], were written in Paris. The series was engraved in 1778 by Sieber in Paris and dedicated to the Electress Marie Elizabeth of the Palatinate.

[2] Probably K. 322 [296a], a Kyrie composed in 1778, was intended to form part of this mass. Otherwise there is no trace of it.   [3] See Köchel, pp. 300, 301.

[4] Johann Christian Bach.   [5] K. 238.

[6] Probably K. 314 [285d], which Mozart rewrote as a flute concerto for De Jean. See Köchel, p. 295, 296.   [7] See p. 448, n. 3.

[8] K. 175, composed in 1773, Mozart's first clavier concerto.

[9] From Mozart's opera *Lucio Silla*.   [10] K. 307 [284d]. See p. 468, n. 1.

(287) *Leopold Mozart to his Wife and Son*

[Extract]   *[Autograph in the Mozarteum, Salzburg]*

SALZBURG, 16 *February* 1778

MY DEAR WIFE AND MY DEAR SON!

I have received your letter of February 7th with the French aria[1] which was enclosed; and my letter of the 12th, written in pain and fear, will have reached you by this time. I began a second letter yesterday, which, however, I do not feel able to finish today. I am saving it up for some other post-day. Your aria has made me breathe a little more easily, for here is one of my dear Wolfgang's compositions and something so excellent that I am sure that it was only some very persuasive tongue which must for the moment have driven you to prefer a knock-about existence to the reputation which you might acquire in a city so famous and so profitable to the talented as Paris. Everyone is right who says that your compositions will be very popular in Paris; and you yourself are convinced, as I am too, that you are able to imitate all styles of composition. It was a good thing that you did not travel with those fellows. But you had long since detected the ⟨*evil streak in their characters*;⟩ and yet all that long time when you ⟨*were associating with them*,⟩ you did not sufficiently trust your father (who is so anxious about you) to write to him about it and ask him for his advice: and it horrifies me to think that your mother did not do so either. My son! You are hot-tempered and impulsive in all your ways! Since your childhood and boyhood your whole character has changed. As a child and a boy you were serious rather than childish and when you sat at the clavier or were otherwise intent on music, no one dared to have the slightest jest with you. Why, even your expression was so solemn that, observing the early efflorescence of your talent and your ever grave and thoughtful little face, many discerning people of different countries sadly doubted whether your life would be a long one. But now, as far as I can see, you are much too ready to retort in a bantering tone to the first challenge—and that, of course, is the first step towards undue familiarity, which anyone who wants to preserve his self-respect will try to avoid in this world. A good-hearted fellow is accustomed, it is true, to express himself freely and naturally; none the less it is a mistake to do so. And it is just your good heart which prevents you from detecting any shortcomings in a person who showers praises on you, has a great opinion of you and flatters you to the skies, and who makes you give him all your confidence and affection; whereas as a boy you were so extraordinarily modest that you used to weep when people praised you overmuch. The greatest art of all is *to know oneself* and then, my dear son, to do as I do, that is, *to endeavour to get to know others through and through*. This, as you

[1] K. 307 [284d].

483

know, has always been my study; and certainly it is a fine, useful and indeed most necessary one. As for your giving lessons in Paris you need not bother your head about it. *In the first place*, no one is going to dismiss his master at once and engage you. *In the second place*, no one would dare to ask you, and you yourself would certainly not take on anyone except possibly some lady, who is already *a good player and wants to take lessons in interpretation*, which would be easy work for good pay. For instance, would you not have gladly undertaken to give Countess von Lützow and Countess Lodron two or three lessons a week at a fee of two or three louis d'or a month, the more so as such ladies also put themselves to a great deal of trouble to collect subscribers for the engraving of your compositions? In Paris everything is done by these great ladies, many of whom are devoted lovers of the clavier and in some cases excellent performers. These are the people who can help you. As for composition, why, you could make money and gain a great reputation by publishing *works for the clavier, string quartets and so forth, symphonies* and possibly a collection of *melodious French arias* with clavier accompaniment like the one you sent me, and finally operas. Well, what objection have you to raise now? But you want everything to be done at once, before people have even seen you or heard any of your works. Read my long list of the acquaintances we had in Paris at that time. All, or at least most of them, are the leading people in that city and they will all be both delighted and interested to see you again. Even if only six of them take you up (and indeed one single one of the most influential of them would be enough), you would be able to do whatever you pleased, I shall have the arias which you want for Mlle Weber copied, and I shall send what I can find. I enclose herewith two unsealed letters of recommendation, which you must keep safely and, when you reach Paris, present to Herr Joseph Felix Arbauer, the big dealer in fancy goods. Mr. Mayer, in whose house Count Wolfegg lived, is Arbauer's agent. I must close. Nannerl and I kiss you both 100000 times and I remain your faithful husband and father

MZT

Grassl Martini, who was Prince Breuner's attendant, was buried today. Wolfgang will remember that he composed for him a little piece for the French horn.[1]

(288) *Mozart to his Father*

[Autograph in the Mozarteum, Salzburg]

MONSIEUR　　　　　　　　　　　　MANNHEIM, 19 *February* 1778
MON TRÉS CHER PÉRE!

　　I hope you received my last two letters safely. In the last one I discussed my mother's journey home, but I now see from your letter of the

---

[1] There is no trace of this composition. See Köchel, p. 47.

12th that this was quite unnecessary. I always thought that you would disapprove of my undertaking a journey ⟨with the Webers,⟩ but I never had any such intention—I mean, of course, *in our present circumstances.* I gave them my word of honour, however, to write to you about it. Herr Weber does not know how we stand—and I shall certainly never tell anyone. I wish my position were such that I had no cause to consider anyone else and that we were all comfortably off. In the intoxication of the moment I forgot how impossible it is at present to carry out my plan, and therefore also—to tell you what I have now done. The reasons why I have not gone off to Paris must be sufficiently evident to you from my last two letters. If my mother had not first raised the point, I should certainly have gone with my friends; but when I saw that she did not like the scheme, then I began to dislike it myself. For as soon as people lose confidence in me, I am apt to lose confidence in myself. Those days when, standing on a chair, I used to sing to you *Oragna fiagata fa* and finish by kissing you on the tip of your nose, are gone indeed; but do I honour, love and obey you any the less on that account? I will say no more. As for your reproach about the little singer in Munich,[1] I must confess that I was an ass to tell you such a palpable lie. Why, she does not yet know what *singing* means. It is true that for a person who had only been studying for three months she sang surprisingly well, and she had, in addition, a very pleasing and pure voice. Why I praised her so much may well have been because I was hearing people say from morning to night 'There is no better singer in all Europe' and 'Who has not heard her, has heard nothing'. I did not dare to contradict them, partly because I wanted to make some good friends, and partly because I had come straight from Salzburg, where we are not in the habit of contradicting anyone; but as soon as I was alone, I never could help laughing. Why then did I not laugh at her when writing to you? I really cannot tell.

What you say so cuttingly about my merry intercourse with your brother's daughter has hurt me very much; but since matters are not as you think, it is not necessary for me to reply. I don't know what to say about Wallerstein. I was very grave and reserved at Beecke's; and at the officers' table also I maintained a very serious demeanour and did not say a word to anyone. Let us forget all that; you only wrote it in a temper.

What you say about Mlle Weber is all perfectly true; and at the time I wrote that letter I knew quite as well as you do that she is still too young and that she must first learn how to act and make frequent appearances on the stage. But with some people one must proceed—by degrees. These good people are as tired of being here as—you know whom and where;[2] and they think that every scheme is practicable. I promised them to write everything to my father; but when the letter was on its way to Salzburg,

[1] Mlle Kaiser. See p. 475.   [2] Mozart and his father in Salzburg.

I kept on telling them: 'She must be patient a little longer, she is a bit too young yet, etc.' They do not mind what I say to them, for they have a high opinion of me. On my advice the father has engaged Madame Toscani (an actress) to give his daughter lessons in acting. Everything you say about Mlle Weber is true, except one thing—that 'she sings like a Gabrielli'; for I should not at all like her to sing in that style. Those who have heard Gabrielli are forced to admit that she was an adept only at runs and roulades; she adopted, however, such an unusual interpretation that she won admiration; but it never survived the fourth time of hearing. In the long run she could not please, for people soon get tired of coloratura passages. Moreover she had the misfortune of not being able to sing. She was not capable of *sustaining* a breve properly, and, as she had no *messa di voce*,[1] she could not dwell on her notes; in short, she sang with skill but without understanding. Mlle Weber's singing, on the other hand, goes to the heart, and she prefers to sing cantabile. Lately I have made her practise the passages in my grand aria,[2] because, if she goes to Italy, she will have to sing bravura arias. Undoubtedly she will never forget how to sing cantabile, for that is her natural bent. Raaff himself (who is certainly no flatterer), when asked to give his candid opinion, said 'She sang, not like a student, but like a master'. So now you know all. I still commend her to your interest with all my heart; and please don't forget about the arias, cadenzas and the rest. Farewell. I kiss your hands 100000 times and remain your most obedient son

WOLFGANG AMADÉ MOZART

I can't write any more for sheer hunger. My mother will display the contents of our large cash-box. I embrace my sister with all my heart. Tell her she must not cry over every silly trifle, or I shall never go home again. My greetings to all our good friends, especially to Herr Bullinger.

(288a) *Maria Anna Mozart to her Husband*

[Autograph in the Mozarteum, Salzburg]

MY DEAR HUSBAND   [MANNHEIM, 19 *February* 1778]

I hope that this letter may find you well again. We are both awfully sorry that our letter horrified you so. On the other hand, your last letter of the 12th distressed us greatly. I implore you with all my might not to take everything to heart in the way you do, for it is bad for your health. Why, everything can be made right again and we have lost nothing but ⟨bad⟩ company. We shall do our very best to make arrangements for

---

[1] i.e. sustained voice.   [2] From *Lucio Silla*. See p. 448, n. 3.

our journey to Paris. Our whole capital now consists of 140 gulden. We shall try to sell the carriage, but I should say that we shall hardly get more than 60 or 70 gulden for it; only the other day someone bought a fine glass carriage with four seats for nine louis d'or. We shall pack all our things into two trunks and travel by mail coach, which will not be very expensive. Quite respectable people travel in this way. But we ought to have rooms engaged, so that we need not stay at the inn for long. If that merchant you told us about would be so kind as to help us to find them, it would be splendid. Meanwhile I am longing for your next letter, so that we may make arrangements in accordance with what you want us to do. Addio. Keep well, both of you. I kiss you both several 10000 times and remain your faithful wife

MARIA ANNA MOZART

All sorts of messages to all our good friends.
What a horrible pen and ink.

(289) *Mozart to his Father*

[Autograph in the Mozarteum, Salzburg]

MONSIEUR   [MANNHEIM, 22 *February* 1778]
    MON TRÉS CHER PÉRE,
    I have been confined to the house for two days and have been taking antispasmodics, black powders and elderberry tea to make me sweat, as I have had catarrh, a cold in the head, headache, a sore throat, pains in my eyes and earache. But, thank God, I am better now and I hope to go out tomorrow, as it is Sunday. I received your letter of the 16th and the two unsealed letters of introduction for Paris. I am glad that you like my French aria. Please forgive my not writing much now, but really I cannot —I am afraid of bringing back my headache, and besides I feel no inclination to write today. It is impossible to put on paper all that we think—at least I find it so. I would rather say it than write it. My last letter will have told you just how things stand. Please believe what you like of me, but not anything bad. There are people who think that no one can love a poor girl without having evil designs; and that charming word maîtresse, wh—e in our tongue, is really much too charming! But I am no Brunetti! no Mysliwecek! I am a Mozart, and a young and clean-minded Mozart. So you will forgive me, I hope, if in my eagerness I sometimes get excited,— if that is the expression I should use, though indeed I would much rather say, if I sometimes write naturally. I have much to say on this subject, but I cannot, for I find it impossible to do so. Among my many faults I have

also this one, a persistent belief that my friends who know me, really do know me. Therefore many words are not necessary: for if they do not know me, oh, then where could I ever find words enough? It is bad enough that one needs words at all—and letters into the bargain. All this, however, is not intended for you, my dear Papa. No, indeed! You know me too well and besides you are too good-natured thoughtlessly to rob anyone of his good name. I only mean those people—and they know that I mean them—who believe such a thing. I have made up my mind to stay at home today, although it is Sunday, because it is snowing so hard. Tomorrow I must go out, for our house nymph, Mlle Pierron, my highly esteemed pupil, is to scramble through my concerto (written for the high and mighty Countess Lützow)[1] at the French concert which is held every Monday. I too, prostitution though it be, shall ask them to give me something to strum and shall contrive to thump it out *prima fista*. For I am a born wood-hitter and all I can do is to strum a little on the clavier. Now please let me stop, for I am not at all in the humour for writing letters today, but feel far more inclined to compose. Once more, please don't forget to do what I asked you in my previous letters about the cadenzas and the aria cantabile with coloratura indications. I am obliged to you already for having had the arias I asked for copied so quickly. That proves that you have confidence in me and that you believe me when I suggest something to you. Well, good-bye. I kiss your hands 1000 times and embrace my sister with all my heart and remain your most obedient son

WOLFGANG AMADÉ MOZART

Mannheim, 22 February 1778.

My greetings to all good friends and especially to my dearest friend Herr Bullinger.

(289a) *Maria Anna Mozart to her Husband*

[Autograph in the Mozarteum, Salzburg]

MY DEAR HUSBAND   [MANNHEIM, 22 *February* 1778]

You say that we have no confidence in you and that we ought to have told you at once about Herr ⟨Wendling's⟩ way of living. The reason why we didn't do so is that for a long time we knew nothing about it. For at first all his friends praised him to us and said that we could not do better than let Wolfgang travel with him; and it is perfectly true that Herr Wendling is the best fellow in the world, only the whole household knows nothing about religion and does not value it. The mother and the daughter never go to church from one end of the year to the other, never go to confession and never hear Mass. On the other hand they are always going

---

[1] K. 246, composed in 1776.

off to the theatre. They say that a church is not healthy. We have heard all this bit by bit partly from their own friends and partly from what Wolfgang himself has seen and heard. I prayed every day that God might prevent this journey and, thank Heaven, He has done so. Most people here have no religion and are out-and-out free-thinkers. No one knows that this is the reason why Wolfgang has not gone off with them, for, if it were known, we should be laughed at. Even our Privy Court Councillor, who is a bird of the same feather, does not know it. We have given him another reason, that is, that Wolfgang has been waiting for letters from Vienna and can't leave until they arrive. They are delighted in the house here that Wolfgang hasn't left, for thus their daughter can make further strides. Thank God, I am well, and I trust that you are the same. Wolfgang has had to stay at home for three days as he had a severe cold and sore throat. But now, thank God, he is well again and is going out tomorrow.

I do hope that Wolfgang will make his fortune in Paris quickly, so that you and Nannerl may follow us soon. How delighted I should be to have you both with us, for nothing could be better. If it is God's will, He will arrange it. Living must be getting harder and harder in Salzburg, and in such circumstances it must be very wretched for everybody. Addio. Keep well, both of you. I kiss you both many 100000 times and remain as always your faithful wife

MARIA ANNA MOZART

Our greetings to all our acquaintances, especially to Monsieur Bullinger, Jungfer Sallerl, Katherl Gilowsky, Herr Deibl, Jungfrau Mitzerl, Frau von Gerlichs. A kiss for Bimperl, who will by this time have forgotten me and will no longer recognize me.

(290) *Leopold Mozart to his Son*

[Extract]   Autograph in the Mozarteum, Salzburg]

MON TRÉS CHER FILS!   SALZBURG, 23 *February* 1778
In order to convince me that in all matters you are careless and in-attentive, you say at the beginning of your letter of the 14th that you see from my letter of the 9th that I have not yet received your last two letters. So on the 9th I should have replied to your wild letter sent off on the 5th, which almost killed me, although you ought to know from my long correspondence with you since you have been in Mannheim, that a letter of mine takes six days to reach you, and although I have told you already that your letters always arrive on *Tuesdays or Fridays*, so that you cannot have a reply from me under a fortnight. But alas! What is the use of all my

precise thinking, all my care, all my consideration and my paternal efforts in pursuance of a most important and necessary enterprise, if (when faced with an apparently serious obstacle which Mamma perhaps may have perceived long ago) you fail to give your father your full confidence and only change your mind when, caught between two fires, you can neither advance nor retreat? Just when I am thinking that things are now on a better footing and taking their proper course, I am suddenly confronted with some foolish, unexpected fancy of yours or else it appears that matters were different from what you represented them to me. So once more I have guessed aright! You have only received 96 gulden instead of 200— and why?—because you finished only two concertos and only three quartets for your client.[1] How many were you to have composed for him, then, since he would only pay you half? Why do you *lie* to me, saying that you had only to compose three short easy concertos and a couple of quartets? And why did you not listen to me when I said *expressly: You ought to satisfy this gentleman as quickly as you possibly can.* Why did I tell you to do so? So that you would be sure of getting those 200 gulden, for indeed I know people better than you do. Have I not guessed everything? It seems that I, who am at a distance, see more and judge better than you do with these people under your very nose. You must be ready to believe me, when I mistrust people, and to act as prudently as I direct. Indeed you have bought experience lately at a somewhat heavy cost to us all. True, you have arranged with Herr Wendling that the sum in question is to be paid to you later and that you will send on your compositions. Yes—and if Wendling can advantageously dispose of what you have now delivered to flautist friends in Paris, then he will try to get a little more. One party has to pay; the other gets the profit. Further, you wrote to me about a couple of pupils and in particular about the Dutch officer,[2] who would pay you three or, as you were inclined to believe, four ducats for twelve lessons. And now it appears that you could have had these pupils, but that you gave them up, simply because on one or two occasions you did not find them at home. You would rather give lessons as a favour.—Yes, of course you would! And you would rather, I suppose, leave your poor old father in need! The effort is too great for a young man like yourself, however good the pay may be; and, no doubt, it is more seemly that your old father of fifty-eight should run round from house to house for a miserable fee, so that he may earn the necessary means of support for himself and his daughter by the sweat of his brow and, *instead of paying off his debts,* support you with what remains over, while you in the meantime can amuse yourself by giving a girl lessons for nothing! My son, do reflect and listen to your common sense! Just think whether you are not treating me

---

[1] The works ordered by De Jean. See p. 481, notes 1 and 2.
[2] De La Pottrie. See p. 429.

more cruelly than does our Prince. From him I have never expected anything, but from you I have expected all. From him I take everything as a
favour, but from you I can hope to receive all by virtue of your duty as
my child. After all, he is a stranger to me, but you are my son. You know
what I have endured for more than five years—yes—and what a lot I have
had to swallow on your account. The Prince's conduct can only bend me,
but yours can crush me. He can only make me ill, but you can kill me.
Had I not your sister and Bullinger, that true friend of ours, I should
probably not have the strength to write this letter which I have been
penning for the last two days. I have to conceal my anxiety from the whole
world; they are the only two persons to whom I can tell all, and who comfort me. I believed that everything you were writing was the truth; and as
everyone here is genuinely delighted when things go well with you and
as people were always asking about you, I, in my joy, gave them a *full
account* of how you were making money and would then go off to Paris.
And as you know how everyone takes delight ⟨in annoying the Archbishop,⟩ a good many people used my story for that purpose. Old Herr
Hagenauer was very sorry that you had to draw 150 gulden in Mannheim,
for these business people naturally want us to earn some money. But when
I told him what you had written, namely, that you had free board and
lodging, that you would be getting 200 gulden and that you had pupils as
well, he was very well pleased. Of course I had to ask him to wait a little
for the repayment of the 150 gulden. Whereupon he replied: '*Don't
mention it! I have every confidence in your Wolfgang. He will do his duty as a
son. Let him get off to Paris and don't worry.*' Well, consider these words and
our present circumstances and tell me whether I can stand any more,
seeing that as an honourable man I cannot leave you in your present
situation, cost what it may. You may rest assured that not a soul knows
that we sent those 150 gulden to Mannheim, for the Hagenauers would
never, never give ⟨the Archbishop⟩ that pleasure. But how disappointed
these friends will be that once more I have to send you money to help you to
get to Paris! All the same, I shall prove to you that you must abide by this
decision. Your proposal to go travelling about, particularly in the present
critical state of Europe, cannot be considered for a moment; very often
you would not even make your travelling expenses; the whole time you
would have to be making enquiries and begging and seeking patrons, so
that your concerts should bring in money; the whole time you would
have to be trying to get letters of introduction from one place to another,
asking for permission to give a concert and facing a hundred incidental
unpleasant circumstances; and in the end you would hardly get enough
money to pay the innkeeper and to meet your travelling expenses, so that
you would have to use your own capital (if you had any) or pawn or even
sell your clothes, watch and rings. Of the former I have had experience.

I had to draw 100 gulden from Herr Ollenschläger in Frankfurt and immediately after my arrival in Paris a further 300 gulden from Turton and Baur, of which, it is true, I used very little, as we soon began to make money. But first of all we had to become known by delivering letters of introduction, etc., and in a large city that takes time, for it is not always possible to meet acquaintances. My dear Wolfgang, all your letters convince me that you are ready to accept, without due consideration and reflection, the first wild idea that comes into your head or that anyone puts there. For example, you say, 'I am a composer. *I must not bury* my talent for composition, etc.' Who says that you ought to do so? But that is precisely what you would be doing, were you to roam about in gipsy fashion. If you want to make your name as a composer, you must be either in Paris, or Vienna or Italy. You are now nearest Paris. The only other question is: 'Where have I most hope of getting on?' *In Italy*, where in *Naples alone* there are at least three hundred maestri and where, from one end of the country to the other, the maestri have contracts (very often two years in advance) with those theatres that pay well? or in Paris, where perhaps two or three are writing for the stage, and other composers may be counted on one's fingers? The clavier must bring you your first acquaintances and make you popular with the great. After that you can have something engraved by subscription, which is slightly more profitable than composing six quartets for an Italian gentleman and getting a few ducats, and perhaps a snuff-box worth three, for your pains. Vienna is even better in that respect, for at least it is possible to get up a subscription for music to be copied for private circulation. You and others have had experience of both. In short, if I could instill into you greater stability and more reflection when these wild ideas occur to you, I should make you the happiest man in the world. I realize, however, that time alone will teach you this, though indeed, as far as your talent is concerned, everything came before its time, while in all branches of knowledge you have always grasped everything with the greatest ease. Why then should it not be possible for you to learn to know people, to fathom their intentions, to close your heart to the world and in every case to think things over carefully, so that you do not always see only the good side of a question or that side which is most flattering to you or which furthers some momentary whim? My dear son, *God has given you excellent judgment*, which (as far as I can see) *only two things* prevent you from using properly. For thanks to me you have learned how to use it and how to know your fellow-creatures. When in the past I used always to guess aright and often foresee the future, you used to say in fun: '*Next to God comes Papa*'. Now what, do you think, are these two things? Examine yourself, my dear Wolfgang, learn to know yourself, and you will discover them. First of all, you have a little too much *pride and self-love*; and secondly, you immediately make

yourself too *cheap* and open your heart to everyone; in short! wishing to
be unconstrained and natural, you fall into the other extreme of being too
unreserved. True, the first failing ought to check the second, for whoever
has pride and self-love will not readily descend to familiarity. Your pride
and self-love, however, are only touched when you do not at once get
the appreciation you deserve. You think that even those who do not know
you, ought to see by your face that you are a man of genius! But when it
comes to flatterers who, in order to bend you to their selfish purposes,
praise you to the skies, you open your heart with the greatest ease and
believe them as you do the Bible. Please do not think that I mistrust your
filial love; the purpose of all my remarks is to make you an honourable
man. Millions have not received the tremendous favour which God has
bestowed upon you. What a responsibility! And what a shame if such a
great genius were to founder! And that can happen in a moment! You
are confronted with far more dangers than those millions who have no
talent, for you are exposed to many more ordeals and temptations. Mamma
must go with you to Paris and you must confide in her, just as you must
confide in me when you write to me. By the next post I shall send you
full particulars, as well as all the addresses you require and also letters to
Diderot, d'Alembert and the rest. I must close. Nannerl and I kiss you
many thousand times and I am your old

MZT

All send greetings, and especially Herr Bullinger.

By the next post I shall get details, I hope, of the amount of money you
have in hand.

By that time our chaise will have been sold, I suppose.

(291) *Leopold Mozart to his Wife and Son*

[*Extract*]   [*Autograph in the Mozarteum, Salzburg*]

SALZBURG, 25 and 26 *February* 1778

MY DEAR WIFE AND MY DEAR SON!

Thank God, I feel somewhat better, though I am still troubled from
time to time with nervous palpitations. This is, however, only natural, for
I cannot shake off my worries. But indeed, I am never depressed by care,
if it is merely due to some misfortune and if I am told everything frankly,
fully and immediately, so that I may contrive and advise; for then I can
think out calmly how to help, propose a remedy and suggest a way out.
But if . . . Well, let us forget it . . . I have told you already, my son, that
you were very wise not to travel to Paris ⟨in that company. A father who
thus sacrifices his daughter⟩ from self-interest is loathsome.[1] How could

[1] Wendling, whose daughter Augusta had been the Elector's mistress.

you rely on his friendship? Meanwhile I shall do my best for Mlle Weber. I suggest that she should keep on very good terms with Signor Raaff and make sure of his support, which will most certainly help her to achieve her object, for he has a tremendous reputation in Italy and has many acquaintances among eminent people there, professors and impresarios. I at once sent for the two copyists to copy those arias which you asked for, o that they might be ready for the Munich mail coach on the 22nd, but to get the work done in time was out of the question. All three copyists have been busy day and night copying Rust's serenata. 'Il Parnasso confuso', as he wants to get away and the serenata has still to be rehearsed under his direction, so that Herr Haydn, who plays the clavier, can conduct it in his absence. However, after a good deal of hunting I found the three arias: *Il tenero momento*; the scena, *Fra i pensieri più funesti di morte*; and *Pupille amate*;[1] and with these I have had to be content. I have also found Bach's aria *Cara*, etc.,[2] but neither the coloratura passages, which your sister copied, nor the various cadenzas which at one time were copied out neatly on small paper. The latter used to be with the little scores. When you were leaving, you bundled everything together in a great hurry, so that it is quite possible that you took them with you. The arias ought to arrive in Mannheim by mail coach during the first week of March. If I had not made the necessary enquiries about the departure of the mail coach, I should not have been able to send them until March 1st, and even then only as far as Munich, '*Learning comes before doing*', as Kessler, our learned trumpeter, declares. I am sending you also five grand arias of Bertoni,[3] Monza, Gasparini, Grétry and Colla.[4] So I have the honour ⟨to make you a present⟩ of five arias and ⟨to pay the expense of having⟩ three of them ⟨copied and posted⟩ to Augsburg, though, by Heaven, I myself ⟨do not possess a farthing. I look like poor Lazarus. My dressing-gown is so shabby⟩ that if somebody calls in the morning, ⟨I have to make myself scarce. My old flannel jerkin⟩, which I have been wearing morning and evening for years, ⟨is so torn that⟩ I can hardly ⟨keep it⟩ on any longer and I cannot afford ⟨to have either a new dressing-gown or a new jerkin made.⟩ Since your departure I haven't had ⟨a single pair of new shoes,⟩ nor have I any ⟨black silk stockings⟩ left. On Sundays I wear ⟨old white stockings⟩ and during the week ⟨black woollen Berlin stockings,⟩ which I bought for 1 gulden 12 kreuzer. If someone had told

---

[1] From Mozart's *Lucio Silla*, nos. 2, 22 and 21.

[2] 'Cara la dolce fiamma', an aria from J. C. Bach's opera *Adriano in Siria*. The coloratura cadenzas K. 293e which Mozart wrote for this and two other arias of J. C. Bach have been preserved. See Köchel, p. 300, 301.

[3] Ferdinando Giuseppe Bertoni (1725–1813), a famous operatic composer in his time. He was trained by Padre Martini and became organist and subsequently maestro di cappella at St. Mark's, Venice.

[4] Giuseppe Colla (1731–1806), was maestro di cappella to the Duke of Parma. He married in 1780 Lucrezia Agujari the famous coloratura soprano. He wrote several successful operas.

me a few years ago that I should have to wear ⟨woollen stockings⟩ and that, when the weather is dry and frosty, I should be glad of your old ⟨felt shoes⟩ to pull on over my ⟨old ones,⟩ and that in order to protect myself from the cold I should have to put on two or three ⟨old⟩ waist-coats—would I ever have believed him? ⟨Plays⟩ and balls are ⟨out of the question⟩ for us. Such is our life, cares within and cares without; and, to make things worse, I have no wife or son with me, and God knows whether—or when—we shall meet again! My one great delight—to hear your compositions—is gone! Everything around me is dead! Your sister alone is now my support, and I try to banish the cares which seem to overwhelm me by a very quiet form of entertainment, which is, to play through on the violin from six to eight every evening, arias, symphonies, masses, vespers, and so forth, while your sister plays the figured bass and gets practice in accompanying. To my amazement she has made such progress that she plays off at sight everything I bring back from the Cathedral, however difficult the fugues may be. By degrees we shall soon have finished playing the contents of the Cathedral chest. Each time I only bring home the organ and violin parts of a few compositions. By means of this practice which she has kept up since your departure, she has acquired such perfect insight into harmony and modulations that not only can she move from one key into another, but she extemporizes so successfully that you would be astounded. And do you know what has inspired her with this determination and terrific industry? *My death!* She realizes and foresees the misery into which she would be plunged, were I suddenly to breathe my last. In that case what do you think would be the future of your Mamma and your sister? Adlgasser's three children have been given 8 gulden a month for one year only. The ⟨Prince⟩ would give my women-folk nothing whatever, for you went off on your own and at the same time he ⟨dismissed⟩ me.[1] He would say that you should support your mother and that your sister should go into domestic service, as he now makes all daughters do who have lost their fathers. So your sister was not crying over a silly trifle, when she wept over your letter: and yet when you told us that you had not got the 200 gulden, she just said: '*Thank God it's no worse!*' Up to the present we have always thought Nannerl rather stingy. But she agrees that to help you both, her own savings must be sacrificed. For how could I, without blushing for shame, ⟨approach⟩ Herr Hagenauer again ⟨for money⟩, without offering him some security? And your sister is doing this willingly and cheerfully, although she knows that if I were to die today she would be absolutely stranded. She gets up daily at six o'clock and goes to Holy Trinity, where she prays so ardently that several people have already spoken to me about it. My dear Wolfgang,

---

[1] Leopold Mozart is referring no doubt to the Archbishop's reply to his son's application or his discharge in the summer of 1777. See p. 268, n. 2.

you are young and you do not worry much, for so far you have never had to bother about anything; you banish all serious thoughts, you have long since forgotten the Salzburg cross, on which I am still hanging; you only listen to praises and flatteries and thus are becoming by degrees insensible and unable to realize our condition or to devise some means of relieving it. In short, you never think of the future. The present alone engulfs you completely, and sweeps you off your feet, although if you would only ponder the consequences of your actions and face them in good earnest, you would I know, be horrified. You will receive this letter on March 4th, and on the 8th you will get another one with particulars about your board and lodging in Paris. We kiss you millions of times and I who still hover between fear and hope, remain your old

MZT

I suppose you know that Noverre is master of the ballet at the Paris opera. Rust has gone away, so once more I am the only Kapellmeister. Ferlendis wants to go off travelling in the spring or he may even leave altogether. Ferrari still wants to get married or to leave Salzburg. Brunetti is in a terrible fix. St. Peter's house, where Haydn lives, used to be his headquarters. But he has now to support Judith and the child, and he has debts amounting to 600 gulden; so people are beginning to think that all of a sudden it will be: Where is Brunetti? The great Luz and Brunetti now take their meals at Spitzeder's, which has become the headquarters of the Italians and a regular gambling den. Addio. Get ready for your journey, so that you may leave as soon as you receive my next letter. The French diligences are not at all draughty and very well sprung. Try to sell our chaise soon for as high a price as possible.

(292) *Mozart to his Father*

[*Autograph in the Mozarteum, Salzburg*]

MONSIEUR,   [MANNHEIM, 28 *February* 1778]
    MON TRÉS CHER PÉRE!

We have received your letter of February 23rd. I hope I shall get the arias next Friday or Saturday, although in your last letter you said nothing more about them, so that I don't know whether you sent them off by the mail coach on the 22nd. I hope you did, for before I leave I should like to play and sing them to Mlle Weber. I was at Raaff's yesterday and brought him an aria which I composed for him the other day.[1] The words are: '*Se al labbro mio non credi, bella nemica mia*', etc. I don't think that Metastasio

---

[1] K. 295.

wrote them.[1] He liked it enormously. One must treat a man like Raaff in a particular way. I chose those words on purpose, because I knew that he already had an aria on them: so of course he will sing mine with greater facility and more pleasure. I asked him to tell me candidly if he did not like it or if it did not suit his voice, adding that I would alter it if he wished or even compose another. 'God forbid,' he said, 'the aria must remain just as it is, for nothing could be finer. But please shorten it a little, for I am no longer able to sustain my notes.' 'Most gladly,' I replied, 'as much as you like. I made it a little long on purpose, for it is always easy to cut down, but not so easy to lengthen.' After he had sung the second part, he took off his spectacles, and looking at me with wide-open eyes, said: 'Beautiful! Beautiful! That is a charming *seconda parte*.' And he sang it three times. When I took leave of him he thanked me most cordially, while I assured him that I would arrange the aria in such a way that it would give him pleasure to sing it. For I like an aria to fit a singer as perfectly as a well-made suit of clothes.[2] For practice I have also set to music the aria '*Non so d'onde viene*,' etc.[3] which has been so beautifully composed by Bach.[4] Just because I know Bach's setting so well and like it so much, and because it is always ringing in my ears, I wished to try and see whether in spite of all this I could not write an aria totally unlike his. And, indeed, mine does not resemble his in the very least. At first I had intended it for Raaff; but the beginning seemed to me too high for his voice. Yet I liked it so much that I would not alter it; and from the orchestral accompaniment, too, it seemed to me better suited to a soprano. So I decided to write it for Mlle Weber. Well, I put it aside and started off on the words '*Se al labbro*' for Raaff. But all in vain! I simply couldn't compose for the first aria kept on running in my head. So I returned to it and made up my mind to compose it exactly for Mlle Weber's voice. It's an Andante sostenuto (preceded by a short recitative); then follows the second part, *Nel seno a destarmi*, and then the sostenuto again. When it was finished, I said to Mlle Weber: 'Learn the aria yourself. Sing it as you think it ought to go; then let me hear it and afterwards I will tell you candidly what pleases and what displeases me.' After a couple of days I went to the Webers and she sang it for me, accompanying herself. I was obliged to confess that she had sung it exactly as I wished and as I should have taught it to her myself. This is now the best aria she has; and it will ensure her success wherever she goes. Yesterday at Wendling's I sketched the aria which I had promised his wife, adding a short recitative. She had chosen the words herself—from 'Didone',

---

[1] The words of the aria were taken from Hasse's opera *Arminio*. According to Köchel, p. 304, the author of the text may have been Giovanni Claudio Pasquini.
[2] The autograph of the aria shows corrections and cuts which Mozart made to suit Raaff.
[3] K. 294, recitative and aria on a text from Metastasio's *Olimpiade*, written for Aloysia Weber. In 1787 Mozart set the same words to music for the famous bass singer, Ludwig Fischer (K. 512).   [4] Johann Christian Bach. See p. 551, n. 2.

'*Ah, non lasciarmi, no*'.[1] She and her daughter are quite crazy about it. I have also promised the daughter some more French ariettas, and began one today.[2] When they are ready I shall send them to you on small paper as I did my first aria. I still have two of the six clavier sonatas to compose,[3] but there's no hurry, for I can't have them engraved here. Nothing is done in this place by subscription; it is a miserly spot, and the engraver will not do them at his own expense, but wants to go halves with me in the sale. So I prefer to have them engraved in Paris, where the engravers are delighted to get something new and pay handsomely and where it is easier to get a thing done by subscription. I would have had these sonatas copied and sent to you long ago; but I thought to myself: 'No, I prefer to send them to him when they have been engraved.' I am looking forward most particularly to the Concert Spirituel in Paris, for I shall probably be asked to compose something for it. The orchestra is said to be so excellent and strong: and my favourite type of composition, the chorus, can be well performed there. I am indeed glad that the French value choruses highly. The only fault found with Piccinni's new opera 'Roland',[4] is that the choruses are too meagre and weak, and that the music on the whole is a little monotonous; otherwise it was universally liked. To be sure, they are accustomed to Gluck's choruses in Paris. Do rely on me. I shall do my very best to bring honour to the name of Mozart and I have not the slightest fear. My last letters will have given you full particulars as to *how things are now*, and as to *what my intentions are*. I do entreat you never to allow the thought to cross your mind that I can ever forget you, for I cannot bear it. My chief purpose was, is and ever shall be to endeavour to bring about our speedy and happy reunion! But we must be patient. You yourself know even better than I do how often things go awry—but they will soon go straight—only do have patience! Let us place our trust in God, Who will never forsake us. I shall not be found wanting. How can you doubt me? Surely it is to your interest that I should work as hard as I can, so that I may have the joy and happiness (the sooner the better too) of embracing with all my heart my most beloved and dearest father? There—you see! Nothing in this world is wholly free from self-interest! If war should break out ⟨in Bavaria⟩, follow us at once, I beg you. I have full confidence in three friends, all of them powerful and invincible, God, your head and mine. Our heads, I admit, are very different, but each in its own way is good, serviceable and useful, and I hope that in time mine will by degrees equal yours in those branches in which it is now inferior. Well, good-bye! Be merry and cheerful. Remember that you have a son who has never,

[1] K. 486a [295a], recitative and aria on a text from Metastasio's *Didone abbandonata*, written for Dorothea Wendling.　　　　[2] Probably K. 308 [295b], 'Dans un bois solitaire'.
[3] K. 301, 302, 303 and 305 [293a–d] were composed at Mannheim, K. 304 [300c] and 306 [300l] in Paris.
[4] *Roland*, the first opera which Piccinni wrote for Paris, was performed on 27 January, 1778.

knowingly, forgotten his filial duty to you, who will endeavour to become more and more worthy of so good a father and who will remain unchangingly your most obedient

WOLFGANG MOZART

I embrace my sister with all my heart!

My greetings to all my good friends, and particularly to Herr Bullinger.

If you have not yet sent off the arias, please do so as soon as possible and you will make me really happy. Ah, if only ⟨the Elector of Bavaria had not died!⟩ I would have finished the mass[1] and produced it and it would have made a great sensation here. I was in excellent humour for composing it when the devil had to trot out that accursed Doctor Sanftl![2]

(292a) *Maria Anna Mozart to her Husband*

[Autograph in the Mozarteum, Salzburg]

MY DEAR HUSBAND,   [MANNHEIM, 28 *February* 1778]

We are now preparing gradually for our departure. I should be glad to pocket a good price for the carriage, but indeed I doubt whether we shall get much for it. However, we shall do our best and keep on until we get at least 50 gulden. These people simply won't value it at more than 4 carolins and keep on finding all sorts of flaws in it. It is always the way when you want to sell an article; and here particularly there are so many selfish people who keep on trying to make double or treble profits and won't do the smallest kindness without pay. I shall be delighted to be out of this and am longing for the day to arrive, which, if it is God's will, will certainly be in a fortnight at latest. Meanwhile I am so looking forward to your letters and to what you have to say to us. Rest assured that everything will be done in accordance with what you want and prescribe. Keep well, both of you. I kiss you both many 10000 times and remain as always your faithful wife

MARIA ANNA MOZART

All sorts of messages to all our good friends.

(293) *Mozart to his Cousin, Maria Anna Thekla Mozart, Augsburg*

[Autograph in the possession of the heirs of Stefan Zweig]

[MANNHEIM, 28 February 1778]

MADEMOISELLE MA TRÉS CHÉRE COUSINE!

Perhaps you think or are even convinced that I am dead? That I have pegged out? Or hopped a twig? Not at all. Don't believe it, I implore you.

[1] See p. 482, n. 2.

[2] The Elector's death was generally considered to be due to the carelessness of his private physician, Dr. Sanftl.

For believing and shitting are two very different things! Now how could I be writing such a beautiful hand if I were dead? How could that be possible? I shan't apologize for my very long silence, for you would never believe me. Yet what is true is true. I have had so many things to do that I had time indeed to think of my little cousin, but not to write, you see. So I just had to let things be. But now I have the honour to inquire how you are and whether you perspire? Whether your stomach is still in good order? Whether indeed you have no disorder? Whether you still can like me at all? Whether with chalk you often scrawl? Whether now and then you have me in mind? Whether to hang yourself you sometimes feel inclined? Whether you have been wild? With this poor foolish child? Whether to make peace with me you'll be so kind? If not, I swear I'll let off one behind! Ah, you're laughing! Victoria! Our arses shall be the symbol of our peacemaking! I knew that you wouldn't be able to resist me much longer. Why, of course, I'm sure of success, even if today I should make a mess, though to Paris I go in a fortnight or less. So if you want to send a reply to me from that town of Augsburg yonder, you see, then write at once, the sooner the better, so that I may be sure to receive your letter, or else if I'm gone I'll have the bad luck, instead of a letter to get some muck. Muck!—Muck!—Ah, muck! Sweet word! Muck! chuck! That too is fine. Muck, chuck!—muck!—suck—o charmante! muck, suck! That's what I like! Muck, chuck and suck! Chuck muck and suck muck!

Now for something else. When the carnival was on, did you have some good fun? One can have far more fun at this time in Augsburg than here. How I wish I were with you so that we could run about together. Mamma and I send our greetings to your father and mother and to you, little cousin, and we trust all three of you are well and in good spirits. Praise and thanks be to God, we are in good health. Don't believe it. All the better, better the all. A propos, how are you getting on with your French? May I soon send you a whole letter in French? You would like one from Paris, would you not? Do tell me whether you still have that Spuni Cuni business? I'm sure you have. Well, I must tell you something before I close, for I must really stop soon, as I am in a hurry, for just at the moment I have nothing whatever to do; and also because I have no more room, as you see; the paper will soon be at an end; and besides I am tired and my fingers are twitching from so much writing; and finally even if I had room, I really don't know what I could tell you, apart from this story which I am proposing to relate. Now listen, it happened not very long ago, it all took place here and it made a great sensation too, for it seemed almost unbelievable; and, between ourselves, no one knows how the affair is going to turn out. Well, to make a long story short, about four hours from here—I have forgotten the name of the place—at some village or other—and indeed it is all one, whether the village was Tribsterill, where muck runs into the sea, or Burmesquik, where the crooked arse-holes are manufactured—in short, it was a village. Now in that village there was a peasant or shepherd, who was well advanced in years, but was still hale and hearty. He was unmarried and very comfortably off and he led a jolly life. But, before I finish my story, I must tell you that when he spoke he had a dreadful voice, so that whenever he said anything, people were always terrified of him. Well to make a long story short, you must know that he had a dog called Bellot, a very fine large dog, white with black spots. Now one day the shepherd was walking along with his sheep, of which he had eleven thousand, and was carrying in his hand a stick with a beautiful rose-coloured ribbon. For he always carried a stick. It was his habit to do this. Well, let's get on. After he had walked for a good hour or so, he got tired and sat down near a river and fell asleep, and dreamt that he had lost his sheep. He awoke in terror, but to his great joy found all his sheep beside him. So he got up and walked on, but not for very long; for he had hardly walked for half an hour before he came to a bridge, which was very long but well protected on both sides in order to prevent people from falling into the river. Well, he looked at his flock and, as he was obliged to cross the river, he began to drive his eleven thousand sheep over the bridge. Now please be so kind as to wait until the eleven thousand sheep have reached the other side and then I shall finish my story. I have already told you that no one knows how the affair is going to turn out. But I hope that before I send you my next letter the sheep will have crossed the river. If not, I really don't care very much; as far as I am concerned, they could have remained this side of the water. So you must just be content with this instalment. I have told you all I know; and it is much better to stop than to make up the rest. If I did so, you would not believe any of the story; but as it is, you will surely believe—not even half of it. Well, I must close, though it makes me morose. Whoever begins must cease, or else he gives people no peace. My greetings to every single friend, and whoever doesn't believe me, may lick me world without end, from now to all eternity, until I cease to be a nonentity. He can go on licking for ever, in truth, why, even I am alarmed, forsooth, for I fear that my muck will soon dry up and that he won't have enough if he wants to sup. Adieu, little cousin. I am, I was, I should be, I have been, I had been, I should have been, oh that I were, oh that I might be, would to God I were, I shall be, if I should be, oh that I should be, I shall have been, oh that I had been, would to God that I had been, what?—a duffer. Adieu, ma chère cousine, where have you been? I am your same old faithful cousin

WOLFGANG AMADÉ MOZART

Mannheim, 28 February 1778.

(294) *Leopold Mozart to his Wife and Son*

[*Extract*]   [*Autograph in the Mozarteum, Salzburg*]

SALZBURG, 28 *February*: 1 *and* 2 *March* 1778

MY DEAREST WIFE AND DEAREST SON!

I have received your letter of February 22nd. Thank God that Wolfgang is better again. When you are travelling, your main concern should be your health. If Mamma has not got enough black powders with her, she will probably get some in Mannheim more easily than in Paris. I am trying to recall the name of the German doctor who is, I think, physician to the Swiss Guard, and who came to see us on the night Wolfgang got his dangerous cold. As far as I can recollect, it was something like 'Herrschwand'.

Well, I must give Wolfgang a description of Baron Bache or Bagge (for I don't know how he spells his name). As far as I know, he was a poor Baron from Prussia or somewhere in those parts, who married the daughter of a wealthy Paris hatter. As time passed by, all sorts of quarrels arose between them and, after we returned to Salzburg, husband and wife drifted into a situation which was followed by a lawsuit, and she is supposed to have entered a convent. He is a passionate lover of music and used to give concerts in his house, as he may still do, for all I know. Further, he always kept a few musicians, such as two players on the French horn (Henno[1] was one), two oboists, a double bass and so forth, to whom he paid a small salary, which they were glad to receive, as it was permanent. Apart from them he did what he could with the help of the foreign virtuosi who came to him for advice and to obtain that opportunity which his house provided, of making acquaintances in a foreign city. Even Parisian virtuosi often go there, some to perform their new compositions, and others to hear foreign music, for Bagge is always on the look-out for new stuff; and finally people go there to listen to these same foreign virtuosi. All that he did for us long ago was to sell some tickets for our first concert, about which Herr von Grimm had badgered him; and for our last concert he sent us his musicians and charged us nothing, so that we had only to pay the singer, Mme Piccinelli, and M. Gaviniés, though indeed in the end the latter refused to take anything. What I noticed about Bagge was that what he liked above all was to pay for a good composition. So, my dear Wolfgang, when first you go to Baron Bagge's, you ought to be rather reserved and you should begin by producing only your very best music, so that you may at once gain credit for yourself. Io Victoria! Now I need not write anything more! Baron Grimm is in Paris! I have this moment received a letter from him, which again contains evidence of

---

[1] Schurig in his note to Leopold Mozart's entry in his *Reiseaufzeichnungen*, p. 69, maintains that this is Heina, who was also a music publisher in Paris.

your usual carelessness. True, Wolfgang was busy and is short-sighted; but did not Mamma see our friend Grimm at the concert at Augsburg?— for it seems that he placed himself in your line of vision. I will quote his letter, or rather the particular passage in German, which is as follows:

I received only the other day your letter of December 25th; and just as I was about to reply to it, your second letter of January 9th arrived. It is perfectly true that I was in Augsburg when Herr Amadeo gave his concert. I was on the point of leaving again at once—but as a matter of fact I went to his concert, where I so placed myself that he and Madame Mozart could see me. But neither recognized me, and as I was in a great hurry to leave and as everyone told me that the Mozarts were on their way to Paris, I decided to remain unrecognized, as we should be sure to meet there. I shall be delighted to see him again; but I am very sorry that he is coming without his father. I see from your letter that he is now on his way; so I may hope to see him any day, and shall then hear everything and decide what I can do for him. He is certainly in good hands with M. Wendling, who can render him most useful services. But no one can take the place of a father (mais personne ne peut remplacer un pére). I returned from my travels three months ago and do not yet know whether my recent journey from Russia will be my last. Il serait temps de songer au repos. Je vous envoie ci-joint mon adresse, pour que vos lettres ne risquent plus de s'égarer. Je suis accablé d'affaires et d'écritures et par conséquent bien mauvais correspondant, mais lorsque M. votre fils sera ici, il sera mon sécrétaire et nous vous tiendrons au courant; en attendant n'ayez point d'inquiétude. Je crois votre fils d'une conduite assez sage pour ne pas redouter pour lui les dangers de Paris. S'il était enclin au libertinage, il pourrait sans doute courir quelques risques; mais s'il a de la raison, il se garantira de tout inconvénient sans mener pour cela la vie d'un ermite, etc. Je suis bien fâché que vous soyez cloué a Salzbourg. Adieu, Monsieur, vous connaissez les sentiments que je vous ai voués. Je vous prie de les regarder comme invariables. Paris, le 21 février, 1778.

He enclosed a card with his address.

Monsieur le Baron de Grimm, Ministre Plénipotentiaire de Saxe-Gotha, rue de la Chaussée d'Antin, près le Boulevard.

In the circumstances I think you ought to drive straight to the Lion d'Argent and, if you arrive late, call on Baron Grimm on the following morning. Who knows but that you might perhaps be able to live quite close to him? I cannot at the moment find the rue de la Chaussée d'Antin. I shall reply, of course, to Baron Grimm at once. I have made arrangements for you to draw four or five louis d'or from Herr Schmalz in Mannheim. So even if you sell our chaise for only five louis d'or, you will have 100 German gulden. When you wrote to me on February 19th, you had only

140 gulden. I gather therefore that Wolfgang has earned nothing by giving lessons and that all that was, as usual, only soap-bubbles. I strongly advise you to leave very soon and hope to hear about this in your next letter. Twice I have been informed that Wolfgang is going to publish clavier duets by subscription; *but whether at Mannheim or Paris I have not yet been told*. He had better do it in Paris. As soon as he gets there, I shall send him from my travelling accounts an item quoting the cost. Addio. We kiss you millions of times. Nannerl and I wish you a pleasant journey. God keep you. Addio.

MZT

(295) *Leopold Mozart to his Wife and Son*

[Extract]   [*Autograph in the Mozarteum, Salzburg*

SALZBURG, 5 *March* 1778

MY DEAR WIFE AND MY DEAR SON!

As you will not receive my letter of March 2nd until the 7th or 8th, I am thinking that you will not be able to leave before the 15th, for I take it that the mail coach leaves once a week. *But you must leave on the 15th.* So I am writing once more, as you will still get this letter on the 11th. In my last I told you that Baron Grimm had written to me and I gave you the contents of his letter. I told you also that I had had a letter sent to Herr Herzog, to enable you still to draw four or five louis d'or in Mannheim. You will probably have sold our chaise by this time for as high a price as you have been able to get. But if once again you have left everything to the last minute—it is your own fault; for indeed I reminded you about everything in good time, that is, about your luggage, the trunks, the mail coach and all your other expenses. You really must think of nothing but your own affairs, do everything immediately and not let yourself be put off by anyone. One important point must not be forgotten, and that is, *to take no other money with you but louis d'or and laubthaler*, for this is the only money that is accepted on the route from Strassburg into France. For Heaven's sake don't waste a moment in getting everything fixed up, for if you reach Paris too late in the season, very little can be done. Besides, it takes time to make acquaintances, as it is such a big place and people are constantly going off to the country. So you must hurry up and make your acquaintances, while people are still in town. If you do not, your prospects will be ruined and we shall have the same story over again of your pulling to pieces whatever plans I have tried to make for you, while your own schemes, which I have done my best to further, have turned out to be impracticable. All that we can do now is to look ahead. Although you have not had to pay for board and lodging in Mannheim, you have spent quite enough money; and as you will now be spending far more, you really must think things out, for you will not be able to earn another farthing there. The parcel of music will no doubt have reached you by this time. You know what our circumstances are and you have ample reason to watch every farthing, for never yet have I been in such a predicament! I pray God that He may send Wolfgang better luck in Paris. Believe me, everything will depend on the skill with which you manage your affairs, wherever you are placed—and you should throw your whole heart into this. It is lucky for Wolfgang that Herr von Grimm is in Paris. He should place complete trust in him and do whatever he advises. Thus must Time be taken by the forelock.

Baron Grimm may be ordered away again soon and may have to undertake some journey in the spring. If so, you would again be left high and dry. If things were to go on in this way, we should be hopelessly in debt and suddenly find ourselves destitute, so that in the end one of us could no longer help the other. In all my letters I have tried to tell you the unvarnished truth; but apparently you have just glanced through them rapidly with half an eye and have then thrown them away. In Heaven's name, I implore you to read them through several times both carefully and attentively; *and in future to consult your own interests only and not always those of other people and to give up being at everybody's beck and call.* Otherwise I swear that you will suddenly be faced with the necessity of having to pawn or even sell your possessions. I have sent a reply to Baron Grimm, explaining fully why Wolfgang did not accompany Wendling to Paris, and telling him that he had to give him some other excuse. Perhaps you will have had a letter from Wendling in the meantime. I mention this so that you may tell Grimm the whole truth. I have arranged for you to draw an extra five louis d'or in Mannheim, but you must be able to draw some louis d'or in Paris on your arrival, for people will not begin to shower money on you at once. So I shall send you a letter of introduction which you can present there. Therefore, as soon as you have moved into your lodgings, send me your new address. At the same time I must think out some other arrangement, so that you may not find yourselves in a fix. But first of all, as soon as you have settled in your new quarters, you must let me know exactly where you are living. Grimm will very probably not be able to put you up; so you should make enquiries from M. Mayer. Keep well. This is my last letter to Mannheim, *as you will surely leave on the 15th.* God keep you and grant you a happy journey. Nannerl and I kiss you millions of times and I remain, faithful unto death, your old

MZT

As a precaution I am sending you again the address of Baron de Grimm, which is:

Rue de la Chausee d'Antin, près le Boulevard.

(296) *Mozart to his Father*

[Autograph in the Mozarteum, Salzburg]

MONSIEUR   [MANNHEIM, 7 *March* 1778]
MON TRÉS CHER PÈRE

We have had no letter from you today, but we hope that the only reason is that owing to the bad weather the post has not arrived punctually, or that you have not written at all. I have received your letter of February 26th. I am very much obliged to you for all the trouble you have taken about the arias. You are indeed punctilious about everything. *Next to God comes Papa* was my motto or axiom as a child, and I still cling to it. Certainly you are right when you say that *Learning comes before doing.* Indeed you must not regret all the bother and trouble this has caused you, for Mlle Weber well deserves your kindness. I only wish you could hear her sing my new aria[1] about which I wrote to you the other day; I say, hear her sing it, for it is absolutely made for her. A man like you who really understands what portamento singing is, would certainly find complete satisfaction in her performance. Once I am happily settled in Paris and, as I hope, our circumstances with God's help have improved and we are all more cheerful and in better spirits, I shall tell you my thoughts more fully and ask you for a great favour. But I must tell you that I was absolutely horrified and that tears came into my eyes when I read in your last letter that ⟨you have to go about so shabbily dressed.⟩ My very dearest Papa! That is certainly not my fault—you know it is not! We ⟨economize⟩ in every possible way here; food and lodging, wood and light ⟨have cost us nothing⟩, and what more can we want! As for dress, you surely know that in places where you are not known, it is out of the question ⟨to be badly dressed,⟩ for appearances must be kept up. I have now set all my hopes on Paris, for the German princes are all skinflints. I mean to work with all my strength so that I may soon have the happiness ⟨of helping you out of your present distressing circumstances.⟩ And now for our journey. A week today, that is, the 14th, we shall leave here. We have been unfortunate about the sale of the carriage, for so far no buyer has turned up. We shall have to be content if we get four louis d'or for it. If we cannot dispose of it, people here advise us to hire a driver and drive in it as far as Strassburg, where we could sell it more easily. However, as it is cheaper to travel by mail coach, I shall leave it here in charge of honest people. Now you must know that, as this is not a commercial town, no carriers go to Paris, and everything is sent by mail coach. I am told that from here to Strassburg the fare for each passenger is half a louis d'or, so I think it should **not** cost us more than fifteen gulden in all. Meanwhile

---

[1] K. 294, 'Non so d'onde viene'.

farewell. Let us put our trust in God, Who will certainly never forsake us. Before I leave I will write one more or even two more letters to you. If only I were in Paris, for I dislike the thought of that tiresome journey. Wendling writes that he was most horribly bored on the journey. Well, I must close so as to leave a little room for Mamma. Adieu. I kiss your hands 100000 times and remain your most obedient son

WOLFGANG MOZART

Mannheim, 7 March 1778.

(296a) *Mozart to his Sister*

[Autograph in the Mozarteum, Salzburg]

MA TRÈS CHERE SŒUR!   [MANNHEIM, 7 *March* 1778]

You must imagine, dearest sister, and that too with a most powerful stretch, that I have written a separate letter to you.

I have turned up to thank you for the 50 gulden you so kindly lent me, and which indeed were very badly needed. And here I congratulate you and tell you how inexpressibly delighted I am that you have such a good heart. I am extremely sorry that I am obliged for some time to rob you of 50 gulden. But, as truly as I am your sincere brother, I shall not rest until I have repaid you for all you have done for me in the goodness of your heart. Happy is that brother who has such a good sister. Please trust me absolutely and never think that I shall forget you; but remember that things do not always turn out, or at least not always exactly, as one wishes. But all will be well in time. Go on practising and whilst scrambling through scores do not forget your galanterie performance, lest I be proved a liar, when people, to whom I have sung your praises, hear you play. For I have always told them that you play with greater precision than I do. Well, adieu, dear sister. I hope that soon we shall be able to embrace one another with joy. I put my trust in God. In my prayers I ask Him for what I believe will be most useful to me and all of us, but I always add: 'Lord, may Thy will be done in earth as it is in heaven'. We mortals often think it is evil and in the end—it turns out to be good. God always knows best how things ought to be. Adieu, my most beloved sister. I kiss you 100000 times and remain your faithful and sincere brother until death.

WOLFGANG AMADÉ MOZART

Now I am happy to set off for Paris because our good friend Grimm is there. I place all my confidence in him and will follow all the advice of such a good friend.[1]

---

[1] This postscript is written on the cover.

(296b) *Maria Anna Mozart to her Husband*

[*Autograph in the Mozarteum, Salzburg*]

MY DEAR HUSBAND,   [MANNHEIM, 7 *March* 1778]

First of all I must tell you that we always receive your letters on Tuesdays and Saturdays. So next Saturday we shall not be able to get any more of them, as the mail coach leaves at six o'clock in the morning and the post only arrives about noon. But if you write next Monday, March 9th, they will forward your letter to Paris. We have not received the arias this week, so we shall expect them next week. The carriage is a great worry to us, for not a soul has turned up even to look at it. People here expect to get everything for a song and to be paid for everything at three times the usual price. I am infinitely delighted that Baron Grimm is in Paris; indeed it is the one thing that comforts me. We can certainly rely on him, as he is a sincere and true friend to us. Wolfgang will very soon do him honour and Grimm will never regret having taken an interest in him. I am frightfully busy this week, and until everything has been settled I shall not know whether I am standing on my head or on my heels. Everything comes on me and, as you may imagine, I have enough things to think about. But I hope that with God's help all will go off well and that we shall arrive in Paris safe and sound. True, this long journey will be very trying for us, but as God wills it, so must it be. Addio. Keep well, both of you. I kiss you both many 1000 times and remain your faithful wife

MARIA ANNA MOZART

All sorts of messages to all our acquaintances, particularly to Monsieur Bullinger and Mlle Sallerl, likewise to Herr Deibl and many others.

(297) *Mozart to his Father*

[*Autograph in the Mozarteum, Salzburg*]

[MANNHEIM, 11 *March* 1778]

MONSIEUR MON TRÉS CHER PÉRE,

I have received your letter of March 5th and am most delighted to hear that our good, kind friend, Baron Grimm, is in Paris.

You are quite right; we are leaving here next Saturday, the 14th, but we have not yet settled whether we shall take the mail coach or whether we shall travel to Strassburg or Metz. However, everything will be fixed up tomorrow morning. Perhaps I shall even be able to send you definite information immediately, for the post doesn't leave until tomorrow

evening and before then we must come to some final decision. We are
having a horrible time trying to sell our chaise. But we must do so, no
matter how little we get for it. For if I were to leave it here, things would
just drag on and after having had the honour of paying storage at a gulden
a month, I might not in the end get more than four louis d'or for it. A
coachman called today and I made him raise his offer from 30 to 38 gulden;
perhaps I shall screw him up to 40. He says that the coach is still quite
good, but that he couldn't make any use of the chassis. He is coming again
tomorrow morning and if he offers me 40 gulden, then in God's name I
shall let him have it. He is the same man who is to drive us from here to
Paris via Metz (which, as you already know, is the shorter route) for
eleven louis d'or. If tomorrow he agrees to do this for ten louis d'or, I
shall certainly engage him, and perhaps even if he demands eleven. For in
any case it is cheaper, which is our chief consideration, and it is more
comfortable for us, as he will use our chaise, that is to say—he will fix the
body on a chassis of his own; and it will be infinitely more convenient for
us, as we have so many odd trifles, which we can easily stuff in our chaise,
but which we could not pack into the mail coach; again, we shall be alone
and able to talk about what we like. For I assure you that if after all I do
travel by mail coach, my only worry will be the boredom of not being
able to talk about what I like and find most convenient; and, because we
really must study economy now, I am very much inclined to do this.
The difference, it is true, will not be very great, but it will be something;
and of course the main thing is to be comfortable, and to this I pay
particular attention on account of my mother. Well, tomorrow I shall
probably be able to write more fully about everything. The difference
amounts to one louis d'or, or one and a half. For we should have to buy
another trunk and a couple of cushions, for people say that the mail coach
jolts you so; which is only natural, as there is a chaussée the whole way.
Please forgive me for writing so little today and so badly, but I have still
so many things to do that I do not know where to begin. Meanwhile
farewell. In about a fortnight's time, after you have read this letter, I trust
that you will have received my first one from Paris. I kiss your hands 1000
times and embrace my sister with all my heart and remain until death
your most obedient son

WOLFGANG AMADÉ MOZART

Mannheim, 11 March 1778.

PS.—A propos. Please send something which I asked you for a long
time ago, and that is, the alphabet, both capitals and small letters, in your
handwriting.[1] Please don't forget this. You asked me the other day to

---

[1] See letter 237a postscript, and p. 530. Mozart wanted to improve his handwriting, the
untidiness of which he continually deplored.

send you Herr Weber's address, so that you might let him have the other arias. If they have not been copied yet, then please have them copied on small paper, that is, if you still have some, so that the postal fee may not be too high.

À Monsieur fridelin Weber
à Mannheim

at the cabinet-maker's,
     opposite the lottery-house.

    Adieu. My greetings to all our good friends and particularly to my best friend, Herr Bullinger.

    We have just this minute come to an agreement with the coachman. He is going to drive us to Paris for eleven louis d'or in our own chaise, which he has bought for 40 gulden. Tomorrow I shall put it down in black and white that, as I have not made him pay me for the chaise, when we reach Paris, I shall only have to pay him seven louis d'or and four gulden.

END OF VOL. I

PRINTED BY R. & R. CLARK, LTD., EDINBURGH